PRODUCTION/OPERATIONS MANAGEMENT

Elsevier Science Publishing Co., Inc.
52 Vanderbilt Avenue, New York, New York 10017

Sole distributors outside the U.S.A. and Canada:

Elsevier Science Publishers B.V.
P.O. Box 211, 1000 AE Amsterdam, The Netherlands

Library of Congress Cataloging in Publication Data

Tersine, Richard J
    Production/operations management: concepts, structure, and analysis
    Second Edition

    Bibliography: p.
    Includes indexes.
    1. Production management. 2. Industrial engineering.   I. Title.
TS155.T456   658.5   79-17770
ISBN 0-444-00923-X

Manufactured in the United States of America

PRODUCTION/OPERATIONS MANAGEMENT:
Concepts, Structure, and Analysis

Second Edition

Richard J. Tersine
The University of Oklahoma

NORTH-HOLLAND
New York • Amsterdam • Oxford

Contents

Preface

I INTRODUCTION   1

1 Production and Operations   3
Service Organizations   6
The Production Function   8
Productivity   12
Production/Operations Decision Levels   14
Conclusion   14

2 Systems Theory and Production   17
Organizational Systems Theory   20
Multiview Systems Concept of an Organization   21
Conclusion   33

3 Decision Theory   39
Aspects of Organizational Decision Making   41
Decision Theory Structure   44
Models   62
Conclusion   67
Appendix A: Model Classifications   72

4 Cost and Capital Analysis   78
Breakeven Analysis   79
Cost Equalization Analysis   84
Incremental Analysis   86
Cost Control   87
Cost Reduction   88
Capital Analysis   89
A Framework for Capital Analysis   104
Conclusion   106

5 Resource Allocation and Linear Programming   **113**

The Simplex Method   114
The Dual Method   128
Sensitivity Analysis   135
The Transportation Method   137
The Assignment Method   152

II POLICY DECISIONS   **169**

6 Policy Decisions   **171**

Objectives   173
Strategies   179
Tactics   183
Conclusion   186
Appendix A: Master Resources Profile   186

III PRODUCT DECISIONS   **191**

7 Product Decisions   **193**

Product Life Cycles   195
Research, Development, and Engineering   197
Feasibility Study   199
Preliminary Design   201
Detailed Design   201
Drawings and Specifications   213
Computer-Aided Design (CAD)   215
Service Design   216
Conclusion   217

8 Network Programming and Project Planning   **225**

Network Development   227
Determination of Activity Times   230
Establishment of Critical Path   232
Probabilistic Statements   237
Project Control   241
PERT/COST   242
Conclusion   242

IV PROCESS DECISIONS   **251**

9 Process and Operation Design   **253**

Product Analysis   256
Make or Buy   261
Capital and Equipment   265
Process Design   268
Operation Design   272
Job Design   273
Conclusion   274

To M.G.T.

10   Job Design   **281**
Division of Labor   284
Job Content   284
Work Methods   285
Job Satisfaction   292
The Physical Environment   295
Job Descriptions   300
Conclusion   301

11   Work Measurement   **305**
Informal Time Standards   306
Stopwatch Time Study   307
Work Sampling   312
Predetermined Time Study   319
Wages and Incentives   319
Conclusion   319

V   PLANT DECISIONS   **325**

12   Plant/Facility Location   **327**
Selection of Region   329
Selection of Community   331
Selection of Site   332
Location Factor Dependences   333
Sources of Assistance   337
Plant Location Trends   337
Quantitative Analysis   338
Foreign and International Considerations   344
Conclusion   345

13   Plant Layout   **351**
Layout Inputs   353
Layout Constraints   353
Layout Design Considerations   356
Layout Outputs   359
Conclusion   368
Appendix A: Line Balancing   369

14   Materials Handling   **381**
Materials Handling Inputs   384
Constraints   387
Flow Factors   392
Materials Handling Decisions   404
Materials Handling Outputs   405
Conclusion   407

VI OPERATIONS DECISIONS   413

15 Forecasting and Market Analysis   415
The Forecasting Function   418
Time Series Analysis   421
Soliciting Opinions   444
Economic Indicators   445
Econometric Models   449
Conclusion   449

16 Production Planning and Master Scheduling   457
Formalized Production Planning   462
Production Planning Methods   462
Master Scheduling   472
Conclusion   484
Appendix A: Master Schedule Format   492

17 Material Requirements Planning (MRP)   497
MRP Inputs   500
MRP Outputs   501
Product Structures   503
MRP Computations   507
MRP Types   517
MRP Overview   518
Capacity Planning and Control   520
Conclusion   524
Appendix A: Bills of Materials (BOM)   525

18 Scheduling and Production Control   541
Production Control Systems   542
Flow Shop Scheduling   544
Job Shop Scheduling   547
In-Process Inventory   569
Just-in-Time   571
Conclusion   574

19 Inventory Control Models   583
Types of Inventory   584
Inventory Costs   584
Independent Versus Dependent Demand   586
Continuous and Independent Demand Items   587
Discrete and Dependent Demand Items   598
Time-Phased Order Point   606
Single Order Quantities   607
Conclusion   613

20   Inventory Control Systems   **621**
Types of Control Systems   623
Selective Inventory Control   633
Inventory System Development   635
Inventory System Improvement   638
Aggregate Inventory Measurement   640
Conclusion   641

21   Purchasing and Procurement   **647**
Purchasing Inputs   651
Constraints   653
Demand Factors   655
Purchasing Decisions   656
Purchasing Outputs   656
Conclusion   670

22   Quality Control   **677**
Control Charts   681
Acceptance Sampling   688
Quality Circles   703
Conclusion   703

23   Maintenance   **709**
Types of Maintenance   711
Individual Versus Group Replacement   716
Internal Versus External Maintenance   718
Crew Size   718
Queuing Theory   718
Monte Carlo Simulation   726
Conclusion   736

Index   **743**

Preface

The study of production and operations is concerned with the creation of goods and services and embodies the collection of knowledge dealing with the design, planning, operation, and control of systems for converting inputs to outputs. It embraces a variety of disciplines and is comprised of a vast number of activities occurring in diverse settings. This text treats P/OM as a major functional area of an organization and emphasizes operational decision making in a management context. Its focus is on the production of quality goods and services at competitive prices and addresses current problems and issues confronting this pursuit.

Historically, P/OM was developed and refined in manufacturing organizations. Today, those basic tenets have been expanded to include service organizations. Since all organizations must face the common production problems of systems design, resource allocation, scheduling of events, and control of operations, the scope of P/OM extends beyond the bounds of its historical foundation in manufacturing and should be recognized for its universality as a basic organizational function. While there are differences, the underlying theory of production is common to both goods and services. Thus, much of the material in this text is as applicable to the management of hospitals and retail outlets as it is to the manufacture of products.

For a study of P/OM to be complete, its topics must be varied, comprehensive, and integrated into a logical framework which includes a policy orientation, concepts, principles, and associated techniques. This text provides such a framework and takes an analytical rather than a theoretical approach. The book relies heavily on graphs, charts, flow diagrams, cases, and numerical examples to convey a substantial introductory framework for production concepts. While quantitative analysis is integral to its approach, advanced quantitative methods and proofs are not presented. Although a knowledge of elementary statistics would be helpful, the only mathematical prerequisite is a proficiency in algebra.

The structure of this text allows flexibility in course content and design. It may be used equally well in either a single semester introductory course or a two semester course sequence. Coverage of preliminary operations topics is basic enough for the fundamental P/OM course; yet, it is broad and analytical enough to also be used in an advanced second semester course that gives an in-depth treatment of specific topics. Furthermore, this text may be used at either the undergraduate or graduate level. It fulfills the production/operations accreditation requirement of the AACSB.

To aid in the presentation of its subject matter, this text includes the following features:

Examples of solved problems to supplement and complement quantitative portions of the chapters. These are detailed but not complex applications of the quantitative techniques cited or discussed.

Figures, diagrams, and charts to further explain and illustrate the concepts and techniques presented. Many of the figures give concise outlines of conceptual logic, while numerous diagrams and flow charts show step-by-step procedures for arriving at problem solutions.

Questions at the end of the chapters to provide summaries and reviews of key points. For the most part, these require qualitative answers and may be used to alert the respondent to central areas which need closer examination.

Problems to facilitate the mastery of quantitative methods used in decision making. These range from simple and direct applications similar to the examples to more challenging and probing problem extensions.

Cases to improve skills in decision making and to promote decision analysis, which incorporates a scope of influencing factors not possible in shorter problem solutions. These demand thoughtful integration of behavioral, quantitative, economic, and other relevant aspects of the problem and can provide a stimulus for deeper investigation of the subject.

Selected bibliography to direct the reader to related works and readings in which the chapter topics are covered more thoroughly.

To accompany this text, support materials are available. An *Instructor's Manual* contains answers to the questions, problem solutions, case suggestions, true/false and multiple choice questions, and examination problems and solutions. An ancillary *Transparency Master Manual* contains charts, graphs, and figures useful for classroom presentation.

I wish to acknowledge the colleagues, students, and reviewers who originally contributed to this text and further to extend my appreciation for the guidance and suggestions donated during its revision. Gratitude is particularly due to Michele Gengler, Rick Toelle, Jack Morris, R. Leon Price, Warren Fisher, and Dan Marrs, who lent their professional skills. A special mention goes to Louise Calabro Gruendel for her editorial contribution.

INTRODUCTION

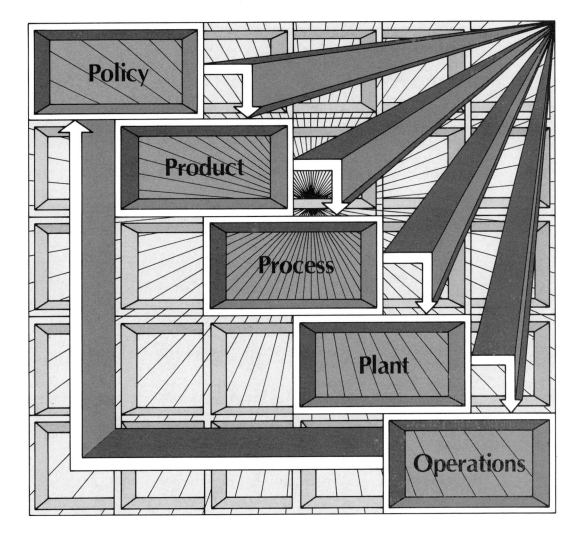

This book is divided into six major sections: the Introduction, Policy Decisions, Product Decisions, Process Decisions, Plant Decisions, and Operations Decisions. The introductory section deals with pervasive topics that are relevant to all the other sections of the book. The policy decisions section deals with *why* the organization exists and what it hopes to accomplish. The product decisions section indicates *what* goods or services the organization plans to provide for society. The process decisions section determines *how* the goods and services will be provided. The plant decisions section establishes *where* to locate the facility as well as its physical layout. Finally, the operations decisions section determines *when* the facility will be activated and operated.

The broad decision levels that structure the major sections of this text are depicted in Figure I. Further explanation and discussion about these decision levels will occur throughout the text.

The Introduction comprises five chapters. The *Production and Operations* chapter introduces and defines the functional area of production and operations. The *Systems Theory and Production* chapter deals with the total organization and its relationship with production and operations. The *Decision Theory* chapter structures the decision making process as it applies to organizations. The *Cost and Capital Analysis* chapter develops the financial aspects that affect organizational decisions. The *Resource Allocation and Linear Programming* chapter outlines several basic linear optimization models that can assist in the efficient allocation of resources. The chapters in the introductory section have broad application in all subsequent sections of the book.

FIGURE I
Production/operations decision levels.

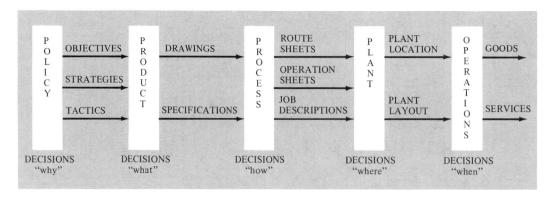

1

Production and Operations

SERVICE ORGANIZATIONS

THE PRODUCTION FUNCTION
Outputs
Inputs
Transformation or Process
Process Characteristics

PRODUCTIVITY

PRODUCTION/OPERATIONS DECISION LEVELS

CONCLUSION

QUESTIONS

SELECTED BIBLIOGRAPHY

Production is a fundamental function in every organization. It embraces those activities responsible for the creation of goods and services that are the outputs of an organization. Since all organizations have an output that is a good and/or a service, all organizations perform a variety of production activities. The basic measure of all the goods and services produced in a nation is called the gross national product (GNP). It reflects the economic health of a nation. Thus, production influences the wealth of a nation and thereby the standard of living of its people.

Production management, as we know it today, had its genesis in the Industrial Revolution of the late eighteenth century. It did exist prior to that time, for somebody had to build pyramids, castles, ships, temples, churches, and roads. However, earlier management was based on slave, serf, authoritarian, and military influence without a scientific technological base. The industrial revolution with its demand for concentration of resources on such a large scale fostered large economic organizations. The movement from family and small scale craft operations to large scale organizations with the substitution of mechanical power for human power gave birth to production management. However, as a continuous and scientific body of knowledge, it is almost totally a product of the twentieth century.

Production management has gone through several phases. The first industrial revolution in the eighteenth century found machines with mechanical power replacing people with muscular power. The second industrial revolution (1945–1980) began with automation and eventually ushered in computers and mathematical models along with the gradual substitution of machines for people as a source of control. The third industrial revolution is now in progress and involves robotics, computer-aided design (CAD), computer-aided manufacturing (CAM), decision support systems (DSS), and automated storage and retrieval systems (ASRS). Production is not a stagnant discipline; it is an evolving function built on a technological base. The need for less expensive production methods, for new products, and for exploiting less accessible sources of raw materials is a motivating force for technological improvements and breakthroughs. As these changes occur, production management is thrust into new arenas.

Production is concerned with the creation of goods and services; it involves the design, planning, operation, and control of the systems that produce goods and services. It is any process or procedure for transforming a set of inputs (the resources purchased by or provided to the organization) into outputs (the products the organization sells or distributes). The inputs are some combination of human beings, materials, money, machines, and methods (technology). The transformation may be physical as in manufacturing, locational as in transportation, temporal as in warehousing (storage), or transactional as in retailing. The outputs may be tangible or intangible, a good or service, or simply satisfaction. The scope of production and operations is exhibited in Table 1.

To many, the term production conjures up images of factories with assembly lines and machinery. Except for the past generation, the focus of production management has been predominantly on manufacturing management, placing substantial emphasis on methods and techniques for operating a factory. In recent years, the focus has broadened to include a wider range of activities that encompass nonfactory (service) operations. Because of the differences in outputs, the kinds of activites performed can vary tremendously from organization to organization.

The management of production is crucial to the successful operation of an organization. First, in most organizations well over fifty percent of the sales dollar is

TABLE 1
The scope of production and operations management

Production & operations classification[a]	Characteristics	Typical examples
Manufacturing 1. Extraction 2. Fabrication 3. Assembly 4. Construction	Physical creation of goods (form utility)	Mining, refining, farming, textiles, vehicles, homes, appliances, buildings, bridges, etc.
Transport[b] 1. Air 2. Water 3. Ground	Change in location (place utility)	Airlines, railroads, taxis, buses, trucks, ships, etc.
Supply[b] 1. Distribution 2. Warehousing 3. Retailing 4. Brokering	Change in ownership (possession utility)	Retail outlets, storage, supermarkets, department stores, gas stations, hardware stores, etc.
Services[b]	Treatment of something or someone (state utility)	Governments, churches, health care, hospitals, education, hotel/motel, banks, entertainment, restaurants, communications (television, radio, newspapers, magazines), utilities (power, water, sewage, telephone), protection (fire, police, legal), etc.

[a]The above classification is not meant to be exclusive, comprehensive, or exhaustive. Several other classifications can be made. It merely exhibits the extent of production and operations management.

[b]Transport and supply can be considered in the services category. There are obvious areas of overlap between them. They are separated above for convenience only.

spent towards production for labor, materials, and overhead expenses. Second, in most organizations over fifty percent of those supervised are in production. Third, in most organizations the majority of the assets such as plant, equipment, and inventory are under the production or operations manager. Fourth, customer satisfaction in terms of quality and on-time delivery is derived from production. Thus, most of the controllable costs and assets in an organiation are managed by the production function.

The analysis of production is concerned with how organizations with a given "state of art" (technology) combine various inputs to produce a stipulated output in an economically efficient manner. Of course, the concept of production is clearer when applied to goods rather than services. Nevertheless, the problems of productivity, resource allocation, and cost control in service industries are just as serious.

Production embraces a wide range of activities and not only the fabrication of goods. Rendering legal service, writing a book, showing a motion picture, and servicing a bank account are all examples of production. Production management is not a random aggregation of tools but rather a synthesis of concepts and techniques that relate directly to and enhance the management of organizations.

Production in a manufacturing organization is conceptually the inner core of the organization and has little *formal* structural contact with the external environment. The other major functional areas (finance and marketing) have much more contact with the external environment. The other functional areas tend to place operating constraints on the production function. Since production is somewhat isolated from the external environment and deals with more tangible aspects, it can plan and control its activities better.

A service organization does not usually produce a physical product as does a manufacturing organization. In service organizations the word "production" is replaced with the word "operations," and the operations manager is responsible for the productive effort. Unfortunately, service industries such as hospitals, universities, governments, and banks are not always thought of as production systems because of the intangible nature of their products.[1] Rising costs and deteriorating service are changing this myopic view. Production methods are increasing the productivity of service organizations and decreasing the waste of resources. Just like manufacturing organizations, service organizations have work to schedule, facilities to lay out, workers to pay, quality to control, and output to deliver. Production occurs in factories, schools, banks, offices, warehouses, retail stores, or any type of organized human endeavor. It is applicable whether the organization is profit or nonprofit, private or public, manufacturing or service.

SERVICE ORGANIZATIONS

There has been a proliferation of organizations that provide service products as opposed to manufactured products. Organizations can be viewed as production systems of two distinct varieties—manufacturing production systems and service production systems. A *manufacturing production system* transforms inputs into a tangible physical product. A *service production system* is based to a greater degree on the processing of knowledge and skills into a product that is not physical in nature. Service generally implies an *act* rather than a physical product. Many organizations are not pure service or pure manufacturing production systems but contain traits common to both. Typical service production systems are found in government, health care, restaurants, retail outlets, hotels, libraries, and prisons.

Service production systems have become an important force in the U.S. economy. Such systems employ the majority of U.S. workers and generate more than fifty percent of the GNP. As societies become more complex, there is a greater need for services, ranging from police protection to education to entertainment.

Physical products often lend themselves to a considerable amount of standardization. This is not the case for many service products for which there is a more pronounced need for personal care. Repairing a vehicle, treating a patient, defending an alleged criminal, and serving a restaurant customer all require special attention to the needs of the particular person receiving the service. Despite the distinctive differences, there are similarities in the problems that arise.

In manufacturing organizations, it is common to find a production manager on the organizational chart. In service organizations, the name production manager infre-

---

[1]Throughout this text, "production management" and "operations management" will be used interchangeably. The separate terms have developed in the literature because of the traditional emphasis on manufacturing in the theory of production.

quently appears, but there are a variety of titles that subsume the same responsibilities. In a retail store, it is the "store manager"; in a hospital, it is the "hospital administrator"; in a university, it is the "chancellor" or "provost"; and in an airline, it is the "operations manager." All of these officers are concerned with the creation of goods and services.

Service systems are very diverse in their operations. Because of this diversity, it is difficult to generalize about them without dealing with a specific type of service. Whereas manufacturing production systems are isolated from the ultimate consumer, service production systems tend to be in direct contact and are therefore more personal.

A service usually involves a higher degree of customer contact than manufacturing; the performance of a service typically occurs at the point of consumption. On the other hand, manufacturing allows a separation of production and consumption, and it occurs in a location remote from the consumer. Services tend to require a higher labor content (labor intensity), while manufacturing can be more mechanized (capital intensity). Higher mechanization generates products with low variability, so manufacturing tends to be smooth and efficient, whereas services sometimes appear slow and awkward with more output variability. Manufacturing systems are dominated by concern for routing, handling, and processing of materials. Service systems are dominated by concerns for meeting and waiting on customers. Processing times are determined primarily by machines and equipment in manufacturing but chiefly by personnel efficiency and the nature of customer needs in services. Table 2 exhibits a comparison of manufacturing and service systems.

Processed knowledge or skill is the product offered for consumption in service production systems. They usually have no finished goods or in-process inventory for smoothing or buffering their operations. The lack of a demand buffer creates significant capacity problems. Peak demand must be met by maintaining excess capacity in facilities and/or personnel. Thus, costly underutilization during slack periods is to be expected. Scheduling of events or services is critical. Consider such examples as stadiums for sports events, beds in a hospital, seats on an aircraft, pews in a church, cells in a prison, and rooms in a motel.

Production planning and control in service organizations is difficult, since services cannot be stockpiled. The product is instantly perishable. If a service facility is waiting to serve and there is no demand, the product is wasted. If either the productive capacity is not large enough to handle peak demand, or it cannot be modified in line with service demands, peak demand is not met and customers may go elsewhere. The usual measure of organizational effectiveness is the level of service that can be offered within some cost constraint.

TABLE 2
Comparisons of manufacturing and service systems

Characteristic	Manufacturing	Service
Output	Tangible	Intangible
Labor content	Low	High
Mechanization	High	Low
Customer contact	Low	High
Output uniformity	High	Low
Capital investment	High	Low

THE PRODUCTION FUNCTION

The production function is the name given to the relationship between the inputs and outputs. It is an expression of the dependent or functional relationship that exists between the inputs (factors or resources) of a production process and the output (product). It is sometimes referred to as an input-output model. The production function is a catalog of output possibilities; it can be shown as a table or, alternatively, as a mathematical equation. Mathematically, it can be written as

output $= f(\text{inputs})$.

Conceptually, it can be depicted as shown in Figure 1. Information flow (dashed lines) may be of several types. It may be reports, memoranda, or spoken words; it may be requests for further information, commands, or instructions; and it may contain routine or extraordinary data from operations.

There are two kinds of production functions or input-output relations. They are *returns to variable proportions* and *returns to scale*. In returns to variable proportions, quantities of some inputs are fixed while quantities of other inputs are variable. In returns to scale, all the inputs are variable.

Returns to variable proportions are mostly confined to short time frames. In the short run, some inputs such as plant and equipment are fixed, while others such as labor can be changed. When an organization expands output by employing more labor, it alters the proportions between fixed and variable inputs and encounters diminishing returns. The law of diminishing returns can be stated as follows: when total output is increased by adding units of a variable input while holding the quantities of other inputs constant, the increases in output after some point will get smaller and smaller. Note that output continues to increase, but at a decreasing (diminishing) rate. The following expression indicates that the output Y is a function of the variable input X_1 while all other inputs are fixed:

$Y = f(X_1 \mid X_2, X_3, \ldots ,X_n)$.

The vertical bar in the above expression indicates that input factors to its right are regarded as fixed while those to its left are varied.

Returns to scale are characteristic of long time frames. In the long run, an organization can expand by changing all its inputs. If the increase in output is proportional to the increase in the quantities of inputs, returns to scale are said to be *constant*. A doubling or quadrupling of inputs causes a doubling or quadrupling of output. If the increase in output is more than proportional, returns to scale are *increasing*. If instead the increase in output is less than proportional, returns to scale are *decreasing*. Organizations frequently expand their capacity to take advantage of economies of scale or advantage of mass production. Because of constraints of demand, technology, and management, organizational size is limited. The following expression indicates that output *(Y)* is a function of variable inputs *(X_i)*:

$Y = f(X_1, X_2, X_3, \ldots ,X_n)$.

Each organization has a production function whose form is structured by the state of its technology. When technology changes, a new production function comes into being. Since there are usually alternative ways to provide a product, management must decide what production function to employ. Different processes, machines, and

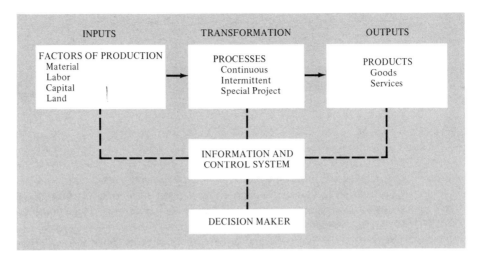

FIGURE 1
The production function.

methods, as well as the substitutability of inputs, complicate the production decision. On a business level, the inputs available to an organization are also influenced by its size and financial (economic) viability.

The notion of the production function is a useful and powerful tool for analysis. It can be applied to situations on all scales: an operation, a job, a department, a process, or an entire organization. The input-output relationship involved in this notion is the foundation of systems theory.

OUTPUTS

An output is the product an organization provides to a customer or society. Outputs constitute a bewildering variety of products, ranging from manufactured goods to public services and from agricultural crops to information. It may take the form of goods, services, information (computer printout), energy (hydroelectric power), waste, or satisfaction. Production systems produce outputs that range on a continuum from highly standardized to highly customized. Standardized products have a high degree of uniformity, and typical examples include television sets, newspapers, refrigerators, computers, car washes, bus rides, and mail service. Customized products are designed for a specific case or individuals; typical examples include eyeglasses, custom drapery, dental care, surgery, taxi service, custom houses, and tailored clothes.

Nearly all organizations have more than one output (product). Usually it is meaningful to speak of product lines that are made up of different sizes, models, or variations of a product.

The starting point for production is the specification of the desired outputs. The demand for outputs comes from customers and the marketplace. Forecasts, sales, orders, predictions, and market analysis measure the structure of demand for an output. The output is expected to have a greater value than the combined values of the inputs, or else the output will not be provided. The demand for an output creates a derived demand for all of the inputs composing it.

The output of a production system is made available to a customer or consumed within the host organization. There are usually undesirable side effects from the production of an output. Since no process is completely efficient, there are bound to be nonfunctional or defective outputs. There are also wastes that must be disposed of, which can enter the ecological system as an input. The elimination of waste or its proper disposal is a challenging task for the manager.

INPUTS

The words "inputs" and "factors of production" are near-synonyms and in many contexts are used interchangeably. In general, the connotation of "inputs" is broader; "factors of production" can refer, in a narrower meaning, to land, labor, and capital alone. In this book, inputs and factors of production will be exact synonyms unless otherwise specified.

The labor (human) input involves both physical labor and intellectual capabilities. The capabilities are often the key asset of an organization, although it is typically not accounted for on the balance sheet. In private organizations, capital becomes available from equity (stock), debt (bond) issues, and reinvested profits. In nonprofit organizations, taxes or contributions are a source of capital. As more capital is allocated, the level of technology typically rises, since equipment tends to replace human labor.

A unit of output normally requires several types of inputs. Inputs to a process consist of land, labor, materials, energy, and capital. They can be measured in physical units or in dollars (their costs). There are varying degrees of difficulty in determining how much of any input is required to make a certain output. Inputs such as direct labor and materials are fully consumed in providing a product and are easily assigned to a given unit of output. The capital input (plant and equipment) is difficult to assign to specific output because it is nearly impossible to measure how much capital is consumed at any point in time. For example, how much of a barber's chair is consumed in providing a single haircut?

The possible physical combinations of the inputs in the production function are determined by technology; they change as technology changes. Each input has a price that the firm must pay. The prices of the inputs, along with their physical productivities, influence the decisions as to how much of each to purchase.

Organizations can handle production decisions by the principle of substitution. This requires surveillance of the production function and input prices. As they change, there should be a substituting of one input for another[2] to keep costs as low as possible. A fall (or rise) in the price of an input causes more (or less) of it to be used. This is the substitution effect. However, for it to be applicable, there must be substitutability between inputs.

In the short run (period of time in which one or more inputs are fixed), input costs can be classified as fixed or variable. A fixed input is one whose quantity cannot readily be changed when an immediate change in output is desirable. A variable input is one whose quantity may be changed almost instantaneously in response to desired changes in output. Fixed costs do not vary as a function of the output rate and include plant and equipment. Variable costs vary as a function of the output rate and include direct labor and materials. In the long run, all costs are variable.

---

[2]The substitution of capital for labor is called mechanization or automation.

TRANSFORMATION OR PROCESS

Inputs are what goes into a process, and outputs are what comes out. It is also necessary to understand what goes on in the process or transformation itself. The transformation is also known by such names as production, process, or operations. We shall use the terms transformation and process to mean the same thing: whatever utility producing activities are performed on the inputs. The transformation may involve change in physical nature, location, possession, or state.

Processes typically require a wide variety of inputs. Many qualitatively different types of each input (labor, capital, and materials) are normally used to produce an output. Technology often offers a choice among a finite number of processes. The processes may or may not use the same inputs.

Processes can be generally classified as continuous, intermittent, or special project. In a *continuous process* the tasks are arranged according to the sequence of operations that are needed to make the product. All products follow a definite progressive sequence from one task to the next. Every product follows the same path, uses the same inputs, and neither skips tasks nor recycles. Examples of continuous processes are assembly lines, chemical plants, paper plants, petroleum refineries, and fast food outlets with standardized products. An *intermittent process* is used for low volume, batch, or customized products each of which requires a different set or sequence of tasks. Examples of intermittent processes are special order fabrication (machine) shops, hospitals, and dental offices. A *special project* is often related to unit production. It involves a unique product or service requiring large amounts of resources that are organized into a single process. Construction, technological development, and new products are examples of special projects.

The specifics of every process are different, but all consist of tasks, flows, and storage. A *task* occurs when there is an addition or change in some input to make it more like the desired output. The two types of *flows* are the flow of products and the flow of information. A *product flow* occurs when the product moves from task to task or to storage and vice versa. [A flow merely changes the position (location) of a product, whereas a task changes the product.] An *information flow* involves records, instructions, and documentation. A *storage* occurs when no tasks are being performed and the product is not being transported. A storage is anything other than a task or a flow. A process can be described by a process flow diagram containing all the tasks, flows, and storages.

Production management is concerned with both the technology of the transformation process and the methodology of managing the process. The technology is usually unique to a given industry and is not the focus of this text. The methodology for managing transformation processes has a theoretical base that is surprisingly similar for most production activities. This thread of commonality provides the base for studying transformations in the production function.

Process Characteristics

Processes can be described by several characteristics such as capacity, efficiency, effectiveness, and flexibility. *Capacity* is the rate of output for a process and is measured in units per time interval. It is frequently referred to as capacity level, maximum capacity, or range of capacity. *Efficiency* is the value of the output of a process divided by the value of the input. The ratio should be greater than one for an economically viable process. Profit can be used as a measure of efficiency. Efficiency can be difficult to measure when it is arduous to allocate inputs to a given output. *Effectiveness* measures actual output against planned output. It requires comparison on the basis of a plan, standard, or goal. *Flexibility* is the ability of a process to produce several different products, or to produce the same product from different mixes or sets of inputs. Flexibility protects a process from the need for change and extends its economic lifetime.

Organizations have an objective of producing and distributing goods and services. They have the characteristics of varying size, growing complexity, specialization of skills, increasing diversity of objectives, adaptability to change, and adaptation to external demands. The idea of the production function can be used as an analytical tool to design, operate, and control organizations.

PRODUCTIVITY

In today's international business environment, increased productivity is a key to the economic success of nations, industries, companies, and workers. Increases in productivity are largely responsible for the high standards of living in industrialized nations. On a national basis, productivity improvement is needed to prevent inflation. Wage, cost, and price increases not supported by productivity increases create inflationary pressures on the economy. Productivity gains are a nation's best defense against inflation and foreign competition, because they contribute to a strong national economy.

Performance is the major criterion in the assessment of organizations. An important performance measure for the comparative study of an organization over time is productivity. It is an important indicator of the ability of an organization to use its scarce resources. An enduring objective of production is to improve productivity, i.e., to reduce the cost per unit of output. Productivity is computed as the ratio of output to input or effort. It measures how much input is required to achieve a given output. It can be applied to measure the performance of an individual worker, crew, machine, process, or department, or the entire organization over a time interval.

The primary factors that determine productivity are technology, work methods, choice of equipment, employees, and management. A common misconception is that workers are the main determinant of productivity. Technological improvements have resulted in the largest productivity gains in recent decades. Mechanized equipment, better tools, and computers have made jobs safer and more productive. However, productivity gains are the result of a number of factors, and this confounding complicates single factor measurements in the productivity equation.

Productivity is the result of the efficiency of labor, the effectiveness of management, and the state of technology. Technology includes new ideas, inventions, techniques, methods, and materials. Management integrates labor with technology to produce outputs. The long run gains in productivity tend to come from the efficiency of technology and the effectiveness of management rather than the efficiency of labor. It is difficult, however, to state precisely what portion of output produced can be attributed to any specific input. Rarely is the output dependent solely upon any single input; it is influenced by the relative quantities of inputs as well as their quality.

Productivity changes usually do not manifest themselves immediately. Effects are more apparent when they are analyzed over a span of years and compared with performance in other organizations, industries, or countries. Annual gains can vary significantly due to the business cycle, technological advances, economic policies, wars, and a variety of other factors.

The basic productivity ratio is output/input. In particular, a macro level index for an organization can be expressed as

$$\text{total productivity} = \frac{\text{goods} + \text{services}}{\text{labor} + \text{materials} + \text{energy} + \text{capital}}.$$

Dollar units are typically used for both the numerator and denominator to allow diverse products and resources to be expressed in equivalent terms. Because organizations employ productivity measures for different purposes, at different levels in an organization, no standard formula exists for calculating a productivity index. Innumerable variations have to be used to carry out the intent of the basic output/input ratio.

As a measure of production efficiency, productivity commonly takes the form of output per worker-hour, where output is measured in dollars or units. An increase in productivity occurs when the output/input ratio rises from one period to the next. When inputs are constant and output increases, resources are being used more efficiently. Greater than proportional increases of output to input tend to conserve resources and may contribute to stable prices (economic stability). Conversely, declining productivity can create inflationary pressures and instability.

The worker-hour is a common unit of input for labor productivity measurements. Productivity in the United States, measured as output per worker-hour, has been increasing in this century at a rate of approximately 3% per year. When output per worker-hour increases with all other inputs constant, it indicates a more efficient utilization of labor. This greater effectiveness can result from more efficient methods, reduced waste, better organization, a faster work pace, improved tools, and so forth. New facilities and equipment are responsible for many large jumps in productivity. For productivity measurements to be valid and comparable in the face of inflation, it is necessary to correct each year's dollar figures to constant values by means of a price index.

Two people work in service industries for every one working elsewhere in the U.S. economy, and the proportion is increasing. Service industries include finance, education, health, wholesale and retail trade, and so forth. Service industries tend to be highly labor intensive, and productivity increases are more difficult to attain there. The principal means for productivity improvement in the service sector are capital intensity and more efficient labor practices. Productivity can be increased by doing things in better ways without any additional cost. Better work methods and scheduling can yield immediate productivity gains. However, there is a point beyond which additional productivity increases are predicated on increased capital investment and technological advances: mechanized equipment, better tools, and computers.

Technology is the knowledge regarding processes, techniques, and methods, by which goods are provided and services rendered. Technology determines the nature of tasks, the flow of tasks within a process, and their relationship to each other. Since technology advances, one refers to the state of technology. As the state of technology changes, it may be possible to change the process and achieve the same output with fewer inputs, or to keep the inputs constant and achieve greater output.

Change means a revision, rearrangement, addition, deletion, or substitution of one thing for another. As such it is inevitable, but the rate and direction of change are not always constant or consistent, nor is it always beneficial and desirable. Organizations make changes to reduce cost, improve products, meet competition, improve processes, streamline operations, provide better service, and so forth. Change should be accepted not only as inevitable but as presenting an opportunity for productivity improvement that can be realized and controlled.

Productivity problems tend to have an operational focus. They may be the effect rather than the cause, or just the tip of the iceberg. Beneath the surface may be strategic or structural problems in an organization. If problems are strategic, they need strategic changes, not merely operational ones. From a strategic point of view, many plants may be too big, attempting to make too many products, based on too many technologies, or directed to the needs of too many markets. Attempts to increase productivity by decreasing cost per unit should be based on a strong strategic position.

PRODUCTION/OPERATIONS DECISION LEVELS

Production and operations management can be subdivided into five broad, interdependent decision levels: policy decisions, product decisions, process decisions, plant decisions, and operations decisions. These decision levels are concerned with *why* the organization exists, *what* products it will provide, *how* the products will be provided, *where* the organization will locate, and *when* the products will be provided:

Why	Policy decisions
What	Product decisions
How	Process decisions
Where	Plant decisions
When	Operations decisions

Formally or informally, all organizations must address these decision levels.

These broad decision levels are highly interdependent. Decisions made on one level tend to influence decisions made in the others. Although these decision levels will be analyzed in five separate sections of this book, their interdependence must be realized. The integration of the decision levels is of paramount importance in an organization.

CONCLUSION

Production describes any organized activity intended to provide goods and services. The concepts and techniques appropriate to the management of production activities in a factory can be effectively applied to service organizations. The problems encountered in the two environments have many similarities as well as subtle differences. The classic production problem in all organizations is the allocation of scarce resources (managerial, natural, technological, and financial) to the benefit of the organization. Productivity is a measure of how efficiently resources have been allocated. Improving productivity is the premier production challenge.

From an ecological point of view, production systems profoundly affect the ecological balance by depleting natural resources to secure production inputs and by generating wastes that can pollute the natural environment. The undesirable environmental impacts of production systems have resulted in new pressures for resource conservation and a cleaner environment. Production systems must be designed and operated in such a fashion as to be in harmony with the natural environment.

Productivity is usually defined as the ratio of output produced per unit of input (worker-hours, machine-hours, quantity of material, or energy units) consumed by a process. It is a measure of performance in acquiring, producing, and distributing goods and services. In order to increase productivity, it is necessary to produce more output for each unit of input. Since it indicates how well resources are utilized, productivity is a measure of production function efficiency.

The primary organizational functions are finance, marketing, and production. Finance generates the capital and funds necessary to support operations; production produces the output; and marketing distributes and sells the output. The focus of this book is on the function called production, which deals with input-transformation-output relationships.

QUESTIONS

1. What is production? What are its two distinct varieties?
2. What are some of the major differences between manufacturing production systems and service production systems? Give examples.
3. What is a production function? Name the two types.
4. Name the three types of processes and give examples of each.
5. A process usually consists of what three categories?
6. What characteristics can be used to describe a process?
7. Define productivity and indicate how it is calculated.
8. What are the primary organizational functions and what are their roles?
9. Name the broad decision levels in production/operations. What questions do they answer?
10. Discuss several organizations with which you are familiar in respect to their inputs, transformation, and outputs.
11. Briefly describe the major stages in the evolution of production management.
12. Why is the management of production crucial to the successful operation of an organization?
13. What factors can influence an organization's choice of inputs?
14. What steps may help an organization to increase its productivity?

SELECTED BIBLIOGRAPHY

Adam, Jr., E. E. and R. J. Ebert. *Production and Operations Management: Concepts, Models, and Behavior,* Englewood Cliffs, NJ: Prentice-Hall, 1982.

Amrine, H. T. et al. *Manufacturing Organization and Management,* Englewood Cliffs, NJ: Prentice-Hall, 1982.

Azadivar, F. *Design and Engineering of Production Systems,* San José, CA: Engineering Press, 1984.

Bedworth, D. D. and J. E. Bailey. *Integrated Production Control Systems,* New York: Wiley, 1982.

Buffa, E. S. *Modern Production/Operations Management,* New York: Wiley, 1983.

———— and J. G. Miller. *Production-Inventory Systems: Planning and Control,* Homewood, IL: Irwin, 1979.

Chase, R. B. and N. J. Aquilano. *Production and Operations Management: A Life Cycle Approach,* Homewood, IL: Irwin, 1981.

Chen, G. K. and R. E. McGarrah. *Productivity Mangement: Text and Cases,* Chicago: Dryden, 1982.

Colley, Jr., J. L. et al. *Production Operations: Planning and Control,* San Francisco: Holden-Day, 1977.

Cook, T. M. and R. A. Russell. *Contemporary Operations Management,* Englewood Cliffs, NJ: Prentice-Hall, 1984.

Dervitsiotis, K. N. *Operations Management,* New York: McGraw-Hill, 1981.

Dilworth, J. B. *Production and Operations Management,* New York: Random House, 1982.

Evans, J. R. et al. *Applied Production and Operations Management,* St. Paul, MN: West Publishing, 1984.

Fitzsimmons, J. A. and R. S. Sullivan. *Service Operations Management,* New York: McGraw-Hill, 1982.

Fogarty, D. W. and T. R. Hoffmann. *Production and Inventory Management,* Cincinnati, Ohio: South-Western, 1983.

Gaither, N. *Production and Operations Management,* Chicago: Dryden, 1984.

Harris, R. D. and R. F. Gonzalez. *The Operations Manager: Role, Problems, and Techniques,* St. Paul, MN: West, 1981.

Hopeman, R. J. *Production and Operations Management,* Columbus, OH: Merrill, 1980.

Laufer, A. C. *Production and Operations Management,* Cincinnati, OH: South-Western, 1984.

Mayer, R. R. *Production and Operations Management,* New York: McGraw-Hill, 1982.

McClain, J. O. and L. J. Thomas. *Operations Management,* Englewood Cliffs, NJ: Prentice-Hall, 1980.

Menipaz, E. *Essentials of Production and Operations Management,* Englewood Cliffs, NJ: Prentice-Hall, 1984.

Meredith, J. R. and T. E. Gibbs. *The Management of Operations,* New York: Wiley, 1984.

Monks, J. G. *Operations Management: Theory and Problems,* New York: McGraw-Hill, 1982.

Moore, F. G. and T. E. Hendrick. *Production/Operations Management,* Homewood, IL: Irwin, 1984.

Peters, M. and T. Oliva. *Operations and Production Management,* Boston: Prindle, Weber, and Schmidt, 1981.

Riggs, J. L. *Production Systems: Planning, Analysis, and Control,* New York: Wiley, 1981.

Sasser, W. E. et al. *Management of Service Operations,* Boston: Allyn and Bacon, 1978.

Schmenner, R. W. *Production/Operations Management: Concepts and Situations,* Chicago: Science Research Associates, 1984.

Schonberger, R. J. *Operations Management,* Plano, TX: Business Publications, 1984.

Schroeder, R. G. *Operations Management,* New York: McGraw-Hill, 1981.

Starr, M. K. *Operations Management,* Englewood Cliffs, NJ: Prentice-Hall, 1978.

Stevenson, W. J. *Production/Operations Management,* Homewood, IL: Irwin, 1982.

Tellier, R. D. *Operations Management: Fundamental Concepts and Methods,* New York: Harper and Row, 1978.

Tersine, R. J. et al. *Problems and Models in Operations Management,* Columbus, OH: Grid, 1980.

———— and J. Campbell. *Modern Materials Management,* New York: North-Holland, 1977.

Vollman, T. E., W. L. Berry, and D. C. Whybark. *Manufacturing Planning and Control Systems,* Homewood, IL: Irwin, 1984.

Wild, R. *Concepts for Operations Management,* New York: Wiley, 1977.

Wight, O.W. *MRP II: Unlocking America's Productivity Potential,* Boston: CBI Publishing, 1981.

2
Systems Theory and Production

ORGANIZATIONAL SYSTEMS THEORY

MULTIVIEW SYSTEMS CONCEPT OF AN ORGANIZATION
Systemic Environmental Model
  Micro Environment
  Linking Environment
  Macro Environment
  Micro-Linking-Macro Factors
Systemic Functional Model
  Policy Decisions
  Product Decisions
  Process Decisions
  Plant Decisions
  Operations Decisions
Systemic Operational Model

CONCLUSION

QUESTIONS
CASES
SELECTED BIBLIOGRAPHY

To understand the internal functioning and operation of organizations, it is necessary to have a framework for analysis. Any theoretical framework must be conceptual in nature and cut across the various environments (internal and external) that impinge on an organization. One must focus on both aggregate structural characteristics and lower-level departmental work units so that both can be integrated into a common network. To accomplish the goal of organizational analysis, it is worthwhile to utilize systems theory.

Constant reference is made in our society to systems (mountain systems, river systems, solar systems, transportation systems, penal systems, political systems, social systems, and so forth). Generally, the term "system" is used to denote something that has numerous interrelated parts or components (subsystems). The whole is not just the sum of the parts; it is much more. A system can be explained only as a totality. It is determined more by interactions than by the things that interact. Instead of explaining the whole in terms of its parts, parts are explained in terms of the whole. For example, a detailed study of each element of a compound such as sodium (Na) and chlorine (Cl) does not ensure an understanding of the combination which is sodium chloride or common table salt (NaCl).

We are surrounded by, live within, and are ourselves systems. All the organizations composing our society and economy are man-made systems. There are systems within systems within systems (hierarchies of systems). The term "system" can mean anything the writer chooses. It is so pervasive and ubiquitous that it can refer to a myriad of phenomena. Anybody using the term must define it so ambiguity can be dispelled.

Systems can be classified in several ways. One categorization is as natural or man-made systems. *Natural* systems behave according to the laws of nature, and their relationships are more predictable in a scientific sense. Examples of natural systems are galaxies, of which our solar system is a part; the human body, which is composed of skeletal, nervous, and circulatory systems; and mountain systems. In contrast, *man-made* systems are those designed and operated by man. They include inputs from natural systems, but are not as scientifically predictable. Examples of man-made systems are economic systems, social systems, and all human organizations in our society.

The systems approach on a macro level (general systems theory) represents an attempt to integrate the knowledge of the physical and social sciences into a unified framework.[1] Boulding established a general classification of systems, which is a theoretical "system of systems" with nine levels of complexity.[2] The nine levels with progressive complexity are frameworks, clockworks, cybernetics, open systems, genetic-societal, animal, human, social organization, and transcendental. The first three levels are made up of physical and mechanical systems and are of particular interest to physical scientists. The next three levels deal with biological systems and are of interest to the biologist, botanist, and zoologist. The remaining three levels (human, social organization, and transcendental) are of particular interest to the social scientist.

Due to the knowledge explosion, disciplines have been breaking up into isolated subdisciplines with nonexistent or tenuous lines of communication. The reduced

---

[1]Kenneth E. Boulding, "General Systems Theory—The Skeleton Of Science," *Management Science,* Vol. 2, April 1956, pp. 197–208.
[2]*Ibid.*

communication among disciplines impedes the total growth of knowledge. The usefulness of a general systems approach lies in the spotlighting of areas where gaps exist in knowledge as well as the transfer of knowledge among disciplines. A simple example is the periodic table in chemistry and how its development was instrumental in new discoveries.[3] The systems approach transcends disciplinary boundaries and is interdisciplinary or multidisciplinary in nature.

For the last few centuries, the sciences have vastly expanded the frontiers of human knowledge by the *process of analysis*. The movement has been towards specialization. Division, dissection, classification, separation, partition, and segmentation characterize the process of analysis. However, research in each of the separate fields of systematic knowledge has resulted in narrowing specialization. Specialists tend to see an organization from their own narrow viewpoint. Walls of ignorance have tended to rise which block the flow of knowledge from discipline to discipline. Synthesis is necessary to assimilate existing knowledge and avoid costly duplication of efforts. Summation, integration, unification, amalgamation, and combination characterize the *process of synthesis*.

Using analysis we take things apart, study the components, and attempt to improve on the components. Analysis is commonplace in organizations, whereas synthesis is not. Analysis is frequently highly mathematical, while synthesis tends to be logical with less mathematical influence.

The systems approach is a philosophical orientation and a desirable goal. It is not something new, but just a change in emphasis that considers internal and external environmental factors. A system receives inputs and, after a transformation of some kind takes place, it produces an output that will be an input to other systems. The input-transformation-output concept is basic to systems theory. The framework establishes hierarchies of relationships by associating activities with other activities so relationships can be identified and classified appropriately. The input to a given system is the output from another system, and the output from a given system is an input to another system. Thus, there are an infinite number of possible systems.

Professors Johnson, Kast, and Rosenzweig demonstrated the application of general systems theory to management practice.[4] Management is the process whereby unrelated resources (men, machines, materials, and money) are integrated through organization into a total system for the accomplishment of objectives. A manager coordinates and integrates the activities (work) of others rather than performing operations himself. Organizations are complex networks of decision processes. There are decision points throughout, from individuals at the operations level to policy makers at the top. Taken together, all the decision points constitute an intricate system.

Organization is a form of activity that is pervasive in our society. A way of life has evolved that is characterized by the proximity and dependency of people on each other and organizations. Organizations can be described as goal oriented (people with a purpose), psychosocial (people working individually and in groups), technical (people using knowledge and techniques), and structurally integrated (people dividing and coordinating their efforts). We shall confine our discussion to organizational systems theory, which is a subset of general systems theory.

---

[3]Mendeleev discovered a system that showed how all basic elements of matter are related by means of the periodic table.

[4]Richard A. Johnson, Fremont Kast, and James E. Rosenzweig, "Systems Theory and Management," *Management Science,* Vol. 10, No. 2, January 1964, pp. 367–384.

ORGANIZATIONAL SYSTEMS THEORY

The systems approach presents the "big picture" as a way of thinking about the job of managing. It provides a framework for relating internal and external environmental factors into an integrated whole. People are organized into groups; groups are organized into departments; departments are organized into divisions; divisions are organized into companies; companies are part of an industry; industries are part of an economy; and so forth. The organization is part of an environment, which it influences and in turn is influenced by. Systems concepts help management expose and to some extent reduce this complexity.

Diversification, growth, consolidation, merger, and the closer interrelationships between organizations and their environment have all contributed to the intricacy of business operations. Organizations must adapt internally by adjusting their information flows, organizational structures, policy patterns, and operating procedures to societal changes. Managerial adaptation requires the acquisition of new knowledge for use in modifying the existing structures and procedures.

An organization is a contrived (man-made) system which interacts dynamically with its environment (customers, competitors, labor unions, suppliers, governments, and many other agencies). It is a system of interrelated parts working in conjunction with each other to accomplish the goals of both the organization and its participants. All organizations receive inputs, transform these in some way, and return outputs to the environment. They have functional subsystems, variously named—procurement, finance, marketing, and production. Since organizations are man-made systems, they tend to be imperfect and involve a great deal of artistry in their design and operation.

It is difficult to identify a complete list of systems characteristics. Any list would be merely a first-order classification, and there would be many second- and third-order characteristics. Generally, however, the characteristics of organizational systems can be categorized as follows:

1. *Boundaries* define what is inside and outside the system. The subsystems are inside, and the external environment is outside. A closed system has rigid, impenetrable boundaries, whereas an open system has permeable boundaries between itself and a broader suprasystem. Boundaries are difficult to delineate in social systems (such as organizations) and are frequently artificial. Arbitrary, traditional boundaries found in many organizations tend more to emphasize the parts and components of the structure than the interrelationships and integration of activities.

2. *Parts or components* define the content of the system. They include:
   a. *Individual*—skills and personality belonging to organizational members.
   b. *Formal organization*—formal structural arrangement of people and functions.
   c. *Informal organization*—the interaction of individuals and informal groups.

3. *Structure* consists of functional, technical, and descriptive relationships among components in the system. Structure deals with interrelationships and interactions among the subsystems. It concerns the division of tasks into operating units and their resultant coordination. It provides for formalization of authority relationships, communications, and work flow. Time lags, amplifications, oscillations, nonlinearities, and distortions compound the determination of key component relationships. Structural components can be classified as:
   a. *Independent variables*, which explain, predict, and cause changes in dependent variables.

        b. Dependent variables, which are influenced by other variables.

        c. Parameters, which represent limiting constraints in descriptive equations, such as the intercept and slope of a straight line.

4. *Balance* refers to the equilibrium of a system:

        a. Stationary balance—the system returns to its previous position after a disturbance. Maintenance forces prevent disequilibrium by keeping the system from changing its direction.

        b. *Dynamic balance*—the system shifts to a new equilibrium position after a disturbance. An adaptable system studies its environment, predicts the future environment, and tries to make changes to remain viable over a time horizon.

5. *Feedback/communications* is the control and coordination mechanism that permits the decision maker to influence the balance of the system in a desirable manner. Feedback is the basis for regulation of a system. Control of the system is maintained through levels and rates. *Levels* (states) are the condition of the system at a given point in time; *rates* (flows) are the condition of the system over a fixed time interval. For example, quantities on a balance sheet are levels because they represent the financial condition at a point in time; quantities on an income statement are rates of flow during a period of time. The system reaction time is an important control feature. Systems are designed with tolerances for variations and changes.

6. *Decision makers* are individuals or groups that determine the goals and service objectives. Organizations tend to have multiple goals and purposes that are espoused by their leaders. The structure and functioning of organizations are the deliberate result of strategic choices made by decision makers.

Organizations are open, dynamic, socio-technical systems. They are in constant interaction with their environment. The systems approach provides a philosophical understanding of organizations, a generalized model for their design, a method for their analysis, and a logic for their management. There is no real alternative to the systems approach for analyzing complex organizations in a dynamic milieu. It meets conceptual, intellectual, philosophical, and practical needs.

MULTIVIEW SYSTEMS CONCEPT
OF AN ORGANIZATION

The model builder faces the dilemma that the more complicated and realistic his model is, the more unwieldy it becomes as a tool for analysis. Once the model builder had to restrict himself to simple models that could be solved by analytical techniques. Now, however, computerized quasi-analytical and heuristic search techniques have increased significantly the probability of finding a near optimum solution to more complex models.

Concepts are only abstractions of reality, but they can help the analyst present constructive explanations of observed behavior. The question is not which version of a model is right or wrong, but whether or not any version is truly explanatory. A conceptual model becomes useful when it assists in making order out of chaotic data. The postulates of any theoretical system must be tested experimentally before they are given operational status.

In viewing an organization, no single model is appropriate in depicting the multiplicity of relationships. Organizations can be studied on a continuum that runs from microscopic to macroscopic levels. Numerous models can be utilized to convey conceptual and functional relationships. A model is neither true nor false; the standard for comparing models is utility, i.e., adequate descriptions and/or successful prediction.

We shall use three models to provide different views of an organization. The three models are the *systemic environmental model,* the *systemic functional model,* and the *systemic operational model.* The models represent perspectives that move from the very broad to the specific, and from the long-term to the short-term time frame. The models assume a physical product is produced, but they are easily adaptable to the production of a service. Because of the great diversity of operations and the particular objectives of different organizations, each system must be unique or at least have some unique elements. Nevertheless, illustrative models can serve as a point of departure.

It is useful to classify the environments that impinge upon an organization. A threefold segmentation includes the micro, linking, and macro environments. The *micro environment* represents the organization itself and its internal affairs; the *linking environment* represents the interfaces the organization has with the macro (external) environment; and the *macro environment* represents the external environment of the organization. The macro environment consists of those factors (influences) that not only are outside the organization's control but determine in part how the organization performs.

The systemic environmental model (SEM) includes the three environments; the systemic functional model (SFM) emphasizes the linking and micro environments; and the systemic operational model (SOM) emphasizes the micro environment. The relationships of the three models (SEM, SFM, and SOM) to the three environments (macro, linking, and micro) are depicted in Figure 1. The following sections will delineate the scope of each conceptual model.

FIGURE 1
Multiview systems concept of an organization.

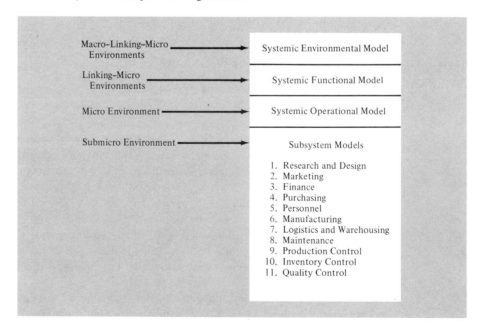

SYSTEMIC ENVIRONMENTAL MODEL

The systemic environmental model abstracts from organizational theories (classical, neoclassical, behavioral, and contingency) and contains elements of scientific management, human relations, small group theory, economics, and decision making (see Figure 2). In this model, each action has a reaction. A change in an input or relationship results in a reorientation of the entire system to some degree. The model does not depict the efficiency of transfer between different sectors, but it does emphasize the path of the flow. The model attempts to unite the micro, linking, and macro environments.

Micro Environment

The micro environment includes the organization and its internal affairs as shown in Figure 3. The interdependence of the formal organization with the informal organization is depicted by their overlap in the transformation section. The organization imports inputs, which it uses in the transformation operation to produce an output. In economic organizations, the value of the output must exceed the value of the inputs or the firm will go out of business.

The formal organization represents the planned arrangements of tasks or duties so as to accomplish its goals efficiently. The formal organization is impersonal and usually defined by job descriptions and organizational charts. The organizational chart gives a static picture of the overall configuration of an organization; it illustrates the division of labor along with vertical and horizontal differentiation. The formal organization is prescriptive; it indicates the way activities should be accomplished.

Under the concept of division of labor, job activities and job relations are determined by job descriptions and organizational charts. Having divided complex jobs into smaller jobs, it becomes imperative that all the operations be coordinated. This is the function of an information system. The information system provides the input to planning and control so that decision makers can coordinate activities to meet the organizational goals.

The informal organization is a product of the formal organization and is derived from the needs and requirements of organizational members. It is the natural groupings of people in work situations not prescribed by the formal structure. The informal organization is not planned formally but arises spontaneously from the activities and interactions of participants. People have needs and objectives that may or may not be congruent with organizational objectives. The informal organization is made up of groups of people with shared orientations. The groups provide support and security to their members. The formal organization usually neglects these needs or does not know how to cope with them.

An organization can be compared to an iceberg. The formal organization is similar to what is above the water level, while the informal organization is like the amorphous mass beneath the water level. Without the informal organization, it is unlikely that the formal organization could stay afloat. If every activity in an organization had to follow rigorous procedures and flow through the formal chain of command, very little would be accomplished, and the organization would choke on bureaucratic rigidity. The informal organization helps to hold the organization together and perform its functions.

Informal relationships are vital for the effective functioning of an organization. Frequently groups develop spontaneous and informal means for dealing with important activities which contribute to overall performance. Although the informal orga-

24

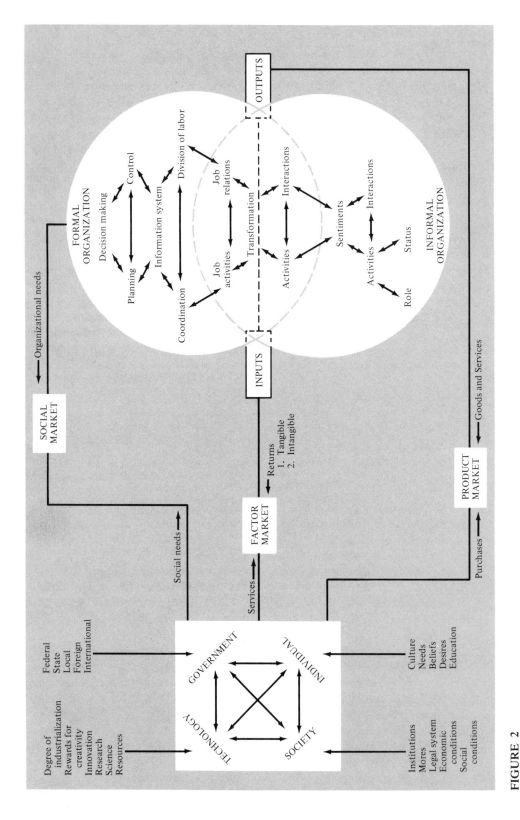

FIGURE 2
A systemic environmental analysis of the firm.

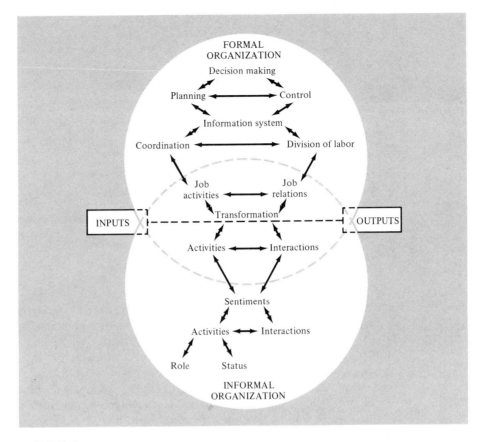

FIGURE 3
Micro environment.

nization can be adaptive and perform innovative functions not adequately met by the formal structure, it also can be counterproductive. Output and performance are influenced strongly by the norms, standards, and behavior of informal work groups.

When people interact due to their activities on the job, they tend to develop positive sentiments (feelings of friendship) towards each other. People who share a common activity are likely to see each other socially, presuming that people who do the same thing are somewhat similar to themselves. Hence, common activity leads to interaction, which in turn increases the strength of sentiments, typically positive ones. People who like each other tend to interact frequently and work well together on common activities. From their activities in the organization, people develop status and roles that may not be legitimated by the formal organization. Operating within the structure of the formal organization we find this "organizational shadow" that accommodates the human needs of its members.

Linking Environment

The linking environment impinges upon the organization at three points—where inputs are obtained from it (factor market); where output is sold to it (product market); and where the goals, objectives, and methods of the organization are sanctioned by it (social market). The factor and product markets are well defined by microeconomics, but the social market is much more vague (see Figure 4).

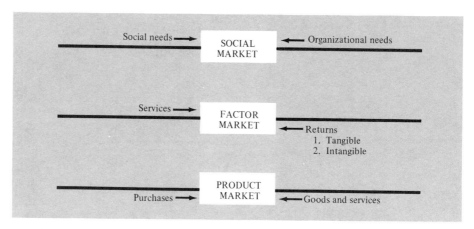

FIGURE 4
Linking environment.

The organization needs certain inputs to meet its goals and objectives. It purchases services and material inputs from the factor market. The output of the organization is sold in the product market, and for it the firm receives revenue. The product market's demand for an organization's outputs and the factor market's cost of inputs for supplying them are the basic elements of the micro economic theory of the firm. The determination of the best level and combination of inputs for the provision of a particular level of outputs is the economic production function problem.

Many social critics have noted the failure of business to behave in socially responsible ways. Society charters (gives life to) corporations through state governments and regulates their behavior through federal, state, and local governments. Society depends upon corporations for employment and income; it supports them by continuing to purchase their goods and services. Achievement of desired levels of social responsibility can add to the cost of production. These costs will ultimately be borne by society in the form of higher prices, higher taxes, lower returns to investors, or some combination thereof.

The social market is where the public puts constraints on the organization to meet its needs or protect itself. Examples of social constraints are laws requiring social security, workman's compensation, minimum wages, overtime pay, safe working conditions, retirement programs, and pollution control devices, as well as antitrust laws, tariffs, and federal, state, and local taxes. The social market is where society, through governments and institutions, sanctions the existence of an organization.

The linking environment represents the connecting systems between the organization and its external environment. Business areas that deal with the linking environment are finance, procurement, personnel, sales, legal, and so forth. Unfortunately, many firms have tended to ignore the social market and overemphasize the more economically oriented factor and product markets.

Macro Environment

The macro environment represents everything outside and beyond the control of the organization. It is difficult to characterize in any great generality. An organization that provides a product to and operates in a single political unit can define the exter-

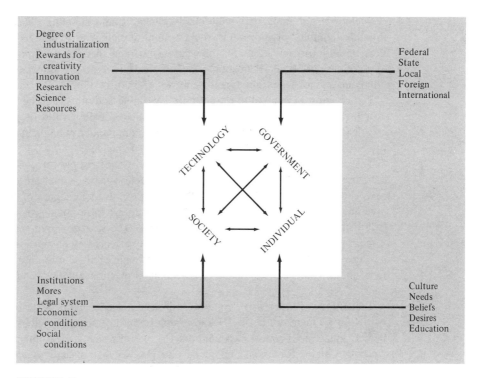

Degree of
  industrialization
Rewards for
  creativity
Innovation
Research
Science
Resources

Federal
State
Local
Foreign
International

TECHNOLOGY   GOVERNMENT

SOCIETY   INDIVIDUAL

Institutions
Mores
Legal system
Economic
  conditions
Social
  conditions

Culture
Needs
Beliefs
Desires
Education

FIGURE 5
Macro environment.

nal environment as that unit. One that operates in, and supplies an output to, numerous geopolitical units must define its macro environment more broadly. Generally, where a firm obtains its inputs and sells its outputs defines its external environment.

The macro environment can be considered a complex interacting mixture of the individual, society, government, and technology, all of which are not mutually exclusive (see Figure 5). It is important to realize that not all organizations have a macro environment of the same composition. As a simple example, a computer hardware firm may be subject to little governmental influence, while technology may be very important; an automobile manufacturer may experience little year-to-year technological change but a great deal of influence by government.

The individual, who is a product of his culture, has needs, beliefs, and desires through which he influences and is influenced by society, government, and technology. Society is a structure of man-made institutions that develops values and norms for acceptable behavior for its members. The existing economic, social, and political conditions modify society's institutions as well as its mores. Government, through statute law (trademarks, patents, antitrust, health, welfare, safety, and labor laws) and its economic purchasing power, has an influence that filters down to the individual level. Technology relates to the application of science to achieve human sustenance and comfort. Technology, through new products and processes, has a great influence on economic conditions. It alters and modifies the composition of the labor force, the design of organization structures, and social relationships. John K. Galbraith describes technology as a major factor directing our lives for the worse.[5]

_____

[5]John K. Galbraith, *The New Industrial State,* Boston: Houghton-Mifflin, 1967.

Society is not static; it is continually changing and adapting. There has been a growth in complex organizations in every field of endeavor. People depend more and more on large organizations for their sustenance and survival. Organizations such as corporations, hospitals, educational institutions, unions, trade associations, and governmental agencies are inextricably interwoven into the fabric of a society.

Participation in community programs, charitable activities, and heavy advertising are conventional organizational techniques used for dealing with the public or society. The role of organizations in a society will come under public scrutiny from time to time, and changes will be requested or even demanded.

The decisions of government can affect the lives of people for generations. Societal pressure groups try to direct government action in areas that are to their advantage. Traditionally, organizations attempt to increase their degree of influence over government via lobbying and financial contributions to political parties in an effort to influence favorable legislation or to prevent excessive governmental surveillance of their activities. Organizations can be seriously affected by changes in policies such as wage and price controls, tax policies, investment credits, foreign exchange rates, trade quotas, currency devluations, consumer protection policies, and judicial decisions.

Technology is a pervasive force in industrial societies, with widespread influence over many of man's activities. A substantial portion of new technology can be attributed to great increases in expenditures for research and development. Technology can create major economic and social changes which impact lives and institutions. Consider such advances as nuclear energy, space exploration, genetics, surgical techniques (transplants), computers, oceanography, transportation, communications (earth satellites), medicine, and electronics in their effect on society. Rapidly advancing technology tends to tax man's organizational and administrative skills while putting emphasis on specialization. Governments expend large amounts of money on research and development for military, social, and scientific purposes.

The interaction of society, government, technology, and the individual provides the structure that defines the macro environment of most organizations. It is important that an organization identify its macro environment, for it has tremendous influence on intermediate and long range planning. For example, changes in the macro environment of the tobacco industry via government influence have modified their long range objectives considerably. As a consequence, these firms have diversified.

The influence of the macro environment through the social market can have a more pronounced effect than through the factor and product markets. An organization will typically acquire (scout) macroenvironmental information (competition, political factors, the economy, the state of technology, labor activities, and so on) in order to reduce the uncertainty of its operation. Through forecasting and scanning, an organization determines changes in its macro environment. Continued existence of an organization is frequently predicated on its ability to forecast and scan environmental changes and its flexibility in adapting to them.

Different environments impose different demands and provide different constraints, threats, and opportunities. Scanning links the organization to its external environment. In scanning, the cost of acquiring information should not exceed the benefits to be derived from it. Scanning can be performed by surveillance or search. *Surveillance* refers to a general watch (monitoring) over an interest; *search* aims at finding a particular piece of information for solving a problem through investigation or research. Scanning increases awareness of and familiarity with an environment.

An organization's involvement in scanning will be influenced by the intensity, degree, and frequency of environmental change.

Micro-Linking-Macro Factors

The key factors of the systemic environmental model are balance and reciprocity. *Balance* refers to the ability of the system to absorb shocks and survive. It deals with the preservation of the character of the organization in the face of changes in the environment. The system can be shocked by the process of decay (for example, if products become technologically obsolete) or by a constriction of flow to and from the markets (caused by an imbalance in the system). It is imperative that the system be able to take various shocks from both inside and outside the organization and still return to a state of balance. Some examples of shocks are merger (takeover) attempts, government bans on the sale of products, strikes, acts of God, failure of a new product to be accepted, and so forth.

Reciprocity can be defined as a mode in which different interests are satisfied. It is the "live and let live" pattern of interacting influences. Complementing, supplementing, and conflicting forces allow the organization to continue its existence because they benefit directly or indirectly from it. The relationships are symbiotic in that two or more dissimilar groups receive mutual benefit. An organization must provide benefits to its owners, creditors, suppliers, and employees and to the public, or its existence will be in jeopardy.

It is clear that adaptation to change over time is necessary to maintain balance and reciprocity. Without balance and reciprocity the organization could not survive long.

SYSTEMIC FUNCTIONAL MODEL

The systemic functional model emphasizes to a greater degree the linking and micro environments. Figures 6 and 7 indicate the structure of the systemic functional model. The perspective of this model is much narrower than that of the systemic environmental model. The concern is for the functions that must be performed by the organization in getting a product to market.

The systemic functional model can be subdivided into five interdependent categories—policy decisions, product decisions, process decisions, plant decisions, and operations decisions.[6] These categories give answers to questions of why make it, what to make, how to make it, where to make it, and when to make it:

Why	Policy decisions
What	Product decisions
How	Process decisions
Where	Plant decisions
When	Operations decisions

These broad decision levels must be addressed, formally or informally, by every organization.

---

[6]The structure and logic of this book are based on the systemic functional model. Policy decisions, product decisions, process decisions, plant decisions, and operations decisions are its major sections.

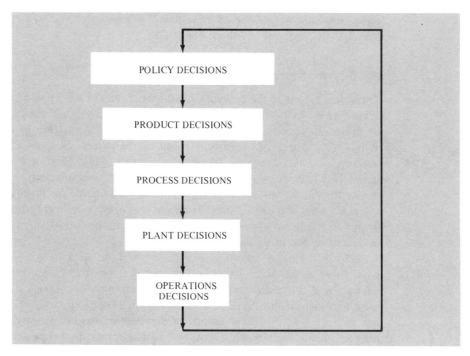

FIGURE 6
Systemic functional model.

Policy Decisions

These begin with the statement of the broad long range objectives of the organization. (Typical examples are growth, market share, sales maximization, market leadership, social responsibility, customer satisfaction, product leadership, survival, and return on investment.) These broad objectives are modified to account for internal and external constraints. These constraints are limiting factors such as technology, financial resources, sources of capital, market conditions, size of the firm, competitor actions, strengths and weaknesses of the existing organization, and so forth. The redefinition of broad long range objectives to a near time frame in line with the capabilities of the organization results in strategies. Then specific tactics or plans are developed to realize the strategies. The tactics are inputs to market analysis, which helps to determine what goods or services the public wants that are within the organization's capabilities.

Product Decisions

Product decisions determine the goods and services an organization will provide to society. Product decisions begin with general specifications from market analysis, which indicate customer requirements. From the general specifications, technical specifications are written, which define the product in much greater detail. Technical specifications are the structure for the functional design, which includes both form and function of the product. The next step is production design, or the effort to

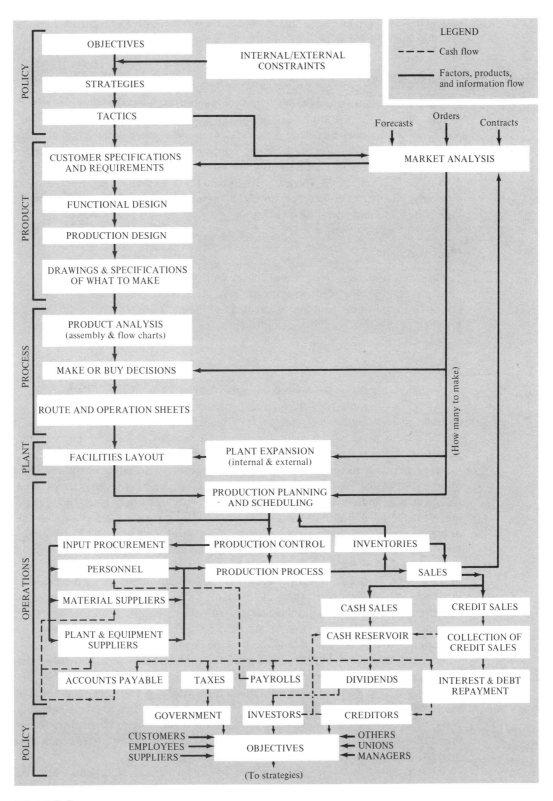

FIGURE 7
A systemic functional analysis of a firm.

design the final product so it can be produced economically. The final release of drawings and specifications of what to make consummates product decisions.

Process Decisions

Process decisions determine how best to produce the product. They begin with product analysis, which utilizes assembly and flow charts for analyzing each component of the product in detail. The decision to subcontract or to build in-house (make or buy) is made. Process decisions, which include a definition of the processes as well as the steps and procedures for each process, are made for all in-house work. Operation sheets are made which specify in detail how to perform each operation of a process. Finally, route sheets are developed to plan the physical flow of the product through the different operating departments.

Plant Decisions

Plant decisions begin with a decision to utilize unused capacity, expand existing plant, or build a new plant to accommodate the product. After this decision, the layout of the physical facilities is decided, including work station design and the selection of materials handling equipment.

Operations Decisions

Operations decisions are concerned with when and how many units to provide. They begin with production planning and scheduling decisions pertaining to the acquisition of men, materials, plant, and equipment. Demand forecasts are translated into production plans, which determine material, personnel, and capital requirements. Activation and organization are achieved during this phase.

Production control concerns itself with the short term scheduling of the resources into the production process. The production process generates inventories of products, which in turn are depleted by sales. Sales, as well as stock issues and borrowing, generate an inflow into the cash reservoir. Many parties have claims on this reservoir—employees, investors, creditors, government, and so forth. These groups have legitimate interests in the activity of any organization.

The board of directors determines the objectives and general policies of an organization. The president and principal officers are usually members of the board of directors. Shareholders with voting interest elect the board of directors and accept or reject proposed amendments to the charter and bylaws.

Management is the group that holds prime responsibility for carrying out the organization's role in society. It sets the priorities and dispenses the rewards. Stockholders and creditors (bond holders) supply the capital. Employees can strike, customers can shift their buying habits, governments can pass restrictive legislation, but management must keep the organization a going concern. If customers don't buy the product, businesses won't supply needed materials, government regulations are too rigid, or financial capital is denied by creditor or equity interests, the organization may cease to exist. For the organization to survive, management must balance the interests of the relevant groups with its role in society.

Objectives are met when group claims are balanced and expectations fulfilled. Any group able to modify the "cash reservoir" can influence the objectives of the organization. A general idea of the groups, people, or parties who have an influence on the objectives of the organization can be ascertained from the inflows and outflows from the "cash reservoir." At this point, the systemic functional model reflects a return to the objectives of policy decisions. Thus, the model recycles and tends to be regenerative.

SYSTEMIC OPERATIONAL MODEL

This model places its emphasis on the micro environment (the firm itself) and is short term in its perspective (see Figure 8). It assumes that the plant and major personnel are already in existence. The optimum operation and control of the system is the paramount consideration. The major decision areas are forecasting, production planning and scheduling, procurement, plant engineering, and control (production control, inventory control, and quality control). The primary emphasis is economic-technical, to achieve efficiency of output within a given structure and technology.

The system operates from forecasts and firm orders which are transmitted to the "brain center," aggregate planning and scheduling. This central decision area determines what must be done to meet the future demand. It establishes the type and mix of inputs and schedules them for the production process. Procurement obtains the desired mix of human and nonhuman inputs. Production uses and transforms the inputs into the output product. Plant engineering maintains, modifies, and installs new plant and equipment. The sales or marketing function provides the successful interaction of the consumer with the output product. The control areas relate to quantity, quality, and cost. Inventory control maintains quantity, and quality control maintains product standards. Cost control is exercised by planning and scheduling.

A close examination of the systemic operational model reveals that many long run decisions are omitted. It does not give adequate attention to the location of the system, physical facility layout, job design, work measurement, selection of equipment and processes, and so forth. The advantages of a short term model are manifested in many short term decisions that must be made but do not require a larger time perspective (should a marginal producer be allowed a line of credit in a slack production period?).

CONCLUSION

This chapter offers a unifying conceptual approach and operational philosophy to understanding systems theory as it applies to modern organizations. Several different models have been developed to define and relate substrata of organizational coexistence, since there are many levels of decision making required in an organization. The conceptual models begin with the macro environmental influences and end with the micro operations occurring within the organization. This modular telescopic treatment is necessary because no single model can appropriately depict the multiplicity of relationships in an organization. The models synthesize environmental forces, organizational functions, economic influences, and behavior into a framework for managerial decision making.

The models developed (systemic environmental model, systemic functional model, and systemic operational model) have been used to emphasize the inadequacy of any single model for all occasions. Different conditions and situations require an adaptive view that can only be obtained from different perspectives. The systems

34

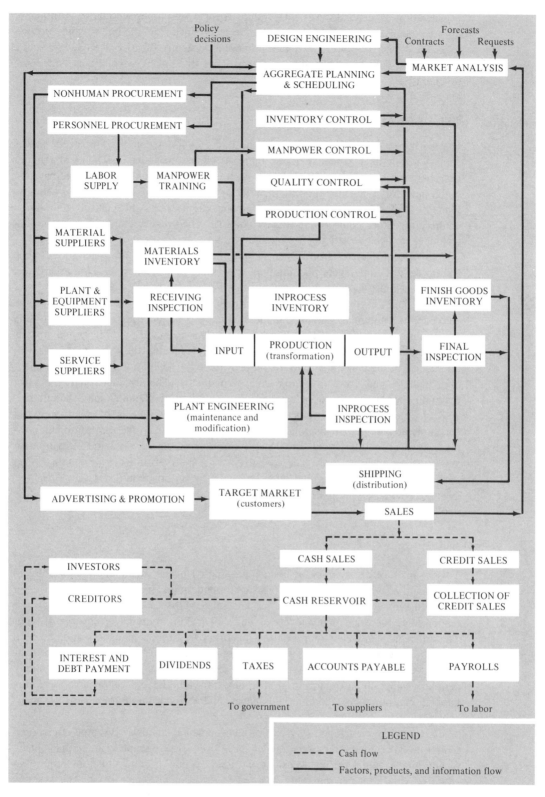

FIGURE 8
Systemic operational analysis of a firm.

approach highlights the objectives of the total system rather than separate departments. This more realistic approach reduces suboptimization (the condition where subsystem or department optimization is not optimum for the total system). Noncongruency of goals leads to suboptimization.

Systems theory is a way of thinking. The models developed herein are not a blueprint for design, but rather a framework for thinking about the elements that go into an organization and how those elements are tied together. They are not "how-to" models, but instead can be used for comparative purposes. They can be used diagnostically to consider where an organization is and why it behaves the way it does. Additionally, they can be used prescriptively to intervene, adjust, or change subsystems that are not performing as they should.

Systems theory can be helpful in designing a new system or redesigning an old system. It can also be helpful in training someone in the use of a system. It can aid in the prediction of behavior when alternatives are available. Systems are much easier to sell to other people or customers than random ideas or unstructured approaches.

There are certain things systems theory cannot do. It cannot improve managerial judgment or identify objectives of the manager or his organization; nor can it predict future conditions and consequences of decisions. It does not indicate what business to pursue, whether to diversify or consolidate, how to divisionalize, or whether to centralize or decentralize operations.

Structuring an organization with the systems concept does not eliminate the need for management functions; rather, there is a change in emphasis. All activities revolve around the system with its objectives, and the functions are executed only to serve this end. Thus the organization is viewed as a set of flows of information, men, materials, and behavior. The systems approach does not replace anything that exists; it merely supplements and extends into additional dimensions.

QUESTIONS

1. What are the general characteristics of organizational systems?
2. In relation to boundaries, what is the difference between an open and a closed system?
3. Name the three models used in the text to provide different views of an organization.
4. What are the three environments that impinge on an organization? How are the environments related to the models in the previous question?
5. Name the three markets that make up the linking environment.
6. Define the terms balance and reciprocity.
7. What are the five interdependent categories of the systemic functional model (SFM)? What questions do they answer?
8. Why are models only abstractions of reality?
9. What purposes do models serve?
10. Using the production function (inputs-transformation-output), describe any system in which you are involved.
11. Does the informal organization serve a useful purpose? If so, then how?
12. What major elements compose the macro environment of most organizations?

CASE 1: EAST IS EAST, AND WEST IS WEST

Sooner Chevrolet, an established automobile dealership, remains number one in sales in the Oklahoma City metropolitan area despite a substantial reduction in the number of vehicles sold over the last several quarters. Sooner always has been successful financially, but is preparing for a slow season, temporarily bracing itself until general economic recovery is fully underway and international commerce resolves its disparities. With the financial collapse of other dealerships on the way, Sooner is reckoning with its own delicately balanced solvency. The firm's management is hoping to ride out the world-wide recession and current trade disputes on the elements of its prior successes—large inventory selections, low prices through volume selling, dependable service, extensive advertising, and a carefully projected image of the "neighborly dealership" with the distinctly western flair.

Heretofore, management always had felt rather comfortably situated in a "boom" location, separated from the more devastated economic environments of other regional areas. They were able to rest, assured of low unemployment rates, in a market sector of consumers better able to finance the newcar sticker prices and still fairly willing to replace their automobiles every three to four years. Here the energy crisis has been viewed as a mixed blessing—negatively impacting the auto industry as a whole but stimulating the wealth and development of the geographical region. Although the local GM Chevrolet plant has scheduled temporary, non-paid employee furloughs in the past, Sooner management has attributed this to national demand factors. This attribution is indicative of management's view that the local operation is insulated from the shrinking national market for all practical purposes.

No doubt Sooner management recognizes that it shares some of the auto industry's woes, but they receive solace in that the firm has been spared the most serious repercussions and the severe plunges in total sales experienced elsewhere. The recurring GM rebates and the low-rate financing arranged through GMAC are outweighing the modest effects of competitors' enticement plans. Although the corporate-backed plans are not eliminating the slump altogether, they offer quick recovery of sales usually lost from interest- and price-sensitive customers.

However, what management views as the greatest problem is not any of the general economic ones which threaten the solvency of rival dealerships—inflated sticker prices, unemployed consumers, and extremely high financing charges—but the unrestrained competition from foreign auto-makers. They feel a large part of their sales is lost to foreign car purchases. Sooner is certain that it needs only to hang on long enough for a Western nation solidarity movement to force the competition in the East to impose export restrictions or to dismantle trade barriers. Sooner's concerns bypass the intermediate national pressures and look to factors external to the American economic situation. Management believes that an allied blitz by Western powers could prevail over the commercial practices of the East by economic means. Hard-hitting negotiations to change international trade practices are seen as the most effective counterpoint to a stronger competitor's unrestrained position. This strategy is left to the political dignitaries and obviously is out of Sooner's domain.

1. Using a systems approach, describe the Sooner operating environment. Specifically include the following factors: labor, supply, financial, competitive, governmental, societal, monetary, and technological.
2. Analyze Sooner's economic and marketing positions.
3. Comment on Sooner's broad view of its environment.

CASE 2: TRAJECTORY UNKNOWN

Quick Shock Electronics manufactures electronic products in the low to medium price range, many with several optional features. The firm is small ($60 million in annual sales), particularly by comparison with its gigantic competitors. QSE is distinguished among small electronics firms solely because it is able to exist at all in an intensely competitive and dynamic industry. The relatively small annual profit is seldom paid out in dividends. QSE stock has a high price/earnings ratio, but speculative investors do buy on the expectation that the firm will experience growth. Its rather mild success thus far depends on innovative changes to existing products of other firms and filling gaps the larger firms leave in their product lines. QSE uses an applications oriented strategy (Chapter 7)—choosing to develop product modifications to serve a particular, specialized, or limited market.

There are frictions within the firm, typically created by rival subsystems, each supporting its own operating strategy and competing for its share of the small capital reserve. Most of the subsystems take repeated stances and hold steadfastly to them. The polarization of positions is never as obvious as at the time the capital budget is prepared. Marketing consistently requests that the firm expand the product line and begin funding of the ad campaigns early in product development so that promotion can begin prior to product release. Production constantly deals with capacity constraints and therefore urges the firm to authorize funding for installation of productivity enhancing equipment. Research and development seek to become more technologically responsive to the consumer, agreeing with marketing on the importance of innovation but disagreeing that responsiveness can come in the form of perceived innovation.

Top management consists mostly of engineers who have been promoted over the last few years. At management meetings, the officers of the firm who do not hold the engineers' philosophy and approach show frustration at the engineers' overall directions. This opposing faction opposes what it holds to be overdesign and unnecessary changes in product design.

A situation is developing which may intensify the conflicting opinions. One R & D expert, an engineer by trade, has an idea for what he believes to be a revolutionary new product. The product would be QSE's first attempt at designing, producing, and marketing an item which is completely distinct from any competitor products.

The initial reactions to the proposed product are not unexpected. Marketing wants to use the product to open new markets. Production now is even more insistent on its need for capital expenditures. Operations emphasizes its past difficulties in adjusting to design variations, and therefore suggests capacity expansion by additional lines, improved in-line equipment, or a move to flexible manufacturing. Finance believes the capital requirements for in-house production will stretch the company's debt limit, but a small amount of funds could be acquired. Accounting is eager to analyze the depreciation benefits and the tax credit possibilities if the project receives the go-ahead. So far most of what is being said is unsubstantiated, but certainly has sparked profound speculation.

1. What information does each subsystem require to analyze its position?
2. Describe how a change in one operating department could affect another. Include competitive issues as well as areas of agreement and mutual convenience.
3. How would the present environment differ from the future if the project were undertaken?

SELECTED BIBLIOGRAPHY

Ackoff, R. L. "Towards a System of System Concepts," *Management Science,* Vol. 17, No. 11, July 1971, pp. 661–667.

Boulding, K. E. "General Systems Theory—The Skeleton of Science," *Management Science,* Vol. 2, April 1956, pp. 197–208.

Churchman, C. W. *The Systems Approach,* New York: Delacorte, 1968.

Forrester, J. W. *Principles of Systems,* Cambridge, MA: Wright-Allen, 1970.

Galbraith, J. K. *The New Industrial State,* Boston: Houghton-Mifflin, 1967.

Hare, V. C., Jr. *Systems Analysis: A Diagnostic Approach,* New York: Harcourt, Brace and World, 1967.

Johnson, R. A. et al. "Systems Theory and Management," *Management Science,* Vol. 10, No. 2, January 1964, pp. 367–384.

————. *The Theory and Management of Systems,* New York: McGraw-Hill, 1973.

Litterer, J. A. *Organizations: Systems, Control, and Adaptation,* New York: Wiley, 1969.

Schoderbek, P. P. et al. *Management Systems: Conceptual Considerations,* Dallas: Business Publications, 1975.

Tersine, R. J. "Production and Operations: A Systems Construct," *Production and Inventory Management,* Vol. 18, No. 4, 1977, pp. 45–53.

————. "Systems Theory in Modern Organizations," *Managerial Planning,* November/December 1973, pp. 32–40.

3
Decision Theory

ASPECTS OF DECISION MAKING

Setting Objectives
The Value Criterion
Planning Horizons
Sequential/Interrelated Decision Making
Dynamic Decision Making
Programmed/Nonprogrammed Decision Making
Cost of Decision Making

DECISION THEORY STRUCTURE

Normative Decision Theory
Decision Making Under Certainty
Decision Making Under Conflict
The Two-Person Zero-Sum Game
The Nonzero-Sum Game
Decision Making Under Risk
Value of Perfect Information
Decision Trees
Decision Making Under Uncertainty
Subjective Probabilities
Principle of Insufficient Reason
Maximin Criterion
Minimax Regret
Coefficient of Optimality
Maximax Criterion

Descriptive Decision Theory
Individual Decision Making
Group Decision Making
Realistic Assessments

MODELS

Model Classifications
The Modeling Process
Model Validity
Overview of Models

CONCLUSION

QUESTIONS

PROBLEMS

CASES

APPENDIX A: MODEL CLASSIFICATIONS

SELECTED BIBLIOGRAPHY

Decision theory studies the tactics and strategies to achieve objectives. It addresses the issue of how men, machines, money, methods, and materials are to be combined, utilized, or expended to achieve a larger (higher) purpose. Technically, it generally involves the use of such analytical tools as models, production functions, incremental analysis, optimization techniques, utility analysis, statistics, and sensitivity analysis. However, decision theory also includes human and behavioral dimensions that frequently defy quantification. Decision theory enters both the quantitative and behavioral domains. It applies to all types of decision situations, but we are concerned primarily with organizational decision theory.

Decision making is at the center of all organizational activities. Managers make decisions about their systems which will achieve their objectives and efficiently use human and material resources. Not only do they make decisions themselves, but they see that effective decisions are made throughout the organization by others. Because of the emphasis in organizations on decision making as a hierarchical right, explorations of the behavioral aspects of the decision process did not occur until the last half of the twentieth century. Even today, there is no unified agreed-upon structure for decision theory. The literature abounds with limited and partial theories that tend to ignore the psychological and sociological characteristics of individuals or the environment in which they live.

The process of management is fundamentally a process of decision making. The functions of management (planning, organizing, and controlling) involve the process of evaluating, selecting, and initiating courses of action. Ansoff classified organizational decisions into three categories:[1]

1. *Strategic decisions* are primarily concerned with external rather than internal problems of the firm.
2. *Administrative decisions* are concerned with structuring the firm's resources to create maximum performance potential.
3. *Operating decisions* are primarily concerned with maximizing the profitability of current operations.

Decision making is vital to the functions making up the management process. The manager makes decisions in establishing objectives; he makes planning decisions, organizing decisions, and controlling decisions. In this sense, modern decision theory is a logical extension of the management process school.

One acting in the capacity of a manager or executive must make choices among various plans and strategies. These choices are made with varying degrees of information. Decision theory gives structure to the different conditions under which decisions are made. The decision making process used by management is becoming more organized and systematic than the intuitive process of the past.

Dahl and Lindblom suggested four broad influencing factors on the decision making processes in organizations:[2]

1. *Hierarchical.* Leaders are influenced by the structure of the hierarchy itself.
2. *Democratic.* Leaders are influenced by nonleaders through such devices as nominations and elections.
2. *Bargaining.* Leaders are to some degree independent of each other and exercise reciprocal controls over each other (labor vs. management).
4. *Pricing system.* Leaders are influenced by the marketplace.

---

[1]H. Igor Ansoff. *Corporate Strategy,* New York: McGraw-Hill, 1965, pp. 5–6.
[2]R. A. Dahl and C. E. Lindblom. *Politics, Economics, and Welfare,* New York: Harper and Row, 1953.

Each decision begins with an awareness that a problem or opportunity exists and continues through the selection of a response. No conscious human act is ever initiated until someone becomes aware that a condition may warrant attention. Thus, all decision making activities are preceded by an awareness episode. Awareness can be related to three temporal modes: it may be anticipatory, concurrent, or reactive. Awareness can be in anticipation of events, while an event is in progress, or significantly after the fact. The *anticipatory stance* is a conscious looking ahead in an effort to anticipate developments before they occur. It is futuristic and involves forecasts or predictions. Particular attention may be given to likely future actions of employees, competitors, customers, suppliers, distributors, legislators, or other significant parties. The *concurrent stance* occurs while events are occurring. The desire is to know about events as soon as they appear. Many control systems in use today fall within this category. The *reactive stance* is a response only after the event has occurred. It reflects a significant delay before awareness takes place. All three awareness stances are common in organizations and influence the quality of decision making.

Basically, a decision must be made when an organization faces a problem, when it is dissatisfied with existing conditions, or when it is given a choice. A considerable amount of managerial activity may be carried on by people other than the decision maker. Staff people and others in the line organization may discover problems, define them, and prepare the alternatives for decision. A manager's task is not only to solve problems, but also to identify and define problems to be solved. The actual decision is only the conclusion of a process. The process in a broad sense includes the activities of (1) discovering and defining things to decide, (2) analyzing the problem, (3) developing alternatives, (4) evaluating alternatives, and (5) implementing the best alternative.

ASPECTS OF ORGANIZATIONAL DECISION MAKING

Organizational decision making has a number of distinguishing features. Some of these are the setting of objectives, value criterion, planning horizons, sequential/interrelated decision making, dynamic decision making, programmed/nonprogrammed decision making, and the cost of decision making. These features will be outlined and discussed in greater detail in the following sections.

SETTING OBJECTIVES

The establishment of the broad organizational objectives of the firm is the basic requirement for all subsequent decisions. From these objectives, strategies and tactics can be set to provide the framework for decision making at lower managerial levels. No logical analysis can proceed to any extent without precise, explicit statements of purpose. All strategies entail certain consequences which require for their assessment a system of values. The values are an image of the objectives and are derived from them. All analyses are based upon some set of objectives, and it is desirable to define them clearly.

Even after organizational goals are set, other problems still exist, such as:

1. *Multiple objectives.* Decision making is complicated by the existence of many diverse objectives. A number of objectives may be difficult to characterize quantitatively. These goals can reflect subjective values rather than objective values. Typical objectives involve growth, diversification, industry position,

profit maximization, sales maximization, social responsibility, personnel development, employee attitudes, etc.

2. *Conflicting objectives.* Any comprehensive list of organizational objectives
will have areas of conflict. Social responsibilities such as pollution control may
adversely affect profit margins. Product diversification may stultify the return
on investment during the introductory period.

3. *Hierarchy of objectives.* Objectives of organizational units must be consistent
with those of higher organizational units. This means there are objectives
within objectives. If the cascade of organizational objectives is inconsistent,
suboptimization results.

THE VALUE CRITERION

Identifying the value criteria for evaluating various courses of action is a vital part
of the decision process. A manager may seek a satisfactory or the best possible
solution. The value system is implied in the objectives of the organization. An optimum decision requires that the objective or its surrogate be expressed as a value
function, that is, a gain or loss that can be maximized or minimized. If the objective
is profit, then the value function is to be maximized. If the objective is expressed in
terms of cost, then the value function is to be minimized.

When several objectives are apparent, they complicate the value function. If the
objectives are conflicting, the major objectives can determine the value function and
other objectives can be established as constraints. The decision maker optimizes the
value function subject to the various constraints. When multiple objectives exist, the
solution may be obtained by goal programming or some other priority-establishing
technique.

One of the most difficult problems in the decision process is the transformation of
objectives into value criteria for evaluating alternatives. Decision makers may not
define objectives clearly for various reasons. For decision making at lower levels in
the organization, the broad objectives may not have much meaning, so that other
more meaningful subobjectives or surrogates must be developed.

PLANNING HORIZONS

Decision making at various levels of management is concerned with various degrees of futurity. Every decision deals with the future, whether it is the next instant
or several time periods removed. Top management decisions involve longer time
periods than do lower level management decisions. Planning horizons denote how
far ahead in the future the decision maker is thinking and planning. There are usually
differences among decisions that are made on a one-month, one-year, five-year, or
ten-year span of time. A period of time must be specified in determining costs and
benefits with different alternatives. Of course, the shorter the time horizon, the more
valid are past operating data, and thus the more accurate and precise the decisions
tend to be. The longer the planning horizon, the higher the uncertainty, and the more
suspect the decisions.

SEQUENTIAL/INTERRELATED DECISION MAKING

Sequential decision making is the process of successively solving interrelated subproblems composing a large complex problem. Because many managerial problems
are extremely complex, organizations resort to specialization of labor by breaking the

problem into many subproblems. Thus, the problem of production is broken down into separate departments: procurement, scheduling, operations, quality control, shipping and so forth. There are hierarchies of decisions ranging from objectives to strategies to tactics. The decisions at the top levels filter down into a myriad of other decisions on the operations level. It is not uncommon for a major decision to involve hundreds of minor decisions before it is accomplished.

DYNAMIC DECISION MAKING

Dynamic decision making emphasizes that management's decisions are not usually one-time events, but are successive over a time frame. Future management decisions are to some degree influenced by past decisions. As additional information and observations are obtained, the decision process can be improved. Changes and refinements are more likely as the data base increases over time.

The past is where the problem is identified and diagnosed. The present is where the alternatives are formulated and a choice made regarding the plan of action. The future is where the decision will be implemented and an evaluation made regarding its outcome. Thus, decision making is dynamic, since it involves multiple time periods.

PROGRAMMED/NONPROGRAMMED DECISION MAKING

Programmed decisions are those that are repetitive or routine. Organizations usually establish definite procedures for making them. In contrast, the nonprogrammed decisions are unstructured and novel; there is no set pattern for handling them. They are custom-tailored to the given situation. Higher levels of management are associated with the unstructured, nonprogrammed decision.

At the broad policy level, decision making relies on techniques and methods that are fairly unsophisticated. The critical issues at this level can often be identified more effectively by a perceptive manager than by a complex computer model. Managers tend to use judgment, experience, intuition, rules of thumb, or specialized models for nonprogrammed decisions. At the more detailed operating level, decision making is based on structured relationships, which are more amenable to quantitative analysis.

COST OF DECISION MAKING

Decision making has a cost, particularly for creating and choosing among alternatives. At increased cost, additional information reduces uncertainty and results in more predictability. Management must determine if the reduced uncertainty is worth the cost of the search. When the costs of wrong decisions are high and long-lasting, the decision deserves serious consideration. Decisions that have significant economic, technological, social, or environmental implications deserve more consideration than those that do not.

In some cases, even with complete information, the cost of solving a problem is greater than the benefits derived from having it solved. For example, many older automobiles burn too much oil. The cost of solving this problem—paying for a valve job and new piston rings—is more of a nuisance to many owners than simply adding a quart of oil approximately every 1,000 miles for the remainder of the useful life of the vehicle. There is a point of diminishing returns, beyond which improvement in the solution is not worth the cost of achieving it.

DECISION THEORY STRUCTURE

One of the primary functions of management is to make decisions that determine the future course of action for the organization over the short and long term. The two general types of broad decision models now in use are *normative* and *descriptive*. The normative framework describes the classical situation where a decision maker faces a known set of alternatives and selects a course of action by a rational selection process. The descriptive framework incorporates adaptive or learning features, and the act of choice spans many dimensions of behavior, rational as well as nonrational.

While there is not any single procedure to follow in arriving at a decision, there are several common elements in the decision process. Six elements common to all decisions are as follows:

1. *The decision maker* is the individual or group making a choice from the available strategies.
2. *Goals or ends to be served* are objectives the decision maker seeks to obtain by his actions.
3. *The preference or value system* comprises the criteria (measure of effectiveness) that the decision maker uses in making his choice. It could include maximization of income or utility and minimization of cost.
4. *Strategies of the decision maker* are the different alternative courses of action from which he can choose. Strategies are based on resources and variables under the control of the decision maker.
5. *States of nature* are possible events not under the control of the decision maker. They are aspects of the uncontrollable environment affecting the choice of strategy.
6. *The outcome* represents the resultant of a given strategy and a given state of nature. When the outcome is expressed in benefit terms, it is called a payoff.

NORMATIVE DECISION THEORY

Normative decision theory is based on rationality. The normative models show how a consistent decision maker should act to be successful. Decision procedures are followed that will optimize something, usually output, income, revenue, costs, utility, etc. The ideal rational person makes a choice on the basis of:

1. a known set of relevant alternatives with corresponding outcomes;
2. an established rule or set of relations that produces a preference ordering of the alternatives;
3. the optimization of something such as money, goods, or some form of utility.

Rationality can be defined as the best selection of means to achieve an objective that is acceptable to the value system of the decision maker. Thus, what is rational depends upon the decision maker. There is no universal standard for judging rationality. It depends on the decision maker's frame of reference, and of course, frames of reference vary among individuals and organizations. What is rational for one individual or group may be irrational for another.

A decision matrix is a convenient way to present the components of a decision. A typical decision matrix is illustrated in Figure 1. The major features of a typical decision structure are the strategies of the decision maker, the states of nature, and

Strategies	States of nature				
	N_1	N_2	• • •	N_j
S_1	O_{11}	O_{12}	• • •	O_{1j}
S_2	O_{21}	O_{22}	• • •	O_{2j}
•	•	•		•
•	•	•		•
•	•	•		•
S_i	O_{i1}	O_{i2}	• • •	O_{ij}

FIGURE 1
A decision matrix.

the outcomes.[3] In a decision matrix, the rows represent strategies available to the decision maker, the columns represent states of nature or conditions that can occur, and entries in the matrix represent the outcomes of the decision. An outcome O_{ij} is a function of the selected strategy S_i and the state of nature N_j.

In mathematical terms, outcomes are called dependent variables, while the strategies (controllable) and states of nature (uncontrollable) are called independent variables. The dependence can be written mathematically as

$$O_{ij} = f(S_i N_j).$$

Strategies (courses of action) are the options available to a decision maker which are based on resources under his control. They are assumed to be mutually exclusive (no two strategies can be in effect at the same time) and collectively exhaustive (all possible strategies are included in the analysis). *States of nature* are variables over which the decision maker has little or no control. They include environmental variables external to the decision such as political actions, climatic conditions, technological innovations, the state of the economy, social conditions, and so forth. They also are assumed to be mutually exclusive and collectively exhaustive. An *outcome* is what occurs when a particular strategy is selected and a particular state of nature occurs. Outcomes are often difficult to predict accurately. They are obtained from estimates, guesses, observations, experimentations, theories, or history. In any decision problem the ingenuity and perceptiveness of the decision maker are required to identify the strategies, the states of nature, and their resultant outcomes.

The dominance principle can be used to eliminate strategies that are not as desirable as others. Any strategy completely dominated by another strategy should be eliminated. A strategy is dominated if there exists another strategy that has at least as desirable an outcome for each state of nature. The dominance principle will seldom single out the best strategy, but it can simplify the selection process by reducing the number of strategies to consider.

The matrix formulation of a decision problem permits recognition and identifica-

---

[3]The decision theorist uses the word ''strategies'' for alternative actions at any level of complexity and organizational involvement. Unfortunately, the word also refers to broad-level policies made by top management, and confusion can result.

FIGURE 2
Rational decision theory continuum.

tion of four distinct kinds of decision situations. They are decision making under certainty, under conflict, under risk, and under uncertainty. The classification is based on what the decision maker knows about the occurrence of the various states of nature. Figure 2 illustrates a rational decision theory continuum.

Decision Making Under Certainty

Decision making under certainty is the simplest kind. The outcome resulting from the selection of a particular strategy is known. There is just one state of nature for each strategy. Prediction is involved, but is assumed to be perfect. There is complete and accurate knowledge of the consequences of each choice. Certainty also implies that relevant parameters such as cost, capacity, and demand have known values. The decision maker simply evaluates the outcome of each strategy and selects the one that best meets his objective.

True certainty is a state or decision situation that seldom exists. The probability that a certain state of nature exists is assumed to be one. The decision maker selects the strategy whose outcome is the best by (1) enumeration of all the possible strategies and selection of the most desirable, (2) progressive improvement of one strategy over another when enumeration of all the strategies is infeasible, or (3) optimization techniques that select the best strategy. Even certainty can present a problem due to the size of the search required; the searching time and expense of deriving all the necessary outcomes can be prohibitive. Examples of decision making under certainty are linear programming, basic inventory models, breakeven analysis, incremental analysis and so forth.

Decision Making Under Conflict

In this case the states of nature are subject to the control of an adverse intellect, as in competitive situations such as bargaining or war. The decision maker is in conflict with intelligent rational opponents whose interests are opposed to his own. The techniques for handling this type of a situation constitute the subject matter of game theory. The states of nature of the decision maker are the strategies of the opponent.

Games are usually classified according to the degree of conflict of interest, the relationship between opponents, and the number of opponents. When one opponent's gains are precisely the other's losses, it is called a zero-sum game. A zero-sum game involves complete conflict of interest. Games with less than complete conflict of interest are termed nonzero-sum games. In nonzero-sum games, the gains of one

		Player Y	
Player X		Strategy Q	Strategy R
		q_1	q_2
Strategy M	p_1	X wins 3	X wins 6
Strategy N	p_2	X wins 4	Y wins 1

$$\text{or } X \begin{matrix} Y \\ \begin{pmatrix} 3 & 6 \\ 4 & -1 \end{pmatrix} \end{matrix}$$

FIGURE 3

competitor are not completely at the expense of the other competitors. The majority of business competitive actions involve nonzero-sum games.

The two-person zero-sum game. The simplest type of game is the two-person zero-sum game. Here the players, *X* and *Y,* are equal in intelligence and ability. Each has a choice of strategies. Each knows the outcome for every possible combination of strategies. The term "zero sum" is used because the sum of gains exactly equals the sum of losses. The individual outcome possibilities are expressed numerically; a positive number indicates a payoff to the player who plays the rows *(X)*, and a negative number indicates a payoff to the player who plays the columns *(Y)*. Each player desires to win, or to minimize his losses if he cannot win. An example conflict matrix is shown in Figure 3.

A *pure strategy* exists if there is one strategy for player *X* and one strategy for player *Y* that will be played each time. The payoff which is obtained when each player plays his pure strategy is called a saddle point. The saddle point is the *value* of the game in which each player has a pure strategy. It represents an equilibrium condition that is optimum for both competitors. A saddle point can be recognized because it is both the smallest numerical value in its row and the largest numerical value in its column. Not all two-person zero-sum games have such a point. When a saddle point is present, complex calculations to determine optimum strategies and game value are unnecessary. The following example illustrates how to determine if a saddle point exists.

EXAMPLE 1

In the two-person zero-sum matrix below the rows are the strategies of player X and the columns are the strategies of player Y. Is there a saddle point? What is the value of the game? What strategies should be selected?

$$\begin{pmatrix} 10 & 15 & 13 \\ 5 & 17 & 6 \end{pmatrix}$$

We have

			row min

$$\begin{pmatrix} 10 & 15 & 13 \\ 5 & 17 & 6 \end{pmatrix} \quad \begin{matrix} 10 \\ 5 \end{matrix}$$

column max 10   17   13

continued

EXAMPLE 1—*continued*

Since the row minimum value of 10 equals the column maximum, there is saddle point. The value of the game is 10. Player X will select his first strategy, which will result in a gain of 10, while player Y will select his first strategy, which will result in a loss of 10.

When a pure strategy does not exist, a fundamental theorem of game theory states that the optimum can be found by using a *mixed strategy*. In a mixed or randomized strategy, each competitor randomly selects the strategy to employ according to previously determined probability of use for each strategy. Using a mixed strategy involves making a selection each time by tossing a coin, selecting a number from a table of random numbers, or using some other probabilistic process.

EXAMPLE 2

Referring to the original matrix in Figure 3, we will determine the mixed strategy. If p_1 and p_2 are the probabilities for player X's strategies, and q_1 and q_2 are the probabilities for player Y's strategies, we can find their values in the following manner:

expected value if Q occurs $= 3p_1 + 4p_2$,
expected value if R occurs $= 6p_1 - p_2$.

The two expected values must be equal. Therefore,

$$3p_1 + 4p_2 = 6p_1 - p_2,$$
$$p_2 = \tfrac{3}{5}p_1.$$

Since

$$p_1 + p_2 = 1,$$

we have

$$p_1 + \tfrac{3}{5}p_1 = 1,$$
$$p_1 = \tfrac{5}{8}, \qquad p_2 = \tfrac{3}{8}.$$

Under these conditions player X would play strategy M five-eighths of the time and strategy N three-eighths of the time. In a similar manner, it can be shown that player Y will play strategy Q seven-eighths of the time and strategy R one-eighth of the time. If Player X uses a chance process with the derived probabilities, his expected benefit will be the same regardless of player Y's strategy:

if strategy Q,   expected value $= \tfrac{5}{8}(3) + \tfrac{3}{8}(4) = \tfrac{27}{8}$,
if strategy R,   expected value $= \tfrac{5}{8}(6) + \tfrac{3}{8}(-1) = \tfrac{27}{8}$.

If Player Y uses a chance process with the desired probabilities, his expected benefit will also be the same regardless of player X's strategy (note that the signs of the matrix elements change when Player Y's choices are considered):

if strategy M,   expected value $= \tfrac{7}{8}(-3) + \tfrac{1}{8}(-6) = -\tfrac{27}{8}$,
if strategy N,   expected value $= \tfrac{7}{8}(-4) + \tfrac{1}{8}(1) = -\tfrac{27}{8}$.

As is always the case in the zero-sum game, player X's gain is player Y's loss and vice versa. The same procedure can be followed when a greater than two-by-two matrix exists, but it is usually easier to obtain the probabilities by using the simplex method linear programming.

When more than two competitors exist, various kinds of coalitions, treaties, and agreements can develop. The best examples of zero-sum games are in military conflicts and various types of athletic competition (football, basketball, hockey, etc.).

The nonzero-sum game. Nonzero-sum games are closer to the actual problems that arise in everyday life and do not lend themselves to straightforward solutions. In most complex games there is no universally accepted solution, for there is no single strategy that is clearly preferable to the others. Games with cooperative and competitive elements are usually complex in this sense. Nonzero-sum games require that the payoffs be given for each player even if there are only two, since the payoff of one player can no longer be deduced from the payoff of the other as in zero-sum games. It is no longer true that a player can only benefit from the loss of his opponent. The outcome of the game is influenced by communication, the order of play, imperfect information, threats, agreements, side payments, personalities of the players, behavioral patterns, and so forth.

Although game models are not of great value in their present form, they do provide a significant conceptual framework for analysis. They offer a meaningful guide for better decision making by focusing on pertinent problems that are prevalent in our everyday lives. They have found application in product development, product pricing, collective bargaining, athletic competition, war strategy, arbitration, foreign policy decisions, voting bloc coalitions, and contract bidding.

Decision Making Under Risk

With decision making under risk the various states of nature can be enumerated and the long-run relative frequency of their occurrence is assumed to be known. The information about the states of nature is probabilistic. Knowing the probability distribution of the states of nature, the best decision is to select the strategy that has the optimum expected value.

Probability means the long-run relative frequency of occurrence. The probability of an event is expressed as a number between 0 and 1. A probability of 0 means there is no possibility of the event occurring; a probability of 1 means that the event is certain to occur. Expected value is merely a weighted arithmetic average which is obtained by multiplying each outcome by its probability and summing these products for the given strategy. In maximization problems the largest expected value indicates the best strategy, whereas in minimization problems the smallest expected value is most desirable.

If there are j states of nature, the sum of their probabilities must equal one, or

$$p_1 + p_2 + p_3 + \cdots + p_j = 1.00.$$

The expected value of any given strategy i can be obtained as follows:

$$EV_i = p_1 O_{i1} + p_2 O_{i2} + p_3 O_{i3} + \cdots + p_j O_{ij}$$
$$= \sum p_j O_{ij}.$$

EXAMPLE 3

An organization must determine what size plant to build to produce a new product. Three different sizes are under consideration—small (S_1), large (S_2), and very large (S_3). The best plant size is dependent upon the level of product demand—low (N_1), medium (N_2), or high (N_3). The possible payoffs and the probabilities of each state of nature, obtained from market research, are listed in the following matrix:

	States of nature		
	N_1	N_2	N_3
Strategy	$\frac{1}{4}$	$\frac{1}{2}$	$\frac{1}{4}$
S_1	$50	$-8	$0
S_2	-10	64	12
S_3	-15	12	66

Hence

$$S_1 \text{ expected value} = \tfrac{1}{4}(50) + \tfrac{1}{2}(-8) + \tfrac{1}{4}(0) = 8.50,$$
$$S_2 \text{ expected value} = \tfrac{1}{4}(-10) + \tfrac{1}{2}(64) + \tfrac{1}{4}(12) = 32.50,$$
$$S_3 \text{ expected value} = \tfrac{1}{4}(-15) + \tfrac{1}{2}(12) + \tfrac{1}{4}(66) = 18.75.$$

The best strategy with the highest expected value is S_2. Using this approach, a large plant would be built to manufacture the new product.

One shortcoming of decision making under risk is that it only represents the average outcome if the event is repeated a large number of times. Such an approach is of little help if the act only takes place once. Typical examples of decision making under risk can be found in queuing theory, statistical quality control, acceptance sampling, the program evaluation and review technique (PERT), and so forth.

Value of perfect information. The expected value gives the unbiased long-run average outcome that will occur when a given strategy is adopted. Under risk, the most desirable strategy has the best expected value. Management may be able to obtain additional information about the situation and determine which state of nature will occur. Of course, the obtaining of additional information usually involves a cost. The additional information is intended to change the situation from decision making under risk to decision making under certainty. How much should management be willing to pay to obtain this additional information on the specific state of nature?

The maximum amount the decision maker would pay to know precisely the state of nature is called the expected value of perfect information (EVPI). It is obtained by subtracting the best expected value under risk (EVR) from the expected value under certainty (EVC). The expected value under certainty is obtained by multiplying the respective probability of occurrence by the best outcome under each state of nature and summing the products. The best expected value is simply the strategy with the most desirable expected value. Mathematically, the maximum cost of information is obtained as follows:

$$\text{EVPI} = \text{EVC} - \text{EVR}.$$

EXAMPLE 4

From the information given in Example 3, how much should management be willing to pay for perfect information (EVPI)?

$$EVC = \tfrac{1}{4}(50) + \tfrac{1}{2}(64) + \tfrac{1}{4}(66) = 61.00.$$

From the solution to Example 3, the EVR is from the best strategy S_2 and is \$32.50. The EVPI is obtained as follows:

$$EVPI = EVC - EVR = 61.00 - 32.50 = 28.50.$$

Therefore, the maximum value of information to management is \$28.50. It would be worth up to \$28.50 to know whether a low, medium, or high demand will occur. A larger expenditure would not be warranted.

Decision trees. A simple way of incorporating probabilistic events into a decision framework is with the use of decision trees. A decision matrix as previously illustrated in Figure 1 is an effective tool to analyze single-phase decisions. For multi-phase decisions, decision matrices are less appropriate, and decision trees are more desirable analytical tools. Decision trees depict possible combinations of alternatives and events in schematic form as branches of a tree.

Decision trees are useful for multi-stage decision problems sequenced over time. The tree is constructed chronologically from left to right using squares for controllable (decision) points and circles for uncontrollable (chance) events. Branches emerging from square nodes represent strategies, while branches which emerge from circular nodes represent states of nature. The probabilities of multiple states of nature are shown on their respective branches, and the probabilities of all branches emanating from any circular node must sum to 1. The outcomes associated with each branch of the tree are stated on the extreme right.

The tree is analyzed backwards in reverse chronological order (from right to left). The expected value of each strategy is the summation of each outcome multiplied by its probability (it is entered in the circle). The optimum expected value from among the circular nodes is then moved to its anterior decision point (it is entered in the square). Branches from square nodes with less desirable expected values are eliminated by cutting off the branch or placing parallel perpendicular lines (‖) through it. The process is continued until the primary (immediate) decision point is reached. Figure 4 illustrates the decision tree for the information in Example 3.

EXAMPLE 5

The Milliburg municipality has an outdated water purification facility. Its water supply frequently falls below minimum acceptable health standards, and at peak usage periods cannot be processed at a rate that supports consumption requirements. The Water Planning Board is deliberating on alternatives that could provide improved water service in the future. Demand for the service will depend upon future regional population growth. Based on population growth estimates, the probabilities of high, moderate, and low levels of demand are 20%, 30%, and 50%, respectively.

continued

EXAMPLE 5—*continued*

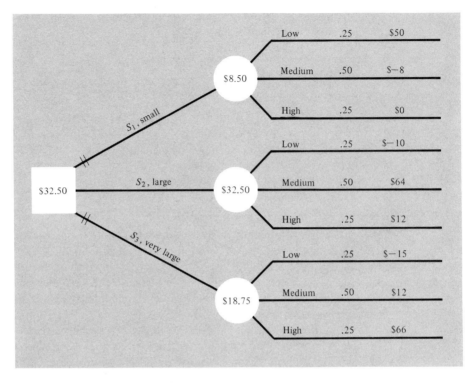

FIGURE 4
Decision tree: Example 3.

A proposal for building a new treatment plant has been submitted. This facility, during a 15-year life, could adequately serve the highest projected level of demand. The net present cost (NPC) for water service and construction, if demand is high, is $70 million; if demand is moderate, is $65 million; and if demand is low, is $55 million.

Alternatively, Milliburg can purchase its entire water supply from Megatown, a nearby metropolitan area. If Milliburg pursues this option now, before Megatown commits its excess capacity elsewhere, it can sign a fixed-price contract for a 15-year period. Purchasing under this contract, Milliburg's water supply has a $90 million NPC for a high demand, $75 million for a moderate demand, and $45 million for a low demand.

A renovation of the existing facility is the third option under consideration. It would have a refurbished life of 15 years but only could meet the requirements of a slowly growing population. Should the city renovate and demand be low, the NPC of water service and plant renovation will be $35 million. If demand proves to be moderate, Milliburg can undergo a small plant expansion at a later date, bringing the NPC to a $75 million total. In lieu of increasing its own processing capacity, Milliburg can purchase its excess water requirements from Megatown. However, Megatown may not offer a fixed-price contract at that time but instead might insist on a cost-plus agreement. The probability that a fixed contract will be available in the future is only 40%. Given a fixed contract in a moderate demand situation, the water supply has a $75 million NPC. If the contract is instead cost-plus, the NPC increases to $85 million for the same level of supply.

Finally, if Milliburg renovates the present facility and demand is high, additional consumption needs can be met by a large scale expansion. The total NPC of this option is

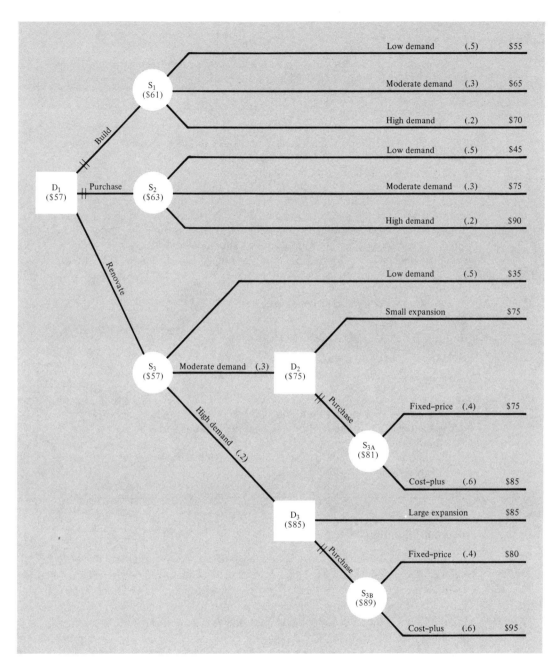

FIGURE 5
Decision tree: Example 5.

$85 million. The city alternatively can purchase the additional supply for $80 million NPC under a fixed-price contract or for $95 million under cost-plus terms.

Which option should the Water Planning Board recommend?

Solution: The appropriate decision tree is shown in Figure 5. Working from right to left, calculate the expected values of the event nodes associated with the dependent

EXAMPLE 5—continued

decisions, D_2 and D_3. The outcomes are multiplied by their respective probabilities and summed to obtain the expected values of strategies (S_{3A}) and (S_{3B}):

$$EV(S_{3A}) = .4(\$75) + .6(\$85) = \$81,$$
$$EV(S_{3B}) = .4(\$80) + .6(\$95) = \$89.$$

The EVs are entered in their respective event nodes and then compared with the expected values of the other strategies emanating from the same decision node. (In this case, the expansion strategies have only one outcome which has a 1.0 probability and becomes the expected value.) The comparison indicates that for both D_2 and D_3 the expansion strategy is preferred, i.e. for D_2, the outcome of the small expansion is less than the expected value of the purchase strategy, $\$75 < \$81$; and likewise for D_3, $\$85 < \$89$. Therefore, strategies (S_{3A}) and (S_{3B}) are eliminated by truncating their branches ($\parallel$). The optimum expected values are moved to the conditional decision squares to become outcomes for their related strategy, S_3, from the primary decision point, D_1 (the expansion costs become the outcomes for the moderate and high states of nature associated with the primary renovation strategy).

With the conditional decisions made, the primary decision strategies are evaluated similarly:

$$EV(S_1) = .5(\$55) + .3(\$65) + .2(\$70) = \$61,$$
$$EV(S_2) = .5(\$45) + .3(\$75) + .2(\$90) = \$63,$$
$$EV(S_3) = .5(\$35) + .3(\$75) + .2(\$85) = \$57.$$

Thus, the alternative to renovate, S_3, has the least expected cost. Its value is moved to the primary decision square, and the other strategies are eliminated. The preferred sequence of decisions is deduced by following the untruncated branches.

Primary decision: Renovate the present facility.

Conditional decisions: If demand is high, expand on large scale. If demand is moderate, expand on small scale.

Decision Making Under Uncertainty

In this case, either you don't know the probabilities associated with the states of nature, or you don't know the states of nature. If you don't know the states of nature, additional research must be conducted before the problem can be approached. If you don't know the probabilities associated with the states of nature, you can use any of numerous techniques in arriving at a strategy. There is no one best criterion for selecting a strategy; a number of plausible ones exist. The choice among the criteria depends upon the decision maker and the attitude or value system embraced. Several approaches to decision making under uncertainty are shown in Figure 6.

Subjective probabilities. This approach assigns probabilities to the states of nature and reduces the problem to decision making under risk. Objective probability flows from the law of large numbers, which asserts that the probability of any specified departure from the expected relative frequency of an event becomes smaller and smaller as the number of events considered becomes larger and larger. The objective or *a priori* probability of an event can be defined as the relative frequency with which an event would take place, given a large but finite number of observations. Unlike objective probability, subjective probability is heavily behavioral in its approach; it

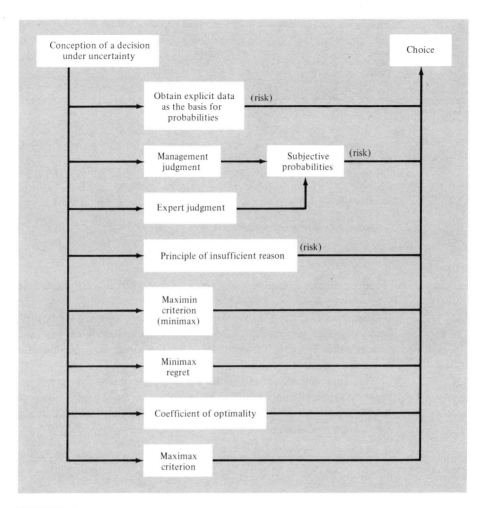

FIGURE 6
Decision making under uncertainty.

interprets likelihoods in terms of personal perception. A decision maker's experience about a situation is, in reality, his probability distribution, and his objectives and values constitute his objective function for it. Objective probability becomes suspect where one of a kind (nonrecurring) decisions have to be made. Bayes' theorem enables a decision maker to start with prior probabilities (which can be subjective) and, by taking into account additional observational information, to emerge with posterior probabilities, i.e., the revised probabilities modified by the additional information.

In problem situations where past data are not available to establish probabilities associated with a future event, the best the decision maker can do is to draw on the judgment of people knowledgable about such events (principally from past experience with similar events). Their quantified judgments are subjective probabilities, which can be analyzed statistically. Subjective probabilities are frequently used in higher level problems such as those associated with strategic choice and long range planning.

Principle of insufficient reason. This approach, also known as the Laplace criterion, assigns equal probabilities to each state of nature and treats the problem as decision making under risk. When there is no particular reason to suppose that one state of nature will occur rather than another, they ought to be considered equally likely (equally probable). This method selects the strategy with the best expected value.

EXAMPLE 6

If the probabilities were not available in Example 3, what strategy would be selected by the principle of insufficient reason?

With the example given earlier of plant size, the probability of demand would be one-third for each state of nature. This method would select the large plant size (S_2), since it has the highest expected value. The calculations are as follows:

expected value of $S_1 = \frac{1}{3}(50) + \frac{1}{3}(-8) + \frac{1}{3}(0) \quad = 14$,
expected value of $S_2 = \frac{1}{3}(-10) + \frac{1}{3}(64) + \frac{1}{3}(12) = 22\leftarrow$,
expected value of $S_3 = \frac{1}{3}(-15) + \frac{1}{3}(12) + \frac{1}{3}(66) = 21$.

Maximin criterion. The maximin criterion says to "pick the best of the worst" or "maximize the minimum." It selects a strategy whose worst outcome is as good as or better than the worst outcome of each other strategy. It is ultraconservative, since it hedges against the worst that might happen.

This approach selects the strategy that maximizes the minimum gain.[4] Observing only the smallest gain that could be achieved for each strategy, the strategy with the largest is selected. This criterion assures the decision maker of a payoff at least as large as the maximin payoff.

EXAMPLE 7

If the probabilities were not available in Example 3, what strategy would be selected by the maximin criterion?

The small plant (S_1) would be selected. The strategy with the largest minimum value is S_1, as shown below:

$S_1 = -8\leftarrow$,
$S_2 = -10$,
$S_3 = -15$.

Minimax regret. For this criterion an opportunity cost matrix (regret matrix) is established. The decision maker attempts to minimize the regret he may experience. Regret is measured as the difference between the actual payoff and the one he could receive if he knew what state of nature was going to occur. The decision maker chooses the strategy whose greatest loss is as small as or smaller than the greatest loss of each other strategy.

Opportunity cost (regret) is the difference between the outcome if the best alternative were chosen and the outcome from the chosen alternative. It is the penalty for

---

[4]When dealing with loss, the criterion becomes minimax, or "minimize the maximum loss."

not selecting the best alternative. The most desirable number in each column is set equal to zero. The regret for each other number in that column is the difference between it and the most desirable number. Thus, the most desirable number has zero regret, and every other number has a higher regret (greater than zero). For maximization, the largest number in each column has subtracted from it each other number in the same column. For minimization, the smallest number in each column is subtracted from each other number in the same column. The strategy that minimizes the maximum regret is chosen.

EXAMPLE 8

If the probabilities were not available in Example 3, what strategy would be selected by minimax regret?

The large plant (S_2) would be selected, as shown in the regret matrix below:

	N_1	N_2	N_3	Maximum regret
S_1	0	72	66	72
S_2	60	0	54	60←
S_3	65	52	0	65

Coefficient of optimality. The coefficient of optimality is a means by which the decision maker can consider both the largest and the smallest outcome, and weigh their importance in the decision by his feeling of optimism. A probability is assigned to the best outcome and also to the worst outcome: the sum of these two probabilities must equal one. The outcomes other than the maximum and minimum are neglected. The probabilities assigned tend to be subjective in nature and reflect how optimistic the decision maker is about the situation. The calculations are straightforward, and the selection is determined by the strategy with the best expected value.

If the coefficient of optimality is one, the decision is the same as in the maximax criterion. If the coefficient is zero, the decision is the same as in the maximin criterion. Thus, a high coefficient reflects an optimistic decision maker, while a low coefficient reflects a pessimistic decision maker. The obvious shortcoming of the coefficient of optimality is the neglect of all intermediate values for each strategy when there are more than two states of nature.

EXAMPLE 9

If the probabilities were not available in Example 3, what strategy would be selected with a coefficient of optimality of 0.7?

With the coefficient of optimality equal to 0.7, the large plant (S_2) would be selected as shown below:

S_1 expected value = 0.7(50) + 0.3(-8) = 32.6,
S_2 expected value = 0.7(64) + 0.3(-10) = 41.8←,
S_3 expected value = 0.7(66) + 0.3(-15) = 41.7.

Maximax criterion. This approach is one of complete optimism and selects the "best of the best." The decision maker assumes the very best will occur, and he selects the strategy with the most desirable outcome. For a maximization problem, the strategy with the largest outcome is chosen. Anybody who employs this approach has a small aversion toward risk and might be categorized as a gambler or "risk taker."

EXAMPLE 10

If the probabilities were not available in Example 3, what strategy would be selected with the maximax criterion?

The very large plant (S_3) would be selected. The large plant has the largest payoff (66) of all the strategies.

DESCRIPTIVE DECISION THEORY

In the normative decision model, a few dimensions of the decision environment were admitted into the decision process, and the decision maker was assumed to be a logical, methodical optimizer. In the descriptive decision model the decision maker is continually influenced by the total environment and also influences the environment. This model is concerned with how decisions are actually made. The decision maker is influenced by his personal values, the time available for making the decision, uncertainty, the importance of the decision, bounded rationality, satisficing behavior, and so forth. There is a great deal of subjective as well as objective evaluation that takes place in decision making. There are limits to human rationality.

Differences between normative and descriptive decision models are:[5]

1. Predetermined goals are replaced by some unidentified structure which is approximated by an aspiration level. Objectives are often vague, in conflict, and not agreed upon.
2. Not all alternatives and outcomes are known; neither are the relationships between specific alternatives and outcomes always defined. Knowledge of the situation is limited.
3. The ordering of all alternatives is replaced by a search routine which considers fewer than all alternatives.
4. The individual does not optimize but seeks to find a solution to "satisfy" an aspiration level.

Individual Decision Making

The descriptive decision model is based on behavioral foundations, and the decision maker is considered a complex mixture of many elements including his needs, culture, skills, personality, and aspirations. Because individuals come from different backgrounds geographically, educationally, socially, economically, and occupation-

---

[5]M. Alexis and C.Z. Wilson. *Organization Decision Making,* Englewood Cliffs, NJ: Prentice-Hall, 1967, p. 161.

ally, they may interpret what they hear and see in a different light from others. The decision maker's behavior reflects his perceptions of people, roles, and organizations in addition to his own values and emotions. The whole collection of experiences and expectations, developed from recurring and nonrecurring situations, forms the premises for individual decisions.

Individuals or groups tend to have established patterns of thought and behavior that can stultify creativity. Habits or inhibitions are developed that filter (block) creative thinking. Some of these filters are perceptual filters, cultural filters, and emotional filters. *Perceptual filters* prevent the decision maker from obtaining the appropriate information about the problem situation. He tends to see only what he wants or expects to see. *Cultural filters* are social inhibitions that cause the decision maker to conform to an acceptable social pattern. *Emotional filters* include fear of making a fool of oneself or merely fear of making a mistake. Communication is easily blocked when there are fears of misinterpretation, distortion, lack of knowledge, criticism, and reprisal. An appropriate organizational climate should be developed to overcome these filtering effects and foster creative decision making.

Every decision maker has a certain set of values that influence his actions. A value is a conception, explicit or implicit, that defines what an individual or a group regards as desirable. It may be a belief, feeling, opinion, conviction, or emotional tone that colors behavior. Whether on a conscious level or not, humans tend to like or dislike, approve or disapprove, want or not want, and position themselves somewhere on a scale from positive to negative feelings with regard to all that is encountered. These feelings may seem unreasonable or irrational, but they still influence behavior.

People are not born with values but acquire and develop them early in life. Clergy, parents, teachers, relatives and others influence an individual's values. A person's values have an impact on the selection of performance measures, alternatives, and choice criteria in the decision process. Typical values can be described as economic, theoretical, political, religious, esthetic, and social.[6] Managers vary considerably in their value profiles. Personal values significantly affect the decision making process.

Four distinct people or groups of people influence how effective or successful a manager's decisions will be. They are the manager himself, his subordinates, his superiors, and his peers. To a varying degree, all of these parties flavor the structure of decisions.

Organizations have the task of channeling person-centered behavior toward group-defined ends. Organizational structures provide status systems with defined roles. These become premises for individual decisions and hence behavior. The organization provides experiences and information through training and communication. These also are premises for decisions and can become powerful means of influencing individuals toward organizational goals.

Group Decision Making

Decisions of major importance or related to policy formulation are typically the product of group interactions. Group decisions are usually by consensus or some type of voting process. Negotiated decisions imply the existence of conflicting factions or

---

[6]W.D. Guth and R. Tagiuri. "Personal Values and Corporate Strategy," *Harvard Business Review,* September-October 1965, pp. 124–125.

power centers, all of which must be satisfied to some degree by the final decision. Much decision making within organizations is negotiated, which accounts for the widespread use of meetings and group discussions. Group processes can coordinate efforts, reduce conflict, aid implementation, and reduce the personal risk to an individual manager.

Groups take longer to make decisions than individuals. However, group decisions are generally advantageous when avoiding mistakes is of greater importance than speed. Participation in the decision making process increases acceptance of the final decision by group members. This is particularly true when change is being contemplated. The group's performance is generally superior to the average group member's, since the total of the group's knowledge is greater and a wider range of problem solving approaches are considered.

There are drawbacks to group decision making. A single or a few dominant members may control the group. This is particularly true when several managerial levels are included in the group. When "higher-ups" are present, many members may be inhibited. Also, competition can develop within the group, so that winning the issue becomes more important than the issue itself. Surprisingly, research has shown that group decisions tend to be more risky than the average of individual members. It may be that individuals feel less responsibility for the outcome of a group decision than when acting alone.

Group decision making is more effective than individual decision making when the following conditions exist:

1. Time constraints are not of crucial importance.
2. The quality of the decision is very important.
3. The problem is unstructured (creative) in nature.
4. Acceptance by subordinates is crucial to implementation.
5. The likelihood of acceptance of a unilateral decision is low.

Realistic Assessments

Identifying the problem can be the most crucial stage in the decision making process. There is a danger that efforts will be directed toward dealing with the symptoms of the problem. When this happens, the problem usually resurfaces.

Another danger is that one or more potentially superior alternatives will be overlooked in the search for alternatives. Finding alternative courses of action requires a high degree of creativity. Because of limitations of time and resources, it may be impossible to explore every feasible option. Consequently, when an alternative is selected it may turn out to be less than optimal.

Decisions usually are based on limited and incomplete knowledge. March and Simon offer a *satisficing model* in contrast to the classical economic rationality model.[7] Their principle of *bounded rationality* states that human beings seldom make any effort to find the optimum strategy in a decision problem. Instead, they select a number of possible outcomes of their available strategies which would be good enough. Then they select a strategy that is likely to achieve one of the good enough outcomes. Bounded rationality is the intuitive selection of a few reasonably appealing alternatives which, in effect, discards all other alternatives. Reduction in the number

---

[7]J.G. March and H.A. Simon. *Organizations*, New York: Wiley, 1958.

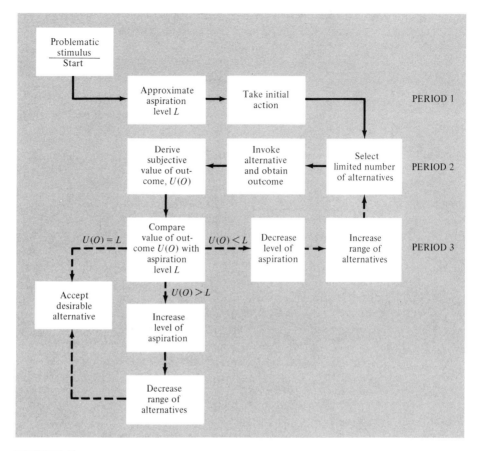

FIGURE 7
Open decision model.

of alternatives makes the analysis more practical and allows adequate study time for the selected options.

Except for the narrowest of problems, it is neither practical nor reasonable to consider all possible alternatives. Even if it were feasible to think of all the possible variations, common sense suggests that some alternatives are not sufficiently different to warrant separate treatment and some are clearly dominated by others. With limited resources, the decision maker must be discriminating in his choice of alternatives to consider. The total effort spent on a decision should not exceed its expected benefit.

In the descriptive models, the decision maker can be characterized as passing through three time periods as shown in Figure 7.[8]

Period 1. The individual starts out with an idealized goal structure. He defines one or more goals as a first approximation to the "ideal goal" in the structure. The action goals may be considered as representative of the decision maker's "aspiration level."

---

[8]K. Lewin et al. "Level of Aspiration," *Personality Disorders,* J. McV. Hunt, ed., New York: Ronald, 1944, pp. 333–378.

Period 2. The individual engages in search activity and defines a limited number of outcomes and alternatives. He does not attempt to establish the relations rigorously. His analysis proceeds from loosely defined rules of approximation. The alternatives discovered establish a starting point for further search toward a solution.

Period 3. Search among the limited alternatives is undertaken to find a satisfactory solution, as contrasted with an optimal one. "Satisfactory" is defined in terms of the aspiration level or action goals.

Descriptive decision theory builds on the rationality of normative decision theory to include specific organizational and political aspects. Organizational aspects require that different dependent departments or groups interact in many decision processes so suboptimization is averted and overall organizational objectives are paramount. This coordinative process is necessary because of the pyramidal structure of most organizations based on mutual dependency. Political aspects relate to the diffusion of power in an organization into several subunits. On complex decisions that affect several subunits, some bargaining is necessary to obtain consensus on the action needed from the various power centers. The rationality approach works well for well-structured problems with a single value criterion. As there is movement from well-structured problems to ill-defined issues, many participants, and multiple value criteria, organizational and political approaches assume greater significance in explaining the behavior of organizations.

Decision makers must consider the distribution of costs and benefits among all groups affected by a decision. Equity considerations require that benefits not accrue to one group at the expense of another; the political nature of a decision often depends on a balanced multilevel perspective that includes the ability to evaluate a decision from organization, group, and individual points of view.

Normative decision models are of most value for recurring decisions that have a historical background; the descriptive decision models are most significant for one-time, nonrecurring decisions. Figure 8 outlines basic approaches to decision making that can be used by organizational members in problem solving situations. The specific approach selected for problem solving will depend upon the given conditions, temporal relationships, and the value system of the decision maker as modified by environmental restraints.

Decision making is not a mechanical endeavor, for it requires imagination with the addition of knowledge and experience. It is an invisible, intellectual task. The personnel involved, the complexity of the decision, and the importance of the decision influence the search, evaluation, and selection. The judgmental aspects of the decision process should be augmented by logic and the methodology of science.

MODELS

The basic goal of decision theory is to make decision making more of a science and less of an art. One major contribution of decision theory has been the development of models that provide a framework for decision making. Models focus on factors that are common to decisions and provide a framework for analysis of situations, problems, and systems. The process of building a model is merely a formal version of the decision process itself. Managers are turning increasingly to models to improve decision making performance.

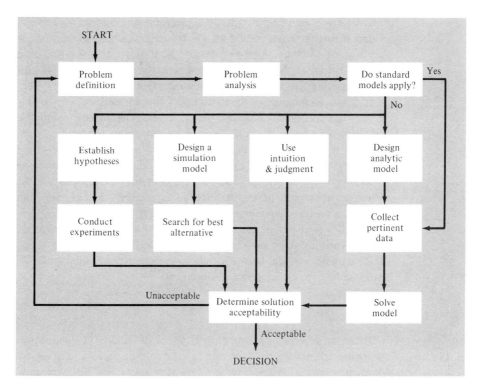

FIGURE 8
Decision making approaches.

Models are pervasively used throughout society for description, explanation, prediction, and control. A model is a synthetic abstraction of reality that can range from a very simple physical model (a child's doll) to a highly complex mathematical model (econometric model of the economy). It is used to capture the essence, but not the nonessential details of a system. It is a thing used to represent something else, and it is always less complex than actual reality.

A model is an invention of the mind, a product of the imagination, and a type of rationalism for an often chaotic world. It does not deal with absolute reality, but only with a limited degree of reality. Models provide the decision maker with the means of tracing out the consequences of potential actions. As such, they constitute a formal approach to decision making.

In modeling, factors that are assumed to have little influence in the situation are omitted. Only those factors believed to be important are included. Model building is not a straightforward, but rather a highly creative activity. In essence, an actual problem or situation is converted into an idealized structure through a process of abstraction. Models produce abstractions in that they simplify and reduce the world to manageable proportions that the human mind can understand. Time is saved by excluding masses of nonessential events and details from examination. Models do not represent every aspect of reality, because of its innumerable and frequently changing characteristics. They are used to parallel reality to the extent that they satisfy the objectives of its designer.

Models are an integral part of organizational decision processes. Managers use models that range from mental images to sophisticated computer programs. If a manager wanted to study the flow of material through a factory, he might construct a scaled diagram of the factory floor, together with the position of equipment, tools, and manpower. He would not include the color of the machines, the heights of the men, or the temperature of the buildings. Only relevant variables with a major impact on the decision situation would be included. The model would then become the vehicle for experimentation to discover the preferred decision.

There are four major benefits provided by models: (1) they permit analysis and experimentation with complex situations to a degree that is impossible with the actual system, (2) they provide economy in representation and inquiry, (3) they significantly reduce the amount of time spent on problem analysis, and (4) they focus attention on the most essential characteristics of the problem.

Models can assist in predicting the outcome of decisions or conditions without actually carrying them out. It is much less expensive and risky to test the results of decisions with a model before actual implementation. Experimentation with real systems can be expensive, slow, and harmful.

MODEL CLASSIFICATIONS

There are several types and classifications of models. A good classification system for models allows the decision maker to choose a model which best fits the situation. More importantly, it can indicate the advantages and disadvantages of a selected model. Model classifications are covered in Appendix A at the end of the chapter.

THE MODELING PROCESS

It is absolutely essential to define the use for which the model is intended. This determines the kind of model (type of abstraction). The model builder must then select the entities or variables to include in the model. Once the entities are chosen, they must be structured (put together) in such a fashion so that their interactions approach reality. The appropriate level of detail for a model is indicated by its intended use. Model development not only requires specialized knowlege, but a creative talent, an ability to focus on significant variables, and skill in synthesizing the interrelationships of system components.

Model development may be viewed as a process of enrichment and elaboration. It begins with very simple models quite different from reality. It moves in evolutionary fashion towards more elaborate models which more nearly reflect the complexity of the actual situation. Analogy or association with previously well-developed logical structures plays an important role in model enrichment and elaboration. Initially, a model is simplified by making variables into constants, eliminating variables, using linear approximations, adding stronger assumptions (restrictions), and suppressing randomness. Model enrichment counterbalances simplification by increasing the amount of detail.

The modeling process is congruent with the scientific method. The scientific method iteratively searches for the most plausible explanation of phenomena through the formation of hypotheses, their verification through experimentation, and their subsequent improvement through test results. Similarly, modeling is iteratively improved by learning from past analyses. In the search for the best model, preliminary ideas must be revised in the light of new insights obtained as analysis proceeds or implementation takes place.

The modeling process is illustrated in Figure 9. It can be visualized as a five-step process as follows:

1. statement of the purpose of the model;
2. formulation of the theory or model;
3. initial verification by comparison with available observations;
4. use of the model to predict future behavior;
5. refinement of the model until behavior can be predicted within an acceptable precision.

Although the five steps are straightforward, the actual process usually involves frequent revisions (looping and cycling). The basic steps are not separate and independent procedures, nor do they always follow in exactly the same sequence. It is possible for the final model to bear little resemblance to the initial model. Even after a model is adopted, it must be subjected to revalidation with the passage of time. Revisions of the model will be predicated on its sensitivity and required level of precision. At all times it is necessary to have a clear understanding of the objectives, assumptions, omissions, and limitations of a particular model.

It is not coincidence that computer technology and models have developed in parallel. In fact, advances in computers have fostered many of the advances in management science. There would probably be little interest in management science were

FIGURE 9
The modeling process.

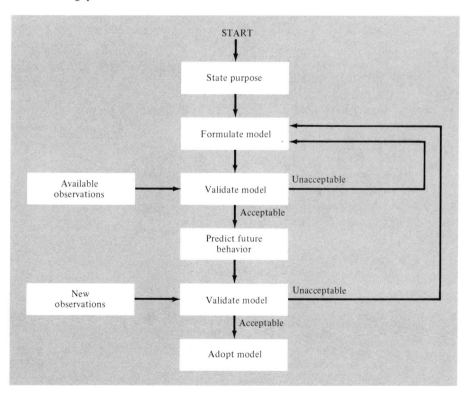

it not for the tremendous data-generating and computational capabilities of the computer. The computer has made it possible to turn previously theoretical models into practical decision aids for managers in all types of organizations.

MODEL VALIDITY

Validation determines how well a model represents the reality it is intended to simulate. Validation can be accomplished by predicting performance with the model for specified conditions and then comparing the results with actual field data. Statistical tests are frequently used to test hypotheses regarding general logic and validity. Of course, the more complex the model, the harder it is to verify its internal logic.

Assessing model validity can be very complicated. Three kinds of validity are technical, operational, and dynamic. *Technical validity* concerns the identification of all the divergences of a model from reality. *Operational validity* deals with the importance or significance of the model divergences. *Dynamic validity* relates to the continuing viability of the model when changes occur.

Technical validity delineates the discrepancies between a model and reality without judging their significance. Implicit or explicit assumptions of the model are highlighted and compared with reality. The accuracy, impartiality, and representativeness of the raw or structured data used in the model development are ascertained. Deviations in the final model between actual and expected outcomes are reported.

Operational validity deals with the importance of the divergences found under technical validity. Since no model can meet all the criteria for being technically valid, the significance of discrepancies must be evaluated. What are the consequences of possible data extremes on operations? What is the probability that the real world will respond as the model indicates? Does the model provide practical decision rules of value to management? What impact will the model have on personnel? The meaning of discontinuities, rigidities, and extremes must be ascertained. Operational validity measures the utility of the model to management.

Dynamic validity attempts to ensure that the model will continue to be valid throughout its intended life cycle. A model is termed robust if changes do not significantly modify its solutions. This is an important property of a model. Sensitivity analysis can be used to judge the effect on the model's output of changes (or errors) in the parameters or input variables.

Provision must be made for reviewing the success of the model over time and making the necessary revisions. Review should be preplanned and regularly scheduled to evaluate the performance of the model throughout its life cycle. Updating allows for revision of parameter values (model structure) as well as modified or expanded coverage.

OVERVIEW OF MODELS

The value of any model depends upon how well it represents what it is supposed to represent for the intended purpose. It is important for a decision maker to be aware of the shortcomings and limitations of any model. By knowing what a given model or technique can do, the manager is more likely to select an appropriate one.

The question of the amount of detail to include in a model involves a balance between accuracy and simplicity. To increase accuracy it is usually necessary to add variables that increase the complexity of relationships. Thus, enhancing realism adds cost. Simpler models are easier to understand and apply. However, an oversimplified model may fail to represent reality and result in misleading if not erroneous outcomes.

"Satisficing" is striving for a given level of achievement while being willing to settle for a lower or slightly less ambitious level. Model formulation frequently involves the satisficing of reality for the sake of workability. Common examples of satisficing are (1) using linear approximations for nonlinear relationships, (2) only considering the major variables to the exclusion of others, and (3) lumping several variables together into a single variable. Most models have satisficing aspects.

Organizational decisions are based on models. The question is not whether to use models or not, but which kinds of models to use. When a manager applies his experience, he compares his model of the present situation with models of similar situations with which he is familiar. The primary danger with models is in the oversimplification of situations to keep the model in workable form.

Models play a significant role in production and operations management; they are extensively integrated into the subject matter of this text. As each model is encountered, try to learn (1) the purpose of the model, (2) how to use the model to generate results, (3) how results are interpreted and used, and (4) what the assumptions and limitations of the model are. The last point is particularly important because virtually every model has an associated set of assumptions that determine the conditions under which the model is valid. If these assumptions are violated, the use of a model will lead to results that are suspect.

CONCLUSION

A framework for organizational decision theory has been outlined which includes normative and descriptive models as well as other pertinent dimensions. Decisions are made with varying degrees of information, and decision theory gives structure and rationale to the different possible environmental conditions. The decision process includes problem definition, discovery of strategies, delineation of states of nature, determination of outcomes, selection of a strategy, and implementation of the strategy (decision).

The manager selects one strategy over others by means of some criteria such as utility, maximum sales, minimum cost, or rate of return. The specific criterion or combination of goals is not entirely the manager's, for the value system is usually modified by groups with special interests such as stockholders, creditors, employers, unions, government, and so forth. In determining feasible strategies, many strategies can be omitted when they are dominated by a previously stated strategy. A decision is made by reducing the number of strategies to one.

The contribution of quantitative techniques to decision theory is mostly in the appraisal stage, the analysis of strategies. Quantitative tools are unable to define problems, suggest hypotheses, or delineate strategies. These abilities are in the domain of the creativity, experience, and personality of the decision maker. However, once the alternatives have been delineated, quantitative techniques can be powerful tools for appraisal and analysis. Thus, quantitative analysis is more often used at the structured operating level than in the unstructured area of upper level policy decisions.

It is essential to an organization that its managers develop rational decision making procedures and strive to improve their decision making capabilities. This can best be accomplished by analyzing their decisions and by obtaining a better understanding of decision theory.

QUESTIONS

1. What are the four broad factors that influence the decision making processes in organizations?
2. Why must objectives be in existence before decisions are made?
3. What is a value criterion?
4. How are the different levels of management influenced by their planning horizons?
5. What are the two types of broad decision models? How do they differ?
6. Name the six elements common to all decisions.
7. What are the four kinds of decision situations in normative decision theory?
8. What is a major shortcoming of decision making under risk?
9. How is a decision under risk made?
10. Do groups or individuals tend to make riskier decisions?
11. Define bounded rationality and satisficing.
12. What are the eight classification dimensions for models?
13. Name the five steps in the modeling process.
14. What are the three kinds of model validity?
15. What models have you used lately to make decisions concerning expenditures of money?
16. What decision awareness stances are common in organizations?
17. In what decision situations would a decision tree be used in lieu of a decision matrix?

PROBLEMS

1. The two-person zero-sum matrix below has rows for the strategies of player X and columns for the strategies of player Y. Is there a saddle point? What is the value of the game? What strategies would each select?

$$\begin{pmatrix} 12 & 7 & 10 \\ 9 & 8 & 12 \\ 15 & 3 & 6 \end{pmatrix}$$

2. A two-person zero-sum matrix is given below. Is there a pure or mixed strategy? What is the value of the game? What strategies would each opponent select?

	Player Y	
	Strategy Q	Strategy R
Player X	q_1	q_2
Strategy M p_1	4	3
Strategy N p_2	3	7

3. Two short term investments are being considered by a firm. From the data in the table below, which investment is more desirable?

Project 1		Project 2	
Probability	Profit	Probability	Profit
.2	$100	.1	$ 80
.4	120	.6	120
.4	140	.3	140

4. The daily demand data below are for a perishable product that sells for $10 per unit and costs $6 to produce. Any product not sold during the day it is produced is discarded at a total loss. What quantity should be produced daily to maximize long term profits?

Demand (units)	20	25	30	35
Probability	0.20	0.30	0.40	0.10

5. From the information given in Problem 4, what is the expected value of perfect information?

6. A player rolls a die and receives a number of dollars corresponding to the number of dots on the face which turns up. What should the player pay for playing, to make this a fair game?

7. A hospital is opening a new maternity wing which will have 59 beds. The administrator must determine the number of full-time nurses to employ. A nurse is paid $10.00 per hour regular time and $15.00 per hour overtime; the average patient load of a nurse is 10 patients per day. There is no difficulty getting nurses from other wings of the hospital to work overtime if they are needed. Based on the following probability distribution of demand, how many full-time nurses should be employed for an 8-hour shift?

No. of beds demanded	Midpoint	Probability
0–10	5	.05
11–19	15	.20
20–30	25	.30
31–39	35	.25
40–50	45	.15
51–59	55	.05

8. From the payoff matrix given below, what is the best strategy?

	States of nature			
	N_1	N_2	N_3	N_4
Strategy	0.2	0.1	0.5	0.2
S_1	50	20	40	10
S_2	10	30	30	20
S_3	−10	−10	20	30
S_4	20	40	10	40

9. You are to establish the inventory level for a product. It is believed that demand will fall in the range from 1 to 6 units, but nothing can be said of the probability over this range. You are informed that the stockout cost per unit is $300 and the storage cost for any unsold units is $100 per unit. What inventory level would you select, based on the principle of insufficient reason?

10. Select the inventory level in Problem 9 based on the minimax criterion.

11. From the payoff matrix below, what strategy would you select based on the (a) maximin criterion, (b) minimax regret, and (c) maximax criterion?

	N_1	N_2	N_3	N_4
S_1	$12	$15	$2	$ 6
S_2	14	8	6	9
S_3	20	12	4	10
S_4	16	9	5	4

12. From the information given in Problem 11, select the best strategy based on a coefficient of optimality of 0.6.

13. A large automobile manufacturer has found that customer complaint letters should be promptly answered by a personal letter. For this purpose the firm employs a number of workers who are paid $6.00 per hour for regular time and $9.00 per hour for overtime. All incoming letters are answered on the same day even if it means overtime work. An average worker can write 5 letters per hour or 40 per eight-hour day. Records indicate the probability distribution of complaint letters per day as follows:

Complaint letters	Probability
120–139	0.06
140–159	0.13
160–179	0.09
180–199	0.21
200–219	0.17
220–239	0.12
240–259	0.08
260–279	0.14
	1.00

How many full-time workers should be employed with the aim of minimizing costs?

14. For quality assurance reasons an organization must select a robot from three alternative models. Each model has a different initial cost, output level, and expected failure rate. The product requiring the robot acquisition sells for $15.00 and will have a $1.00 variable cost per unit regardless of the model purchased. The product's daily demand is subject to chance but can be increased if the firm advertises at a cost of $20.00 per day. On the other hand, an entire day's demand will be lost if a robot breakdown occurs. Any operating failure that does occur can be repaired within one working day at a cost of $100.00. Given the demand and operating data below, which robot should be purchased? Should the firm advertise the product?

Robot	Daily fixed cost	Maximum daily output	Probability of failure (each day)
A	$200	30	.1
B	100	25	.2
C	70	20	.2

	Daily demand level					
Adver-tising	High		Medium		Low	
	Demand	Probab.	Demand	Probab.	Demand	Probab.
Yes	40	.4	25	.5	15	.1
No	30	.3	20	.5	10	.2

15. What robot would be selected in Problem 14 if the daily demand distributions were not known and the selection were based on the principle of insufficient reason?

16. If the organization in Problem 14 could hire a consultant to obtain perfect information, how much should management be willing to pay for this service?

17. What decision would be made in Problem 14 based on the maximin criterion?

CASE 1: AN OLD STANDARD

Tom Wright, production manager of the Mohawk Plant of Carbonics Incorporated, recently attended an advanced management seminar conducted at the Sloan Business School. The seminar was devoted primarily to the topic of executive decision making. One of the speakers, Professor Knowit, particularly impressed Tom with her lectures on decision making. Research and experience had convinced Professor Knowit that employees, if given the chance, would intelligently analyze problems and make quality decisions.

Upon returning to Mohawk, Mr. Wright decided to practice some of the methods he learned at the seminar. Monday morning he summoned the fifteen workers of the assembly department to his office. He told them that in view of the recent installation of new equipment in their department, production standards are too low. He charged them with analyzing the situation and then deciding, among themselves, what the new standards should be. Tom assumed his workers would establish much higher output standards than those currently used by the department.

After several hours of deliberation, the workers reached their decision. Much to Tom's surprise the group did not agree with his assessment that the production standards are too low. Their consensus was that the standards had been accurate when the previous equipment was first installed, but that they became too high after the equipment became worn. Therefore, they decided the standards should remain the same as before, since new equipment again had just been installed. They also felt that these standards should not remain in effect after the equipment had been in operation a few years. Their contention was that the standards should again be loosened after the new equipment had worn down.

The decision was completely unacceptable in light of upper management directives. However, Tom knew it would be detrimental if he refused to abide by his workers' decision.

1. Is group decision making a viable management technique?
2. Must Tom Wright abide by his workers' decision to keep the current production standards?
3. How would you resolve Tom's dilemma?

CASE 2: ASPIRATION LEVELS

A group of investors, all businessmen from diverse backgrounds and dissimilar educational experiences, has decided to pool resources and invest jointly. They are all excited about the joint investment, for they feel there are better opportunities for large investors or investment groups than for individuals. Separately none is able to afford investment projects that potentially return above-average profits, and typically they place their own extra capital in guaranteed, minimum- to average-return notes and bonds.

A financial analyst has recommended four investment opportunities for the group. She has chosen an eclectic selection, partially because she has not handled their financial matters before and as yet cannot determine exactly the type of investments they are seeking, and partly because the group itself is a motley collection of investors. The analyst has used the rate of return basis for investment analysis. Also presented was a cautionary statement that the assigned rates of return are not guaranteed but are inexactly forecasted and therefore cover a range from a loss of 5% to a gain of 20%. The analysis also included a short description of the degree of risk entailed with each to account for the variation in returns and the probability of achieving a designated return. Each of the investments on the recommended list has the same capital requirement, which is approximately the amount of the group's consolidated resources. The four investments she has suggested are outlined below in terms of each one's probability of earning a given rate of return:

	Rate of return (%)					
Investment	−5	0	5	10	15	20
A₁	.10	.10	.15	.20	.30	.15
A₂	.20	.15	.10	.10	.10	.35
A₃	0	.10	.50	.30	.10	0
A₄	.1̄66	.1̄66	.1̄66	.1̄66	.1̄66	.1̄66

Except for the fact that the investments require the same invested capital and are forecasted over the same 25 percentage point range, there are striking dissimilarities. The first investment has expected returns that cover the entire range as shown and has a relatively high probability of earning over 10%. This prediction is forecasted from similar franchise investments undertaken by other clients. The second alternative is an investment in an oil-related production opportunity, and its returns are also those generally revealed by examinations of previous returns on similar investments. The third's predictions show less variation but solidly reflect earnings received in portfolio investments of equally wide diversification. The fourth is a new venture, and the assigning of equal earnings probabilities over the range arises from insufficient predictive data.

Selection is difficult, due to the different investor philosophies and risk adversions held by group members. The analyst has tried to assuage the uneasiness of certain members by explaining the use of probabilities in frank but descriptive terms. She has stressed that the ROIs are forecasted, involve risk, and are appealing to different investors, depending on the decision maker's prejudice and viewpoint. She has advocated group analysis by whatever means or techniques they deem useful and urged them to identify and use the approach most consistent with their levels of optimism.

1. Analyze the alternatives according to several decision principles. Apply a decision principle or approach not used in the text.
2. What are the chances that the use of multiple techniques could complicate the selection process? How does the selection process become more complicated by group decision making?
3. Is there a preferred strategy? Which do you recommend?

APPENDIX A. MODEL CLASSIFICATIONS

Models can be classified several different ways. There are eight classification dimensions that appear to adequately define most models. They are depicted in Figure 10 as function, structure, dimensionality, temporal reference, degree of certainty, degree of generality, degree of closure, and degree of quantification. Any given model can be classified by these dimensions. These eight descriptive classifications will be outlined in the subsequent sections.

Function

Models can be classified according to their function as descriptive, predictive, or normative. *Descriptive models* merely describe a present or past set of conditions or activities and make no attempt to predict or recommend. They provide a representation of a situation without any prescription. Descriptive models are used to define a situation more clearly, identify possible areas of change, and investigate the consequences of various decision alternatives. They do not identify the best choice of all the possible alternatives. They provide a framework that aids the decision maker in selecting a strategy. Typical descriptive models are maps, organizational charts, photographs, and financial statements.

Predictive models indicate the consequences of various strategies. They can predict the outcome of decisions. This type of model will relate dependent and independent variables in

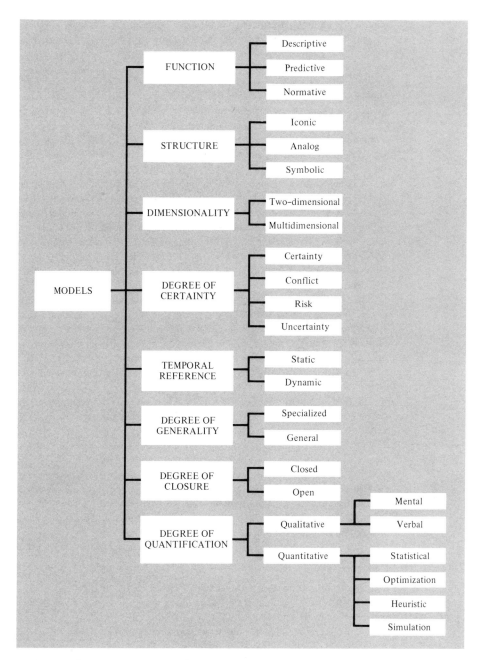

FIGURE 10
Model classifications.

such a manner as to forecast the results of specific circumstances. Management can obtain the answer to "what if" types of questions. However, predictive models cannot provide information as to the desirability of each outcome. Typical predictive models are annual budgets, decision trees, market forecasts, and queuing theory.

Normative models indicate what should be done to achieve an objective. This type of model selects the best answer or solution from the available alternatives. All optimization procedures are normative. The primary problem in using normative models is the choice of the proper criteria for choosing the best solution. Typical normative models are linear programming, inventory economic order quantities, integer programming, and quadratic programming.

Structure

Models can be classified according to their structure as iconic, analog, and symbolic. *Iconic models* are physical replicas that retain some of the physical relationships of the things they represent. These models are generally the simplest to conceive and provide a degree of concreteness not available with other models. They are the least abstract. However, they are severely limited in their ability to represent causal relationships. These models visually look like the real thing, but are usually scaled up or down.

As children most of us enjoyed models of spaceships, homes (dollhouses), racing cars, trucks, guns, aircraft, and children (dolls). These models look very much like their real counterparts although they are scaled-down versions. The interior features are usually neglected on toy models. Some features of the real object are included while others are excluded. Typical iconic models are photographs, planetariums, engineering blueprints, and children's toys.

Another structural type is an *analog model*. These models use a characteristic of one system to represent some characteristic of another system. Unlike the iconic model, the components representing the system no longer physically resemble it. Analog models are like the object or situation they represent, but only abstractly. Thus, the model is analogous but not physically representative. Analog models allow complex or cumbersome components to be represented by components that are easier to analyze. However, there must be a strong correspondence between the model elements and the actual system for the representation to be effective. Typical analog models are a graph using distances to represent interrelationships among variables, an electrical schematic diagram which uses lines to show electrical connections, flow charts, network graphs, and scheduling charts.

The final structural category is the *symbolic model,* which uses various types of symbols to represent aspects of the actual system. Symbolic models have no physical resemblance to the actual system under study. The relationships among variables are represented by symbols. Since most organizational problems do not lend themselves to representation in physical form, these models are of greatest interest and application. These models are the most general, flexible, and abstract—often being mathematical. For this reason, a symbolic model is often difficult to conceive and develop. It is most effective in determining the effects of changes on an actual system. A person's written or spoken version of his thoughts is a symbolic model. Other typical symbolic models are Monte Carlo simulation, statistical acceptance sampling, linear programming, breakeven analysis, and game theory.

Dimensionality

Models can be categorized by dimensionality, that is, the number and kinds of variables used in its construction. *Two-dimensional models* are the simplest and are exemplified by simple regression analysis, blueprints, maps, and photographs. *Multidimensional models* have more than two dimensions and include scaled prototypes of ships, bridges, aircraft, automobiles, buildings, etc.; multiple regression analysis; simulation; and pilot plant operations.

When models have so many variables that it is impossible to categorize them, they are called *n*-dimensional models. Two-dimensional models are designed to convey information, and do so with a minimum of effort and confusion. Three-dimensional models permit the examination of the physical characteristics of a problem. With an increase in the number of dimensions, more interaction can be represented. However, there is a point of diminishing returns.

Temporal Reference

Models can be classified according to their temporal reference as static or dynamic. Temporal reference refers to the influence of time in the model. A *static model* ignores time (none of the relationships vary with time). Typical static models are inventory economic order quantities, breakeven analysis, organization charts, marginal analysis, and queuing theory. A *dynamic model* has interactions that are time dependent. Typical dynamic models are dynamic programming, exponentially weighted moving averages, growth models, and forecasting techniques. Static models reduce the number of variables under consideration by eliminating time. Dynamic models are particularly effective in examining problems when interactions, outputs, and inputs vary with time. These models can become very cumbersome, however.

Degree of Certainty

Models can be classified according to their degree of certainty: certainty, conflict, risk, and uncertainty. Degree of certainty refers to the knowledge the decision maker possesses about the states of nature influencing the system under analysis. States of nature are those aspects of the environment in which the system operates over which the decision maker has little or no control.

With the *certainty model,* there is only one state of nature for each strategy. In essence, the probability that the specific state of nature will occur is one (perfect knowledge). The decision maker simply selects the strategy with the most desirable outcome via enumeration of all strategies, progressive improvement, or use of optimization techniques. Typical certainty models are present value techniques, basic inventory models, marginal analysis, and scheduling techniques.

In *conflict models,* the states of nature for the decision maker are under the control of an opponent or competitor. The technique for handling conflict constitutes the subject matter of game theory. The conflict of interest can be total or partial and may involve one or more competitors. Typical conflict models are athletic competition (football, basketball, hockey), war, bargaining, and labor negotiations.

With *risk models,* the states of nature are known and can be described probabilistically (stochastically). The decision maker selects the strategy with the optimum expected value. Examples of risk models are decision trees, statistical control charts, statistical acceptance sampling, and actuarial tables.

In *uncertainty models,* future conditions and their corresponding probabilities are not known. The decision maker must be able to ascertain the relevant states of nature. Solution procedures require a selection based on judgment, utility, or risk via subjective probabilities.

Pure certainty models are most applicable in situations where there is a high degree of predictability. They are usually less complicated and therefore economical to use, but perfect predictability is seldom possible. Conflict models consider situations in which the states of nature are under the control of an opponent. So far they have been of little value with the possible exceptions of labor negotiations and warfare. Risk models lessen the degree of certainty necessary, but still assume a relatively high degree of knowledge about the states of nature and their respective probabilities. Uncertainty models reduce the level of knowledge assumed and are more realistic. However, they incur the limitation of a lack of knowledge about the states of nature and associated probabilities.

Degree of Generality

In degree of generality, models may be specialized or general purpose. Generality means the extent to which models can be applied to different situations. *General models* can be used for many different types of decision problems. Examples of general models are linear programming, waiting line analysis, statistical quality control, and financial reports. *Specialized models* can be applied only to a particular kind of problem. If the problem can be adequately represented by general purpose models, it is usually more economical and less time consuming to use them. However, in many cases general models do not provide satisfactory representation and there is sufficient justification for the more demanding task of constructing a special purpose model. Computer simulations are an example of special purpose models, since they are designed to simulate a particular system.

Degree of Closure

Models may be open or closed. Closure refers to the extent to which the model is influenced by its environment. Influences from the external environment are essentially uncontrollable, while those from the internal environment may be considered controllable. An *open model* has one or more exogenous variables (supplied from the external environment). In a *closed model* all the variables are endogenous (supplied from the controllable, internal environment). A closed model has no interactions with its external environment. It is difficult to find a system that is completely closed. It is more useful to think of systems in terms of the degree to which they are closed. However, it is possible to represent a system with a closed model when its interactions are largely endogenous. This procedure is generally more economical and less time consuming than using an open model. Input-output models take open systems into consideration, but most models are of the closed variety.

Degree of Quantification

Models can be categorized according to their degree of quantification as qualitative or quantitative. A *qualitative model* avoids mathematical description or measurement. As such, qualitative models are less precise, rational, and consistent than quantitative models; however, they are usually more flexible, robust, and reflective of reality. Quantitative models employ equations and yield numerical outcomes, while qualitative models are usually not related to numbers.

Qualitative models frequently consider intangible, human, and behavioral factors that are ignored in quantitative models. Qualitative models can be subdivided into mental and verbal models. *Mental models* are usually the first level of abstraction of a decision maker as he conceptualizes a problem or situation. Whenever somebody thinks about something, he makes a mental model. Of course, different people can possess different mental models for the same phenomenon. *Verbal models* may follow mental models; they exist when a situation is described in either speech or writing. Verbal models attempt to communicate and improve on mental models, but still tend to be imprecise. An example is a manager conveying the interactions of a problem to an employee via a memorandum.

A *quantitative model* involves the use of the language of mathematics (equations and mathematical statements). The weaknesses of the qualitative model are overcome to a great degree by the logic of mathematics. It is extremely precise, and it lends itself to testing. Quantitative models are derived from qualitative models and are found more often in the physical sciences than in the social sciences. It is not uncommon for quantitative models to be developed from qualitative models or to be used to test the validity of qualitative relationships. The rapid development and sophistication of quantitative modeling has resulted in the new organizational areas of operations research, quantitative analysis, and management science. Quantitative models are of great benefit because they allow us to measure behavior objectively. Their limitations are caused by inadequate measuring techniques, the nature and number of variables, and the complexity of the relationships being considered.

Quantitative models can be subdivided further into statistical, optimization, heuristic, and simulation models. *Statistical models* describe or make inferences about data obtained from different phenomena. Probability distributions, described by measures of central tendency, dispersion, peakedness, and skewness, are encountered. Typical examples of statistical models are mortality tables, control charts, acceptance sampling, queuing theory, and Markov chains. It is necessary that the probability distributions used adequately describe the pattern of behavior with a minimum of error for this type of model to be effective.

Optimization models determine the most desirable strategy from the various possible alternatives. This is usually accomplished by the maximization or minimization of some measure of utility. Optimization models are either analytical or algorithmic. An *analytical optimization model* arrives at the best solution by a direct, nonrepetitive process. Typical examples of analytical optimization models are economic order quantities, marginal analysis, incremental analysis, and mathematical functions that are optimized by differential and integral calculus. *Algorithmic optimization models* usually arrive at the best solution by a repetitive (iterative) process. Typical examples are linear programming, integer programming, and quadratic programming. An iterative process begins with an initial solution and a computational procedure to arrive at an optimum solution. Both of these optimization procedures can be extremely complex and expensive.

Heuristic models do not ensure optimum solutions, but employ decision criteria that simplify the research process and result in favorable solutions. Heuristics are "rule of thumb" approaches that use logic and common sense derived from observation and introspection. The essence of heuristics is in the application of selective routines that reduce the size of the problem. If an optimum solution is computationally or economically infeasible, a heuristic rule can incrementally test alternatives and improve on a given solution. Heuristics simplify the search process and reduce the number of alternatives tested. A reasonable rather than an optimum solution is usually obtained. Typical examples of heuristic models have been developed for the traveling salesman problem, job-shop scheduling, line balancing of assembly lines, and plant layouts.

Simulation models attempt to recreate the essence of a system's behavior over time. Like heuristic models, simulation models attempt to obtain reasonable rather than optimum solutions. Simulation is particularly useful for very complex problems where other models are either impractical, uneconomical, or unavailable. Simulation models are specialized to particular circumstances. These models are well suited for answering "what if" questions and testing changes in the system before they are implemented (if we do this, what will occur?). However, there is no guarantee that a good, much less an optimal, solution will result.

SELECTED BIBILOGRAPHY

Alexis, M. and C. Z. Wilson. *Organization Decision Making,* Englewood Cliffs, NJ: Prentice-Hall, 1967.

Ansoff, H. I. *Corporate Strategy,* New York: McGraw-Hill, 1965.

Cyert, R. M. and J. G. March. *A Behavioral Theory of the Firm,* Englewood Cliffs, NJ: Prentice-Hall, 1963.

Dahl, R. A. and C. E. Lindblom. *Politics, Economics, and Welfare,* New York: Harper and Row, 1953.

Guth, W. D. and R. Tagiuri. "Personal Values and Corporate Strategy," *Harvard Business Review,* September/October 1965.

Lewin, K. et al. "Level of Aspiration," *Personality Disorders,* J. McV. Hunt, ed., New York: Ronald, 1944.

March, J. G. and H. A. Simon. *Organizations,* New York: Wiley, 1958.

Raiffa, H. *Decision Analysis,* Reading, MA: Addison-Wesley, 1968.

Schlaifer, R. *Analysis of Decisions Under Uncertainty,* New York, McGraw-Hill, 1969.

Steiner, G. A. and J. B. Miner. *Management Policy and Strategy,* New York: Macmillan, 1977.

Tersine, R. J. and W. E. Riggs. "Models: Decision Tools for Management," *Journal of Systems Management,* October 1976.

Tersine, R. J. "Organization Decision Theory: A Synthesis," *Managerial Planning,* July/August 1972.

4

Cost and Capital Analysis

BREAKEVEN ANALYSIS
  Linear Breakeven Analysis
  Contribution Margin
  Nonlinear Breakeven Analysis

COST EQUALIZATION ANALYSIS

INCREMENTAL ANALYSIS

COST CONTROL
  Product Costing Systems
  Cost Standards
  Budgets

COST REDUCTION

CAPITAL ANALYSIS
  Present Value of a Single Payment
  Present Value of an Annuity
  Capital Analysis Techniques
    Payback Period
    Payback Reciprocal
    Average Rate of Return (ARR)
    Net Present Value (NPV)
    Uniform Equivalent Annuity
    Internal Rate of Return (IRR)

  Capital Analysis Disparities
  Depreciation

A FRAMEWORK FOR CAPITAL ANALYSIS

CONCLUSION

QUESTIONS

PROBLEMS

CASES

SELECTED BIBLIOGRAPHY

Costs are usually the most manageable aspect of operations and involve the greatest number of managerial decisions. In profit-making organizations, costs must be kept below revenues or no profit will result. Nonprofit organizations are funded with budget appropriations which limit their operations to certain cost levels. Cost analysis and control are never ending managerial responsibilities that form the basis for economic analysis.

A cost function indicates the relationship between costs and output. The production function and the prices paid for inputs determine an organization's cost function. Since production functions exhibit different forms with one, some, or all inputs variable, cost functions also exhibit different forms. Because almost all organizations (including service and nonprofit organizations) must operate within budgetary constraints, they are all concerned with costs. Technology and competitive characteristics of an organization's environment can elevate the significance of cost analysis.

A convenient analytical fiction can be introduced by segmenting time into the short run and the long run. The *long run* is reasonably clear; it is a period of time of sufficient length such that all inputs (factors of production) can be fully adjusted. The *short run* is a more nebulous concept; it may be an hour, day, month, or year. There are obviously many "short runs," and the longer the time, the greater the possibility for factor substitution and adjustment. In the short run certain types of inputs cannot be changed (increased or decreased). In the long run, all inputs can be varied so as to obtain the most efficient input combination.

In the short run, some inputs are fixed, so expansion or contraction can take place only by varying the amounts of the other (variable) inputs. The fixed inputs in the short run are plant, equipment, and some unique kinds of skilled labor. Output can range from zero if operations are halted to some maximum capacity limited by the fixed inputs. In the long run, all inputs are variable, so output can range from zero to an indefinitely large quantity. The long run is only a planning horizon. Organizations operate in the short run and plan in the long run.

The short and the long run are not definite periods of calendar time; they are sets of conditions. Between the short run and long run there can be no sharp or exact distinction. The two merge into each other and are industry and technology dependent.

In the short run, costs are divided into fixed costs and variable costs. The fixed costs are mainly plant and equipment; they are costs that continue even if operations are temporarily shut down, producing nothing at all. The variable costs are those that vary with the level of output; they are mainly direct labor and material. If a firm ceases operations, variable costs are not incurred but fixed cost obligations continue.

Profit is the difference between total revenues and total costs. Revenues are output related, while costs tend to be input and process related. Many operations in an organization contribute only to costs and do not directly influence revenues. If costs can be reduced and revenues maintained, profits can be increased. To control costs, firms employ cost accounting systems. The ultimate aim of a cost control system is to maintain and improve the spread between revenues and costs.

BREAKEVEN ANALYSIS

The study of the behavior of revenues and costs in relation to output is called breakeven analysis. Its purpose is to estimate the profit of an organization that will result under different operating conditions or output levels. Although it is not a requirement, most breakeven charts assume that there are linear relationships and that all costs are either fixed or variable. The breakeven point is the level of output at which profit is equal to zero; it is also the point at which total revenue equals total cost.

LINEAR BREAKEVEN ANALYSIS

In its basic form, breakeven analysis uses a graphic chart on which total cost and total revenue are plotted in relation to output. The ordinate represents fixed costs, variable costs, and revenue in dollars; the abscissa represents output, expressed as the number of units of product that can be supplied in a given time period. Total cost and total revenue are depicted by straight lines, which intersect at the breakeven point; profit and loss are indicated by the vertical distance between the revenue and cost lines as shown in Figure 1. The breakeven point is the level of output at which total costs are equal to total revenue. To the right of the point, the vertical distance between the two lines represents the profit; to the left, the loss.

Total cost is subdivided into variable costs and fixed costs. *Variable costs* are those that vary directly with the output volume; *fixed costs* tend to remain constant

FIGURE 1
Linear breakeven chart.

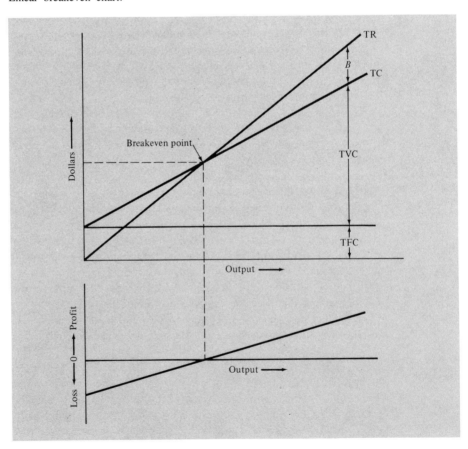

regardless of the output level. While fixed costs are shown graphically as a horizontal line on a breakeven chart, variable costs are usually shown as a straight line with a positive slope. Typical variable costs are raw materials, direct labor, freight cost, and sales commissions. Typical fixed costs are rent, property taxes, depreciation, and interest on bonds. In practice, it is sometimes difficult to decide whether a particular cost belongs in the fixed or variable category.

Usually a breakeven analysis is conducted for a single product in a fixed plant. In the short run the size of the plant, amount of equipment, and management remain constant. Total revenue is equal to the unit price times the output quantity. An algebraic model for cost and revenue relationships is as follows:

$$\text{total revenue} = \text{TR} = pq,$$
$$\text{total cost} = \text{TC} = \text{TFC} + \text{TVC} = \text{TFC} + vq,$$
$$\text{profit} = B = \text{TR} - \text{TC} = pq - (\text{TFC} + vq) = q(p - v) - \text{TFC}.$$

At the breakeven point, $B = 0$ and $\text{TR} = \text{TC}$. Thus

$$\text{breakeven point in units} = q = \frac{\text{TFC}}{p - v},$$
$$\text{breakeven point in dollars} = pq = \frac{p(\text{TFC})}{p - v} = \frac{\text{TFC}}{1 - v/p} = \frac{\text{TFC}}{1 - \text{TVC/TR}},$$

where

TR	= total revenue,	B	= profit,
TC	= total cost,	q	= quantity produced,
TFC	= total fixed cost,	v	= variable cost per unit,
TVC	= total variable cost,	p	= selling price per unit.

EXAMPLE 1

A shoe manufacturer with total fixed costs of $200,000 sells a product for $24 per unit. The product has a variable cost of $20 per unit. What is the breakeven point in units and dollars? How many units must be sold for a profit of $80,000?

We have

$$\text{breakeven point} = q = \frac{\text{TFC}}{p - v} = \frac{200,000}{24 - 20} = 50,000 \text{ units},$$
$$\text{breakeven point} = pq = 24(50,000) = \$1,200,000.$$

For a profit of $80,000,

$$q = \frac{B + \text{TFC}}{p - v} = \frac{80,000 + 200,000}{24 - 20} = 70,000 \text{ units}.$$

The breakeven point is 50,000 units or $1,200,000. For a profit of $80,000, the manufacturer must sell 70,000 units.

CONTRIBUTION MARGIN

The difference between the revenue per unit and the variable cost per unit ($p - v$) is called the contribution per unit. Whenever the variable cost per unit is less than the selling price, the product can make a contribution to profit and fixed costs. The economist defines the contribution per unit as the difference between marginal revenue and marginal cost. The amount by which the total contribution exceeds the total fixed costs is called profit. If fixed costs exceed the total contribution, a loss is incurred. When total contribution and fixed costs are equal, the organization breaks even for the period. The most profitable products are those with the largest difference between total revenue and total variable cost. Overhead or fixed costs are irrelevant in the short term, since they continue regardless of the level of output. In the long run, an organization must cover all its costs or it will cease operations; in the short run, a firm operates as long as it has a positive contribution. Products with the largest contribution are the most desirable:

$$\text{Total contribution} = C = \text{TR} - \text{TVC} = \text{TFC} + B = pq - vq = q(p - v).$$

NONLINEAR BREAKEVEN ANALYSIS

Several modifications can be made to traditional breakeven analysis to make it more realistic. Many costs are partly fixed and partly variable. Such costs as heat, light, power, and maintenance are semifixed.

Total cost and total revenue functions may not be linear, but curvilinear with multiple breakeven points. The total revenue curve may not be linear because of quantity discounts, trade discounts, or cash discounts offered to customers. Increasing market saturation can also depress the price and thus reduce the slope of the total revenue curve, while sales promotion and advertising can increase the slope. The total cost function may be nonlinear because of raw material quantity discounts, inventory carrying costs, overproduction, multiple shifts, overtime, and decreasing marginal returns to variable factors.

The assumption of linearity can be dropped with no adverse effect on the usefulness of the breakeven model provided the equations can be written or plotted for the pertinent range of the total cost and total revenue curves. The breakeven point can still be obtained by equating total cost to total revenue. The point of maximum profits can be found by setting the first derivative of the profit equation (total revenue–total cost) equal to zero.

Figure 2 shows a case of multiple breakeven points. Total revenue is shown as linear to represent a fixed price per unit of output. Total costs are depicted as curvilinear to indicate a changing cost per unit of output. Profits are earned over the range of outputs between the breakeven points; at output levels below and above the profitability range, losses are incurred.

This condition is typical for many firms in the short run that are operating with fixed plant and equipment. They experience economies as output is increased up to a point, and then diseconomies as production is increased further. After the first breakeven point, profits continue to increase as overhead costs are allocated over more units of output. Profits start to decrease as the reductions in fixed costs per unit are outweighed by rising variable costs per unit. Variable costs per unit tend to increase as more production is crowded into the fixed plant, as labor becomes less efficient, and as mechanical breakdowns occur more frequently.

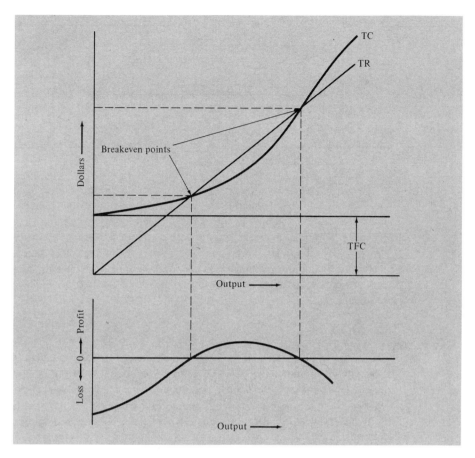

FIGURE 2
Nonlinear breakeven chart.

EXAMPLE 2

An organization has a total revenue function equal to $30q$, and a total cost function equal to $2q^2 - 30q + 250$. What are the breakeven quantities, the profit maximizing production level, and the fixed costs?

At breakeven, total revenue equals total cost:

$$30q = 2q^2 - 30q + 250,$$
$$0 = 2q^2 - 60q + 250,$$
$$0 = q^2 - 30q + 125,$$
$$0 = (q - 5)(q - 25).$$

$\therefore$ Breakeven points are 5 and 25 units.

$$\text{profit} = \text{total revenue} - \text{total cost},$$
$$B = 30q - 2q^2 + 30q - 250,$$
$$= -2q^2 + 60q - 250.$$

Taking the first derivative of profit with respect to output, setting it equal to zero, and solving for q, we obtain the following:

$$\frac{dB}{dq} = -4q + 60 = 0,$$

$$q = 15 \text{ units.}$$

$\therefore$ Profit maximizing output is 15 units. Fixed costs are $250, the constant value in the total cost function.

Breakeven analysis indicates the level where total cost and total revenue cancel. It is a valuable aid in uncovering profit potential. Breakeven analysis indicates to management the fluctuations in profits which occur at various levels of output. Changes in output, revenues, product mixes, labor performance, material utilization, prices, and technology can be analyzed by this technique. Cost data are available in historical accounting records, or if not available can be estimated. The major advantages of breakeven analysis are that it is quick and easy to compute as well as simple to understand.

COST EQUALIZATION ANALYSIS

Cost equalization analysis (CEA) determines the quantity of production (or purchase) at which the cost for one decision alternative equals the cost for other decision alternatives. It finds the cost tradeoff points by examining total cost relationships. By knowing the cost equalization point, it is possible to select the alternative that will minimize cost.

There is a striking similarity between breakeven analysis and cost equalization analysis. Breakeven analysis is a comparison between total revenue and total cost to determine when they are equal (the breakeven point). Cost equalization analysis is a comparison between two or more costs to determine when they are equal—hence the name. The method for breakeven and cost equalization analysis is fundamentally the same.

Given two processes, products, or situations, the cost equalization (breakeven) point is obtained by equating the total costs as follows:

$$TC_1 = TC_2,$$

$$TVC_1 + TFC_1 = TVC_2 + TFC_2,$$

$$v_1 q + TFC_1 = v_2 q + TFC_2,$$

$$q = \frac{TFC_2 - TFC_1}{v_1 - v_2}.$$

If the cost equalization point q is to be positive, then it must be that $TFC_2 > TFC_1$ and $v_1 > v_2$: this is the typical case that arises from the use of a more expensive automated process that reduces the direct labor requirement. However, if $TFC_2 > TFC_1$ and $v_2 > v_1$, then the cost lines diverge without a cost equalization point and process 2 cannot be justified economically. Cost equalization analysis is depicted graphically in Figure 3. When a cost equalization point exists, output levels above it

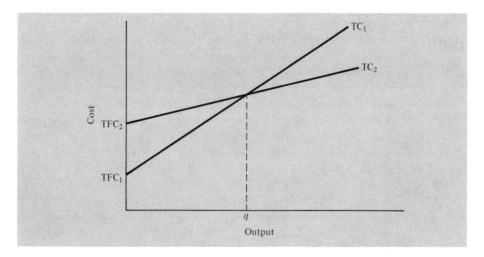

FIGURE 3
Cost equalization analysis.

would favor the selection of process 2; output levels below it, process 1. A good rule of thumb is to select the alternative with the smallest fixed cost for output levels below the cost equalization point, and the alternative with the largest fixed cost for output levels above the cost equalization point.

Cost equalization analysis determines the quantity, or output, where the cost for one alternative equals (crosses over) the cost for another alternative. It displays the cost relationships among alternatives, using either an algebraic or a graphical approach. It is a decision guide for minimizing cost.

EXAMPLE 3

A manager is comparing two machines for purchase. Machine A has a purchase cost of $12,000 and a variable cost per unit estimated at $7.50; machine B has a purchase cost of $20,000 and a variable cost per unit estimated at $5.00. What is the cost equalization point? What decision rule should be applied to the purchase?

We have

$$TC_A = TC_B,$$
$$7.50q + 12,000 = 5.00q + 20,000,$$
$$q = \frac{20,000 - 12,000}{7.50 - 5.00}$$
$$q = 3200 \text{ units.}$$

If output will be below 3200 units, then machine A should be purchased; if above, then machine B.

INCREMENTAL ANALYSIS

Incremental analysis compares the differences among the alternatives being considered. When cost or benefit elements are common to each alternative considered, they are irrelevant (can be neglected in the analysis). Incremental benefits or costs vary as a function of the alternatives considered. An incremental cost may be fixed or variable. Incremental analysis is situational, and each situation is unique. Many management problems require comparing one cost against another, or the payment of some cost to achieve a benefit. Incremental analysis offers wide application for testing proposed actions. It can be used for plant capacity decisions, equipment replacement decisions, make or buy decisions, machine utilization decisions, inventory control, quality control, and process selection.

Incremental analysis is not confined to cost analysis; it can include benefits as well as costs in its comparisons. Thus it is also a cost-benefit or tradeoff analysis procedure. However, in production situations it most frequently involves cost comparisons. While there is no exact procedure for incremental analysis, there are some general guidelines that can be followed:

1. Select the decision variable that will be used to measure cost and benefit changes. Typical examples might be the production run size, the order quantity, the sample size, the crew size, and so forth.
2. Determine all costs that change as the decision variable is increased or decreased. Any costs that do not vary with the decision variable can be ignored. Summing all of the relevant cost changes will give the total incremental cost.
3. Determine all benefits that change as the decision variable is increased or decreased. Summing all the relevant benefit changes will give the total incremental benefit.
4. Subtract the total incremental cost from the total incremental benefit to obtain the net benefit.
5. Of the alternatives considered, the best selection will have the largest net benefit. If only costs are being compared, the alternative with the lowest cost is selected.

EXAMPLE 4

The Walbash Publishing Company must set the price for a new book. The marketing manager is considering sales prices of $8.00, $6.00, and $5.00. The fixed costs allocated to the book are $8,000; the variable costs per book are $3.00. Sales forecasts are for 4,000 books at $8.00 per book, 6,000 books at $6.00 per book, and 11,000 books at $5.00 per book. At what price should the book be sold?

We have

$$B = pq - (\text{TFC} + vq),$$
$$B_8 = (8)4{,}000 - 8{,}000 - (3)4{,}000 = \$12{,}000,$$
$$B_6 = (6)6{,}000 - 8{,}000 - (3)6{,}000 = \$10{,}000,$$
$$B_5 = (5)11{,}000 - 8{,}000 - (3)11{,}000 = \$14{,}000.$$

The book should be sold at $5.00, since that results in the highest profit of $14,000.

"Incremental analysis" and "marginal analysis" are sometimes used interchangeably. More precisely, however, marginal analysis indicates what happens if conditions are changed by a single unit, whereas incremental analysis is not limited to any such small quantity. Realistically, organizations do not usually change their operations by a single unit. Expansion or contraction usually occurs in large quantities (lumps). Thus, marginal analysis can be considered a limiting case of incremental analysis.

COST CONTROL

Costs form the basis for a large number of managerial decisions. They are also one of the most manageable aspects of organizational operations. For an organization to be successful, its costs must be controlled within budgeted limits. Control is basically a comparison of actual performance with planned or standard performance. When results fail to measure up to expectations, the causes are identified and action is taken to rectify the situation.

The costs typically associated with producing an output are direct materials, direct labor, and operations overhead. *Direct material cost* is the cost of the materials included in the finished product. It includes raw materials and components transformed in the processing into the final output. Of course, there are no direct material costs if the output is a service. *Direct labor cost* is the cost of the labor used in producing the output. It does not include indirect labor costs of personnel who do not take part in the actual processing of the output. *Operations overhead costs* are all those costs associated with operations except direct material and direct labor.[1] The sum of the three costs (direct material, direct labor, and operations overhead) is the operations cost, which is also referred to as manufacturing cost or cost of goods produced. Added to operations cost would be such costs as sales cost and administrative cost, as shown in Figure 4.

Cost data must be accumulated, processed, and reported in a meaningful way. Cost collection and allocation is basically a cost accounting function. The method of collecting costs depends on the type of production system involved. The two general classifications are job costing and process costing.

PRODUCT COSTING SYSTEMS

Product costing can be accomplished by either job costing or process costing. *Job costing* is used where costs can be allocated to a specific job or product. The costs are gathered (summed) together for each individual product or service. Job costing is widely used where a number of different kinds of output are produced, as in intermittent production systems. *Process costing* is used where costs are gathered for a period of time and allocated equally to the units of output produced for the period. Process costing is common where a single type of output is produced over a long period of time, as in continuous production systems. Job costing is more precise and less arbitrary in assigning costs, while process costing is a less cumbersome system. A product cost system that is purely job or purely process is difficult to find. Elements of both are usually found in most organizations.

---

[1]In manufacturing organizations, operations overhead is also referred to as manufacturing overhead.

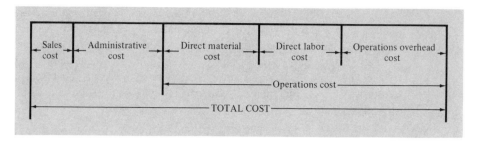

FIGURE 4
Product costs.

COST STANDARDS

Cost standards are established for direct labor, direct material, and operations overhead. Most standards are stated in terms of a single unit of output. Direct labor costs are determined from time standards, and direct material costs are calculated from the average quantity of material used in a unit. A cost standard gives an indication of "normal" or 100% efficiency.

Cost standards may be derived from historical costs, intelligent estimates, or an analytical buildup of cost components. They must be revised when the prices of inputs change or the production process is modified. Cost standards become the basis for evaluating performance. Management can compare actual cost with standard cost and concentrate its effort on discrepancies.

BUDGETS

A budget is a statement of expected performance in some quantitative measure (usually money) for future periods. It is both a planning and a control device. Budgets are made for all major activities of an organization. They can be fixed or variable. A fixed budget is determined for a specific level of output or activity. Variable budgets are more flexible and are developed for several levels of output. Knowing the organization's standard costs, the manager can then calculate his budgetary expenditures for any given level of output.

COST REDUCTION

Cost reduction begins where cost control ends. Cost control is concerned with maintaining costs in accordance with established standards. The standards are goals. Cost reduction, on the other hand, continually challenges these goals in an attempt to achieve lower and lower costs. The ability to reduce costs and not just control them is essential in a competitive environment.

Cost control seeks the lowest possible cost under existing conditions, whereas cost reduction recognizes no condition as permanent. A change in conditions can result in lower cost. Cost control is never finished, while cost reduction can be finished because of its project orientation. Cost control is limited to items that have standards, but cost reduction applies to every aspect of the organization whether or not standards exist. Cost control emphasizes the past and present; cost reduction emphasizes the present and future.

An organization with good cost control is not necessarily cost efficient. Management devotes considerable attention and resources to cost control. Such common activities as general accounting, budgeting, cost accounting, and industrial engineering are committed to cost control methods and techniques on a continuing basis. However, the best cost accounting and control system does no more than maintain the status quo. In a changing environment, the status quo is not good enough.

The amount of cost reduction that can be achieved is related to the characteristics of the given cost and the degree of management effort expended. Realistically, a point of diminishing returns can be reached where the cost of the additional effort outweighs the potential savings. It is unwise to concentrate on minor cost elements while major costs are neglected. Accordingly, it is essential to identify those areas where cost reduction efforts should be concentrated.

Every organization tends to have a distinctive cost structure or cost profile. The cost profile indicates where cost reduction efforts should start or can be most successful. The cost profile is obtained by expressing every cost element as a percentage of budget, sales dollars, or cost of sales. Efforts should be concentrated in those categories that could reduce cost the most. That is, those categories with the highest contribution to cost should be studied first. Usually a few cost categories represent the majority of total costs.

Cost reduction does not always involve only reducing current cost levels; it also includes achieving greater productivity at existing cost levels. Cost reduction is obtained when higher productivity is attained from an existing production unit. When unused (idle) productive resources are utilized, cost reductions are possible.

There is a tendency for organizations to attempt to produce everything possible in-house when many items could be purchased. This is one aspect of the important and much-discussed *make or buy decision*. The "make" option is pursued in the belief that such a practice will increase the overhead (burden) absorption. In fact, it may be more economical to reduce the overhead rather than to absorb it. Frequently, janitorial services, equipment maintenance, legal services, and so forth can be subcontracted at a lower cost to local suppliers. Organizations should concentrate in their own areas of expertise and not try to perform all activities.

Standardization refers to uniformity in components, work methods, procedures, equipment, and processes. Standardization reduces variety. Any organization with numerous or lengthy bills of material is a candidate for standardization analysis. Lack of standardization creates tremendous burdens in design engineering, manufacturing setups, inventory levels, parts replacement, and so forth. It is just as relevant in paperwork forms, clerical effort, and data processing. Standardization is desirable for products, components, processes, work methods, and job design. It will be discussed more thoroughly in subsequent chapters.

It is impossible to give a complete list of cost reduction options. We have barely scratched the surface. Any cost is a candidate for improvement, and the possibilities are endless. The number of techniques and options available for potential cost reduction is limited only by the imagination of the analyst. Cost reduction does not mean merely reducing the amount of money spent. It means getting better results for the same amount of money or the same results for less.

CAPITAL ANALYSIS

Managers make decisions concerning the allocation of capital to acquire capabilities for improving the strategic position of the organization. Usually they are beneficial in revenue generation or cost reduction. They might include proposals for new products, technologies, facilities, or equipment. Sometimes they involve proposed replacements of existing equipment, processes, or facilities. Since the supply of funds to all organizations is limited, the use of funds should be carefully evaluated to ensure that the best choices are made.

New investment proposals are among the most important decisions that management may be called upon to make. These decisions are important not only because they involve a large commitment of capital, but also because such a commitment, once made, is largely irreversible. Mistakes in investment analysis affect the operation of a business for years to come, and they can be expensive if not ultimately disastrous.

A capital good can be defined as a good that provides a stream of benefits for a time period of longer duration than one year. It includes machinery, plant, and equipment. For accounting purposes the purchase price of the capital good is depreciated over several years. The need for capital expenditures comes from three sources:

1. *Depreciation.* Fixed assets (other than land) are continually wearing out and need to be replaced.
2. *Obsolescence.* New products and more efficient methods may render an asset obsolete even though it functions as designed (technological obsolescence).
3. *Expansion.* The economy as a whole is growing (as evidenced by the GNP). Most individual companies grow year after year, and so keep buying more plant and equipment.

A capital investment is a commitment of resources with an expectation of benefits over some future period. When a capital investment is made, costs are incurred in the expectation of future returns, and the future naturally involves uncertainty or risk. Every decision involves alternatives, even if the alternative is simply to do nothing.

Traditionally, industry has obtained the majority of the billions of dollars each year to pay for its capital investment needs from internally generated funds ("net cash flow"). It also obtains funds externally from equity and debt. Equity capital comes from the funds obtained from stock sales. Debt capital is obtained by borrowing, as with bonds, notes, and other liabilities. Nonprofit organizations obtain capital from gifts, donations, taxes, or operating income. Internally, an organization can increase its available funds by retaining earnings from profits. "Net cash flow" for an investment is earnings (net income or net benefit) after income taxes plus depreciation (EAT + depreciation).

Capital budgeting is the decision making process concerned with whether or not to add to or replaced fixed assets. Funds are committed in the present in return for an expected stream of future cash benefits. Many times these capital expenditures are of considerable magnitude and may affect the future existence of the company. Investments can be limited by the following three factors:

1. scarcity of available funds;
2. limited investment opportunities;
3. disproportionate increase in organizational costs due to rapid growth (organizational indigestion).

The concepts of opportunity cost and the time value of money are important in capital expenditure decisions. Opportunity costs are the benefits the organization could have realized had it invested its capital in an alternative. The time value of money simply means that a dollar today is worth more than a dollar received in the future.

Capital investment decisions usually merit the attention of top management. There are several important reasons for this high-level attention:

1. A large amount of money is being committed.
2. Resources are being committed for a long period of time.
3. Decisions are not easily reversible without great expense.
4. Success or failure of the company may depend on the quality of the decision.
5. Risks and uncertainty increase with the length of the time horizon.
6. Lower level attention might result in the suboptimization of the overall system.

PRESENT VALUE OF A SINGLE PAYMENT

The present value technique of analysis discounts all relevant cash flows to the current time period. Money to be received in the future is worth less in the present. This is because the money could be invested in something else and a return earned on it. Present values are used to determine the current value of a sum or stream of receipts (or payments) expected to be received (or paid) in the future. Assume a principal sum P is invested at interest rate i which will yield a future total sum S in n years if all the earnings are retained and compounded annually. Then

$$S = P(1 + i)^n,$$
$$P = \frac{S}{(1 + i)^n} = S(PV_{sp}),$$

where

$$PV_{sp} = \text{present value factor for a single payment} = \frac{1}{(1 + i)^n}.$$

Fortunately, it is not necessary to calculate the present value factors; they can be looked up in tables such as Table 1. By multiplying the present value factor by the future sum, the present value is obtained. The practice of reducing future sums or income streams to present values by using specific interest rates is often referred to as discounting.

PRESENT VALUE OF AN ANNUITY

An annuity is a series of equal payments (receipts) to be paid (or received) at the end of successive periods of equal time. The present value of an annuity is the value of the annuity over a future period expressed in terms of the present. We shall use the notation PV_a for the present value factor of an annuity, and S_a for the yearly annuity payments. It can be shown that the present value of an annuity payment of size S_a is as follows:

$$P_a = \frac{S_a}{i}\left(1 - \frac{1}{(1 + i)^n}\right) = S_a \frac{1 - (1 + i)^{-n}}{i} = S_a (PV_a).$$

Annuity present value factors are given in Table 2. By multiplying the present value factor by the annuity amount, the present value is obtained.

TABLE 1

Present value of a single payment[a]

Years hence	1%	2%	4%	6%	8%	10%	12%	14%	15%
1	0.990	0.980	0.962	0.943	0.926	0.909	0.893	0.877	0.870
2	0.980	0.961	0.925	0.890	0.857	0.826	0.797	0.769	0.756
3	0.971	0.942	0.889	0.840	0.794	0.751	0.712	0.675	0.658
4	0.961	0.924	0.855	0.792	0.735	0.683	0.636	0.592	0.572
5	0.951	0.906	0.822	0.747	0.681	0.621	0.567	0.519	0.497
6	0.942	0.888	0.790	0.705	0.630	0.564	0.507	0.456	0.432
7	0.933	0.871	0.760	0.665	0.583	0.513	0.452	0.400	0.376
8	0.923	0.853	0.731	0.627	0.540	0.467	0.404	0.351	0.327
9	0.914	0.837	0.703	0.592	0.500	0.424	0.361	0.308	0.284
10	0.905	0.820	0.676	0.558	0.463	0.386	0.322	0.270	0.247
11	0.896	0.804	0.650	0.527	0.429	0.350	0.287	0.237	0.215
12	0.887	0.788	0.625	0.497	0.397	0.319	0.257	0.208	0.187
13	0.879	0.773	0.601	0.469	0.368	0.290	0.229	0.182	0.163
14	0.870	0.758	0.577	0.442	0.340	0.263	0.205	0.160	0.141
15	0.861	0.743	0.555	0.417	0.315	0.239	0.183	0.140	0.123
16	0.853	0.728	0.534	0.394	0.292	0.218	0.163	0.123	0.107
17	0.844	0.714	0.513	0.371	0.270	0.198	0.146	0.108	0.093
18	0.836	0.700	0.494	0.350	0.250	0.180	0.130	0.095	0.081
19	0.828	0.686	0.475	0.331	0.232	0.164	0.116	0.083	0.070
20	0.820	0.673	0.456	0.312	0.215	0.149	0.104	0.073	0.061
21	0.811	0.660	0.439	0.294	0.199	0.135	0.093	0.064	0.053
22	0.803	0.647	0.422	0.278	0.184	0.123	0.083	0.056	0.046
23	0.795	0.634	0.406	0.262	0.170	0.112	0.074	0.049	0.040
24	0.788	0.622	0.390	0.247	0.158	0.102	0.066	0.043	0.035
25	0.780	0.610	0.375	0.233	0.146	0.092	0.059	0.038	0.030
26	0.772	0.598	0.361	0.220	0.135	0.084	0.053	0.033	0.026
27	0.764	0.586	0.347	0.207	0.125	0.076	0.047	0.029	0.023
28	0.757	0.574	0.333	0.196	0.116	0.069	0.042	0.026	0.020
29	0.749	0.563	0.321	0.185	0.107	0.063	0.037	0.022	0.017
30	0.742	0.552	0.308	0.174	0.099	0.057	0.033	0.020	0.015

[a]Present value of $1 received at the end of the specified period.

EXAMPLE 5

Should a machine be rented for $7,500 a year or purchased for $40,000 if the useful life is ten years and the cost of capital is 14% (neglect tax considerations)?

We have

$$P_a = S_a \,(PV_a) = 7,500(5.216) = \$39,120,$$

where the present value factor of 5.216 is obtained from Table 2 for 10 years at a rate of 14%. It is more advantageous to rent the machine, since the present value of the rental ($39,120) is less than the purchase price ($40,000).

TABLE 1 *(continued)*

	16%	18%	20%	22%	24%	25%	26%	28%	30%
	0.862	0.847	0.833	0.820	0.806	0.800	0.794	0.781	0.769
	0.743	0.718	0.694	0.672	0.650	0.640	0.630	0.610	0.592
	0.641	0.609	0.579	0.551	0.524	0.512	0.500	0.477	0.455
	0.552	0.516	0.482	0.451	0.423	0.410	0.397	0.373	0.350
	0.476	0.437	0.402	0.370	0.341	0.328	0.315	0.291	0.269
	0.410	0.370	0.335	0.303	0.275	0.262	0.250	0.227	0.207
	0.354	0.314	0.279	0.249	0.222	0.210	0.198	0.178	0.159
	0.305	0.266	0.233	0.204	0.179	0.168	0.157	0.139	0.123
	0.263	0.225	0.194	0.167	0.144	0.134	0.125	0.108	0.094
	0.227	0.191	0.162	0.137	0.116	0.107	0.099	0.085	0.073
	0.195	0.162	0.135	0.112	0.094	0.086	0.079	0.066	0.056
	0.168	0.137	0.112	0.092	0.076	0.069	0.062	0.052	0.043
	0.145	0.116	0.093	0.075	0.061	0.055	0.050	0.040	0.033
	0.125	0.099	0.078	0.062	0.049	0.044	0.039	0.032	0.025
	0.108	0.084	0.065	0.051	0.040	0.035	0.031	0.025	0.020
	0.093	0.071	0.054	0.042	0.032	0.028	0.025	0.019	0.015
	0.080	0.060	0.045	0.034	0.026	0.023	0.020	0.015	0.012
	0.069	0.051	0.038	0.028	0.021	0.018	0.016	0.012	0.009
	0.060	0.043	0.031	0.023	0.017	0.014	0.012	0.009	0.007
	0.051	0.037	0.026	0.019	0.014	0.012	0.010	0.007	0.005
	0.044	0.031	0.022	0.015	0.011	0.009	0.008	0.006	0.004
	0.038	0.026	0.018	0.013	0.009	0.007	0.006	0.004	0.003
	0.033	0.022	0.015	0.010	0.007	0.006	0.005	0.003	0.002
	0.028	0.019	0.013	0.008	0.006	0.005	0.004	0.003	0.002
	0.024	0.016	0.010	0.007	0.005	0.004	0.003	0.002	0.001
	0.021	0.014	0.009	0.006	0.004	0.003	0.002	0.002	0.001
	0.018	0.011	0.007	0.005	0.003	0.002	0.002	0.001	0.001
	0.016	0.010	0.006	0.004	0.002	0.002	0.002	0.001	0.001
	0.014	0.008	0.005	0.003	0.002	0.002	0.001	0.001	0.001
	0.012	0.007	0.004	0.003	0.002	0.001	0.001	0.001	

CAPITAL ANALYSIS TECHNIQUES

What techniques can be used to compare capital investment alternatives? Several techniques exist, and each has advantages and disadvantages. Paramount in the use of these techniques is the maxim that the output will be only as good as the input. The methods are simple, but gathering relevant and accurate inputs is frequently difficult. The basic techniques for ranking investment alternatives are the payback period, payback reciprocal, average rate of return, net present value, uniform equivalent annuity, and the internal rate of return.

Payback Period

The payback period is the length of time required for the net cash flow to equal the investment. It is also known as the cash breakeven period. Thus, the payback period is not a gauge of prospective profitability but of the rate of turnover or liquid-

TABLE 2

Present value of an annuity[a]

(N) (Years)	1%	2%	4%	6%	8%	10%	12%	14%	15%
1	0.990	0.980	0.962	0.943	0.926	0.909	0.893	0.877	0.870
2	1.970	1.942	1.886	1.833	1.783	1.736	1.690	1.647	1.626
3	2.941	2.884	2.775	2.673	2.577	2.487	2.402	2.322	2.283
4	3.902	3.808	3.630	3.465	3.312	3.170	3.037	2.914	2.855
5	4.853	4.713	4.452	4.212	3.993	3.791	3.605	3.433	3.352
6	5.795	5.601	5.242	4.917	4.623	4.355	4.111	3.889	3.784
7	6.728	6.472	6.002	5.582	5.206	4.868	4.564	4.288	4.160
8	7.652	7.325	6.733	6.210	5.747	5.335	4.968	4.639	4.487
9	8.566	8.162	7.435	6.802	6.247	5.759	5.328	4.946	4.772
10	9.471	8.983	8.111	7.360	6.710	6.145	5.650	5.216	5.019
11	10.368	9.787	8.760	7.887	7.139	6.495	5.937	5.453	5.234
12	11.255	10.575	9.385	8.384	7.536	6.814	6.194	5.660	5.421
13	12.134	11.343	9.986	8.853	7.904	7.103	6.424	5.842	5.583
14	13.004	12.106	10.563	9.295	8.244	7.367	6.628	6.002	5.724
15	13.865	12.849	11.118	9.712	8.559	7.606	6.811	6.142	5.847
16	14.718	13.578	11.652	10.106	8.851	7.824	6.974	6.265	5.954
17	15.562	14.292	12.166	10.477	9.122	8.022	7.120	6.373	6.047
18	16.398	14.992	12.659	10.828	9.372	8.201	7.250	6.467	6.128
19	17.226	15.678	13.134	11.158	9.604	8.365	7.366	6.550	6.198
20	18.046	16.351	13.590	11.470	9.818	8.514	7.469	6.623	6.259
21	18.857	17.011	14.029	11.764	10.017	8.649	7.562	6.687	6.312
22	19.660	17.658	14.451	12.042	10.201	8.772	7.645	6.743	6.359
23	20.456	18.292	14.857	12.303	10.371	8.883	7.718	6.792	6.399
24	21.243	18.914	15.247	12.550	10.529	8.985	7.784	6.835	6.434
25	22.023	19.523	15.622	12.783	10.675	9.077	7.843	6.873	6.464
26	22.795	20.121	15.983	30.003	10.810	9.161	7.896	6.906	6.491
27	23.560	20.707	16.330	13.211	10.935	9.237	7.943	6.935	6.514
28	24.316	21.281	16.663	13.406	11.051	9.307	7.984	6.961	6.534
29	25.066	21.844	16.984	13.591	11.158	9.370	8.022	6.983	6.551
30	25.808	22.396	17.292	13.765	11.258	9.427	8.055	7.003	6.566

[a]Present value of $1 received annually at the end of each period for N periods.

ity of the investment. The recovery of the investment must be completed before there is a return on the investment. The return depends on the service life of the asset and the value of its services beyond the payoff point. If the firm is desperately short of cash, the financial manager uses the payback method to emphasize investments that produce a quick return of cash funds. The liquidity objective is stressed at the expense of profit objective. Organizations characterized by instability, uncertainty, and rapid technological change may adopt the payback approach on the grounds that the future is too unpredictable. This method does not consider the time value of money.

When the net cash flows are the same each time period, the payback period is calculated as follows:

$$\text{Payback period} = \frac{\text{investment}}{\text{net cash flow}} = \frac{I}{F} = \frac{I}{\text{EAT} + \text{depreciation}}.$$

When the net cash flows vary (are not the same for each period), the payback period

TABLE 2 *(continued)*

16%	18%	20%	22%	24%	25%	26%	28%	30%
0.862	0.847	0.833	0.820	0.806	0.800	0.794	0.781	0.769
1.605	1.566	1.528	1.492	1.457	1.440	1.424	1.392	1.361
2.246	2.174	2.106	2.042	1.981	1.952	1.923	1.868	1.816
2.798	2.690	2.589	2.494	2.404	2.362	2.320	2.241	2.166
3.274	3.127	2.991	2.864	2.745	2.689	2.635	2.532	2.436
3.685	3.498	3.326	3.167	3.020	2.951	2.885	2.759	2.643
4.039	3.812	3.605	3.416	3.242	3.161	3.083	2.937	2.802
4.344	4.078	3.837	3.619	3.421	3.329	3.241	3.076	2.925
4.607	4.303	4.031	3.786	3.566	3.463	3.366	3.184	3.019
4.833	4.494	4.192	3.923	3.682	3.571	3.465	3.269	3.092
5.029	4.656	4.327	4.035	3.776	3.656	3.544	3.335	3.147
5.197	4.793	4.439	4.127	3.851	3.725	3.606	3.387	3.190
5.342	4.910	4.533	4.203	3.912	3.780	3.656	3.427	3.223
5.468	5.008	4.611	4.265	3.962	3.824	3.695	3.459	3.249
5.575	5.092	4.675	4.315	4.001	3.859	3.726	3.483	3.268
5.669	5.162	4.730	4.357	4.033	3.887	3.751	3.503	3.283
5.749	5.222	4.775	4.391	4.059	3.910	3.771	3.518	3.295
5.818	5.273	4.812	4.419	4.080	3.928	3.786	3.529	3.304
5.877	5.316	4.844	4.442	4.097	3.942	3.799	3.539	3.311
5.929	5.353	4.870	4.460	4.110	3.954	3.808	3.546	3.316
5.973	5.384	4.891	4.476	4.121	3.963	3.816	3.551	3.320
6.011	5.410	4.909	4.488	4.130	3.970	3.822	3.556	3.323
6.044	5.432	4.925	4.499	4.137	3.976	3.827	3.559	3.325
6.073	5.451	4.937	4.507	4.143	3.981	3.831	3.562	3.327
6.097	5.467	4.948	4.514	4.147	3.985	3.834	3.564	3.329
6.118	5.480	4.956	4.520	4.151	3.988	3.837	3.566	3.330
6.136	5.492	4.964	4.524	4.154	3.990	3.839	3.567	3.331
6.152	5.502	4.970	4.528	4.157	3.992	3.840	3.568	3.331
6.166	5.510	4.975	4.531	4.159	3.994	3.841	3.569	3.332
6.177	5.517	4.979	4.534	4.160	3.995	3.842	3.569	3.332

is determined by counting the time periods until the accumulated net cash flows equal the investment.

The reasons for using the payback period are as follows:

1. It emphasizes liquidity needs rather than profitability.
2. Future returns are highly uncertain.
3. Firms do not maximize, but earn a satisfactory return, so a rough gauge is all that is necessary.
4. It is easy to measure, compute, and explain.

The disadvantages of the payback period are as follows:

1. It neglects the time value of money.
2. It neglects the return on investment after payback is completed.
3. It neglects the cost of obtaining funds (cost of capital).
4. It neglects the timing of inflows.

Payback Reciprocal

A project with an infinite lifetime and equal net cash flows has an internal rate of return equal to the payback reciprocal.[2] If the project does not have an infinite life, the payback reciprocal is greater than the internal rate of return. Under certain conditions the payback reciprocal is an adequate approximation to the internal rate of return. These conditions are:

1. The useful life of the project is at least twice the payback period.
2. Benefits are constant over the investment life.
3. There is no salvage value.

Average Rate of Return (ARR)

The average rate of return method eliminates some of the faults of the payback method. This method ranks projects according to their average rates of return over their useful lives. One method for calculating the average rate of return is to divide the average annual income (earnings after depreciation and taxes) by the average investment. Like the payback method, this method is easy to understand and to calculate. In addition, it considers earnings over the life of the project. However, it fails to consider the timing of these inflows.

This rate is based upon reported accounting income and is also called the accounting rate of return. It is given mathematically by

$$\text{Average rate of return} = \frac{\text{average earnings after taxes}}{\frac{1}{2}(\text{investment})}$$

$$= \frac{\frac{1}{n}\sum_{i=1}^{n}E_i}{\frac{1}{2}I} = \frac{\overline{E}}{\frac{1}{2}I}.$$

Net Present Value (NPV)

None of the previous techniques consider the time value of money. A dollar today is worth more than a dollar one year from today because it can be earning interest, or other income, over the time period. If a savings account pays 6% interest annually, a dollar invested today will be worth $1.06 one year from today. Thus, one can readily see that money has a value in relation to time. The net present value, uniform equivalent annuity, and internal rate of return methods for ranking capital investments consider the time value of money by giving greater weight to the income of the earlier years of a project. The farther in the future the income is, the lower will be the weight assigned to that income. The weight assigned is called the "present value factor."

In the net present value technique, the future cash inflows are discounted at a predetermined discount rate (cost of capital), and the sum of the present values is compared with the cost of the investment. This method assumes some minimum

[2]For a mathematical proof, see C. T. Horngren, *Cost Accounting*, Englewood Cliffs, NJ: Prentice-Hall, 1982, Chapter 12.

desired rate of return (cost of capital) is required and that net cash flow can be reinvested at this rate. All expected cash flows are discounted to the present using the minimum desired rate of return. If the result is positive, the investment is desirable because its return exceeds the desired minimum. If the result is negative, the investment is undesirable. The mathematical formulation is as follows:

$$P = -I_0 + \frac{F_1}{1 + k} + \frac{F_2}{(1 + k)^2} + \cdots + \frac{F_n}{(1 + k)^n}$$

$$= -I_0 + \sum_{j=1}^{n} \frac{F_j}{(1 + k)^j}$$

where

P = net present value,
I_0 = investment required at time 0,
F_j = net cash flow in time period j,
k = minimum required rate of return (cost of capital),
n = lifetime of the project.

The NPV is equal to the present value of inflows minus the present value of outflows. The discount rate is determined first and applied to the expected net cash flows to determine their present value. The present values are summed, and the investment outlay is subtracted. If the result is positive, the project is acceptable. If it is negative, the project should be rejected. Acceptable projects will be undertaken in accordance with capital rationing. The discount rate selected may reflect costs of capital, the average return on investment, or some other minimum standard. The higher the selected rate, the lower will be the present value.

Fortunately, it is not necessary to work with the mathematical formulation of net present value. The present value factors needed are those in Table 1 and Table 2. If the net cash flows are the same for each year, the appropriate present value factor is found in Table 2 as the present value of an annuity. If the net cash flows are different for each year, the appropriate present value factors are found in Table 1 as the present value of a single payment.

A profitability index is frequently used for ranking different projects by the net present value technique. The index is calculated by dividing the gross present value of a project by the required investment. The index makes different size projects comparable. Projects with profitability indexes greater than one are desirable. The mathematical formulation is as follows:

$$\text{Profitability index} = \frac{\text{gross present value}}{\text{investment}} = \frac{P + I_0}{I_0}$$

For some evaluations, such as replacement studies, only costs are considered, and benefits are neglected. In these instances, the NPV selects the alternative with the minimum present value of initial and future disbursements.

Some managers object to discounting techniques because the underlying estimates are so rough that the refinement of discounting them is considered more work than it is worth. Those who do use them argue that the extra work involved is small and the results are better than not attempting to allow for the time factor.

Uniform Equivalent Annuity

The uniform equivalent annuity technique is sometimes used in place of the net present value technique. It is especially useful for comparing projects with different economic lives, because it offers comparable benefit or cost per year figures. Instead of converting all figures to the present value, this method converts all figures to an equivalent annuity. Both techniques are internally consistent, and either will give the same final results in the comparison of investment alternatives. Since the two are equivalent, we shall favor the net present value technique and not develop the uniform equivalent annuity technique.

Internal Rate of Return (IRR)

The internal rate of return technique is a method for deriving the rate of return implicit in a set of forecasted cash flows. The yield to maturity on a contractual obligation is derived by finding the rate of return at which the flow of future receipts has a present worth equal to the capital investment required. It can also be stated as that rate of return which equates the present value of inflows to the present value of outflows. If capital could be obtained at less than this rate, the investment would provide a benefit equal to the difference between the rate of return earned and the cost of capital. If the cost of capital is higher that the rate of return, the receipts generated from the investment would be insufficient to cover costs.

The internal rate of return equates the present value of future periodic cash inflows with the present value of the capital investment expenditure required to undertake the project. Projects are ranked in descending order of IRR. All those with an IRR greater than a given ''hurdle rate'' are acceptable, subject to capital budget constraints. IRR can be determined from the following formula:

$$I_0 = \frac{F_1}{1 + r} + \frac{F_2}{(1 + r)^2} + \cdots + \frac{F_n}{(1 + r)^n}$$
$$= \sum_{j = 1}^{n} \frac{F_j}{(1 + r)^j},$$

where

I_0 = investment required at time 0,
F_j = net cash flow in time period j,
r = internal rate of return,
n = lifetime of the project.

If the computed internal rate of return (r) is greater than the firm's cost of capital, the project is desirable. Present value tables make available a method of solution that does not require the mathematical solution from the above formula. To obtain the IRR for unequal cash flows, it is necessary to use a trial-and-error approach and interpolate between the returns. The payback reciprocal gives a rough indication of the approximate internal rate of return.

Unlike the NPV, which also can be used for cost comparisons, the IRR requires estimates of benefits as well as costs. Moreover, the NPV's reinvestment rate is assumed to be the firm's cost of capital, whereas the IRR technique implicitly assumes that the net cash flows are (or can be) reinvested at the calculated internal rate of return.

EXAMPLE 6

A new machine can be purchased for $200,000. The pertinent capital analysis data are as follows:

Year	(1) Depreciation	(2) Earnings before taxes	(3) Taxes	(4) Earnings after taxes (2−3)	(5) Net cash flow (4 + 1)
1	40,000	20,000	8,000	12,000	52,000
2	64,000	30,000	12,000	18,000	82,000
3	48,000	40,000	16,000	24,000	72,000
4	32,000	24,000	9,600	14,400	46,400
5	16,000	20,000	8,000	12,000	28,000
Salvage	—	10,000	4,000	6,000	6,000

The cost of capital is 15%, and the salvage value at the end of the fifth year is $10,000. What are the payback period, average rate of return, net present value, and internal rate of return? Should the machine be purchased?

Payback Period:

$$52,000 + 82,000 + 66,000 = \$200,000$$
$$\text{Payback period} = \quad 1 \quad + \quad 1 \quad + \quad 0.92 \quad = 2.92 \text{ years.}$$

Average Rate of Return:

$$\text{Average rate of return} = \frac{\overline{E}}{\frac{1}{2}I_0}$$
$$= \frac{(12,000 + 18,000 + 24,000 + 14,400 + 12,000 + 6,000)/5}{\frac{1}{2}(200,000)}$$
$$= 0.173, \text{ or } 17.3\%.$$

Net Present Value:

$$P = -I_0 + \sum_{j=1}^{n} \frac{F_j}{(1 + k)^j}$$
$$= -200,000 + 52,000\,(0.870) + 82,000\,(0.756) + 72,000\,(0.658)$$
$$+ 46,400\,(0.572) + 34,000\,(0.497)$$
$$= -200,000 + 198,047$$
$$= -\$1953.$$

Internal Rate of Return:

$$I_0 = \sum_{j=1}^{n} \frac{F_j}{(1 + r)^j},$$

$$200,000 = 52,000\,PV_{sp} + 82,000\,PV_{sp} + 72,000\,PV_{sp} + 46,400\,PV_{sp}$$
$$+ 28,000\,PV_{sp} + 6,000\,PV_{sp}$$

From the present value table

$$r = 14\%, \quad I_0 = \$202,377,$$
$$r = 15\%, \quad I_0 = \$197,583.$$

Interpolating between 14% and 15%,

$$r = 0.14 + \frac{(202,377 - 200,000)(0.01)}{(202,377 - 197,583)}$$
$$r = 0.145, \quad \text{or } 14.5\%.$$

In summary, the payback period is 2.9 years; the average rate of return is 17.3%; the net present value is $-\$1953$, and the internal rate of return is 14.5%. Since the rate of return is less than the cost of capital and the net present value is negative, do not purchase the machine.

EXAMPLE 7

An investment of $200,000 in a machine will have a salvage value of $60,000 after an economic life of 5 years. Maintenance and operating costs are $40,000 the first year and increase by $2,000 per year thereafter. If the firm's cost of capital is 10%, what is the net present value cost of the investment before tax considerations?

Present value of investment:	$200,000

Present value of operations:

Year 1: 40,000 (0.909)	36,360	
Year 2: 42,000 (0.826)	34,692	
Year 3: 44,000 (0.751)	33,044	
Year 4: 46,000 (0.683)	31,418	
Year 5: 48,000 (0.621)	29,808	
	165,322	165,322

Present value of salvage:	
Year 5: 60,000 (0.621)	-37,260
Net present value cost:	$328,062

CAPITAL ANALYSIS DISPARITIES

Although there are advantages and disadvantages to each of the capital analysis techniques, there are disparities that exist among the methods of analysis. Several disparities are as follows:

1. *Size disparity*. Some of the techniques compare benefits generated with investment required in arriving at an index of desirability. The absolute quantities of investment and benefit are neglected in favor of a rate or index. For example, analyses of two mutually exclusive investments could give conflicting results. A small investment could have a higher IRR but a lower NPV than a competing investment of a larger size. According to the indexing method, the firm would choose the small investment and forego the greater benefit of the large investment. One method of avoiding this dilemma is to rank projects based on their NPV.

2. *Time disparity*. For comparison purposes, not all projects have the same expected lifetime. An appropriate analysis requires the project lifetime be normalized or investment at project termination be forecasted. When alternatives considered differ in their expected lives, one approach is to extend the evaluation over a planning horizon equal to the smallest common multiple for the life of all alternatives.

3. *Risk disparity*. The risk and uncertainty of future cash flows do not receive sufficient treatment in many instances. Should a project with a higher return be considered more desirable if the risk involved is larger? How should risk and return be considered? The life of an asset, the cost of capital, and an asset's salvage value are all subject to unpredictable changes due to economic, technological, or other environmental factors.

4. *Nonmonetary disparity*. Not all pertinent factors can be quantified and compared mathematically. Difficulties in measuring certain types of benefits or sacrifices do not justify their exclusion from analyses. Human, behavioral, and social factors cannot be completely ignored.

5. *Dependence disparity*. Many investment proposals are not independent, since they are influenced by past decisions and acceptance will influence future decisions. Contributions of individual pieces of equipment in an operating system are difficult to establish, since they contribute to the earning power of the total system.

DEPRECIATION

The allocation of the cost of a capital good (long-lived asset) to the individual accounting periods of its life is termed depreciation. It is a charge that reflects the decrease in value of an asset over time. Since a capital good provides benefits for many years, it is expensed over several periods of time rather than all at once, when the asset is purchased.[3] Depreciation has an important effect on income tax payments. Different depreciation methods can substantially alter the pattern of cash flows and thus influence capital investment decisions.

The value of a physical asset normally decreases with time because of physical and functional deterioration. The life of an asset can be measured in several different ways. The *physical life* of an asset is the length of time it is capable of performing its intended function satisfactorily. The *economic life* of an asset is the length of time it can perform its intended function not only satisfactorily but also competitively compared with available alternatives. Technological innovation may render an asset obsolete before it reaches the end of its physical life. The *accounting life* of an asset is the length of time over which the asset is depreciated. The accounting life is based on tax laws and governmental requirements. It may or may not reflect the true decrease in the value of the asset.

Depreciation is an accounting scheme to recover the initial investment of an asset over successive periods of its life. It is the part of each period's income set aside as an expense in order to recover the initial investment, possibly for its eventual replacement. Since depreciation is an expense, the larger the depreciation charged the smaller the income, and hence the smaller the taxes that must be paid. It is desirable

---

[3]Land is not depreciated, since it will last indefinitely.

TABLE 3
Recovery property class lives under ACRS

Class life	Type of recovery property
3 year	Automobiles, light trucks, machinery and equipment used for research and development, and other short-lived tangible personal property.
5 year	All other tangible personal property not included in the other personal property recovery classes; this includes most machinery and equipment and public utility property with a useful life of 4 to 18 years.
10 year	Public utility personal property with a life of more than 18 but not more than 25 years, theme and amusement park property, residential manufactured homes, railroad tank cars, and certain coal utilization properties.
15 year public utility	All public utility personal property with a life in excess of 25 years.
15 year real property	All depreciable real property other than that included in the 10 year class.

for an organization to depreciate an asset as rapidly as possible to defer tax payments and to protect against obsolescence in the event of unforeseen technological improvements.

The Economic Recovery Act of 1981 introduced a new system of tax depreciation. This system, the Accelerated Cost Recovery System (ACRS), provides recovery of the cost of property in a manner which bears no relationship to the period during which the asset is actually used. Depreciable assets are now referred to as *recovery property,* and depreciation is referred to as *cost recovery.* The Act categorizes all depreciable assets as one of five types and allocates the original cost of the asset over a 3, 5, 10, or 15 year period. The property classes are shown in Table 3.

Each class of property has a predetermined schedule for cost recovery (depreciation), as shown in Tables 4 and 5. If an organization desires not to use Tables 4 and

TABLE 4
Recovery percentage of personal property

Recovery year	Property class			
	3 year	5 year	10 year	15 year public utility
1	25%	15%	8%	5%
2	38	22	14	10
3	37	21	12	9
4	—	21	10	8
5	—	21	10	7
6	—	—	10	7
7	—	—	9	6
8	—	—	9	6
9	—	—	9	6
10	—	—	9	6
11	—	—	—	6
12	—	—	—	6
13	—	—	—	6
14	—	—	—	6
15	—	—	—	6

TABLE 5
Recovery percentage of 15 year real property

Year of ownership	Month of first year when property was placed in service											
	1	2	3	4	5	6	7	8	9	10	11	12
1	12%	11%	10%	9%	8%	7%	6%	5%	4%	3%	2%	1%
2	10	10	11	11	11	11	11	11	11	11	11	12
3	9	9	9	9	10	10	10	10	10	10	10	10
4	8	8	8	8	8	8	9	9	9	9	9	9
5	7	7	7	7	7	7	8	8	8	8	8	8
6	6	6	6	6	7	7	7	7	7	7	7	7
7	6	6	6	6	6	6	6	6	6	6	6	6
8	6	6	6	6	6	6	5	6	6	6	6	6
9	6	6	6	6	5	6	5	5	5	6	6	6
10	5	6	5	6	5	5	5	5	5	5	6	5
11	5	5	5	5	5	5	5	5	5	5	5	5
12	5	5	5	5	5	5	5	5	5	5	5	5
13	5	5	5	5	5	5	5	5	5	5	5	5
14	5	5	5	5	5	5	5	5	5	5	5	5
15	5	5	5	5	5	5	5	5	5	5	5	5
16	—	—	1	1	2	2	3	3	4	4	4	5

5, it can use an optional straight-line method. However, the period over which the straight-line cost recovery may be used is predetermined and again bears no relation to the actual useful life. The straight-line method depreciates an asset on a uniform annual basis. The straight-line options available for each class of recovery property are as follows:

Property class	Optional straight-line recovery periods (years)
3 year	3, 5, or 12
5 year	5, 12, or 25
10 year	10, 25, or 35
15 year public utility	15, 35, or 45
15 year real property	15, 35, or 45

If the optional straight-line method of cost recovery is chosen, the half-year convention must be strictly followed. For example, if five years is chosen as the recovery period, then 10% (one-half of a year's allowance) would be allowed in years 1 and 6, and 20% would be allowed for years 2 through 5. The effect is that the actual recovery period is always one more year than that elected from the table. Also, the full cost of the asset is recovered; salvage value, if any, is ignored.

An investment tax credit is a direct deduction in income tax in the year an acquisition is made. It affects the cost of an asset to be recovered. The cost of an asset to be recovered will be reduced by one-half of the amount of such credits. For example, if a 10% investment tax credit is in effect and the investment is $100,000, a deduction of $10,000 from taxes due in the first year is permitted, and the recovery cost of the asset will be $95,000 [100,000–(10,000/2)].

EXAMPLE 8

A new machine costs $120,000 and has a cost recovery of five years. What is the annual cost recovery (depreciation) with ACRS? What is the annual cost recovery with the 5 year optional straight-line method? If the tax rate is 40%, what is the annual tax benefit?

For ACRS, the recovery percentages are taken from Table 4:

Year	Recovery percentage	Cost to be recovered	Annual cost recovery	Tax rate	Annual tax benefit
1	15	$120,000	$18,000	.40	$ 7,200
2	22	120,000	26,400	.40	10,560
3	21	120,000	25,200	.40	10,080
4	21	120,000	25,200	.40	10,080
5	21	120,000	25,200	.40	10,080
			$120,000		$48,000

For the optional straight-line, the half year convention is followed, so the cost recovery is over six years.

Year	Recovery percentage	Cost to be recovered	Annual cost recovery	Tax rate	Annual tax benefit
1	10	$120,000	$12,000	.40	$ 4,800
2	20	120,000	24,000	.40	9,600
3	20	120,000	24,000	.40	9,600
4	20	120,000	24,000	.40	9,600
5	20	120,000	24,000	.40	9,600
6	10	120,000	12,000	.40	4,800
			$120,000		$48,000

A FRAMEWORK FOR CAPITAL ANALYSIS

Asset purchases or replacements should not be handled in a haphazard manner. Many significant factors are difficult to quantify and may not be apparent from the investment analysis techniques already delineated. Figure 5 outlines in a flow diagram important considerations in discounted cash flow capital investment analysis. The flow diagram emphasizes the information inputs required from the various areas of an organization.

Capital investment analysis begins with the submission of proposals for capital expenditures. The proposals may come from specific planning areas within the organization or functional departments. Competition may be the incentive for proposals. All proposals must delineate the prospective outflow and inflow of funds over their lifetimes. The initial outflow is usually the required investment, while the inflow is the periodic net cash flows. To rank the proposals, it is necessary to adopt an analysis technique. Either the net present value or internal rate of return technique is

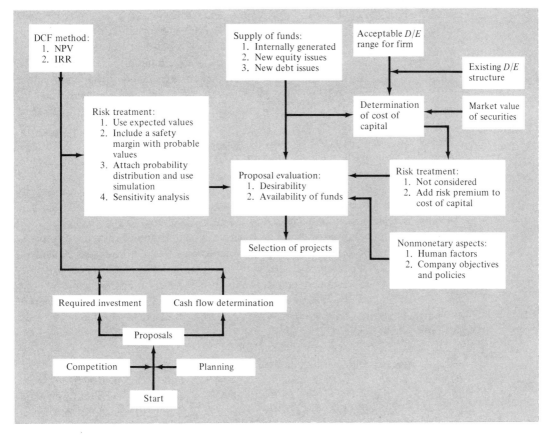

FIGURE 5
DCF capital investment analysis.

appropriate, since both consider the time value of money. For consistency and simplicity we assume that the net present value technique is selected.

The risk treatment for net cash flows can be handled in several ways. The simplest treatment is to use single point estimates or expected values and ignore risk altogether. On risky proposals a safety margin to probable values would lower the periodic net cash flow estimates. A more involved approach would attach a probability distribution to each periodic net cash flow and simulate its performance. Another approach is to test several different extremes of net cash flow and see if it influences the proposal's relative position. This approach is called sensitivity analysis.

The supply of funds for capital expenditures comes from internally generated funds, new equity issues, and new debt issues. An organization is usually part of an industry of several competing organizations. There is usually an acceptable range of debt to equity ratio for the industry as well as for an individual organization. The debt to equity range is usually historical and becomes a financial constraint in obtaining new sources of capital for expansion. If an organization exceeds its acceptable debt to equity range, it can experience difficulty with its suppliers, creditors, and owners. For example, suppliers may only deliver on COD terms, creditors may increase the cost of debt or refuse to lend altogether, and owners of equity issues may sell their stocks, which can depress their market value and increase the cost of equity. Knowing the existing debt to equity ratio, the acceptable debt to equity range, and the market value of securities, the organization can determine its cost of capital. The cost of capital is the minimum rate of return that an organization must attain before it will consider the capital investment desirable. Any proposal above the cost of capital is economically desirable; any proposal below the cost of capital is undesirable.

Previously we considered risk in the net cash flows. It can also be considered through adjustments in the cost of capital. Usually risk is considered only in one (either in net cash flows or the cost of capital). Risk can be ignored in the cost of capital by using a single point estimate. To consider risk via the cost of capital, its percentage is assigned a premium for risky projects. For example, if the normal cost of capital is 15%, it may be increased to 20% for risky proposals.

Several nonmonetary aspects are relevant in the evaluation of investment proposals. Human factors such as the response of personnel to the proposals should be considered. Since operating personnel will be required to make the adopted proposals successful, they are an important factor. Strong resistance to change can drive any proposal into the undesirable category. Company objectives must also be considered. A financially desirable proposal may threaten to expand the organization into new areas it does not desire.

The final selection of proposals involves the supply of funds, the ranking of competing proposals, and consideration of nonmonetary aspects. The supply of funds means the amount of money available. Proposals cannot be accepted if they exceed the supply of funds. The aggregate of accepted proposals must be within this amount. The capital analysis technique will rank all the proposals with respect to their financial desirability.

Financial data and analysis techniques tend to emphasize the quantitative aspect of an organization, but an organization has other, qualitative dimensions. These must also be considered in the selection process. The final selection of acceptable projects involves a balancing of the quantitative and qualitative aspects of the organization.

CONCLUSION

All organizations operate with a limited supply of funds. This means there are more things that funds can be expended upon than there are funds for. Since there are many ways to use funds, the uses should be evaluated to ensure the best choices are made. Several cost and capital analysis techniques have been outlined with the goal of improving the decision process. Many decisions justify the use of more than one technique, for each provides a slightly different perspective.

Cost control is almost a universal responsibility of managers. Control implies the existence of standards for measuring performance. Cost standards specify what an activity, component, or product should cost under normal operating conditions. Standards are typically established for labor, material, and overhead. Cost variance analysis is a common management by exception device. From expected levels of deployment and standards, budgets can be developed. Cost reduction is an attempt to challenge standards and find more efficient methods of operation.

Before any new investment is undertaken, it should be able to pass four tests:

1. It should serve the objectives of the organization.
2. Its economic benefits should exceed its costs.
3. It should be desirable from the nonmonetary point of view, which includes human, behavioral, and qualitative aspects.
4. It should be more desirable than other investment possibilities.

If any of the above tests are not passed, the investment should be suspect.

QUESTIONS

1. Differentiate between a cost function and a production function.
2. Contrast the long run and the short run periods of time.
3. What is breakeven analysis?
4. What impact does increasing fixed cost have on the contribution margin of a product?
5. Differentiate between breakeven analysis and cost equalization analysis.
6. What system of product costing should be used in a continuous production system? An intermittent production system?
7. Define standard cost.
8. Contrast cost control and cost reduction.
9. What is capital budgeting?
10. Why is the present value concept important in capital analysis?
11. What are the five capital analysis techniques outlined in the text?
12. What is the selection decision rule associated with the IRR technique of capital analysis?
13. What is cost recovery (depreciation)?
14. What is the influence of salvage value on the cost recovery of an asset?
15. What risk adjustments can be made in discounted cash flow methods?
16. Why would the federal government legislate the Accelerated Cost Recovery System (ACRS), despite the fact that it defers payment of federal taxes?
17. What reinvestment rate assumptions do the NPV and IRR techniques have?
18. What tests should a new investment pass before it is undertaken?

PROBLEMS

1. The Jones Manufacturing Company produces chairs. An analysis of their accounting data reveals:

Fixed cost	$50,000 per year
Variable cost	$2 per chair
Capacity	20,000 chairs per year
Selling price	$7 per chair

   a. Compute the breakeven point in the number of chairs.
   b. Find the number of chairs Jones must sell to show a profit of $30,000.
   c. What is the fixed cost per chair at 75% of capacity?

2. An operations manager must determine the profit or loss which will result from productive operations, given the following information. Fixed costs are $400 per week, variable

costs are $2.50 per unit, sales revenue is $5 per unit, and the present level of production is 100 units per week.

    a. What is the profit or loss at this level of production?

    b. What must the production level be to break even?

3. Assume that a company is producing and selling 5000 units of its product per year and that the following data are associated with its operations:

Fixed costs	$3,000.00
Variable cost per unit	.50
Selling price per unit	1.00

    a. How much profit or loss is expected at this volume?

    b. Assume that fixed costs are reduced to $2,000. What effect will this have on the profit?

    c. Assume that fixed costs remain at $3,000 and that the variable costs per unit increase to $.75. What volume would be necessary to make a profit of $1,000?

4. A producer of electrical equipment is considering the installation of one of two types of machines. A long-range sales forecast indicates that sales will not fall below 8,200 units per year for the next 5 years, the expected life of each machine. Machine 1 will increase fixed costs by $20,000 per year, but will reduce variable costs by $6 per unit. Machine 2 will increase fixed costs by $4,000 per year, but will reduce variable costs by $4 per unit. Variable costs now amount to $20 per unit.

    a. At what point are you indifferent as to which machine to purchase?

    b. Which machine should be purchased?

5. A company's variable costs average 60% of its sales volume. What must the dollar volume of sales be if the company is to cover its fixed costs of $500,000 and make a net profit before taxes of $100,000?

6. The normal productive capacity of the Starland Corporation is 170,000 units per year. Standard variable manufacturing costs are $11 per unit. Fixed factory overhead is $350,000 per year. Variable selling expenses are $3 per unit, and fixed selling expenses are $260,000 per year. The unit sales price is $20.

    a. What is the breakeven point in dollars?

    b. How many units must be sold to earn an income (before taxes) of $50,000 per year?

    c. How many units must be sold to earn a net income (before taxes) of 10% on sales?

7. The Green Manufacturing Company has leased facilities to manufacture a new product. The following data have been formulated from cost and market studies:

Estimated annual sales	24,000 units
Estimated costs:	
Materials	$96,000
Direct labor	14,400
Overhead	24,000
Administrative expenses	28,800

Selling expenses are expected to be 15% of sales. The required profit is $1.02 per unit.

    a. What should the selling price be per unit?

    b. What is the breakeven point in dollars and units if overhead and administrative expenses are fixed but other costs are variable?

8. The mathematical equation for the total cost of a business is $6x^3 + 2x^2 + 4x + 27$, where x is the production volume. What is the marginal cost function for the business? What is the significance of the 27 in the total cost equation?

9. Compute the present value of the following stream of payments assuming a 10% rate of return:

Year	Amount
1	$ 1,000
2	2,000
3–5	4,000
6	10,000

10. Your great aunt, with a life expectancy of 15 more years, promises to give you $1,000 in her will if you will give her a car you are about to sell.
   a. If money is worth 12% to you, at what price would you have to sell your car to beat her offer?
   b. Would you be better off if she gave you $500 now and left you $500 in her will?

11. A machine costing $150,000 has a cost recovery of 5 years and an estimated salvage value of $15,000 at the end of the sixth year. Its pattern of estimated benefits is as follows:

Year	EBT + depreciation
1	$60,000
2	80,000
3^a	0
4	60,000
5	30,000
6	20,000 + salvage

^{a}A major overhaul will be required.

Assuming straight-line cost recovery, a 40% tax rate, and 16% cost of capital, determine: (a) payback period, (b) average rate of return, (c) net present value, and (d) internal rate of return.

12. Two mutually exclusive proposals of equal risk have been received for the purchase of a new machine. Data on each are as follows:

	Machine A	Machine B
Investment	$84,000	$60,000
Salvage value	0	0
EBT + depreciation:		
1–3 years	30,000	24,000
4–5 years	20,000	24,000

Assume 3 year straight-line cost recovery, a corporate tax rate of 40%, and a 20% cost of capital. Rank each project according to (a) payback period, (b) average rate of return, (c) net present value, and (d) internal rate of return.

13. Bascom Manufacturing Company can purchase a new robot at a cost of $50,000 that will replace an existing machine with a book value of $12,000. The robot will reduce operating costs by $10,000 per year and have a ten-year life with no salvage value. The disposal value of the old machine is $6,000. If the robot has a five year straight-line cost recovery, the corporate tax rate is 40%, and the cost of capital is 14%, would you recommend purchasing the robot based on its net present value?

14. The Unitron Company is considering bidding on a contract to produce a special fixture for the government. This would require the purchase of a new mold that would cost $50,000, have a freight and setup cost of $10,000, and have a $3000 salvage value at the end of its 5 year life. If the contract is obtained, it will increase revenues by $70,000 and increase expenses by $30,000 during each of the 5 years. An initial recoverable investment in inventory of $20,000 will be required during the 5 year life of the contract. The cost recovery of the mold is 33%, 45%, and 22% respectively over three years. If the corporate tax rate is 40%, and the cost of capital is 15%, determine the average rate of return and the net present value of the contract.

15. Paritron is considering two mutually exclusive proposals for the purchase of an office machine. Data on each are as follows:

	Machine A	Machine B
Original cost	$18,000	$27,000
Freight & installation	2,000	1,000
Estimated life (years)	3	4
Salvage value	0	2,000
Net cash benefits before taxes & depreciation:		
Year 1	10,000	17,000
2	10,000	17,000
3	10,000	17,000
4	10,000	17,000

The cost recovery for both machines is 33%, 45%, and 22% respectively over three years. If the tax rate is 40%, and the cost of capital is 12%, which machine should be selected, using the net present value?

CASE 1: REAP WHAT IS SOWN

Mid-America Harvest has under contract one of the principal theoreticians of CAD/CAM (computer aided design/computer aided manufacturing). Dr. Monroe's services are enlisted by the farm implement manufacturer because the organization's operation is becoming so complex it seems unmanageable, its labor force expenditures are excessive, and its costs are growing precipitously. Under the direction of Dr. Monroe and his assembled team of specialists, Harvest is planning its CAD/CAM implementation. The eventual ends are sophisticated factory automation, the integration of the functions of its manufacturing process, and the description of all its subsystems in programmable terms. The present aim is to test and plan modifications in Harvest factories prior to major investments in facilities and computer software. The planning sequence is taking steps to eliminate unwanted circumstances that could result when the CAM phase becomes the final stage in the reorganization.

A CAD/CAM system generally is implemented in modular phases because of the difficulties in arraying its dynamic interaction. Harvest executives, otherwise hopeful of the prospects for the total system, still are eager to utilize part of the process. They want to phase in parts that are proving useful elsewhere and not wait for the full development of total CAD/CAM linkage. Therefore, before CAM becomes forged, the issue lies with the acquisition of its logical predecessor, CAD.

Dr. Monroe is advising that CAD can start paying impressive dividends in increased production, reduced costs, better quality products, and greater manufacturing flexibility. He promises that a software CAD program can be written to speed up the work of drafting, and if properly programmed, subject the assemblages to simulated real life conditions; e.g., an electronic image can simulate the stress and strain on a combine design as it extracts its wheels from mud on one side and slips on ice on the other. This capability could save unbelievable time and expense consumed as a consequence of current methods that fabricate prototypes, test, modify specifications, refabricate, and retest.

Inasmuch as other firms boast 5:1 reductions in labor and 3:1 decreases in lead time with their CAD programs, Dr. Monroe insists that Harvest purchase a $150,000 CAD software package capable of similar achievements. He feels that a number of design engineers and draftsmen will become redundant, and their employment vacancies and relinquished wages would more than cover the positions and wages required by computer specialists. At least six craftsmen could be dismissed who presently earn approximately $14/hr. He further estimates materials usage savings of $30,000 a year. These figures do not even include the savings from CAD generated tapes which would automatically program the numerically controlled machines and supplant the manually prepared instructions.

Dr. Monroe does note that already a more capable but more expensive CAD is on the way. Whereas Harvest's contingent CAD system is relatively small and displays images that are networks of lines resembling a wire mesh, the future CADs will be more realistic representations. They will appear as solid objects with internal structures and external shapes and will provide vital information with greater clarity and precision than is possible with the mesh modeling. Nevertheless, solid modeling is just becoming commercially available, and Dr. Monroe is enthusiastic about the savings that can be obtained immediately from the commercially successful mesh modeling available from Applicon of Massachusetts.

1. Describe the capital investment scenario at Harvest.
2. Identify the factors that are critical to the technological reorganization that is occurring.
3. Should Harvest purchase the CAD system from Applicon?

CASE 2: HOT AIR?

Thermal Corporation is forced either to terminate production of its largest room air-conditioner or to find an option that will rectify its consistent financial losses. The product has been carried for several periods in order to offer distributors a complete line, but management has reluctantly decided not to carry any product that does not at least break even. The metal-clad unit's sagging sales are a consequence of the increasing popularity of competitive models which are lighter and cheaper but have equivalent BTU ratings. Fifty percent of the production capacity once allocated to the large-size portable stands idle: only 6,250 units are produced on a line that has a 12,500 unit yearly production rate at full capacity. A decision has to be made soon. Rather than abruptly discontinue the product, the firm is evaluating the following executive staff suggestions for improving the product's competitive position.

Option 1: Modify the product. Two process engineers have determined that preformed plastic parts and exterior panels could be subcontracted and then assembled in the plant by most of the personnel currently employed to manufacture the metal unit. A large number of the assets devoted to the metal unit could be retained for use on other room units or modestly converted to central-air production. Moreover, only incidental new equipment would be required for the plastic fabrication process. The researchers presented the following figures in their endorsement of the modification proposal:

	Plastic unit (proposed)	Metal unit (current)
Sales	$4,750,000	$2,750,000
Variable costs	3,750,000	2,000,000
Fixed costs	500,000	1,000,000
Profit	400,000	−250,000

To ensure that a comprehensive study was done, the engineers also investigated data on related products. The only information pertinent to the product planning question was their estimate that fixed costs for the other metal products collectively would increase $700,000, since part of the capital would be converted to their use. Revenues and variable costs of the other products were excluded from the report, because they were deemed to remain unchanged.

Option 2: Reduce fixed costs. A cost accountant felt that since the rest of the products are doing well on a financial statement basis, an accounting change could be in order. She decided the unprofitable product is bearing a disproportionate share of total factory fixed costs, e.g. depreciation on unproductive equipment. Therefore, she recommended reducing the product's fixed cost allocation by redistributing a portion of its costs to profitable products or by selling off the most obsolete of the idle equipment.

Option 3: Reduce variable costs. A production engineer, scoffing at the fixed cost suggestion, stated in strong terms that variable costs would be more amenable to a cost-cutting strategy. His calculations estimated a $50 shaving of the variable cost per unit would return the product to profitability. Subsequently, he outlined changes in work methods that, if instituted, would cut variable costs by that amount.

Option 4: Utilize excess capacity. Another production specialist was in favor of increasing output. He explored the strategy of utilizing the current excess capacity. The specialist felt that a $200,000 maintenance expenditure would update the line and transfer equipment so that the 12,500 unit production rate could be met smoothly and efficiently at present employment levels. The proposal also included two means for disposing of the additional output. The units could either be "dumped" in another geographical market, if the company would lower the price by $20 a unit; or the firm could spend $20 a unit on an ad campaign to boost sales at the current price within the present marketing network.

1. Analyze the alternatives.
2. Suggest other options.
3. Which option is best?

SELECTED BIBLIOGRAPHY

Chase, R. B. and N. J. Aquilano. *Production and Operations Management,* Homewood, IL: Irwin, 1981.

Hertz, D. B. "Risk Analysis in Capital Investments," *Harvard Business Review,* January–February 1964, pp. 95–106.

Horngren, C. T. *Cost Accounting,* Englewood Cliffs, NJ: Prentice-Hall, 1982.

Monks, J. G. *Operations Management: Theory and Problems,* New York: McGraw-Hill, 1982.

Moriarity, S. R. and C. P. Allen. *Cost Accounting,* New York: Harper and Row, 1984.

Tersine, R. J. and W. Rudko. "A Bivariate Stochastic Approach to Capital Investment Decisions," *The Engineering Economist,* May 1972.

5
Resource Allocation and Linear Programming

THE SIMPLEX METHOD
Mathematical Notation
Slack and Artificial Variables
Maximization
Minimization
Additional Explanation
Unusual Situations

THE DUAL METHOD
Mathematical Notation
Dual Variables: Interpretation
Additional Explanation

SENSITIVITY ANALYSIS

THE TRANSPORTATION METHOD
Northwest Corner Rule
Dummy Locations
Degeneracy
Modified Northwest Corner Rule

THE ASSIGNMENT METHOD

QUESTIONS

PROBLEMS

CASES

SELECTED BIBLIOGRAPHY

Linear programming consists of a group of mathematical methods for optimization in planning, scheduling, and allocating resources. It deals with the allocation of scarce resources to competing ends each of which holds varying degrees of utility. Linear programming optimizes a value system subject to a set of constraints. The objective function expresses the value system or goals. Constraints are limitations of the environment such as capacity, a priori rules, and capabilities.

The method is called linear programming because it uses only linear equations (no logarithmic, trigonometric, exponential, or parabolic functions). An optimization model is linear when the variables are raised no higher than the first power. If it costs $20.00 for 5 units of labor, then it must cost $40.00 for 10 units of labor. This requirement is the principle limitation of the technique. Additionally, no provisions are made for risk or uncertainty. The stated relationships are assumed to follow precisely (deterministically) the given mathematical expressions. The values of the decision variables are assumed continuous, so they may take on fractional or integer values.

If an organization must select a strategy and its resources are in limited supply and interrelated, it can use linear programming provided it can express its objective and limitations as linear mathematical equations or inequalities. One cannot in fact expect direct costs or overhead costs to remain constant at all levels of output. When some resources are held constant, increases in other resources yield a diminishing increment of output. Frequently, however, a linear relationship is an excellent approximation of the actual situation. When linear assumptions are suspect, nonlinear programming techniques can be applied. In specific cases linear programming can be supplemented with integer programming, quadratic programming, dynamic programming, or calculus-based methods.

There is no algebraic formula for calculating the solution to a linear programming problem. All available methods are iterative. This means the same type of operation must be repeated until a desired optimal solution is achieved. Linear programming is easily adaptable to the logic of a computer, and standard programs are readily available.

THE SIMPLEX METHOD

The simplex method is an iterative technique that is a successive-improvement method. Essentially, it establishes an initial solution and then repeats the process to form improved solutions until no further improvement is possible and the optimal solution is found. The formal procedure ensures that a better solution will be found at each iteration and an optimal solution will be obtained in a finite number of iterations. Matrix algebra is the foundation for the simplex method of linear programming. Underlying the simplex method is the Gauss-Jordan complete elimination procedure for solving systems of simultaneous linear equations. This procedure transforms an initial matrix $(A \mid I \mid B)$ into the form $(I \mid A^{-1} \mid X)$ by row operations.

Row operations are performed on the total matrix $(A \mid I \mid B)$ until A is transformed into the identity matrix. An identity matrix is a square matrix with 1's down its principal diagonal and 0's as its other elements. The following is a list of row operations which can be utilized in arriving at the identity matrix in the Gauss-Jordan complete elimination procedure.

1. You can multiply a row vector by any whole number or fraction (positive or negative).
2. You can replace a row vector by itself plus or minus another row vector.
3. You can replace a row vector by itself plus or minus a whole number or fraction times another row vector.

EXAMPLE 1

Solve the following simultaneous equations for a and b:

$1a + 1b = 5$,
$2a + 3b = 13$.

Let

$$A = \text{matrix of detached coefficients} = \begin{pmatrix} 1 & 1 \\ 2 & 3 \end{pmatrix},$$

$$I = \text{identity matrix of } A = \begin{pmatrix} 1 & 0 \\ 0 & 1 \end{pmatrix},$$

$$B = \text{column vector of constants} = \begin{pmatrix} 5 \\ 13 \end{pmatrix},$$

$$A^{-1} = \text{inverse of matrix } A,$$

$$X = \text{solution vector}.$$

Starting with

$$\begin{array}{cc|cc|c} 1 & 1 & 1 & 0 & 5 \\ 2 & 3 & 0 & 1 & 13 \end{array}$$

subtract two times row 1 from row 2 to obtain

$$\begin{array}{cc|cc|c} 1 & 1 & 1 & 0 & 5 \\ 0 & 1 & -2 & 1 & 3 \end{array}$$

Subtract row 2 from row 1 to obtain

$$\begin{array}{cc|cc|c} 1 & 0 & 3 & -1 & 2 \\ 0 & 1 & -2 & 1 & 3 \end{array}$$

Thus $a = 2$, $b = 3$.

The solution vector X contains the solution. Since the 1 in the identity appears in the first column of the final matrix, it indicates that $a = 2$. (The first column in the matrix represented the detached coefficients of a, and the second column represented the detached coefficients of b.) The other 1 in the identity of the final matrix is in column 2, so $b = 3$.

MATHEMATICAL NOTATION

The simplex method utilizes the Gauss-Jordan complete elimination procedure and uses an objective function in tandem to indicate when optimization has been achieved. In equation notation the simplex model can be stated as follows:

Optimize $Z = C_1 x_1 + C_2 x_2 + \cdots + C_n x_n$

subject to $A_{11} x_1 + A_{12} x_2 + \cdots + A_{1n} x_n \leq B_1,$

$\qquad\qquad A_{21} x_1 + A_{22} x_2 + \cdots + A_{2n} x_n \leq B_2,$

$$\cdot$$
$$\cdot$$
$$\cdot$$

$\qquad\qquad A_{m1} x_1 + A_{m2} x_2 + \cdots + A_{mn} x_n \leq B_m,$

where

$\quad B_i \geq 0, \qquad i = 1, 2, \ldots, m,$

$\quad x_j \geq 0, \qquad j = 1, 2, \ldots, n,$

A_{ij}, B_i, and C_j are known constants,

$\quad n =$ number of decision variables,

$\quad m =$ number of constraints.

The variables x_j are the decision variables whose values are determined when the LP model is solved. Decision variables represent choices available to the decision maker in terms of either input or output quantities. The objective function coefficients C_j, the constraint coefficients A_{ij}, and the right-hand side coefficients B_i are parameters of the model. The parameters of the model must be known or accurately estimated in order to determine the final solution to the decision variables. Since there are m constraints on n unknown decision variables, only m variables will be in the solution, and $n - m$ variables always will be equal to zero (out of the solution). In matrix notation the simplex model can be stated as follows:

Optimize $Z = Cx$

subject to $Ax \leq B,$

where A, B, and C are known constants, A is an $m \times n$ matrix, B is an $m \times 1$ matrix, and C is a $1 \times n$ matrix.

The simplex method provides a systematic procedure for finding values for x_j's such that the objective function Z is optimized within the solution space defined by the linear constraints $Ax \leq B$.

SLACK AND ARTIFICIAL VARIABLES

From the equation and matrix notation above it can be seen that the constraints are in inequality form. To utilize the Gauss-Jordan procedure it is necessary to have equalities (equations). To make this transformation to equality form and to automatically add an identity matrix (as is necessary to get the $A \mid I \mid B$ matrix), slack and artificial variables must be utilized. Slack variables are used to make inequalities into equalities. Artificial variables are used when the slack variables do not create the necessary $+1$ coefficient for the identity matrix. The slack variable represents unutilized capacity, while the artificial variable is a mathematical convenience to achieve $a + 1$ element for the identity matrix. Since the artificial variable is a mathematical convenience, it is necessary to ensure that it never appears in the final solution.

Constraints are limitations on the alternatives available to decision makers. There are three types: less than or equal to ($\leq$), greater than or equal to ($\geq$), and simply equal to ($=$). A "less than or equal to" condition implies an upper limit on the amount of some scarce resource (materials, machine hours, or labor hours) available for use. A "greater than or equal to" condition specifies a lower bound that must be achieved in the final solution. An "equal to" condition is more restrictive in the sense that it specifies exactly what a decision variable(s) should equal. In addition to constraints peculiar to a specific problem, there is a general nonnegativity condition that applies to all problems. It means that negative values of decision variables cannot be used. Since nonnegativity is a part of each LP problem, it can be disregarded in the problem formulation.

Below is an example of the modification required on the constraints prior to their introduction into the linear programming tableau. A positive slack variable is added to all "less than or equal to" constraints; a negative slack and a positive artificial variables are added to all "greater than or equal to" constraints, and a positive artificial variable is added to all equality constraints:

from	to
$x_1 + x_2 \leq 10$	$x_1 + x_2 + S_1 = 10,$
$2x_1 + x_3 \geq 5$	$2x_1 + x_3 - S_2 + A_1 = 5,$
$x_2 + x_3 = 8$	$x_2 + x_3 + A_2 = 8.$

Slack variables are attached to inequalities to obtain an equality. In the "greater than" inequalities the slack variable is subtracted to obtain an equality, so its coefficient is -1. Since coefficients in the identity matrix must be all $+1$'s, an artificial variable is added to obtain the $+1$. To ensure that no artificial variables are in the final optimum solution, the coefficient of the artificial variable in the objective function is assigned either a $+M$ or $-M$, designating a very large positive or negative amount. Since no slack variable is required for an equality constraint, an artificial variable is added to get the identity element for the matrix. In maximization problems, the value of the artificial variable is $-M$, which is equivalent to a loss, and this ensures it will not be in the final solution. In a minimization problem, the value is $+M$, which is equivalent to an extremely high cost, and this similarly ensures its absence. Thus, the slack and artificial variables are used to automatically set up the identity matrix and obtain the form $A \mid I \mid B$.

Slack and artificial variables help to introduce the initial solution. Any variables that occur in one equation must appear in all equations. The variables that do not affect an equation are written with a zero coefficient.

The following table will be helpful in dealing with inequalities and assigning objective function values to slack and artificial variables:

	Objective function value	
Type of constraint	**Max problem**	**Min problem**
1. $\leq$ inequality (add a positive slack variable)	A zero coefficient to the slack	A zero coefficient to the slack
2. $\geq$ inequality (add one negative slack and one positive artificial variable)	A zero coefficient to the slack and $-M$ to the artificial	A zero coefficient to the slack and M to the artificial
3. $=$ equality (add a positive artificial variable)	$-M$ coefficient to the artificial	M coefficient to the artificial

EXAMPLE 2

The following constraint conditions have been modified so they could be entered into the simplex tableau:

from	to
$10a + 9b + 8c \leq 400$	$10a + 9b + 8c + S_1 \qquad\qquad\qquad = 400,$
$a \qquad\qquad \geq 6$	$a \qquad\qquad -S_2 \quad + A_1 \quad = 6,$
$b + c \leq 30$	$b + c \qquad + S_3 \qquad = 30,$
$c = 15$	$c \qquad\qquad\qquad + A_2 = 15.$

MAXIMIZATION

Once the constraint equations are written with the appropriate slack and artificial variables, the objective function is written and the problem is set up in a standard simplex tableau. The simplex method has the advantage of determining an optimum solution when there are more unknown variables than equations. At this point, a simple maximization problem will be solved to explain the simplex algorithm. Figure 1 illustrates a flow diagram of the simplex maximization procedure.

EXAMPLE 3

Solve the following problem by the simplex method:

Maximize   Profit $= 8a + 6b$
subject to $4a + 2b \leq 60,$
$\qquad\qquad 2a + 4b \leq 48.$

The first step is to convert the inequalities to equations by adding slack variables:

$4a + 2b + S_1 \qquad = 60,$
$2a + 4b \qquad + S_2 = 48.$

Objective function: $8a + 6b + 0S_1 + 0S_2 = $ max.
We now fit the equations into a standard simplex tableau:

C_j		8	6	0	0	
	Solution vector	a	b	S_1	S_2	B_0
0	S_1	④	2	1	0	60←(leaving vector)
0	S_2	2	4	0	1	48
	Z_j	0	0	0	0	0
	$C_j - Z_j$	8	6	0	0	

$$\begin{pmatrix} \text{entering} \\ \text{vector} \end{pmatrix}$$

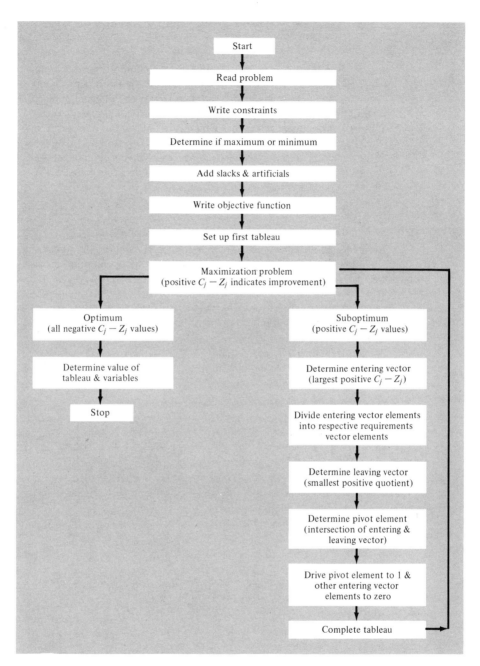

FIGURE 1
Simplex method of linear programming: maximization.

Z_j is obtained for each variable by multiplying each element in the column by the corresponding value in the C_j column and summing the resultant products. (Z_j for the entering vector column is obtained by multiplying 4 by zero and 2 by zero and summing the products, which gives zero for Z_j. The same procedure is used for each column vector in obtaining Z_j values.) To arrive at an optimum solution the $C_j - Z_j$'s must be negative

continued

EXAMPLE 3 — *continued*

or zero in the maximization problem. The *a* column vector is the entering vector, since it has the largest positive value and represents the greatest per unit increase in the objective function. The leaving vector is determined by dividing each element in the entering vector into the corresponding element value in the requirements vector (B_0) and selecting the smallest nonnegative number which is the maximum number of the variable that can enter based on the most restrictive constraint. The smallest nonnegative number is selected to ensure the nonnegativity of numbers in the requirements vector. In business applications only the first quadrant is meaningful to the manager. In the example S_1 is the leaving vector; thus

$$S_1: \quad \frac{60}{4} = 15; \quad S_2: \quad \frac{48}{2} = 24.$$

The intersection of the entering vector and the leaving vector indicates the pivot element. The pivot element will be driven to one by the row operation of division by itself into all the row vector elements. In this case, all elements in row vector S_1 will be divided by four. After the pivot element is driven to one, row operations must be performed to make the other values in the entering vector equal to zero. Every other row must now be recalculated. To find the new elements for the rows the following formula is used:

$$\begin{pmatrix} \text{Elements in} \\ \text{row to be} \\ \text{replaced} \end{pmatrix} - \left[\begin{pmatrix} \text{Intersectional} \\ \text{element of old row} \\ \text{to be replaced} \end{pmatrix} \begin{pmatrix} \text{Corresponding} \\ \text{element of} \\ \text{replacing row} \end{pmatrix} \right] = \begin{pmatrix} \text{New} \\ \text{row} \end{pmatrix}$$

In the example, row S_2 must be revised:

$$\begin{pmatrix} \text{Elements in} \\ \text{row to be} \\ \text{replaced} \end{pmatrix} - \left[\begin{pmatrix} \text{Intersectional} \\ \text{element of old row} \\ \text{to be replaced} \end{pmatrix} \begin{pmatrix} \text{Corresponding} \\ \text{element of} \\ \text{replacing row} \end{pmatrix} \right] = \begin{pmatrix} \text{New} \\ \text{row} \end{pmatrix}$$

2	− [	2	×	1	] =	0
4	− [	2	×	$\frac{1}{2}$	] =	3
0	− [	2	×	$\frac{1}{4}$	] =	$-\frac{1}{2}$
1	− [	2	×	0	] =	1
48	− [	2	×	15	] =	18

The above values are for the new S_2 row and go into the next tableau.

At this point, the new tableau is completed and the same iterative process continued until the $C_j - Z_j$ row indicates an optimum solution has been obtained:

C_j			8	6	0	0	
		Solution vector	*a*	*b*	S_1	S_2	B_0
8		*a*	1	$\frac{1}{2}$	$\frac{1}{4}$	0	15
0		S_2	0	③	$-\frac{1}{2}$	1	18←
		Z_j	8	4	2	0	120
		$C_j - Z_j$	0	2	−2	0	
				↑			

b is the entering vector, and S_2 is the leaving vector. Thus

$$a: \quad \frac{15}{\frac{1}{2}} = 30; \quad S_2: \quad \frac{18}{3} = 6.$$

The pivot element in the previous tableau is 3. Row vector S_2 is divided by 3 to make the pivot equal to one. To drive the other entering vector element to zero, one-sixth of old row vector S_2 is subtracted from row vector a and the new tableau is completed as follows:

C_j		8	6	0	0	
	Solution vector	a	b	S_1	S_2	B_0
8	a	1	0	$\frac{1}{3}$	$-\frac{1}{6}$	12
6	b	0	1	$-\frac{1}{6}$	$\frac{1}{3}$	6
	Z_j	8	6	$\frac{5}{3}$	$\frac{2}{3}$	132
	$C_j - Z_j$	0	0	$-\frac{5}{3}$	$-\frac{2}{3}$	

Since all the $C_j - Z_j$ elements are negative or zero, the optimum solution is obtained. The solution vector, which indicates the identity matrix variables, reveals the decision variables that are in the solution. The requirements vector elements reveal the magnitude of each optimal decision variable. The last element in the Z_j row gives the optimum value of the problem. The solution is $a = 12$ and $b = 6$ for a maximum profit of \$132.

Maximizing profits is frequently stated as the objective function in LP problems. Profit functions are not usually linear functions, but contribution functions are. Therefore in maximizing profits, we really mean maximizing the contribution, which is profit plus fixed costs. The concept of contribution is explained in the previous chapter on cost and capital analysis.

MINIMIZATION

Example 3 illustrated the simplex method for a maximization problem. The procedure for a minimization problem is similar except for two differences:

1. The value of the artificial variable in the objective function is $+M$. (In the maximization problem it is $-M$.)
2. The criterion for selecting the entering vector is now reversed. The entering vector is the most negative element in the $C_j - Z_j$ row. The optimum solution is reached when all the elements in the $C_j - Z_j$ row are positive or zero. (In the maximization problem the optimum is reached when all the elements are negative or zero.)

Except for the above conditions, all the procedures are the same. Figure 2 illustrates a flow diagram for the simplex minimization procedure.

EXAMPLE 4

A dog food processor received an order for 2000 pounds of a mixture consisting of cereal and beef parts. The cereal costs \$.30 per pound, and the beef parts cost \$.80 per pound. No more than 800 pounds of cereal can be used, and at least 600 pounds of beef parts

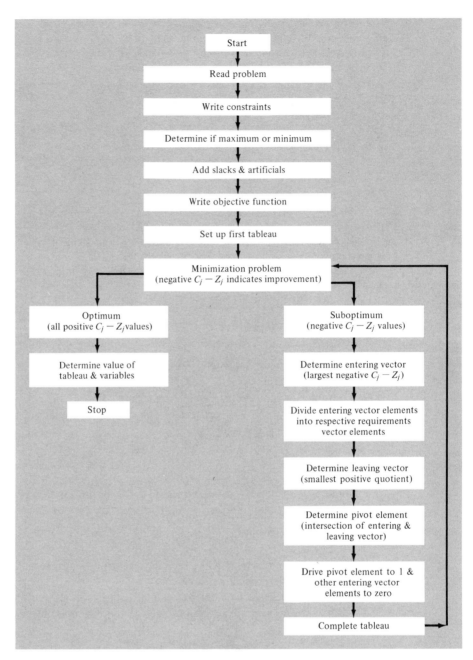

FIGURE 2
Simplex method of linear programming: minimization.

EXAMPLE 4 — *continued*

must be used. How much of each ingredient should be used to minimize cost?
Let

x_1 = no. of pounds of cereal,
x_2 = no. of pounds of beef parts.

Constraints:

$$x_1 \leq 800,$$
$$x_2 \geq 600,$$
$$x_1 + x_2 = 2000.$$

We introduce slack and artificial variables as required:

$$x_1 \quad + S_1 \qquad\qquad\qquad = 800,$$
$$x_2 \quad - S_2 + A_1 \qquad = 600,$$
$$x_1 + x_2 \qquad\qquad + A_2 = 2000.$$

Objective function:

$$0.3x_1 + 0.8x_2 + 0S_1 + 0S_2 + MA_1 + MA_2 = \min.$$

For computation convenience, we will not carry the decimal point in the objective function, but we will correct the final tableau to account for it. The initial tableau is

C_j	Solution vector	3	8	0	0	M	M	
		x_1	x_2	S_1	S_2	A_1	A_2	B_0
0	S_1	1	0	1	0	0	0	800
M	A_1	0	①	0	-1	1	0	600 ←
M	A_2	1	1	0	0	0	1	2000
	Z_j	M	$2M$	0	$-M$	M	M	$2600M$
	$C_j - Z_j$	$3 - M$	$8 - 2M$	0	M	0	0	
			↑					

x_2 is the entering vector and A_1 is the leaving vector. Thus

$$S_1: \frac{800}{0} = \text{undefined}; \qquad A_1: \frac{600}{1} = 600; \qquad A_2: \frac{2000}{1} = 2000.$$

The second tableau is

C_j	Solution vector	3	8	0	0	M	M	
		x_1	x_2	S_1	S_2	A_1	A_2	B_0
0	S_1	①	0	1	0	0	0	800 ←
8	x_2	0	1	0	-1	1	0	600
M	A_2	1	0	0	1	-1	1	1400
	Z_j	M	8	0	$M - 8$	$8 - M$	M	$1400M + 4800$
	$C_j - Z_j$	$3 - M$	0	0	$8 - M$	$2M - 8$	0	
		↑						

x_1 is the entering vector and S_1 is the leaving vector. Thus

$$S_1: \frac{800}{1} = 800; \qquad x_2: \frac{600}{0} = \text{undefined}; \qquad A_2: \frac{1400}{1} = 1400.$$

continued

EXAMPLE 4 — *continued*

The third tableau is

C_j		3	8	0	0	M	M	
	Solution vector	x_1	x_2	S_1	S_2	A_1	A_2	B_0
3	x_1	1	0	1	0	0	0	800
8	x_2	0	1	0	-1	1	0	600
M	A_2	0	0	-1	①	-1	1	600 ←
	Z_j	3	8	$3 - M$	$M - 8$	$8 - M$	M	$600M + 7200$
	$C_j - Z_j$	0	0	$M - 3$	$8 - M$	$2M - 8$	0	

The entering vector is S_2 and the leaving vector is A_2. Thus

$$x_1: \quad \frac{800}{0} = \text{undefined}; \quad x_2: \quad \frac{600}{-1} = -600; \quad A_2: \quad \frac{600}{1} = 600.$$

The fourth tableau is

C_j		3	8	0	0	M	M	
	Solution vector	x_1	x_2	S_1	S_2	A_1	A_2	B_0
3	x_1	1	0	1	0	0	0	800
8	x_2	0	1	-1	0	0	1	1,200
0	S_2	0	0	-1	1	-1	1	600
	Z_j	3	8	-5	0	0	8	12,000
	$C_j - Z_j$	0	0	5	0	M	$M - 8$	

Since $C_j - Z_j$ contains all positive or zero values, the optimum solution has been obtained. The best strategy is to mix 800 pounds of cereal with 1200 pounds of beef parts for a minimum cost of $1200. (The value 12,000 is corrected to $1200 because the decimal point was deleted for computational simplicity.)

ADDITIONAL EXPLANATION

In summary, the simplex method encompasses the following steps:

1. Formulate the constraints and objective function for the problem.
2. Add the necessary slack and artificial variables, and establish the initial tableau.
3. Check the solution for optimality. If optimal, stop. If not, continue.
4. Select the variable to enter to improve the solution and the variable to leave the solution.
5. Perform row operations to revise the solution.
6. Return to step 3 and continue until optimality is achieved.

When a tie exists for the entering or for the leaving vector, it may be chosen arbitrarily.

When the $C_j - Z_j$ row indicates an optimum solution, the solution is obtained by observing those variables that are in the identity matrix or the solution vector. It is possible for a final solution to have a slack variable; this indicates no action is to be taken. In no instance should a final solution have an artificial variable, for this would indicate no feasible solution exists. If an artificial variable occurs in a final solution, the constraint equations should be reevaluated for errors, inconsistencies, or impossible conditions.

Each simplex tableau represents a possible solution to the problem, but an optimal solution has not been obtained until the signs of the coefficients in the $C_j - Z_j$ row indicate it. Each possible solution is indicated by those variables that occur in the identity matrix. With each iteration, the value of the new tableau should be an improvement over the prior tableau's value. The variables in the identity matrix define the basis of the tableau. The basis of each tableau contains those variables that are in the feasible solution space. The basis of the optimal tableau is also called the optimal feasible solution. Variables not in the basis are at the zero level.

The solution of a linear programming problem may be considered as the optimum use of the available scarce resources to achieve the objectives. The objectives of the organization are represented by a linear objective function, and the constraints—such as capital, labor, and other resources—within which the organization operates usually are represented by several linear inequalities. The simplex method is an algorithm for solving linear programming problems. The initial feasible solution usually starts at the zero activity level (none of the resources being utilized). For each successive iteration there generally is improvement in the value of the tableau until an optimum solution is indicated.

In a simplex *maximization* problem: C_j is the unit gain for variable j, Z_j (opportunity cost) is the loss that results from bringing one unit of variable j into the solution, and the net gain achieved by introducing one unit of variable j into the solution is expressed by $C_j - Z_j$. Positive values for $C_j - Z_j$ indicate further improvement can be made in the tableau, which will provide additional benefits. Negative values for $C_j - Z_j$ indicate that a loss of benefits would result from entering these variables in the solution. The largest positive $C_j - Z_j$ value is chosen when determining which variable to enter into the solution, since it provides the maximum benefit. When all of the $C_j - Z_j$ values are zero or negative, an optimum solution has been obtained.

In a simplex *minimization* problem: C_j is the unit cost for variable j, Z_j is the reduction in cost that results from bringing one unit of variable j into the solution, and the net benefit achieved by entering one unit of variable j into the solution is expressed by $C_j - Z_j$. Negative values for $C_j - Z_j$ indicate further improvement can be made in the tableau, which will provide additional benefits (cost reductions). Positive values for $C_j - Z_j$ indicate that a decrease in benefits (increased cost) would result from entering these variables in the solution. The largest negative $C_j - Z_j$ value is chosen when determining which variable to enter into the solution, since it provides the maximum benefit (reduces cost the most). When all $C_j - Z_j$ values are zero or positive, an optimum solution has been obtained.

All simplex problems can be solved by the maximization procedure outlined in Figure 1. A simplex minimization problem can be solved by multiplying the minimization objective function by -1 and proceeding with the maximization procedure. Any simplex maximization problem can also be solved by the minimization procedure, by multiplying its objective function by -1 and proceeding as outlined in Figure 2.

UNUSUAL SITUATIONS

Not all simplex problems have feasible solutions. The following types of conditions may be observed:

1. *No feasible solution.* No solution will satisfy all the constraints. This can also occur when $C_j - Z_j$ indicates the solution is optimum, but artificial variables are still in the solution.

2. *Infeasible solutions.* All variables in a basis are required to be nonnegative. The existence of negative variables in a solution indicates the solution is infeasible. (The rule for selecting the leaving vector is designed to prevent the solution from straying into the infeasible region.)

3. *Infinite solutions.* When all the numbers in the entering vector column are zero or negative, an infinite (unbounded) solution exists. This indicates the problem has not been defined properly, since there are always limitations on resources and production activities. This situation usually develops when a misstated constraint describes an unbounded solution space.

4. *Degenerate solutions.* Any solution in which there are equally acceptable choices (a tie between two or more variables) for the leaving vector is degenerate. One of the variables is arbitrarily chosen. If a solution cannot be reached and looping occurs, another variable can be selected. Degenerate solutions frequently occur when redundant constraints exist. However, the simplex method usually works through them to a final optimum solution.

5. *Redundant constraints.* A redundant constraint lies entirely within a region made infeasible by other constraints. It is dominated by other constraints in the set.

6. *Multiple solutions.* Zero-valued nonbasic variables in the $C_j - Z_j$ row indicate other equally desirable solutions. When a variable not in the basis has a $C_j - Z_j$ value equal to zero, that indicates that the variable can be entered into the basis without any change in the value of the tableau. This may be important when intangible factors indicate certain solutions may be more desirable although quantitative weights do not reveal it.

EXAMPLE 5

A school store sells calculators at a profit of $.50 each and shirts at a profit of $.40 each. It takes 2 minutes of a salesgirl's time and 2 minutes of a cashier's time to sell a calculator. It takes 3 minutes of a salesgirl's time, but only 1 minute of a cashier's time, to sell a sweatshirt. The store is open for 2 hours a day, and there are 1 cashier and 2 salesgirls on duty. How many of each item should the store attempt to sell each day in order to earn a maximum profit?
Let

X_1 = no. of calculators; X_2 = no. of sweatshirts.

Then we have

	X_1	X_2	Capacity (min.)
Cashier	2	1	120
Salesgirls	2	3	240
Profit/unit	$.50	$.40	

Constraints:

$$2X_1 + X_2 \leq 120,$$
$$2X_1 + 3X_2 \leq 240.$$

To obtain equalities we now introduce slack variables which have a zero contribution to profits:

$$2X_1 + X_2 + S_1 \quad = 120,$$
$$2X_1 + 3X_2 \quad + S_2 = 240.$$

Objective function:

$$0.50\, X_1 + 0.40\, X_2 + 0S_1 + 0S_2 = \text{max.}$$

Then we have the tableaus

C_j		0.50	0.40	0	0	
	Solution vector	X_1	X_2	S_1	S_2	B_0
0	S_1	②	1	1	0	120←
0	S_2	2	3	0	1	240
	Z_j	0	0	0	0	0
	$C_j - Z_j$	0.50	0.40	0	0	
		↑				

C_j		0.50	0.40	0	0	
	Solution vector	X_1	X_2	S_1	S_2	B_0
0.50	X_1	1	$\frac{1}{2}$	$\frac{1}{2}$	0	60
0	S_2	0	②	-1	1	120←
	Z_j	0.50	0.25	0.25	0	30
	$C_j - Z_j$	0	0.15	-0.25	0	
			↑			

C_j		0.50	0.40	0	0	
	Solution vector	X_1	X_2	S_1	S_2	B_0
0.50	X_1	1	0	$\frac{3}{4}$	$-\frac{1}{4}$	30
0.40	X_2	0	1	$-\frac{1}{2}$	$\frac{1}{2}$	60
	Z_j	0.50	0.40	0.175	0.075	39
	$C_j - Z_j$	0	0	-0.175	-0.075	

The best strategy is 30 calculators and 60 sweatshirts for a maximum profit of $39.

THE DUAL METHOD

Every linear programming problem has associated with it another linear programming problem called the dual. The initial problem is called the primal, and the related (shadow) problem is called the dual. The two paired together are termed dual problems, since both are formed from the same set of data. The optimum basic feasible solutions to these problems are such that one can easily be used to obtain solutions to the other.

What is the use of the dual, if the optimal solution of the primal contains, in itself, the solution of the dual? The solution of the dual of a linear programming problem may be easier to obtain (less computation) than that of the primal problem, or it may allow a check on the primal solution. The size of the linear programming problem influences the selection between the primal and the dual. If the primal has more constraint equations than unknown variables, it is often easier to solve the dual problem, since fewer iterations will be required.

If the primal problem has a solution, its dual will have a solution. If the primal has a finite optimum solution, so will the dual. If the primal problem has an unbounded optimum solution, the dual will not have any feasible solution.

After the dual problem is formulated, the solution procedure is exactly the same for any linear programming problem. Mechanically, the dual problem is formulated from the primal problem in the following manner:

1. If the primal is a maximization problem, the dual is a minimization problem, and vice versa.
2. The coefficients of the primal objective function become the constants of the dual constraints.
3. The constants of the primal constraints become the coefficients of the dual objective function.
4. The coefficients for the dual variables in the constraint equations are obtained by transposing the matrix of coefficients for the primal (the column coefficients in the primal become row coefficients in the dual, and the row coefficients in the primal become column coefficients in the dual).
5. The inequality signs are reversed.
6. The n variables X_n of the primal are replaced by m new variables Y_m in the dual.

MATHEMATICAL NOTATION

From the above conditions, it is apparent that if the primal has m constraints and n variables, the dual will have n constraints and m variables. The matrix notation of the model where T indicates the transpose of a matrix is as follows:

Primal: Maximize CX *Dual:* Minimize $B^T Y$
         subject to $AX \leq B,$ subject to $A^T Y \geq C^T,$
         where $X \geq 0.$ where $Y \geq 0.$

The following table shows the structure of the primal and dual problems when all the primal constraints are of the ''less than or equal to'' ($\leq$) type:

Dual \ Primal	X_1	X_2	·	·	·	X_n	$\leq$
Y_1	a_{11}	a_{12}	·	·	·	a_{1n}	B_1
Y_2	a_{21}	a_{22}	·	·	·	a_{2n}	B_2
·	·	·				·	·
·	·	·				·	·
·	·	·				·	·
Y_m	a_{m1}	a_{m2}	·	·	·	a_{mn}	B_m
$\geq$	C_1	C_2	·	·	·	C_n	minimize / maximize

The following table shows the structures of the primal and dual problems when all the primal constraints are of the "greater than or equal to" ($\geq$) type:

Dual \ Primal	X_1	X_2	·	·	·	X_n	$\geq$
Y_1	a_{11}	a_{12}	·	·	·	a_{1n}	B_1
Y_2	a_{21}	a_{22}	·	·	·	a_{2n}	B_2
·	·	·				·	·
·	·	·				·	·
·	·	·				·	·
Y_m	a_{m1}	a_{m2}	·	·	·	a_{mn}	B_m
$\leq$	C_1	C_2	·	·	·	C_n	maximize / minimize

A simple example will illustrate the formulation of the dual from the primal.

EXAMPLE 6

In the simplex method section, Example 5 gave a problem with the following conditions:

Maximize $0.50X_1 + 0.40X_2$
subject to $2X_1 + X_2 \leq 120$,
$2X_1 + 3X_2 \leq 240$.

Formulate and solve the dual problem.
We have

Dual \ Primal	X_1	X_2	$\leq$
Y_1	2	1	120
Y_2	2	3	240
$\geq$	0.50	0.40	minimize / maximize

continued

EXAMPLE 6—*continued*

The resulting dual conditions are as follows:

Minimize $120Y_1 + 240Y_2$
subject to $2Y_1 + 2Y_2 \geq 0.5,$
$\quad\quad\quad Y_1 + 3Y_2 \geq 0.4.$

The first simplex tableau is as follows:

C_j	Solution vector	120 Y_1	240 Y_2	0 S_1	0 S_2	M A_1	M A_2	B_0
M	A_1	2	2	-1	0	1	0	0.5
M	A_2	1	③	0	-1	0	1	0.4 ←
	Z_j	$3M$	$5M$	$-M$	$-M$	M	M	$0.9M$
	$C_j - Z_j$	$120 - 3M$	$240 - 5M$ ↑	M	M	0	0	

The entering vector is Y_2 and the leaving vector is A_2. The second tableau is as follows:

C_j	Solution vector	120 Y_1	240 Y_2	0 S_1	0 S_2	M A_1	M A_2	B_0
M	A_1	⑴⅓	0	-1	$\frac{2}{3}$	1	$-\frac{2}{3}$	0.234 ←
240	Y_2	$\frac{1}{3}$	1	0	$-\frac{1}{3}$	0	$\frac{1}{3}$	0.133
	Z_j	$80 + 1\frac{1}{3}M$	240	$-M$	$\frac{2}{3}M - 80$	M	$80 - \frac{2}{3}M$	$31.9 + 0.234M$
	$C_j - Z_j$	$40 - 1\frac{1}{3}M$ ↑	0	M	$80 - \frac{2}{3}M$	0	$1\frac{2}{3}M - 80$	

The entering vector is Y_1, and the leaving vector is A_1. The third tableau is as follows:

C_j	Solution vector	120 Y_1	240 Y_2	0 S_1	0 S_2	M A_1	M A_2	B_0
120	Y_1	1	0	$-\frac{3}{4}$	$\frac{1}{2}$	$\frac{3}{4}$	$-\frac{1}{2}$	0.175
240	Y_2	0	1	$\frac{1}{4}$	$-\frac{1}{2}$	$-\frac{1}{4}$	$\frac{1}{2}$	0.075
	Z_j	120	240	-30	-60	30	60	39
	$C_j - Z_j$	0	0	30	60	$M - 30$	$M - 60$	

Since all the $C_j - Z_j$ values are positive, the optimum solution to the dual problem has been obtained. The optimum solution to the primal problem as obtained from Example 5 is as follows:

C_j	Solution vector	0.50 X_1	0.40 X_2	0 S_1	0 S_2	B_0
0.50	X_1	1	0	$\frac{3}{4}$	$-\frac{1}{4}$	30
0.40	X_2	0	1	$-\frac{1}{2}$	$\frac{1}{2}$	60
	Z_j	0.50	0.40	0.175	0.075	39
	$C_j - Z_j$	0	0	-0.175	-0.075	

The optimum value of the primal is always the same as the optimum value of the dual. Here the optimum value was 39 for both problems.

The solution to the primal problem is found in the optimum dual tableau under the slack variables in the $C_j - Z_j$ row. The absolute value of the slack variables in the optimum dual tableau in the $C_j - Z_j$ row represents the solution to the primal problem. In a similar manner, the absolute value of the slack variables in the optimum primal tableau in the $C_j - Z_j$ row represents the solution to the dual problem. In the optimum primal tableau $X_1 = 30$ and $X_2 = 60$; in the $C_j - Z_j$ row of the optimum dual tableau you find 30 under S_1 and 60 under S_2. Likewise, in the optimum dual tableau $Y_1 = 0.175$ and $Y_2 = 0.075$; in the $C_j - Z_j$ row of the optimum primal tableau you find the absolute values 0.175 under S_1 and 0.075 under S_2. Generally, the slack variables in the $C_j - Z_j$ row of the optimum primal tableau reveal the optimum solution to the dual problem, and vice versa. Thus, the above example has illustrated that the primal solution contains the dual solution and vice versa.

DUAL VARIABLES: INTERPRETATION

The solution to the dual problem represents an economic interpretation that is a form of marginal analysis (what will happen if one more unit of input is employed?). The dual variables, Y_m, in a profit maximization primal problem are the marginal profits of each additional input or output. (The dual variables are sometimes called opportunity costs or shadow prices.) The dual variables Y_m in a cost minimization primal problem are the marginal costs of each additional input or output. The constant B in the primal constraint equations determines if the dual variables relate to marginal input or output. If the constant in a constraint equation limits the factors of production, the marginal analysis refers to input. If the constant in a constraint equation limits output, the marginal analysis refers to output. Knowledge of how much profits would increase or costs would decrease with an additional unit of each of the various scarce resources is valuable information.

In a primal maximization problem, the dual variables indicate how much profit is being forgone for lack of additional units of scarce resources. In Example 6 the restraining constant was capacity, which was stated in minutes (120 minutes for cashiers and 240 minutes for salesgirls). The marginal analysis of the problem reveals that marginal profit could be obtained by increasing capacity by one minute. If the cashier time were increased from 120 to 121 minutes, marginal profit would be increased by $.175. In a similar manner, if salesgirl time were increased from 240 to 241 minutes, marginal profit would be increased by $.075. When the slack variables in the C_j-Z_j row of the primal have nonzero absolute values, they indicate how much marginal benefit can be derived by employing an additional unit of each resource. When the slack variables in the $C_j - Z_j$ row of the primal have zero values, no marginal benefit can be derived by making additional resources available. The zero value indicates that the resources are not currently being fully utilized to their capacity. Thus, the dual variables measure the value or worth of relaxing a constraint by acquiring an additional unit of that factor of production.

EXAMPLE 7

Formulate and solve the dual problem from the following primal problem:

Minimize $\$8X_1 + \$9X_2$

subject to $2X_1 + X_2 \geq 200,$

$X_1 + 3X_2 \geq 200,$

$X_1 \qquad \geq 60,$

$X_2 \geq 40.$

We have

Primal Dual	X_1	X_2	$\geq$
Y_1	2	1	200
Y_2	1	3	200
Y_3	1		60
Y_4		1	40
$\leq$	8	9	maximize / minimize

The resulting dual conditions are as follows:

Maximize $200Y_1 + 200Y_2 + 60Y_3 + 40Y_4$

subject to $2Y_1 + Y_2 + Y_3 \leq 8,$

$Y_1 + 3Y_2 + Y_4 \leq 9.$

Adding the necessary slack variables, the first simplex tableau is as follows:

C_j		200	200	60	40	0	0	
	Solution vector	Y_1	Y_2	Y_3	Y_4	S_1	S_2	B_0
0	S_1	②	1	1	0	1	0	8 ←
0	S_2	1	3	0	1	0	1	9
	Z_j	0	0	0	0	0	0	0
	$C_j - Z_j$	200	200	60	40	0	0	
		↑						

The entering vector is Y_1, and the leaving vector is S_1. The second simplex tableau is as follows:

C_j		200	200	60	40	0	0	
	Solution vector	Y_1	Y_2	Y_3	Y_4	S_1	S_2	B_0
200	Y_1	1	$\frac{1}{2}$	$\frac{1}{2}$	0	$\frac{1}{2}$	0	4
0	S_2	0	②$\frac{1}{2}$	$-\frac{1}{2}$	1	$-\frac{1}{2}$	1	5 ←
	Z_j	200	100	100	0	100	0	800
	$C_j - Z_j$	0	100	-40	40	-100	0	
			↑					

The entering vector is Y_2, and the leaving vector is S_2. The third simplex tableau is as follows:

C_j		200	200	60	40	0	0	
	Solution vector	Y_1	Y_2	Y_3	Y_4	S_1	S_2	B_0
200	Y_1	1	0	$\frac{3}{5}$	$-\frac{1}{5}$	$\frac{3}{5}$	$-\frac{1}{5}$	3
200	Y_2	0	1	$-\frac{1}{5}$	$\frac{2}{5}$	$-\frac{1}{5}$	$\frac{2}{5}$	2
	Z_j	200	200	80	40	80	40	1000
	$C_j - Z_j$	0	0	-20	0	-80	-40	

Since all of the quantities in the $C_j - Z_j$ row are negative or zero, an optimum dual solution has been obtained. Since the value of the final optimal tableau is the same for the dual and the primal, the minimum cost of the primal is $1000. The absolute slack variable values in the $C_j - Z_j$ row of the optimum dual tableau indicate the solution to the primal problem (S_1 corresponds to X_1, and S_2 corresponds to X_2). The optimum size of X_1 is 80 and the optimum size of X_2 is 40 in the primal problem. The dual solution variables ($Y_1 = 3$ and $Y_2 = 2$) represent the marginal cost of changing the constants of the primal constraints by one. It would decrease the cost by $3 if the first primal constraint equation had its constant term decreased from 200 to 199. It would increase the cost by $2 if the second primal constraint equation had its constant term increased from 200 to 201.

ADDITIONAL EXPLANATION

The dual problem solved in Example 7 required two iterations before an optimum solution was obtained. If the primal problem had been solved, it would have required a minimum of four iterations. The computational efficiency of the dual in certain situations is apparent.

The inequality restrictions of the primal problem must all be pointed in the same direction. If, in the original formulation of the problem, one or more restrictions have their inequalities pointed in the other direction, they must be reversed. An inequality can be reversed by multiplying through by -1. For example, the constraint $2X_1 + 3X_2 - 4X_3 \geq 10$ can be written as $-2X_1 - 3X_2 + 4X_3 \leq -10$.

If a primal constraint involves an equality, two inequalities must be substituted for it. One of the inequalities is a "less than or equal to," and the other is "a greater than or equal to." For example, the equation $X_1 + X_2 + 2X_3 = 10$ can be rewritten as the two constraints:

$$X_1 + X_2 + 2X_3 \leq 10,$$
$$X_1 + X_2 + 2X_3 \geq 10, \quad \text{or} \quad -X_1 - X_2 - 2X_3 \leq -10.$$

Using the above conventions, all constraints can be made to point in the same direction. To clarify the point, we work an example of a problem with the three types of constraints.

EXAMPLE 8

In the Simplex Method section, Example 4 gave a problem with the following conditions:

Minimize $\$0.3X_1 + \$0.8X_2$
subject to $X_1 \leq 800,$
$X_2 \geq 600,$
$X_1 + X_2 = 2000.$

The constraints can be rewritten as follows:

$-X_1 \geq -800,$
$X_2 \geq 600,$
$X_1 + X_2 \geq 2000,$
$-X_1 - X_2 \geq -2000.$

	X_1	X_2	$\geq$
Y_1	-1		-800
Y_2		1	600
Y_3	1	1	2000
Y_4	-1	-1	-2000
$\leq$	0.3	0.8	maximize / minimize

The resulting dual conditions are as follows:

Maximize $-800Y_1 + 600Y_2 + 2000Y_3 - 2000Y_4$
subject to $-Y_1 + Y_3 - Y_4 \leq 0.3,$
$Y_2 + Y_3 - Y_4 \leq 0.8.$

Adding the necessary slack variables, the first tableau is as follows:

C_j		-800	600	2000	-2000	0	0	
	Solution vector	Y_1	Y_2	Y_3	Y_4	S_1	S_2	B_0
0	S_1	-1	0	①	-1	1	0	0.3 ←
0	S_2	0	1	1	-1	0	1	0.8
	Z_j	0	0	0	0	0	0	0
	$C_j - Z_j$	-800	600	2000	-2000	0	0	
				↑				

The entering vector is Y_3, and the leaving vector is S_1. The second tableau is as follows:

C_j		-800	600	2000	-2000	0	0	
	Solution vector	Y_1	Y_2	Y_3	Y_4	S_1	S_2	B_0
2000	Y_3	-1	0	1	-1	1	0	0.3
0	S_2	①	1	0	0	-1	1	0.5 ←
	Z_j	-2000	0	2000	-2000	-2000	0	600
	$C_j - Z_j$	1200	600	0	0	-2000	0	
		↑						

The entering vector is Y_1, and the leaving vector is S_2. The third tableau is as follows:

| C_j | | -800 | 600 | 2000 | -2000 | 0 | 0 | |
	Solution vector	Y_1	Y_2	Y_3	Y_4	S_1	S_2	B_0
2000	Y_3	0	1	1	-1	0	1	0.8
-800	Y_1	1	1	0	0	-1	1	0.5
	Z_j	-800	1200	2000	-2000	800	1200	1200
	$C_j - Z_j$	0	-600	0	0	-800	-1200	

Since all of the quantities in the $C_j - Z_j$ row are negative or zero, an optimum dual solution has been obtained. The minimum cost for the primal is $1200, and it is the same as the maximum of the dual. The absolute slack variable values in the $C_j - Z_j$ row of the optimum dual tableau indicate the solution to the primal problem (S_1 corresponds to X_1, and S_2 corresponds to X_2). The optimum size of X_1 is 800, and of X_2 is 1200. The dual solution variables ($Y_1 = 0.5$ and $Y_3 = 0.8$) represent the marginal cost of increasing or decreasing the constants of the primal constraints by one. If the constant in the first primal constraint ($X_1 \le 800$) were increased from 800 to 801, the cost would decrease by $.50. If the constant in the third primal constraint ($X_1 + X_2 = 2000$) were increased from 2000 to 2001, the cost would increase by $.80; if it were changed from 2000 to 1999, the cost would decrease by $.80.

The dual problem solved in Example 8 required two iterations before an optimum solution was obtained. The solution to the primal problem required three iterations (see Example 4 in the Simplex Method section). The computational efficiency of the dual is again apparent.

The optimal dual variables indicate the advisability of modifying the existing resource base. They indicate the bottleneck areas and the modifications in resources that will achieve the most benefit. The dual variables are the marginal values of an additional unit of each resource in the constraint limits denoted by B in the primal. The dual variables indicate how a change in one unit in the input of a resource will affect the value of the objective function if the additional factor input is used optimally.

The marginal values obtained from the dual are valid only within certain ranges of capacity. Changing the availability of a resource by one unit or more may change the whole structure of an optimal solution. As more and more capacity is made available by increasing one factor, eventually another factor will become the bottleneck. The single unit change applies only if other things remain constant.

SENSITIVITY ANALYSIS

The final (optimal) simplex tableau provides additional information beyond the quantities of the decision variables needed to optimize an objective function. The dual variables, as shown earlier, can tell management the impact on the objective function of a marginal (one unit) change in the constraint constants (B). If a change in one unit is desirable, then management may want to find if a change of 2, 3, or more units is feasible with respect to the dual variable. Specifically, it is desirable to know the range over which the dual variable will remain valid. This information reveals to management the amount of spending that would be justified to obtain additional units of scarce resources.

Sensitivity analysis is a form of post-optimality analysis, since it is applied after the optimum solution to the primal problem is obtained. An important phase of sensitivity analysis is the study of the effect of changes on the right-hand side of a constraint in the initial simplex tableau on the optimal solution. By changes of the right-hand side, we mean changing the values of one of the elements in the B column of the linear programming problem. The range of feasibility will indicate the amount of change that can be made in one element of the right-hand side while still maintaining a valid dual variable. The range is obtained by dividing the appropriate slack or artificial column elements into the respective requirements column elements in the optimal tableau. The following table indicates the right-hand ranges for each type of constraint:

	Right-hand side ranges	
Type of constraint	Allowable increase	Allowable decrease
1. $\leq$ inequality	Least positive $(-B_o/S_i)$	Least negative $(-B_o/S_i)$
2. $\geq$ inequality	Least positive (B_o/S_i)	Least negative (B_o/S_i)
3. $=$ equality	Least positive $(-B_o/A_i)$	Least negative $(-B_o/A_i)$

EXAMPLE 9

Determine the range of feasibility for the dual variables in (a) Example 3 and (b) Example 4.

(a) Example 3:

First constraint: $4a + 2b \leq 60$.

S_1	B_o	$-B_o/S_1$
$\frac{1}{3}$	12	-36
$-\frac{1}{6}$	6	36

Upper limit $= 60 + 36 = 96,$
Lower limit $= 60 - 36 = 24.$

Second constraint: $2a + 4b \leq 48$.

S_2	B_o	$-B_o/S_2$
$-\frac{1}{6}$	12	72
$\frac{1}{3}$	6	-18

Upper limit $= 48 + 72 = 120,$
Lower limit $= 48 - 18 =\ \ \ 30.$

(b) Example 4:

First constraint: $X_1 \leq 800$.

S_1	B_o	$-B_o/S_1$
1	800	$-$ 800
-1	1200	1200
-1	600	600

Upper limit $= 800 + 600 = 1400$,
Lower limit $= 800 - 800 = 0$.

Second constraint: $X_2 \geq 600$.

S_2	B_o	B_o/S_2
0	800	$+ \infty$
0	1200	$+ \infty$
1	600	600

Upper limit $= 600 + 600 = 1200$,
Lower limit $= 600 - \infty \quad = 0$.

Third constraint: $X_1 + X_2 = 2000$

A_2	B_o	$-B_o/A_2$
0	800	$- \infty$
1	1200	-1200
1	600	$-$ 600

Upper limit $= 2000 + \infty \quad = \infty$,
Lower limit $= 2000 - 600 = 1400$.

THE TRANSPORTATION METHOD

The transportation method, or the distribution method (as it is also called), of linear programming is a tool for allocation of goods from a set of origins to a set of destinations so as to optimize an objective function. All transportation problems can be solved by the simplex method, but the transportation method is considerably easier and simpler. "Transportation method" is a misnomer: though the technique was developed in connection with problems dealing with the physical shipment of goods, it is adaptable to any linear source-to-destination problem. The technique is particularly useful for an organization producing the same product at numerous plants and shipping to numerous distribution centers (warehouses). It has found applications in distribution, scheduling, plant location analysis, and machine loading.

Various approaches have been developed for solving the distribution problem—the northwest corner rule with stepping stone method, the modified distribution method (MODI), the Vogel approximation method (VAM), the mutually preferred method, the simplex method, etc. In this section, the northwest corner rule with the stepping stone method and the modified northwest corner rule will be introduced.

For a problem to be suitable for solution by the transportation method, it must meet three conditions:

1. The items being distributed must be expressed in common units that are uniform and interchangeable. The coefficients of all variables in the constraints

FIGURE 3
Transportation method of linear programming.

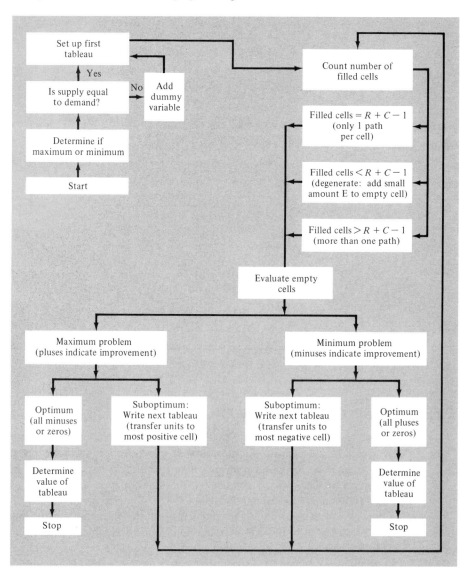

must be zero or one. This ensures a one-to-one rate of substitution between variables.

2. The objective function and constraint equations must be linear.
3. The sum of source capacities must equal the sum of destination requirements. If inequalities exist, a dummy location can be created to obtain equality.

Like the simplex method, the transportation algorithm starts with an initial solution and moves to increasingly improved solutions in a finite number of iterations. In the transportation method, however, the initial solution may be developed by alternate methods. It will not be the zero feasible solution, but one possible solution closer to the final solution, if not the final solution itself.

NORTHWEST CORNER RULE

The northwest corner rule illustrates how to obtain a very quick feasible initial solution. It begins at the upper left-hand cell (northwest corner) of the table and fills the cells as needed to meet the source and destination requirements (rim conditions) in a stair-step fashion without regard to costs or benefits. The results of this rapid assignment rule is usually a rather high cost or low benefit solution that requires numerous iterations for optimization.

Figure 3 contains a flow diagram that illustrates the transportation method algorithm. It consists of basically three major steps:

1. Set up the first feasible solution.
2. Test for optimality.
3. Improve the solution until optimality is obtained.

To illustrate the northwest corner rule with the stepping stone method, a simple cost minimization problem will be solved.

EXAMPLE 10

A company manufactures a given product in three plants (A, B, and C) from which four markets (1, 2, 3, and 4) are supplied. The market requirements, plant capacities, and unit costs from each plant to each market are given below. What shipping strategy will minimize cost?

Plant	Market				Unit capacity
	1	2	3	4	
A	$9	$6	$4	$7	35
B	2	4	6	3	20
C	8	1	8	6	45
Unit requirements	30	40	10	20	100

Figure 3 contains the algorithm for solving transportation problems. The problem is a minimization of cost. The supply from the plants, 100 (35 + 20 + 45), is equal to the market demand, 100 (30 + 40 + 10 + 20). The next basic step is to set up the first feasible tableau. We begin in the upper left-hand corner of the matrix (the northwest corner) and note that plant A has 35 units available and market 1 needs 30 units. We assign 30 units from A to 1. We have not used up A's supply, so we move to the right under market 2 and assign the balance of A's supply of 5 units to market 2. Looking at the requirements for 2, we note that it has a total requirement of 40 units. We drop down to plant B, which has a capacity of 20 units, and assign all of B's capacity of 20 units to market 2. Since we have only satisfied 25 units (5 from A and 20 from B) of market 2's demand for 40 units, we drop down to plant C with a capacity of 45 units and assign 15 units of its capacity to market 2. Having satisfied markets 1 and 2, we move to market 3 with a demand for 10 units and satisfy it from plant C. The next market is 4, with a demand for 20 units, which receives all the remaining capacity from plant C. Having assigned all of the plant capacity to markets, we complete the first transportation tableau by placing the unit costs in the upper right-hand corner of each cell.

The first transportation tableau, as shown in Figure 4, is a possible solution to the problem. The next step is to test the solution for optimality by evaluating each empty cell to determine if a lower cost routing is possible. The number of filled cells in Figure 4 is six. If the number of rows plus the number of columns minus one is equal to the number of filled cells, there is only one pathway to evaluate for each empty cell (R + C − 1 = number of filled cells). In the example 3 + 4 − 1 = 6, so there is only one pathway to evaluate for each empty cell. In evaluating empty cells for possible improvement, a closed pathway is selected. The pathway is similar to the moves of the rook in the game of chess except that empty or filled cells can be skipped in moving to a suitable filled cell. With the exception of the empty cell being evaluated, every other cell on the pathway must have an allocation of units. Right angle turns are made at each cell on the pathway, which results in the addition of one unit and the subtraction of one unit from each row and column included in the pathway. The addition and subtraction ensure that the unit capacity and unit requirement constraints will not be violated.

Every empty cell must be evaluated after each iteration to see if it represents a potential improvement in the solution or cost advantage by serving as an alternative route. An empty cell is evaluated by summing the changes in cost that would occur if a single unit were placed in the empty cell through a unitary redistribution of its present allocation. For each possible redistribution path, the cells that will receive an additional unit are positive, as their allocation represents a cost; cells that will lose a unit are negative, as their replacement represents a savings. The result is a signed (+ or −) amount by which the objective function will be changed for each unit reallocated to the empty cell. To the cell that indicates the most improvement, the greatest possible quantity is added without violating the rim requirements.

In the example shown in Figure 4, the unfilled cells are A3, A4, B1, B3, B4, and C1. If the evaluation of all the empty cells gives positive values, the solution is optimum. If the cell evaluation gives a negative value for any empty cell, it indicates cost reduction can be achieved by transferring as many units as possible to that cell. The empty cell evaluations are as follows:

$$A3 = A3 - C3 + C2 - A2 = 4 - 8 + 1 - 6 = -9, \leftarrow$$
$$A4 = A4 - C4 + C2 - A2 = 7 - 6 + 1 - 6 = -4,$$
$$B1 = B1 - A1 + A2 - B2 = 2 - 9 + 6 - 4 = -5,$$
$$B3 = B3 - C3 + C2 - B2 = 6 - 8 + 1 - 4 = -5,$$
$$B4 = B4 - C4 + C2 - B2 = 3 - 6 + 1 - 4 = -6,$$
$$C1 = C1 - A1 + A2 - C2 = 8 - 9 + 6 - 1 = +4.$$

FIGURE 4
Northwest corner—initial tableau.

The last step in the solution of the transportation problem requires that suboptimum solutions be improved. The numerous empty cell evaluations with negative signs indicate that the cost can be reduced by transferring units. The cell that is the most negative, A3, is chosen for improvement, and the −9 indicates the cost will be reduced by $9.00 for each unit transferred to cell A3. To determine the maximum number of units that can be transferred to cell A3, examine the number of units in the cells that had their unit cost subtracted in the cell evaluation of A3. The negative values were −8 for cell C3 and −6 for cell A2. Choose the cell with the smallest number of units, since any larger transfer would result in a cell with negative units. C3 has 10 units and A2 has 5 units, so 5 units will be transferred to cell A3. (5 units are added to cell A3, 5 units are subtracted from cell C3, 5 units are added to cell C2, and 5 units are subtracted from cell A2.) See Figure 5 for the new, improved solution. No other cells have been changed except those along

FIGURE 5
Stepping stone method—2nd tableau.

continued

EXAMPLE 10— *continued*

the improved pathway. The empty cell evaluation of the second tableau shown in Figure 5 is as follows:

$$
\begin{aligned}
A2 &= 6 - 4 + 8 - 1 &&= +9, \\
A4 &= 7 - 6 + 8 - 4 &&= +5, \\
B1 &= 2 - 9 + 4 - 8 + 1 - 4 &&= -14, \leftarrow \\
B3 &= 6 - 8 + 1 - 4 &&= -5, \\
B4 &= 3 - 6 + 1 - 4 &&= -6, \\
C1 &= 8 - 9 + 4 - 8 &&= -5.
\end{aligned}
$$

The existence of negative values indicates that further cost reduction is possible. The most negative cell is $B1$, so units will be transferred to it. The cells that had their unit cost subtracted in the cell evaluation of $B1$ are $A1$, $C3$, and $B2$. $A1$ has 30 units, $C3$ has 5 units, and $B2$ has 20 units. The smallest amount is in cell $C3$, so 5 units will be transferred to cell $B1$. (5 units are added to cell $B1$, 5 units are subtracted from cell $A1$, 5 units are added to cell $A3$, 5 units are subtracted from cell $C3$, 5 units are added to cell $C2$, and 5 units are subtracted from cell $B2$.) See Figure 6 for the improved solution. The empty cell evaluation of the third tableau shown in Figure 6 is as follows:

$$
\begin{aligned}
A2 &= 6 - 4 + 2 - 9 &&= -5, \\
A4 &= 7 - 6 + 1 - 4 + 2 - 9 &&= -9, \leftarrow \\
B3 &= 6 - 2 + 9 - 4 &&= +9, \\
B4 &= 3 - 6 + 1 - 4 &&= -6, \\
C1 &= 8 - 2 + 4 - 1 &&= +9, \\
C3 &= 8 - 1 + 4 - 2 + 9 - 4 &&= +14.
\end{aligned}
$$

Negative values indicate that further cost improvement is possible. The most negative cell is $A4$. The cells that had their unit cost subtracted in the cell evaluation $A4$ are $C4$, $B2$, and $A1$. $C4$ has 20 units, $B2$ has 15 units, and $A1$ has 25 units. The smallest quantity

FIGURE 6
Stepping stone method—3rd tableau.

Plant	Market 1	Market 2	Market 3	Market 4	Unit capacity
A	25 [9]	[6]	10 [4]	[7]	35
B	5 [2]	15 [4]	[6]	[3]	20
C	[8]	25 [1]	[8]	20 [6]	45
Unit requirements	30	40	10	20	100

| Plant | Market | | | | Unit capacity |
	1	2	3	4	
A	9 10	6	4 10	7 15	35
B	2 20	4	6	3	20
C	8	1 40	8	6 5	45
Unit requirements	30	40	10	20	100

FIGURE 7
Stepping stone method—4th tableau.

is in cell $B2$, so fifteen units will be transferred to cell $A4$. (15 units are added to $A4$, 15 units are subtracted from $C4$, 15 units are added to $C2$, 15 units are subtracted from cell $B2$, 15 units are added to cell $B1$, and 15 units are subtracted from cell $A1$.) See Figure 7 for the improved tableau. The empty cell evaluation of Figure 7 is as follows:

$$A2 = 6 - 7 + 6 - 1 \qquad\qquad = +4,$$
$$B2 = 4 - 2 + 9 - 7 + 6 - 1 = +9,$$
$$B3 = 6 - 2 + 9 - 4 \qquad\quad = +9,$$
$$B4 = 3 - 2 + 9 - 7 \qquad\quad = +3,$$
$$C1 = 8 - 9 + 7 - 6 \qquad\quad = 0,$$
$$C3 = 8 - 4 + 7 - 6 \qquad\quad = +5.$$

Since none of the values has a negative sign, an optimum solution has been achieved in three iterations. When a zero value is obtained in an empty cell evaluation, it indicates the existence of an alternative route with the same cost. The optimum routing schedule is shown in Figure 7. The cost of the optimum solution is obtained by multiplying the cost by the number of units assigned to each filled cell and summing these values. In the example, the minimum cost is

$$9(10) + 4(10) + 7(15) + 2(20) + 1(40) + 6(5) = \$345.$$

In situations where a tie exists between two or more empty cell evaluations, the selection may be made arbitrarily or based upon the greatest number of units that can be redistributed. In this case, the greatest aggregate reduction is preferred.

The only important difference between the procedure for solving a minimization problem and for a maximization problem lies in the rule for improvement based on the empty cell evaluations. In maximization, the sign rule is reversed and an optimum solution is obtained when the cell evaluations give all negative values; a positive sign indicates additional benefit can be obtained by transferring units to the corresponding cell location. As in minimization, the cell that is introduced into the solution is the one that offers the greatest benefit per unit.

EXAMPLE 11

A manufacturer must build 100 units of product *A*, 60 of product *B*, and 30 of product *C* over a given time period. Each product order, or any part of an order, may be fabricated on any of three machines. The capacity of all the machines is the same for all three products, but incremental unit profits are different for product-machine combinations:

Machine	Product A	Product B	Product C
1	$20	$10	$8
2	5	9	7
3	5	3	6

The open (unscheduled) capacity of the machines for the given time period is 90 units for machine 1, 50 units for 2, and 50 units for 3. What combinations maximize profit?

Figure 3 contains the algorithm for solving this problem. The initial tableau is as follows:

Machine	Product			Unit capacity
	A	B	C	
1	20 90	10	8	90
2	5 10	9 40	7	50
3	5	3 20	6 30	50
Unit requirements	100	60	30	190

$$1B = 10 - 9 + 5 - 20 \qquad\quad = -14, \quad 2C = 7 - 6 + 3 - 9 \qquad = -5,$$
$$1C = 8 - 6 + 3 - 9 + 5 - 20 = -19, \quad 3A = 5 - 5 + 9 - 3 \qquad = +6.\leftarrow$$

Machine	Product			Unit capacity
	A	B	C	
1	20 90	10	8	90
2	5	9 50	7	50
3	5 10	3 10	6 30	50
Unit requirements	100	60	30	190

$$1B = 10 - 3 + 5 - 20 = -8, \qquad 2A = 5 - 9 + 3 - 5 \quad = -6,$$
$$1C = 8 - 6 + 5 - 20 \quad = -13, \qquad 2C = 7 - 6 + 3 - 9 \quad = -5.$$

Produce 90 A on 1, 50 B on 2, 10 A on 3, 10 B on 3, 30 C on 3.

Maximum profit $= 90(20) + 50(9) + 10(5) + 10(3) + 30(6) = \$2510$.

Every transportation method problem of LP can be solved by the simplex method. However, the transportation method is a more efficient algorithm. The objective function and constraints for Example 11 are as follows:

Maximize $20X_{1A} + 10X_{1B} + 8X_{1C} + 5X_{2A} + 9X_{2B} + 7X_{2C} + 5X_{3A} + 3X_{3B} + 6X_{3C}$

subject to
$$\begin{aligned} X_{1A} + X_{1B} + X_{1C} &= 90, & X_{1A} + X_{2A} + X_{3A} &= 100, \\ X_{2A} + X_{2B} + X_{2C} &= 50, & X_{1B} + X_{2B} + X_{3B} &= 60, \\ X_{3A} + X_{3B} + X_{3C} &= 50, & X_{1C} + X_{2C} + X_{3C} &= 30. \end{aligned}$$

It can be seen that the above simplex problem would require 6 artificial variables and at least 6 iterations before an optimum solution could be attained. Thus, the computational efficiency of the transportation method is apparent.

DUMMY LOCATIONS

The transportation method requires that the sum of source capacities equal the sum of destination requirements. In Examples 10 and 11, supply equaled demand, so the above condition was met. If supply does not equal demand, a dummy location can be created to obtain equality. The dummy location is assigned zero objective function values and is neglected if the final solution indicates a dummy location assignment. If demand exceeds supply, the dummy location can represent an imaginary plant. If supply exceeds demand, the dummy location represents an imaginary warehouse. The dummy location is similar to the slack variable in the simplex method.

EXAMPLE 12

A firm produces a product in three plants (A, B, and C) and it ships the product to three warehouses (X, Y, and Z). The incremental unit profit for the different plant to warehouse combinations is shown below. What routing schedule would you recommend to maximize profits?

Plant	Warehouse			Supply (units)
	X	Y	Z	
A	$20	$ 7	$10	140
B	5	0	8	50
C	6	10	9	60
Demand (units)	100	50	30	

continued

EXAMPLE 12—*continued*

Plant	Warehouse X	Warehouse Y	Warehouse Z	Warehouse S	Unit capacity
A	[20] 100	[7] 40	[10]	[0]	140
B	[5]	[0] 10	[8] 30	[0] 10	50
C	[6]	[10]	[9]	[0] 60	60
Unit requirements	100	50	30	70	250

FIGURE 8
Northwest corner—initial tableau.

Figure 3 contains the flow diagram for the maximization procedure. Since supply and demand are not equal (180 units are required, but the plants can produce 250 units), a dummy variable must be introduced. The dummy warehouse, S, is introduced with a zero contribution to profit, and any units allocated in its cells will be ignored in the final solution. The first tableau is established by the northwest corner rule in Figure 8. The empty cell evaluation of the first tableau in Figure 8 is as follows:

$AZ = 10 - 8 + 0 - 7 = -5,$ $\quad CX = 6 - 20 + 7 - 0 + 0 - 0 = -7,$
$AS = 0 - 0 + 0 - 7 = -7,$ $\quad CY = 10 - 0 + 0 - 0 = +10,\leftarrow$
$BX = 5 - 20 + 7 - 0 = -8,$ $\quad CZ = 9 - 8 + 0 - 0 = +1.$

FIGURE 9
Stepping stone method—2nd tableau.

Plant	Warehouse X	Warehouse Y	Warehouse Z	Warehouse S	Unit capacity
A	[20] 100	[7] 40	[10]	[0]	140
B	[5]	[0]	[8] 30	[0] 20	50
C	[6]	[10] 10	[9]	[0] 50	60
Unit requirements	100	50	30	70	250

Plant	Warehouse				Unit capacity
	X	Y	Z	S	
A	20 100	7 10	10 30	0	140
B	5	0	8	0 50	50
C	6	10 40	9	0 20	60
Unit requirements	100	50	30	70	250

FIGURE 10
Stepping stone method—3rd tableau.

The largest positive value is 10 for cell CY. Cells BY and CS had their unit profits subtracted, so the cell with the smallest quantity indicates the transfer amount of 10 units (10 units are added to CY, 10 units are subtracted from BY, 10 units are added to BS, and 10 units are subtracted from CS). Figure 9 shows the new tableau. Its empty cell evaluation is as follows:

$$AZ = 10 - 7 + 10 - 0 + 0 - 8 = +5,\leftarrow \quad BY = 0 - 0 + 0 - 10 \qquad = -10,$$
$$AS = 0 - 0 + 10 - 7 \qquad\qquad = +3, \qquad CX = 6 - 20 + 7 - 10 \quad = -17,$$
$$BX = 5 - 20 + 7 - 10 + 0 - 0 = -18, \qquad CZ = 9 - 8 + 0 - 0 \qquad = +1.$$

The largest positive value is 5 for cell AZ. The cells AY, CS, and BZ had their unit profits subtracted, so the cell with the smallest quantity indicates the transfer of 30 units (30 is added to AZ, 30 is subtracted from AY, 30 is added to CY, 30 is subtracted from CS, 30 is added to BS, and 30 is subtracted from BZ). Figure 10 shows the revised tableau. Its empty cell evaluation is as follows:

$$AS = 0 - 0 + 10 - 7 \qquad\qquad = +3,\leftarrow$$
$$BX = 5 - 20 + 7 - 10 + 0 - 0 = -18,$$
$$BY = 0 - 10 + 0 - 0 \qquad\qquad = -10,$$
$$BZ = 8 - 0 + 0 - 10 + 7 - 10 = -5,$$
$$CX = 6 - 20 + 7 - 10 \qquad\quad = -17,$$
$$CZ = 9 - 10 + 7 - 10 \qquad\quad = -4.$$

The only positive value is 3 for cell AS. Cells AY and CS had their unit profits subtracted, so the cell with the smallest quantity indicates the transfer of 10 units (10 is added to AS, 10 is subtracted from AY, 10 is added to CY, and 10 is subtracted from CS.)

Figure 11 shows the revised tableau. Its empty cell evaluation is as follows:

$$AY = 7 - 10 + 0 - 0 = -3, \qquad\qquad BZ = 8 - 0 + 0 - 10 = -2,$$
$$BX = 5 - 20 + 0 - 0 = -15, \qquad\qquad CX = 6 - 20 + 0 - 0 = -14,$$
$$BY = 0 - 10 + 0 - 0 = -10, \qquad\qquad CZ = 9 - 0 + 0 - 10 = -1.$$

continued

EXAMPLE 12— *continued*

Plant	Warehouse				Unit capacity
	X	Y	Z	S	
A	20 100	7	10 30	0 10	140
B	5	0	8	0 50	50
C	6	10 50	9	0 10	60
Unit requirements	100	50	30	70	250

FIGURE 11
Stepping stone method—4th tableau.

Since all of the empty cells have a negative sign, the optimum solution has been reached. The optimum solution is to ship 100 from A to X, 30 from A to Z, and 50 from C to Y. The maximum profit is

$$100(20) + 30(10) + 10(0) + 50(0) + 50(10) + 10(0) = \$2,800.$$

DEGENERACY

If more than $R + C - 1$ cells are filled, there will be more than one pathway for one or more cells. All of the possible pathways must be evaluated in determining optimality. If less than $R + C - 1$ cells are filled, the problem is degenerate and not all empty cells will have a closed path. The degenerate condition may occur in the initial solution, or it may arise when two cells of equal allocation go out of the solution when a transfer of units is made to a lower cost cell.

There are several ways to handle degeneracy. The difficulty can usually be overcome by placing a quantity E, representing an infinitesimal allocation, in the number of cells required to bring $FC = R + C - 1$. The following rules will prove helpful:

1. If degeneracy occurs in an *initial* tableau, assign the small quantity E to any of the unfilled locations present where a filled cell does not have any other allocations in the row and column in which it is the intersecting member.
2. If the above condition does not exist for an initial tableau, place the small quantity E in any unfilled cell (preferably a high cost cell in a minimization problem or a low profit cell in a maximization) that will allow complete cell evaluation.
3. If degeneracy occurs *beyond* the initial tableau, assign the small quantity E to one of the cells that was filled in the previous tableau and that became empty when redistribution was completed. Again, the assignment can be based on the relative cost (or profit) of the cells that were reduced to zero units.

The cell with the small allocated quantity E is treated like a filled cell, but it is neglected as an allocation in the final optimal solution. Degeneracy can appear and disappear many times before a final optimal solution is obtained.

EXAMPLE 13

A company has factories A, B, and C which supply warehouses D, E, F, and G. Weekly factory capacities are 190, 250, and 150 units; weekly warehouse requirements are 90, 80, 110, and 160 units, respectively. Unit shipping costs are as follows:

	D	E	F	G
A	$1	$2	$3	$6
B	6	5	2	3
C	7	3	4	9

If production costs are the same at each factory, what is the minimum cost distribution schedule?

Figure 3 contains the algorithm for solving the problem. The initial tableau is as follows:

Factory	Warehouse					Unit capacity
	D	E	F	G	Dummy	
A	1 / 90	2 / 80	3 / 20	6	0	190
B	6	5	2 / 90	3 / 160	0	250
C	7	3	4 / E	9	0 / 150	150
Unit requirements	90	80	110	160	150	590

Since the number of filled cells is 6 and $R + C - 1 = 3 + 5 - 1 = 7$, the problem is degenerate. A small amount E is placed in cell CF. The empty cell evaluation is as follows:

$$AG = 6 - 3 + 2 - 3 = +2, \quad B\ dummy = 0 - 0 + 4 - 2 = +2,$$
$$A\ dummy = 0 - 0 + 4 - 3 = +1, \quad CD = 7 - 1 + 3 - 4 = +5,$$
$$BD = 6 - 1 + 3 - 2 = +6, \quad CE = 3 - 2 + 3 - 4 = 0,$$
$$BE = 5 - 2 + 3 - 2 = +4, \quad CG = 9 - 4 + 2 - 3 = +4.$$

Since all the empty cell evaluations are zero or positive, the tableau is optimum. The best distribution schedule is 90 A-D, 80 A-E, 20 A-F, 90 B-F, and 160 B-G. Do not produce any units in factory C. The minimum cost is

$$90(1) + 80(2) + 20(3) + 90(2) + 160(3) = \$970.$$

MODIFIED NORTHWEST CORNER RULE

The stepping stone method with the northwest corner rule can be a long and tedious process with numerous iterations. A short-cut approach is the stepping stone method with the modified northwest corner rule. The modified northwest corner rule requires a reorientation of the initial table with the optimum allocation placed in the northwest corner cell, and other more desirable cells selected as the rim requirements are satisfied. This rule attempts to obtain a very good first solution so less iterative computations will be necessary. The rule does not ensure optimality of the first feasible solution, but generally only a limited number of iterations are needed. The approach tends to place the more desirable situations in the northwest corner. The difference between it and the stepping stone method with the northwest corner rule is the development of the first feasible tableau. All other procedures are identical. In essence, more time is spent arriving at the first solution so less time will be required in obtaining the final optimal solution.

EXAMPLE 14

Solve the problem in Example 10 using the stepping stone method with the modified northwest corner rule.

In the cost table, cell C2 gives the lowest cost of $1.00, so it will be placed in the northwest corner of the first feasible solution table. Market 2 has a demand for 40 units, and plant C can produce 45 units. So as not to violate the rim conditions, 40 units are placed in cell C2, which satisfies market 2.

Plant C still has 5 units unallocated. Selecting the market with the lowest cost of the three remaining markets, assign market 4 to receive units from plant C. Since market 4 has a requirement for 20 units, it can take the 5 units from C and satisfy the capacity requirements of plant C.

Market 4 still has a requirement for 15 additional units. From the remaining plants (A and B), plant B is placed in the table, since it has the lowest cost ($3.00) under market 4. Cell B4 gets 15 units, which satisfies market 4.

Plant B still has 5 units unallocated. Selecting the market with the lower cost of the two remaining markets, assign market 1 to receive units from plant B. Since market 1 has a requirement for 30 units, it can take the 5 units from B and satisfy the capacity requirement of plant B.

Market 1 still has a requirement for 25 additional units, so they are assigned from the only remaining plant, plant A.

Plant A still has 10 units unallocated, and these are assigned to the final market, market 3. Thus, the initial feasible solution has been obtained by the modified northwest corner rule as shown in Figure 12.

After the initial feasible solution is determined, the procedure is exactly the same as in the stepping stone method with the northwest corner rule. At this point, we have completed the first of the three steps required for solution of the distribution problem. In performing the second step, it is necessary to evaluate each empty cell in Figure 12 to determine if a lower cost routing is possible. The empty cell evaluation of the first tableau is as follows:

$$
\begin{aligned}
C1 &= 8 - 2 + 3 - 6 & &= +3, \\
C3 &= 8 - 4 + 9 - 2 + 3 - 6 &= +8, \\
B2 &= 4 - 1 + 6 - 3 & &= +6, \\
B3 &= 6 - 4 + 9 - 2 & &= +9, \\
A2 &= 6 - 1 + 6 - 3 + 2 - 9 &= +1, \\
A4 &= 7 - 3 + 2 - 9 & &= -3.\leftarrow
\end{aligned}
$$

The last step in the solution of the problem requires that suboptimum solutions be improved. The -3 indicates the cost will be reduced by $3.00 for each unit transferred

Plant	Market				Unit capacity
	2	4	1	3	
C	1 40	6 5	8	8	45
B	4	3 15	2 5	6	20
A	6	7	9 25	4 10	35
Unit requirements	40	20	30	10	100

FIGURE 12
Modified northwest corner—initial tableau.

to cell $A4$. To determine the maximum quantity of units that can be transferred to cell $A4$, examine the number of units in the cells that had their unit cost subtracted in the cell evaluation of $A4$. The negative values were -3 for cell $B4$ and -9 for cell $A1$. Choose the cell with the smallest number of units, since any larger transfer would result in a cell with negative units. $B4$ has 15 units and $A1$ has 25 units, so 15 units will be transferred to cell $A4$. (15 units are added to cell $A4$, 15 units are subtracted from $B4$, 15 units are added to $B1$, and 15 units are subtracted from $A1$.) See Figure 13 for the new improved solution. No other cells have been changed except those along the improved pathway. The empty cell evaluation of the tableau shown in Figure 13 is

$$C1 = 8 - 9 + 7 - 6 \qquad = 0, \qquad B4 = 3 - 2 + 9 - 7 \qquad = +3,$$
$$C3 = 8 - 4 + 7 - 6 \qquad = +5, \qquad B3 = 6 - 4 + 9 - 2 \qquad = +9,$$
$$B2 = 4 - 1 + 6 - 7 + 9 - 2 = +9, \qquad A2 = 6 - 1 + 6 - 7 \qquad = +4.$$

FIGURE 13
Modified northwest corner–2nd tableau.

Plant	Market				Unit capacity
	2	4	1	3	
C	1 40	6 5	8	8	45
B	4	3	2 20	6	20
A	6	7 15	9 10	4 10	35
Unit requirements	40	20	30	10	100

continued

EXAMPLE 14 — *continued*

> Since none of the cell evaluations are negative, an optimum solution has been obtained in one iteration. The minimum cost is
>
> $1(40) + 6(5) + 2(20) + 7(15) + 9(10) + 4(10) = \$345.$

In Example 14 it took one iteration to get the optimum solution using the modified northwest corner rule, whereas it took three iterations in Example 10 with the northwest corner rule. The modified northwest corner rule is a more desirable approach that usually requires significantly fewer computations and iterations.

THE ASSIGNMENT METHOD

The assignment method is a linear programming technique for determining an optimal allocation of resources. It is an efficient iterative technique that finds an optimal assignment schedule without explicit consideration of all the possible alternatives. The assignment algorithm guarantees an optimal combination of agents to tasks. The technique has been used for the assignment of orders to machines (machine loading), workers to machines, personnel to jobs, salesmen to territories, etc.

The assignment method is a simple type of linear programming where n tasks can be performed by any one of n agents. Each agent is assigned to one and only one task. This method can be considered a special case of the transportation method where the number of rows equals the number of columns and supply equals the demand for each allocation. The assignment method provides a link between linear programming and integer-valued, combinatorial problems.

One infallible procedure for determining optimal assignments would be to try all possibilities and select the best. This procedure is appropriate for small matrices, but it is impractical for large ones. If there are seven agents and seven tasks, there are 5040 different possibilities to consider ($7! = 5040$). The assignment of ten agents to ten tasks would involve more than 3.6 million possible assignments ($10!$). The assignment method is an easy and quick procedure for making agent assignments without the investigation of all the alternatives.

The assignment method requires a one-to-one allocation between agents and tasks. This condition results in a square matrix where the number of agents equals the number of tasks. The solution procedure does not allow for the possibility of assigning one of the agents to two or more tasks. If the number of agents (rows) is not equal to the number of tasks (columns), dummy agents or tasks with a zero value can be used to obtain a square matrix. If all agents cannot perform every task, a very large cost can be allocated to the forbidden assignments, to ensure that they will not be in the solution. Fictitious dummy assignments are ignored in the final solution.

The assignment method algorithm is flow diagrammed in Figure 14. Essentially, the technique minimizes opportunity costs. The opportunity cost matrix is manipulated until the algorithm indicates an optimal solution. The optimal assignment will have zero opportunity cost, and it will be indicated by cells with zeros in the matrix. The zeros specify the lowest level of cost attainable with the given resources, technology, and economic conditions.

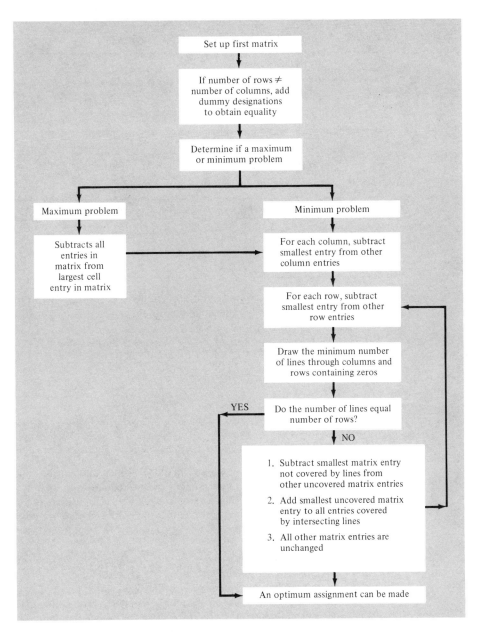

FIGURE 14
The assignment method algorithm.

EXAMPLE 15

The Continuous Company mass produces four products, which can be produced at any of four machine centers. Because of expensive setup costs, each product will be produced at only one machine center for the next year. Determine the best assignment of products to machine centers based on the following operating costs per unit:

continued

EXAMPLE 15— *continued*

Product	Center 1	Center 2	Center 3	Center 4
A	$4	$6	$3	$9
B	6	3	6	4
C	8	6	4	6
D	7	5	6	8

The opportunity costs can be developed for each column. They are obtained by subtracting the lowest cost cell entry in each column from the other costs in the same column. The result is the following matrix:

Product	Center 1	Center 2	Center 3	Center 4
A	0	3	0	5
B	2	0	3	0
C	4	3	1	2
D	3	2	3	4

The next step is to subtract the lowest opportunity cost in each row from all the opportunity costs in the same row. This operation results in the following matrix:

Product	Center 1	Center 2	Center 3	Center 4
A	0———————3———————0———————5			
B	2———————0———————3———————0			
C	3	2	0	1
D	1	0	1	2

In the next step we draw the minimum number of lines through the rows and columns containing zeros.[1] If the minimum number of lines equals the number of rows (or columns), an optimal assignment has been achieved. There are usually other ways of drawing the lines, but the only requirement is that the number be the minimum. Since there are four lines in the above matrix and four rows, a minimum cost assignment can be made.

The last step is to scan each row and select the zero cell in those rows where there are no other zeros; similarly scan each column and select the zero cell in those columns where there are no other zeros. The rows with single zero cells are C and D, so product C will be assigned to center 3 and product D to center 2. The columns with single zero cells are center 1 and center 4, so product A will be assigned to center 1 and product B to center 4. The final assignments are as follows:

Product	Machine Center	Unit Cost
A	1	$4
B	4	4
C	3	4
D	2	5

[1]When the matrix is large an algorithm can be used to determine the minimum number of lines. See M. Sasieni, A. Yaspan, and L. Friedman, *Operations Research: Method and Problems,* New York: Wiley, 1959, pp. 189–190.

Assignments are made by selecting zero cells. Hence, the minimum cost is attained via a zero opportunity cost. The actual cost of the assignments is determined from the original matrix that contains the actual cost data.

EXAMPLE 16

Five men are being interviewed for four positions in a firm. The personnel manager has administered four tests to measure the applicants' aptitudes for each position. The highest possible score on each test is 10. Based on the aptitude scores, indicate the men you would hire and specify their positions.

Man	Position 1	Position 2	Position 3	Position 4	Position 5
A	6	9	5	7	0
B	5	1	7	5	0
C	2	6	9	9	0
D	2	9	7	3	0
E	4	5	6	6	0

Since the original matrix was not square, a dummy position 5 was added. The man assigned to position 5 will not be hired by the firm. The objective of the personnel manager is to maximize aptitudes for all the positions. Since it is a maximization problem, subtract all cell entries in the matrix from the largest cell entry (this operation converts a profit matrix into a cost matrix). The largest cell entry is 9. The modified matrix is as follows.

Man	Position 1	Position 2	Position 3	Position 4	Position 5
A	3	0	4	2	9
B	4	8	2	4	9
C	7	3	0	0	9
D	7	0	2	6	9
E	5	4	3	3	9

The opportunity costs for each column are obtained by subtracting the lowest cost cell entry in each column from the other costs in the same column. The result is the following matrix:

Man	Position 1	Position 2	Position 3	Position 4	Position 5
A	0	0	4	2	0
B	1	8	2	4	0
C	4	3	0	0	0
D	4	0	2	6	0
E	2	4	3	3	0

Since there are 5 rows, and 4 lines can be drawn through all zero-cells, the final solution has not been attained. Subtracting the smallest cell entry in each row will not change the matrix, since column 5 contains all zeros.

continued

EXAMPLE 16—*continued*

The next step requires the subtraction of the smallest cell entry not covered by the lines from every other uncovered cell entry and the addition of the smallest uncovered cell entry to all intersecting line cell entries. The smallest uncovered cell entry is one:

Man	Position 1	Position 2	Position 3	Position 4	Position 5
A	0	0	4	2	1
B	0	7	1	3	0
C	4	3	0	0	1
D	4	0	2	6	1
E	1	3	2	2	0

There are still 5 rows, and 4 lines can cover all zero cells. The smallest uncovered cell entry is again subtracted from all uncovered cells and added to all intersecting line cell entries. The smallest uncovered cell entry is one. The result is the following matrix:

Man	Position 1	Position 2	Position 3	Position 4	Position 5
A	0	0	3	1	1
B	0	7	0	2	0
C	5	4	0	0	2
D	4	0	1	5	1
E	1	3	1	1	0

Since 5 rows and 5 lines are required to cover all zero cell entries, an optimum assignment has been secured.

The final step requires that rows and columns with only one zero be scanned to determine assignments. Rows *D* and *E* have single zero entries, and column 4 has a single zero entry. Therefore, man *E* will be assigned to position 5, man *D* to position 2, man *C* to position 4, man *B* to position 3, and man *A* to position 1. Since man *E* was assigned to the dummy position 5, he will not be offered a position with the firm. The final assignments are as follows:

Man	Position	Aptitude score
A	1	6
B	3	7
C	4	9
D	2	9
		31

It is not uncommon for the assignment method to indicate numerous feasible solutions. This can occur if numerous rows and columns have more than single zero cell entries in the final matrix. The decision maker can select any combinations with zero cell entries and be confident that no better assignment exists.

The assignment method represents decision making under certainty. Risk factors such as cost variances, machine breakdowns, unscheduled maintenance, man-machine interactions, absenteeism, measurement irregularities, and other disturbances are considered negligible or left till later. The comparative evaluation procedure is dependent upon the accuracy of the point cell entries, and no allowance is made for error of estimation.

Assigning an agent for a fairly long period is the most popular use of the assignment method. The assignment of personnel to jobs on an assembly line, the hiring of personnel for permanent organizational positions, and the long-term allocation of separate production facilities to products are the prevalent applications for this method.

When agents are to be assigned to tasks that require frequent restructuring, the assignment method is less desirable. Whenever numerous products are manufactured on the same equipment, production rates are variable, job priorities exist, setup and teardown costs are low, and production is intermittent, simulation or other heuristic methods are used. The assignment method requires a stable system, and it is not readily adaptable to a volatile changing environment.

All problems that can be solved by the assignment method can be solved by the simplex method, but the amount of computation is excessive. The appropriate mechanics for a simplex solution is as follows:

$$\text{Optimize} \quad \sum_{i=1}^{n} \sum_{j=1}^{n} C_{ij} X_{ij},$$

$$\text{where} \quad \sum_{j=1}^{n} X_{ij} = 1 \qquad \text{for} \quad i = 1, 2, \ldots, n,$$

$$\sum_{i=1}^{n} X_{ij} = 1 \qquad \text{for} \quad j = 1, 2, \ldots, n,$$

$$X_{ij} = 0 \text{ or } 1 \qquad \text{for all } i \text{ and } j.$$

QUESTIONS

1. What is the major limitation of linear programming?
2. What is an identity matrix?
3. What purposes do slack and artificial variables serve in the simplex method?
4. What are the three types of constraint conditions?
5. What must be done to a "less than or equal to" constraint before entry into the simplex tableau? A "greater than or equal to" constraint? An equality?
6. What is the value of a slack variable in the objective function?
7. What is the value of an artificial variable in the objective function?
8. How do you determine the entering vector in a simplex maximization problem? A minimization problem?
9. How do you determine the leaving vector in a simplex problem? What is the pivot element?

10. When is a simplex maximization problem optimum? A minimization?

11. Why would anybody solve the dual problem when the same solution can be obtained from the primal?

12. What is the economic significance of the dual variables?

13. What is the difference between the initial tableaus in the simplex method and transportation method?

14. If supply does not equal demand in the transportation method, what must be done?

15. In the transportation method, why is it necessary that the number of filled cells be equal to rows plus columns minus one?

16. Why does the assignment method require a square matrix?

17. How is a degenerate simplex solution handled?

18. What is the purpose of sensitivity analysis conducted for simplex problems?

19. What is the purpose of evaluating empty cells in the transportation method?

20. Distinguish between the zero cost allocations and actual costs with respect to the assignment method.

PROBLEMS

1. You are given the following initial linear programming tableau:

C_j		$20	$80	0	0	
Profit	Solution vector	X_1	X_2	X_3	X_4	B
0	X_3	1	2	1	0	100
0	X_4	1	1	0	1	80
	Z_j	0	0	0	0	0
	$C_j - Z_j$	20	80	0	0	

a. Is this a maximization or minimization problem?

b. What vectors (X_1, X_2, X_3, or X_4) are in the above solution?

c. What is the entering vector?

d. What is the leaving vector?

e. Where is the pivot point?

f. What is the value of the tableau?

g. Write the objective function without slack or artificial variables.

h. Write the constraint equations without slack or artificial variables.

2. You are given the following linear programming tableau:

C_j		$3	$8	M	0	M	0	
	Solution vector	X_1	X_2	X_3	X_4	X_5	X_6	B
M	X_3	4	6	1	0	0	0	120
0	X_4	1	0	0	1	0	0	12
M	X_5	0	1	0	0	1	-1	16
	Z_j	$4M$	$7M$	M	0	M	$-M$	$136M$
	$C_j - Z_j$	$3 - 4M$	$8 - 7M$	0	0	0	M	

    a. Is this a maximization or minimization problem?
    b. What vectors are in the above solution?
    c. What is the entering vector?
    d. What is the leaving vector?
    e. What is the value of the tableau?
    f. Write the objective function.
    g. Write the constraint equations without slack or artificial variables.

3. The Derrick Manufacturing Company makes three products. The contribution per unit is $2 for X_1, $4 for X_2, and $3 for X_3. Each product passes through three manufacturing centers as a part of the production process. The process time (in hours) required in each center for one unit of each product is as follows:

		Center	
Product	1	2	3
X_1	3	2	1
X_2	4	1	3
X_3	2	2	2

The total production capacity available next week is 60 hours in center 1, 40 hours in center 2, and 80 hours in center 3.
    a. Write the constraint equations without slack or artificial variables.
    b. Write the constraint equations with slack and artificial variables, as required.
    c. Would you solve this as a maximization or a minimization problem?
    d. Write the objective function.
    e. Write the first linear programming tableau.

4. The Fargo Corporation produces two industrial products, A and B. Each product requires processing in three different departments of the plant. The contribution of product A is $10, and for product B $12. The processing time required for each product and total time available in each department are as follows:

Department	Hours required		Monthly hours available
	Product A	Product B	
1	2	3	1500
2	3	2	1500
3	1	1	600

    a. Assuming the firm can sell all of the products it can produce, what is the most profitable output combination?
    b. What is the total contribution?

5. The Office Lounge is a retail lounge that specializes in jumbo five ounce martinis for the exhausted-after-work executive. The lounge sells four types of martinis. The subsequent table shows the name of the drinks, the recipe per drink in ounces, and the retail (selling) price.

Drink name	Premium gin	Cheap gin	Premium vermouth	Cheap vermouth	Retail price
Fair day		2		3	$ .40
Rough day		3	2		.70
Crying jag	3			2	.80
Pushover	4		1		1.10

Because of liquor controls, the manager cannot obtain more than the following weekly quantities of liquor, purchased at the constant prices shown:

Ingredient	Ounces per week	Price per ounce
Premium gin	500	$.20
Cheap gin	2600	.10
Premium vermouth	1000	.15
Cheap vermouth	400	.05

Consumer behavior imposes limits on the number of drinks that can be sold using cheap gin, premium gin, or cheap vermouth as part of the mixture. Up to 100 drinks per week can be sold using cheap gin, up to 200 drinks per week using premium gin, and up to 150 drinks per week using cheap vermouth. There is no constraint on premium vermouth. The relative proportions of ingredients in any particular type of drink do not influence the marketing limitations noted above. Lay out a buying and selling program for the firm that will optimize profit.

6. A small plant makes two products. The plant has two departments, grinding and plating, and each product requires processing in both departments. The capacities of the departments are different for the two products and the profit per item is also different. The relevant data are summarized in the table below. How many units of each product should be produced in achieving maximum profit?

Product	Capacity per day		Profit per unit
	Department 1 Grinding	Department 2 Plating	
A	400	250	$1.00
B	200	400	1.25

7. The Gerald Manufacturing Company produces many products, but only C, D, E, and F pass through the following departments: planing, milling, drilling, and assembly. The requirements per unit of product in hours and the contribution are as follows:

Product	Department				Contribution per unit
	Planing	Milling	Drilling	Assembly	
C	0.5	2	0.5	3	$8
D	1	1	0.5	1	9
E	1	1	1	2	7
F	0.5	1	1	3	6

The minimum sales requirements and available monthly department capacities are as follows:

Department	Capacity (hours)	Product	Minimum sales (units)
Planing	1800	C	100
Milling	2800	D	600
Drilling	3000	E	500
Assembly	6000	F	400

Your position as production manager requires that you specify production quantities of each product for the coming month.
a. Write the constraint equations and objective function.
b. Set up the first tableau. (Do not solve this problem manually, since it is very long and tedious.)

8. A manufacturer desires to determine how to manufacture six orders in the least possible time. The orders are

Order No.	Quantity
1	10
2	40
3	60
4	20
5	20
6	30

These orders are manufactured in one operation on *any one* of three machines. The production routing department supplies the following data:

Machine	Hours available	No.	Production time (hours per unit)					
			1	2	3	4	5	6
A	80		3	3	2	5	2	1
B	30		4	1	1	2	2	1
C	160		2	2	5	1	1	2

The most efficient routing and the minimum time to process all orders would normally be what is desired. *Do not solve this problem,* but:
a. State the constraints in inequality form.
b. State the objective function.
c. Remove the inequalities by adding the appropriate slack and artificial variables.

Hint: Let X_{ij} be the number of units from order number i produced on machine j ($i = 1, 2, 3, 4, 5, 6; j = A, B, C$).

9. Solve the following linear programming problem by the dual method:

Maximize $X_1 + 2X_2$
subject to $-X_1 + 3X_2 \leq 10,$
$X_1 + X_2 \leq 6,$
$X_1 - X_2 \leq 2,$
$X_1 + 3X_2 \geq 6,$
$2X_1 + X_2 \geq 4.$

10. Solve the following linear programming problem by the dual method:

Maximize $3X_1 + 2X_2$
subject to $\quad X_1 + \quad X_2 \geq 1,$
$\quad\quad\quad\quad X_1 + \quad X_2 \leq 7,$
$\quad\quad\quad\quad X_1 + 2X_2 \geq 10,$
$\quad\quad\quad\quad\quad\quad\quad\quad X_2 \leq 3.$

  a. What is the solution to the primal problem?
  b. What will be the effect on the value of the solution of increasing the constant term in the second constraint equation from 7 to 8? Of decreasing it to 6?

11. Any one of three numerically controlled machines can be used to process four different jobs in approximately the same time. However, the programming time per machine varies for the different jobs. Given the total cost matrix in dollars per hour, how should the jobs be assigned so that total costs are minimized?

	Job				Machine hours
NC machine No.	A	B	C	D	available
1	$10	$20	$30	$30	50
2	10	15	22	25	150
3	15	10	10	15	300
Machine hours required	100	50	50	300	

12. A company has four factories from which it ships to four foreign countries. The production costs and capacities in each of the four factories are

Factory	Cost/100	Capacity (100s)
A	$40	140
B	43	260
C	39	360
D	45	220

The demand in each country is

Country	Demand (100s)
1	180
2	150
3	280
4	200

Transportation costs in dollars per 100 units between the factories and countries are

	1	2	3	4
A	48	56	60	58
B	47	53	57	59
C	51	61	63	63
D	51	55	63	61

What production and distribution schedule will minimize costs?

13. Four jobs (1, 2, 3, and 4) must be performed by four employees (*M, N, O,* and *P*). Each employee can only do one of the tasks. The values given in the matrix below are error rates for each employee and task. Assign the workers so the error rate is minimized.

	1	2	3	4
M	18	17	19	19
N	16	12	17	18
O	16	10	15	19
P	12	13	12	16

14. Mr. McMillin owns four secluded nightclubs, all located quite a distance from the city. He has hired four entertainment groups for the clubs, but has no idea which group should be assigned to which club. One of the local college students developed the projected revenue matrix below from historical data, but the student then went on vacation.

	Club			
Group	*1*	*2*	*3*	*4*
A	$280	$310	$325	$305
B	245	260	305	305
C	280	270	280	285
D	295	260	300	290

Mr. McMillin must pay each group a salary, shown in the table below, and travel expenses, shown in the travel expenses matrix. How should he assign the groups to maximize profits?

Group	Salary (per night)
A	$50
B	60
C	50
D	50

		Travel expenses per night club			
Group	Club	*1*	*2*	*3*	*4*
A		$20	$35	$20	$10
B		10	10	15	25
C		10	35	20	10
D		25	15	15	40

15. A consultant has recommended that a manufacturer have his mechanics specialize rather than have each mechanic perform the complete overhaul. The consultant has developed the subsequent cost matrix based on historical plant records. Any mechanic can be assigned to any one job. What assignment will result in the total minimum cost?

Mechanic	Job segment number									
	1	2	3	4	5	6	7	8	9	10
Fred	10	12	11	9	8	13	15	14	9	10
Carl	11	13	12	8	10	9	12	11	12	9
Lou	12	10	10	10	13	14	9	8	11	12
Pat	13	9	14	9	8	13	11	15	13	11
George	14	8	12	8	15	12	13	9	15	14
Tim	15	11	9	10	13	11	14	8	13	9
Jeff	9	12	11	11	14	9	8	11	8	10
Cliff	10	13	10	9	8	8	8	10	11	11
Mac	9	12	14	8	13	8	11	9	12	12
John	11	14	13	12	8	10	9	8	13	9

CASE 1: DEADLY COURTSHIP

One of the best cotton producing areas in Arkansas is in the lower Mississippi flood plain area. The tobacco budworm and cotton bollworm, rather than the commonly known boll weevil, are the major pests in this area. The development and spread of pesticide resistant strains of these pests, and other problems associated with heavy applications of pesticides (extermination of natural enemies) mark the onset of what has been termed the "crisis phase" of cotton production. With bankruptcy and ecological ruin in its wake, a "pest war" is underway to implement many of the research developments of the NSF/EPA cotton research teams. Within an integrated pest management (IPM) program built on the use of sophisticated methods and a mini-computer network is Arkansas's local pilot system known as BUGNET. The first project in the BUGNET pilot is a federally funded opportunity to reduce the area's pest population. The federal stipulation pursuant to the BUGNET funding is that newer technologies which control pests by ecologically safer means be used in conjunction with proven commercial pesticides.

Prior to BUGNET and the establishment of other local programs, the research has been used to develop and upgrade the pest control decision-making techniques for implementation at the farmer level. The upgrading requires the use of simulation and optimization models for the growth of the cotton crop, the dynamics of the insect pests, and the insect impact on cotton production. Of particular importance for BUGNET are simulation experiments in which bollworm and tobacco budworm damage is imposed on the cotton crop model. These experiments indicate that in arriving at appropriate economic thresholds for the pests (acceptable levels of insect populations), the farmers must consider the development of that year's crop as well as the future environment and management practices. The thresholds then can be used to determine when intervention actions should be taken for the purpose of delaying interference with nature until populations exceed acceptable limits. Moreover, the research links models for the two insect species with the cotton model to simulate the effects of different insecticides, natural treatment substances, and spraying patterns on cotton yield. A simplified version of the overall integrated pest management system follows. It depicts a trivial representation of the complex problem in population ecology. However, because the crops are grown for profit, the output is necessarily a monetary one.

Now the stage is set for adoption by the farmers. County agents enthusiastically inform area farmers that the IPM strategy compares favorably with the production costs and benefits of traditional treatment programs. The particular IPM strategy the Arkansas agents have selected combines usage of synthetic sex pheromone (behavior-modifying) compounds for interfering with sexual communication and harsher, nonresistant pesticides. Although early failure of pheromones turned off farmers, the county agents now are convincing some farmers that

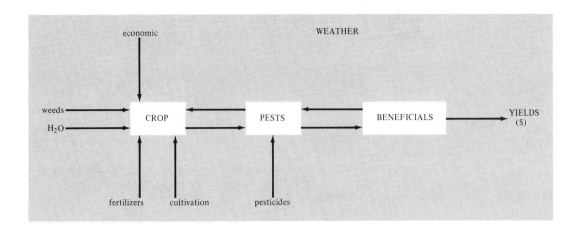

the newest pheromone (virelure) can be perfected so that it will reduce infestations to levels that can be contained by the commercial insecticides. The pheromone causes chaos and fatal mating between the two species' mismatched genitalia and thereby reduces and delays the need for chemical insecticides.

The pilot study covers 18,600 hectares (approximately 46,000 acres) planted in cotton. The county agents suggest spending the $300,000 grant in a two phase treatment—application of virelure followed at a later date by an application of methyl parathion (the harsh chemical will be applied when population levels exceed economic thresholds). The methyl parathion is research validated as giving twice the effectiveness per hectare sprayed from the ground as does an individual ground application of virelure. Moreover, an aerial permeation technique renders either substance twice as effective as ground application. In order for either substance to reach its effectiveness level, two-thirds of the area under observation must receive treatment. However, county restrictions on aerial spraying of chemicals (pheromones also legally hold a chemical classification) forbid that application technique in 5,000 hectares within the pilot study area.

Treatments must be completed within a five day (round the clock, if necessary) time span due to climactic and biological factors. One hundred sixty hectares can be sprayed per hour from the air, while only a third of that area can be ground sprayed in that same time. While methyl parathion is more effective, it also is more expensive. Virelure application costs $8.00 per hectare if sprayed aerially, and methyl parathion is an additional $2.00 per hectare. Furthermore, labor costs increase ground application of either substance by $5.00 per hectare over aerial application.

Thus, the county agents and the local farmers need to formalize the BUGNET strategy. The county agents base their preferences on their model of the cotton production system and their desire to apply substances according to stipulated effectiveness levels and in compliance with the terms of the grant. The farmers would like to see other control methods analyzed and take the attitude that unless the degree of control results in economic benefit, it is of no importance. They would like to see statistics on

1. crop rotation benefits,
2. herbicides and defoliants,
3. biological control (parasites, predators, pathogens),
4. profits when resistant cotton varieties have been planted,
5. effects of total elimination of insect species,
6. short season crops which allow less time for infestation of mature plants.

The county agents rebuttals to these requests are the time pressures for utilizing the grant, grant stipulations, usefulness of their model, and impossibility of totally integrating all these aspects, as well as the impracticality of some of the suggestions (e.g. the harm in eliminating the pests altogether).

1. Can LP be used to structure the BUGNET program suggested by the county agents? How would changes in the number of hours allowable, the amount of the fund, the aerial restrictions, and other constraints affect the plan?
2. What other objective functions may be appropriate? What other variables may be used in an LP analysis?
3. Discuss the integrated approach and the use of quantitative techniques. Address implementation problems, influence of other disciplines, forecasting techniques, and the farmers' suggestions in reference to IPM.

CASE 2: TRAGIC FLAWS

Several tragic accidents occurred this year in the Tulsa public schools which produced fatalities, disabilities, and other traumata. A water heater explosion and structural collapses of facilities were the most serious. The freak water heater explosion would have caused enough alarm, but the repeated mishaps due to physical defects in plant and equipment hardly were considered coincidental misfortunes. All of the accidents were traced to unsafe and dilapidated physical conditions, and each accident site was judged unfit for habitation in its present state.

Community leaders and parent groups participated in public displays of concern. Those particularly aroused at the School Board meetings were citizens residing in areas which had suffered catastrophies. The School Board recognized their needs and sympathized with their losses, but also ordered a study of other aged structures. The study group found that several other public properties were in violation of minimum health and safety standards and should not house students and faculty members in the upcoming term without mandatory renovations.

The State of Oklahoma cooperated in the effort. After some juggling of books, the State Appropriations Committee found that the amount funded to Tulsa for building construction and maintenance was $3 million short of the total that should have been appropriated under enrollment guidelines. The State also contributed $2 million from a budget surplus fund ahead of its scheduled allocation to the city government (on the basis of its allocation to a school renovation fund).

With $5 million available, the Tulsa School Board compiled a list of schools that are in critical need of repair and qualify as primary targets for the renovation fund. Five schools qualified for emergency repairs, and the School Board requested bids from six contractors for each of the designated schools. Separate bids for each target school were requested, because the renovations must be completed in the three-month summer closing and no one contractor can complete more than one school renovation in that time. Each contractor promised completion by the fall and submitted the bids (in $100,000) that follow:

Contractor	School				
	1	2	3	4	5
A	11.0	11.0	12.5	14.0	13.0
B	12.0	11.5	13.0	16.0	17.0
C	13.5	13.0	11.5	15.0	14.0
D	12.5	12.0	13.5	15.5	13.0
E	13.0	13.5	12.0	14.5	15.0
F	11.5	12.5	14.0	16.5	16.0

Upon opening of the bids, the School Board postponed the contract conferment date. The board realized that the renovation costs were inflated beyond its original estimates and exceeded the state appropriation. Either additional funds would have to be raised or one or more of the target schools would be eliminated from the renovation project. Additional funds would have to come in the form of increased local tax revenues, so the School Board made an appeal to the city managers.

Unless an emergency tax measure were voted, a local tax referendum could not be passed in time for the city to allocate to the renovation fund. If the city managers felt that a tax referendum had a strong chance of passing during the next election, the city would loan the money to the renovation fund from another city account (on the assumption that the incoming revenue would start to accrue during the next fiscal year). However, the city managers do not believe a tax proposal would pass. Except for those residing in stricken areas, public sentiment is weak. The majority of Tulsa residents see no benefit for their communities, and in all probability, will defeat this measure as resoundingly as they defeated the last tax increase referendum.

With a general lack of support, the money will have to be raised elsewhere or come from some other part of the school budget. Alternatively, the aged schools will be closed and students bused to safer structures.

1. How much more money is needed?
2. If the funds are acquired, which contractor should be given each target school contract?
3. If the funds are limited to the $5 million state appropriation, which school(s) should be eliminated, based on costs? Should cost be the primary decision factor?
4. Comment on limitations of optimization models.

SELECTED BIBLIOGRAPHY

Ackoff, R. L. and M. W. Sasieni. *Fundamentals of Operations Research,* New York: Wiley, 1968.

Chase, R. B. and N. J. Aquilano. *Production and Operations Management: A Life Cycle Approach,* Homewood, IL: Irwin, 1981.

Hopeman, R. J. *Production: Concepts, Analysis, and Control,* Columbus, OH: Charles E. Merrill, 1980.

Lee, S. M. and L. J. Moore. *Introduction to Decision Sciences,* New York: Petrocelli/Charter, 1975.

Levin, R. I. and C. A. Kirkpatrick. *Quantitative Approaches to Management,* New York: McGraw-Hill, 1982.

Sasieni, M. W. et al. *Operations Research: Method and Problems,* New York: Wiley, 1959.

Tersine, R. J. et al. *Problems and Models in Operations Management,* Columbus, OH: Grid, 1980.

Thompson, G. L. *Linear Programming,* New York: Macmillan, 1971.

Turban, E. and J. R. Meredith. *Fundamentals of Management Science,* Plano, TX: Business Publications Inc., 1981.

II

POLICY DECISIONS

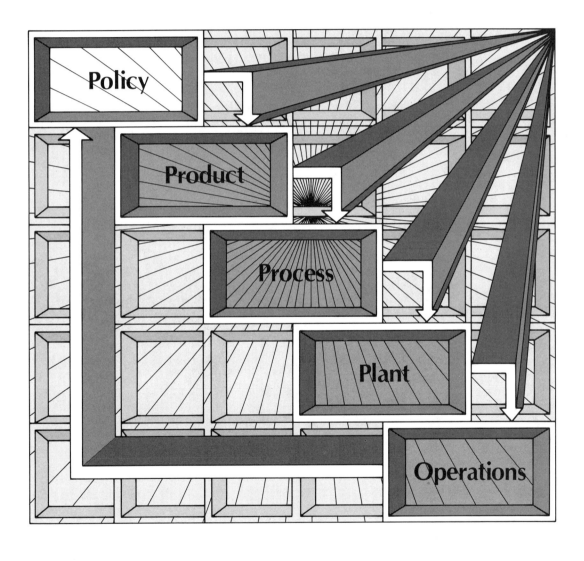

The previous, introductory section covered the ubiquitous areas of systems theory, decision theory, cost and capital analysis, and resource allocation. This section, on policy decisions, will establish the reasons for existence of an organization. The purposes and goals of an organization will influence all the subsequent decisions to be made within it. All actions taken within an organization should derive their legitimacy from preestablished policy decisions. Thus, policy matters are the compass or direction-determining device for an organization. This section consists of a single chapter, titled "Policy Decisions." It will delineate the objectives, strategies, and tactics of an organization, as shown in the policy function in Figure I.

FIGURE I
The policy function.

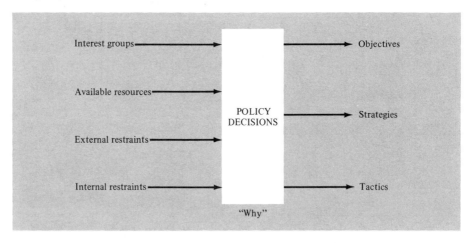

6
Policy Decisions

OBJECTIVES
  Interest Groups
  Available Resources
  Restraints
    External Restraints
    Internal Restraints

      STRATEGIES
        Congruency of Strategies
        Organizational Structure

          TACTICS
          Budgets

            CONCLUSION

              APPENDIX A: MASTER RESOURCES PROFILE
              QUESTIONS
              CASES
              SELECTED BIBLIOGRAPHY

Policy decisions give identity and direction to the hopes, aspirations, and thinking of an organization. They provide a comprehensive and unified picture of the present and future directions for the organization to those who must operate and function within it. Policy decisions begin with a statement of the broad, long range objectives of the organization. Objectives can be termed a "statement of purpose," for they are the goals of the organization as a whole.

The establishment of organizational objectives is the basic requirement for all subsequent decisions to be made on a lower level. Since there are many different types of organizations in a society, it should be no surprise that objectives can be varied and diverse (typical examples are growth, survival, market share, social responsibility, profit maximization, return on investment, product leadership, and so forth). Objectives indicate why the organization exists. They are not subject to frequent revisions, but are guideposts to direct the movement of the organization over time (the future), which is characterized by risk and uncertainty.

Policy decisions include the overall organizational objectives, strategies, and tactics. As illustrated in Figures 1 and 2, policy decisions are a progressive movement from objectives to strategies to tactics, with various influences being exerted. The most prevalent influencing factors are special interest groups, available resources, external restraints, and internal restraints. Objectives, strategies, and tactics include "what you want to achieve" and "how you want to achieve it." They are essential for survival, continuation, and growth of an organization.

FIGURE 1
Policy decisions.

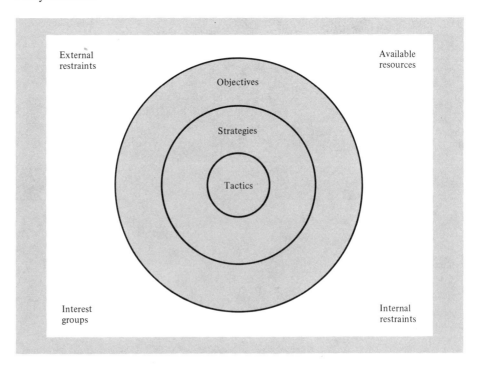

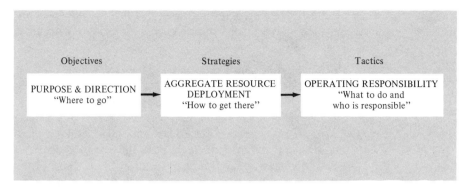

FIGURE 2
The flow of policy decisions.

OBJECTIVES

Policy decisions are made in order to determine where an organization is going and how well it is doing in getting there. An objective is a desired condition or state that an organization seeks to achieve. Objectives are goals or ends that explain the reason for the organization's existence. They provide the framework for decision making at all levels, and relate what the institution's role should be in society. Objectives tend to be directional, but not specific as to magnitudes. It is generally more meaningful to refer to a set of organizational objectives than to a single objective. Since organizations are subject to complex influences from varied groups or parties, objectives rarely tend to be simple and straightforward.

Objectives are necessary in the management of any enterprise, whether it is a profit-making firm, an agency of government, or any type of nonprofit organization. They are general and enduring statements of purpose that express management's intentions while providing guidelines for the further development of the institution. Organizations are never identical. They have different histories, traditions, resources, reputations, management styles, and abilities, and often different objectives.

There is no standard classification of objectives nor any fixed number an organization should have. Objectives range widely from organization to organization, but they generally fall into the three general categories of service to owners and investors (profit), service to customers (satisfaction), and service to society (social responsibility). *Service to owners and investors* tends to rely on profit as an overall financial measure of performance. *Service to customers* justifies the existence of the organization in terms of its product market. *Service to society* emanates from the ethical and moral codes set forth by the society in which the organization operates. Various combinations of objectives covering each of the three categories are found in most organizations.

Objectives are usually established by organizations to assist decision making, to provide incentives for its members, to direct growth, or to judge performance. To achieve effectiveness an organization must set goals and measure performance vis-à-vis a control system moderating goal deviations. In any event, the objectives of an institution must be known before measures of effectiveness can be delineated. Measures of effectiveness are those measures that indicate how well an organization is meeting its objectives. Some common criteria for measuring organizational effectiveness are as follows:

1. *Production*—the ability of the organization to produce the quantity and quality of output demanded by society.
2. *Efficiency*—the efficacy of transfer between inputs and outputs. Examples may include rate of return, profit, cost per unit, revenue per patient, and so forth.
3. *Satisfaction*—the meaningful work relationships and life experiences shared by organizational members. It can be stated in terms of attitudes, turnover, absenteeism, tardiness, or grievances.
4. *Adaptiveness*—the ability of the organization to respond to internal and external changes.
5. *Development*—the organization's investment in itself to enhance its capability to survive in the long run. It can relate to research, products, processes, or human development programs.

Once organizational objectives are developed, other problems exist, such as:

1. *Multiple objectives.* Many diversified objectives may exist which are difficult to characterize quantitatively. These goals frequently reflect subjective values rather than objective values. They may be independent or interdependent, qualitative or quantitative, general or specific, and objective or subjective. The optimization of one objective may result in a lower level of attainment for others.
2. *Conflicting objectives.* Any comprehensive list of objectives will have areas of conflict. With multiple, conflicting objectives, it is feasible to treat some conflicting objectives as restraints. It is then possible to optimize the remaining objectives subject to the restraints. When changing an objective to a restraint, it is necessary to establish its minimum level of performance. For example, it is impossible to maximize the quality of a product and at the same time minimize the cost of manufacturing it. However, it is possible to minimize cost subject to a quality restraint, or to maximize quality subject to a cost restraint.
3. *Hierarchy of objectives.* Objectives of organizational units must be consistent with objectives of other units (goal congruence). Since there are objectives within objectives, this means the cascade of objectives should be consistent. The major goals of an organization are typically segmented into divisional goals, which are fragmented further into plant goals, department goals, group goals, and individual goals.

INTEREST GROUPS

Objectives are prescribed by management, but they emanate from many different sources. An organization consists of and is influenced by many groups. These groups may be complementing or opposing the others' interests, but management establishes goals so as to reconcile differences and provide mutual benefit. The groups are not the same in number and influence for all organizations.

An organization is a coalition of individuals and groups seeking to improve or maintain their interests. Diverse interest groups may have symbiotic relationships and vested interests. The organization cannot function (or survive) without mutual cooperation. Many decisions are not made in a rational or formal way, but rather through compromise, accommodation, and bargaining. In an organization, it is important to identify the major interest groups and coalitions.

Interest groups include managers, customers, investors, creditors, suppliers, unions, and so forth. Customers influence objectives by their decisions concerning purchases of the institution's output. Employee productivity affects the efficiency of process transformation and thus performance. Government, through regulation and taxes, modifies the cash reservoir. Investors determine the ease of access to capital markets for expansion and growth. Creditors constrain change through restrictive covenants and interest charges. Suppliers represent a drain on cash resources that affect costs and thus profits. Managers influence objectives by their personal value systems and attitudes toward operation of the entity. There are many other groups that can influence goals or press management for more favorable consideration. Management must reconcile differences and harness the energies of its diverse pressure groups in order to survive.

With diverse individuals and groups conflict is inescapable. Conflicts (where one group seeks to advance its own interests at the expense of another group) arise in organizations when interdependent subunits have inconsistent goals, have different perceptions of how to reach a common goal, or must share scarce resources. Conflict is resolved through bargaining, compromise, or consensus. Conformity to objectives is attained by incentives or payments (wages, compensations, interest, status, dividends) to members. Changes and adjustments usually involve a bargaining process among the major group members. Interest groups are not all of the same stature or prominence, and several may be passive most of the time. Past bargains become precedents for future bargains, and the process can become formally institutionalized. For an organization to be successful, it is necessary to identify the needs of each interest group, to establish some balance among them, and to designate policies which permit satisfaction of needs.

People at the helm of an organization have explicit or implicit aspirations and values. The personal values of those "in control" have a significant bearing on future directions. A personal value system can be considered a permanent perceptual framework that shapes and influences the general nature of an individual's behavior. Values are similar to attitudes, but they are more ingrained, permanent, and stable. The power of personal values to select, filter, and influence what an individual sees, hears, and does is an important behavioral phenomenon. Every individual participant within an organization brings to his work activity a multitude of personal goals and motives that influence his professional behavior. The diversity of objectives of individual participants creates problems of goal integration and congruence. Personal values influence decisions throughout an organization. Feelings, sentiments, and aspirations are part of a manager's own behavior as well as that of those around him. While an organization may have an identity of its own, its present health and future development surely depend on the individuals and groups who guide its activities.

In systems analysis the efficiency of transfer from inputs to outputs is paramount, and the most common measure of value is benefit or profit. When profitability is not relevant, control of cost is substituted. Although profit is a necessary objective of profit making organizations, it is not sufficient when conglomerate influences of different parties are influential. Survival is perhaps the most predominant influence that unites heterogeneous groups. When survival is not in doubt, other objectives become apparent. However, other objectives tend to be subservient to the survival of the organization. The goals of an organization can range on a continuum from survival (perhaps, infinite life) to service to society. Most goals are somewhere in between the extremes.

Every organization develops traditions, habits, and a character separate from its constituents. The character of an organization is complex and multifaceted. Financial analysis deals with only a portion of organizational activities. Although it reflects many objectives, it does not deal with the substantive activities underlying monetary data. Financial analysis is only one view of a complex organizational domain, for it neglects many other human and intangible factors. Organizational objectives are an amalgamation of the goals of the individuals and groups that are influential with the organization.

Because of the many and varied groups of human beings affected by modern organizations, they are thrust into the role of social institutions. Corporations have been undergoing significant changes that are modifying their historical role. Some of these changes are as follows:

1. The separation of management and ownership has affected corporate structure and relationships among the different subgroups. Although directors are elected by stockholders, they tend to be a self-perpetuating body. Due to dispersion and lack of organization, stockholders are almost without power to bring pressure on management.
2. Certain groups other than stockholders are better situated to exert influence on management. These groups include customers, governments, unions, employees, creditors, and the general public (all of which make demands on the corporation).
3. Subject to the varied demands, management tends to be less and less responsible to the owners, and more and more responsible to the corporation as a whole. Management attempts to balance the needs of all groups, not just those of the owners.
4. The first task of management is to create a successful product with widespread use and salability. The second task is the division of the proceeds of success among those groups responsible for its success. All of the groups compete for as large a share of the "success pie" as possible. The groups do not have equal influence, and stockholders frequently are far from the most effective.

Interest groups usually want institutions to behave in a manner calculated to benefit them. Often new pressures are designed to change traditions and procedures that have proven to be unresponsive to needs. People are devising new ways to demand consideration in the making of decisions that affect their lives. Both public and private institutions are experiencing an increase in pressure from the bottom up rather than from the top down. Decisions that once were made privately and were regulated by the profit motive now are being profoundly affected by public policy and the political process.

AVAILABLE RESOURCES

Every organization has limits on its resources (amount and sources of capital, number and quality of key personnel, physical production capacity, etc.). The issue is how to use these limited resources to their best advantage. Over a period of time an organization develops distinctive competencies in various areas. The personnel in every organization will have a distinctive area of competence; there is something they do well. To stray far from the common areas of expertise involves additional risks.

Every organization must find the things it does best and build its strategies around these strengths. This is what is known as leading from strength. Organizations that do not lead from strength—that hold back and respond defensively—may spend an inordinate amount of time "spinning their wheels."

An analysis of internal resources will indicate what the organization is capable of doing in view of its resource profile. The analysis can be assembled from available information such as reports, facts, opinions, statements, and observations. Interviews with key personnel can be a fertile source of information. In essence, the analysis develops the capabilities inventory of all the resources at an organization's disposal.[1]

RESTRAINTS

Just as an individual is a product of heredity and environment, so is an organization. An organization can affect its environment by analyzing it, predicting it, attempting to change it, adapting to it, or even leaving it. The environment can change to the benefit or detriment of an organization. A failure to respond in some way to changes in the environment can result in the eventual failure of the institution or deterioration in its relative position. An organization must forecast the future characteristics of the environment with which it will interact.

In varying degrees all organizations are dependent upon their environment for survival. The immediate external environment includes the organizations and parties in the factor markets that supply the input resources, and the recipients in the product markets that obtain the organization's output products or services. An organization is a part not only of markets but also of an industry, an economy, a community, a nation, and other systems. An analysis of its environment involves the examination and detection of international, national, political, social, economic, and technological trends. The environment is always changing, and the greater the change, the more important it is for the organization to gather data about it.

Broad organizational objectives must be modified to account for internal and external restraints operating on the organization. Restraints narrow the alternatives available to an organization because of the "realities" or "facts of life" peculiar to the entity. The restraints are limiting factors such as technology, financial resources, market conditions, sources of capital, size of the organization, and so forth. Celestial objectives must be filtered through terrestrial realities.

External Restraints

An organization must be analyzed both internally and externally to determine its special strengths and weaknesses so strategies can be developed for new and better goal attainment. External restraints are from the external environment and can be classified as social, political, technological, and economic influences.

Social influences relate to the values and norms of a people and how they change over time. Such items as size and location of the population, education, disposable income, and so forth can be important factors. An assessment of the impact of broad social changes on an organization's products, services, and employees will reveal

---

[1]Appendix A at the end of this chapter contains a master resources profile for assessing an organization.

possible limitations or opportunities. The potential impact of social change can restrict an organization's decision space and limit its alternatives. For example, equal
opportunity, ecology, and consumerism are important issues in our society.

Since organizations are controlled by more than one level of government, *political
influences* can be variegated. Federal, state, and local governments impose various
forms of regulation and taxes. Governments may compete with, protect, or regulate
an organization. Governments compete with many private organizations in the services they provide (insurance, government arsenals, military commissaries, power
generation). Governments protect organizations by direct subsidy, tariffs, price supports, and special tax privileges. Governments regulate organizations by controlling
entry (atomic energy), competition (antitrust and monopoly), product standards
(safety and quality), pricing (utilities), hiring practices (civil rights), working conditions (OSHA), wages (minimum wage), accounting practices (income tax regulation), issuance of stock (SEC), and so forth.

In general, government influence is far-reaching and increasing. Some organizations are subject to more regulation than others. For some firms, government influences product design and composition (drugs), processing (meat packing), distribution (liquor), labeling (furs), advertising (cigarettes), pricing (electric utilities),
transportation (sulfuric acid), etc. Laws are constantly being modified, superseded,
or reinterpreted, and their impact must be reascertained.

Technological influences can be felt through various avenues. It is a rare organization that is not influenced by technology. New products and refinements render
older products obsolescent. New and substitute materials can force replacement of
old configurations. Advanced procedures and methods can drastically change production techniques. New equipment and computers can change the nature of operations.
The level of technical expertise within an organization can restrict its future directions. Demonstrations of new products, announcements of research projects, patent
awards, trade and professional journals, government sponsored research, and professional society reports on new technology deserve scrutiny. Management must not
only be aware of developments of technological consequence; it must attempt to
accurately assess their impact.

Economic considerations have several influences. The present and future state of
the economy as revealed by the business cycle affects most organizations. The number of competitors, nature of the competition, ease of market entry, and size of
investment required for market entry may place limitations on maneuverability. The
financial structure of an organization in conjunction with its access to financial resources will determine growth potentials. The availability of good suppliers and
channels of distribution are important at various stages in a product's life cycle. A
ready supply of manpower with high productivity provides flexibility, and vice versa.

An organization can obtain information about its external environment from many
sources, such as employees, board members, colleagues, professional societies, conferences, friends, meetings, books, customers, reports, journals, consultants, and
governments. An assessment of an organization's position in its industry and environment is necessary before strategies can be developed.

Internal Restraints

Internal restraints are based on the resource and technical capabilities within the
organization. An organization can determine its "sphere of competence" by analyzing its internal operations. An internal appraisal of the areas of finance, sales, pro-

duction, engineering, and personnel will reveal strengths and weaknesses. A review of the mix and performance of an organization's assets (human and nonhuman) indicates future potentials. A detailed assessment of performance in internal operations provides data for the development of strategies.

Financial analysis consists of studying the historical influences of income figures, operating statements, and balance sheet relationships. Ratios can be calculated and various formulas applied to "look behind the figures" and "make the figures talk." It is implicitly assumed that future performance is based on trends and experiences of the past. For stable organizations without substantial change, financial analysis can be very meaningful. However, for growth or high technology organizations the past helps little in prognostication. Although financial analysis may indicate the results, it may not indicate the underlying causes. But even though it is neither adequately comprehensive nor oriented to the future, financial analysis is a very important starting point.

To adequately evaluate an organization, it is necessary to look at the present and future as well as the past. From a *product point of view,* it is necessary to analyze products, product lines, markets, distribution channels, and the competitive position. From a *technological point of view,* it is necessary to analyze research and development, equipment, processes, quality, and manufacturing capabilities. From a *financial point of view,* it is necessary to analyze liquidity, cash flow, working capital, capitalization structure, sources of funds, and operating efficiency. From a *managerial point of view,* it is necessary to analyze the composition, age, talent, background, and capabilities of personnel. Overall, the evaluation of an organization requires clinical judgment of the highest order.

STRATEGIES

An analysis of the breadth and depth of an organization is a precondition for the development of strategies. The analysis should provide a profile of strengths and weaknesses within, between, and among various departments and functional areas. Key talents or capabilities are identified. Before deciding "where it wants to go," it is desirable to establish "where it is now." Figure 3 outlines the genesis and development of strategies. They are developed to fill the gap between the organization's present and desired position.

A strategy is a broad course of action that involves a significant amount of resources. The development of strategies is an attempt to introduce rationality into an environment of vested interests, bureaucratic rigidities, political influences, and many uncertainties. Strategies are the ways an organization deploys its primary skills and resources. Each strategy should be defined and identified to include its:

1. purpose,
2. consequence or impact,
3. alternative courses of action,
4. costs and benefits,
5. measures of performance.

Strategies are the means by which an organization makes use of its primary skills and resources to select the most logical route to achieve its stated ends (objectives) while considering the forces in its environment. They provide direction to the activities of an organization and the people associated with it. They must be formulated, implemented, and evaluated. Strategies should be committed to paper and made ex-

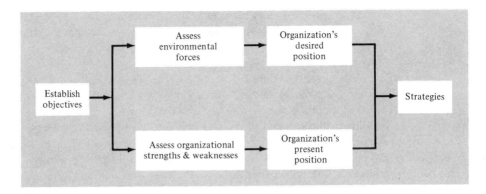

FIGURE 3
Strategies: genesis and development.

plicit. That lessens the danger of their being incomplete or misunderstood, and it simplifies delegation and coordination. The formulation of strategies requires an analytical view with the conceptual and integrative ability to visualize the potential and direction of the organization.

After an organization has assessed its strengths, weaknesses, and restraints, it can develop its marketing strategies, financial strategies, operating strategies, organizational strategies, and personnel strategies. Strategies must be developed for its entire environment and sphere of interest. To meet future personnel needs, it is necessary to develop hiring, incentive, and training programs. To meet future plant and equipment needs, it is necessary to make investments, mergers, and divestments. To meet future technical needs, it may be necessary to establish research and development programs.

Strategies integrate the functional purpose with desired aspirational levels and they are based on the following modes:

1. contraction,
2. stability,
3. growth,
4. combinations.

Contraction is a regressive mode based on reduction of operations, sale of part of the organization, or captive combination with a stronger organization. Contraction may be best when there is little hope of achieving success with other strategies because of inadequate resources and little likelihood of obtaining the resources. It may be chosen by default when there is no other way to attain objectives. It may be chosen as a temporary action until resources are obtained and growth is pursued. In contraction one cuts costs via personnel layoffs, elimination of all but the most profitable products, reduction of product variety, reduction in marketing expenditures, emphasis on purchasing and production efficiency, and so forth. During difficult or bad times such as recessions and depressions, contraction can be quite common. The ultimate contraction involves the sale or abandonment of the organization.

Stability is a status quo mode based on maintaining the present course or direction. The organization continues to do what it has been doing the way it has been doing it, with only minor modifications or changes. It can be very effective in unchanging or very slowly changing environments.

Growth is an aggressive mode of expansion through internal or external means. It can be obtained by increasing a share of a static (or even declining) market, by retaining or increasing a share of an expanding market, and by entering new markets. Growth can be set at a measured rate by some indicator such as assets, sales, product lines, profit, and so forth. Several avenues for growth are available: vertical or horizontal integration, diversification, multinationalism, or conglomeration. Growth can occur through internal expansion of present products and services or externally through merger and acquisition. Mergers and acquisitions are a means of achieving growth through synergism by better utilization of physical facilities, new product lines, additional distribution channels, more technical expertise, a stronger financial position, geographic penetration, and so forth. A growth mania can be deleterious, since bigger is not always better.

Combination is a mixed mode where contraction, stability, and growth are mixed to meet a particular need. It is possible for an organization to contract on one product, stabilize on another, and grow with another. An organization may also change its strategies in view of environmental realities.

When they are explicit, strategies become multi-use tools in appraisal of performance, control, and coordination as well as in all phases of the decision process. Strategies are needed in every major area where performance and results directly affect the survival and prosperity of an organization. They guide and measure progress towards goals. They do not necessarily fit convenient time frames, but are by their nature rather opportunistic (often made in reaction to a perceived opportunity or threat). Problems, opportunities, and "ideas" do not arise according to some set timetables; they must be dealt with whenever they happen to be perceived.

CONGRUENCY OF STRATEGIES

When strategies have been developed, they should be evaluated in light of the following:

1. internal consistency,
2. consistency with the environment,
3. capabilities of available resources,
4. acceptable level of risk,
5. appropriate time horizon,
6. overall feasibility.

Internal consistency refers to the cumulative impact of strategies on organizational objectives. Do the strategies complement and supplement each other by fitting into an integrated pattern? *Consistency with the environment* refers to their compatibility with what is going on outside the organization. Do the strategies integrate with what exists now and what is expected in the future? One must be concerned with the current position as well as what is likely to occur (speed and direction of movement). *Capabilities of available resources* refer to what an organization has to help it achieve its objectives. Resources are, in gambling terms, a bundle of chips available for the serious game of business. It is frequently desirable to isolate the critical resource(s) in short supply that limits possible maneuverability. Balance must be achieved between strategies and resources.

The *acceptable level of risk* refers to the uncertainty of strategies. An impulse to protect against all risk is understandable but imprudent, infeasible, and uneconomical. Different strategies involve different risks, and management must establish its risk preferences. As time horizons increase, risk increases, particularly in unstable markets. Diversification can be used to lower risk. High payoffs are usually associated with high risk strategies. *Appropriate time horizon* refers to the time period over which the strategies will be followed. Frequently, the larger the organization, the longer the time needed to implement and adjust to contingencies. As organizations get larger, the time horizon for strategies usually expands. The *overall feasibility* refers to the workability of strategies on a practical level. Organizations deploy expensive, limited, and complex resources in pursuit of transitory opportunities. Time and room to maneuver are desirable.

There should be a preference for the strategies with greater flexibility. Strategies that permit corrective action are preferred to those that cannot be changed once they are made. A strategy that has even a small likelihood of producing a catastrophic outcome should be avoided although it may have a high benefit expectation. The penalty for irreversibility can outweigh benefit considerations.

If nothing has been stated specifically by management to identify strategies, the prevailing strategies must be assumed from an analysis of actual events. Current strategies must be reappraised from time to time. If the reappraisal discloses that major problems exist, it may be advisable to revise, change, or abandon existing strategies. Changes in strategies frequently necessitate changes in organizational structure.

Strategies are more subject to change than objectives, since they apply to an intermediate time frame. Strategies redefine the objectives and make them more realistic in view of environmental conditions. Strategic planning involves constant surveillance of the environment so that potential opportunities, threats, and problems can be identified and the necessary strategies formulated to exploit opportunities or neutralize threats. Even though drastic modifications to strategies may be unnecessary, frequent incremental changes may be warranted to keep abreast of the times.

ORGANIZATIONAL STRUCTURE

Organizations are not designed *in toto* as we see them. They are usually a product of design, development, modification, and redesign as conditions change and evolve. The general organizational environment (opportunities and risks) and the organization's resources (personnel, money, machines, material, and methods) help to establish strategies. In turn, strategies serve as the basis for the development of organizational structure. Structure outlines the formal relationships among employees. It is set forth by organizational charts, job descriptions, rules, and procedures.

Organizational structure is the nature and scope of an organization as it appears on an organizational chart. It is the manner in which the whole is organized into divisions and/or hierarchical levels. It concerns the arrangement of individuals and their interrelationships and functions. It shows the authority relations of individuals to one another based on their formal roles in the organization.

The organizational chart gives some indication of the hierarchical nature of positions and indicates the major activities performed. It prescribes certain patterns of formal interaction among positions. However, it does not indicate informal relationships, the interactions between equals, or the significance of personality. Emphasis is placed on superior-subordinate relationships and the formal structure.

Each situation must be analyzed in order to determine the most appropriate structure. Should work be divided by product, function, customer, or geography? Is a narrow or wide span of control more desirable? These questions and many others must be answered before a decision on structure can be delineated. The division of labor and the subsequent coordination of work activities into a meaningful composite is a creative task of management. Structure includes the formal hierarchy, plans, procedures, role specifications, committees, project teams, or any other operating mechanisms.

The best organizational structure will vary according to the situation. There is no one pattern or style that is universally appropriate. Structure should reinforce the thrust of strategies. A change in strategies usually leads to a realignment of the organization. When a strategy is altered, the fabric of relationships that ties the work of employees together may need readjustment. Complexity and size will also influence structure. In essence, management must search for the "right fit" among the personnel, organizational characteristics, and the task requirements. Sometimes a flexible design is needed, and at other times a more structured one. The establishment of an organizational structure is less than an exact science.

TACTICS

Tactics involve the further definition and implementation of strategies. Tactics deal with the specific allocation of resources. While strategies are paths to objectives, tactics are paths to strategies. Tactics are derivatives of strategies, and strategies are derivatives of objectives. Strategies guide the formulation of period tactics which serve as the specific directional and evaluative devices of an organization. While strategies tend to apply to the organization as a whole, tactics are related to specific functional and operational areas. Each strategy will give birth to numerous tactics. A summary of the differences between strategies and tactics is contained in Table 1.

Strategies set the direction for the organization, but tactics or plans are needed to implement strategies. Tactics develop the details of how strategies will be implemented. Tactics spell out the meaning of strategies to the subsystems or lower levels of an organization. A tactic is a guide for carrying out a phase of a strategy. Thus, each strategy will have numerous tactics emanating from it.

Top management develops strategies, whereas tactics tend to come from operating functions at lower organizational levels. Tactics are usually developed by operating

TABLE 1
A contrast of strategies and tactics[a]

Characteristic[b]	Strategies	Tactics
Managerial level	Highest	Lower
Point of view	Organizational	Functional
Degree of structure	Unstructured	Highly structured
Degree of objectivity	Subjective	Objective
Time horizon	Long term	Short term
Risk level	High	Low
Range of alternatives	Numerous	Few
Information needs	Large	Limited
Degree of detail	General	Specific
Degree of importance	Major	Minor

[a]The differences between strategies and tactics are clear. However, the specific line of demarcation (boundaries) between them can be blurred.

[b]This list of characteristics is not meant to be exhaustive.

subsystems. They are extensive in detail, but limited in scope to specific activities. Management in upper levels should be greatly concerned with objectives and strategies, while lower levels focus mainly on tactics.

Strategies are factored, or broken down, into tactics by the middle or lower levels of management. Thus strategies flow down from top management and tactics flow up from lower management. The process permits all levels of management to be involved in policy decisions. Discrepancies and inconsistencies in strategies and tactics must be reconciled by various levels of management.

BUDGETS

Management translates strategic considerations into management considerations for specific time periods. These tactics or plans will establish what things are to be done, in what time frames, and who is responsible for actions and results. The primary and most commonly used planning device is a budget which transforms tactics into a common numerical or financial denominator. Budgets are also used as control devices to compare performance with plans and report deviations.

A budget is a plan specifying anticipated results in numerical or quantitative terms. It is also a control device that provides for follow-up, evaluation, and feedback. Since a budget is a short range plan, it is a natural tool for measuring conformance or nonconformance. A budget is composed of a group of subsidiary budgets which express the tactics for operating functions within an organization. Thus, projected budgetary figures are compiled by function for coordination into a master budget of operations for the upcoming fiscal period.

Budgets are concerned with the coordination and control of internal flows of resources. They analyze in financial detail the many activities an organization must perform in implementing tactics. They relate the outputs desired to the inputs required. Traditional budgeting approaches emphasize inputs and start at the lower organizational levels. Both bottom-up and top-down approaches to budgeting are in common use today. Budgeting should start with the expected demand as revealed by forecasts and market analysis.

As shown in Figure 4, there are various kinds of budgets in use today. In essence, they can be classified into five basic categories as follows:

1. *Revenue and expense budgets.* These are the most common types of budgets. The revenue budget consists of estimated sales revenue to be obtained during the period. The expense budget contains the estimated total operations cost, which comes from sales/administrative expenses and from the estimated production cost. The revenue and expense budgets are sometimes called the operating budget. Of course, revenue minus expense gives the estimated profit or loss (income statement).

2. *Production budgets.* Some budgets may be expressed in physical rather than monetary terms because it is easier to control operations on this basis. Material and production output, for example, are often budgeted in terms of units. Manpower is expressed in terms of man-days or labor-hours. Eventually, of course, these are translated into monetary quantities, but for control purposes physical terms are employed.

3. *Cash budgets.* These budgets are simply forecasts of cash receipts and expenditures. They report the planned sources and uses of cash throughout the pe-

riod. They predict the flows into and out of the cash reservoir, which indicates
liquidity or the ability to pay bills as they come due.

4. *Capital expenditure budgets.* These budgets are the plans for replacing, improving, or adding to plant and equipment. Investments constitute long-run
   commitments and are for extended periods of time.
5. *Balance sheet budgets.* A balance sheet budget forecasts the assets, liabilities,
   and net worth of the organization at the end of the particular period. It provides
   an estimated financial picture at a given point in time.

Just as forecasts need not be perfect, budgets need not be perfect in order to be
effective. Both positive and negative discrepancies should be expected from day to
day for a number of reasons. They should not be considered disturbing unless they
are excessive or persistent.

Since they deal with the future, many of the elements in a budget are estimates or
forecasts which will not materialize exactly in the way planned. *Fixed budgeting* is
the predominant system used at the present time. It estimates operations at an expected output level or volume for the budget period. In contrast, *variable budgeting*
estimates operations at several levels of output. With *zero based budgeting,* every
expense or item must be justified and historical levels do not justify future continuation or existence. There are numerous other types of budgets or sub-budgets (departmental) that supplement the basic budgets.

Because objectives and strategies are broad and encompassing (involve more art
than science), their development rarely uses quantitative techniques. Tactics are more

FIGURE 4
Financial budgeting.

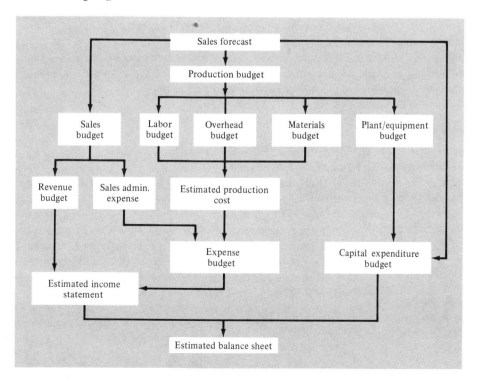

short term and specific, which makes them more amenable to quantitative analysis. Even here, although analytical techniques can be of great value, vision, imagination, and keen judgment remain essential.

CONCLUSION

A purpose of organizations is to serve certain segments of society in a productive, efficient manner. Policy decisions establish objectives, develop programs (strategies) for their accomplishment, consider the costs and benefits of various alternative approaches, and utilize a budgetary process to reflect program activity (tactics). Objectives are similar to the trunk of a tree, while strategies are the branches emanating from the trunk and tactics are the twigs emanating from the branches. Policy decisions establish the boundaries for all subsequent organizational decisions.

Objectives assist in separating the important from the unimportant. They zero in on the desirable achievements. Strategies help to direct energy toward accomplishment of objectives. Tactics are the step-by-step action plan for making strategies meaningful on the lower operational levels. The flow of policy decisions from objectives to strategies to tactics unites the organization into an overall master plan for a given time period.

Performance is the ultimate criterion in the assessment of organizations. Performance is a value judgment and frequently involves a comparative study of effectiveness and efficiency over a time horizon. Effectiveness indicates the ability of an organization to attain its objectives. Efficiency is the ratio of product outputs to resource inputs or effort. Productivity indicates efficiency and the ability of an organization to use its scarce resources.

Efficiency indicates the economic or technical proficiency of an organization's operations. Efficiency is evidenced at a lower organizational level than effectiveness. An organization can be effective and not efficient. Likewise, an organization can be efficient and not effective. Effectiveness is measured at the objectives and strategies levels, while efficiency is determined at the tactical level. It is desirable for an organization to be both effective and efficient.

APPENDIX A. MASTER RESOURCES PROFILE

I. Name of the Organization
   A. General statement of the purpose and objectives of the organization
   B. Historical background
      1. Date of organization
      2. Present legal structure (date and state of incorporation)
      3. Historical changes in organizational structure by mergers, acquisitions, and spin-offs
      4. Any major changes in organizational purpose or objectives
   C. Brief description of goods and services offered
   D. Brief description of product markets served

II. External Environment
   A. Size and nature of product market
   B. Statute laws pertaining to the organization
   C. Nature of competition or cooperation with other organizations

    III. Goods/Services Offered
        A. Detailed description of products
        B. Competitive advantages and disadvantages
           1. Technological position (obsolescence, patents)
           2. Design, styling, trademarks
           3. Quality, product life, reliability, maintainability
           4. Depth and breadth of product lines
           5. Costs and pricing

    IV. Marketing
        A. Market location, coverage, and penetration
        B. Channels of distribution and methods of sale
        C. Advertising and publicity
        D. Type, quality, and availability of salespersons and distributors
        E. Training and development of personnel

    V. Production/Operations
        A. Location of facilities
        B. Plant and equipment capabilities
        C. Raw material sources and costs
        D. Material, quality, manpower, and cost controls
        E. Research and development efforts
        F. Expertise and distinctive abilities

    VI. Finance
        A. Summary of financial condition
        B. Historical and pro forma income statements, balance sheets, and cash flow statements
        C. Major equity interests
        D. Current debt (lenders and terms)
        E. Return on investment, equity, and sales
        F. Financial comparison with other, similar organizations
        G. Major capital investments

    VII. Management
        A. Senior management personnel
           1. Resumes and qualifications
           2. Functions, competencies, and age profile
           3. Levels of compensation
        B. Training and development programs
        C. Employee benefits and perquisites

QUESTIONS

1. What are the three major outputs from policy decisions?
2. What are the most prevalent factors influencing policy decisions?
3. Name the three general categories of objectives.
4. What is meant by hierarchy of objectives?
5. Name some of the major interest groups and how they influence an organization's objectives.
6. Why is it important for an organization to stay within its areas of competence?
7. What are the major external restraints on an organization?
8. What is a strategy?

9. Name the four modes upon which strategies are based.

10. What is organizational structure?

11. What is a tactic?

12. Tactics are developed at what managerial level in an organization?

13. Contrast strategies and tactics.

14. Are budgets planning or control devices?

15. Name the five basic kinds of budgets.

16. Discuss any occasions where you have come in contact with budgeting or budgets.

CASE 1: FIGURATIVELY SPEAKING

Lannie LaLean Spas is a national chain of health, nutrition, and fitness clubs which operates local centers restricted to female clienteles. The home organization has appropriated special funds to each of its local clubs based on their relative size, need, and marketing potential. The Athens, Georgia club will receive $35,000 for the purpose of improving its service operations in line with company objectives. The terms of the special appropriations prohibit the acquisition of plant and equipment; capital improvements are excluded, because another company source allocates for fixed assets, no physical improvements are deemed necessary, and the stated purposes of the special fund are to promote customer appeal, heighten marketing efforts, and improve individual customer service. Since one objective alone cannot encompass the organization's simultaneous and somewhat ambiguous service goals, the following three tactical aims delineate the operating objectives:

1. *To increase membership.* This applies to signing new members for services, renewing contracts for existing members, and signing present members for additional programs. It relates to local club service from an aggregate clientele perspective and gives an overall measure of an individual club's revenue generating capability.

2. *To speed average customer processing time.* This is aimed at reducing delays (the average amount of time a customer must wait to use equipment in the completion of an exercise program) and at efficient utilization of equipment and facilities. It also relates to customer satisfaction and bears on attracting and retaining members.

3. *To increase the attendant (instructor) to customer (A/C) ratio.* The intent is to have the average number of instructors on duty increase in proportion to the number of customers utilizing the facility. It is felt that a higher ratio improves the quality of the service, allows for instructor-led "free" group exercise routines, and enables instructors to sign members for additional services and to recruit prospective members.

The final expenditure of special funds to meet these goals is left to the discretion of the club manager. Inga Svelte, the Athens manager, has three alternatives, and each could consume all or a major portion of the $35,000. Only one alternative could be implemented intact; the others could only be partly completed with the remaining funds. Each of the alternatives will have a positive impact on at least one of the three objectives, and in practice could fail to help, or even set back, the other two. Of the objectives to be satisfied, the company ranks the increase in membership and/or service contracts as top priority.

Inga would like to conduct a campaign for new members similar to an ambitious one conducted five years ago. The cost of the new search would be set at $25,000; it would attract new clients by means of a series of open houses, local TV ads, promotions sponsored through existing members, and introductory discounts. The campaign is expected to increase membership from 1000 to 1160 signed customers. On the negative side, the new membership probably would bring about a 10 minute increase in average processing time and decrease the attendant/customer ratio by 15%; both of these would adversely effect future renewals.

A second alternative is to hire two new attendants for approximately $35,000 in salaries and commissions. Presently, there are five instructors on duty for an average of 40 customers. The new hires could increase the number of instructors on duty by one. Each new instructor is expected to sign five new members a month. The addition of new attendants in the past has had no significant effect on customer processing time, since there are speed-ups and interruptions associated with instructor intervention.

The third option frequently is suggested by the new members—to extend the number of operating hours by opening on Sundays. This could draw membership from a sector unable to schedule workouts during existing hours and potentially could lure 100 new members. The rescheduling of instructor hours would decrease the A/C ratio by 20%, and processing time could be slimmed down from 50 minutes at present to 35 minutes. The new operating hours would cost LLL $35,000 in overtime and operating expenses.

Inga must reconcile the disparities among the alternatives with regard to goal accomplishment. At this time, she sees no alternative that clearly dominates the others. However, she feels that there is some relationship between the alternatives that can be translated into operating terms (criteria). Attracting members is preeminent to the organization; both average processing time and the attendant/customer ratio bear on the membership goal. In Inga's assessment, a five minute reduction in average processing time is as worthwhile as a 1% increase in membership; similarly, a 10% increase in the A/C ratio is equivalent to a 1% increase in membership. In order to allocate her special fund, Inga believes that it is necessary to gauge all of the goals on the same basis. Even then, she is forced to make tradeoffs and choose a program that best meets her criteria but is not superior on all measures.

1. Discuss LLL goals, priorities, and tradeoffs.
2. Try to express the criteria in terms of one scale (a baseline criterion) or on an index system, if possible.
3. Select an alternative according to results from item 2 or from some incorporation of other methods of analysis.

CASE 2: AFTER DEREGULATION

Atlantic Airlines has just declared bankruptcy. The company's last desperate move to win passengers by slashing prices further failed, and the last-minute sale of some of its overseas routes was too little too late. Merger talks with other airlines and solicitations of new cash from investors also proved futile. Its passenger load factor, a measure of how much money a given flight is making, had dropped to 45% and less, whereas the airline needed 70% to meet cash-flow requirements.

Atlantic's demise was attributed to its overly ambitious expansion program. What was a small regional airline ballooned after the Airline Deregulation Act. The trendy carrier paid exorbitant amounts of money to well-known designers for interior schemes, dressed its employees in Pucci-styled uniforms, and painted its fuel-guzzling aircraft conspicuously fashionable colors. Moreover, enormous sums were needed for the quick inauguration of service to a host of new cities. Atlantic borrowed millions of dollars to buy jumbo jets to offer its premium first-time services. Expansion was so spectacular that debt obligations doubled within one operating year. As the economy turned sour and oil-producers sweetened their prices, Atlantic soared swiftly to its final destination.

The removal of Atlantic's capacity from the marketplace would allow an increase of nearly 2% in industry-wide passenger load factors, if the other airlines refrained from adding capacity. Each additional percentage point is estimated to contribute $600 million in industry operating profits. But some of the other carriers are taking the opportunity to gain Atlantic's market share and are bidding for the vacant airport slots in order to increase their service to these markets. Investors see the end of Atlantic as the chance for much-needed profits for the surviving lines that also are deeply in debt and showing current operating losses.

Public Airlines was Atlantic's most avid competitor in many southeastern cities. When Atlantic went to price-slashing in order to solve its liquidity crisis, Public began a price-fare competition in its determination not to be undersold. Because of its relative solvency and profit generation in other geographical regions, Public operated below cost on the routes it shared with Atlantic. Public was able to hold out and now sees the Atlantic failure as a perfect opportunity to move to number one in the larger cities and gain monopolistic presence in the smaller ports-of-call.

Public has added several nonstops to service the southeastern hub city and has called back all laid-off reservations personnel as well as several flight and cabin crews. It also has hired reservations agents and will take delivery of some of its delayed orders for jumbo jet aircraft. Even though the price-fare schedules manipulated during its war with Atlantic at times cost Public $12 million per month, the carrier will continue price wars with the lesser lines serving the larger cities so that it is sure to gain the majority of Atlantic's market share. It also is planning to be a big bidder for the slots vacated by Atlantic. Public does plan to raise fares for the less traveled routes and to offer discounts on bookings far in advance of service.

Central Airlines also is following an aggressive strategy. It bought a smaller line at an inflated price to provide a feeder service for international flights, some of which it purchased from Atlantic. The acquisition put an end to the low expenses that were so favorable when the small line was independent. Labor costs have risen unbelievably now that the employees of the acquired line benefit from Central's high-cost labor contract. Central is manipulating fares up and down to attract business on one hand and to satisfy nervous shareholders on the other. Its air-fare manipulation has caused frequent schedule changes and cancellation of some flights and routes without notification. Central is awaiting the addition of new slots at some of the major airports and is appealing to others to expand, as many of the airlines are constrained by the present terminal space.

Not all of the airlines are engaging in air-fare wars or expansion programs. Air South and Appalachia, southeastern regional carriers, are delaying any moves to add new service because of fears that too many airlines will enter their market. Air South, which had been forced to withdraw from some of the routes it shared with Public and Atlantic during the fare war, has decided not to reenter, in expectation that others will aggressively vie to be Atlantic's replacement. Appalachia has cut one of its three routes that served the southeastern hub because of full aircraft utilization and slow delivery on its newer aircraft. Both Air South and Appalachia intend to offer discounts to corporate customers and will drop time restrictions and advance booking policies.

Another small carrier that traditionally served as a low-fare alternative to Atlantic's shuttle service is switching to a normal-fare strategy that attempts to offer better service to its customers. The change involves a complete service overhaul and repricing system. The changes include more spacious seating, food service, newspapers, departures on the half-hour rather than the hour (the remaining competitor schedules on the hour), and on board ticketing. The shuttle will stress convenience rather than price sensitivity as its major demand factor.

1. Comment on the collapse of and the strategies used by Atlantic.
2. Contrast the goals of the other airlines in response to the failure of a competitor.
3. List some effects of airline deregulation on airline policy, and discuss objective and strategy selection for a highly competitive and capital intensive industry.

SELECTED BIBLIOGRAPHY

McCarthy, D. J. et al. *Business Policy and Strategy,* Homewood, IL: Irwin, 1979.

McNichols, T. J. *Executive Policy and Strategic Planning,* New York: McGraw-Hill, 1977.

Newman, W. H. and J. P. Logan. *Strategy, Policy, and Central Management,* Cincinnati, OH: South-Western, 1976.

Steiner, G. A. and J. B. Miner. *Management Policy and Strategy,* New York: Macmillan, 1977.

Tersine, R. J. "Policy Decisions: The Organization's Future," *Industrial Management,* January–February 1978.

Tersine, R. J. and E. M. Cross. "Towards a Theory of Policy: A Conceptual Model Approach," *Managerial Planning,* September–October 1977.

III

PRODUCT DECISIONS

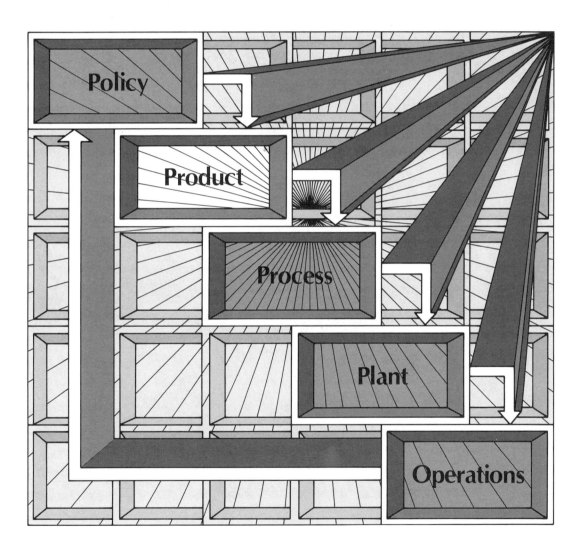

The previous section on policy decisions determined the reasons for an organization's existence. It outlined the objectives, strategies, and tactics of the organization. This section will develop the product decisions that are made under the umbrella of policy decisions. Product decisions determine the goods and services that will be provided by the organization to its customers. The product function establishes the drawings and specifications of the product as shown in Figure I.

This section on product decisions comprises two chapters. The *Product Decisions* chapter establishes the structure necessary to develop products from their initial conception to their final definition (product configuration). The chapter on *Network Programming and Project Planning* relates to large, nonrepetitive special projects.

FIGURE I
The product function.

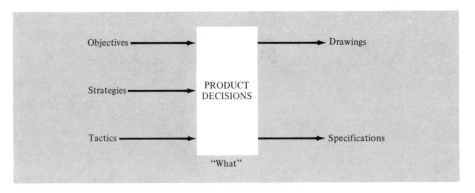

7

Product Decisions

PRODUCT LIFE CYCLES

RESEARCH, DEVELOPMENT, AND ENGINEERING
Research
Development
Engineering
Product Strategies

FEASIBILITY STUDY

PRELIMINARY DESIGN

DETAILED DESIGN
Functional Design
Market Quality Level
Materials Selection
Reliability
Maintainability
Warranties and Guarantees
Patents, Copyrights, and Trademarks

Form Design
Packaging

Production Design
Product Simplification
Product Diversification
Standardization
Modularity
Value Analysis

DRAWINGS AND SPECIFICATIONS

COMPUTER-AIDED DESIGN (CAD)

SERVICE DESIGN

CONCLUSION

QUESTIONS

PROBLEMS

CASES

SELECTED BIBLIOGRAPHY

Product decisions determine the goods and services an organization will provide to society. They entail the systematic gathering of a number of proposed projects and the selection of those products that satisfy the objectives of the organization. A product is defined as the output (good or service) from a productive system made available to a customer. Products are normally thought of as physical goods, but services also are products. Since products are the major output of organizations and are usually its prime source of revenue, their design and selection should be identified closely with organizational objectives. Although product design involves engineering considerations and selection involves marketing considerations, production capabilities have a strong influence on both design and selection.

Demands due to customers, technology, and competition continually increase the number of different products, options, and special features. New products are necessary for survival and growth in a dynamic economy. Product decisions are a never-ending task. Since more new products fail than succeed, the development of new products is a costly and risky business. Organizations must develop new products, but the odds weigh heavily against their success. Better theory and decision procedures at each stage of the new product development process are an attempt at risk and cost reduction. The long term survival of an organization depends on its continued ability to satisfy consumer and public needs through the goods and services offered.

Sometimes products must be modified or redesigned to conserve resources, reduce energy consumption, improve safety, or control pollution. There are impacts on the environment on both the input side for resource conservation and the output side through pollution. Recycling may reduce the pressure for new materials and the amount of solid waste after disposal.

Most organizations have many products. A variety of products is usually necessary in order to survive over an extended period of time. A variety of products protects against patent expirations, competitive products, new technologies, and the risks of "putting all your eggs in one basket." A product line is not fixed; it is always undergoing change.

An organization should not view its products as independent and unrelated to each other. It should consider the role of each product in the larger system of all organizational products or product lines. Products should complement or supplement each other with respect to production and/or distribution.

A foremost consideration in product decisions is the market the organization plans to serve. The market includes any user of the goods or service as well as other organizations serving the same market. All organizations (profit or nonprofit) must consider their markets. Market research tests customer acceptance of products and compiles new ideas for development. It interfaces between the organization and its markets (existing and potential).

The reason for the constant concern for product decisions is that a product tends to have a life cycle. Product decisions manifest themselves through entirely new products, major modifications to existing products, and minor modifications (improvements) to existing products. Competitive marketplace pressure exists to provide higher quality and better performance products without an increase in price. The final design of a product is never fully frozen in an organization. Thus, organizations, unlike individuals who inevitably age and die, can maintain an ageless vigor by the continual development of new products and services.

PRODUCT LIFE CYCLES

All products have a life cycle, but those of different products have different characteristics. For some products (high technology and fashion items) the entire cycle may last for as little as one or two years, whereas other products have survived for decades. Strategic planning is influenced substantially by the relative position of an organization's products in their life cycles. An organization's portfolio of products as manifested by their life cycle positioning provides a rationale for allocating scarce resources among them. Cost, price, and production strategies for a product line are a function of life cycle location, and not all product lines should be treated alike.

All products have a finite life span and progress through a sequence of fairly well-defined stages of development. The product life cycle describes the evolution of a product as measured by its sales over time. At any given time, a product is at a certain stage. Although the universal applicability of life cycle planning is debatable, several successful organizations have incorporated it into their strategic planning. In this strategic style, emphasis is placed on maintaining a balanced portfolio of products in various stages of development. Products with declining product missions are phased out and replaced with products associated with new and growing product missions.

The four common life cycle stages, as shown in Figure 1, are introduction, growth, maturity, and decline. The commercial history of many products shows an initial slow growth in sales while the market is being conditioned (introductory phase), followed by a rapid growth in sales as the product gains market acceptance (growth phase), followed by a tapering off in the rate of growth as the market becomes saturated (maturity phase). Finally, for most products there is a drop in demand as the product is superseded by new products (decline phase). The cycle time span and the time in each stage vary greatly among products. The life cycle of a product has much similarity with the human life cycle of birth, growth, maturation, and demise. From a marketing viewpoint, the division of the product life cycle into four distinct stages makes it possible to study the characteristics of the market in each stage and develop appropriate strategies.

After its birth, the product passes through a low sales volume *introductory stage*. During the following *growth stage,* volume and profit both rise. Volume stabilizes during the *maturity stage,* and unit profits start to fall. Eventually, in the *decline stage* of the product, sales volume declines because the need for the product disappears or a substitute product is developed to fill the same need. The length of the life cycle, the duration of each stage, and the shape of the curve can vary widely for different products.

The profit cycle of a product is quite different from its sales cycle. During introduction, it may not earn any profit because of high initial startup costs. In the growth stage, unit profits typically attain their peak and then start declining, although total profits may continue to climb for a time on rising sales volume. During late growth and early maturity, increasing competition cuts deeply into profit margins and ultimately into total profits. Finally in the decline stage, declining volume eventually pushes costs up to a level that substantially eliminates profit.

It is important to identify the transition from one life cycle stage to the next, because marketing strategies will change with the stage. Product development and design are crucial in the introductory stage. During the growth stage, a well-grounded reputation based on product reliability is paramount. Promotion, service, and marketing are vital during the maturity stage. Cost control is the key factor during the decline.

The fundamental progressions of product life cycles are not inevitable but can be altered by careful management. The object is to control product life cycles by (1) controlling individual product life cycles, (2) controlling the mix of products in the product line according to their location in their life cycle (adding and pruning products to obtain a desired mix), and (3) allocating funds and manpower among products in accordance with their benefit potential. A product's introduction stage can be shortened by increasing marketing expenditures or securing national distribution more quickly. The growth stage can be hastened by exploiting additional markets, lowering product pricing, and initiating more productive sales efforts. The maturity stage can be radically modified by product improvements, repackaging, and product revitalization. The object is to reshape the life cycle so decline and demise are avoided. Of course, not all products can be revitalized, so it is important to recognize the fact

FIGURE 1
General product life cycle.

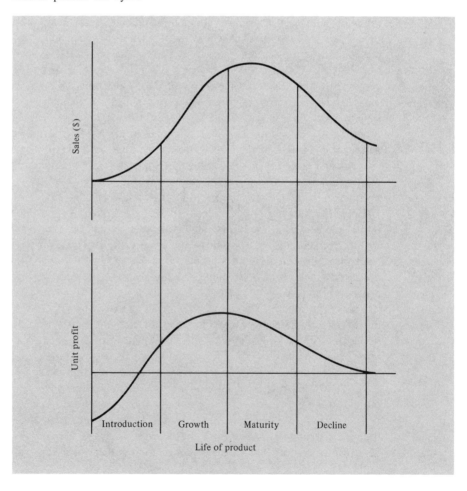

and make the necessary time and monetary adjustments. If a product can be effectively differentiated and "distinguished by brand," it may have found an elixir that extends its lifetime and suspends its life cycle.

Before product decisions are covered further, we indicate the overall role of research, development, and engineering in an organization. These activities are usually important for its continued existence. They are particularly significant to product decisions.

RESEARCH, DEVELOPMENT, AND ENGINEERING

The development and improvement of new and old products as well as processes is vital to the survival of many organizations. *Research* seeks to make basic discoveries and uncover new principles. Research may be pure (no foreseeable practical application) or applied (directed towards the solution of a practical problem). *Development* usually follows applied research and focuses on economically feasible applications. *Engineering* implements the work of research and development groups for commercial benefit. The cumulative impact of research, development, and engineering is illustrated in Figure 2.

Some of the purposes of research, development, and engineering are as follows:

1. discover and advance knowledge,
2. develop new products,
3. develop new production processes,
4. improve existing products and processes,
5. find uses for by-products or waste products,
6. provide technical service to functional departments,
7. analyze competitive products.

The importance of research, development, and engineering varies with the nature of the organization in question. Its significance is underlined by the fact that many entities are making only a few of the products that made up their lines only eight or ten years ago. Although research, development, and engineering are being discussed under product decisions, they have equal significance in other major decision cate-

FIGURE 2
Research, development, and engineering.

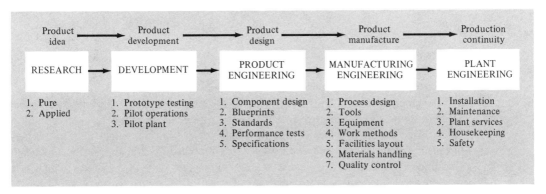

gories (process, plant, and operations decisions). Their treatment under product decisions is for convenience only, and their broader implications for other areas should be noted.

RESEARCH

Pure research (fundamental research) is undertaken primarily for the sake of knowledge itself with no consideration of commercial possibilities. Its objective is to contribute to man's general knowledge of his environment by clarifying the cause-and-effect relationship in natural phenomena. It attempts to explain why things happen. Pure research often results in ideas with little or no commercial application, at least at the time of discovery. With few exceptions, pure research is not undertaken by industrial organizations. Very large organizations, governments, universities, and independent research agencies conduct pure research. The expense is too great and the return too small for most organizations.

In contrast, *applied research* is concerned almost entirely with practical applications and the solution of practical problems. Its objective is the design of a product or process that will have some economic value. Applied research is more suited to industrial organizations. It frequently uses the results of pure research. It usually takes place in the laboratory and the library.

Applied research can be further subdivided into product research, manufacturing research, materials research, market research, and operations research. *Product research* is directed towards new products, new uses for present products, or by-product utilization. *Manufacturing research* is directed towards improvement of manufacturing processes and reduction in costs. *Materials research* seeks the discovery and improvement of materials constituting a product. *Market research* seeks to learn the needs, desires, and purchasing behavior of customers. It tests customer acceptance of products and provides a source of new ideas for development. *Operations research* is the organized application of the techniques of science (usually mathematical) to solve the operating problems in organizations.

DEVELOPMENT

Development fills the gap between research and engineering. Development is a directed trial and error process through successive designs until general specifications are met as economically as possible. Successive trials progressively eliminate problems and introduce design improvements. Pilot operations, pilot plants, and prototype testing can be part of a development effort. Laboratory experiments using small equipment must be validated before large-scale production can commence.

Development can be subdivided into product development and process development. *Product development* usually involves testing several designs and evaluating their feasibility. *Process development* has to do with machines, tooling, layout, methods, and the design of special manufacturing devices.

Development usually involves prototype testing and pilot operations. *Prototype testing* studies the performance of the physical product in various design configurations. The objective is to arrive at an economical design that adequately meets performance requirements. *Pilot operations* are simply the manufacture of the new product under simulated factory conditions. A pilot plant may be employed which is a scaled down model of plant operations. Generally a small quantity is produced to study the process and uncover any product defects or process inefficiencies that may exist. Defects can be in the product itself or they can stem from manufacturing difficulties.

ENGINEERING

Engineering involves the implementation and activation of the development effort. Engineering functions fall into the categories of product engineering, manufacturing engineering, and plant engineering. *Product engineering* is the design of the product for manufacturing purposes. The product engineer must confirm component design, blueprints, standards, specifications, and product performance testing. *Manufacturing engineering* is the design of the manufacturing processes. The manufacturing engineer must design processes, tooling and equipment, work methods, materials handling devices, layout of facilities, and quality standards. *Plant engineering* is responsible for continued production after the facility is operational. The plant engineer must install equipment, perform repairs and maintenance, operate plant services (power, steam, air, water), care for buildings and grounds, and perform overall plant housekeeping.

PRODUCT STRATEGIES

Organizations can follow various types of strategies concerning their product lines. The four major product strategies can be termed market leader, follow the leader, applications oriented, and production efficient. Most organizations will adopt a mix of these strategies based on their particular circumstances.

The *market leader strategy* involves an intense research, development, and engineering effort. Technical leadership is exerted through large financial investments. It involves a high degree of risk-taking, and usually only large organizations with substantial resources can adopt this posture. The organization must be able to absorb mistakes and recoup without endangering its well-being.

The *follow-the-leader* strategy involves minor research but strong development and engineering effort. It requires a rapid technical response to new products developed by market leaders. Manufacturing and marketing expertise are also vital to its success. It enters the market with a competing model during the growth stage of the product. Large and medium size organizations usually pursue this strategy.

The *applications oriented strategy* involves minor research and development but strong engineering effort. It develops product modifications to serve a particular, specialized, or limited market segment. It enters the market during the maturity stage of the product. This strategy is common to small and medium size organizations.

The *production efficient strategy* involves little research, development, and engineering but a strong manufacturing effort. It is based on superior manufacturing efficiency and cost control. Competition in price and delivery are paramount. It enters the market during the maturity stage. This strategy is common in small organizations with low overhead.

FEASIBILITY STUDY

Product decisions usually begin with general or customer specifications from market analysis which indicate customer needs or requirements. Internal research, employee suggestions, individual inventors, distributors, or suppliers may also be sources of new product ideas. At periodic points in time, all new products or projects are subjected to a feasibility study to establish their economic, technical, and operational plausibility. Unfeasible products or projects are discarded, and feasible selections are sent to preliminary design. An outline of the flow of effort for product decisions is contained in Figure 3.

In translating a product idea into an actual product, the organization must consider its areas of major strength. It is desirable to select products that do not divert effort from the structure that has made the organization successful. By a process of exclusion, top organizational officers should define the boundaries of the organization beyond which new product developments should not stray. A product may be considered unacceptable if it (1) lacks benefit (profit) potential, (2) is incompatible with organizational goals, (3) exceeds capital availability, (4) exceeds managerial or technical skills, or (5) is not as desirable as other available opportunities.

After a new product idea has been reviewed and found to be compatible with an organization's objectives and resources, its financial impact must be determined. An organization can use cost-benefit analysis by ascertaining the costs and pricing of potential products. New products can be compared on the basis of risk. Should the risk judgment be positive, the product idea can be sequenced for further development. Should the risk judgment be negative, the product idea is shelved. In evaluating potential products, an organization can use breakeven analysis, incremental analysis, marginal analysis, simulation, or decision theory. Where cash flows and capital investment are paramount considerations, net present value or internal rate of return methods can be adopted. Generally, products with the greatest expected return on

FIGURE 3
Product decisions. [From Richard J. Tersine and John H. Campbell, *Modern Materials Management,* New York: North Holland, 1977, p. 26.]

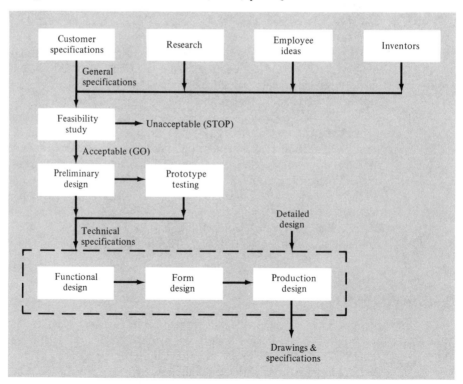

investment are given priority. Of course, any feasibility study will involve considerations that defy quantification.

PRELIMINARY DESIGN

Preliminary design involves the transition from concept to reality. General product specifications established in the idea stage must be transformed into a technically efficient, marketable product. General or customer specifications must be formulated that will define the product in much greater detail. Prototypes frequently are used to evaluate design alternatives and typically undergo extensive testing to determine the performance characteristics of optional designs. Once a model has been constructed, laboratory tests of physical properties, behavioral outcomes, and overall deficiencies can be made. As deficiencies are revealed, a prototype design is modified until satisfactory performance is obtained. A large number of tradeoffs among cost, quality, and performance are considered. Prototype testing also can include market testing of different product configurations.

The process of finding the best design is called optimization. It can be obtained by trial and error modifications of successive designs, by experimental methods in which parameters are changed in a consistent manner, or synthetically by computer simulation. If the experimental construction and test program have not dealt too harshly with the original design, the work of redesign may be only minor. However, if major flaws have been exposed, redesign may reach major proportions. The aim of preliminary design is to work out the "bugs" from an engineering viewpoint and arrive at a viable design.

In preliminary design, the specifics of a product are tentatively established. After preliminary design, the product is subjected to detailed design (functional design, form design, and production design). The detailed design will result in drawings and specifications that completely define the product and its characteristics.

DETAILED DESIGN

Detailed design, sometimes referred to as final design, comprises functional design, form design, and production design. *Functional design* is concerned with how the product works (its performance). *Form design* is concerned with how the product appears. *Production design* is concerned with how the product will be produced. All these detailed design efforts occur in parallel.

FUNCTIONAL DESIGN

Functional design is concerned with the performance of the product. Management must be concerned with the relationships among market quality level, reliability, and cost in deciding on technical specifications. Through various research means, management can determine market quality level and reliability relative to competitive products, and relate these factors to cost. Market surveys and other means can determine how the market for a given product is structured. The various market segments may represent different quality levels of the product.[1]

---

[1]Market quality levels and production quality levels are sometimes confused. Market quality level relates to the type of market segment desired. Production quality level relates to the ability of the manufactured product to meet its design specifications.

Because of the interaction of design features, there is no obvious starting point in the network of functional design criteria. A good design will balance criteria and values. The criteria may be economic in relation to markets and demand, behavioral in relation to customer behavior, or technological in relation to materials, methods, and processes.

Market Quality Level

Market quality level is related to the market segments the product will serve. A product may serve high, moderate, or low quality markets. These market quality levels will be reflected in the selection of materials used in production and in the specified degree of reliability of the final product. Likewise, production costs will vary with the market quality level. Higher quality products tend to cost more to produce and have more value in the marketplace. However, there is a point of diminishing returns where costs increase beyond value. Functional design will establish specifications for the product in terms of these variables. In some cases, process decisions will be affected to a greater or lesser extent by specified market quality and reliability standards.

Materials Selection

With a stated market quality level, the decision process may proceed to materials selection. A major cost component of many products is the materials used in production. The quality and reliability of the materials should meet specifications as prescribed by the standards set for the final product. The alternative combinations of inputs to the conversion processes must be weighed from an economic standpoint. There are usually numerous alternative materials to consider for any given product.

For this reason, consideration must be given to those materials that have the most likely appeal to the targeted customers. For example, a buyer of a luxury car is likely to select leather over vinyl seats, but the buyer of an economy car probably would not. Additionally, alternative materials are chosen from the standpoint of processing costs. This concerns detailed knowledge of material properties and the capabilities of the production system to process them. For example, titanium metals are expensive and difficult to process, while wood and aluminum are easier to process on various types of equipment. The choice frequently is based on the relative acquisition and processing costs of the materials. By no means does the low cost material always win. Frequently, the low cost material cannot be processed equally well; its high scrap rate and excessive processing costs may work against it.

Reliability

It is a rare product that will not eventually fail. The life of a product is dependent on its design, the manufacturing quality, the conditions under which it is used, and chance. Thus, failures emanate from several sources, and it is impossible to predict them precisely.

A consumer rates quality subjectively according to how well a product satisfies a number of functional and psychological needs. To a great extent, a customer's idea of quality flows from the reliability of a product as revealed by its performance in use. Buyers frequently compare reliability before purchasing competing products. It can significantly influence repeat sales, reflect on an organization's image, and result in legal complications if it is too low.

Reliability refers to a product performing its intended function for a specified period of time (consistency of operation). Often it is expressed as a number that indicates the probability that a product will perform its intended function under given conditions satisfactorily (without failure) for a specified time period or number of cycles. The reliability of a product, so measured, may be anywhere between 0 (indicating certainty of failure) and 1 (indicating certainty of operation). If an item has a reliability of 0.90, it means the probability that it will function as intended is 90%, and the probability that it will fail is 10%. Thus, it is expected that on the average 1 of every 10 items will fail, or equivalently, that the item will fail on the average of once in every ten trials.

A failure can be defined as a change from operational to nonoperational status. Three types of failures may occur when components or systems are in operation. These failure types are:

1. early failure (infant mortality),
2. chance or random failure,
3. wearout failure.

Early failure is more a design problem than a reliability consideration. Its cause should be identified and corrected. It may be due to defective material, improper assembly, incorrect adjustments, and so forth. Factory testing may remove early failures. Chance failures usually occur infrequently and are not caused by any one thing in particular. Wearout failures are caused by components reaching the end of their "design life." Once the failure rate pattern of a product is known, steps can be taken to improve its reliability.

Reliability involves both individual parts and the whole product. A product can fail when any critical part fails; therefore a system's reliability is not better than that of its most unreliable part. The more critical parts there are, the less the reliability of the product. Failures may follow a statistical distribution such as the normal or Poisson.

The determination of the degree of reliability should be a joint decision by marketing, production, and engineering segments of the organization. Designers attempt to increase reliability by designing simplicity into products, adding redundant components, and building products with greater potential than required (overdesign). It is necessary to design components for the system that have reliabilities beyond the requirements of the system as a whole. However, overdesign can be a futile and costly endeavor. There is usually a positive correlation between simplicity and reliability. With simplicity, there are fewer things to go wrong. Simplicity in design is extremely advantageous. It is desirable to use as few components as possible and to ensure that each component in the product is reliable.

As a product becomes more complex, its very complexity tends to make it less reliable. The greater the number of parts or components in a product, the greater the probability that one of them will fail and cause the product to malfunction. When a product is comprised of a number of components in series, its overall reliability is obtained by multiplying together the probabilities of all the components that can cause failure:

$$R_p = R_1 \cdot R_2 \cdot R_3 \cdot \cdots \cdot R_n,$$

where

R_p = overall product reliability,
R_i = reliability of component i ($i = 1, \ldots, n$),
n = number of components in series in the product.

Where the failure of a part is critically important, designers often add a redundant part or subsystem as insurance. Redundancy (independent parallel subsystems) serves to make the system fail-safe. The need for redundancy depends upon the seriousness of a failure. Hospital emergency power sources and dual automobile braking systems are examples of redundancy. Where high reliability is necessary, redundancy is common. When a product or system has a parallel redundancy, its overall reliability is

$$R_p = R_1 + R_1(1 - R_2) = 1 - (1 - R_1)(1 - R_2).$$

The reliability of n parallel components is

$$R = 1 - [(1 - R_1)(1 - R_2) \cdots (1 - R_n)].$$

EXAMPLE 1

A flow control system consists of three components in series, with individual reliabilities $R_1 = 0.90$, $R_2 = 0.95$, and $R_3 = 0.85$. A failure of the system results in a cost of \$5,000. (a) What is the reliability of the system? (b) What is the long run expected cost of failure? (c) What would be the reliability of a complete parallel backup system? (d) What is the maximum amount of funds that should be expended for a parallel system?

(a) $R_p = R_1 \cdot R_2 \cdot R_3 = (0.90)(0.95)(0.85) = 0.73.$
(b) The probability of failure is $1 - 0.73 = 0.27$. The long run expected cost of failure is $(0.27)(\$5,000) = \$1,350.$
(c)

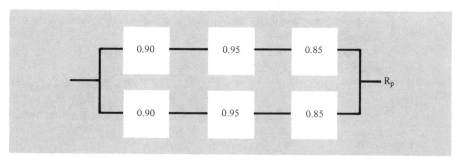

The redundant system is expected to be reliable 73% of the time, just like the primary system. The redundant system should be activated only when the primary system fails. So the reliability of the combined system would be the reliability of the primary system plus 73% of the expected 27% failures, or $R_p = 0.73 + (0.27)(0.73) = 0.93.$

(d) The probability of failure of the combined (primary and backup) system is $1 - 0.93 = 0.07$. The long-run expected cost of failure is $(0.07)(\$5,000) = \$350$. The expected failure cost has been reduced from \$1,350 to \$350. If the parallel system costs less than $\$1,350 - \$350 = \$1000$, it will be desirable.

Another method of improving reliability is through maintenance. Frequently, preventive maintenance can result in high reliability for a product even though long-term reliability is not designed into the parts of the product. Periodic inspection and replacement of worn parts can reduce operational failures significantly. Preventive maintenance can be worthwhile when it increases the operating time by reducing the frequency or severity of failures (breakdowns). Frequently, preventive maintenance can be performed in off-peak periods when operational needs are minimal.

Reliability can be calculated in several ways. Although its overall measure is usually a probability, it can be expressed as a product failure rate, or the mean time between failures. The failure rate (FR) measures (1) the number of failures during an operating period, or (2) the number of failures among the products tested. The first approach focuses on the *length of service* and is commonly used in product warranties which pertain to a given period of time after the purchase of a product. The second approach, as illustrated in Example 1, focuses on a *point in time* when a system must operate for one or a few uses:

$$FR = \frac{\text{number of failures}}{\text{operating time}} \text{ or } \frac{\text{number of failures}}{\text{number tested}}.$$

The mean time between failures (MTBF) is calculated as follows:

$$MTBF = \frac{\text{operating time}}{\text{number of failures}} = \frac{1}{FR}.$$

EXAMPLE 2

One hundred artificial heart valves were tested for 20,000 hours at a laboratory research center, and 6 valves failed during the test. (a) What is the percentage of failures? (b) What is the number of failures per unit-year? (c) How many failures can be expected per year for every 100 installations? (d) What is the mean time between failures?

(a) $FR = \dfrac{\text{number of failures}}{\text{number tested}} = \dfrac{6}{100} = 0.06$, or 6%.

(b) Operating time = total time − nonoperating time
$$= (100)(20,000) - 6(20,000)/2$$
$$= 1,940,000 \text{ unit hours};$$

$$FR = \frac{\text{number of failures}}{\text{operating time}} = \frac{6}{1,940,000}$$
$$= 0.000003 \text{ failures per unit-hour};$$

$(0.000003)(24 \text{ hr/day}) (365 \text{ day/yr}) = 0.026 \text{ failures per unit-yr.}$

(c) $(0.026 \text{ failures per unit-yr})(100 \text{ units}) = 2.6 \text{ failures per year.}$

(d) $MTBF = \dfrac{\text{operating time}}{\text{number of failures}} = \dfrac{1,940,000}{6}$
$$= 323,333.3 \text{ unit-hours per failure.}$$

Reliability can be measured during pilot runs to uncover potential problems, by endurance tests to determine performance characteristics (life expectancy), and by tests under actual operating conditions. Establishing product reliability involves cost tradeoffs. A highly reliable product is usually high in cost. The cost tradeoff involves original product cost and maintenance cost. The original product cost is usually excessive for perfect reliability, just as maintenance cost is excessive for the unreliable product. The original product cost tends to increase with reliability, while the maintenance cost tends to decrease with increasing reliability. Management should search for the reliability level that results in the minimum of the combined costs.

Life testing is the continuous testing (operation) of the product until it fails. The testing should reveal the probability distribution of product failures. It should also reveal what component or feature of the product usually fails first. Life testing may be real (under actual operating conditions) or simulated (under artificial or laboratory conditions).

Maintainability

Maintainability refers to the ability of a product or system to stay in operating condition with a reasonable amount of effort. It is frequently expressed as a number that indicates the probability that, when a specified maintenance action is initiated, the failed device will be restored to operable condition in a specified downtime. It may involve customer repair facilities, service from the manufacturer, provisions for replacement parts, and written maintenance or repair procedures.

Maintainability relates to maintenance costs, frequency of repair, service, and operational costs. It can be expressed in terms of ease of repair and maintenance, availability, safety, and accuracy. The objective of maintainability is to design systems that can be kept operational with the least time, expense, and expenditure of support resources.

Maintainability can be expressed quantitatively as the mean time to repair a product. The average availability of the product is obtained as follows:

$$\text{Average availability} = \frac{\text{MTBF}}{\text{MTBF} + \text{MTTR}},$$

$$\text{MTBF} = \frac{\text{operating time}}{\text{number of failures}},$$

$$\text{MTTR} = \frac{\text{nonoperating time}}{\text{number of failures}},$$

where

MTBF = mean time between failures, or how long on the average the product operates before it fails,

MTTR = mean time to repair, or how long on the average it takes to correct a failure.

There is an obvious tradeoff between reliability and maintainability. It is desirable to increase MTBF and decrease MTTR, but increased reliability (increased MTBF)

and increased maintainability (decreased MTTR) increase cost. Thus, it is desirable to obtain the mix of reliability and maintainability that results in minimum cost.

Breakdown and preventive maintenance are the two major types of maintenance. Breakdown maintenance is only performed after the product fails or otherwise does not work. Preventive maintenance is performed to delay or prevent failures via periodic checking of the product and replacing components prior to failure. The preferred type of maintenance for a product is situational and depends on the costs and consequences of failure.

Since any mechanical or electrical device is subject to breakdown, accessibility for service is an important design feature for many products. Modular construction permits maintenance by substitution of submodules. Reliability is not as critical when prompt repair and recovery can be assured. Maintainability can involve reducing the severity of failures as well as their frequency.

Maintainability deals with the reestablishment of product performance when anomalies occur. Adequate research and design must be performed to establish repair schedules and the general or special maintenance (overhauls) required to assure performance. The maintainability criterion includes the proper planning of replacement parts production. Emphasis is placed on standardization of components within product lines to reduce costs associated with carrying replacement parts inventory for both producer and consumer. Maintenance will be more thoroughly covered in Chapter 23.

Warranties and Guarantees

Reliability (product) engineering establishes sound design, evaluates product performance, and reflects the stated quality level. As evidence of the importance of product assurance to consumers, warranties and guarantees are provided by the producer. The warranty may serve as a competitive device; however, it is primarily designed to reflect stated quality and reliability standards. Management must give special attention to warranties to assure protection to the buyer and themselves. Expensive lawsuits and customer dissatisfaction may result from inadequate attention to specifications in the warranty.

Warranties guarantee, at least partially, the operation of an item over a specified length of time. If the product fails, the organization must take steps as outlined in the warranty to repair or replace the product. The extent of liability ranges from partial to total. At an extreme, the product is replaced or all repairs are performed by the manufacturer; more usually, only a portion of the repair or replacement cost is provided. The warranty may apply to the whole product or only certain components of the product.

For complex products, an organization may provide the customer with a service or operations manual. It serves as a guide for the operation, repair, and replacement of the product. Warranties and guarantees are frequently included in the manual, as well as places to obtain service. The longer the time period over which a product is intended to function, the greater the need for some type of warranty.

There has been growing concern from the consuming public about product quality. Consumers have increased their strength through legislation, consumer groups, and new governmental bodies. These efforts have tended to increase the producer's liability for his product's quality and safety.

Patents, Copyrights, and Trademarks

An important consideration in functional design is the protection of a new product by a patent, copyright, or registered trademark. Patents are granted for the invention of new and useful machines, processes, and goods. New discoveries of fact or principle are patentable when practically applied in products. A patent is a grant by the Federal government providing an inventor legal protection against infringement for a certain number of years. Patents applicable to manufacturing are those which relate to mechanical, chemical, or electrical characteristics (features which affect the operation of the product), and they are granted for 17 years. A patent provides a monopoly position to an organization by precluding competitors from infringing on unique product features. After a patent term expires, inventions become public property.

The intention of patent laws is to encourage the development of new ideas and their implementation. Without the patent law, there would be little incentive to expend large sums of money for the development of new products. An imitator could copy the design and reap the benefits of the development effort without any expenditure. The patent law is intended to protect the innovator. Patents are offered by the U.S. Patent Office, which is under the U.S. Department of Commerce.

A patent is not a guaranteed protection until its infringement has been proven valid by litigation (court action); however, it is usually a substantial deterrent to the unauthorized use of the invention.

A patent holder has exclusive production rights to the new product or processing method and may license the rights to others for the patent duration. It is advisable early in the development phase to make sure that the proposed design does not infringe on the rights protected by earlier patents. Sometimes the effective life of a patent can be extended by patenting improvements. In this case, competitors may use the basic patent but may not use the improvement patent without permission. Frequently products appear with "patent applied for" or "patent pending" markings. These are attempts at preventing prospective competitors from entering the field. Since patents give protection for only seventeen years, some organizations attempt to keep their ideas secret rather than apply for patents. If a secret is discovered, however, there is nothing a company can do to prevent its use.

Patent law is a complex legal specialty and requires the services of a competent patent attorney. Large organizations usually employ patent attorneys; small organizations and individuals can easily obtain the services of a patent attorney for a fee.

The protection of creations such as printed matter, maps, charts, drawings, paintings, and photographs is through *copyrights*. Copyrights provide exclusive right to reproduce, publish, and sell the work for the author's life plus an additional 50 years after the author's death. A *trademark* is an identifying device, name, or symbol used to distinguish a product from those produced by others. Trademarks are legally protected for 20 years and are renewable. A trademark is important for customer identification of a product.

FORM DESIGN

Form design relates to the physical appearance or shape of the product. According to a traditional design maxim, form follows function. However, aesthetic aspects enter into the physical shape of the final product which may have little to do with functional requirements. Form design is much more important for consumer goods than for industrial goods. With consumers, color, style, and fashion may be more important than function. Personal identification and image may also be significant factors to a consumer. The packaging of a product may be an extension of its form and contribute to its acceptance.

Packaging

When an item is sold to the ultimate consumer, it is almost always delivered in some kind of package. The package may be a bag, box, can, tube, vial, envelope, jar, bottle, cylinder, pail, drum, tote bin, or even a rail car, barge, truck, or ship. The customer is usually primarily interested in the contents of the package. Since the package is ultimately discarded, recycled, or destroyed, it is usually advisable to employ the most economical packaging available.

Packaging is the use of containers, wrapping materials, decorations, and labeling to protect, promote, secure, preserve, containerize, and increase the utility of a product. To package a product so it gets through the distribution cycle safely and economically is a major challenge. Before a product package is designed, information should be known about the product's properties, its customers, statute laws, distribution requirements, and the materials available.

Packaging is not just another manufacturing operation; it must serve many purposes. The needs of the customers, retailer, distributor, marketing department, and transportation department must be considered as well. The final selection usually will represent a compromise that economically balances the various interest groups.

The basic materials of packaging are paper, cardboard, cellophane, steel, aluminum, glass, wood, and plastic. Paper and cardboard are the most widely used, since they are cheap, lightweight, and easy to print on. They can be corrugated for additional strength or wax-treated for protection against moisture. Glass, plastic, and metal are used extensively for liquid products. The selection of the type of packaging will depend on such factors as:

1. susceptibility of the product to damage,
2. normal hazards to which it will be exposed,
3. the length of time it must remain in the package,
4. the promotional role of the package,
5. the likelihood of product tampering.

Packaging can be part of the promotional effort supporting the sale of a product. In self-service operations, it can be a silent salesperson. Many products are very similar, so the only real difference is the package which can distinguish the product and create a brand identification. Package redesign is often used to increase the appeal of a well-established product. The appearance of a package should satisfy point of sale and other marketing demands.

The immediate package is not the only aspect that must be considered. Inner packaging and shipping containers may also be required. In some instances, as many as four different packages may be necessary—an inner wrapping, the visible package, a corrugated box containing a few dozen packages, and finally a much larger shipping container of more durable construction. The mode of transportation adopted will influence the design of the shipping container. For some items, including hazardous materials, the transportation medium establishes shipping and container specifications.

PRODUCTION DESIGN

Product decisions lead to a product that is acceptable in performance (function), style (form), and producibility. Since the design engineers are concerned primarily with the performance and style of a product, they may overlook the producibility problems of processing, assembly, tools, and equipment. Products can very easily be overdesigned, which increases their cost. A product may be designed in such a manner that it is difficult or impossible to build. Production designers review drawings and make changes to improve the economy of manufacture. For example, the original design may be altered for simplicity of manufacture if it requires excessive machining or finishing.

Production design is concerned with production at the desired quality level and at an acceptable cost. It is concerned with the producibility of a product within cost limitations. There are almost always alternatives of design that will meet functional requirements. Specific areas that can influence cost are materials selection, methods of joining parts, tolerances, product complexity, and product variability.

Production design focuses on the economies of production. The design of a product tends to commit the productive systems to specific processing methods; thus, the greatest opportunity for cost savings occurs during the design of the product. The available modes of production can affect the final cost of a product. Production design is the conscious effort to consider how a product will be built during the design phase. If no consideration is given to production modes during the design phase, the cost of an item will frequently be excessive. The minimum production cost of an item is determined by its design. Production design does not determine how the product will be manufactured, but it does consider such modes in establishing the final product design.

Functional design means creating something that functions according to specifications. Once the functional design has been accomplished there are usually alternatives of design that will meet functional requirements. At this point, production design becomes very important. The goal is to select a detailed design that provides the greatest functional benefit at the lowest cost. Product simplification, product diversification, standardization, modularity, and value analysis are important considerations in production design.

Product Simplification

One of the most perplexing problems facing management is a determination of the optimum degree of product variety. Too much variety raises costs, while too little may retard sales. Products that offer unnecessary variety and immaterial differences should be discontinued. Product simplification means reducing the number and variety of products. It involves the elimination of marginal product lines, types, and models. Simplification will reduce design complexity and the range of products, which results in less varied purchases, smaller inventories (less investment), and lower production costs. Of course, product simplification also means fewer customer choices, which can influence revenues. While industrial buyers are more concerned with performance and economy, individual consumers are influenced by many other factors including product variety.

A simplification program is usually undertaken when product diversification has been carried beyond its practical limits. When style is not a dominant factor, product lines can easily become too broad and uneconomical. An application of Pareto's law, also known as the ABC concept, often indicates that a large amount of sales is concentrated in a few products. Conversely, a large number of products account for a very small portion of sales. Therefore, serious consideration should be given to the elimination of many of the products that contribute little to sales volume and profit.

Product Diversification

Product diversification is the opposite of product simplification, and it results in a proliferation of product lines, types, and models. Highly competitive organizations are frequently compelled to diversify to attract and hold customers. Less competitive or monopolistic organizations are more likely to concentrate on simplification. With diversification overall costs will be higher, but the important consideration is not costs but the gap between revenues and costs. When diversification can widen the gap between revenues and costs, it is very desirable.

Diversification may be competitively necessary for organizations that must offer their customers a "full line." It can also be a stabilization tool for sales and production of seasonal products. Excess or idle capacity can be allocated by balancing operations with additional compatible products. Diversification spreads the risk and protects against a decline in demand for a single product or the loss of a major customer. Excess or idle capacity can be a strong impetus for diversification.

The three approaches to product diversification are horizontal diversification, vertical diversification, and lateral diversification. *Horizontal diversification* expands into similar and complementary products that use the same equipment, facilities, or channels of distribution. *Vertical diversification* expands by making rather than buying. It may be directed forward into the channels of distribution or into retailing. It can also be backward into the raw materials supply and other purchased services. *Lateral diversification* expands outside the confines of a given industry into unrelated products. This usually takes place through mergers and acquisitions. The benefits of diversification come largely from a broader product line, more complete utilization of resources, or possibly a better seasonal balance of operations.

There are disadvantages to diversification. Increased variety often means products must be manufactured in small volume using batch processing methods that are inherently more costly than high volume or assembly line methods. Costs for labor, materials, tooling, and setups are all increased. Furthermore, increased variety increases inventory levels for the manufacturer, distributor, and retailer, so supply problems are compounded.

Standardization

Standardization refers to the attempt to gain uniformity in the characteristics of a product such as size, shape, color, quantity, and performance. It also refers to uniformity in work methods, equipment, machine parts, procedures, and processes. The hidden costs of unnecessary variety include excess requirements for paperwork, records, space, and tools, as well as small production runs, high purchase prices, and additional order processing. Standardization makes possible mass production through interchangeability of parts.

Standardization plays an important economic role in production design. Nonstandard or specialized treatment is usually more costly because of its lower volume and individualized design. Standard materials, processes, methods, and packaging are highly desirable. Standardization permits interchangeability of parts and simplifies maintainability of the product. Procurement is easier and less production difficulties are encountered; inventory investment is less.

With standardization, parts and subassemblies can be used interchangeably, which reduces production cost without impairing quality. There is less design work and lower tooling cost. Items purchased outside are bought in large quantities to take advantage of price breaks. There are fewer purchase orders to process and fewer items to stock.

Standardization should not be confused with product simplification. Standardization deals with specific materials and processes applied to a given product, whereas simplification/diversification deals with the range of different products and their variety.

The four basic types of standards are (1) international standards, (2) national standards, (3) industry standards, and (4) company standards. Specific standards can be obtained from organizations that have developed them, such as:

National Bureau of Standards

American National Standards Institute (ANSI)

American Society for Testing and Materials

Underwriters' Laboratories

Society of Automotive Engineers

American Society of Mechanical Engineers

Federal Bureau of Specifications

National Lumber Manufacturers' Association

Modularity

It is possible to achieve a broad product line and at the same time enjoy the fruits of standardization through the utilization of modular design. Modularity involves the development of component "building blocks" that can be assembled in many different combinations and configurations in order to provide a variety of products. The essence of modularity is to design, develop, and produce parts which can be combined in a multitude of ways (maximize the combinatorial variety of assemblies). It provides reasonably high product variety and low component variability at the same time. It is an attempt to reconcile the need for product diversification with low processing cost.

Each individual order can be translated into a unique assembly configuration. Although each assembly is unique, the final product is composed of standardized parts and components. Modularity provides for uniformity and high volume production of parts. The uniformity of parts pleases the production department, while the product variety pleases the marketing department. Potential conflicts between production and marketing are thus overcome. Modularity permits a much greater variety at a reasonable cost than would otherwise be possible. The classic example is today's automobile, which is produced to customer order, but it is made up of standardized parts.

Value Analysis

Value analysis aims at ensuring that every element of cost contributes proportionately to the function of the product. The goal is to improve the product at a given cost, or to provide the same or better performance at lower cost without impairing quality or reliability. Although value analysis is important in initial design, it is also useful in redesign, changes in processing methods, and selection of components and materials. The usual approach is as follows:

1. Divide the product into separate parts and operations.
2. Establish the cost of each part and operation.
3. Determine the relative value of each part or operation to the product.
4. Search for a new approach to high-cost, low-value items.

Value analysis will be more thoroughly covered in Chapter 21 on purchasing and procurement.

DRAWINGS AND SPECIFICATIONS

The final release of engineering drawings and specifications terminates product decisions. There will be engineering drawings for each part or component, for each subassembly, and for the final assembly (end item). For example, an exploded assembly drawing of a water pump is shown in Figure 4. Of course, various types of engi-

FIGURE 4
Exploded assembly drawing.

WATER PUMP

NO.	REQ.	DESCRIPTION
1	4	$\frac{5}{8}$"x1" HEX-HEAD BOLTS
2	1	OUTLET FLANGE
3	2	STEEL BALLS
4	1	PUMP BODY
5	1	PACKING RING
6	1	PUMP PACKING GLAND
7	1	PUMP PLUNGER
8	1	COTTER PIN

NO	REQ	DESCRIPTION
9	1	PLUNGER BOLT
10	1	ECCENTRIC STRAP
11	1	ECCENTRIC (INSIDE)
12	1	ECCENTRIC (OUTSIDE)
13	1	FLAT HEAD SCREW
14	1	CAMSHAFT REAR BEARING
15	2	NO.9 WOODRUFF KEYS
16	1	INTAKE FLANGE

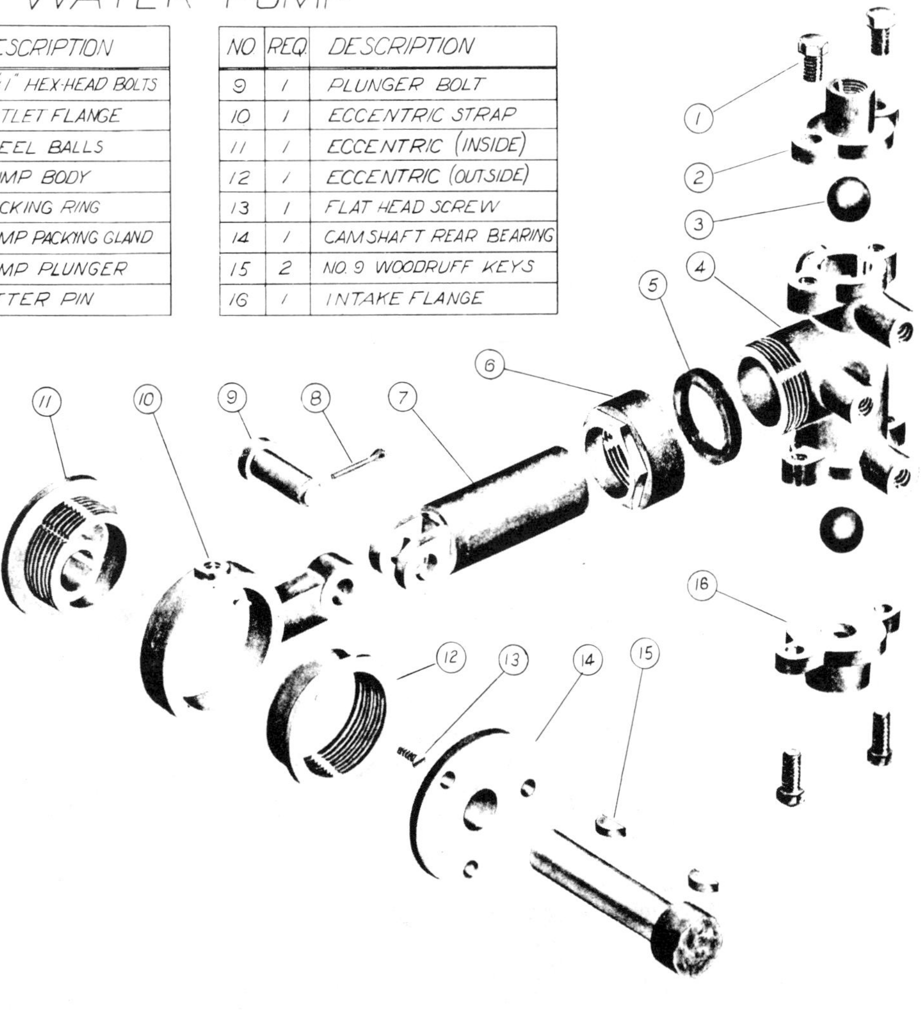

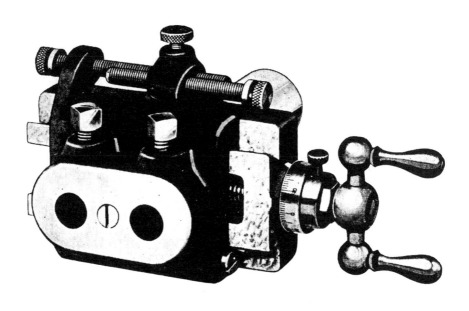

PARTS LIST

NO. OF SHEETS __2__ SHEET NO. __1__ MACHINE NO. *M-219*

NAME __NO. 4 SLIDE TOOL (SPECIFY SIZE OF SHANK REQ'D.)__

LOT NUMBER

NO. OF PIECES

TOTAL ON MACH	NO. PCS.	NAME OF PART	PART NO.	CAST FROM PART NO	TRACING NO	MATERIAL	ROUGH WEIGHT PER PC	DIA.	LENGTH	MILL	PART USED ON	NO.REQ FINISH
	1	Body	219-12		D-17417	A-3-S D.F.						
	1	Slide	219-6		D-19255	A-3-S D.F.					219-12	
	1	Nut	219-9		E-19256	#10 BZ.					219-6	
	1	Gib	219-1001		C-11129	S.A.E. 1020					219-6	
	1	Slide Screw	219-1002		C-11129	A-3-S					219-12	
	1	Dial Bush	219-1003		C-11129	A-1-S					219-1002	
	1	Dial Nut	219-1004		C-11129	A-1-S					219-1002	
	1	Handle	219-1011		E-18270	(Buy from Cincinnati Ball Crank Co.)					219-1002	
	1	Stop Screw (Short)	219-1012		E-51950	A-1-S					219-6	
	1	Stop Screw (Long)	219-1013		E-51951	A-1-S					219-6	
	1	Binder Shoe	219-1015		E-51952	#5 Brass					219-6	
	1	Handle Screw	219-1016		E-62322	X-1315 C.F.					219-1011	
	1	Binder Screw	219-1017		E-63927	A-1-S					219-6	
	1	Dial	219-1018		E-39461	A-1-S					219-1002	
	2	Gib Screw	219-1019		E-52777	A-1-S		$\frac{1}{4}$-20	1		219-6	
	1	Binder Screw	280-1010		E-24962	A-1-S					219-1018	
	2	Tool Clamp Screws	683-F-1002		E-19110	D-2-S					219-6	
	1	Fill. Hd. Cap Scr.	1-A			A-1-S		$\frac{3}{8}$	$1\frac{3}{8}$		219-6 219-9	
	1	Key	No.404 Woodruff								219-1002	

FIGURE 5
Slide tool and parts list.

neering drawings and product specifications may be required. The product specifications will include any special verbal instructions that are not conveyed by the engineering drawings. The drawings and specifications completely define the product. The specifications indicate the functional characteristics of the item and how it should perform. The engineering drawings or blueprints will contain the following information:

1. materials,
2. material standards,
3. dimensions,
4. tolerances,
5. surface finishes.

For service systems, the equivalent of an engineering drawing is a detailed statement of methods and procedures. Depending upon the type of product, the complete design may be presented in drawings, formulas, description sheets, bills of material, or other types of specifications.

Engineering drawings contain a bill of materials or parts list, as shown in Figure 5, to identify each item in the product. It usually shows the way a product is constructed from parts into subassemblies and then into the final assembly. The bill of materials for each product will be a basic production planning document to determine what parts, supplies, and components must be available before production can be scheduled. Bills of materials will be discussed in more detail in Chapter 17 on material requirements planning.

Configuration management identifies and documents the configuration of a product through its life cycle. It documents all the changes to a product. Product changes are manifested through formal revisions to drawings and specifications.

COMPUTER-AIDED DESIGN (CAD)

In the past, product designs had to be laboriously drawn, component by component, and numerous revisions were required as changes were made. Designs had to be tested with prototypes, and significant delays were encountered while design errors and component mismatches were corrected. Any problems discovered during prototype testing required design changes and expensive rework.

In an attempt to reduce costs and speed up the new product development process, many organizations are using computer-aided design (CAD), that is, design executed with a computer on a video screen. A CAD system uses a typewriter-like alphanumeric keyboard for entering command statements and input data. In addition, devices are used to create and manipulate images on a CRT screen. These devices include a lightpen applied directly to the screen, a pencil-like electronic stylus maneuvered on a sensitized tablet, joysticks, pushbuttons, or thumbwheels. As the user creates the CRT image with any of these devices, the coordinated data are stored in the memory. The computer is programmed to combine geometric and numerical data so the sketch can be transformed rapidly into a precise engineering drawing and displayed graphically on the screen. Modifications and design changes can be easily made and rapidly incorporated. When the design is completed, the engineer can request that paper drawings be printed using a plotter. The new technology is simplifying the engineering tasks required for new product development.

CAD originally was envisioned as a sophisticated drafting tool that could improve productivity. Instead of designing by drawing lines on a piece of paper, designers "draw" electronically on a screen. Once the drawing is completed, the computer allows the designer to rotate objects and look at them in any orientation, at any scale, in any cross section. The boring repetitive details are minimized, and the designer is free to concentrate on more creative aspects of design.

Perhaps the most impressive aspect of CAD is its capability of electronically assembling components and testing a design. CAD can simulate the performance characteristics of the product. Engineering analysis can be performed on several design alternatives. The product's response to various kinds of stresses can be ascertained. Since the computer can tell the designer what would happen under certain performance conditions, it allows the testing of new ideas before expensive prototypes are built. If a part is to be mated with other parts during assembly, the designer can move the parts about on the screen to check for compatibility, tolerance, and suitability for intended use. Alternative designs can be quickly tested and compared. Hence many prototypes and engineering models can be eliminated. The overall influence of CAD is a superior product design and a substantially shorter product development lead time. Vastly increased productivity is the most attractive feature of CAD systems.

SERVICE DESIGN

In the United States, over half of the employed people are engaged in producing services rather than goods. Typical service industries include government, education, transportation, finance, health care, and so forth. In a service organization, the service it renders is the actual product. Services are usually more esoteric and less subject to exact definition than the design of a physical good. Actually "services" covers a broad variety of activities not directly involving a physical product.

In many ways, producing services and producing physical products are similar. However, service industries usually place heavy emphasis on the personnel needed to provide the service. In other words, they tend to be labor intensive rather than capital intensive. Services are usually perishable and cannot be stockpiled (an empty airline seat does not translate into an additional seat on the next day).

Both service and goods producing organizations are interested in service levels. A *service level* is the ability to meet customer demands, usually expressed as a percentage of demands met. Goods producing organizations meet their customer demand from goods carried in inventory. Thus, they have more flexibility in scheduling their operations. Service organizations have to strike a balance between the cost of making customers wait and the cost of idle personnel or facilities. Services cannot rely on inventories, so they adjust their service levels by adding personnel and/or facilities.

Services do not have actual drawings, but they do have specifications. These tend to be more imprecise due to the variability of services and their strong dependence on human factors. The service time in a restaurant, at an airline counter, or at a bank typically displays considerable variability from customer to customer because of unique requirements. As services become more standardized, however (fast food outlets, medical laboratories, and machine-operated bank services), specifications approach the precision found in manufactured products. Services are greatly affected by the number of servers, the abilities and pace of the servers, the length of the waiting line, the physical layout of the service facility, and the variety of the services rendered.

The difficulty in discussing service organizations is due to their broad diversity. They are a potpourri of organizations, each having its own pecularities. However, queuing theory and simulation can be powerful tools of analysis in establishing economic levels of service for such organizations.

CONCLUSION

Product design and development (product decisions) rarely follow the concise, discrete sequences suggested herein. Typically, there are frequent recycling loops to prior steps, and certain activities may be performed out of sequence or concurrently. The extent of formalization varies from organization to organization and depends upon the type of product being developed.

If existing facilities will be used to produce a product, the product design will be influenced by the capabilities of the existing production system. If new facilities are to be acquired, the number of product design alternatives is increased or, at least, not limited by existing capabilities. Thus, there is a strong interaction between product design and the design of the production system. Product decisions will influence process decisions and vice versa. The decision process tends to be more iterative than segmented.

A customer rarely buys merely a physical product. Other attributes of the transaction include delivery, credit terms, return privileges, repair services, operating instructions, and the like. Problems dealing with prices, channels of distribution, discounts, guarantees, and maintenance must be solved. Salesmen, service men, and field representatives directly influence the image of an organization and its products. Thus, every "good" really contains a "service" component.

The degree of effort spent on product decisions will be related to the expected value of benefits. For high volume products, the effort may be tremendous; for low volume products it may be minimal. In very small organizations, one person may be responsible for the whole range of decisions. In large organizations, a large number of people from numerous departments may be involved.

QUESTIONS

1. What are product decisions and what do they entail?
2. Briefly describe the concept of a product life cycle, and name the four common life cycle states.
3. What are the two types of research? Describe each type.
4. Name the five subdivisions of applied research.
5. Describe the development process.
6. What are the three functional areas of engineering? Briefly describe each.
7. What are the basic inputs to detailed design, and what area of product decisions do they come from?
8. What are the coexisting activities comprised in detailed design?
9. What is meant by functional design and what are its major concerns?
10. Define form design and list its major features with regard to consumer goods.
11. What major factors influence the type of packaging selected?
12. Briefly describe the most important considerations in production design.
13. What information can be obtained from engineering drawings or blueprints?
14. Name four major product strategies.
15. What are the advantages of CAD for new product development?

PROBLEMS

1. A manufacturer is considering the production of a new type of clock-radio. Demand for the unit is expected to be at least 12,000 units. The research department has developed the following equation for the cost of production for each 100 units produced (relevent production range is 6,000 to 12,000 units):

$$C = 40Q^2 - 6400Q + 480,000 = \text{total cost,}$$

where Q = number of units produced in hundreds. In order to minimize the cost of production, how many units should be produced? What is the cost per unit at the minimum cost of production?

2. At a meeting of the Corporate Planning Board a proposal is submitted to add a new line of video recording equipment. An extensive analysis of the product has been completed, and the results are shown below. The cost of capital for the corporation is 12% and the tax rate is 50%. What is the net present value of the project? Should it be undertaken?

	Investment (thousands)
Production equipment	$1260[a]
Marketing expenses	175
Personnel (inclusive training)	35
Inventory	197
Total	$1667

Year	Sales (thousands)
1	$ 840
2	1250
3	1300
4	1050
5	900
6	480

[a]Depreciation is $210,000/year with direct expenses of $115,000/year. The cost of goods sold is 30% of yearly sales.

3. The research department of a large corporation determined the demand and cost functions for an electrical relay to be

$$Q = 64 - 2P,$$
$$TC = 144 + 12Q,$$

where

Q = quantity demanded in units,
P = price per unit,
TC = total cost.

Assume that the corporation is trying to maximize current profits and that the price of the relay will not affect the sale of other products. What price should be charged for the relay to maximize profit?

4. A young enterpreneur is considering investing $10,000 in a new type of snow removal machine. If the snowfall next winter is over thirty inches his product will be purchased by the city, and he will make a net profit of $25,000. If the snowfall is less than thirty inches he will lose $6,000. The chances of having over thirty inches of snow are 20%. The young man can invest his money for 6 months at 8% per year in another investment. Should he invest in the snow removal machine?

5. A large corporation has just completed design of a specialized pocket calculator designed to help shoppers convert to the metric system. The total factory cost per unit is $4.00. The customary markup in the pocket calculator industry is 100% above production cost. However, the executive vice president desires to know the effect of pricing above and below the normal markup price. The proposed alternatives are $12.00 and $6.75; the appropriate cash flows are projected below. If the cost of capital is 10% and the firm uses the net present value technique, what price should be selected?

	Net cash flows (thousands)		
Year	at $12.00	at $8.00	at $6.75
0	($1,200)	($1,800)	($2,300)
1	900	800	700
2	700	750	800
3	500	700	900
4	400	500	900
5	100	250	600
6	0	150	450
7	0	50	300

6. A manufacturer of all-purpose household cleaners is considering producing a new type of spray cleaner. The contribution margin is $.90 per unit, and the required investment in equipment is $350,000. Promotional expenses will be $90,000. The estimate of demand is as follows:

Demand (cases[a])	Probability
20,000	0.05
30,000	0.10
40,000	0.15
50,000	0.30
60,000	0.25
70,000	0.15
	1.00

[a]Of one dozen units.

Should the new product be produced? If the rate of return the manufacturer could earn on another investment is 25%, should the product be produced?

7. A manufacturer of processed soybean feed for livestock has derived the following demand and probability schedule for next season:

Quantity demanded (bushels)	Probability
10,000	0.20
20,000	0.20
30,000	0.20
40,000	0.20
50,000	0.20

The incremental cost is $18 per bushel, and the selling price is $28 per bushel. The processed feed will not keep and has a zero salvage value. The son of the manufacturer reasons, "Since there is equal chance of demand above and below 30,000 bushels, we should produce 30,000." How many bushels would you produce?

8. An airplane hydraulic control system consists of 3 units in series with reliabilities of $R_1 = 0.95$, $R_2 = 0.90$, and $R_3 = 0.92$. A failure of the system could result in loss of the aircraft.
   a. What is the reliability of the system?
   b. What would be the reliability with one backup system installed?
   c. What would be the reliability with two backup systems installed?

9. A manufacturer has determined that a drill press experiences a failure rate of 0.002 for every 1000 hours of operation. The mean time to repair (MTTR) is 5 hours.
   a. What is the number of failures per 1000 hours of operation?
   b. What is the average availability of the drill press?

10. An electronics manufacturer has designed a product containing a combination of series and parallel parts as shown below. What is the reliability of the product?

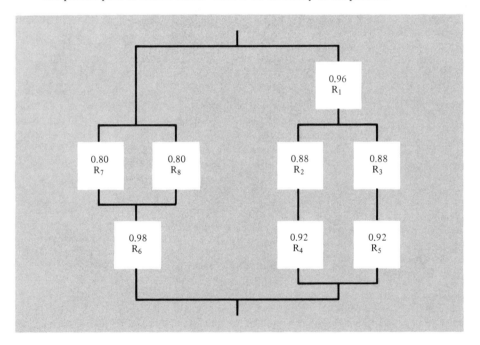

11. The manufacturer of a small radio places twelve radios on test for 3000 hours. Six fail after 300, 800, 900, 1200, 1900, and 2300 hours, respectively.
    a. What is the MTBF?
    b. What is the failure rate?
    c. How many failures can be expected in one year if 10,000 radios are sold and each is played two hours every day?

12. An automatic processing system is made up of 4 components as shown below.
    a. What is the reliability of the system?
    b. If an interconnection is installed between points A and B, is the reliability of the system changed?

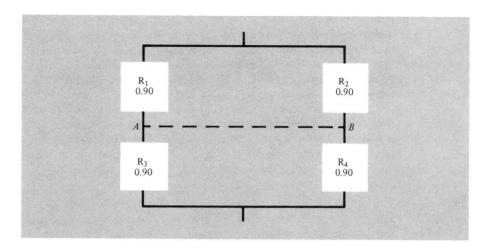

13. An electrical manufacturer desires to determine the reliability of a new type circuit breaker. Four hundred circuit breakers were placed on test. The results of the test are shown below.

No. of operations	No. of failures	No. of operations	No. of failures
0–1,000	20	8,000–9,000	10
1,000–2,000	18	9,000–10,000	9
2,000–3,000	17	10,000–11,000	8
3,000–4,000	16	11,000–12,000	7
4,000–5,000	15	12,000–13,000	6
5,000–6,000	13	13,000–14,000	6
6,000–7,000	12	14,000–15,000	5
7,000–8,000	11		173

a. What is the probability that a circuit breaker will fail between 5000 and 6000?
b. What is the probability that a circuit breaker will fail between 5000 and 15,000?
c. If the circuit breaker is designed to operate 12,000 times, what is its reliability?

14. The reliability of a hydraulic press is determined to be 0.88 for a designed operating time of 10,000 hours. A failure of the hydraulic press will cost $28,000. The reliability of the press can be increased to 0.96 by 20 hours of preventive maintenance at a cost of $65.00 per hour. Should be preventive maintenance be performed?

15. A part can be fabricated from three metals: brass, steel, or aluminum. The same machinery and equipment can be used for either metal, but the machining rates are different. In addition, the part made of steel requires a surface finish to retard rusting and corrosion. Estimates of time and costs are as follows:

	Steel	Aluminum	Brass
Raw material cost (per pound)	$0.50	$0.80	$1.00
Gross weight per part (pounds)	2.	1.5	1.75
Labor cost (per machine hour)	$15.00	$15.00	$15.00
Machine time per part (hours)	0.8	0.5	0.6
Surface finishing (hours)	0.2	0	0
Labor cost for finishing (hours)	$20.00	$20.00	$20.00
Overhead rate (per machine hour)	$40.00	$20.00	$20.00

Which material results in the lowest total cost per part?

CASE 1: ZIRON—A BLURRED IMAGE

Ziron, the preeminent power in the plain paper duplicator business, is losing its fast hold on the copier market. The company's market share has been trimmed from 65% to 40% in just five years. It also is beset with declining profit increases. In a previous ten-year span, Ziron's net income grew 25% yearly on 30% annual revenue gains. In the next five years, revenues grew 15% a year while earnings grew 13%. For the nine months just ended, Ziron revenues increased 9% and net income rose 8.5%. To contribute to its abated earnings increases, Ziron has acquired a number of "hi-tech" companies—the most successful of which lie outside the reprographics and office machines fields. Ziron's estimated income (in millions of dollars) is shown below:

	19X7	19X6	19X5	19X4
Reprographics				
Rentals and services	$4900	$4850	$4300	$3850
Sales	1370	1200	990	790
Operating profit	1280	1400	1300	1150
Other businesses[a]				
Rentals and services	420	410	350	300
Sales	1500	1250	950	750
Operating profit	140	130	110	110
Ziron, Inc. &				
Subsidiaries				
Total operating revenue	8700	8200	7000	6000
Net income	670	620	570	490

[a]Includes the Office Systems Group in addition to supplies, toner, publishing, etc.

Copiers and other reprographic products still provide nearly 80% of total revenue. These products now compete with some 240 various models of 40 competitor companies. Revenues of competitors accrue mainly from sales, whereas Ziron has rented or leased as much as 90% of its units. Foreign competition has established a national network of dealers and distributors which successfully attract small businesses as first-time purchasers. The low-volume end of the market (customers who make less than three to ten thousand copies per month) has gone from renting domestic copiers to owning foreign products, because the imports reduce production costs by at least 20%, have a perfected liquid toner process, and sell for 50% under the nearest Ziron product. After witnessing 80% of the new business in the low-volume market pass into foreign competitors' hands, Ziron has countered with pricing plans on low-volume copiers that should attract some new buyers. It also has introduced a number of new products and its first low-cost unit in fifteen years.

Corporate officials drafted a new copier-duplicator sales structure that is divided into smaller, more independently managed units. The sale of individual component machines (those not sold as part of an integrated office system) is organized under the Business Machine Group (BMG). The BMG is composed of two main divisions: the Office Products Division (OPD) markets reprographic equipment, and the Information Services Division (ISD) is responsible for more specialized component products and services. Both divisions are divided further into marketing operations for large and small accounts.

The company is experimenting with a number of sales and distribution methods. Following the foreign lead, it has widened its own dealer-distribution network and introduced direct mail and telemarketing. Even though the firm has been pleased with the effectiveness of the direct sales approach, it is cutting part of the sales force and retraining the rest in order to rebalance direct and indirect selling. The paring of salaried salespeople and the move to part-time straight-commission personnel is based on rising wages of direct sales staff and manpower requirements in its expanded retail chain.

Even with these changes, Ziron's low-volume sales stand a chance of retaining only 30% of the market. The situation is different at medium and high volume. Ziron holds 38% at the medium level and 70% at the high level. However, competition is seen to be getting stronger in both segments. In the medium range, competitors are starting to use techniques similar to those used for their remarkable success with the low-volume business. Consequently, Ziron has taken price reductions on three medium-volume models and increased the cost of service maintenance agreements. At the high end, one domestic firm is said to have a superior product and is announcing a price increase on this model. Ziron plans no countermove. Since Ziron spearheaded extensive services and support networks to accompany sales and rentals at the high-price end, management is sure that the company's fine reputation in these areas will remain as its competitive edge over other high-volume vendors.

As opposed to component sales and service, the other main product group at Ziron centers around complete office automation. The Office Systems Group (OSG) offers technology for tying office systems together and has products which include word processors, personal computers, professional workstations, and electronic typewriters. The outlook for Ziron integrated systems is more favorable than for its copiers with respect to growth. The company's integrated systems are expected to grow at least 25% annually compared to its overall copier growth of 13% (Ziron's projections range from a 10% growth rate at the low end to a 15% rate at the high end, while the industry average is expected to be 18% overall). Although the objective of OSG is to become a complete systems supplier for the electronic office of the future, the group has shown only one profitable quarter in its six-year history and lost $40 million during the last fiscal year.

Thus, the principal product groups are struggling. The older line is trying to retain a large portion of the industry share it once held. The new product group is fighting to secure a role in what could become a lucrative field in the future. Both are vying for position in highly competitive areas.

1. Describe Ziron's principal product groups (include analysis of product positioning, life cycle, etc).
2. What might be appropriate strategies for the product lines?
3. Make other recommendations and/or observations concerning the competitive office products field.

CASE 2: PHOTO-ALCHEMY

Five years ago a British conglomerate bought 55% of Blomquist Chemical Corporation's shares and initiated a hard-fought turnaround of the failing chemical company. The parent corporation now has 65% of the stock and is restructuring Blomquist by trimming costs, closing inefficient plants, upgrading production, and realigning management. Recently a marketing VP was promoted to company president, three marketing divisions were split into five, and five company executives were appointed to serve jointly as marketing VPs and divisional general managers.

Blomquist generally has tried to enter markets where there are a limited number of competitors, no matter what their relative strength or dominance. When Blomquist enters an area, it tries to hit the market with something new. In the graphics business, Blomquist introduced itself with the first liquid developer when others still were using powder mixes. The company now claims 10% of the whole market and remains second only to the industry giant, Kodiak. Most of the revenue earned by the Photo-Graphics Division comes from sales of developers and fixers to the photo-processing and graphic-arts industries, and the division's salespeople regularly call on large clients such as Berkey, Fotomat, Technicolor, and Colorcraft. Blomquist's Photo-Graphics Division provides nearly one-third of the company's sales and has experienced less prosperity than usual as sales of photo-finishing chemicals and products have been relatively flat. The sales plateau is a consequence of a recessionary climate and is not a phenomenon unique to Blomquist. All industries connected with photographic equipment or photoprint finishing have sustained stagnant revenues during the cyclical downswing. In preparation for the upswing, the division is considering other stirring entries into related technological fields.

One concept under consideration is a direct investment in the latest photo-finishing market, the minilab. These labs are small retail outlets that process film in-house in less than 1 hour. These quick-finish enterprises have 8% of the print processing business in less than three years and expect to command 25% within two more years. Blomquist presently has made half of the sales of developers to the 1300 operating minilabs. Blomquist has outflanked others in developer sales by offering the minilabs a bimonthly newsletter with technical tips, a toll-free hotline for technical advice, regular monthly seminars on processing for lab employees, and a national network to market products especially packaged for the labs. Now this is not enough. Since Blomquist has heard that Kodiak will open its own minilab program, it wants to do the same. The marketing management feels this is necessary even though the company has been able to maintain strong bonds not only with minilab managers but with Noritsu, the original equipment supplier to the majority of the 1300 minilabs.

In keeping with a policy of introducing new concepts as a way to enter and substantially change a market, Blomquist is planning an investment in the micro minilab market. The micro units will be manufactured abroad and marketed through the domestic network. The new equipment will be able to process photos of quality similar to the standard minilabs but will be only the size of a desktop copier. They probably will be sold to diverse retailers such as dry cleaners, drug stores, beauty shops, etc., and will cost $30,000, compared to $250,000 for a conventional minilab. Even without a direct investment in the concept, Blomquist will be the sole supplier of pre-packaged chemicals for the units, since other suppliers have shown no interest.

Revenue growth for silver-based products should be good once the upswing starts. Profits have been robust in the past as long as conventional photography has enjoyed increasing enthusiasm. Blomquist is married to standard camera technology, and the new disc cameras will make use of the minilab processes. The only blotch on the company pro formas is the possibility of electronic photography. The video-based, "filmless," systems may catch on, but Blomquist marketing personnel think the impact will be minimal for at least a decade.

1. Discuss Blomquist product strategies.
2. Describe Blomquist's opportunities to get in on the ground floor of the minilab market.
3. How is Blomquist trying to place itself on the leading edge of technology? How aggressive should or can the company be?

SELECTED BIBLIOGRAPHY

Asimow, M. *Introduction to Design,* Englewood Cliffs, NJ: Prentice-Hall, 1966.

Gorle, P. and J. Long. *Essentials of Product Planning,* New York: McGraw-Hill, 1973.

Goslin, L. N. *The Product-Planning System,* Homewood, IL: Irwin, 1967.

Leech, D. J. *Management of Engineering Design,* New York: Wiley, 1972.

Miles, L. D. *Techniques of Value Analysis and Engineering,* New York: McGraw-Hill, 1972.

Ostrofsky, B. *Design, Planning, and Development Methodology,* Englewood Cliffs, NJ: Prentice-Hall, 1977.

Starr, M. K. *Product Design and Decision Theory,* Englewood Cliffs, NJ: Prentice-Hall, 1963.

Tersine, R. J. "Forms of Industrial Research, Development, and Engineering," *Industrial Marketing Management,* Vol. 6, No. 6, 1977.

8

Network Programming and Project Planning

NETWORK DEVELOPMENT

DETERMINATION OF ACTIVITY TIMES

ESTABLISHMENT OF CRITICAL PATH

PROBABILISTIC STATEMENTS

PROJECT CONTROL

PERT/COST

CONCLUSION

QUESTIONS

PROBLEMS

CASES

SELECTED BIBLIOGRAPHY

A network is a view of a system that depicts the interconnections and interactions of its various constituents. Network programming is a useful systems technique for identifying and recognizing relationships among interdependent subsystems. It is a valuable tool for system design, analysis, and control that permits continuous reevaluation of a program. Network programming provides a vehicle for assessment of existing systems and a framework for the design of new systems.

A special project is a unique product or service which requires significant resources to accomplish an objective in a limited period of time. It typically involves one-of-a-kind, large scale, terminable, and nonrepetitive production. Areas of application are in the construction of highways, bridges, tunnels, dams, pipelines, airports, ships, planes, missiles, skyscrapers, homes, processing plants, amusement parks, camping grounds, and refuges. It is also used for R&D projects (new products, space shuttles, weapon systems, etc.), conferences, motion pictures, conventions, banquets, political campaigns, advertising campaigns, and organizational audits. Most projects are designed for a limited lifetime. The usual life cycle is characterized by an early buildup of resources, a leveling off as work nears completion, and a cutting back as project termination approaches.

A special project is used for unique, one-time production. It applies to a wide range of manufacturing and service situations. Organizations often use special teams or organizational structures for such undertakings. It is not uncommon for a special project to take months or even years to complete.

Program evaluation and review technique (PERT) is the most popular type of network programming for planning, scheduling, and controlling complex projects which occur infrequently.[1] A PERT network is a schematic model that depicts the sequential relationships among the tasks that must be completed to accomplish a project. It can determine the total expected time to complete a project and identify "bottleneck" activities that have a critical effect on project completion.

PERT focuses on the project as a whole, with regard to coordination of work activities, schedules, and resource deployment. The network approach provides a means of dovetailing the totality of activities, problems, decisions, and operations that constitute a project. PERT contributes directly to the optimum utilization of resources, particularly time, manpower, and money.

Perhaps its greatest benefit is that it forces the manager to plan the project in explicit detail. After the project is planned, the technique can be used throughout the project lifetime as a control mechanism. Periodically, it can be used to monitor progress and call attention to any delays that threaten the successful completion of the project. Additionally, it can assist in making decisions concerning time and cost tradeoffs of specific project activities.

Two basic types of PERT are PERT/TIME and PERT/COST. On any given project, two significant variables are time and resources (personnel, equipment, funds). The time required for project completion is dependent upon resource utilization. Additional resources allocated to a project can reduce the completion time; resource reduction can result in project elongation. PERT/TIME assumes that resources are at a given level (or unlimited) and considers time as the only relevant network variable. PERT/COST considers time and cost as variables and attempts to obtain an optimum

---

[1]PERT and its variant CPM are essentially the same. Since the terms are used almost interchangeably, we will use the more common term PERT.

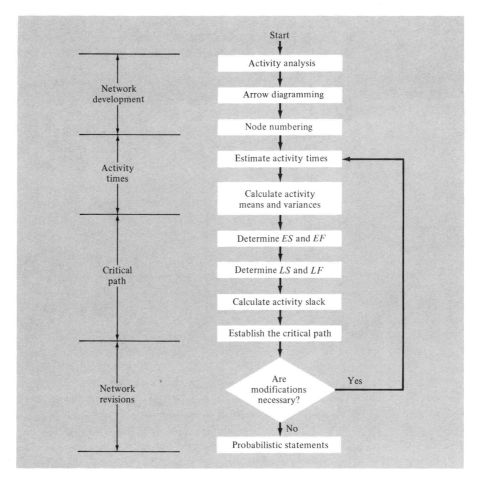

FIGURE 1
The PERT procedure.

tradeoff. PERT/COST begins where PERT/TIME ends. It determines if it is advantageous to shorten activity times by applying additional resources.

The PERT procedure is outlined in Figure 1. It requires the decision maker to develop the network, determine activity times, establish the critical path, and make network revisions.

NETWORK DEVELOPMENT

A network depicts the sequence of activities necessary to complete a project. It provides a composite picture of an entire undertaking. The development of a PERT network may be divided into three phases:

1. *Activity analysis*. This involves a detailed delineation of the operations, work methods, and subtasks that must be performed to complete the project. Essen-

tially, the total project is subdivided into activities. An activity is any portion of a project that consumes time and resources and has an identifiable beginning and end. Activity analysis breaks a project down into its component operations to form a complete list of essential activities.

2. *Arrow diagramming*. This develops a graphical network representation of the project that shows the precedence relationships among the activities. It requires a knowledge of which activities must be completed before other activities can be started, which activities can be performed in parallel, and which activities immediately succeed other activities. Precedence requirements specify the order or sequence in which the various activities can be performed.

FIGURE 2
Common PERT network symbolisms.

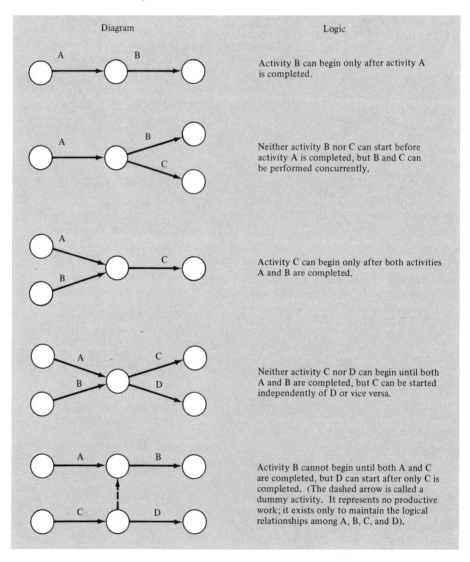

Diagram	Logic
	Activity B can begin only after activity A is completed.
	Neither activity B nor C can start before activity A is completed, but B and C can be performed concurrently.
	Activity C can begin only after both activities A and B are completed.
	Neither activity C nor D can begin until both A and B are completed, but C can be started independently of D or vice versa.
	Activity B cannot begin until both A and C are completed, but D can start after only C is completed. (The dashed arrow is called a dummy activity. It represents no productive work; it exists only to maintain the logical relationships among A, B, C, and D).

An *activity* is the work necessary to complete a particular event, and it usually consumes time and resources. An *event* is a point in time (a milestone), and its occurrence signifies the completion of all activities leading up to it. All activities originate and terminate at events; they are identified by their start and end events. Several activities may emanate from or lead into an event. Activities are normally represented by arrows or lines in a network, while events are represented by circles or nodes. Each arrow symbolizes a distinct activity and connects two events. Each event is a specific point in time marking the beginning and/or end of an activity. The sequence of activity arrows shows the expected consecution of the work effort.

Dummy activities, which are assigned zero performance time, are used to facilitate node numbering (differentiate activities with the same starting and ending nodes) and to provide logical sequencing relationships that cannot be shown otherwise. Dummy activities are represented by a dashed arrow in a network. See Figure 2 for common PERT network symbolisms.

3. *Node numbering*. Each activity arrow is identified by its tail *(i)* and head *(j)* numbers. The nodes are numbered so that for each activity *i* is always less than *j (i < j)*. The numbers for each arrow are progressive, and no backtracking through the network is allowed. This convention in node numbering is useful in computer programs to develop the logical network relationships and to prevent cycling. Each activity should have a different *i-j* number for identification purposes. Computerized PERT systems usually identify activities only by their beginning and ending node numbers.

Certain basic rules apply to PERT network development. There is only one initial (starting) event and one terminal (ending) event. Arrows imply logical sequencing only, and their length has no significance. There can be no doubling back, no loops, and no either-or options. Before an activity begins, all activities or paths leading to its start must be completed. Networks are easier to check if all arrows flow from left to right and as many arrow crossovers as possible are eliminated. Unnecessary (redundant) dummies do not impair the logic of the network, but they do create extra calculations and network complications, and therefore should be avoided. Node numbers should not be assigned until the entire network is drawn and verified.

EXAMPLE 1

From the information given below construct a PERT network, labeling activities, activity times, and nodes.

Activity	Description	Immediate predecessors	Time (days)
A	Receive production authorization	—	0
B	Determine parts requirements	A	2
C	Determine production factors	B	4
D	Determine material availability	C	6
E	Determine manpower availability	C	3
F	Determine equipment availability	C	5
G	Prepare operation schedule	D,E,F	8
H	Prepare and issue shop forms	G	7

continued

EXAMPLE 1—*continued*

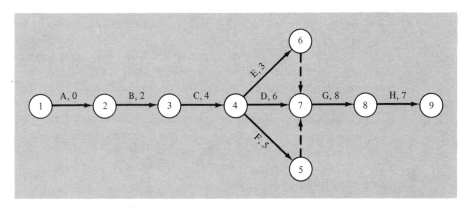

When sequencing events, several types of dependences between and among activities must be considered. Among them are natural, resource, and policy dependences. *Natural* or *technological dependence* occurs when one activity cannot take place until another is completed—for example, the roof cannot be put on a house until the frame has been erected. *Resource dependence* occurs when different activities require the use of the same resource and therefore cannot take place simultaneously. *Policy dependence* results from an organization's operational policies such as not beginning construction until all materials are on site.

DETERMINATION OF ACTIVITY TIMES

Activity time can be treated in one of two ways—either deterministically or probabilistically. Deterministic methods use a single time estimate for each activity; probabilistic methods use activity times that are derived from a probability distribution. The probability distribution of activity times is based on three time estimates for each activity, which may emanate from time studies, past performances, or educated guesses. The time estimates are obtained from people who have some knowledge about the work and the length of time it typically takes. Judgment and experience are vital ingredients in establishing time estimates.

A beta distribution is used to represent the probability distributions of uncertain activity times. The following three time estimates define the range and the mode of activity times:

1. *Optimistic (a)*. This is an estimate of the minimum time an activity will take— a result that can be obtained only if unusually good luck is experienced and everything "goes right the first time." As a general rule, there should be a 1% probability that the activity will take less time than the optimistic estimate.
2. *Pessimistic (b)*. This is an estimate of the maximum time an activity will take—a result that can occur only if unusually bad luck is experienced. It should not include "catastrophic events" or "acts of God" unless these hazards are inherent risks in the activity. As a general rule, there should be a 1% probability that the activity will take more time than the pessimistic estimate.

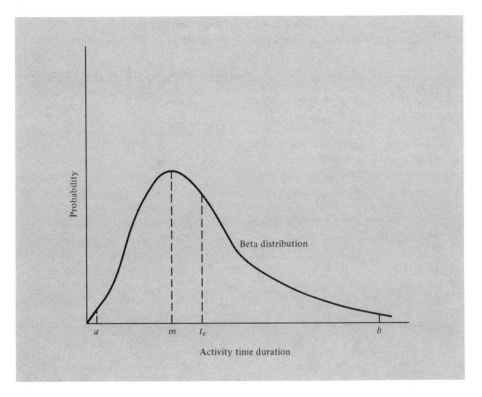

FIGURE 3
PERT activity times.

3. *Most likely (m)*. This is an estimate of the modal time an activity will take. It is the result that would occur most often if the activity could be repeated a number of times under similar circumstances.

The beta distribution is used in PERT to describe activity time duration because it is extremely flexible. It is a unimodal distribution that can acquire a wide variety of shapes between any two finite values. It can be made symmetrical, skewed, peaked, or flat, so as to describe many environmental phenomena. This flexibility of form renders the beta a useful distribution to fit to empirical data when no theoretical justification for another distribution exists. Also, the two parameters of the distribution (mean and standard deviation) can be easily approximated by conversion of the three time estimates. An illustration of beta distributed activity times is shown in Figure 3.

The three time estimates are reduced to a single expected time, t_e. Most PERT applications give the most likely time (m) a weight of four and the optimistic (a) and pessimistic (b) times a weight of one in arriving at the expected time. Thus the expected time and variance of each activity are calculated in the following manner:

$$t_e = \frac{a + 4m + b}{6} = \text{mean or expected time,}$$

$$s^2 = \left[\frac{b - a}{6}\right]^2 = \text{variance.}$$

The size of the variance reflects the degree of uncertainty associated with an activity's time. The larger the variance, the greater the uncertainty.

EXAMPLE 2

The three time estimates for an activity are as follows:

optimistic = 3 days,
most likely = 6 days,
pessimistic = 15 days.

What are the mean and standard deviation for the activity?

$$t_e = \frac{a + 4m + b}{6} = \frac{3 + 4(6) + 15}{6} = 7,$$

$$s = \frac{b - a}{6} = \frac{15 - 3}{6} = 2.$$

The mean is 7 days, and the standard deviation is 2 days.

Single time estimates for activity duration are appropriate when sufficient historical data are available. Expected time estimates for activity duration are appropriate for unfamiliar or experimental projects with insufficient historical data. After the single or expected time estimates are obtained for each activity, they are entered beside the appropriate activity arrow in the network.

ESTABLISHMENT OF CRITICAL PATH

With the PERT network completed and activity times estimated, it is a simple matter to develop the important schedule data for each activity and for the project as a whole. A path is a sequence of activities which leads from the starting node to the finishing node. The length of time for any path is the summation of the expected times of the activities on the path. The path with the longest time is called the critical path, and it is of particular interest because it governs the project completion time. If there are delays along the critical path, there will be corresponding delays in the project completion time.

To determine the critical path, it is necessary to obtain data on the earliest start and earliest finish times, the latest start and latest finish times, and the available slack:

1. *Earliest start and finish times.* The earliest start (ES) is the earliest time an activity can begin: when all preceding activities are completed. The earliest finish (EF) for each activity is its ES plus the activity time. When two or more parallel activities are immediate predecessors to another activity, the ES for the activity is the largest of the EF of its predecessors. In other words, the ES for an activity equals the latest EF of immediate predecessors to the activity.

This indicates that successor activities cannot begin until the completion of all prior activities. ES and EF are developed by starting with the first activity and working through the network to the final activity.

2. *Latest start and finish times*. The latest finish time (LF) of the project is the scheduled time when the total project must be completed. This date is often fixed independently of the network, from a date set by the customer or established by contract. The latest start time (LS) is the latest time at which an activity can be started if the project schedule is to be maintained. The latest start time of an activity is its LF minus the activity time. The LS and LF are developed by starting with the final activity and working backward through the network. To determine the LF for an activity that has two or more parallel successors, select the smallest LS of its successors. In other words, LF for an activity equals the earliest LS of the immediate successors for that activity.

3. *Slack*. After both the forward pass (ES, EF) and backward pass (LS, LF) have been completed, the slack can be computed for each activity. The total slack for an activity is the maximum time it can be delayed beyond its earliest start without delaying the completion of the total project. The slack will be the same for all activities on the critical path; activities along the critical path have zero total slack if the target completion date is the same as the earliest finish for the last network activity. *Total slack* is the difference between the latest start and the earliest start of an activity (LS-ES), or the difference between its latest finish and earliest finish (LF-EF). *Free slack* is the amount of time an activity can be delayed without delaying the earliest start of another activity. Free slack is the difference between the earliest finish of an activity and the earliest start of its immediate successor activities. The free slack for an activity is less than

FIGURE 4
Network time parameters.

1. EARLIEST START (ES):
   (a) Initial activity, $ES_{ij} = 0$
   (b) Successor activities, ES_{ij} = maximum EF of immediate predecessor activities
2. EARLIEST FINISH (EF):
   (a) Initial activity, $EF_{ij} = t_{ij}$
   (b) Successor activities, $EF_{ij} = ES_{ij} + t_{ij}$
3. LATEST FINISH (LF):
   (a) Terminal activity, LF_{ij}, management assigned
   (b) Predecessor activities, LF_{ij} = minimum LS of immediate successor activities
4. LATEST START (LS):
   (a) Terminal activity, $LS_{ij} = LF_{ij} - t_{ij}$
   (b) Predecessor activities, $LS_{ij} = LF_{ij} - t_{ij}$
5. TOTAL SLACK (TS):
   $TS_{ij} = LS_{ij} - ES_{ij} = LF_{ij} - EF_{ij}$
6. FREE SLACK (FS):
   (a) Terminal activity, $FS_{ij} = 0$
   (b) Predecessor activities, $FS_{ij} = (ES$ of immediate successors$) - EF_{ij}$

or equal to its total slack. Total slack is shared by all activities on a given path, while free slack refers exclusively to a single activity.

ES and EF times are developed by a forward pass (via addition) through the network. Calculation of LS and LF times reverse the procedure for ES and EF; they are obtained by a backward pass (via subtraction) through the network. The information obtained from the forward and the backward pass can be used to identify the critical path and to calculate slack. The total slack is the difference between the two start times or the two finish times; these differences are the same for each activity. All activities along the critical path will have the same amount of slack. It will either be zero or the minimum amount of slack for all the activities. The critical path activities are crucial to the on-time completion of the project, because a delay in any of them results in a delay in the entire project. They should receive the greatest amount of management attention. Network time parameters are outlined in Figure 4.

EXAMPLE 3

If the completion time for the project in Example 1 is 27 days, what are the ES, LS, EF, and LF for each activity?

The ES, LS, EF, and LF can be placed in a block adjacent to each activity in the format of $\boxed{\text{ES,LS} \mid \text{EF,LF}}$.

The ES and EF are determined by a forward pass (via addition) through the network. The EF of each activity is equal to the ES plus the activity time:

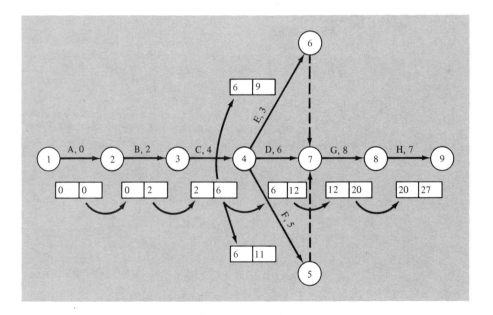

The LS and LF are determined by a backward pass (via subtraction) through the network. The LS of each activity is equal to the LF minus the activity time:

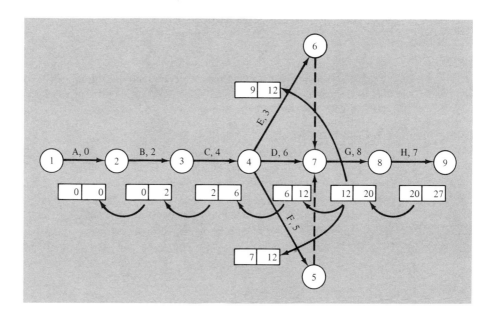

When moving forward (forward pass) in the network with activities *D*, *E*, and *F* converging on activity *G*, the ES for activity *G* is the largest EF, which is 12 days from activity *D*. When moving backward (backward pass) in the network with activities *D*, *E*, and *F* converging on activity *C*, the LF for activity *C* is the smallest LS, which is 6 days for activity *D*. The final network combines the forward pass and backward pass and appears as follows:

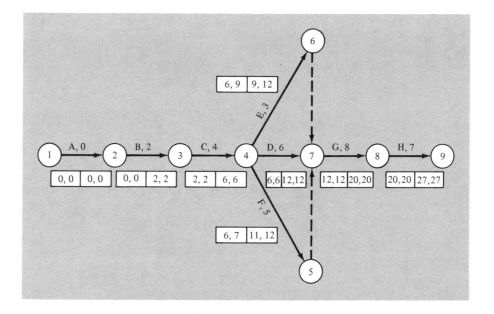

EXAMPLE 4

From the information given below develop a PERT network, labeling activities and activity times and nodes. If the target date for completion of the project is three days longer than the critical path time, calculate the earliest start, latest start, earliest finish, and latest finish for each activity, i.e.,

ES,LS	EF,LF

What activities are on the critical path? Give the total and free slack for each activity.

Activity	Immediate predecessors	Time (days)
a (start)	—	0
b	a	2
c	a	1
d	b	3
e	b	4
f	c	2
g	e,f	3
h	d	1
i (finish)	g,h	0

The PERT network is as follows:

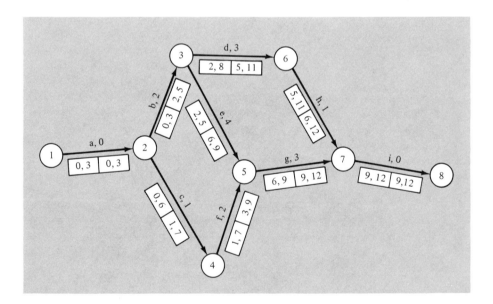

The earliest start is time 0, and you work through the network until the last activity. The LF for the project is three days longer than the EF of the last activity (i), so the LF for the project is 9 + 3 or 12. Note that the ES for activity g is the later earliest finish (EF) of its predecessors e and f, so it is the 6 from activity e. Note also that the LF for activity a is the smaller latest start (LS) of its successors b and c, so it is the 3 from activity b. The critical path contains those activities with three days of slack, and it is the path *a, b, e, g, i*. The total and free slack for each activity are as follows:

Activity	Total slack	Free slack	Critical path
a	3	0	*
b	3	0	*
c	6	0	
d	6	0	
e	3	0	*
f	6	3	
g	3	0	*
h	6	3	
i	3	—	*

On complex projects a computer is used to search the pathways and determine the critical path through the network. The critical path (the pathway that takes the longest time through the network) indicates the least time required to complete the total project. The project can only be shortened by reducing the time of the activities along the critical path. All the paths and activities that are not on the critical path contain slack.

The decision maker can shorten the project if he can utilize resources from noncritical path activities. Since noncritical path activities can be delayed without affecting the project completion time, the reallocation of resources to critical activities could result in a reduction in the lifetime of the project. Any delay or acceleration of critical path activities will directly affect the completion of the project.

PROBABILISTIC STATEMENTS

PERT allows the decision maker to develop probabilistic information concerning project completion. The completion times of every activity in the network are assumed independent of one another and beta distributed. When independent probability distributions are added together, the mean and variance of the resulting distribution are equal to the sums of the means and variances for the individual distributions. PERT makes use of the central limit theorem to conclude that the distribution of the overall project time will be normal. The duration time of the project is a random variable which is normally distributed around the project's expected duration. The mean of the normal distribution is the expected critical path time, and the variance is the sum of the variances for each activity along the critical path.

The probability of the project being completed within the expected critical path time is 0.5. Similarly, the probability of the project taking longer than the expected critical path time is 0.5. The normality assumption postulates the existence of a large number of independent random variables (activities on the critical path). For rough approximations, 30 random variables (activities) are usually considered acceptable.

The probability of a project requiring a given time for completion can be deter-

238

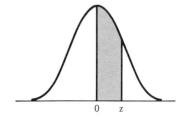

0   z

TABLE 1
Areas of a standard normal distribution[a]

z	0.00	0.01	0.02	0.03	0.04	0.05	0.06	0.07	0.08	0.09
0.0	0.0000	0.0040	0.0080	0.0120	0.0160	0.0199	0.0239	0.0279	0.0319	0.0359
0.1	0.0398	0.0438	0.0478	0.0517	0.0557	0.0596	0.0636	0.0675	0.0714	0.0753
0.2	0.0793	0.0832	0.0871	0.0910	0.0948	0.0987	0.1026	0.1064	0.1103	0.1141
0.3	0.1179	0.1217	0.1255	0.1293	0.1331	0.1368	0.1406	0.1443	0.1480	0.1517
0.4	0.1554	0.1591	0.1628	0.1664	0.1700	0.1736	0.1772	0.1808	0.1844	0.1879
0.5	0.1915	0.1950	0.1985	0.2019	0.2054	0.2088	0.2123	0.2157	0.2190	0.2234
0.6	0.2257	0.2291	0.2324	0.2357	0.2389	0.2422	0.2454	0.2486	0.2517	0.2549
0.7	0.2580	0.2611	0.2642	0.2673	0.2703	0.2734	0.2764	0.2794	0.2823	0.2852
0.8	0.2881	0.2910	0.2939	0.2967	0.2995	0.3023	0.3051	0.3078	0.3106	0.3133
0.9	0.3159	0.3186	0.3212	0.3238	0.3264	0.3289	0.3315	0.3340	0.3365	0.3389
1.0	0.3413	0.3438	0.3461	0.3485	0.3508	0.3531	0.3554	0.3577	0.3599	0.3621
1.1	0.3643	0.3665	0.3686	0.3708	0.3729	0.3749	0.3770	0.3790	0.3810	0.3830
1.2	0.3849	0.3869	0.3888	0.3907	0.3925	0.3944	0.3862	0.3980	0.3997	0.4015
1.3	0.4032	0.4049	0.4066	0.4082	0.4099	0.4115	0.4131	0.4147	0.4162	0.4177
1.4	0.4192	0.4207	0.4222	0.4236	0.4251	0.4265	0.4279	0.4292	0.4306	0.4319
1.5	0.4332	0.4345	0.4357	0.4370	0.4382	0.4394	0.4406	0.4418	0.4429	0.4441
1.6	0.4452	0.4463	0.4474	0.4484	0.4495	0.4505	0.4515	0.4525	0.4535	0.4545
1.7	0.4554	0.4564	0.4573	0.4582	0.4591	0.4599	0.4608	0.4616	0.4625	0.4633
1.8	0.4641	0.4649	0.4656	0.4664	0.4671	0.4678	0.4686	0.4693	0.4699	0.4706
1.9	0.4713	0.4719	0.4726	0.4732	0.4738	0.4744	0.4750	0.4756	0.4761	0.4767
2.0	0.4772	0.4778	0.4783	0.4788	0.4793	0.4798	0.4803	0.4808	0.4812	0.4817
2.1	0.4821	0.4826	0.4830	0.4834	0.4838	0.4842	0.4846	0.4850	0.4854	0.4857
2.2	0.4861	0.4864	0.4868	0.4871	0.4875	0.4878	0.4881	0.4884	0.4887	0.4890
2.3	0.4893	0.4896	0.4898	0.4901	0.4904	0.4906	0.4909	0.4911	0.4913	0.4916
2.4	0.4918	0.4920	0.4922	0.4925	0.4927	0.4929	0.4931	0.4932	0.4934	0.4936
2.5	0.4938	0.4940	0.4941	0.4943	0.4945	0.4946	0.4948	0.4949	0.4951	0.4952
2.6	0.4953	0.4955	0.4956	0.4957	0.4959	0.4960	0.4961	0.4962	0.4963	0.4964
2.7	0.4965	0.4966	0.4967	0.4968	0.4969	0.4970	0.4971	0.4972	0.4973	0.4974
2.8	0.4974	0.4975	0.4976	0.4977	0.4977	0.4978	0.4979	0.4979	0.4980	0.4981
2.9	0.4981	0.4982	0.4982	0.4983	0.4984	0.4984	0.4985	0.4985	0.4986	0.4986
3.0	0.4987	0.4987	0.4987	0.4988	0.4988	0.4989	0.4989	0.4989	0.4990	0.4990

[a]An entry in the table is the proportion under the entire curve which is between $z = 0$ and a positive value of z. Areas for negative values of z are obtained by symmetry.

mined by using a standard normal table where Z represents the deviation from the mean in standard deviation units, or

$$Z = \frac{T - T_e}{S},$$

where

$T_e = \Sigma t_{ec}$ = expected critical path time,
$S^2 = \Sigma s_c^2$ = critical path variance,
t_{ec} = expected time of a critical path activity,
s_c^2 = variance of a critical path activity.

The decision maker can determine the probability of a project being completed in time T by obtaining the Z-value in the above formula and consulting the standard normal table. The standard normal table will give the area under the normal curve that represents Z standard deviations from the mean. The areas of a standard normal distribution are given in Table 1.

EXAMPLE 5

Activity	Predecessor	Expected time t_e	Optimistic time a	Most likely time m	Pessimistic time b
A	—	8	7	8	9
B	—	12	5	10	27
C	—	7	5	7	9
D	A	3	1	3	5
E	A	12	5	13	15
F	A	5	4	4.5	8
G	C,F	4	3	3.75	6
H	C,F	2	1	2	3
I	B,D	7	4	6	14
J	B	9	6	8.5	14
K	E,G,I	6	4	6	8
L	H,K	10	3	10.5	15

Listed in the above table are activities, sequence requirements, and activity times for a project. The project completion date is 36 days after the project begins. Perform the following:

a. Draw the PERT network, labeling activities and computing ES, EF, LS, and LF for each activity.
b. Determine the critical path for the network as well as the total slack and free slack for each activity.
c. What is the probability the project will be completed within 34 days?
d. What is the probability the project will require more than 39 days for completion?

The following network contains the information for item a. The subsequent table contains the critical path, total slack, and free slack for item b.

continued

EXAMPLE 5—*continued*

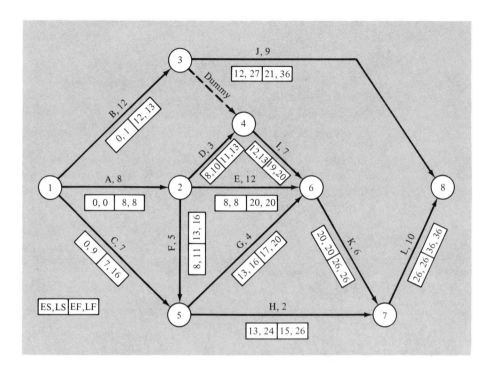

| | Sequence | | | | | Total slack | Free slack | Variance |
Activity	i	j	t_e	EF	LF	LF–EF		s^2
A^a	1	2	8	8	8	0	0	0.111
B	1	3	12	12	13	1	0	13.444
C	1	5	7	7	16	9	6	0.444
Dummy	3	4	0	12	13	1	0	—
D	2	4	3	11	13	2	1	0.444
E^a	2	6	12	20	20	0	0	2.777
F	2	5	5	13	16	3	0	0.444
G	5	6	4	17	20	3	3	0.250
H	5	7	2	15	26	11	11	0.111
I	4	6	7	19	20	1	1	2.777
J	3	8	9	21	36	15	—	1.777
K^a	6	7	6	26	26	0	0	0.444
L^a	7	8	10	36	36	0	—	4.000

[a]Activities along the critical path.

c: The probability of completion within 34 days is determined as follows:

$T_e = \Sigma t_{ec} = 8 + 12 + 6 + 10 = 36$ days,

$S^2 = \Sigma s_c^2 = 0.111 + 2.777 + 0.444 + 4.000 = 7.332,$

$Z = \dfrac{T - T_e}{S} = \dfrac{34 - 36}{2.71} = -0.74.$

From Table 1, a Z of 0.74 gives a probability of 0.2703. The probability of completion within 34 days is 0.2297 (0.5000 − 0.2703 = 0.2297).

d: The probability that the project will require more than 39 days to complete is determined as follows:

$$Z = \frac{T - T_e}{S} = \frac{39 - 36}{2.71} = 1.11.$$

From Table 1, a Z of 1.11 gives a probability of 0.3665. The probability of the project requiring more than 39 days is 0.1335 (0.5000 − 0.3665 = 0.1335).

PERT accounts for project time variability based only upon the critical path activities (it ignores noncritical path activities). A path which is shorter than the critical path could end up with a longer actual time than the critical path, particularly if its expected time is close to the critical path time and it has a large variance. When this condition occurs, Monte Carlo simulation can be employed to estimate the probabilities of different completion times.

PROJECT CONTROL

All projects go through planning, scheduling, and control phases. The planning phase establishes the objectives of the organization and the resources for the project. The scheduling phase establishes the time and resource assignments. Finally, the control phase monitors the progress of the project in terms of time, cost, and performance; it also corrects the plan as necessary to achieve project objectives. Replanning is inherent in control, and it is greatly facilitated by computerized information systems which are timely and accurate. The task of developing and updating project networks can become complex for projects of even moderate size.

After a project network is completed, management can answer the following questions:

1. What is the shortest time to complete the entire project?
2. Which activities are critical and must be monitored closely?
3. How much flexibility (slack) is there with noncritical activities?
4. Can resources be shifted from noncritical to critical activities?
5. If activity duration is uncertain (probabilistic), what is the probability of meeting specific schedule deadlines?

Once the project begins, the emphasis shifts to coordination and control. Effective project control requires quick and reliable feedback of the progress to date. Periodic revisions are necessary to update the network diagram in an attempt to anticipate "bottleneck" situations. Contingency planning is performed for resource diversion to alleviate bottlenecks which delay successor activities.

It is not uncommon to have multi-level diagrams with the highest level composed of only broad activities and the lowest level being detailed diagrams of each broad activity. The focus of management's attention is centered on critical and near-critical activities with emphasis on activities that can be rescheduled to improve resource utilization. As the project moves forward in time, there will be delays and unexpected occurrences that require network revision. When a significant discrepancy exists between actual results and the plan, corrective action should be taken. These corrective actions might include revision of the plan, reallocation of funds, personnel changes, and other changes in resources. As a result of corrective actions, the plan should once again be feasible and realistic.

PERT/COST

PERT/COST is an extension of basic PERT which focuses attention upon costs as well as time. It is concerned with how best to shorten a project's completion time. In many situations, it is possible to reduce the length of a project by injecting additional resources. The impetus to shorten projects may reflect efforts to avoid late penalties, to take advantage of monetary incentives for timely completion of a project, or to free resources for use on other projects. Additionally, project abbreviation may be an attempt to reduce indirect costs associated with the project such as supervision, labor and personnel costs, and facilities or equipment costs. Project length can be shortened by reducing individual critical activity times through the use of more personnel, more or better equipment, overtime, and so forth. Unfortunately, some activities cannot be shortened at all (cement takes a certain time to harden), so that no amount of money can reduce their activity times.

Basic PERT also deals with time and cost tradeoffs. If the overall time of a project can be shortened, costs may be reduced. When there are limited resources that can be utilized in these tradeoffs, one often can speed up an activity only at the expense of slowing down another. However, since some activities are "more critical" than others, such tradeoffs may improve overall project performance.

PERT/COST begins by focusing on those activities on the critical path, since shortening noncritical activities would not influence the total project duration. Critical activities are "crashed" by starting with the lowest cost per unit time first. The process continues to the next lowest cost activity as long as the cost to crash is less than the benefits received from crashing. When there are multiple critical paths, they must all be reduced simultaneously. After each critical activity is crashed, the critical path is shortened and must be redetermined, since the path may change. The analysis can get quite complicated, since the critical path often shifts and multiple critical paths frequently result.

Before crashing can commence, the following information is needed:

1. Regular time and crash time estimates for each activity.
2. Regular cost and crash cost estimates for each activity.
3. The list of activities on the critical path.

Critical activities are crashed in order of increasing costs as long as crashing costs do not exceed the benefits. Crashing activities reduces indirect project costs while increasing direct project costs. The optimum amount of crashing results in minimizing the sum of direct and indirect costs.

CONCLUSION

To utilize PERT all of the individual tasks to complete a given project must be put in a network consisting of events and activities. An event represents a specified activity accomplishment at a particular instant in time. An activity represents the time and resources that are necessary to progress from one event to the next. Emphasis must be placed on defining events and activities with sufficient precision so there is no difficulty in monitoring actual accomplishments as the project proceeds.

Events and activities must be sequenced in the network under a logical set of ground rules (technological order), which allow the determination of important critical and subcritical paths. No successor event can be considered completed until all of its predecessor events have been completed, and no looping is allowed. (Looping occurs when a successor event can have an activity dependence that leads back to a predecessor event.)

Time estimates are made for each activity of the network on a point estimate or a three-way basis (i.e., optimistic, most likely, and pessimistic). The three time estimates are a gauge of the uncertainty of the activity, and represent full recognition of the probabilistic nature of many of the tasks in nonrepetitive projects. The three time estimates are reduced to a single expected time and a variance, which are used to indicate the probability of meeting an established schedule date.

The important results of the calculations involved in PERT are the determination of the critical path and slack times for the network. The critical path is the longest time path through the system. It can be defined as that set of interrelated activities, the delay of any one of which would delay the project's completion by an equal amount of time. Slack means surplus time or "time to spare" on an activity. It provides an opportunity to transfer manpower, materials, equipment, or supervision to an activity that lies on the critical path, and thereby perhaps shorten the total project time. There can be slack on the critical path, but the critical path has the least arithmetic value of slack. An activity with slack time need not commence at its earliest possible schedule date; it can be delayed and still not hold up the project.

Manual calculations are feasible for smaller projects, but computer assistance is a necessity for larger ones. Computer programs for network programming are widely available.

There are numerous network scheduling techniques. In this chapter, the focus has been on PERT only. The reader interested in other techniques should consult the bibliography.

QUESTIONS

1. Name several areas of application for PERT.
2. What are the three basic phases in the development of a PERT network?
3. Define an activity. What is the purpose of activity analysis?
4. What is accomplished in arrow diagramming?
5. Differentiate between an activity and an event.
6. Explain the function of a dummy activity.
7. Describe the convention for node numbering in PERT, and state its use.
8. In what ways can activity times be derived for critical path scheduling techniques?
9. Why is the beta distribution chosen in PERT to represent activity time variation?
10. How is the expected time obtained from beta distributed activity times?
11. What is the significance of the critical path?
12. Distinguish between total slack and free slack.
13. What is meant by a "forward pass" and a "backward pass" through the network?

14. How can probability statements be made concerning completion times for the entire project?

15. What impact can noncritical activities have on project completion?

16. Explain the basis for time and cost tradeoffs in order to reduce project completion time.

17. How should the process for project reduction (crashing) be executed?

18. Develop a PERT network for the completion of a term paper.

19. List several projects in your area which might have used some type of network programming for planning and control.

PROBLEMS

1. What is the critical path time for a small maintenance project which consists of the following job activities?

Job	(Initial node, final node)	Estimated duration (days)
a	(1,2)	2
b	(2,3)	3
c	(2,4)	5
d	(3,5)	4
e	(3,6)	1
f	(4,6)	6
g	(4,7)	2
h	(5,8)	8
i	(6,8)	7
j	(7,8)	4

2. What is the earliest project completion time for the project listed below?

Activity	i,j	Estimated duration (days)
a	1,2	2
b	1,3	4
c	1,4	3
d	2,5	1
e	3,5	6
f	4,6	5
g	5,6	7

3. What is the critical path time for the following network?

Activity	i,j	Estimated duration (days)
a	1,2	7
b	1,6	6
c	2,3	14
d	2,4	5
e	3,5	11
f	4,5	7
g	6,7	11
h	5,8	4
i	7,8	18

4.

Activity	Immediate predecessor	Expected time t_e	Optimistic time a	Most likely time m	Pessimistic time b
A	—	3	2	3	4
B	A	6	4	6	8
C	A	5	4	4.75	7
D	—	5	3	5	7
E	C	2	1	2	3
F	D	8	7	8	9
G	B,E,F	6	5	6	7

Assume a project completion time of nineteen days after the project begins. From the above data, perform the following:
a. Draw the PERT network, labeling activities, and compute ES, EF, LS, and LF for each activity.
b. Determine the critical path for the network as well as the total slack and free slack for each activity.
c. What is the probability the project will be completed within seventeen days?
d. What is the probability the project will require more than twenty days for completion?

5.

Activity	Immediate predecessor	Expected time t_e	Optimistic time a	Most likely time m	Pessimistic time b
A	—	5	4	5	6
B	—	3	1	3	5
C	A	2	2	2	2
D	A	4	3	4	5
E	B	9	7	8	15
F	C	2	1	2	3
G	D,F	1	1	1	1
H	G	7	6	6	12
I	E,H	2	1	2	3

Assume a project completion time of nineteen days after the project begins. From the above data, perform the following:
a. Draw the PERT network, labeling activities, and compute ES, EF, LS, and LF.
b. Determine the critical path as well as the total slack and free slack.
c. What is the probability the project will be completed within eighteen days?
d. What is the probability the project will require more than twenty days?

6.

Activity	Immediate predecessor	Expected time t_e	Optimistic time a	Most likely time m	Pessimistic time b
A	—	6	5	6	7
B	—	5	2	5	8
C	A	8	6	7	14
D	B	2	1	2	3
E	C,D	3	3	3	3
F	B	8	6	8	10
G	E	4	1	4	7
H	F,G	5	4	5	6

Assume a project completion time of twenty-six days after the project begins. From the above data, perform the following:
a. Draw the PERT network, labeling activities, and compute ES, EF, LS, and LF.
b. Determine the critical path as well as the total slack and free slack.

c. What is the probability the project will be completed within twenty-four days?
d. What is the probability the project will require more than thirty days?

7.

Activity	Immediate predecessor	Optimistic time a	Most likely time m	Pessimistic time b
A	—	1	2	3
B	A	4	6	8
C	A	7	8	15
D	B	2	5	8
E	C,B	3	6	9
F	E	3	4	11
G	D	9	9	15
H	F,G	4	7	16

Assume a project completion time of thirty-one days after the project begins. From the above data, perform the following:
a. Draw the PERT network, labeling activities, and compute ES, EF, LS, and LF.
b. Determine the critical path as well as the total slack and free slack.
c. What is the probability the project will be completed within thirty days?
d. What is the probability the project will require more than thirty-three days?

8.

Activity	Immediate predecessor	Expected time t_e	Optimistic time a	Most likely time m	Pessimistic time b
A	—	7	4	6	14
B	—	8	7	8	9
C	A	3	3	3	3
D	A	7	5	6	13
E	D	6	5	6	7
F	B,C	5	2	5	8
G	B	9	7	8	15
H	E	2	1	2	3
I	G,F,H	1	1	1	1

Assume a project completion time of twenty-three days after the project begins. From the above data, perform the following:
a. Draw the PERT network, labeling activities, and compute ES, EF, LS, and LF.
b. Determine the critical path as well as the total slack and free slack.
c. What is the probability the project will be completed within twenty days?
d. What is the probability the project will require more than twenty-five days?

9.

Activity	Immediate predecessor	Optimistic time a	Most likely time m	Pessimistic time b
A	—	1	3	5
B	—	4	4	4
C	—	5	6	7
D	A	4	5	12
E	C	3	3.5	7
F	B,C,D	2	5	8
G	B	4	5.5	10
H	E	6	8	10
I	F,H	1	2	3
J	F,G	3	4	5
K	G	7	8	9
L	I,J,K	3	4	5

Assume a project completion time of twenty-four days after the project begins. Using the data above, perform the following:

a. Draw the PERT network, labeling activities, and compute ES, EF, LS, and LF.

b. Determine the critical path as well as the total slack and free slack.

c. What is the probability the project will be completed within twenty-two days?

d. What is the probability the project will require more than twenty-five days?

CASE 1: SHOWPLACE

Two residential contractors incorporated to build a suburban housing project which will be featured in the annual "Parade of Homes." So far they have completed their preliminary site study, feasibility studies, and a forward planning phase (which includes legal organization of the company, obtaining governmental subdivision approvals, commissioning and directing the design of the site and the structures, setting up contracts and purchasing, organizing the accounting system, and financing the project). They also have finished their cost and profit analyses and prepared their budgets (including a separate budget for the construction of model homes). In a few days, the contractors will receive their permits and sign the finalized subcontractors' and suppliers' agreements.

The contractors now are becoming involved with the construction phase of the project. The townhouse complex that is to be constructed must be built within the allocated budget, on schedule, and with sufficient quality to minimize callbacks and legal problems. They are concerned most with time performance after the construction phase commences because of efficient resource utilization and because project completion can affect the opening of the show homes as well as the starting dates for subsequent projects. Both contractors have well-organized field operations. They are confident that the townhouse project will be a predictable, finely tuned operation with realistic goals and dependable outcomes.

The construction of the subdivision tract will be planned and controlled by a very simple form which denotes all subdivision operations in chronological order (from clearing the land to final pavement and city acceptance). The contractors feel the secret to subdivision work is the scheduling of the staking activities which precede the work of the necessary construction components. Their subdivision form is designed to take the construction through the intricacies of a subdivision and should result in a successful tract if the various stages are followed closely. An incomplete example of the subdivision schedule is shown in Table A-1.

They also intend to lay out the construction schedules for the four-unit model in chronological order. Although their construction superintendent has his own way of scheduling and his own preference concerning the amount of detail, the contractors prefer a greater degree of detail to ensure that proper lead time is given for scheduling materials and labor. It will be their duty to notify subcontractors when to commence work and suppliers when to deliver materials. In order to plan these events, the contractors have devised a weekly construction schedule for the model homes as shown in Table A-2. A separate form will be used for each

TABLE A-1
Subdivision schedule

Item No.	Description of activity	Sub-contractor	Original Start	Original Comp.	Revised Start	Revised Comp.	Revised Start	Revised Comp.	Deviation (days)	Days allowed	Days actual
	Clearing										
	Remove irrigation lines										
	Stake pad & streets										
	Round grade										
	Stake storm										
	Install storm										
	Stake sanitary										

unit within the model. The precedence of operations is indicated, and overlap of activities performed on the same day can be construed.

Because the contractors recognize that unanticipated events are common, they used statistical methods to obtain estimated performance times and allowable variances. Based on their calculations, they have promised the Homebuilders Association that the models will be completed three days before the home show opens, which is 60 days after their scheduled start date.

While they feel their time estimates will allow them enough flexibility in activity scheduling, they are less pleased with the latitude in deploying labor. Their needs for construction crews vary over the course of the project. At times workers may be idle as they await completion of subcontracted activities. Occasionally overtime may be paid when redeployed workers return late from intermediary projects. Moreover, some operations require smaller crews to lessen confusion and redundancy. Others can employ increasing numbers working simulta-

TABLE A-2
Weekly construction schedule—Project: townhouse unit

Item	Activity	Job No. →	9	10	11	Precedence	t_e	s^2
a	Lay out lot; locate services; grade (rough)					—	2	0.33
b	Lay out house; trench					a	2	0.50
c	Drill, clean, & inspect piers; pour concrete					b	3	1.00
d	Set forms & pour foundations; pour garage slab					c	2	1.00
e	Erect mudsill, girders, & floor joists (1st floor)					d	3	1.00
f[a]	Install drains & rough plumbing; hook up sewer					d	4	1.67
g	Erect subfloor & frame (1st floor)					e,f	3	0.80
h	Erect subfloor & floor joists (2nd)					g	3	1.67
i	Erect frame (2nd) & stairs					h	4	1.22
j	Complete roof trusses; do sheathing; construct fascia & verge					i	5	2.11
k[a]	Install rough plumbing (2nd)					h	2	0.33
l[a]	Install sheet metal, windows, doors					i	2	1.50
m	Hang exterior laths for brickwork					l	3	1.67
n[a]	Lay brickwork					m	6	2.67
o	Finish roof & flashing; tile roof					j	4	1.89
p[a]	Install heating & air conditioning					j	3	1.00
q[a]	Install rough electric					j	3	1.67
r	Insulate					m,k,p,q	2	1.33
s	Fasten sheetrock; tape, top, texture					r	10	3.56
t[a]	Finish flooring					s	3	1.23
u[a]	Finish carpentry					t	4	2.67
v	Fasten gutter, downspouts; trim					n,o	2	1.11
w[a]	Install appliances					t	2	1.11
x[a]	Install finished plumbing					t	2	1.67
y[a]	Paint; enamel; hang wallpaper					u,w,x	6	3.44
z	Sand & varnish floors					y	2	2.00
aa[a]	Install finished electric					y	1	1.34
bb	Lay storm drains					d	1	0.50
cc	Finish grading					v,bb	2	0.34
dd	Pour walks & driveway					cc	3	1.78
ee[a]	Landscape					dd	2	0.89
ff[a]	Install linoleum & carpeting					z,aa	2	1.00
gg[a]	Inspect (final)					u,ff	1	0.50

[a]Subcontracted.

neously; in some of these cases, an activity can be completed by three crew members working ten days or by five crew members working six days. Since the workload is unevenly dispersed and the establishment of crew sizes a key variable, the allocation of labor and the possible labor deployment alternatives are the aspects of project planning that provoke their greatest efficiency concerns.

1. Discuss the use of scheduling documents such as those shown. Would the use of more sophisticated PERT techniques enhance project planning, scheduling, and control?
2. Discuss the construction phase in relation to the entire subdivision project. Analyze the model home construction's relationship to the other phases of the subdivision project, the transition between the phases, the reliance upon suppliers and subcontractors within and between phases, and the contractors' view of the accuracy of large project outcomes.
3. Is the 60 day project duration realistic? What is the probability that the project will take longer than 60 days to complete? Is project completion contingent only upon construction activities? What actions can prolong or reduce the amount of time necessary to complete the project?
4. Discuss the deployment of resources and, in particular, the deployment of labor. Generate alternatives for meeting deadlines when the size of the work force is allowed to fluctuate. Also discuss the actual costs of work force fluctuation.

CASE 2: A CONCESSION STAND

The Construction Company of Moore (CCM) and Moore city officials are disputing over a 50-meter swimming pool project that was completed one operating season behind its scheduled opening. The $700,000 municipal pool, according to CCM, was delayed because of heavy rains, foulups in the delivery of materials, and a walkout by a plastering subcontractor late in the project. Although no completion deadline was set in the pool contract, a $100,000 retainage due to CCM at project completion has not been paid, in retribution for revenues lost during the past summer. Since no specific date was set to obligate payment of the retainage, the paperwork which confirms completion and releases the retainage is being withheld by the city.

A willingness to accept some responsibility for project tardiness and economic hardships incurred from nonreceipt of the retainage have CCM ready to strike a compromise. The city of Moore has only $13,000 left of the funds from its general obligation issue used to build the pool. A city architect and CCM representatives have priced out a concession stand that could be added to the pool complex for $17,000. CCM has offered to build the concession stand for $13,000, if it is paid the retainage due from the late construction on the pool. The city will accept the offer provided the agreement includes a $200-a-day penalty if work extends beyond May 25 and $300 daily after May 29, and stipulates payment of the retainage will be made upon final acceptance of the concession stand project.

CCM supervisors estimate that out-of-pocket construction costs for the stand actually will be $14,500. The project is temporarily scheduled to start May 1 and is expected to be finished just in time for the May 25 opening. If the project takes the entire 24 days to complete, it will consume the total $14,500 estimate. However, CCM supervisors assume that the project can be shortened so that it will cost only the $13,000 contract price. Based on the project time and cost estimates in Table B-1, the supervisors calculate that the $300 per day fixed costs (including lost interest on the retainage) which can be saved for each day the project is expedited will cover the discount given on the concession stand.

1. Qualitatively discuss the terms of the pool project and the agreement under analysis for the concession stand project.
2. What is the probability that the concession stand will be built by May 25? By May 29?
3. Will expediting be necessary to (a) avoid the penalties, (b) reduce the cost of the project to break-even? If so, which activities should be expedited?

TABLE B-1
Concession Stand Project

Activity	Immediate predecessor	Expected time (days)	Variance	Cost per day to expedite	Maximum days that can be expedited
a	—	4	1.50	$160	1
b	a	3	1.00	100	1
c	a	6	1.80	200	3
d	a	2	1.00	—	—
e	b	2	0.50	300	1
f	b	4	2.00	180	2
g	d	4	1.33	100	2
h	d	3	0.90	—	—
i	e	5	2.44	210	2
j	e	3	1.44	320	1
k	c,f,g,j	7	3.00	150	4
l	c,f,g,h,j	6	2.80	100	3
m	i,k,l	4	1.67	170	2
n	m	2	0.50	180	1

4. What recommendations would you make to CCM concerning legal implications, cost analyses, terms for compromise, etc.?

SELECTED BIBLIOGRAPHY

Archibald, R. D. and R. L. Villoria. *Network-Based Management Systems,* New York: Wiley, 1967.

Battersby, A. *Network Analysis for Planning and Scheduling,* New York: Wiley, 1970.

Britney, R. R. "Bayesian Point Estimation and the PERT Scheduling of Stochastic Activities," *Management Science,* Vol. 22, No. 9, May 1976, pp. 938–948.

Buffa, E. S. *Operations Management,* New York: Wiley, 1972.

Burman, P. J. *Precedence Networks for Project Planning and Control,* New York: McGraw-Hill, 1972.

Elmaghraby, S. B. *Activity Networks: Project Planning and Control by Network Models,* New York: Wiley, 1977.

Hoare, H. R. *Project Management Using Networks,* New York: McGraw-Hill, 1973.

Iannone, A. *Management Program Planning and Control,* Englewood Cliffs, NJ: Prentice-Hall, 1967.

Levin, R. I. and C. A. Kirkpatrick. *Planning and Control with PERT/CPM,* New York: McGraw-Hill, 1966.

Moder, J. J. and C. R. Phillips. *Project Management with CPM and PERT,* New York: Reinhold, 1970.

Moore, L. J. and E. R. Clayton. *GERT Modeling and Simulation,* New York: Petrocelli/Charter, 1976.

Pritsker, A. A. B. *Modeling and Analysis Using Q-GERT Networks,* New York: Wiley, 1979.

Whitehouse, G. E. *Systems Analysis and Design Using Network Techniques,* Englewood Cliffs, NJ: Prentice-Hall, 1973.

Weist, J. D. and F. K. Levy. *A Management Guide to PERT/CPM,* Englewood Cliffs, NJ: Prentice-Hall, 1977.

IV
PROCESS DECISIONS

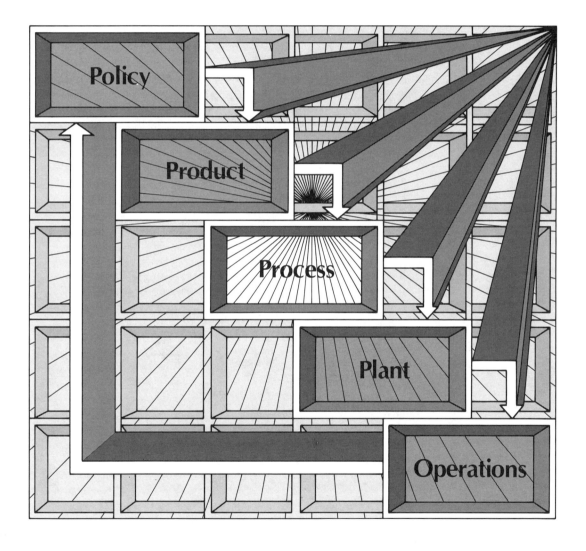

The previous section, on product decisions, determined what goods or services the organization is going to provide to society. This section, on process decisions, will determine how the organization is going to provide the products. The selection of the processes, operations, and work methods necessary for product creation will involve economic, technological, and behavioral considerations. Process decisions are concerned directly with the transformation of inputs into outputs. They establish the route sheets, operation sheets, and job descriptions as shown in Figure I.

This section on process decisions comprises three chapters. The *Process and Operation Design* chapter outlines the technical work methods to be adopted. The next chapter, *Job Design,* integrates the human factor into the production system. The final chapter, *Work Measurement,* deals with the establishment of production standards for performance.

FIGURE I
The process function.

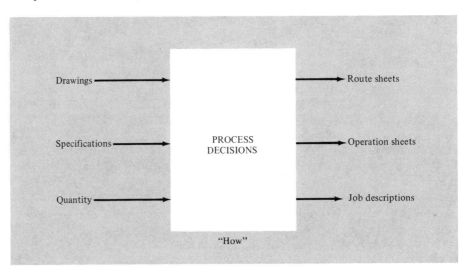

9

Process and Operation Design

PRODUCT ANALYSIS

MAKE OR BUY

CAPITAL AND EQUIPMENT
Robotics
Computer-Aided Manufacturing (CAM)

PROCESS DESIGN

OPERATION DESIGN

JOB DESIGN

CONCLUSION

QUESTIONS

PROBLEMS

CASES

SELECTED BIBLIOGRAPHY

Whereas product decisions determine what will be produced, process decisions establish how the product will be produced, offered, or supplied. Process decisions, also known as process planning, begin after product decisions are made. The outputs of product decisions (drawings and product specifications) along with quantity forecasts from market analysis are the inputs to process decisions. Their aim is to devise the best economical production techniques and work methods consistent with capital, equipment, and manpower availability. They select the methods of combining materials, information, energy, capital, and personnel into goods and services. Process decision relationships are schematically represented in Figure 1.

A process contains a series of operations that transform inputs into outputs. It may be performed by members of the organization, a machine, an individual, a computer, or nature. A process may be a fabrication or assembly whereby an array of inputs is transformed into one output (automobile plant); it may be a disassembly where one input is converted into several outputs (meatpacking plant); it may be a service (education or retailing). The transformation capabilities of an organization are constrained by both their resource base and the existing level of technology.

Process decisions are concerned directly with the transformation of inputs into outputs. The goal of process decisions is to achieve the desired output and quality level at least cost. The introduction of new products, product improvements, and model changes makes it mandatory that adequate organization be provided for process decisions. Every time a new output is designed or an existing output is redesigned, process decisions are undertaken. Additionally, existing processes are reviewed when technological advances are available.

Process selection, like product design, can greatly influence the cost and quality of the product. During product decisions, preliminary considerations for process decisions are made at the production design stage. Product decisions will influence and

FIGURE 1
Process decisions.

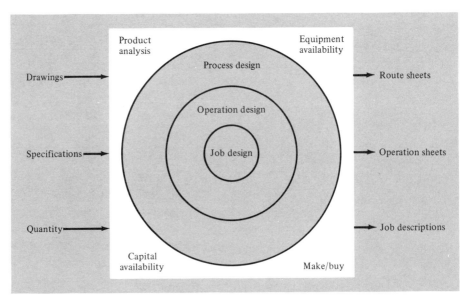

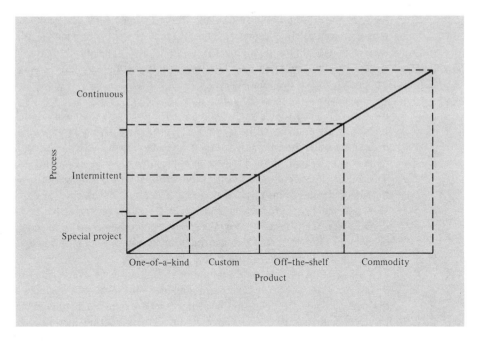

FIGURE 2
Process selection.

sometimes dictate the process required to produce a product. The product category and its impact on process selection are generalized in Figure 2.

The basic factors that affect the selection of a process are:

1. the required volume or quantity of the product,
2. the desired quality of the product,
3. the equipment that is available or can be obtained.

The volume to be produced is related to a given time period and indicated as the rate of production. It indicates the capacity requirements for the system. Production methods vary widely with the volume to be provided. In terms of quality the dimensional requirements, types of surfaces, and other characteristics of a product must be matched to the capabilities of different types of machines and methods. Generally, the higher the required quality level of a product, the higher is the cost to produce it. Quality considerations will be discussed in greater detail in the subsequent chapter on quality control. Frequently, processes are designed to be compatible with existing equipment. If product requirements overload the productive capacity of certain equipment groups, new or more productive equipment may be acquired.

The transformation process is usually different for organizations producing goods than for those producing services. The transformation process requires machines, methods, and people. With a manufacturing organization, it is typical to have a greater amount of capital (machines, tools, equipment). In contrast, service industries tend to be people (labor) intensive. However, the difference is becoming less clear; service industries are increasing their capital investment and adopting mechanized processes similar to manufacturing industries. Typical service industries that have become more capital intensive in an effort to reduce costs are health care (hospitals), transportation (airlines), and fast food outlets (hamburger chains). While service industries may not provide a physical product, they do encounter several problems very similar to goods producing industries. Usually services cannot be stored (inventory) or consumed in a physical sense.

The business of many organizations fluctuates seasonally, or according to some other cycle. Faced with such fluctuations, an organization may synchronize operations with its demand so it does not carry product inventory in excess of its immediate demand. Unfortunately, seasonal production usually means unstable employment. Other organizations produce at approximately a level rate throughout the year. This means the accumulation of a product inventory during periods of slack demand to satisfy demand during peak periods. There are advantages and disadvantages to seasonal and level production rates. Level production rates that produce inventory must reckon with obsolescence, deterioration, storage costs, and financing. Seasonal production rates to match demand must reckon with fluctuating plant utilization and high employment costs (hiring, firing, and training).

To help alleviate seasonal undulations, organizations use various stabilization devices. A stable work force can be maintained and seasonal demand satisfied through the use of overtime. The product line can be expanded to include complementary products with opposite seasonal patterns. Subcontracting at times of peak demand can reduce excessive capacity needs. The independent organization with little competition can make its customers wait longer, raise prices to decrease demand, or simply refuse the additional business.

Process decisions outline the steps for the fabrication of each part, the construction of each subassembly, and the assembly of the product. The product must be broken down into its subassemblies, components, and parts. A decision must be made on whether to fabricate or purchase each part, as well as how each assembly will be performed. Each part or component is studied for the best methods of manufacture and assembly. Product analysis means the analysis of the different process alternatives.

PRODUCT ANALYSIS

A product analysis studies the engineering drawings or plans to determine the overall scope of the project. If the product is complicated, considerable effort may go into exploding it into its component parts and assemblies. The analysis may take the form of special drawings that show relationships of parts, cutaway models, and assembly diagrams. The procedures for describing, analyzing, and evaluating a process can be assisted by a number of useful graphic aids. The basic charts used in product analysis are:

1. *Assembly or "gozinto" charts*—schematic models that define how parts go together, the order of assembly, and the overall structure of the product. As shown in Figure 3, such a chart portrays the proposed sequence of assembly operations required to synthesize a product.

2. *Operation process charts*—schematic models specifying the step-by-step operations required to produce an item. Only productive activities are included on this chart (transportation and storage are excluded). It shows the operations performed and their sequence from where the raw materials enter to where the

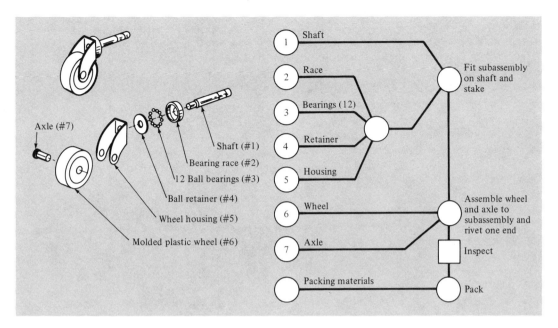

FIGURE 3
Assembly chart for a caster.

finished product emerges. As shown in Figure 4, only two symbols are used in constructing the chart. A circle designates an operation, and a square an inspection.

3. *Flow process charts*—schematic models with similar information to the operation process charts, but transportation and storage activities are also included. These charts yield detailed information on five classifications: operations, transportations, inspections, delays, and storages. The time required and the distances moved are also recorded. Flow process charts are standard ASME (American Society of Mechanical Engineers) symbols (Figure 5) to denote what happens to a product as it progresses. Flow process chart examples are shown in Figures 6 and 7.

Flow charts and diagrams are used to aid in detecting and eliminating inefficiencies in a process by analyzing the sequence of tasks in a step-by-step fashion. The overall objective is to specify in detail the most economical operations and sequences required to make the product or provide the service. The value of visual aids in understanding a problem is tremendous. Diagrams, charts, and other graphical representations contribute to better communication by efficiently collecting, classifying, and analyzing data. A standardized format provides a common language so several people can visualize problems together. Charts are excellent tools for presenting proposals to all management levels. It is a common practice for a chart portraying present conditions to be compared with charts illustrating competing alternatives (see Figure 8).

A process planner will question the details of a proposed process. He will attempt to eliminate operations, substitute operations, combine operations, or develop a better

258

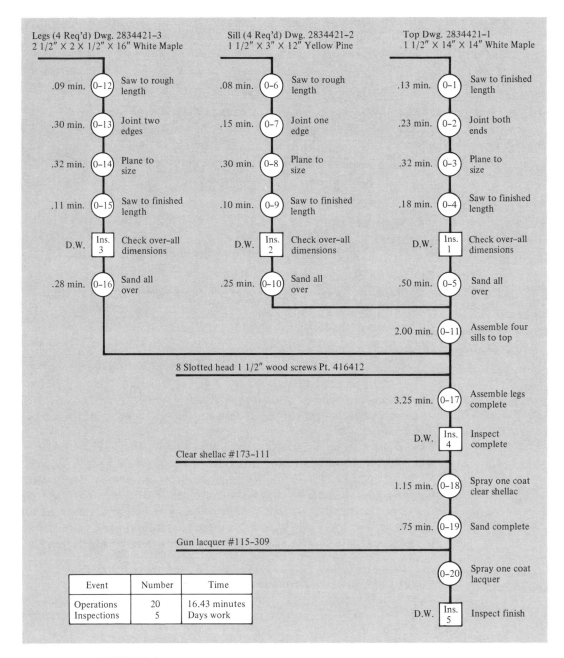

FIGURE 4

Operation process chart for a wood table. [From B. W. Niebel, *Motion and Time Study*, 7th ed. Homewood, IL: Irwin, 1982, p. 25. Copyright 1982 by Richard D. Irwin, Inc.]

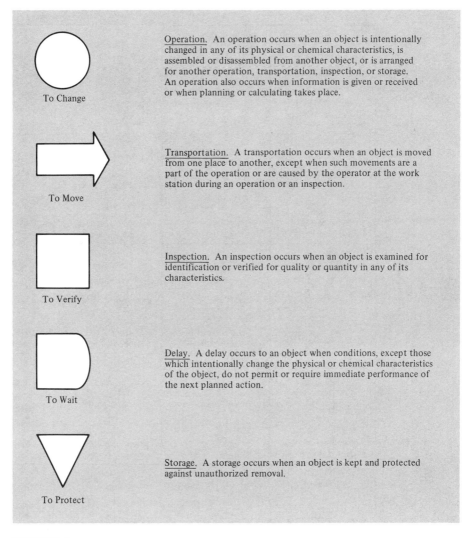

Operation. An operation occurs when an object is intentionally changed in any of its physical or chemical characteristics, is assembled or disassembled from another object, or is arranged for another operation, transportation, inspection, or storage. An operation also occurs when information is given or received or when planning or calculating takes place.

To Change

Transportation. A transportation occurs when an object is moved from one place to another, except when such movements are a part of the operation or are caused by the operator at the work station during an operation or an inspection.

To Move

Inspection. An inspection occurs when an object is examined for identification or verified for quality or quantity in any of its characteristics.

To Verify

Delay. A delay occurs to an object when conditions, except those which intentionally change the physical or chemical characteristics of the object, do not permit or require immediate performance of the next planned action.

To Wait

Storage. A storage occurs when an object is kept and protected against unauthorized removal.

To Protect

FIGURE 5
Flow process chart symbols.

sequence of operations. Transportation, storage, and delay activities should be minimized. Typical questions and potential actions are as follows:

Question	Followed by	Potential action
What is the purpose?	Why?	Eliminate unnecessary activity
Where should it be done?	Why?	Combine or change place
When should it be done?	Why?	Combine or change sequence
Who should do it?	Why?	Combine or change person
How should it be done?	Why?	Simplify or improve method

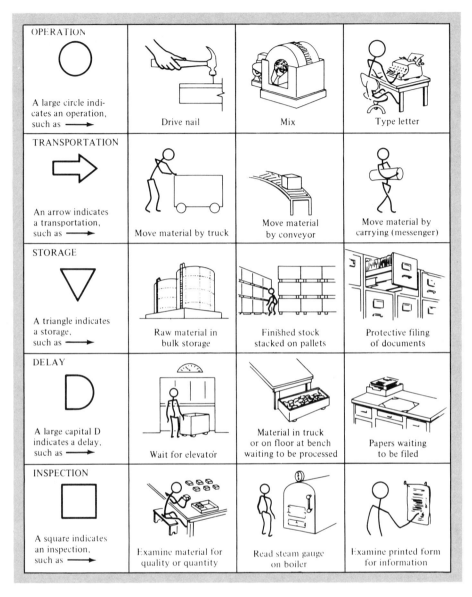

FIGURE 6
Flow process chart examples. [From B. W. Neibel, *Motion and Time Study,* 7th ed., Homewood, IL: Irwin, 1982, p. 29. Copyright 1982 by Richard D. Irwin, Inc.]

The aim of the questioning approach is to spur the imagination. One question may lead to a chain reaction of new ideas. The search is for a better way to perform the activities. Typical inefficiencies might involve work duplication, backtracking, handling problems, or uneven work distribution.

Charts have no inherent analytical power; they are merely recording devices. When processes are not very complex, charts are not required. However, when processes involve scores of operations, charts are an orderly method of analysis. They make relationships explicit and easier to understand.

IDENTIFICATION										
SUBJECT CHARTED	SPARK PLATE ASSEMBLY FOR MODEL OMF					CHART NUMBER				
DRAWING NUMBER		PART NUMBER				TYPE OF CHART				
POINT AT WHICH CHART BEGINS			LOCATION/SHOP	BLDG.		SHEET NUMBER _____ OF _____ SHEETS				
POINT AT WHICH CHART ENDS			LOCATION/SHOP	BLDG.		CHARTED BY			DATE	
QUANTITY INFORMATION						APPROVED BY			DATE	
						YEARLY PRODUCTION				
						COST UNIT				

QUANTITY UNIT CHARTED	SYMBOLS	DESCRIPTION OF EVENT	DIST MOVED IN FT.	UNIT OPER. TIME IN MIN.	UNIT TRANSP. TIME IN MIN.	UNIT INSPECT. TIME IN MIN.	DELAY TIME IN MIN.	STOR TIME IN MIN.
	O⇨□D▽	Material in Storage						
	O⇨□D▽	Move material to work area	20		.077			
	O⇨□D▽	Temporary Storage						
	O⇨□D▽	Pickup washers & spark plate		.065				
	O⇨□D▽	Press four washers to plate		.160				
	O⇨□D▽	Temporary Storage						
	O⇨□D▽	Pickup plates & insulators		.060				
	O⇨□D▽	Stack spark plates–30/board		.175				
	O⇨□D▽	Temporary Storage						
	O⇨□D▽	Inspect				.005		
	O⇨□D▽	Temporary Storage						
	O⇨□D▽	Move to Dept. 109–10 boards/trip	200		.007			
	O⇨□D▽	Temporary Storage						
	O⇨□D▽	Pickup plate & wrap–around		.035				
	O⇨□D▽	Rivet to wrap–around		.055				
	O⇨□D▽	Inspect				.119		
	O⇨□D▽	Return empty boards to Dept. 105	200		.006			
	O⇨□D▽							
	O⇨□D▽	TOTAL	420	.550	.090	.124		
	O⇨□D▽							

FIGURE 7
Flow process chart for spark plate.

MAKE OR BUY

Process decisions begin with a product analysis that extends to every subassembly, component, or raw material composing the item. In view of the quantity demanded and the resources available to the organization, a make or buy decision is made on each material or component required by the finished product.[1] A buy decision means the purchase of components from external suppliers. A make decision means internal production.

Should we manufacture what we sell, or should we buy it? If we manufacture, should we just assemble purchased parts, or should we make the parts? Should we

---

[1]The make or buy decision is sometimes called the make, buy, or lease decision. Actually, leasing is a kind of buying where ownership is not transferred.

FIGURE 8
Comparative flow process chart.

IDENTIFICATION

SUBJECT CHARTED			CHART NUMBER
DRAWING NUMBER	PART NUMBER		TYPE OF CHART
POINT AT WHICH CHART BEGINS	LOCATION/SHOP	BLDG.	SHEET NUMBER ___ OF ___ SHEETS
POINT AT WHICH CHART ENDS	LOCATION/SHOP	BLDG.	CHARTED BY DATE
QUANTITY INFORMATION			APPROVED BY DATE
			YEARLY PRODUCTION
			COST UNIT

SUMMARY

	PRESENT		PROPOSED		DIFFERENCE	
	NO.	TIME IN....	NO.	TIME IN....	NO.	TIME IN....
OPERATIONS						
TRANSPORTATIONS						
INSPECTIONS						
DELAYS						
STORAGES						

UNIT COST – DIRECT LABOR & INSP.
DISTANCE TRAVELED IN FT.
TOTAL YEARLY SAVING DIRECT LABOR
INSTALLATION COST OF PROPOSED METHOD
ESTIMATED NET SAVINGS–FIRST YEAR

PRESENT METHOD

QUANTITY UNIT CHARTED	SYMBOLS	DESCRIPTION OF EVENT	DIST. MOVED IN FT.	UNIT OPER. TIME IN....	UNIT TRANSP. TIME IN....	UNIT INSPECT. TIME IN....	DELAY TIME IN....	STOR. TIME IN....

PROPOSED METHOD

QUANTITY UNIT CHARTED	SYMBOLS	DESCRIPTION OF EVENT	DIST. MOVED IN FT.	UNIT OPER. TIME IN....	UNIT TRANSP. TIME IN....	UNIT INSPECT. TIME IN....	DELAY TIME IN....	STOR. TIME IN....

make or buy raw materials for the parts? The answer to these questions will indicate the degree of vertical integration in an organization.

Very few organizations make all the needed components for their products from basic raw materials. They lack the expertise, diversified skills, and facilities required to do so. Usually, some components are fabricated from raw materials and others are procured from suppliers. Economically, a component is considered for in-house production if the firm has sufficient capacity and its value is sufficient to cover all variable costs as well as make some contribution to fixed costs and profit. As capacity becomes more fully utilized, the make decision should be reviewed, since alternative items may offer a higher contribution.

Many of the components specified for a product may be standardized and mass produced by other firms. It would not be economical to produce a small quantity of such items. In these instances, the buy decision is straightforward. In other instances, the best decision is not so clear and additional analysis is necessary.

Make or buy decisions must be made periodically by nearly every manufacturing organization. Every component of the product is a potential candidate for purchase, and conversely every purchased item is a potential candidate for production. Normally, the ultimate decision may be assumed to rest upon an analysis of comparative costs. However, there are a number of factors other than cost that may be of overriding significance, and many of them are difficult to quantify. No simple rule can be applied to all cases. Each case must be decided on its own merits, and the important issues may vary in different cases or at different times.

The level of production activity has a bearing on the make or buy decision. When workload is high with maximum plant utilization, there is a tendency to purchase items. When workload is low with idle plant capacity, there is a tendency to make more items. Organizations with high overhead or fixed costs normally attempt to keep their production facilities fully utilized, whereas those with low fixed costs are prone to purchase items elsewhere. Internal production helps stabilize the work force and ensure a more reliable supply source.

Some of the factors influencing "make or buy" are as follows:

1. Idle plant capacity
2. In-house capabilities
   a. Personnel
   b. Equipment
   c. Future capabilities
3. Economic advantage
   a. Incremental cost
   b. Overhead allocation
4. Reliability of supply
5. Trade relations (reciprocity)
6. Employment stabilization
7. Alternative resource uses

In general, a growing new company will tend to buy more items than a mature company. The growing organization understandably concentrates its efforts on increasing its output by emphasizing its major product lines. A mature company tends to have facilities, capital, and personnel that can be used for making more readily than buying. The growing and mature companies are thus expanding in a mode most appropriate to their circumstances.

Internal supply will require additional process decisions on the production process as well as the steps and procedures necessary to produce the item. In some circumstances, there may be no alternative but to make the item. This occurs when the technology is unavailable elsewhere or when the process is protected by patents.

The make or buy decision is not an irrevocable act. It is desirable to review the options periodically, or when the events surrounding the initial decision have changed.

EXAMPLE 1

Should you make or buy the following three items composing a product?

	Item A	Item B	Item C
Quantity needed	4,000	700	12,000
Total material cost	$ 600	$10,000	$ 9,000
Total direct labor hours	200	1,500	2,000
Lowest supplier bid	$ .80	$ 50.00	$ 2.00
(price per unit)			

The cost accounting department indicates that the direct labor cost per hour is $8.00 and the fixed overhead rate per direct labor hour is $6.00. The fixed overhead continues even if there is no production.

Item A:

$$\text{Total cost to buy} = (\$.80)(4,000) = \$3200$$
$$\text{Total cost to make} = \$600 + (\$8.00)200 + (\$6.00)200 = \$3400$$
$$\text{Variable cost to make} = \$600 + (\$8.00)200 = \$2200$$

If unused capacity is available, it is desirable to make the item, since variable costs are much less than the buy price and overhead is allocated irrespective of the level of production.

Item B:

$$\text{Total cost to buy} = (\$50)(700) = \$35,000$$
$$\text{Total cost to make} = \$10,000 + (\$8.00)1500 + (\$6.00)1500 = \$31,000$$
$$\text{Variable cost to make} = \$10,000 + (\$8.00)1500 = \$22,000$$

The make alternative is much less costly than the purchase from a supplier.

Item C:

$$\text{Total cost to buy} = (\$2.00)12,000 = \$24,000$$
$$\text{Total cost to make} = \$9,000 + (\$8.00)(2000) + (\$6.00)2000 = \$37,000$$
$$\text{Variable cost to make} = \$9,000 + (\$8.00)(2000) = \$25,000$$

The lowest cost alternative is to purchase the item from the supplier.

Thus, item B should be a "make" and item C should be a "buy," while item A should be a "make" if sufficient unused capacity is available.

CAPITAL AND EQUIPMENT

More and more work once done by people is being transferred to machines. Machines are very desirable for routine and repetitive operations. They can apply great force uniformly and precisely while responding quickly to control signals. There are thus a number of tasks where machines are superior to people. However, they are inferior to people when it comes to developing new methods, exercising more than limited judgment, and responding to unforeseen events.

Machines and equipment are very costly. Yet their allocated cost per unit will be small if a large enough volume is produced. For large volumes, large investments in special purpose equipment can be justified. *Special purpose equipment* is designed to do a limited range of work and is not readily adapted to other uses. For small volumes, *general purpose equipment* is desirable because it can perform several functions and is suited to a wide range of operations.

Besides being more flexible, general purpose equipment is not as costly. However, it requires skilled manpower to set up as well as to operate. It is usually relatively slow in operation. Special purpose equipment requires skilled manpower to set up, but can usually be operated without human surveillance or with semiskilled or unskilled labor.

Automation is the mechanization of work by replacing manual activity with machine activity. It is difficult to distinguish between automation and mechanization; the terms frequently are used interchangeably. Automation, however, implies more than mechanization in that it includes feedback control which permits automatic corrections or adjustments for variations from preset conditions. Thus in automation, machines provide both power and control.

There are specific technologies which underlie the processes for given industries. These technologies deal with the relative relationship between power and control. Since technologies are changing, it is meaningful to speak of "levels of technology." Capacity requirements often indicate the requisite technological level as revealed by capital investment analysis. General technological levels are segmented in Table 1.

Machines are frequently linked together and integrated in such a fashion that they perform many functions automatically. Automatic control, or cybernetics, has machines controlling the operation of machines. Automation has been referred to as the second industrial revolution. Generally there are four areas of automation development in organizations: (1) automatic machinery, (2) integrated materials handling and processing equipment, (3) control mechanisms, and (4) computers and data processing equipment.

Automation is the application of special purpose machines in an integrated manner. It can range from simple mechanization to a continuous flow process where machines replace human beings in the direction, operation, and control of a system.

TABLE 1
General technological levels

	Manual	*Mechanized*	*Automated*
Power	Human	Machine	Machine
Control	Human	Human	Machine

Automation can be applied to product fabrication, product synthesis (assembly), office procedures (data processing) or product handling (storage, retrieval, and transfer). Automation applications abound in process industries that handle bulk solids, liquids, or gases in some form and modify them (physically or chemically) to produce a final product. Organizations that have made the transition to automation are characterized by relatively uniform products, high volume production, and continuous processes.

ROBOTICS

A key element of automation technology is robotics. More and more companies are turning to robots for productivity improvements. Prognosticators foretell of the ultimate impact of robotics technology as being the total redesign of manufacturing facilities—a transfiguration to completely automated and computerized complexes that minimize the role of human labor and have a physical appearance foreign to present technology.

Robots have been used for decades but the first models were huge machines designed for heavy, hazardous activities. The new breed of robots is smaller, more mobile, and can perform various functions. Robots can be dedicated to special purposes at high output while retaining the ability to be reprogrammed to operate as general purpose equipment. They are a competitive weapon to increase reliability, improve quality, and add flexibiilty. Their great flexibility and ability to do special purpose work has the potential to change the form of appropriate equipment for intermittent processes. Robots offer a more cost effective approach in moderate volume areas than manual or hard automation methods. Some proponents describe the robot revolution as being as momentous to industry as the conversion from horses to tractors in agriculture.

Robots can set the stage for the long-awaited, pervasive shift to flexible automation. Instead of buying expensive, new equipment when a product is changed or undergoing massive, complex setups when changing over production, robots can be inexpensively and quickly reprogrammed to do the new jobs. With robotics, the reaction time can be shortened to minimize changeover time and costs. The largest impact of robotics may be felt in the estimated 75% of all goods that are produced in batches too small to be economical for automated assembly. Contrary to popular belief, the majority of U.S. products are not mass-produced but are assembled in small batches as styles and sizes change. At present, these products are put together largely by hand because extensive mechanization of the traditional kind is prohibitively expensive. It is now believed that robots can take over many of these batch operations. In these numerous and varied industries, robots are estimated to be able to reduce manufacturing costs by at least 50%.

Industry estimates set the average up-time for a robot at approximately 95%, compared to 75% for the average blue-collar worker. In addition, the robot worker can work three shifts a day, takes no coffee breaks or vacations, does not call in sick, does not come to work intoxicated or hung over, and does not become sluggish or bored with the work routine. A robot is not bothered by such hazards as heat, noise, nuclear radiation, and noxious fumes. It can perform dangerous jobs, and in so doing, decrease the firm's expenses for safety equipment and workman's compensation. They also can replace workers now relegated to menial, dirty, and degrading jobs. The advantages of robot workers over human workers are listed in Table 2.

TABLE 2
Advantages of robot workers over human workers

Increase productivity

> *Work more reliably:*
> Set standards of 95% uptime
> Can work three shifts
> Take no vacations
> Take no coffee breaks

> *Work more consistently and accurately:*
> Improve product quality
> Reduce scrap rates
> Make production more predictable
> Contribute to higher capital utilization
> Self-diagnose departures from efficiency
> Can design improved work methods

> *Work less expensively:*
> Work for lower wages
> Eliminate need for workman's compensation
> Eliminate need for retirement plans and social security
> Eliminate need for insurance programs

> *Work in less controlled environments:*
> Work in poor climactic conditions
> Ignore noise
> Do hazardous or dangerous jobs

> *Work solely for the organization:*
> Do not moonlight
> Do not engage in industrial espionage
> Do not sabotage operations
> Do not become proselytized
> Do not commit internal theft
> Do not strike

COMPUTER-AIDED MANUFACTURING (CAM)

A significant trend in manufacturing is the increasing use of the digital computer in the design and manufacture of products. This application is referred to as CAD/CAM, which stands for computer-aided design and computer-aided manufacturing. CAD was introduced in Chapter 7 on *Product Decisions* and uses computer interactive graphics to design a product. CAM is the computer control of production machines (numerically controlled machines and robots) that can be reprogrammed to perform a variety of tasks. The CAD/CAM linkage greatly shortens the time between design and production, with magnified productivity gains. The ultimate goal is computer integrated manufacturing (CIM), or the automated factory.

CAM can provide users of intermittent processes with the efficiencies long enjoyed by continuous processes. In essence, it is more flexible than special purpose equipment and results in lower unit costs than general purpose equipment. These efficiencies are possible because CAM systems can process numerous different parts and need not be as dedicated as the hard automation found in continuous processes. Currently, most industrial parts produced in the U.S. are made in small lots of 100 pieces or less. In these intermittent processes, 95% of throughput time is spent in waiting, moving, or storing items, and only 5% is spent in actual productive transformations. CAM can substantially improve productivity by reducing the nonproductive portion of throughput time.

The emphasis of CAM is on coordinating the operations of various machines and controlling the flow of work through the shop. Typically each machine is controlled by a microcomputer; several machines are linked by a minicomputer; and several minicomputers are tied in turn to a large mainframe computer. The programs for the manufacture of each part can be stored in a central data base and transferred from the mainframe computer to any of the machine tools in the network. The trend is to disperse microcomputers to individual workers for data entry and processing control. The computers are then linked to one another and to the central data base by telephone lines or another telecommunications network.

PROCESS DESIGN

Process design, or the selection of the overall plan for producing a product, will be affected by volume (quantity), quality, and cost. It encompasses a series of decisions on the general nature of the processing system, the specific equipment to be utilized, and the specific routing through which the product must flow. If the expected volume of processing economically justifies it, a fully automated system may be used. If the expected volume does not justify this level of investment, a manual or man-machine system may suffice. Process design for a manufacturer converts raw materials into finished goods; for a hospital, it converts sick patients into healthy persons; and for a university, it converts entering students into educated graduates.

Before process design can take place, the analyst must have some idea of the manner in which output will be scheduled for production (production quotas). Will the production rate be seasonal or at a steady rate all year? Will single or multiple shifts be required? What will be the lot size or the number of units produced per run?

Will production be to stock or to order? If production is to stock, products will be produced in anticipation of demand and inventories maintained. If production is to order, products will be produced only when customer orders are received, and product inventories will not exist. An organization can use either a continuous or intermittent process for production to stock, whereas an intermittent process is suited to production to order.

The process designer must have a considerable knowledge of processes, equipment, machines, and men. Besides determining each machine required, he must list the proper tools, jigs, and fixtures. The operations must be listed for each fabricated part, each subassembly, and each assembly.

Process design concentrates on the set of operations as well as their interrelationships. It identifies the operations required and their sequence. It selects the work stations and work flow system. A work station is the physical site where an operation is performed and consists of equipment and machines. The work flow system organizes the flow of work between the work stations. The work flow system can be continuous, intermittent, or some combination of both. In work station selection, the dimensional requirements, surface finishes, and other characteristics of items to be provided must be matched to the available machines and methods (technology). A comparison of process characteristics is contained in Table 3.

For a *continuous process,* there is constant production, and it usually is capital intensive (high capital-to-labor ratio). The volume of output is high, so considerable analysis and expense are involved in arriving at a specialized process. All the work

TABLE 3

Relative process characteristics

	Intermittent	Continuous
Products:	Diverse variety	Limited variety
	Nonstandardized	Standardized
	Make to order	Make to stock
	Lumpy demand	Stable demand
	Small orders	Large orders
	High profit margin	Low profit margin
	Custom market	Mass market
Facilities:	Flexible	Dedicated
	General purpose equipment	Special purpose equipment
	Medium investment	High investment
	Utilization important	Utilization critical
Manpower:	High skill	Low skill
	Labor intensive	Capital intensive
	Labor dependent	Labor independent
Scheduling:	Material driven	Capacity driven
	Long throughput time	Short throughput time
	Large queues	Few or no queues
	Bottlenecks change	Bottlenecks designed away

stations are devoted exclusively to a few products, and they are grouped according to process requirements of the product. A continuous process dictates specialized equipment, methods, and procedures.

Continuous processes produce the same standardized products day in and day out. Repetitive manufacturing is the continuous fabrication and assembly of standardized units produced in (mass) volume, or of products assembled to order in volume from standard (mass produced) options. Another class, usually referred to as the process industries, deals with fluids, gases, powders, and processes involving chemical change. Although repetitive manufacturing measures output in discrete units and process industries in units of volume or weight, both are considered continuous processes. Typical repetitive manufactured products include automobiles, televisions, refrigerators, home furnishings, and apparel. Typical process industry products include oil, beer, detergents, sulfuric acid, and paper.

In an *intermittent process,* the item being processed (product, part, person, information) goes through a processing sequence, but the work performed and its sequence vary with the item. Thus, the routes through the system will vary with the job, and the processing required at each work station may also vary. To adequately utilize personnel and equipment, each work center must perform a given function. Each work center involves a degree of specialization in a field of activity which can include considerable variety. Trades, crafts, and broad specialties are typical work center activities. The central problem of layout design in intermittent production systems is the relative location of each work center or department.

For an intermittent process, there is discrete production on any given job, and it is more labor intensive than a continuous process. There are usually several products processed on the same equipment, and flexibility is more important than specialization. Machines and equipment of the same category are grouped together into work stations. The work stations are determined by function rather than by the dictates of a given product. General purpose equipment and machines are employed, which results in a smaller capital investment. The final selection of a process usually becomes a capital investment analysis of the available alternatives. Both economic and non-economic factors must be weighed before making the final decision.

In practice there are few instances of purely continuous or purely intermittent processes; most organizations strike a balance between these extremes. Continuous processes usually involve the following:

1. large volume production of standardized products,
2. specialized machines and equipment,
3. fixed path materials handling systems such as conveyors and cranes,
4. unskilled and semiskilled workers.

Intermittent processes usually involve the following:

1. low volume production of a wide variety of products,
2. general purpose machines and equipment,
3. variable path materials handling systems such as trucks and forklifts,
4. relatively highly skilled workers.

EXAMPLE 2

An organization can produce a product by two different processes. The relevant cost data are as follows:

	Process A	Process B
Variable cost	$20/unit	$50/unit
Fixed cost	$500,000	$200,000

a. For what levels of demand would the processes be desirable?
b. What process should be selected, and how should the unit be priced if demand forecasts for possible prices are as follows:

   5,000 units at $120 per unit,
   14,000 units at $100 per unit,
   20,000 units at $ 70 per unit?

a: Cost equalization analysis can be used to find the economic range of production for each process. At their cost equalization point both are equally desirable:

$$TC_A = TC_B,$$
$$20X + 500,000 = 50X + 200,000,$$
$$X = 10,000 \text{ units.}$$

From 0 to 10,000 units, process B is desirable. Above 10,000 units, process A is more desirable.

b: The maximum profit level will indicate the best price and process:

$$profit = total \ revenue - total \ cost;$$

for \$120:   profit = 120(5000) − 50(5000) − 200,000   = \$150,000,
for \$100:   profit = 100(14,000) − 20(14,000) − 500,000 = \$620,000,
for \$70:   profit = 70(20,000) − 20(20,000) − 500,000 = \$500,000.

To maximize profits, the price should be set at \$100 per unit and process A selected. It will result in an estimated profit of \$620,000.

A process comprises a set of operations. An operation is performed at a specific work station or physical site. Process design selects a process that will achieve the design and performance requirements of the product at low cost. It identifies the operations required and their sequence. Certain operations may be performed concurrently (parallel) while others may have precedence requirements (series). The output from process design will be a *route sheet* for the product. It will specify the sequence of operations in a process by name, number, location, and any other additional descriptive information required. Examples of route sheets are shown in Figures 9 and 10.

The route sheet is an important scheduling document. For continuous processes, a permanent route sheet is developed when the facility is designed. For intermittent

FIGURE 9
Typical route sheet.

ROUTE SHEET	Part Description:				Part No.			Sheet _____ of _____ Order No. _____ Quantity _____ Sch. Comp. Date _____			
	Material										
Operation No.	Operation Description	Work Center	Machine No.	Tools Required	Standard Time			Finish Date	Inspection		
					Set-up	Per Unit	Per 100		Number	Date	Inspector
									Inspected	Rejected	

ROUTE SHEET	Part Description: Motor Housing		Part No. EMH 4421MC		Sheet 1 of 1 Order No. 3508 Quantity 30 Sch. Comp. Date 12/18					
	Material: Per attached drawing									

Operation No.	Operation Description	Work Center	Machine No.	Tools Required	Standard Time			Finish Date	Inspection			
					Set-up	Per Unit	Per 100		Number		Date	Inspector
									Inspected	Rejected		
10	Mill & Finish	432	4324	A17/B62	2	4	400					
20	Bore	436	4361	A4	3	6	600					
30	Drill	390	3903		4	2	200					
40	Face	440	4401	C19/B20	2.5	3	300					
50	Drill	390	3902		4	2	200					
60	Face	440	4402	C19/B20	2.5	3	300					
70	Inspect	999	N/A	D932/940	—	12	1200					

FIGURE 10
Route sheet for motor housing.

processes, a different route sheet may be developed for each new order. Custom orders will require unique route sheets.

OPERATION DESIGN

Process design concentrates on the set of operations as well as their interrelationships. Operation design concentrates on the aspects of each individual operation in the process, but not the interrelationships among operations. Operation design is composed of operation content and operation methods. Process design will tend to dictate operation content but not the operation methods.

An operation can be broken down into several steps; the steps can be subdivided into elements (man or machine elements); the elements can be further subdivided into motions; and finally the motions can be broken into micromotions (very small portions of a motion). The subdivision of an operation is undertaken for the purpose of analyzing the content to determine the least cost method of performing the operation. Additionally, standards for output control can be developed for performance evaluation and employee training.

The content of each operation in the process and the method of performing each step are the province of operation design. The content of an operation will include a combination of inputs such as the material, manpower, work station, and tools required to produce or process a product. It is sometimes difficult to separate content

---

Operation Sheet HPC 6403

HIGH PRESSURE STAMPING MACHINE COMPRESSOR

1. Obtain authorization from supervisor before starting.
2. Before starting the high pressure stamping machine, the following actions must be performed:
   a. Open valve A to high pressure air line.
   b. Open valves on stages 1 through 4 and drains on stages 1 through 4.
   c. Open the moisture separator drain valves (valves J through M).
   d. Ensure valves to the lube oil and circulating water pressure gauges are open (valves N through Q).
   e. Ensure oil level in compressor reservoir sight glass is in area marked by green stripe.
3. Open circulating water suction and discharge valves (valves AA and BB).
4. Ensure rheostat is turned in full counterclockwise direction.
5. Start compressor by shifting master switch to *On* position.
6. Shift lube oil alarm to test position. If alarm does not sound, shut down compressor. If alarm sounds, shift to *Run* position.
7. Write down lube oil pressure and circulating water pressure in Operating Log Book and initial. If oil pressure is below 25 PSI, secure machine and notify supervisor.
8. Ensure that all air drains are clear of water and discharging dry air.
9. When all drains are clear of moisture, close the drains and increase the compressor speed to 550 RPM.
10. Observe all pressure gauges and thermometers for each stage Normal readings are:

	Pressure	*Maximum temperature*
First Stage	31 to 38 PSI	245
Second Stage	170 to 185 PSI	235
Third Stage	800 to 850 PSI	330
Fourth Stage	3000 PSI	285

11. Never allow Fourth Stage pressure to exceed 3200 PSI. If pressure or temperatures exceed above limits, secure compressor at once and notify supervisor.
12. While compressor is running, open stage drains every 20 minutes. Valves will be opened and closed slowly to avoid initiating a shock wave in system.
13. For stopping compressor, refer to operating sheet HPC 6404.

FIGURE 11
Operation sheet.

and method, since they interact. By subdivision of the content of each operation, alternative methods of performance can be ascertained. The objective is to determine the least cost method of performing the operation. Operation design involves the influences of both technology and economics in establishing production methods and procedures. The final output from operation design will be *operation sheets* at each work station that delineate exact methods and procedures required to process a product. A typical operation sheet is shown in Figure 11.

JOB DESIGN

Job design involves the role of the human element in the design of systems. The next chapter will deal exclusively with job design. Although job design will be treated independently, it is a subset of process decisions.

The final output of job design will be *job descriptions* delineating the quantity and type of personnel required by the production system. The work methods established will supplement or improve the procedures outlined on the operation sheets. Job descriptions specifically outline the role of personnel and how they will be integrated into production operations.

CONCLUSION

Process decisions may be thought of as a series of decisions on the alternative ways of making a product, the type of process to adopt, the equipment to be employed, the work flow system for the product, and the work methods to be incorporated. Process decisions determine the type of process (continuous or intermittent), the machines to employ, the components to make, the components to buy, the work methods, and the manpower requirements. The spatial aspects of process decisions are considered, but their final analysis is delegated to plant decisions. Although process decisions utilize scientific approaches, they are still more art than science. The amount that should be spent on process decisions depends on the potential benefits.

The selection of the most desirable process, or operations to make up the process, can be aided by economic analysis. Capital investment analysis, linear programming, marginal analysis, breakeven analysis, and incremental analysis are basic tools for selecting the more desirable alternatives. Motion and time study, work standards, and work measurements are tools for integrating the human factor into the process equation.

The outputs from process decisions are operation sheets, route sheets, and job descriptions. *Operation sheets* specify in detail how to perform each operation of a process. The operation sheets are maintained at the work stations so technicians can refer to them for direction. The *route sheets* show the physical flow of the product through the different operating departments or work stations. Route sheets determine what shall be done and where, by establishing the operations, their sequence, and manpower and equipment requirements. The route sheet is essentially a map for guiding the product through production. *Job descriptions* include the job requirements, duties, and a brief description of working conditions as well as personal qualifications required to give the highest probability of success. The personnel department can use the job descriptions in their recruitment of personnel for the prospective productive effort.

QUESTIONS

1. What are the goals of process decisions?
2. Name the inputs to and the outputs from process decisions.
3. List the basic factors that affect the selection of a process.
4. What are the disadvantages to level production rates when product demand is seasonal? What devices can be used to help alleviate seasonal undulations?
5. Briefly describe three charts used in product analysis. Include the chief differences among them.
6. How are flow charts used in product analysis?
7. Illustrate and define the common flow process chart symbols.
8. What circumstances would favor a buy decision over a make decision?
9. Synopsize the concept of automation.

10. Name the four areas of automation development in organizations.

11. In what types of manufacturing are robotics expected to have the greatest impact?

12. List some of the advantages of robot workers over human workers.

13. How will CAM improve production efficiency?

14. Contrast the three design phases of process decisions.

15. Give a brief comparison of the relative characteristics of intermittent and continuous processes.

16. Into what steps is an operation broken? Why?

17. From your own experience, describe a process or procedure for producing a product.

18. Draw a flow process chart of the student registration procedure. How could it be improved?

PROBLEMS

1. An organization has forecasted sales for the upcoming time period of $87,000 for a given product. The forecast was based on a selling price of $12.50 per unit. Soon after the forecast was made, management decided to increase the price by 10%, with the result that dollar sales are expected to increase by 6%. What impact will the price increase have on the production level for the period?

2. The Slippery Shoe firm manufactures shower clogs at a variable cost of $2.10 per pair. The fixed costs for a month are $90,000. If the clogs are sold to a distributor for $3.00 per pair, how many pairs must be produced monthly for the firm to break even?

3. A single-product company operates at 100% capacity with annual sales of $2,400,000, fixed costs of $800,000, and variable costs of $1,200,000. The product sales price is $80 per unit. Plant capacity is scheduled to increase by 30% after the purchase of additional equipment, which will increase fixed costs by $200,000 with no change in the variable cost per unit. At what percentage of plant capacity must the expanded plant operate to maintain the same return on sales? (Assume the sales price is constant.)

4. The Sputter Company has an order for 450 two-cylinder lawnmower engines. Each piston requires two piston rings, which are made at the company's Waybelow Casting Works. Currently, there are 50 engines in stock that can be applied to the order. Additionally, Waybelow needs to supply 700 rings to its service outlets. The average time to produce the ring is 2.85 minutes with a 15% scrap loss and a 90% labor efficiency. What is the workload in hours for the piston ring department for the upcoming period?

5. A proposed assembly line is to have an output of 2,000 units per week. The route sheet for the product indicates that a milling operation is required that will take 0.072 hours per unit. If the line will operate 40 hours per week, how many milling machines should be purchased?

6. A specific department is to be laid out on a process basis. The equipment to be located in the department will require 950 square feet of floor space. An analysis of a similar layout of a department reveals that it occupies a total space of 48,000 square feet, of which 12,000 is utilized for equipment. In general, the department does not appear to be congested, nor does it seem to contain wasted space. What might be a good estimate of the total space requirement for the department under consideration?

7. Materials are being moved continuously from one location in the plant to another. The quantity to be handled is such that equipment can be assigned solely to the transportation of material. The two locations are separated by a distance of 0.2 mile. The materials are stacked on pallets, and one loaded pallet weighs 500 pounds. A forklift truck is being considered for this activity. Its load capacity is two loaded pallets per trip, and its average speed would be 5 miles per hour. This average was obtained by taking into account

the speed under load, the speed without load on the return trip, delays, and downtime for repairs and maintenance. If 105 tons of material are to be moved from one location to the other during an eight hour day, how many forklift trucks should be acquired?

8. Castings loaded on skids are to be moved continuously from one department to another by means of a truck. The departments are 660 feet apart. Each casting weighs 20 pounds, and 30 such castings can be loaded on one skid. The trucks to be used can carry one skid per trip at an average speed of 2 miles per hour. If 24,000 castings are to be moved from one location to the other during a 40 hour week, how many trucks will be required for this activity? (Neglect loading and unloading time as well as downtime per truck.)

9. A part can be purchased for $30.00. To make the part would require a $50,000 investment in equipment and $14.00 variable manufacturing cost per unit. What is the cost equalization point for the make or buy decision?

10. An automatic machine costs $600,000 to install. It would eliminate the need for three man-hours per piece produced. Current labor rates are $10 per hour. At what demand level would the automatic machine become undesirable? If the annual demand is 5,000 units, what will be the payback period?

11. A product requires five machining operations on five different machines. Demand for the item is stable with a mean value of 4,000 per week. The average machining time for each machine is given below:

Machine	Average time per part (hours)
1	.020
2	.025
3	.100
4	.500
5	.050

Given that there are 40 productive hours per week, how many of each machine should the organization employ?

12. An industrial laundromat utilizes three types of machines in its production operation— washers, extractors, and dryers. After the laundry is washed, it is spun dry in an extractor and then processed through the dryer. The laundromat has three washing machines, each of which can wash 100 pounds in 30 minutes. The single extractor can spin dry 200 pounds in 10 minutes. The two dryers each handle 100 pounds in 40 minutes. The firm has been working at capacity, and it frequently does not complete its orders on time. If additional capacity is desired, what additional equipment should be bought?

13. An organization is introducing a new product that will sell for $100 per unit. It is considering three alternative ways to make the product, with the following cost structures:

Process	Tooling cost	Variable cost/unit
A	$25,000	$30
B	40,000	20
C	50,000	16

The forecasted demand estimates are as follows:

Quantity	1500	2000	2500	3000	3500	4000
Probability	0.10	0.30	0.25	0.15	0.12	0.08

Which process should be selected?

14. Your firm has just received a contract to build a product that you have not produced in the past. As a process planner, you are analyzing one component of the product to determine if it should be manufactured in-house or subcontracted. A job shop down the street will produce the component at a cost of $2.50 per unit. By working with the cost accounting section you develop the following breakdown of costs based on whether you manufacture with excess plant capacity or expand plant capacity:

Unit cost time	Existing plant capacity available	Expanded plant capacity
Variable manufacturing	$2.20	$2.20
Additional plant and equipment	.00	.25
Additional handling equipment[a]	.10	.10
Factory overhead[b]	.70	.75
Total unit cost	$3.00	$3.30

[a]Handling equipment is treated as separate from direct plant and equipment used in manufacturing.
[b]Factory overhead does not change if existing plant capacity can be utilized.

a. If existing plant capacity is available, would you make or buy the component, and what is the unit cost benefit?
b. If you must expand plant capacity, would you make or buy the component, and what is the unit cost benefit?

15. A decision must be made to repair or replace an important piece of equipment. It will cost about $5000 to refurbish the existing unit and about $0.25 per hour to operate it thereafter. A new advanced unit can be purchased for $18,000 with the old unit used as a trade-in. The new unit will only cost about $0.15 per hour to operate. It is estimated that approximately 150,000 hours of operation will be required on the equipment. Would you repair or replace the equipment?

CASE 1: URBANE

The Urbane Company, which produces and sells a highly successful line of ten-horsepower motors to wholesalers, is faced with an equipment decision. The company's old equipment for making subassemblies is worn out, and the firm must decide how to maintain a steady supply of the components. Urbane is considering two main directions; one involves a choice between conventional supply methods, and the other entails a major organizational changeover to a more controversial system.

The traditional alternatives under consideration are: (1) to completely replace the old equipment with new equipment which could mesh with existing capital assets, or (2) to buy subassemblies from a reliable outside supplier who has quoted a unit price of $22.00 for a minimum of 8000 units per year and $20.00 per unit on a minimum of 12,000 units annually over a 5-year contract period.

Production of the subassembly was 12,000 units in each of the past two years. Future needs (projected for a 5-year planning horizon) are expected to be 10,000 units per year if the current recession continues and 14,000 units annually if the recession is ameliorated by counteracting business policies. By most estimates, the recession is projected to have a 40% chance of lingering well through the next few years.

The new equipment will be technologically obsolete in five years, will cost $500,000 cash, and probably will have no appreciable salvage value at the end of its viability. The equipment vendor states assuredly that the increased machine speeds of the replacement equipment over the old equipment will reduce labor and variable overhead by $7.00 a unit. One of the vendor's other clients, who used identical equipment to produce 15,000 units last year, showed the following unit costs:

Direct material	$5.00
Direct labor	2.00
Variable overhead	1.00
Fixed overhead[a]	9.50
	$17.50

[a]This includes $2.00 allocated as direct department overhead that can be avoided by not making and a $7.50 amortization of depreciation calculated over the expected life of the investment.

The new models of the subassembly equipment will be compatible with the present facility layout and are contemporaneous with the automation levels of the rest of the operating machinery. If the company chooses to install the replacement equipment, the subassembly operation is expected to have an annual capacity of 20,000 units. If the company decides to purchase the subassemblies, its present assembly line will be unsuitable for other production tasks because of its age and inflexibility. (The old line has a scrap value equal to the cost of its removal.)

The second main direction Urbane can take is to move into flexible manufacturing. Installation of a highly automated subassembly line would be the first step toward a totally automated facility. The new assembly line would be composed of automated materials handling equipment that feeds parts to numerically controlled machines. The manufacturing system would be interspersed with programmable robots which are capable of basic assembly tasks.

An experimental model of a similar assembly line is under surveillance at another organization's manufacturing plant. The company with the prototype line has fairly complete information regarding raw materials costs and machining requirements for its component operation. Since actual assembly time and output studies of the prototype operation have been made, it is believed that it would be easy to obtain accurate estimates of the necessary machining operations for the Urbane proposal. The main unsolved problems are to make final choices of prototype equipment to be included in an analysis, develop a precise layout for the equipment chosen, and determine the assembly costs relevant for the planned design.

1. Ignoring taxes and interest, compare the conventional alternatives on a per unit basis for the expected annual demand. At what volume would Urbane be indifferent between manufacturing with the replacement equipment and buying?
2. Assuming a 14% cost of capital and a 40% tax rate for Urbane, indicate which of the conventional alternatives is more desirable according to the net present value technique.
3. Discuss possible evaluative processes which could be used to compare the flexible system with the conventional alternatives.
4. What factors should be brought into the decision process other than those above? Include considerations that must be applied to all three courses of action.

CASE 2: SMALL PRODUCTION UNITS

A group of foreign production experts identified what they believe to be the real weakness in most modern economies—poor production management. They asserted that current productivity problems primarily are caused by adherence to production philosophies and practices of the past which make it impossible to increase present levels of efficiency. To prove their theory, they tested the production efficiency of a number of batch production plants in their native country and compared the findings with performance results obtained for the same plants several decades ago. The objective measures used to determine the production efficiency of the plants in the previous studies were the same measures used by the team of experts. The measures consisted of:

1. *Throughput time*—the amount of time for materials to pass through the plant (from incoming materials to shipment as final goods).
2. *Inventory turnover*—the dollar amount of products sold from the plant to the average dollar amount tied up in stocks and work in process.
3. *Order processing*—
   a. number of orders produced by a given completion date which meet quantity and quality requirements,
   b. number of orders delivered to the plant in the quantities required and by the specified dates.

The performance findings of the initial studies were extremely poor. Quite remarkably, those achieved in the recent study were almost identical. Although important advances in technology had occurred in the interval between the studies, it appeared that the advances aimed at productivity improvement had almost insignificant effects. The experts attributed the similarities between the findings to the continued acceptance of outdated production management beliefs. They itemized the beliefs which were felt to have undergone little change in the last several decades as follows:

1. Line production is inherently virtuous and can be applied extensively.
2. Process organization is the most acceptable transformation method when line production is impossible.
3. Production management should be structured as a functional unit.
4. The larger an organization grows, the more efficient it can become.
5. Multi-cycle ordering of production parts is the most economically sound purchasing strategy.

The research team maintained that for many reasons these long-held beliefs are inaccurate and counterproductive. They instead upheld an approach which contradicts the efficacy and applicability of the practices stipulated above. The new approach has three main features. First, organizational units must be small and based on products rather than processes; units must specialize in the total process by completing whole products or groups of parts. Second, all units should be as autonomous as possible; each should have the authority to make decisions about matters which concern it directly. Third, materials should be ordered for single production cycles; that is, materials should be purchased only as needs for particular production cycles occur.

The new approach for production organization into small semi-autonomous units is similar to operating small separate businesses rather than operating a large, centralized organization. If taken to an extreme case, it could mean obsolescence for long machine paced assembly lines in certain industries. At the very least, it means the introduction of startling methodological changes for improving efficiency.

1. Comment on the studies used to substantiate the research team's position.
2. Discuss the validity of each of the production beliefs said to exist for decades.
3. Evaluate the new approach by analyzing the strengths and weaknesses of each of its main features.

SELECTED BIBLIOGRAPHY

Barnes, R. M. *Motion and Time Study,* New York: Wiley, 1968.

Gunn, T. G. "The Mechanization of Design and Manufacturing," *Scientific American,* Volume 247, No. 3, 1982. pp. 115–30.

Maynard, H. B. *Industrial Engineering Handbook,* New York: McGraw-Hill, 1971.

Mermet, J. *CAD in Medium Size and Small Industries,* New York: North-Holland, 1981.

Neibel, B. W. *Motion and Time Study,* 7th ed., Homewood, IL: Irwin, 1982.

Ostrofsky, B. *Design Planning and Development Methodology,* Englewood, Cliffs, NJ: Prentice-Hall, 1977.

10
Job Design

DIVISION OF LABOR

JOB CONTENT

WORK METHODS

JOB SATISFACTION

THE PHYSICAL ENVIRONMENT
Human Factors
Temperature
Illumination
Noise
Color
Safety

JOB DESCRIPTIONS

CONCLUSION

QUESTIONS

CASES

SELECTED BIBLIOGRAPHY

The industrial revolution of the late eighteenth century used machines to replace man's toil and energy. Man became a controlling mechanism in a man-machine era. Twentieth century automation replaced man as a control mechanism with automatic feedback control and relegated him to a "watchdog" or maintenance function. Modern automation systems via computers have taken over the office, as labor-dependent processes are now done more efficiently by machines. Similarly, highly sophisticated automation via robotics already has replaced laborers in many routine and hazardous blue collar manufacturing jobs. In each successive phase, increased mechanization, automation, and computerization have brought about worker displacement and initiated the redesign of jobs.

Job redesign has resulted in the creation of new jobs, the relocation of workers to different jobs, and the redistribution of workers among the various segments of the job force. As automation replaced workers in the manufacturing industries, many moved from the manufacture of goods to the production of services. Many just coming into the work force were assimilated by the expanding service industry. The movement from unskilled factory labor to white collar work reflected the industrial trend toward service and informational work often called the post-industrial revolution. As machines changed the nature of manufacturing jobs and workers shifted from manual labor into service positions, man's role became more complex and specialized. As these work systems changed, they dramatically modified the traditional roles of work and its design.

In spite of all the modern technological advancements and the recomposition of the work force, man is still a vital factor in production and operations. While his role has changed, his importance has not. Even in automated and computerized systems, man is necessary in a surveillance role. In manual, semi-automated, man-machine, and automated work systems, job design is important to the overall effectiveness of operations. The significance of labor cost to an organization depends on whether it is labor or capital intensive. If value (cost) is added largely through the use of manpower rather than machines, then labor supply, wages rates, and labor efficiency become critical factors.

Job design determines the role of the human element in production systems. It specifies the structure of each job and determines the distribution of work within an organization. Whereas process design and operation design tend to be product-oriented, job design is human-oriented. Man is the most complex of all factors of production. His physical, mental, and social characteristics as well as his capabilities and limitations must be considered in job design.

A man-machine system may consist of one man and one machine, a number of men and one machine, one man and several machines, or several men and several machines. The specific man-machine relationship can vary considerably, but it is restrained by available resources, technology, and economics. A machine in this sense is a device that permits or aids a worker to accomplish his job. The design of the man-machine relationship involves a great deal of latitude and discretion.

Just as process design tends to limit the alternatives for operation design, job design is limited in alternatives by operation design. The selection of the operation methods narrows job design considerably. Operation design determines what operations (human and nonhuman) are necessary at each work station to produce a product. Job design is only concerned with the human activities specified in operation design.

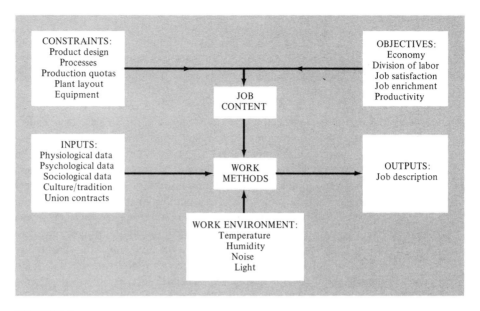

FIGURE 1
Job design. [From Richard J. Tersine and John H. Campbell, *Modern Materials Management,* New York: North Holland, 1977, p. 32.]

"A job" is the aggregate of all the potential work assignments a worker may be asked to perform. A worker usually expects guidance or instructions on how to perform his assignments. Job design should provide the worker with a carefully planned work station where he can perform at peak effectiveness with maximum comfort. The basic content of many jobs (usually trade, professional, and skilled) is established by tradition and customs. Union contracts may also define job content. A job can be classified in terms of the following:

1. physical effort required,
2. physical skill required,
3. intelligence and mental skill required,
4. responsibilities that must be assumed,
5. working and physical conditions.

Job content and work methods constitute job design. While job content defines what must be accomplished, work methods specify how the worker should perform his assignments. Operation design will essentially dictate job content at each work station or area. Constraints and objectives of an organization also influence job content, as shown in Figure 1.

Division of labor and job enrichment are opposing factors in establishing job content. The greatest degree of freedom in job design is in the selection of work methods to accomplish a given job content. Job design is based on both economic and noneconomic needs, and particular organizational philosophies greatly affect how jobs are designed. Job design is not a science; considerable judgment is involved.

DIVISION OF LABOR

The division of labor results in job specialization by segregating tasks into fewer jobs. This makes it possible to fill many positions with less skilled personnel, which in turn makes recruiting easier because qualified workers are easier to find. Since fewer skills are required, wage rates generally are lower. This has tremendous cost advantages when coupled with a high volume output, where indirect or fixed costs per unit also are typically low. Cost advantages also arise from shorter worker training time, consistent worker assignments, and shorter production times due to learning curve effects. Furthermore, higher degrees of automation are made possible.

Minute division of labor is uncommon in modern organizations because of the development of machinery to replace workers in the performance of very simple tasks. One notable exception is in assembly lines, where labor remains the predominant mode of operation. The nature and extent of the division of labor may be dictated by the machinery and equipment employed. In highly mechanized and automated facilities, technology determines the assignment of work; the worker performs those residual tasks that have not been incorporated in the machinery. In organizations where manual labor predominates and only small tools are utilized, the situation is reversed. Instead of the worker being an adjunct of the machine, tools are an adjunct of the worker. Such is the case in assembly work that is predominantly manual, and for high skill and craft jobs.

There are technical and economic limits to the division of labor. Low production volume, for example, does not favor an intricate division of labor.

Jobs can be structured in terms of specialization, standardization, discretion, and expertise. The fewer the different tasks performed by each individual, the greater the *specialization*. Conversely, personnel are *generalists* when each performs many different job titles (classifications). *Standardization* refers to the degree to which the performance of tasks and work methods is specified in detail. *Discretion* indicates the degree of freedom the personnel have over how they perform their job. *Expertise* refers to the degree of knowledge or skills required by the job holder. It indicates a level of professionalism measured by level of education, experience, or exhibited proficiency required to perform certain job requirements.

There are interrelationships among the four dimensions of specialization, standardization, discretion, and expertise. A change in one can affect the others. For example, specialization increases standardization because a narrower range of tasks simplifies the job to a smaller set of more frequent operations. The narrower range of tasks and their standardization decreases the amount of decision making discretion, which also reduces the training and skills (expertise) required to perform them.

JOB CONTENT

Job content establishes the scope and depth of the job, while work methods establish how it is to be performed. Job enlargement and job enrichment are attempts to broaden the job content and make it more meaningful for employees. Job enlargement counteracts the trend toward greater specialization by increasing the number of tasks (greater variety) performed. Job enrichment affects specialization by vertical expansion of responsibility to such areas as inspection, scheduling, and planning of the work. The work method should be the best way of performing a particular job. Motion study determines the necessary motions and movements for a task and designs the most efficient method for putting the motions and movements together.

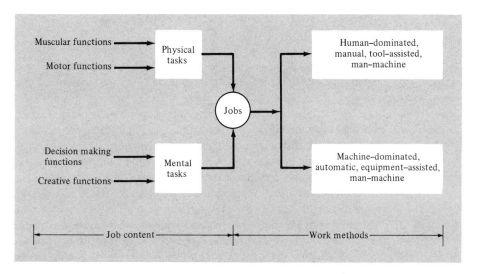

FIGURE 2
Job design extremes.

Job scope refers to the number of different operations performed. In performing a job with narrow scope, the worker performs few operations and repeats the cycle frequently. Job enlargement expands the job scope horizontally: it adds a few more duties to increase the variety and reduce the monotony, but it does not increase job responsibility. *Job depth* refers to the freedom of the worker to plan and organize his own work. Job enrichment expands the job depth vertically and increases job responsibility. Job scope and depth can only be altered by changing the basic job structure or the job content.

Simple, routine, and repetitive jobs can be performed more quickly and uniformly by machines than by people in most cases. People cannot match the force and consistency of machines. However, people are usually more flexible than machines. In jobs involving thinking and variability, people are usually far superior. When creativity, conceptualization, and judgment are required, the human is more desirable. Machines with humanlike (''thinking'') features are frequently expensive and difficult to build.

When jobs are designed, the role of people and machines should be carefully analyzed. It is important to recognize those areas where people and machines are superior. It is also important to determine how people and machines can be integrated into an effective, coordinated system. Job design extremes are illustrated in Figure 2.

WORK METHODS

A main objective of work methods is to maximize productivity and efficiency by determining the best way to perform the tasks of a job. The quantity and quality of employees needed will depend on the work methods. Work methods are dramatically influenced by the tools, materials, and equipment associated with a given operation.

When changes are made, work methods usually are altered, as are productivity and efficiency.

As was stated earlier in the chapter, a *job* is the aggregate of all the potential work assignments an employee may be asked to perform. The job can be subdivided further into tasks, elements, and micromotions. A *micromotion* is the smallest of job activities. It includes basic movements such as reaching, grasping, releasing, or positioning an object. An *element* is composed of two or more micromotions. It is a more complete entity, such as transporting, filling, or tightening an item. A *task* is an aggregation of two or more elements into a complete operation, such as monitoring, controlling, or adjusting. A job is the summation of all the tasks an employee will be required to perform. Usually it involves some combination of physical and intellectual capabilities. Work methods are concerned with how the tasks of a job are performed.

A job can be anything from processing mail orders to treating patients, from making pencils to making ice cream. Some jobs have few options in their performance; others have many options. What is accomplished may not be as important as the way it is done. However, certain principles concerning how things can be done are easily transferable from job to job.

For a given technology on a scientific basis, work methods depend largely on various tools of motion study. These tools tend to be of two types. The first type consists of charts, tables, or graphic devices for visualizing the job. The second type includes traditional and proven principles of motion economy that are guidelines for efficiency. The usual procedure is to use the graphic devices to record the method and then attempt to improve it by the principles of motion economy.

Motion study is the systematic analysis of the human motions used to perform an operation. The purpose is to eliminate unnecessary motions and to identify the best sequence of motions for maximum efficiency. In developing work methods, the motion analyst tries to:

1. eliminate unnecessary motions,
2. combine activities,
3. reduce fatigue,
4. improve the work station arrangement,
5. improve tool and equipment design.

Work methods are often described in charts that depict in detail the precise tasks for a job. There are several kinds of charts that can be used in designing a job and indicating ways to improve it. Charts similar to those used in process design and operation design are also useful in work methods design. The charts used in work methods design show more detailed work elements than do flow charts, which represent an entire process. A chart by itself does not design or improve a job; it takes a person to make improvements. All a chart can do is depict relationships. Nearly all charts have symbols for each detail. They usually include the time to do tasks as well as the distances moved.

Since jobs occur with a great deal of variation, it is necessary to analyze them separately. Usually schematic and graphical charts are used to design and improve jobs. Several work analysis tools are outlined in Figure 3. The assembly chart, operation process chart, and flow process chart have been previously mentioned. The operation chart depicts the elementary motions of the right and left hands. The Simo

ACTIVITY	OBJECTIVE	TOOLS
Overall system	Optimize operations (eliminate/combine steps)	Assembly chart, operation process chart, & flow process chart
Stationary worker (fixed work place)	Minimize motions (simplify method)	Operation chart, Simo chart, principles of motion economy
Man/machine	Minimize the cost of man and machine (minimize idle time)	Activity chart (man/machine chart)
Team (Man/men)	Maximize productivity (minimize interferences and delays)	Activity chart, gang process chart

FIGURE 3
Work analysis tools.

(simultaneous motion) chart is similar to the operation chart, but it employs high speed motion pictures for analysis. An activity chart, also called a man/machine chart, outlines work that involves a worker interfacing simultaneously with a machine or machines. Gang process charts study work activities dependent upon a crew or gang of men working together. Charts are used as data organizers that permit a scientific evaluation of the situation in comparison with other potential alternatives. An operation chart, activity chart, and Simo chart are illustrated in Figures 4, 5, and 6.

In micromotion analysis, the work performed by each hand is broken down into fundamental hand motions called "therbligs." The motions are recorded in motion pictures. The information ultimately is transferred to a Simo chart. This type of analysis is very specialized and expensive. It is extremely detailed and usually limited to short cycle, repetitive tasks.

Other types of tools exist, but those mentioned are the most common types in use. Repetitive job activities are those most frequently subjected to analysis.

Over the years, industrial engineers have established several general statements, called principles of motion economy, that outline efficient work methods. The principles of motion economy are applied to the appropriate schematic or graphical chart in finalizing job design. These principles can be very helpful in original design or in improving existing methods. Figure 7 contains typical principles of motion economy that apply to the human body, work place arrangement, and tool design.

The high labor content of most service industries renders them a prime target for work methods analysis. Simple charting techniques can substantially improve productivity in financial institutions, retail establishments, hospitals, and so forth. Unfortunately, these organizations tend to perceive themselves as being "nonproduction" in orientation. The more progressive organizations are correcting this myopic view.

288

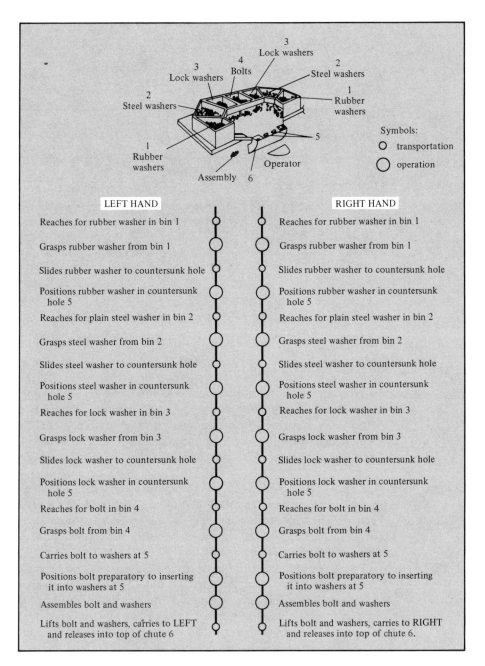

FIGURE 4
Operation chart. [From Ralph M. Barnes, *Motion and Time Study,* New York: Wiley, 1968, p. 114. Copyright 1968, John Wiley and Sons.]

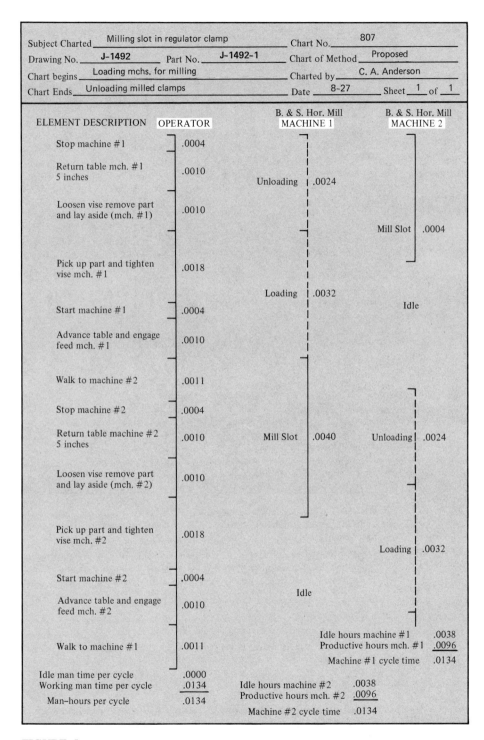

FIGURE 5
Activity chart. [From B. W. Niebel, *Motion and Time Study,* 7th ed., Homewood, IL: Irwin, 1982, p. 136. Copyright 1982 by Richard D. Irwin, Inc.]

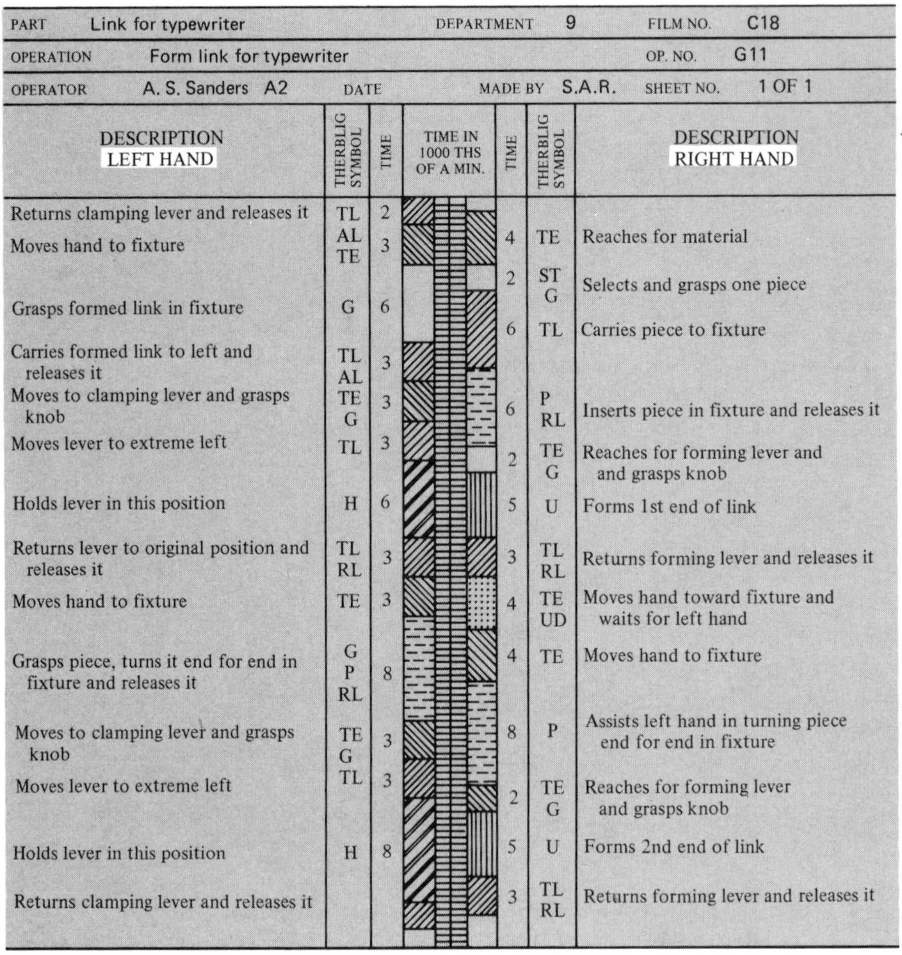

PART	Link for typewriter			DEPARTMENT 9			FILM NO. C18
OPERATION	Form link for typewriter					OP. NO.	G11
OPERATOR	A. S. Sanders A2	DATE		MADE BY S.A.R.		SHEET NO.	1 OF 1

DESCRIPTION LEFT HAND	THERBLIG SYMBOL	TIME	TIME IN 1000 THS OF A MIN.	TIME	THERBLIG SYMBOL	DESCRIPTION RIGHT HAND
Returns clamping lever and releases it	TL	2				
Moves hand to fixture	AL TE	3		4	TE	Reaches for material
				2	ST G	Selects and grasps one piece
Grasps formed link in fixture	G	6		6	TL	Carries piece to fixture
Carries formed link to left and releases it	TL AL	3				
Moves to clamping lever and grasps knob	TE G	3		6	P RL	Inserts piece in fixture and releases it
Moves lever to extreme left	TL	3		2	TE G	Reaches for forming lever and and grasps knob
Holds lever in this position	H	6		5	U	Forms 1st end of link
Returns lever to original position and releases it	TL RL	3		3	TL RL	Returns forming lever and releases it
Moves hand to fixture	TE	3		4	TE UD	Moves hand toward fixture and waits for left hand
Grasps piece, turns it end for end in fixture and releases it	G P RL	8		4	TE	Moves hand to fixture
Moves to clamping lever and grasps knob	TE G	3		8	P	Assists left hand in turning piece end for end in fixture
Moves lever to extreme left	TL	3		2	TE G	Reaches for forming lever and grasps knob
Holds lever in this position	H	8		5	U	Forms 2nd end of link
Returns clamping lever and releases it				3	TL RL	Returns forming lever and releases it

FIGURE 6
Simo chart. [From Ralph M. Barnes, *Motion and Time Study,* New York: Wiley, 1968, p. 183. Copyright 1968, John Wiley and Sons.]

FIGURE 7
Principles of motion economy. [Abstracted from Ralph M. Barnes, *Motion and Time Study,* New York: Wiley, 1968, p. 220. Copyright 1968, John Wiley and Sons.]

Use of the human body

1. The two hands should begin as well as complete their motions at the same time.
2. The two hands should not be idle at the same time except during rest periods.
3. Motions of the arms should be made in opposite and symmetrical directions, and should be made simultaneously.
4. Hand and body motions should be confined to the lowest classification with which it is possible to perform the work satisfactorily.
5. Momentum should be employed to assist the worker wherever possible, and it should be reduced to a minimum if it must be overcome by muscular effort.

6. Smooth continuous curved motions of the hands are preferable to straightline motions involving sudden and sharp changes in direction.
7. Ballistic movements are faster, easier, and more accurate than restricted or "controlled" movements.
8. Work should be arranged to permit easy and natural rhythm wherever possible.
9. Eye fixations should be as few and as close together as possible.

Arrangement of the work place

10. There should be a definite and fixed place for all tools and materials.
11. Tools, materials, and controls should be located close to the point of use.
12. Gravity feed bins and containers should be used to deliver material close to the point of use.
13. Drop deliveries should be used wherever possible.
14. Materials and tools should be located to permit the best sequence of motions.
15. Provisions should be made for adequate conditions for seeing. Good illumination is the first requirement for satisfactory visual perception.
16. The height of the work place and the chair should preferably be arranged so that alternate sitting and standing at work are easily possible.
17. A chair of the type and height to permit good posture should be provided for every worker.

Design of tools and equipment

18. The hands should be relieved of all work that can be done more advantageously by a jig, a fixture, or a foot-operated device.
19. Two or more tools should be combined wherever possible.
20. Tools and materials should be prepositioned whenever possible.
21. Where each finger performs some specific movement, as in typewriting, the load should be distributed in accordance with the inherent capacities of the fingers.
22. Levers, crossbars, and hand wheels should be located in such positions that the operator can manipulate them with the least change in body position and with the greatest mechanical advantage.

EXAMPLE 1

A machine operator can load a machine in 2 minutes and unload it in 1 minute. Several machines of this type are available, and their automatic run time is 4 minutes. Each operator is paid $12 per hour, and the cost per machine is $50 per hour.

a. Construct an activity chart for a single operator with two machines.
b. Determine the cycle time.
c. What is the idle time of the worker per cycle?
d. What is the idle machine time per cycle?
e. What is the total cost per hour?
f. What is the total cost per cycle?
g. What is the cost of idle time per hour?

continued

EXAMPLE 1—*continued*

a: The operator does not reach a steady state condition until the ninth minute, as shown in the figure below.

Time (min)	Worker	Machine 1	Machine 2
	Load 1	Load	Idle
2	Load 2	Run	Load
4	Idle	Run	Run
6	Unload 1	Unload	Run
8	Load 1	Load	Idle
10	Unload 2		Unload
	Load 2	Run	Load
12	Idle		Run
	Unload 1	Unload	Run
14	Load 1	Load	Run
16	Unload 2		Unload
18	Load 2	Run	Load
20	Idle		Run

(Cycle = 7 min, between 9 and 16 minutes)

b: The cycle time is the steady state time it takes to load and unload both machines. It is 7 minutes.
c: The worker idle time per steady state cycle is 1 minute.
d: Machines are not idle in steady state.
e: Cost per hour = (worker cost) + (machine cost) = 12 + 2(50) = $112/hour.
f: Cost per cycle = [112/(60 minutes)](7 minutes/cycle) = $13.07/cycle.
g: Idle time cost per hour = $\dfrac{(1 \text{ min/cycle})(\$12/\text{hour})}{7 \text{ min/cycle}}$ = $1.71.

JOB SATISFACTION

Job satisfaction and motivation are not synonymous. Motivation is a drive to perform, while satisfaction reflects the individual's attitude or happiness with the situation. The result of motivation is increased effort, which in turn increases performance as modified by abilities. The result of satisfaction is increased commitment to the organization, which may or may not result in increased performance.

Many approaches have been suggested for creating "satisfying" jobs. Some of these approaches are as follows:

1. *Job rotation* is the practice of periodically changing job assignments. It does not require that jobs be redesigned. Personnel are shifted from one job assignment to another.
2. *Job enlargement* makes a job structurally larger by increasing its scope (number of different operations performed). A greater variety of tasks are performed.
3. *Job enrichment* increases both job scope (diversity) and job depth (freedom to plan and organize the work). The employee is given greater responsibility for how to perform his job responsibilities.
4. *Participative management* solicits employee advice on job related decisions. The employee is considered a partner with a valuable input to the decision making process.
5. *Industrial democracy* places worker representatives on all decision making bodies of the organization. Industrial democracy can encompass much more than job related matters.
6. *Organizational development* attempts to change attitudes and values to improve communication and reduce conflicts. Group processes and sensitivity training are associated with the organizational development approach.
7. *Variable work schedules* (flextime) permit employees a certain amount of freedom in selecting work hours as long as they put in a full day's work.
8. *The four-day workweek* consists of four ten-hour days. The worker has a long weekend for leisure activities and spends less time per week on transportation.
9. *Job-splitting* occurs when two persons share one full time job.
10. *Quality circles* are formed from voluntary groups of six to twelve workers who do the same or similar work in the same work area. They meet on a regularly scheduled basis (usually an hour a week on company time) to discuss problems and potential improvements in quality and productivity. To identify, analyze, and arrive at solutions to problems, circles use group dynamics, brainstorming, cause and effect analysis, sampling, control charts, histograms, and scatter diagrams. The group makes presentations to management on their findings, and approved recommendations are implemented.

All of the above approaches have a behavioral orientation. They attempt to solicit employee involvement and interest by increasing stimuli, job variety, job freedom, and behavioral awareness or by permitting the employee to have a voice over those matters that affect his role within the organization. The choice of strategy and the tactics depends upon the particular situation in the organization. People have different social and cultural backgrounds. These differences must be considered when jobs are designed in different regions or countries.

Technology is probably the largest determinant of the design of jobs. It has not been uncommon for machines, tools, materials, and processes to receive more attention than the worker in an organization. Frequently only residual consideration is given to the human element. Behaviorists have tended to overcompensate for this myopic view. The sociotechnical approach attempts to integrate all the work dimensions in their proper proportion without bias. It considers other alternatives than the two extremes of technical domination and human satisfaction. It is necessary to balance the technical and social elements of any work system.

Job performance and effort are not necessarily synonymous. Job performance re-

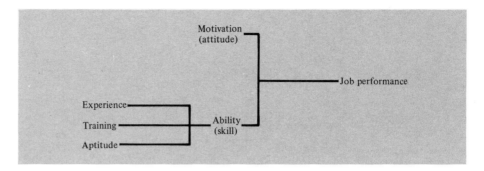

FIGURE 8
Job performance.

FIGURE 9
A job satisfaction–productivity audit.

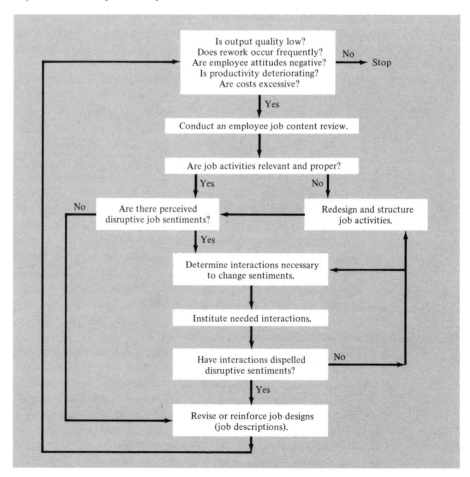

fers to the accomplishment of the tasks that make up the individual's job, and it results from a person's efforts and abilities. Effort is the amount of energy (physical or mental) used by the individual in performing a task. For effort to be meaningful it must be supported by a level of proficiency. Figure 8 indicates the basic components of job performance.

A person's ability can be considered a product of his experience, training, and aptitude. Experience is the knowledge and skills acquired in work pursuits. Training may be from a formal academic or technical institution as well as from in-house training programs. Aptitude is usually measured by some type of dexterity or intelligence test. However, job performance is a function of both ability and motivation. Most organizations focus only on a person's ability (experience, training, and aptitude) and ignore the significance of motivation when hiring personnel. It is very difficult to ascertain a person's motivational level fairly. Previous associates and peers are an excellent source of information on motivational traits.

It is desirable to relate job satisfaction to productivity. Increased job satisfaction does not mean increased productivity. However, a decrease in job satisfaction can be translated into decreased productivity. Difficulties in job satisfaction and productivity can sometimes be linked to inadequate or inappropriate job designs. It is desirable to review job activities on a periodic basis, as in a six month or one year employee merit review. A possible job satisfaction–productivity audit that could be applied on a periodic basis is outlined in Figure 9.

When job designs or job descriptions are not revised periodically, they tend to become outdated and misrepresentative. As methods, techniques, products, and personnel change, it is only natural that job activities are modified. If revisions are not made, improper or inefficient methods will be perpetuated. A periodic update can remove potential conflicts and disruptive sentiments. These necessary revisions are helpful in coordinating overall organizational activities. They are also useful in training new employees when growth or turnover occurs.

For job design to be effective, it should be:

1. performed by experienced personnel with the necessary training and background,
2. consistent with organizational goals,
3. documented in written form,
4. understood and agreed to by both management and employees, and
5. revised periodically as changes occur.

Because of their intimate involvement, employees frequently are a valuable source of suggestions for job improvement.

THE PHYSICAL ENVIRONMENT

The physical work environment, which includes factors such as temperature, humidity, ventilation, noise, light, and color, can have an important impact on work performance in terms of productivity, quality of output, and accidents. Thus, the physical environment is an important consideration in the design of the job. While studies clearly show that adverse physical conditions do have a negative effect on performance, the degree of influence frequently varies from individual to individual. The importance of safety considerations in the design process was magnified by the passage of the Occupational Safety and Health Act of 1970 (OSHA). Designed to reduce the incidence of job injuries, the Act outlines very specific federal safety guidelines which must be followed by U.S. organizations. The purpose of the act is to assure every worker a safe and healthy work environment.

HUMAN FACTORS

A body of knowledge has developed that is known as human factors engineering. It is also referred to as ergonomics, engineering psychology, biomechanics, and so forth. The principal focus of human factors engineering has been the development of principles and data to be used in adapting equipment and the work environment to the human element. It relates to sensorimotor processes, physical stress and fatigue, and associated environmental phenomena.

Physical activity and stresses of work cause changes in heart rate, oxygen consumption, and blood pressure, as well as other metabolic functions. By using physiological measurements, the effects of different types and levels of work can be measured. The energy or physiological cost of work can be measured and expressed in calories per unit of time. The energy consumption of a worker varies from around 2 calories per minute for clerical activity to approximately 10 calories per minute for heavy work. The heart rate can double from its normal 70 beats per minute to over 140 during strenuous physical activity. While there is no complete agreement on an energy standard, attempts have been made to utilize energy data in the establishment of work standards.

Physical activities involving large muscle masses, such as are common in moderate to heavy manual labor, are suitable for physiological measurement. However, environmental factors such as temperature and humidity can dramatically influence these measurements. If these factors are not constant over the work period, the measurements will be spurious. Tasks that involve a high level of localized fatigue are not suitable for heart rate or oxygen consumption analyses.

Job designers have gradually shifted human efforts from physical labor to decision making and equipment control. Current trends indicate that a substantial portion of jobs will be less physical in nature. There will be a larger portion of jobs involving sensorimotor performance. Of particular importance in these jobs will be the perceptual capacity of the worker. While fatigue reduces performance where heavy physical activity is involved, reduction in performance efficiency for less physical jobs is more likely to be psychological than physiological. The problem of fatigue is usually combated with rest periods.

TEMPERATURE

Although human beings can function under a wide range of temperatures, work performance can be adversely affected unless they are kept within a narrow comfort zone. Increased fatigue is experienced for physical jobs outside the comfort zone, while more errors are encountered for mental jobs. In general, temperature control involves consideration of relative humidity and rate of air flow as well as the temperature itself. The combination of all three must be considered in establishing a desirable work environment.

A human has a homeostatic average body temperature of 98.6 degrees Fahrenheit. This temperature is automatically maintained by physiological changes. In hot environments, perspiration is generated to cool the body. In cold environments, much more energy is expended to maintain the body's temperature. It is desirable to have a work environment that does not require the body to respond to temperature extremes. Although it depends on the nature of operations, a temperature from 60 to 70 degrees is acceptable in most cases. Workers engaged in manual operations prefer lower temperatures than sedentary workers. Temperature extremes may significantly increase the physiological cost of performing any job.

Where temperature control is impractical or impossible, appropriate support equipment or clothing can be made available. In cold areas, insulated boots, trousers, parkas, and gloves may be desirable. In warm areas, light clothing tends to dissipate body heat. Cold liquids and salt tablets should be available in warm areas, and warm liquids in cold areas.

The humidity level is an important factor in temperature control. Humidity is measured as the ratio of the moisture content of air to that which it could contain at a given temperature. If the humidity is low, more heat can be endured. A dry environment of less than 50% humidity is usually more pleasant for work.

ILLUMINATION

The amount of illumination desirable for a job depends on the individual involved and the nature of the work. Jobs that require exacting discrimination demand more illumination than less detailed work. The standard measure of light intensity is the footcandle (the amount of light cast by a standard candle on a one foot square panel at a distance of one foot). Recommended illumination levels for a multitude of situations are published by the Illuminating Engineering Society (IES). Some recommended levels of illumination for various tasks are as follows:

Light intensity (foot-candles)	Task, application, or places
1000	Extremely fine machining and assembly, precision surgical operations
200	Fine machining, drafting, close inspection
150	Accounting, tabulating, business machine operation
100	Filing, sorting, assembly
70	Reading, studying, typing
50	Ordinary inspection, general office work, wrapping
30	Interviewing, shipping and receiving
20	Stairways, elevators, washrooms

An employee cannot function effectively without an adequate amount of light. Research has shown that illumination levels lower than the recommendations lead to fatigue and errors in job performance. However, increases in illumination far above the recommendations do not eliminate fatigue and errors.

The quantity of light is only one significant measurement. The quality of light (such as the amount of glare and the contrast) may also be important. Glare is an undesirable effect of illumination. It can affect visual performance and cause discomfort. Glare may be direct (caused by the primary light source) or reflected (caused by reflection from bright and glossy surfaces). Light should be cast on the work area rather than in the line of vision of the employee. Dull surfaces and light-colored walls tend to reduce glare. Strong contrasts in light intensity in the work area are also undesirable.

NOISE

Noise refers to sound that is unwanted because it is sudden, unpleasant, or loud. It is a health hazard, an annoyance, and an environmental pollutant both inside and outside the work environment. It contributes to hearing loss, speech interference, activity disruption, and stress. Almost everyone is exposed daily to noise from a number of sources.

Sound is measured by its intensity (or amplitude) and its frequency (or pitch). The human auditory system is extremely sensitive to sound pressure, and can accommodate sounds with intensities 10 billion times greater than a barely audible sound. Since the range of amplitudes encountered in the everyday environment is so great, a logarithmic scale, called the decibel (dB) scale, is used to measure sound pressure. The softest sound that can be heard (20 micropascals) corresponds to zero decibels. With this sound level as a baseline, each time the intensity is increased by a factor of 10, the corresponding decibel value increases by 10 decibels. Thus, a sound with a pressure 10 times as large as the barely audible level would be at 10 dB, a pressure 100 times as large would be at 20 dB, and a pressure 1000 times as large would be at 30 dB.

When the sound pressure becomes very great, pain will normally be experienced. This occurs at between 120 and 140 dB. However, sound levels well below the pain threshold can cause permanent damage to the hearing mechanism with extended exposure; they can result in hearing impairment or even total deafness.

Some typical noise levels as measured on the decibel scale are as follows:

Pressure level (decibels)	Noise source
130	Approximate pain threshold
115	Jet engine
110	Riveter
100	Noise in car passing truck at 60 mph
95	Pneumatic drill
90	$3\frac{1}{2}$ hp lawn mower
80	Phone ringing
70	Electric alarm clock
60	Typical office
50	Quiet office
20	Whispered conversation
0	Sound threshold

The frequency of sound, measured in cycles per second (hertz) is also significant for the effect of noise on an individual. The range of human hearing extends from 20 to 20,000 cycles per second. The high and low frequencies are relatively inaudible. Sound pressure level and frequency interact in establishing the threshold of hearing sensitivity. Noise with only low frequency components is less annoying than noise with predominately high frequencies (shrill sounds such as sirens).

Noise affects some people more than others. Most people's hearing deteriorates as they get older, perhaps because they have been overexposed to noise. Employees have an ability to adapt to noisy conditions within reasonable limits without decreasing their performance. As the level gets higher, it becomes annoying, potentially damaging, and finally physically painful. Hearing loss results from subjection to high noise levels over long periods of time. However, there is little agreement as to how long is long or how high is high. Most experts believe that harmful effects can be expected from noise levels above 90 dB.

Nuisance noise, well below the level of physical harm can contribute to lowering worker performance. Infrequent, irregular, high pitched, or resounding sounds are annoying and distracting. Workers tend to become irritable, nervous, and more easily fatigued in a noisy environment. However, a degree of accommodation may result from continued exposure.

Noise abatement procedures usually involve:

1. elimination or reduction of the noise at its source (redesign, reduction of vibration, and the use of noise insulation devices for the mounting of moving parts),
2. isolation of the noise from the workers by barriers (baffles, enclosures, distance, or sound absorption devices),
3. dampening or absorption of noise by protective devices for workers (helmets, earplugs, or ear covers).

COLOR

Color in the work environment has an effect on employee performance; it is additionally used for plant safety and color coding. Light colors reflect light better and improve the level of illumination. Human reaction to color is not uniform, but the "cool colors" (greens, blues, beige) are usually restful and unobtrusive. The "warm colors" (red, orange, yellow) draw attention and create excitement which can result in eventual fatigue. Most workers feel cooler in light green or blue surroundings and warmer in red or dark orange. Color on walls and equipment is usually in dull or flat finishes, rather than glossy finishes, which can create glare.

Emergency equipment is usually painted red. Potentially dangerous areas are often outlined in yellow. Color coding is also used to help differentiate valves, pipes, wires, and hazardous materials.

SAFETY

At one time or another all employees are subjected to hazards on the job. An important consideration in job design must be the safety of employees. Accidents occur for two basic reasons: first, employees are careless on the job, and second, unsafe conditions exist in the work environment. Safety programs and training to instill safety consciousness can help reduce employee carelessness. In safety education, instruction is provided on the proper and safe ways to perform tasks.

Safety is not one problem but many. The potential hazards are so varied that there is no single solution. Any work environment has conditions that can result in personal injury. It is impossible or uneconomic to protect against all risks. Statistically, a person is safer on the job than in his own home. Even with safe working conditions, however, accidents can occur from unsafe human practices.

Unsafe working conditions may pertain to facilities, toxic materials, machines, materials handling, layout, maintenance, and general housekeeping. Workers are often protected against hazards through the use of protective devices. Typical examples of such devices are respirators, safety eyeglasses, hard hats, earplugs, steel toed shoes, and protective clothing.

Toxic materials are a constant source of danger to personnel. Chemicals, irritating fluids, noxious fumes, and various kinds of dust are health hazards. Some materials create health problems with prolonged human exposure. Polyvinyl chloride, asbestos, and certain insecticides are known cancer causing agents. Many substances can impair body functions and damage human organs.

Machinery and equipment are a common source of accidents. Moving parts or components can sever or mangle human appendages. Loose clothing or jewelry can become entangled in moving parts. Moving parts should be housed or encased and have guards.

Materials handling equipment by its nature involves motion. Improper operation of materials handling equipment can result in serious accidents. Education of operators on proper utilization is an endless task. Inspection and repair of handling equipment can reduce hazards. Conveyors, cranes, trucks, and special handling devices are responsible for a significant portion of industrial accidents.

Good layout of facilities can contribute to accident prevention. Typical layout hazards include narrow aisles, blind corners, sharp edges, protruding obstacles, and overhead obstructions. Entrances, exits, stairways, and elevators are frequent accident areas. Well lighted, marked, and color coded designations can improve safety conditions.

Lack of proper maintenance frequently results in mishaps. Machinery and equipment should be serviced properly. Vehicles and moving stock should be well maintained and checked periodically. Preventive maintenance is frequently preferable to failure maintenance.

General housekeeping refers to keeping a clean and orderly facility. Poor housekeeping results in many injuries in organizations as well as in homes. Dirty floors lead to falls. Cluttered and littered work areas lead to fires as well as injuries. There should be a place for everything and everything should be in its place.

JOB DESCRIPTIONS

A job description is a written statement outlining the contents and essential requirements of a job. The tasks and activities that are part of the job are defined and described. Many job descriptions contain three general parts:

1. a summary of duties, responsibilities, and working conditions,
2. the details of key tasks and responsibilities,
3. qualifications for employees in the job.

A job description's scope and content depend on its intended use. It usually contains the job title, a description of the job itself, a statement of the duties and responsibilities required, and sometimes the minimum experience, skill, education, physical abilities, and so forth. For some jobs, it delineates such factors as working conditions, supervision required, and tools and equipment used in performance of the job. A job description may be written by industrial engineers, managers, supervisors, foremen, the personnel department, or the workers themselves. Wage and salary ranges may also be listed. Generally, the more skill, education, and responsibility required in a job, the more it is worth.

CONCLUSION

Job design is the planned structuring of human work effort. It is a continuous effort as opposed to a one-time requirement. Job design is manifested through job descriptions. The task of designing and improving (redesigning) jobs never ends. Probably the time will never come when it is not possible to make further improvements.

QUESTIONS

1. Generally speaking, how have work systems changed?
2. How does operations design affect job design?
3. Distinguish between job content and work methods.
4. Give some advantages of division of labor.
5. Define specialization, standardization, discretion, and expertise as they relate to job structures.
6. Contrast job scope and job depth.
7. What is motion study? How does a motion analyst accomplish the purposes of motion study?
8. Describe the major work analysis tools.
9. To what general categories do the principles of motion economy apply?
10. Cite some of the suggested approaches for creating "satisfying" jobs.
11. Job performance can be shown to be a function of what components?
12. What does human factors engineering contribute to job design?
13. What significance do illumination studies have for job design?
14. What information regarding sound pressures is of interest in job design?
15. How can some accidents be prevented in the workplace?
16. Briefly outline the contents of a job description.

CASE 1: DRACONIAN

At Draconian Industries, Hannibal, Mo., quality circles were started after President Reinhardt "Reiny" Tumbach completed a quality-circle (QC) study program sponsored by the International Association of Quality Circles (IAQC) in Midwest City, Oklahoma. Reiny wanted to avail himself of the QC approach, because it held the promise of improving productivity and involved the least time and expense of all the techniques seen as responsible for Japan's success. At the conference, the Draconian CEO was impressed by the other attendees' testimonials of quick, visible improvements (proponents claimed that QCs could do just about anything—increase productivity, improve quality, reduce costs, boost employee morale, and brighten the company's image). For example, the chairman of an iron and steel company declared that 25% of his company's profits were due to QCs, and another chief executive reported 70% cost reductions on two post-QC projects. By the conclusion of the conference, Reiny was confident in the behavioral technique and sure that Draconian would achieve financial benefits soon after its own QC implementation.

The management of Draconian Industries typically played conventional roles. The company's organizational structure had developed into a vertical arrangement (long chains of command). Most company information was tightly held by staff members, and operating departments functioned autonomously. Reiny realized that this situation was quite distinct from the harmonious work force situations popularized at the conference. He felt an abandonment of curt directives for more democratic methods would result in anywhere from 4:1 to 10:1 direct return on the QC investment (the payoff ratio publicized in the QC literature). The move to participative management styles was to lead to cost reductions through the elimination of scrap materials, the labor required to rework or replace poor-quality parts, and the time required to rectify the mistakes in records and other similar functions.

The initial structure of Draconian's QCs was a standard composition in an effort to duplicate the prescribed Japanese format. There were groups of eight volunteers who held regular QC meetings; each group's members worked in the same area and all were day-shift employees. Reiny served as the first facilitator and was responsible for scheduling meetings, providing training for members, keeping meetings on course, and fulfilling the liaison position between the circles and the organization. Top-level executives formed the steering committee which meshed the circles with the corporate structure. They set the objectives for the program (e.g. better equipment utilization, unit output per hour, cost reduction, damaged goods scrappage, etc.); established the ground rules; determined the funding methods; developed guidelines (such as what to do about "weak" members); set up a reporting system; and determined where circles were to be started and how they would be evaluated. In its implementation, the QC approach became the fastest single system put into operation at Draconian.

The most tangible evidence of the system at work was the "management presentation session" where members presented their solutions to problems. All involved parties, such as representatives of other departments and the top management of the company, tried to attend. Usually about 50 people heard each presentation, and management generally would give its final decision within two weeks. Almost 70% of the proposals were accepted without alteration, and only 10% were rejected outright.

During the second quarter of QC operation, Reiny became dissatisfied with this esteemed management tool. No cost-effective productivity increases had been measured. In fact, the introduction of QCs actually reduced productivity by 2.5%, which typically corresponded to the amount of time workers spent conducting the business of the circle. Already discouraged about the money and effort spent on the program, Reiny was more disconcerted by the cost elements of funds allocated to the continuation of the program—training sessions and materials, loss of productive time for training and circle meetings, and prospective consultants' fees. Reiny considered the initial QC effort a failure and thought desuetude its logical end.

The members of the steering committee wanted the program to remain in existence. Moreover, they had hoped to inaugurate the following actions within the next program phase:

a. Persuasion of the reluctant first-line supervisors to participate as circle leaders.
b. Establishment of a task force (separate from the steering committee) to cope with many of the lesser problems (particularly those where quick payoffs were expected).
c. Abbreviated meetings.
d. Solicitation of outsiders (mild pressure on nonmembers).
e. Creation of a method for gain-sharing (means to extrinsically reward circle members who contribute—preferably in the form of financial recognition restricted to spending on work-related projects).
f. Establishment of training programs for statistical quality control (segregated according to previous experience and level of sophistication).

Given the opposing attitudes of the CEO and his executive steering committee, the future of QCs at Draconian was problematic.

1. Did the QC program fail? Why or why not?
2. How tenable are the proposed changes? What recommendations would you have made?
3. Comment on a QC program's ability to hike productivity. Make particular references to issues in the case.

CASE 2: DOMICILIARY "SWEATSHOPS"

Janet Stickrod had been to upstate Vermont many times as a "flatlander" there to gaze at autumn's splendor. But her latest visit to the Lake Champlain countryside was as a representative of the U.S. Labor Department to assist exploited workers and squelch egregious labor violations. Janet was sent to investigate breaches of the Fair Labor Standards Act being perpetrated by knitwear companies. Yarns were consigned to local women to knit into ski caps for pay. Although the work apparently was done voluntarily, governmental statutes prohibiting "homework" were broken in the process. Specifically, the infractions included violations of minimum wage standards, premiums for overtime, restrictions on working hours, and legal record-keeping and reporting requirements.

The practice of working at home was outlawed 40 years earlier when "sweatshop" conditions prevailed in the garment industry. The homework issue resurfaced when the growth in homework proceeds became almost unchecked and when unions and other interest groups openly objected to its lawlessness. Janet, who personally held the time-honored view of sweatshops, was a leader in the public crusade to abolish the practice. She went to Vermont to uncover the culprits, end unfair competitive practices, secure workers their rights under the law, and in general, provide genuine and substantive relief for the workers.

During the course of her investigation, Janet conducted interviews with the women employed to do homework. She recorded the following responses regarding her efforts:

"I enjoy my work at home, because I work when I want, as fast as I want, and where I want."

"You have no right to tell me what I can do in my own home—I'm a consenting adult in a capitalistic country."

"This isn't Miami or New York. I know what I'm doing. I am not being taken advantage of because I don't have citizenship papers or speak the language."

"I don't understand denying me the opportunity for honest labor. This is the first time in my life that I've worked leisurely and enjoyed my family at the same time. There must be a dollars-and-cents reason you are doing this."

The Labor Department wanted to put them out of business to spare them any possible misuse at the expense of their employers. The department maintained that if the majority of the people protected under a law would otherwise be subjected to abuse, exploitation, or other such unsafe or unjust practices, then that piece of legislation is warranted and worth enforcing in a democratic society. Even though social legislation which requires that all workers be paid a minimum wage or that workers refrain from industrial homework may be detrimental to a few, the law combats the previous and potential injustices inflicted on the masses.

Janet had seen horrid examples of what could develop in the absence of enforced social legislation. Some of her accounts to the Vermont women resembled descriptives of 19th century practices. The modern sweatshops flouted federal laws—workers were paid trifling wages for 12 hour days in their own deplorable work places. Moreover, these employees, who were treated so inhumanly, often worked illegally. These undocumented workers filled many jobs in the needle occupations that legitimately should have employed American workers.

The employers, the knitwear companies, had their own hardship story. The industry had a difficult time finding workers, because the work was hard and tedious but required basic skills. The trade was extremely competitive, margins were low, work was seasonal, and members barely could afford to pay welfare wages and still remain in business. Many firms easily entered the industry but were forced out through rapid style changes and poor cash returns.

Janet, while preparing for the hearings on the homework issue, kept mulling over and over the positions of the ladies, the Labor Department, the industry, the unions, and all of the other critics and reform groups. Life in Vermont no longer was simple.

1. Outline the pros and cons of homework and minimum wage laws.
2. Are the laws misapplied in this case? Is reform necessary? If so, what course should it take?
3. What implications for job design are present in this case?

SELECTED BIBLIOGRAPHY

Altimus, Jr., C. A. and R. J. Tersine. "Chronological Age and Job Satisfaction: The Young Blue Collar Worker," *Academy of Management Journal,* March 1973.

Barnes, R. M. *Motion and Time Study,* New York: Wiley, 1968.

Chapanis, A. *Man–Machine Engineering,* Belmont, CA: Wadsworth, 1965.

Dickson, P. *The Future of the Work Place,* New York: Weybright and Talley, 1975.

McCormick, E. J. *Human Engineering,* New York: McGraw-Hill, 1976.

Neibel, B. W. *Motion and Time Study,* Homewood, IL: Irwin, 1982.

Steers, R. M. and R. T. Mowday. "The Motivational Properties of Tasks," *The Academy of Management Review,* Vol. 2, No. 4, October 1977.

Terkel, S. *Working,* New York: Pantheon, 1972.

Tersine, R. J. and C. A. Altimus, Jr. "Job Satisfaction: High and Low Job-Skill Level Blue Collar Workers," *Journal of Business Research,* January 1974.

Vroom, V. H. *Work and Motivation,* New York: Wiley, 1964.

11

Work Measurement

INFORMAL TIME STANDARDS

STOPWATCH TIME STUDY
    Elemental Analysis
    Time Measurement
    Sample Size
    Performance Rating
    Standard Time Development

WORK SAMPLING

PREDETERMINED TIME STUDY

WAGES AND INCENTIVES

CONCLUSION

QUESTIONS

PROBLEMS

CASES

SELECTED BIBLIOGRAPHY

Technology, automation, and computers are changing work habits and relationships, but labor remains a predominant factor in the work environment. Work measurement is a tool for evaluating and planning labor utilization in production systems. It is the methodical analysis of tasks for the purpose of establishing standard times for their performance using specified methods under prescribed conditions.

Work measurement, known also as time study, determines the amount of time required to perform a unit of work. It establishes the amount of time required by a qualified worker, using a standard method and working at a standard work pace, to perform a specified operation. When properly utilized, work measurement can increase overall efficiency, which can make possible higher wages for labor, lower prices for consumers, and higher profits for equity interests.

Before work measurement commences, job design and work relationships must be established and standardized. Standards permit a comparison of actual and planned manpower performance. They also assist in determining other resource requirements used as inputs to a system.

The output from work measurement is production time standards. A time standard usually includes the working time of an employee, with allowances for personal delays, unavoidable delays, and fatigue. If management is to utilize labor inputs efficiently, it must formulate standard methods of work performance.

Production time standards are used for many purposes in an organization. The application of even the most basic of quantitative techniques requires work measurement data. Estimates of labor costs (how much output can be expected per unit of time) are needed in numerous calculations. A few decisions in which production standards play a vital role are as follows:

1. determination of manpower levels,
2. make or buy decisions,
3. equipment replacement decisions,
4. product pricing,
5. contract bids and estimates,
6. estimation of delivery dates,
7. labor cost control,
   a. performance comparisons,
   b. employee compensation,
8. scheduling of jobs and machines.

Work measurement techniques have developed into several distinct categories. The most common work measurement techniques are stopwatch time study, work sampling, and predetermined time studies. These techniques will be discussed in this chapter.

INFORMAL TIME STANDARDS

All organizations have some type of production standards. Even when they do not exist formally, there are informal standards based on knowledge of the work and past performance. Many organizations make do with simple judgmental estimates based on past experience. Such estimates are inexpensive to derive and are quickly and easily formulated, but may not be sufficiently accurate.

They are also subjective, inconsistent, and subject to bias. Since the work method is not standardized, it is difficult to establish a time rate. If past performance is based on numerous work methods, the time standard will be inconsistent. It's like trying to measure something that keeps changing. Also, past experience tends to be based on the working speeds of certain individuals. Were those workers high or low performers? Were they using the proper work methods? When informal time standards are used by an organization, their pitfalls should be as carefully ascertained as are their benefits.

STOPWATCH TIME STUDY

Stopwatch time study is a technique of work measurement in which work is observed directly while it is being performed. An analyst takes a sample of one worker's activity and uses it to derive a standard for the entire organization. A stopwatch is used to determine the time required for a qualified and well-trained worker to accomplish a specific task while working at a normal pace. A qualified worker is one who is physically and mentally suited to the job and who possesses the necessary training, skills, and knowledge to carry out the job with sufficient safety, quality, and speed. Stopwatch time studies are usually confined to repetitive, short-cycle tasks that are currently being performed.

There is no set procedure for constructing a stopwatch time study, but the following basic steps must be completed:

1. Select and record information about operation and operator.
2. Verify standard work methods and conditions.
3. Divide the operation into job elements.
4. Record the observed (actual) time required for each element.
5. Determine the sample/cycle size for the desired level of accuracy and precision.
6. Determine the average time for each job element.
7. Performance rate the operator for each job element.
8. Determine the normal operation time (summation of 6 × 7).
9. Determine the allowances associated with the operation.
10. Determine the standard time for the operation.

In the initial phase the time study analyst will record pertinent information such as the name of the operator, the location of the study, the date, and a description of the operation. Additionally he usually sketches a layout of the workplace and lists all equipment, materials, fixtures, jigs, and tools. This descriptive information may be essential at a later date to determine if a methods change has occurred and a revision is needed in the time standard.

ELEMENTAL ANALYSIS

The operation being studied should be standardized as to method, materials, and conditions. It makes little sense to time study operations that are changing or non-standardized. The operation should be broken down into separable elements. The elements contain a series of motions that can be identified, described, and recorded. In subdividing an operation into elements, it is recommended that (1) the elements have distinct beginning and end points, (2) the elements be as short as can conveniently be timed, (3) human times and machine times be separated, (4) constant elements be separated from variable elements, and (5) repetitive elements appearing in each cycle be separated from intermittent elements that appear less frequently.

After all the work elements of an operation are identified, a complete description of each element is entered on a time study record in the sequence of its occurrence. Each element should be sufficiently described so it can be duplicated at a later date. For any given job, a number of different elemental breakdowns are possible. The elemental breakdown serves as a detailed job description of the operation for future purposes. Additionally, the element data can be cataloged for a handbook of standard data times that can be used on jobs with similar elements. Thus it can be helpful for predetermined time studies.

TIME MEASUREMENT

After the operation has been divided into its elements, the measurement of element times can commence. Element times are taken directly at the workplace with stopwatches or from motion pictures. Stopwatch studies are far more numerous than camera studies owing to their greater versatility and lower cost. The continuous and the snapback stopwatch are the two most common measurement devices.

With the *continuous stopwatch,* the analyst records the time when an element starts and when it finishes on the time study sheet. The watch is started from zero at the beginning of the study and is not stopped until all the cycles being timed are completed. At no point is the watch reset to zero; as it runs without interruption, the analyst records the reading at the end of each element. The elapsed time for each element is obtained at the end of the study by taking the difference between successive readings. With the *snapback stopwatch,* no subtraction is necessary. Each element starts at time zero and its duration is recorded; the device is snapped back to zero for the next element. The process is repeated for each element for as many cycles as necessary in the study. Each device has its advantages and each probably results in about the same degree of accuracy. Some believe that continuous is best because it includes the overall time for the study, eliminates the requirement for snapping back to zero, and eliminates the possibility of deleting delays.

Stopwatches in use today include a variety of timing devices. The older decimal-minute stopwatches are being superceded by digital electronic devices. These newer devices range from pushbutton ones with visual display (similar to hand calculators) to ones with keyboard entry recorded on magnetic tape that can be computer-processed immediately or stored for later retrieval.

SAMPLE SIZE

The time required to perform an operation can be expected to vary from cycle to cycle. Since work measurement is a sampling process, the analyst must include a sufficient number of cycles to give an adequate representation of the statistical population from which the time values are chosen. To determine the adequate size of the sample for a time study it is necessary to consider the variability of each element in the study. It is also necessary to conduct a preliminary study so some data are available to make an estimation. A preliminary study usually consists of a sample of 5 to 20 successive cycles of the operation.

The number of cycles that must be timed is a function of three things: (1) the variability of observed times, (2) the desired precision, and (3) the desired confidence level. A 95% confidence and 5% precision level mean the analyst wants the sample average to be within 5% of the population average 95 out of 100 times. A different sample size may be required for each element. Thus, the sample size will be governed by the element that calls for the largest sample size. The element with the greatest variability will tend to control the size of the sample necessary to give the required confidence. The usual desired confidence is 95% with a precision of ± 5%. The following formula will give the sample size for a desired confidence and precision level based on a normal distribution:

$$N = \frac{nZ^2[n\Sigma X^2 - (\Sigma X)^2]}{(n - 1)p^2(\Sigma X)^2} = \text{required sample size,}$$

where

n = preliminary sample size,
X = elemental stopwatch time,
p = precision level fraction,
Z = confidence level factor ($Z = 1$ for 68.3% confidence level, $Z = 2$ for 95.5% confidence level, and $Z = 3$ for 99.7% confidence level).

If the required sample size is less than the preliminary sample size, the study can be concluded. However, if the required sample size is more than the preliminary sample size, the study must be repeated until the cycle size equals the required sample size. After the study is completed, it is necessary to recheck the data to see if the sample size was adequate.

PERFORMANCE RATING

Each element of an operation must be performance rated. The performance rating, which is also called leveling, is the rate an experienced time study analyst assigns to the operator to indicate his work pace in relationship to what a normal worker would accomplish. The particular operator under study must be rated as above average, average, or below average on each element. Elemental ratings are desirable because (1) the worker's proficiency may not be the same for all elements of the job, (2) some elements may not be performed in every cycle, and (3) it develops a file of standard elemental times which can be used to set times synthetically for other jobs. The time study analyst passes judgment on the operator's efficiency in assigning the rating. The performance rating is applied because the work measurement is to determine what a normal worker would be expected to accomplish. Without the performance rating, there would be no transferability of the standard to other workers; it would apply only to the operator involved in the study. For a normal worker, the performance rating is 100%. A performance rating above 100% means the worker is faster than normal; below 100%, that he is slower.

Time study is a skill. The use of the stopwatch requires training and practice. The art of performance rating requires the analyst to retrain periodically, usually with training machines and motion pictures of standard rates and speeds.[1] These motion pictures show operations being performed at different paces for which consensus

---

[1]One source of such films is the Society for the Advancement of Management.

ratings have been developed. Examples of these rating standards are walking at a rate of 3 miles per hour on a smooth level surface, and dealing a standard deck of 52 playing cards into four equal piles in 0.5 minutes.

When an analyst is conducting a time study, he rates the operator for the job element by comparing the tempo with the normal tempo from films of activities of comparable difficulty. As you might suspect, performance rating is a controversial aspect of stopwatch time studies. The rating factor is influenced by the effort and skill of the operator as well as the job difficulty.

STANDARD TIME DEVELOPMENT

There are three different kinds of time; actual time, normal time, and standard time. *Actual time* is the mean time it takes for the operator to perform each element in the operation. *Normal time* is the time required to perform the operation by an operator who is working at 100% efficiency (100% performance rating) with no delays (avoidable or unavoidable). Finally, *standard time* is the time required to perform the operation by an operator who is working at 100% efficiency with unavoidable delays but no avoidable delays.

All stopwatch time studies involve the measurement of the actual observed time, the adjustment of the observed time to a normal time by means of a performance rating, and the adjustment of the normal time to the standard time to include allowances (interruptions, fatigue, personal needs) for the operation. The allowances include all unavoidable delays, but exclude avoidable delays. The performance rating adjusts the observed time to what a normal worker could be expected to accomplish.

Since unavoidable delays do not occur with regularity on every cycle of the job, the adjustments are not made for each element. Instead, they are made as one allowance which is applied to the normal time of the operation. The allowance factor includes time lost because of fatigue, faulty materials, breaks for personal needs, machine breakdowns, maintaining the work area, supervisory direction, and so forth. The allowance factor can be determined statistically from work sampling, by judgment, or sometimes by collective bargaining.[2]

When all of the elemental times have been computed, average elemental times can be determined. Once the elemental performance ratings are established, they are multiplied by the average elemental times. The total (summation) of the average elemental times adjusted for efficiency by the performance rating is the normal time for the operation. The inclusion of the allowance time with the normal time results in the standard time for the operation.

The normal time and standard time are determined by the following formulas:

$$\text{normal time} = \sum \left[(\text{average element time}) \frac{\text{performance rating}}{100} \right],$$

$$\text{standard time} = \text{normal time} + \text{allowance time}$$

$$= \frac{\text{normal time}}{1 - \text{allowance fraction}}.$$

---

[2]The allowance factor is taken as a fraction of standard time in this section. Sometimes it is defined as a fraction of normal time.

EXAMPLE 1

An operation consisting of three elements has been subjected to a stopwatch time study. The raw data are contained in the table below. The allowance for the operation is 20%. What is the standard time for the operation? What should the standard be in hours per 1000 units?

Job element	Performance rating (%)	Observations (seconds/element)										Mean time (sec)	Normal time (sec)
		1	2	3	4	5	6	7	8	9	10		
1	90	7	7	8	9	8	10	10	8	9	7	8.3	7.47
2	100	14	14	18	15	14	14	15	16	16	14	15.0	15.00
3	110	8	7	8	9	9	7	7	8	7	8	7.8	8.58
													31.05

$$\text{standard time} = \frac{\text{normal time}}{1 - \text{allowance fraction}}$$

$$= \frac{31.05}{1 - 0.20} = 38.81 \text{ sec/unit,}$$

$$(1000 \text{ units}) \cdot (38.81 \text{ sec/unit}) \cdot \frac{1}{60 \text{ sec/min}} \cdot \frac{1}{60 \text{ min/hr}} = 10.78 \text{ hr.}$$

The standard time is 38.81 seconds/unit, and the standard for 1000 units is 10.78 hours.

EXAMPLE 2

The time study analyst in Example 1 wants to determine if his sample size was large enough. A confidence of 95.5% with a precision of ± 5% is desired. What is the required sample size?

Sample or cycle	Element 1		Element 2		Element 3	
	X	X^2	X	X^2	X	X^2
1	7	49	14	196	8	64
2	7	49	14	196	7	49
3	8	64	18	324	8	64
4	9	81	15	225	9	81
5	8	64	14	196	9	81
6	10	100	14	196	7	49
7	10	100	15	225	7	49
8	8	64	16	256	8	64
9	9	81	16	256	7	49
10	7	49	14	196	8	64
Total	83	701	150	2266	78	614

continued

EXAMPLE 2—*continued*

Element 1: $N = \dfrac{nZ^2[n\Sigma X^2 - (\Sigma X)^2]}{(n-1)p^2(\Sigma X)^2} = \dfrac{10(4)[10(701) - 6889]}{9(0.0025)\,6889} = 31.2$, or 32.

Element 2: $N = \dfrac{10(4)[10(2266) - 22,500]}{9(0.0025)22,500} = 12.6$, or 13.

Element 3: $N = \dfrac{10(4)[10(614) - 6084]}{9(0.0025)6084} = 16.4$, or 17.

The first element gives the largest required sample size of 32. The analyst should take 22 more samples of the operation, so the total sample size is 32.

WORK SAMPLING

Work sampling is a work measurement technique that requires direct observation of the work but does not require a stopwatch time study analyst to establish output standards. The absence of stopwatches and highly visible analysts reduces some of the negative psychological influences of direct observation. Work sampling can also be used for intermittent tasks where stopwatch time study is inadequate or too costly. The cost of work sampling is less than for formal stopwatch studies, and work samplers do not have to be as highly trained as stopwatch analysts. Many nonmanufacturing (service) operations are well adapted to work sampling measurement.

Work sampling is sometimes referred to as ratio-delay study. It is a statistical technique based upon the laws of probability and random sampling. It consists of taking a number of intermittent, randomly spaced, and instantaneous (brief) observations of an activity and from them determining the percentage of time devoted to each category. If an adequate number of observations are taken, this percentage can be considered accurate. Work sampling is used extensively in the following ways:

1. To measure working and nonworking time for delay allowance purposes.
2. To estimate the percentage utilization of machines and equipment (cranes, forklifts, tools).
3. To estimate the percentage of time devoted to various job activities.
4. To measure an operation and establish a time standard for it.

Work sampling has been used in repair and maintenance activities, janitorial service, retailing, health care, and warehousing.

The analyst simply records for each random observation whether the operative is working or idle. After all the observations have been taken, the proportion of working observations is determined. From information obtained from the sample, inferences are made about the universe of work activity. The key to the accuracy of the technique is in the number of observations. A greater number of observations provides a higher degree of accuracy. The number of observations required in work sampling can be large, ranging from several hundred to several thousand, depending on the operation and the desired degree of accuracy.

Determining the sample size required necessitates a statement concerning the desired confidence and precision level. Just as with the stopwatch study, a preliminary sample must be taken to obtain estimates of parameter values. The usual desired confidence is 95% with a precision of $\pm 5\%$. The following formula will give the sample size for a desired confidence and precision level:

$$N = \frac{Z^2 \, (1 - f)}{p^2 f} = \text{required sample size,}$$

where

$$
\begin{aligned}
f &= \text{proportion of time spent in an activity,} \\
1 - f &= \text{proportion of time not spent in an activity,} \\
p &= \text{precision level fraction,} \\
Z &= \text{confidence level factor } (Z = 1 \text{ for } 68.3\% \text{ confidence level, } Z = 2 \text{ for} \\
& \quad 95.5\% \text{ confidence level, and } Z = 3 \text{ for } 99.7\% \text{ confidence level).}
\end{aligned}
$$

Note that as the confidence level factor increases and/or the precision level fraction decreases, the size of the sample increases. The 95% confidence level and $\pm 5\%$ precision level have the following meaning: you are confident that in 95 cases out of 100 the proportion of time in an activity will be correct within $\pm 5\%$ of f.[3]

EXAMPLE 3

An organization wants to know the percentage of time an operation is idle with a confidence of 95.5% and a precision of $\pm 5\%$. A preliminary random sample of 100 observations indicates 25% idleness. What further analysis is required?

It is necessary to determine the required sample size for the confidence level and precision desired. The required sample size is determined as follows:

$$N = \frac{Z^2(1 - f)}{p^2 f} = \frac{4(1 - 0.25)}{0.0025(0.25)} = 4800.$$

Since 100 observations have been taken and 4800 are required, another 4700 observations should be made. After the additional observations have been taken, the precision level should be verified. For example, suppose the idle fraction is 0.28 after all of the observations. The precision level would be as follows:

$$4800 = \frac{4(1 - .28)}{p^2(0.28)},$$

$$p = \pm 0.046, \text{ or } \pm 4.6\%.$$

Since the $\pm 4.6\%$ precision is below the required 5%, the number of observations is sufficient. This means the results are correct within $\pm 4.6\%$ of 28% ($\pm 4.6 \times 28\% = \pm 1.3\%$), so that the operator idle time is between 26.7% and 29.3%.

---

[3]The sample size formula above is based on a precision level that has a range of $f \pm pf$. When an absolute precision level with a range of $f \pm p$ is desired, the appropriate sample size formula is $N = Z^2 f(1 - f)/p^2$.

As with stopwatch studies, work sampling also can be used to set production standards. For certain operations, work sampling will probably be better than other methods. This is true for long cycle operations, some group activities, and work that involves indirect labor. The analyst does not concern himself with the elements of the operation being studied. He simply records whether the operator is working or idle at random points over a given period of time. The analyst also performance rates the operator each time he is observed and obtains an average performance rate for the job. Once all the observations have been recorded, the normal time can be determined by the following formula:

$$\text{normal time} = \frac{(\text{total study time})(\text{working time fraction})(\text{perf. rating})}{\text{number of units produced}}.$$

The standard time is the normal time plus allowance time, or

$$\text{standard time} = \text{normal time} + \text{allowance time}$$

$$= \frac{\text{normal time}}{1 - \text{allowance fraction}}.$$

Work sampling is very valuable on noncyclical and long cycle jobs where stopwatch time studies are of little help. The time study analyst requires great skill, whereas the work sampling observer can be relatively unskilled. One major drawback of work sampling is that it does not provide the complete and detailed breakdown of elements that stopwatch time studies do.

EXAMPLE 4

A work sampling study of a warehouseman revealed the following information:

Total time of study	24 hr = 1440 min
No. of orders processed	320
Total no. of observations	1000
No. of observations working	850
Average performance rating	105%

Company policy is to give allowances of 10% of total time on the job. What is the standard time per order?

$$\text{normal time} = \frac{(\text{total study time})(\text{working time fraction})(\text{perf. rating})}{\text{number of units}}$$

$$= \frac{(1440)(0.85)(1.05)}{320} = 4.02 \text{ minutes/order},$$

$$\text{standard time} = \frac{\text{normal time}}{1 - \text{allowance fraction}}$$

$$= \frac{4.02}{1 - 0.10} = 4.47 \text{ minutes/order}$$

EXAMPLE 5

The organization in Example 4 desires a 95.5% confidence and a $\pm 3\%$ precision level on all work sampling. Was the sample size sufficient in Example 4?

$$N = \frac{Z^2(1-f)}{p^2 f} = \frac{4(1-0.85)}{0.0009(0.85)} = 784.3, \text{ or } 785.$$

Since the original sample size was 1000 and the required sample size for the given confidence and precision is 785, the sample size was sufficient.

PREDETERMINED TIME STUDY

The concept behind predetermined time studies is that work can be broken down into elemental motions. The average time for a person to perform a basic motion should be fairly constant. Predetermined or synthetic time studies consist of tables of standard time values for performing various types of basic motions, such as reach, move, turn, grasp, and position. Various predetermined time systems have been developed by organizations and consulting firms. To establish the time standard, the operation is divided into basic motions and the sum of their time values becomes the normal time for the operation.

An elemental analysis of many different jobs reveals that many elements are similar. An operation that is broken down into common elements can be described by time estimates from standard time data. The elemental time standards are determined from previous stopwatch time studies or from a specialized predetermined time system. The operation is broken into elements, appropriate time values are selected from the data file, suitable allowances are added, and the result is a time standard for the operation. The advantage of this technique is that the standard can be set in advance of the performance of the operation. Thus, it is quicker, less expensive, and more consistent than a specialized study.

Standard time data can be obtained from internal or external sources. After taking a number of stopwatch time studies, an organization will have normal times for a variety of elements. Eventually, many of the elements appearing in new jobs will be ones that have already been determined. When this happens, there is no need to make a stopwatch time study of a new job. Instead, the analyst can simply list the elements of the operation and refer to his files to determine the normal times.

Some of the more popular external predetermined time systems are *methods time measurement (MTM), work factor, method time analysis, basic motion times,* and *basic time survey.* Some of the standard time values used in methods time measurement are shown in Figure 1. An operation is recorded or synthesized by listing the constitutent movements. Time values are extracted from the appropriate table in Figure 1 and summed to obtain the normal time. Allowances are then applied and the result is the standard time.

In MTM, times are measured in time-measurement units (TMU); one TMU equals 0.0006 minutes. These values were obtained from extensive research on basic motions. Motion pictures were taken of people performing the several categories of

TABLE I – REACH – R

Distance Moved Inches	Time TMU				Hand in Motion		CASE AND DESCRIPTION
	A	B	C or D	E	A	B	
3/4 or less	2.0	2.0	2.0	2.0	1.6	1.6	A Reach to object in fixed location, or to object in other hand or on which other hand rests.
1	2.5	2.5	3.6	2.4	2.3	2.3	
2	4.0	4.0	5.9	3.8	3.5	2.7	
3	5.3	5.3	7.3	5.3	4.5	3.6	B Reach to single object in location which may vary slightly from cycle to cycle.
4	6.1	6.4	8.4	6.8	4.9	4.3	
5	6.5	7.8	9.4	7.4	5.3	5.0	
6	7.0	8.6	10.1	8.0	5.7	5.7	
7	7.4	9.3	10.8	8.7	6.1	6.5	C Reach to object jumbled with other objects in a group so that search and select occur.
8	7.9	10.1	11.5	9.3	6.5	7.2	
9	8.3	10.8	12.2	9.9	6.9	7.9	
10	8.7	11.5	12.9	10.5	7.3	8.6	
12	9.6	12.9	14.2	11.8	8.1	10.1	
14	10.5	14.4	15.6	13.0	8.9	11.5	D Reach to a very small object or where accurate grasp is required.
16	11.4	15.8	17.0	14.2	9.7	12.9	
18	12.3	17.2	18.4	15.5	10.5	14.4	
20	13.1	18.6	19.8	16.7	11.3	15.8	
22	14.0	20.1	21.2	18.0	12.1	17.3	E Reach to indefinite location to get hand in position for body balance or next motion or out of way.
24	14.9	21.5	22.5	19.2	12.9	18.8	
26	15.8	22.9	23.9	20.4	13.7	20.2	
28	16.7	24.4	25.3	21.7	14.5	21.7	
30	17.5	25.8	26.7	22.9	15.3	23.2	
Additional	0.4	0.7	0.7	0.6	0.4	0.75	TMU per inch over 30 inches

FIGURE 1
Elemental motion time system. (Copyright by the MTM Association for Standards and Research. Not to be reprinted without written consent from MTM Association, 16-01 Broadway, Fair Lawn, NJ 07410.)

motions. This approach yielded precision in measurement that could not be attained with a stopwatch.

Increasingly, organizations are using computers to store and retrieve standard data. Computer-based systems store standard times for different elements or motions and then provide a coding system for retrieving the appropriate data. The retrieval process is automatic and requires only the input of the suitable code numbers.

Predetermined time studies are adaptable to computerization. They can treat non-repetitive, long-cycle, and noncyclical jobs, as well as jobs that are not being performed. Additionally, the performance rating is bypassed, and the elemental times

TABLE II – MOVE M

Distance Moved Inches	Time TMU			Hand In Motion B	Wt Allowance			CASE AND DESCRIPTION
	A	B	C		Wt. (lb) Up to	Dynamic Factor	State Constant TMU	
3/4 or less	2.0	2.0	2.0	1.7	2.5	1.00	0	
1	2.5	2.9	3.4	2.3				
2	3.6	4.6	5.2	2.9	7.5	1.06	2.2	A Move object to other hand or against stop
3	4.9	5.7	6.7	3.6				
4	6.1	6.9	8.0	4.3	12.5	1.11	3.9	
5	7.3	8.0	9.2	5.0				
6	8.1	8.9	10.3	5.7	17.5	1.17	5.6	
7	8.9	9.7	11.1	6.5				
8	9.7	10.6	11.8	7.2	22.5	1.22	7.4	
9	10.5	11.5	12.7	7.9				B Move object to approximate or indefinite location.
10	11.3	12.2	13.5	8.6	27.5	1.28	9.1	
12	12.9	13.4	15.2	10.0				
14	14.4	14.6	16.9	11.4	32.5	1.33	10.8	
16	16.0	15.8	18.7	12.8				
18	17.6	17.0	20.4	14.2	37.5	1.39	12.5	
20	19.2	18.2	22.1	15.6				
22	20.8	19.4	23.8	17.0	42.5	1.44	14.3	
24	22.4	20.6	25.5	18.4				C Move object to exact location
26	24.0	21.8	27.3	19.8	47.5	1.50	16.0	
28	25.5	23.1	29.0	21.2				
30	27.1	24.3	30.7	22.7				
Additional	0.8	0.6	0.85	0.75	TMU per inch over 30 inches			

EFFECTIVE NET WEIGHT			
	No. of Hands	Spatial	Sliding
Effective Net Weight (ENW)	1	W	W × F_C
	2	W/2	W/2 × F_C

W = Weight in pounds
F_C = Coefficient of Friction

FIGURE 1—*continued*

are reliable by virtue of the large samples from which they were derived. The biggest advantage, of course, is the ability to develop a standard time for an operation before it is ever performed. Some organizations plan operations by using predetermined time studies and then follow up with stopwatch time studies after the operations have been going for a period of time.

TABLE III A – TURN – T

Weight	Time TMU for Degrees Turned										
	30°	45°	60°	75°	90°	105°	120°	135°	150°	165°	180°
Small–0 to 2 Pounds	2.8	3.5	4.1	4.8	5.4	6.1	6.8	7.4	8.1	8.7	9.4
Medium–2.1 to 10 Pounds	4.4	5.5	6.5	7.5	8.5	9.6	10.6	11.6	12.7	13.7	14.8
Large–10.1 to 35 Pounds	8.4	10.5	12.3	14.4	16.2	18.3	20.4	22.2	24.3	26.1	28.2

TABLE III B – APPLY PRESSURE – AP

FULL CYCLE			COMPONENTS		
SYMBOL	TMU	DESCRIPTION	SYMBOL	TMU	DESCRIPTION
APA	10.6	AF + DM + RLF	AF	3.4	Apply Force
APB	16.2	APA + G2	DM	4.2	Dwell Minimum
			RLF	3.0	Release Force

TABLE IV – GRASP – G

TYPE OF GRASP	Case	Time TMU	DESCRIPTION	
PICK–UP	1A	2.0	Any size object by itself, easily grasped	
	1B	3.5	Object very small or lying close against a flat surface	
	1C1	7.3	Diameter larger than 1/2″	Interference with Grasp
	1C2	8.7	Diameter 1/4″ to 1/2″	on bottom and one side of
	1C3	10.8	Diameter less than 1/4″	nearly cylindrical object.
REGRASP	2	5.6	Change grasp without relinquishing control	
TRANSFER	3	5.6	Control transferred from one hand to the other	
SELECT	4A	7.3	Larger than 1″ × 1″ × 1″	Object jumbled with other
	4B	9.1	1/4″ × 1/4″ × 1/8″ to 1″ × 1″ × 1″	objects so that search
	4C	12.9	Smaller than 1/4″ × 1/4″ × 1/8″	and select occur.
CONTACT	5	0	Contact Sliding, or Hook Grasp.	

TABLE V – POSITION* – P

CLASS OF FIT		Symmetry	Easy To Handle	Difficult To Handle
1–Loose	No pressure required	S	5.6	11.2
		SS	9.1	14.7
		NS	10.4	16.0
2–Close	Light pressure required	S	16.2	21.8
		SS	19.7	25.3
		NS	21.0	26.6
3–Exact	Heavy pressure required	S	43.0	48.6
		SS	46.5	52.1
		NS	47.8	53.4

*Distance moved to engage–1″ or less

METHODS-TIME MEASUREMENT
MTM-APPLICATION DATA

1 TMU = .00001 hour
= .0006 minute
= .036 seconds

FIGURE 1—*continued*

WAGES AND INCENTIVES

Wages and salaries constitute a substantial percentage of the value of goods and services consumed. There are two basic wage systems in common use today: *time-based systems* and *output-based systems.* Wage systems based on time are the most common in industry. With time-based systems the employee is usually paid at a fixed time interval (every week, two weeks, or month). The level of wages does not change as output increases or decreases, and there is little incentive for increased output. With an output-based system there is an incentive: the employee is paid at a higher level for increased output. There are numerous types of output-based systems. Incentive systems require more time, effort, and paperwork to install and use than do time-based systems. The popularity of output-based systems has diminished as output has come to depend more on groups and machines than on individuals.

The time-based and output-based systems are the two general categories of wage systems. However, there are numerous systems that are hybrids of the two. Additionally, there are participative plans where profit-sharing is involved. The object of participative plans is to get the employees directly involved with the objectives of the organization and permit them to share in the fruits of their effort.

CONCLUSION

Work measurement results in production standards that indicate the expected productivity of a particular job or operation. Most forms of organizational and quantitative analysis require production standards as a basic input. Work measurement data are an integral part of an organization's information system. They influence decision making throughout an organization. Work measurement techniques apply to physical activities. They are not applicable to nonphysical processes such as thinking, planning, or other mental processes (you cannot accurately time what you cannot see).

Work measurement and the establishment of production time standards occur after job design. Standards or rates are dependent upon work methods, and work methods are an integral part of job design. Of course, work measurement should not be undertaken until work methods and operating procedures are standardized.

The work measurement techniques outlined in this chapter are stopwatch time studies, work sampling, and predetermined time studies. Each technique has its own advantages and disadvantages. The choice of one over the others depends on the circumstances and conditions surrounding the selection. The objective is to select the technique to fit the occasion.

QUESTIONS

1. What is the primary purpose of work measurement?
2. What are the potential benefits of work measurement to an organization?
3. Give several uses of production time standards.
4. List some weaknesses of informal time standards.
5. What types of task lend themselves to stopwatch time studies?
6. What level of worker should be observed in stopwatch time studies?
7. Why must each element be performance rated in stopwatch time studies?
8. Differentiate among actual time, normal time, and standard time.
9. What affects the required sample size?

10. What is the purpose of the allowance factor and how is it established?

11. List some uses of work sampling.

12. What are some of the advantages of predetermined time studies over other work measurement techniques?

13. Briefly describe how synthetic time standards are derived.

14. Give a concise description of the two basic wage systems most commonly used.

15. Can work measurement be applied to all jobs?

16. List a few examples of informal time standards used in planning your personal activities.

17. Outline a work sampling plan which could be used to determine how nurses on duty in a hospital ward spend their time.

PROBLEMS

1. A work operation consisting of three elements has been subjected to a stopwatch time study. The raw data are contained in the following table. The total allowance for the operation has been set at 25% by the union contract. Determine the standard time for the work operation.

Job element	Performance rating	Observations (min/part)					Mean time[a] (min)	Normal time (min)
		1	2	3	4	5		
1	90%	.15	.18	.17	.16	.19	_____	_____
2	100%	.22	.23	.24	.22	.24	_____	_____
3	120%	.15	.14	.39	.16	.16	_____	_____

[a]Excluding unusual times.

2. A work operation of six elements has been analyzed using stopwatch time study techniques. The following data were collected. Management has decided to allow a 20% allowance. Determine the standard time for the operation.

Job element	Performance rating	Observations (min/part)										Mean time (min)	Normal time (min)
		1	2	3	4	5	6	7	8	9	10		
1	0.80	.12	.14	.17	.22	.18	.12	.16	.18	.15	.16	_____	_____
2	0.90	.22	.24	.27	.25	.18	.30	.23	.18	.30	.23	_____	_____
3	1.00	.30	.30	.30	.30	.30	.30	.30	.30	.30	.30	_____	_____
4	1.10	.25	.27	.35	.40	.35	.42	.28	.38	.34	.36	_____	_____
5	0.75	.50	.57	.63	.65	.52	.56	.67	.51	.73	.56	_____	_____
6	0.95	.73	.65	.85	.62	.64	.70	.72	.80	.75	.64	_____	_____

3. From the information given in Problem 1, determine the approximate sample size for a 95% confidence and a ±5% precision level.

4. From the information in Problem 2, determine the approximate sample size for a 68% confidence and a ±5% precision level.

5. A work study sample of an operation yields the data below. Determine the required sample for a 68% confidence level and a ±10% precision level.

Observations of operator working	130
Observations of operator idle	70
Total observations	200

6. An operation was subjected to a work study analysis. The observer found the workers were working in 324 observations and idle in 76 observations. Determine the required sample size if the company demands a 99% confidence level and a ±4% precision level.

7. A work sample study conducted over the 80 hours of a 2-week period yielded the following data. The idle time was 20%, the performance rating was 100%, and the total number of parts produced was 225. The allowance for this part is 25%. Determine the standard time per part.

8. A work study sample was conducted over a month of four weeks each having 40 hours. The idle time was found to be 30%, the performance rating was 90%, and the total number of parts produced was 476. The allowance for this part is 20%. Determine the standard time per part.

9. Using the data from Problem 7, what sample size must be taken if the company requires a 68% confidence level with a ±4% precision level?

10. Using the information from Problem 8, what should be the sample size required to give a 99% confidence level with a ±3% precision level?

11. The normal time for a grinding operation is 3.512 hours per 100 units. It is estimated that unavoidable delays will account for 20% of the total operating time and that labor efficiency will be 90%.
   a. What is the standard time for the job?
   b. What is the mean time for the job?

12. A time study was taken of a drill press operator drilling a hole in a flat plate, using the continuous-timing method. The stopwatch readings in minutes at the transition points between each operation element were as follows:

Operation element	1	2	3	4	5
Load piece into jig and clamp	0.08	0.60	1.16	1.69	2.20
Place jig under drill and lower spindle	0.14	0.66	1.21	1.74	2.25
Drill (automatic feed)	0.44	1.00	1.53	2.05	2.55
Raise spindle of drill	0.46	1.02	1.56	2.07	2.57
Remove piece from jig	0.52	1.04	1.62	2.13	2.63

The average time was used as the base time for each operation element. The time-study man rated the overall performance on the study at 115%. The allowances determined from an interruption study were 5% for personal and fatigue together, and 5% for other unavoidable delays. Determine the standard time.

13. a. In making a time study of turning the outside diameter of a shaft for an engine, a time-study man recorded a spindle speed of 500 rpm, a depth of cut of $\frac{1}{32}''$, and a feed of 0.010'' per revolution. The shaft was 10'' long and was turned from 1'' stock. Determine the machine time for this operation if the final diameter is to be $\frac{30}{32}''$.
   b. From the time study, the mean time in minutes for each of the manual elements associated with the above machine time was determined to be as follows:

Pick up dogged part and place between centers	.10
Position tool post	.07
Turn outside diameter [see part a]	
Clear tool post	.05
Remove part from center	.05

This performance was rated at 100%. The allowances that were added to the normal time were: personal 3%, fatigue 2%, other unavoidable delays 10%. Calculate the standard time for this operation.

CASE 1: WHERE IS MY ENTITLEMENT?

The U.S. Secret Service, an agency of the U.S. Treasury Department, is best known as the agency responsible for the protection of the presidential family. It is also assigned to investigate and make arrests in matters involving missing or stolen government checks and bonds and in cases pertaining to the printing and circulation of counterfeit currency. All agents are trained to perform every agency function; they typically spend part of their careers on permanent protective assignments in Washington and the rest of their careers on field office duties where they may be transferred among the many regional offices. When on field assignments, the agents handle check, bond, and counterfeit cases, do surveillance and compile information pertinent to protection efforts, and serve on temporary protective details. The temporary details usually consist of short stints at diplomatic functions within their field office territory, travel with visiting dignitaries, or additional support or relief of headquarters agents on permanent assignments.

Field agents usually are given a geographical area within their field office district and are responsible for all check cases which occur in that area. A check case occurs in an area if the complainant resided there at the time of the alleged theft. Although case assignments are based on geographical boundaries not necessarily fixed by statistical analysis, disproportionate case numbers tend to balance out because caseloads are kept fairly level. Each field office has its own method of leveling, but most methods essentially establish maximum caseload levels for each agent.

Cases first received at field offices are classified as "open." A case is reclassified from "open" to "active" when it is assigned to an agent. It subsequently becomes "closed" when it is solved and an arrest or restitution is made. When an agent deems a case unlikely to be solved, he usually closes it as unsolved. However, he may reopen it if a new lead is obtained, or may leave it as "active" pending the discovery of more revealing information. As agents close cases from their active files, they add "open" cases based on the age of the cases in their "open" pool or according to some other priority method. Otherwise, the Special Agents-in-Charge (SACs) of the field offices designate "open" cases to be placed in agents' working files when active case levels drop. When a backlog of cases for a particular agent becomes too large, the SACs may assign other agents to work some of the "open" cases. The agents given cases outside of their own area usually have fewer incoming cases or low caseloads presently in their active files.

The SACs of the field offices are complaining to headquarters that their districts are experiencing staffing problems and need additional manpower to manage the workloads. The backlogs of unassigned check cases are growing large, especially in dense population areas. Headquarters is aware that the number of incoming cases per month is growing and expected to increase for the next operating period. However, headquarters is concerned that the increasing backlogs may be resulting more from poor utilization of manpower and inefficient policies and practices used in field office investigations.

Headquarters does not want to respond immediately to the SACs' complaints. It is reluctant to relieve agents of temporary assignments (many of which are done voluntarily) or to ask for dispensation from current federal hiring freezes. Therefore, headquarters feels that casework analysis and check case standards are needed. The purpose is to obtain casework information so that staffing decisions can be made on a basis other than guesswork. Within the proposed analysis, the average time per working unit (case) is to be calculated. Once the average time is derived, it can be multiplied by a forecast of the number of cases for each regional office. This then can be converted into staff needs.

In assessing staff needs, two other important factors are to be taken into account. First, each agent on field assignment typically works a ten-hour day. The agents are paid for 25% overtime (2 hours/day) on a regular basis and are required to show their working hours on their daily reports. Given the nature of their work, the Treasury Department seldom questions the "automatic" overtime. Second, the agents are evaluated on check case performance. Although some agents maintain that merit increases and promotions are more heavily weighted on other functions, the working unit (check case) is used as a determinant in performance standings. Measures such as the number of cases closed, the number of arrests, the conviction rate on arrests, and the quality and thoroughness of case reports are included in the agents' civil service written evaluations.

There are many field offices and over 1800 agents. Headquarters intends to send agency representatives to two of the field offices to conduct casework studies. The two selected are San Diego and Norfolk. These cites were chosen as bases for comparison, because they are separated geographically but share some of the same physical and demographic characteristics. Both are in coastal metropolitan areas where transit times are factors in field investigations. Both have large concentrations of federal employees and significant numbers of federal retirees in their areas. Norfolk specifically was selected because of its proximity to Washington, D.C. It frequently supplies agents to headquarters for temporary assignments and is used as a stop-over by many visiting heads of state. Furthermore, its location on the eastern seaboard has made it a prime target for passing counterfeit money as shipments of bogus bills are made between the crime centers in the Northeast and Miami.

1. Analyze the work analysis situation for the agency by (a) discussing the applicability of time studies; (b) describing the type of work standards that should be developed.
2. How does the proposed study compare with work sampling? What problems would stem from the use of work sampling and work analysis in general?
3. How might the work situation be improved? Would techniques such as specialization result in improved efficiency?
4. What factors are especially important in setting standards for services and for government agencies? What practices can improve the efficiency of these sectors?

CASE 2: QUICK-STOP

Bill Timely is the manager of three local convenience stores which are franchises of the national Quick-Stop Shops. He has received frequent complaints from customers and letters from regional headquarters concerning the operation of his stores. Most are criticisms involving slow checkout service, long waits for the gas pumps to be switched on from inside the stores, dirty stores, depleted stocks of basic food items, outdated and shopworn inventory left on dusty shelves, and personnel who become insolent when interrupted in their private conversations.

Bill is aware of these flagrant conditions and more. He faces extremely large staff turnover and constant morale problems. It generally takes Bill two months to train one full-time staff member, and the typical length of employee service is just over one year. Because of company policy and high operating costs, Bill tries to keep operating crews at a minimum. He always has two operating personnel on duty during late night hours, but he schedules only one staff member per store during the slowest daytime hours.

It is the duty of operating personnel (full and part-time) to check out customers, watch the gasoline pumps and clear them for the next sale, stock shelves, participate in inventory counts, and perform housekeeping duties. The employees admit they fall short on many of the duties and insist they do not have adequate time to perform all of the shop maintenance and selling functions. They stress security reasons for spending the majority of the time at the checkout counter, watching customers, and observing the gasoline pumping stations. Many of the clerks who work in the afternoon say that surveillance of adolescents keeps them from any other prescribed chores. All of the employees have asked to be given more relief and designated break times; the lack of relief personnel forces them to be stranded at the counter and unable to take necessary personal breaks.

Bill always has felt that adequate hours are scheduled to accomplish the totality of shop tasks. He nevertheless decided to conduct a work sampling study to determine the amount of time that actually involved productive chores and to estimate the standard time to handle a customer transaction. He took a sample of 300 observations over the course of a three week period. One of the three stores was selected as the site of the sampling study by drawing straws. To remove any effect of sampling bias, the hours of the day were chosen by random numbers. All of the 24 daily operating hours over the 21 day period were given an equal chance of being chosen. The number of workers on duty at any given time and the schedules of many of the workers varied. The table below shows the results of the work sampling at the end of Bill's study.

Week	Total no. of observations	No. of observations when work was being performed
1	90	74
2	95	82
3	115	96

Bill performance evaluated his employees at 110% by averaging the performance ratings he had assigned throughout the course of the study. During that time, the store being sampled recorded 6000 cash register transactions (including gasoline sales). At the regional managers meeting, he found that other managers estimated their employees' productive time to be approximately 90% for operations which handled nearly the same number of transactions.

1. Assuming that Bill requires a 95.5% confidence level and a ±5% precision for his study, did he take enough samples?
2. What was his standard time per transaction?
3. Given the limited information in the case, evaluate the results of the work sampling study. Make any recommendations based on the findings or the description of the convenience store operation.

SELECTED BIBLIOGRAPHY

Barnes, R. M. *Motion and Time Study,* New York: Wiley, 1980.

Maynard, H. B. et al. *Methods Time Measurement,* New York: McGraw-Hill, 1948.

Mundel, M. E. *Motion and Time Study: Principles and Practice,* Englewood Cliffs, NJ: Prentice-Hall, 1978.

Nadler, G. *Work Design,* Homewood, IL: Irwin, 1970.

Niebel, B. W. *Motion and Time Study,* Homewood, IL: Irwin, 1982.

PLANT DECISIONS

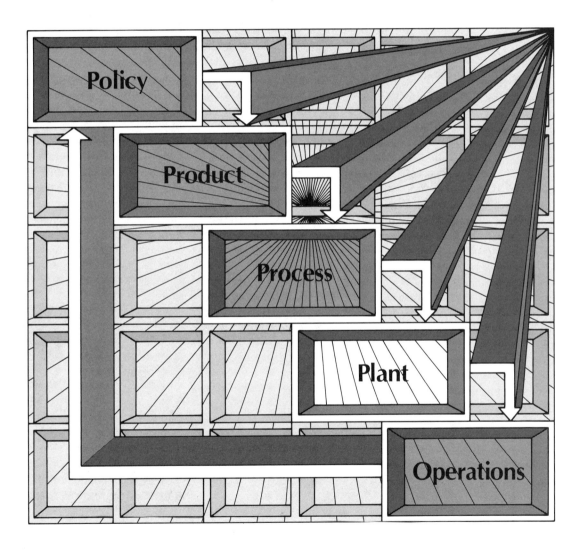

While product decisions determine what will be produced, and process decisions determine how the product will be produced, plant decisions determine where the product will be produced as well as the physical plant layout. The word "plant" is used in a very broad sense here. Its usual connotation is of a factory or some form of manufacturing facility. Here plant may refer to a factory, manufacturing facility, distribution center, warehouse, service center, or retail outlet.

As shown by the plant function in Figure I, decisions on facility location and layout are extremely important. They establish the capacity of physical facilities. For most organizations the establishment, abandonment, or relocation of facilities occurs infrequently. Once a location is chosen, an organization usually remains there for many years. Thus, errors in location often lead to long term problems that are difficult to overcome. Substantial expansion or contraction in an organization necessitates plant decisions. Despite its infrequency, an inappropriate location or an uneconomical capacity level can result in ultimate failure. Organizations exist in a dynamic environment with changing economic conditions, markets, products, and sources of inputs. The need for flexibility and adaption requires a review of plant decisions on a periodic basis.

This section on plant decisions contains three chapters. The *Plant/Facility Location* chapter develops those considerations necessary in locating the organization's operations. The *Plant Layout* chapter establishes the configuration of the facility so that efficient operations are possible. The final chapter, *Materials Handling,* concentrates on the flow of materials within the facility.

FIGURE I
The plant function.

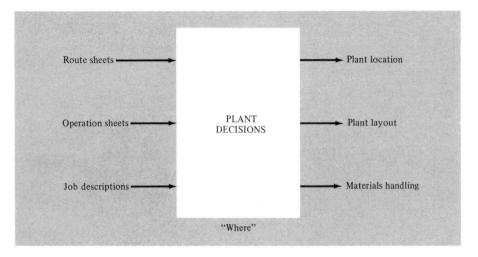

12
Plant/Facility Location

SELECTION OF REGION

SELECTION OF COMMUNITY

SELECTION OF SITE

LOCATION FACTOR DEPENDENCES

Input Dependence
Process Dependence
Output Dependence
Owner/Executive Preference
General Cost Factors

SOURCES OF ASSISTANCE

PLANT LOCATION TRENDS

Movement to Suburbs
Industrial Parks
Competition for Industry
Decentralization
Pollution Concerns

QUANTITATIVE ANALYSIS

FOREIGN AND INTERNATIONAL CONSIDERATIONS

CONCLUSION

QUESTIONS

PROBLEMS

CASES

SELECTED BIBLIOGRAPHY

Several possibilities for expanding capacity when the existing facility is overcrowded are to do the following:

1. subcontract work,
2. add additional shifts,
3. work overtime,
4. expand the present facility,
5. move to another larger facility,
6. keep the current facility and add another facility elsewhere.

Plant/facility location begins with a decision to utilize unused plant capacity, expand existing plant capacity, or build a new plant to accommodate the product. If an existing plant is operating at less than full capacity, the product may be integrated into the present facility. If market analysis indicates a potential demand that exceeds existing facilities, either internal or external expansion may be warranted. Internal

FIGURE 1
Plant location.

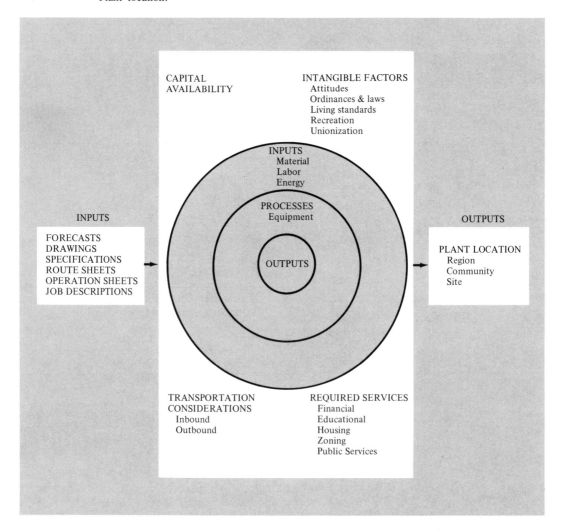

expansion means building onto the existing facility at the current site. External expansion involves a plant location study to determine the site of a completely new facility.

The need for a new plant location can arise from many sources. A newly formed organization must decide the location of its operating facilities. When the demand for an organization's output increases beyond the capacity of its existing facilities, expansion is necessary. Sometimes single plant operation becomes inefficient and decentralization of operations is desirable to control costs or improve service. Obsolescence or technological advance may render an existing facility inoperable. Various economic factors that change with time may dictate a reevaluation of an existing facility's location.

The location of the plant is significant because of its influence on revenues and costs. A plant location decision should consider the total supply-production-distribution system. Modes of available transportation and the costs of labor, taxes, land, construction, and fuel, as well as many other factors, contribute to the overall competitive position of an organization. The addition of a new plant is not a matter of determining a location independent of existing plants. Each potential location results in a new allocation of capacity to market areas; the solution from the economic viewpoint is one that optimizes profits for the network of plants rather than for the additional plant being considered.

The plant location decision is depicted in Figure 1. The inputs to the decision are forecasts, drawings, specifications, route sheets, operation sheets, and job descriptions. An analysis of the production inputs, processes, and outputs will indicate the needs of operations. Capital availability will dictate the financial limits on plant location. Both inbound and outbound movements will involve transportation considerations. The required services are those support activities necessary for the organization and its members. Finally, the intangible factors have to do with the general desirability of a given location. The final output of the plant location decision is the selection of the region, the community, and the site for the new facility.

There is usually no such thing as a plant location that is clearly superior to all others.[1] There are many tangible and intangible factors that are not readily quantifiable. A selection must be made involving tradeoffs among the different locations. A comparative cost analysis of various locations may point toward settling in one community, but an appraisal of intangible factors may result in a decision to select another. Table 1 outlines the major factors that influence plant location.

A standardized checklist of some kind is extremely worthwhile to ensure that potentially critical factors are not overlooked. The list contained in Table 1 is by no means exhaustive. Certain factors assume more importance than others, depending on the product, organization, industry, and so forth. Also, some factors lend themselves to quantitative analysis more readily than others.

SELECTION OF REGION

The selection of the region depends upon the scope of the organization. For a multinational organization, it is a country or region of the world. For a national organization, it is the region within the geopolitical unit (northeast or the like). A given country may be segmented into broad general areas identified by population, cultural

---

[1]Locating a facility is sometimes compared to selecting a mate. While it is possible to change later, the change can be both expensive and unpleasant.

TABLE 1
Plant location factors

Factor	Region	Community	Site
Market proximity	X		
Raw material proximity	X		
Transportation availability			
Highways	X	X	X
Waterways	X	X	X
Railroads	X	X	X
Airports	X	X	X
Labor supply		X	
Climate	X		
Power and fuel supply	X	X	
Water supply and waste disposal	X	X	
Wage scales	X	X	
Tax structure and incentives		X	
Pollution control		X	
Community attitudes		X	
Living standards	X	X	
Land availability and cost		X	X
Zoning restrictions			X
Medical and hospital facilities		X	
Financial institutions and services		X	
Schools, churches, and recreation		X	
Police, fire, refuse collection		X	
Soil characteristics & drainage			X
Universities & higher education		X	

similarities, natural boundaries, geography, or some other means. The organization segments the regions on a basis that meets its particular needs. The selection of a region is frequently influenced by market proximity, raw material proximity, transportation availability, public services (power, fuel, water), or climate.

Organizations can view plant location in terms of capital investment analysis. The important financial terms are revenue, operating costs, and investment; location may affect all three. Organizations dealing directly with consumers, such as retailers, banks, restaurants, and supermarkets, locate close to their markets because location affects revenue much more than it affects operating cost and investment. For manufacturing and wholesaling organizations, revenues are not as strongly influenced by location. However, operating cost and investment are highly sensitive to location. In this chapter, we will focus on manufacturing and wholesaling organizations and exclude retailing organizations, which are usually the subject matter of marketing. An analysis of revenue, operation cost, and investment will indicate those regions that are most economically desirable.

The location of a plant directly influences production costs and marketing effectiveness. Decentralization of industries indicates that many good locations exist. Sometimes it is easy to select the region for a new facility because certain factors dominate the decision. For example, extraction (mines, seas, farms, and forests) is raw materials oriented; beer is water oriented; aluminum is power oriented. Services, on the other hand, are customer oriented: their location is dictated by the location of users, clients, and consumers. If technology or customers do not specify location, then organizations may be transportation oriented, since raw materials must in any event be brought in and products distributed.

Usually the closer a product moves to the ultimate consumer, the greater the transportation cost it has accumulated. A material when first extracted from nature has accrued a negligible transportation cost. From this point on the basic material cost is the same, but each successive move adds labor and other costs, so the total transportation cost in the product continually increases. In general, a product that experiences a substantial weight gain should be produced near the market (assembly industries). Likewise, a weight-losing product should generally be produced near the source of supply (extracting industries).

Many American cities and industrial sites are located on waterways (coastal ports, rivers, man-made canals, or lakes). Water transportation is the least costly form of transport per ton-mile. It is slow by modern standards, but organizations that process heavy, bulky items with a low value per ton (grain, logs, petroleum, iron ore) still consider water transport an important location factor.

Railroads permitted expansion of industries into areas not served by water routes. Although the cost per ton-mile is greater than water transport, it offers additional speed and flexibility of shipment. Trucks offer a greater degree of flexibility and speed, but they are even more costly. Air transport is the most costly form of transportation. It is used for low-weight, high-cost items; perishable products such as flowers; and critical replacement parts for maintenance.

When labor is important, the number of potential employees available is not an adequate indicator of labor supply. Frequently, particular skills or training require the consideration of the pool of labor available. Skilled and technical personnel can be difficult to find, so location near cities may be necessary. The extent and character of unionization influences some organizations, and they may prefer states that have right-to-work laws. When only unskilled or semiskilled workers are required, there are fewer encumbrances on the labor supply. The composition, stability, productivity, and cost of labor are important considerations.

An analysis of the cost structure of a product will indicate major plant location factors. An attempt should be made to reduce or control the major cost factors. If the cost of labor is major, a location near an abundant and low cost labor supply is important. With a bulky, low-value product, transportation cost may dictate a location near major markets. With a low-weight, high-value product, location near the market is unimportant and some other cost factor than transportation will influence the decision. For products requiring large quantities of energy or water, location must be near adequate supplies of these resources.

The considerations mentioned above are not exhaustive. Each organization has its own needs and its own assessment of their relative importance.

SELECTION OF COMMUNITY

Once the region is selected, one looks for a specific community or locality within the region. For several types of organizations, such as hospitals, educational institutions, or prisons, the community may be the major location decision to be made. The selection of a community is frequently influenced by labor supply, wage scales, tax structure, community attitudes, living standards, and financial or other inducements.

A community should have adequate highways, streets, and public transportation. If personnel must be attracted to the area, community services such as schools, churches, residential housing, medical facilities, recreation, and police and fire protection are important. Some organizations place an emphasis on education and locate near universities and technical schools.

Competent, honest, and cooperative governmental officials are desirable. Local legislation affecting the organization will be in their hands. Zoning ordinances, taxation, and waste disposal are just a few types of local legislation with great impact. Most attention usually is focused on property taxes, but other types of taxation such as sales taxes, income taxes, licenses, and workman's compensation contributions should be investigated. A favorable political climate can be an important asset. With a good community attitude, an organization can grow and prosper; with a poor community attitude, problems and difficulties may be on the horizon.

Many communities offer inducements to organizations to operate facilities in their area. These may take on many different forms. The community may build the plant and lease it back to the organization on a long term lease. Paved access roads or parking lots may be provided at no cost. Railroad spurs may be built. Exemptions from local taxes for a specified period of time are not uncommon. Unfortunately, the communities that offer the most usually have undesirable features associated with their location, and they should be carefully investigated. When concessions are offered, they usually hide disadvantages that may more than equal the concession.

SELECTION OF SITE

After the community has been selected, the exact site within the community must be chosen. Several sites are usually considered. They are compared with respect to the following:

1. transportation access (highways, railroad sidings),
2. availability of services (water, electric, gas, sewers),
3. zoning restrictions,
4. land availability and cost,
5. space for expansion,
6. soil characteristics (bearing and drainage),
7. construction costs,
8. compatibility with surrounding land use.

A site five times the actual plant area is considered minimal to meet the needs of future expansion, parking spaces, and so forth.

Transportation is frequently an important consideration. Raw materials and components must be brought in and final products shipped out. The ideal site for transportation would be on a major waterway, with a railroad siding, with access to a highway, and in proximity to a major air terminal.

Topography and geological structure affect the type of construction. Though construction methods have advanced to the point where a building can be built almost anywhere, costs often become prohibitive if the underlying structure cannot support the building without extra substructure. This is particularly important if heavy machinery or equipment generating vibration will be used. Geological fault zones should be avoided as well as sites subject to flood or landslide.

Many organizations move to well-developed industrial areas to be near suppliers, parts houses, equipment suppliers, and tool distributors. Location of a facility within an industrial park can simplify the site selection decision. Unfortunately only small and medium size operations can locate in industrial parks. Large operations usually must select their site irrespective of organized industrial areas. Because of their need for vast land areas and their high demands on transportation systems, they must find and develop a site that is compatible with their individual needs.

Site selection cannot correct the error of poor region selection. Site selection is a type of engineering problem, while region selection is more of an economic problem.

Environmental impact statements are becoming commonplace for facilities that deplete natural resources or release some type of effluent. It is not uncommon for environmental groups to oppose specific locations.

LOCATION FACTOR DEPENDENCES

Location factor dependence refers to a dominant factor that determines where a plant will be located. A dominant factor means a single factor that overrides any further considerations. A list of the major location factor dependences is as follows:

1. input dependence,
2. process dependence,
3. output dependence,
4. owner/executive preference,
5. general cost factors.

Each of these factor dependences will now be discussed and explained.

INPUT DEPENDENCE

Input dependence occurs when location is determined by the source of factor inputs or the sources of raw materials. This may be necessary because of input perishability or transportation costs. This is typical where bulky or heavy raw materials are involved. Analytical-type industries that take a basic raw material and decompose or transform it into numerous products are usually limited in their location by their major inputs. Organizations that reduce the bulk or weight of a product tend to locate near the source of supply. Examples of industries that are input dependent are oil, steel, farming, lumber, dairy, mining, and fishing.

Being near its raw materials allows an organization to get better supplier service and to save on incoming freight. However, when there are numerous geographically dispersed suppliers, it is difficult to locate near all of them. On the other hand, it is frequently possible to find nearby suppliers no matter where a facility is located.

PROCESS DEPENDENCE

Process dependence occurs when location is determined by process requirements. When production processes have unique characteristics that require specialized processing, they can limit the location. If processes require a large quantity of water, as in nuclear reactors and breweries, they must be near a source of sufficient quality. When processes require substantial amounts of power, as aluminum extraction does, locations are similarly restricted. Sometimes processes emit noise, odors, or other irritants that require location in isolated areas.

OUTPUT DEPENDENCE

Services are produced and consumed simultaneously, so they tend to be highly dependent upon the locations of their customers. Goods usually are standardized products that can be produced, stored, and transported to customers for use at a later date. Manufacturing tends to be more influenced by inputs and processing technology, whereas services are influenced more by the outputs and proximity to the market.

Output dependence occurs when location is determined by product markets. Synthetic-type industries that take numerous inputs and combine or transform them into a few products are usually located near their customers. Service industries also locate close to their customers. If the final product is perishable, it may require a location near its markets. A fragile product that cannot risk long shipments may be located in a similar manner. Custom-made products usually require location near the customer. Examples of industries that are output dependent are automobiles, appliances, banks, cement, transportation, hotels, health care, and soft drinks.

Being near the market lets an organization give better service to its customers and often saves on outgoing freight cost. If the market is nationwide or international, however, the facility cannot always be near its markets. In many cases, the facility location determines the market area more than the market area determines the facility location.

OWNER/EXECUTIVE PREFERENCE

Owner/executive preference occurs when location is determined by the personal preferences of the organization's leaders. Managers may have a strong preference to remain in a given locality. Frequently, desires to be in a certain type of environment for family, social, cultural, or educational reasons will influence the desirability of alternatives. Small or owner-operated organizations are usually located in this manner by the preferences of the top executive officer.

GENERAL COST FACTORS

New plant location represents a sizable investment and creates heavy sunk costs. The relevant costs are those that will be incurred in the future operation of the facility. It is difficult to measure or precisely estimate these costs, so there is an element of risk. Costs can be segmented into tangible costs and intangible costs. The tangible costs are more readily measured; the intangible costs must be judged more subjectively. Typical tangible costs are as follows:

1. land,
2. rental, purchase, or construction,
3. input transportation,
4. output transportation,
5. labor,
6. fuel, power, and water,
7. taxes and insurance,
8. relocation.

Comparison of tangible costs may be facilitated by listing the relevant factors as follows:

Factor	City A	City B	City C
Rent	$ 30,000	$ 25,000	$ 23,000
Labor	235,000	230,000	260,000
Freight	90,000	74,000	30,000
Taxes	15,000	23,000	8,000
Power	100,000	100,000	90,000
Total operating costs	$470,000	$452,000	$411,000

On the basis of operating costs alone, City C appears to be the best location. Of course, intangible factors must also be considered which might change the location. Although an economic cost analysis does not make the final location decision, it is useful in marshalling the facts.

Sometimes it is useful to segment costs into inbound costs, inplant costs, and outbound costs for analysis purposes. *Inbound costs* are principally the cost of freight from the source (suppliers) to the plant. *Inplant costs* are labor and production costs. *Outbound costs* are primarily the cost of freight from the plant to its destination. An analysis of these costs reveals their significance to total product cost. Costs that contribute the most to total product cost are usually important locational considerations.

Intangible costs can be extremely important even though they defy quantitative measurement. The tangible costs can be compared, since they can be expressed in the common denominator of dollars. There are no universal common denominators for comparing intangible costs. Typical intangible costs are

1. community attitude and culture,
2. weather and other natural phenomena (hurricanes, floods, earthquakes),
3. transportation availability,
4. labor situation,
5. statute laws, ordinances, and regulations,
6. union activities and attitudes,
7. supporting institutions (banks, schools, churches, universities),
8. housing and general living conditions.

Decisions related to intangible costs present measurement difficulties. There are two approaches that can be used to resolve the problem. The first approach relies totally on the subjective evaluation of the decision makers. The second approach is quasi-objective and relies on preference ratings for the various intangible factors. Weights or dimensionless index numbers can be used to express importance, and the various factors are then compared in some objective manner.

One approach to qualitative factor analysis is as follows:

1. Develop the list of relevant factors (perhaps from a checklist).
2. Establish a numerical preference rating scale for each factor (perhaps 1 to 5 or 1 to 10).
3. Assign a preference rating or score to each factor.
4. Weight each factor relative to its overall importance to the decision.
5. Mulitply the preference rating by the weight for each factor.

6. Sum the total points for each location.
7. The location with the maximum number of points is the most desirable.

Preference rating has the same purpose as the tangible cost comparison. It substitutes a point value for a monetary value when monetary values are unobtainable or their determination is prohibitive. Equal or variable weights can be assigned to each intangible factor based on their perceived significance. A numerical point assignment for a given factor is obtained by multiplying the rating for the factor by its weight. The summation of the point assignments for each intangible factor gives the total point value for each location being considered. The location with the greatest number of points is the most desirable in relation to the intangible factors.

EXAMPLE 1

A company conducted a comprehensive study of three alternative locations for a new manufacturing facility. For each location, the company compiled subjective ratings of the relevant location factors. In addition, it ranked the factors according to their overall importance to the location decision. Based on the following results of the study, which location is the most acceptable?

Factor	Weight	Site		
		A	B	C
Community receptivity	0.3	Excellent	Good	Average
Labor availability	0.2	Average	Good	Excellent
Transportation quality	0.3	Average	Average	Good
Cost of living	0.1	Below average	Excellent	Average
Proximity to suppliers	0.1	Good	Poor	Excellent
	1.0			

Each location is assigned a rating of 1 to 5 points for each factor, with 1 representing poor and 5 representing excellent. The rating points then are multiplied by the weight of the respective location factor to obtain the site factor value. The sums of the weighted-factor values for each location are used to compare the sites and to make the final selection. The following table summarizes the weighted-factor process:

Factor	Weight	Site[a]		
		A	B	C
Community receptivity	.3	$5 \times .3 = 1.5$	$4 \times .3 = 1.2$	$3 \times .3 = 0.9$
Labor availability	.2	$3 \times .2 = 0.6$	$4 \times .2 = 0.8$	$5 \times .2 = 1.0$
Transportation quality	.3	$3 \times .3 = 0.9$	$3 \times .3 = 0.9$	$4 \times .3 = 1.2$
Cost of living	.1	$2 \times .1 = 0.2$	$5 \times .1 = 0.5$	$3 \times .1 = 0.3$
Proximity to suppliers	.1	$4 \times .1 = 0.4$	$1 \times .1 = 0.1$	$5 \times .1 = 0.5$
Total		3.6	3.5	3.9

[a]The five point rating scale is: 5 = excellent, 4 = good, 3 = average, 2 = below average, and 1 = poor.

Site C has the largest sum of weighted-factor values, 3.9. Therefore, it is the most acceptable location in terms of the subjective comparison.

SOURCES OF ASSISTANCE

States, regional authorities, and communities are interested in enticing organizations to locate in their jurisdiction. Usually an expansion of the tax base and employment opportunities for its residents are among the stimuli for attracting new facilities. Most states have industrial development agencies that furnish assistance to organizations considering location in the state. Regional authorities and local chambers of commerce are fountains of information on location in their community. Public utilities, banks, real-estate agencies, and transportation companies will cooperate willingly with the hope of expanding their area of business. Management consulting firms can provide services and advice. There are a number of excellent sources of information pertaining to plant locations.

PLANT LOCATION TRENDS

Several trends have been taking place in plant location. It is impossible to predict to what extent they will be important in the future. However, no drastic changes are apparent at this time. Some of the major trends are as follows:

1. movement to the suburbs,
2. industrial parks,
3. competition for industry,
4. decentralization of operations,
5. pollution concerns.

Each of these trends will now be discussed and outlined.

MOVEMENT TO SUBURBS

Perhaps no trend is as pronounced as the movement of organizations out of the cities into the suburbs. The declining cities often achieved their prominence because of water and rail transportation that are no longer as important to industry. Cities tend to have higher taxes on homeowners and organizations. Land is more expensive in the city than in the suburbs. With less expensive land outside the cities, it is possible to achieve further economies with less expensive, more efficient single story facilities.

The decay of the cities has brought about serious social problems. Crime rates are higher in central city areas, so higher insurance rates are charged for such locations. The middle class of people have moved into the suburbs for many reasons, which has left the cities with a lower socioeconomic class population. Some cities have limited land areas and have been built to capacity. The larger the city, the longer the work trip becomes, the worse the air pollution is, the higher the cost of government is, and the more social problems there are. People who can afford to have rebelled against these conditions by moving out. Organizations have followed. Thus, there has been a general movement of industry into the suburbs as well as to smaller cities and rural communities.

INDUSTRIAL PARKS

These are havens where separate tracts of land have been zoned and built to meet the needs of industry. Because of the design of industrial parks, they are usually occupied by small and medium size assembly plants, light manufacturing, service centers, warehouses, and distribution centers. The parks are private or local government owned. All the necessary services are usually provided, so industry is separated into a desirable location that meets the land use requirement of the area. There is no encroachment of industry on residential areas and vice versa. Location in these industrial districts can simplify the selection of a site.

COMPETITION FOR INDUSTRY

State, regional, and city governments actively seek new businesses to locate in their area. *The Wall Street Journal* and other periodicals frequently contain advertisements intended to attract industry. The search for new businesses can even lead them to foreign lands. Various types of inducements are used to attract and entice an organization to locate a new facility or expand an existing operation. Tax breaks, rent free facilities, sharing of construction costs, and training of employees are typical concessions made by eager or economically depressed communities.

Communities that offer rent-free or tax-free buildings or even free sites usually attract new organizations. Generally, these incentives are for limited periods after which regular charges are assessed. Temporary inducements should not overshadow the basic merits of alternative locations.

DECENTRALIZATION

Decentralization has become increasingly feasible as telecommunications and transportation have improved. An organization may operate several similar facilities in numerous locations. This can occur when organizational growth beyond a certain size in a given location becomes inefficient and unwieldy. It can occur because an organization desires to provide better service via local operations. It can also be a natural response to local competition. Decentralization can protect the organization when local strikes or disruptions occur. Unaffected facilities can continue to satisfy market demands.

POLLUTION CONCERNS

The control of waste, discharges, and undesirable irritants became a national goal in the 1970s. Air pollution by industry has been abated by stringent legislation. Water pollution standards have increased substantially. The Environmental Protection Agency (EPA) has established strict standards for all forms of environmental pollution. These standards have influenced organizations to such an extent that it is not uncommon for 5–20% of the capital budget to be expended on pollution control equipment.

QUANTITATIVE ANALYSIS

The quantitative analysis approaches to location studies usually are some form of incremental analysis, simulation, transportation, or assignment methods of linear programming. The incremental analysis approach applies to the single plant model. The linear programming and simulation models are useful for multiplant analysis where a common product is provided. Quantitative models tend to be highly restrictive in their assumptions. They tend to neglect the intangible location factors. However, they are an excellent starting point for an analysis.

Proft-making organizations tend to prefer locations that will maximize revenues and minimize costs (maximize profits). When comparing several alternative locations, only revenues and costs that vary from one location to another need to be considered. If revenue per unit for a given market is the same regardless of where the product is produced, revenue can be eliminated from consideration. Likewise, if cost per unit for a given market is the same, it can be neglected. When both revenue per unit and cost per unit for a given market vary, comparisons should be based on a profit analysis.

EXAMPLE 2

Potential locations A, B, and C have the cost structure listed below. At what level of output would each facility become attractive? If the expected output is 75,000 units, what facility is most desirable?

Location	Fixed cost/year	Variable cost/unit
A	$100,000	$3.00
B	150,000	2.00
C	250,000	1.00

At the cost equalization point, two sites are equally desirable:

$$TC_A = TC_B,$$
$$100,000 + 3.00X = 150,000 + 2.00X,$$
$$X = 50,000 \text{ units};$$
$$TC_B = TC_C,$$
$$150,000 + 2X = 250,000 + X,$$
$$X = 100,000 \text{ units}.$$

The following table gives the decision rule for location selection:

Location	Output level (units)
A	0–50,000
B	50,000–100,000
C	≥100,000

For an expected output level of 75,000 units, location B results in the lowest total cost.

Capital investment analysis can be used to compare location alternatives. The following example illustrates the use of net present value for comparison purposes.

EXAMPLE 3

Dynatech Industries is capable of producing 10,000 units of output annually and presently is utilizing nearly all its production capacity. The company is a rapid growth firm and anticipates that its demand will double over the next ten years. Dynatech estimates that the growth will be steady rather than sporadic and wants to expand its capacity in advance of the increasing demand. Two options, both of which provide the same overall capacity but at different time intervals, are under consideration:

continued

EXAMPLE 3— *continued*

Alternative A: Acquire and refurbish another facility at a separate but nearby location. The new location could provide an additional 10,000 units of capacity immediately following a hasty refurbishment. The cost to acquire and renovate the facility is $1,600,000 (including $100,000 for the land), and the equipment to operate the facility costs $600,000.

Alternative B: Expand the present facility and subcontract. The present facility can be expanded in the immediate future to provide an additional 6000 units of capacity. The remainder of the 10,000 unit requirement could be provided by subcontractors as it is needed. The expansion costs $1,000,000, and the additional equipment costs $500,000.

The acquisition, expansion, or equipment purchases are allowed five year optional straight-line depreciations. Dynatech's effective tax rate is 40%, and its computed cost of capital is 12%. Both the acquisition and the refurbishment have the same expected life and will be fully depreciated before the end of the ten year planning period. The salvage values for the two options are deemed unimportant in the analysis. Operating benefits for both alternatives are assumed to be identical. Operating expenses (excluding depreciation) for the next ten years are projected as follows:

	Alternative	
Year	A	B
1– 2	$150,000	$120,000
3– 4	225,000	195,000
5– 6	285,000	260,000
7– 8	330,000	420,000[a]
9–10	360,000	565,000[a]

[a]Includes subcontracting expenses.

Using the information given, decide whether option A or B is more desirable.

The alternatives can be evaluated according to their net present value costs. The analysis shows:

Alternative A	
Initial investment	$2,200,000
Present value of operating expenses	
150,000(.6)(1.690) + 225,000(.6)(1.348)	
+285,000(.6)(1.074) + 330,000(.6)(.856)	
+360,000(.6)(.683)	834,750
Present value of depreciation tax savings	
210,000(.4)(.893) + 420,000(.4)(2.712)	
+210,000(.4)(.507)	−573,216
Net present value cost	$2,461,534
Alternative B	
Initial investment	$1,500,000
Present value of operating expenses	
120,000(.6)(1.690) + 195,000(.6)(1.348)	
+260,000(.6)(1.074) + 420,000(.6)(.856)	
+565,000(.6)(.683)	894,189
Present value of depreciation tax savings	
150,000(.4)(.893) + 300,000(.4)(2.712)	
+150,000(.4)(.507)	−409,440
Net present value cost	$1,984,749

The cost difference in favor of Alternative B is ($2,461,534 − 1,984,749) $476,785.

The previous decision to commit to an expansion project which entails the subsequent use of subcontractors is based strictly on cost factors. Other facility decision factors also might support its selection over the acquisition alternative. For example, liquidity concerns favor its lower initial costs; risk of technological obsolescence or failure to reach estimated demand levels lessens because of its smaller capital formation and built-in capability to quickly reduce external production capacity; materials handling and transportation, scheduling, stocking of inventories, layouts, and other operations functions can achieve certain economies not feasible in the operation of multiple facilities; and site factors such as zoning, utilities and services, land use, security, etc. are less critical when constructing on the same site rather than on a second location.

The following considerations counter the favorableness of the expansion alternative over the acquisition: less control over the entire production process is possible; the advantages of decentralization are lost; economies achieved by bulk purchasing and shipping over long distances are foregone when outside sources are used; and interim uses for the excess capacity are overlooked. These and other factors show that capital investment analysis is not almighty. The technique is extremely useful for comparisons of cost factors, but the final decision usually results in tradeoffs and compensations involving a multitude of factors.

The transportation method can be useful in making factory and warehouse location decisions. When a company has several factories and/or warehouses and is thinking of expanding capacity by the addition of a new facility, this method is appropriate. For the mechanics associated with the transportation method, the reader is referred to Chapter 5 on resource allocation and linear programming. A simple example will be used to illustrate the technique.

EXAMPLE 4

Demand has been increasing for the Horizon Corporation with present plants in St. Louis and Boston. The company is considering the addition of a third plant in Denver or Dallas to produce its major product. The fixed costs for the two prospective plants are essentially the same. After considerable study, the following pertinent data were obtained:

| | Distribution cost/unit | | | | Expected Annual Demand (units) |
| | From Existing Plants | | From Proposed Plants | | |
To Warehouse	St. Louis	Boston	Denver	Dallas	
New Orleans	$5	$8	$6	$4	20,000
San Francisco	6	10	3	9	20,000
Atlanta	8	7	10	6	26,000
Baltimore	9	6	11	10	24,000
Plant capacity (units)	35,000	30,000	25,000	25,000	
Production cost/unit	$15	$18	$16	$17	

On the basis of the above data, should the new plant be located in Denver or Dallas?

To solve the above problem it is necessary to use the transportation method and test which of the two alternatives (St. Louis, Boston, and Denver; or St. Louis, Boston, and Dallas) results in the minimum cost. The relevant unit cost for each assignment is the sum of distribution cost per unit and production cost per unit.

continued

EXAMPLE 4 — *continued*

The first tableau for the Denver option is shown in Figure 2. After a few iterations, the optimum tableau for the Denver option is shown in Figure 3. The first tableau for the Dallas option is shown in Figure 4. After a few iterations, the optimum tableau for the Dallas option is shown in Figure 5. The cost of the Denver option in thousands of dollars is as follows:

$$20(15) + 23(20) + 25(6) + 24(24) + 22(5) + 19(20) = \$1,976.$$

Warehouse	Plant			Demand
	St. Louis	Boston	Denver	
New Orleans	20 / 20,000	26	22	20,000
San Francisco	21 / 15,000	28 / 5,000	19	20,000
Atlanta	23	25 / 25,000	26 / 1,000	26,000
Baltimore	24	24	27 / 24,000	24,000
Supply	35,000	30,000	25,000	90,000

FIGURE 2
Initial tableau—Denver alternative.

FIGURE 3
Optimum tableau—Denver alternative.

Warehouse	Plant			Demand
	St. Louis	Boston	Denver	
New Orleans	20 / 15,000	26	22 / 5,000	20,000
San Francisco	21	28	19 / 20,000	20,000
Atlanta	23 / 20,000	25 / 6,000	26	26,000
Baltimore	24	24 / 24,000	27	24,000
Supply	35,000	30,000	25,000	90,000

Warehouse	Plant			Demand
	St. Louis	Boston	Dallas	
New Orleans	20 20,000	26	21	20,000
San Francisco	21 15,000	28 5,000	26	20,000
Atlanta	23	25 25,000	23 1,000	26,000
Baltimore	24	24	27 24,000	24,000
Supply	35,000	30,000	25,000	90,000

FIGURE 4
Initial tableau—Dallas alternative.

FIGURE 5
Optimum tableau—Dallas alternative.

Warehouse	Plant			Demand
	St. Louis	Boston	Dallas	
New Orleans	20 15,000	26	21 5,000	20,000
San Francisco	21 20,000	28	26	20,000
Atlanta	23	25 6,000	23 20,000	26,000
Baltimore	24	24 24,000	27	24,000
Supply	35,000	30,000	25,000	90,000

The cost of the Dallas option in thousands of dollars is as follows:

$$20(15) + 21(20) + 25(6) + 24(24) + 21(5) + 23(20) = \$2,011.$$

The lowest cost option is Denver with a cost of $1,976,000. It is $35,000 lower in cost than the Dallas option.

FOREIGN AND INTERNATIONAL CONSIDERATIONS

The growth of multinational corporations that operate or have facilities in several countries requires foreign plant considerations. Foreign plant location differs in some respects from domestic location. It infuses more factors, and worse-known ones, into its analysis because of different cultures, laws, and political influences. Language barriers, customs, and indigenous business practices can present operating, control, and even policy problems. As in the domestic situation, a systematic analysis of location alternatives is necessary.

The growth in multinational operations in the last generation is evidence of the importance of foreign locations. Some organizations are attracted to foreign locations because of abundant natural resources. Others are interested in ample supplies of labor at lower costs. Many firms desire foreign locations to expand their markets. Developing countries may offer financial incentives as part of economic development programs for improving their standard of living.

Some major factors in considering a plant location in another country are as follows:

1. U.S. government regulations on capital investment in foreign countries.

2. Host country regulations concerning foreign investment:
   a. requirements for setting up a local corporation,
   b. percentage of capital that can be foreign,
   c. percentage of employees that can be foreign,
   d. feasibility of joint operations with local firms,
   e. taxation of foreign-owned firms,
   f. convertibility of currency,
   g. transfer of earnings out of the country.

3. Political situation in the country:
   a. stability of the government,
   b. attitude towards foreign capital,
   c. protection against expropriation of foreign firms.

4. Economic situation in the country:
   a. standard of living or per capita income,
   b. trends in gross national product,
   c. fiscal stability,
   d. trends in foreign investment.

The checklist is far from complete, but it does provide initial guidance for some of the significant concerns.

In selecting a foreign plant location, a firm must eliminate those countries that look upon foreign investment with disfavor and those countries with unstable political and social structures that pose a threat to continued growth and profitability.

Lower wage rates are sometimes an inducement to foreign locations for products with high labor content. Products in industries with a high labor content have lower costs in some countries abroad. However, firms whose cost structure is dominated by capital, materials, and energy tend to have higher costs abroad. The important consideration is productivity. While the domestic worker is usually paid at a higher rate, the larger capital investment in tools and mechanization tend to make him highly productive. Of course, each situation is different and must be evaluated on its own merits.

CONCLUSION

Location decisions are a vital part of the strategic planning process of virtually every organization. They confront both new and existing organizations. Factors such as growth, market shifts, depletion of inputs, and the introduction of new products are typical reasons for location analysis. The significance of location is highlighted by its long-term commitment, and its influence on operating efficiency and on customer service.

Plant location is far from being a scientific exercise. Because of the uncertainties associated with the analysis, there is no such thing as the best plant location. Location choice is as much avoiding all seriously negative features as it is choosing the most positive factors. A thorough analysis of plant location factors will identify potential locations as acceptable or unacceptable. The final selection can be made from those in the acceptable category.

A primary objective of plant location is to select the location that will optimize profits or minimize the cost of the product delivered to the customer. Numerous attempts have been made to quantify the location analysis procedure, but so many individual and institutional value judgments enter into this type of decision that a totally objective analysis is virtually impossible. No fully satisfactory quantitative formulation of the location problem is available. The quantitative techniques and models that have been utilized have been restricted to limited and specialized conditions. Nevertheless, it is desirable to bolster intangible and subjective elements with whatever quantitative data are available.

More guesswork is used in determining plant location than one would imagine. The research that is conducted involves a lot of intuition and rules of thumb. The locational requirements for any given organization tend to be unique. In analyzing the pertinent factors, some weigh more heavily than others, and the mix can vary from organization to organization. The general factors have been outlined in this chapter, but they must be tailored to fit the situation. While plant location is not a science, it certainly can be made more scientific.

QUESTIONS

1. List several possibilities by which an organization can increase its capacity when it is experiencing overcrowding.
2. What is the significance of a plant's location?
3. What conditions may give rise to a plant location decision?
4. Give the inputs to and the outputs from a plant or facility location decision?
5. What major considerations influence the selection of a region for a facility?
6. Cite several influences present in the selection of a community.
7. What factors typically are important in the selection of a facility site?
8. What factor(s) does the selection of a region, community, and site have in common?
9. Describe input, process, and output dependence, and give examples of each.
10. List several tangible and intangible cost factors involved in location decisions.
11. What are two approaches to the measurement of the intangible costs of a new location?
12. What are some sources of assistance in selecting a community for a new facility?
13. Outline some major trends in facility location.
14. What technique can be used to locate a new facility within an existing organizational network?

15. What factors should be considered when analyzing another country for a plant location?

16. Discuss important considerations in the location of prisons, fire stations, state employment offices, banks, hospitals, fish canneries, and oil refineries.

PROBLEMS

1. A new plant must be located to produce a new product. The location selection will be based solely on the lowest cost facility. The expected annual demand is 25,000 units. Three locations are being considered. Where should the plant be located?

Location	Fixed cost/year	Variable cost/unit
Norfolk	$200,000	$50
Japan	400,000	30
Korea	800,000	10

2. A firm is considering three alternative locations for a new facility. The facility will have a useful life of ten years and be designed for an annual demand of 100,000 units. The relevant cost data are as follows:

Cost	A	B	C
Construction & equipment	$6,000,000	$6,100,000	$6,200,000
Labor/unit	2.10	2.20	2.00
Materials/unit	4.20	4.00	4.10
Utilities/year	40,000	38,000	42,000
Transportation cost/unit	0.50	0.55	0.40
Taxes/year	30,000	25,000	40,000

What location results in the lowest total cost?

3. The market research department of the firm in Problem 2 developed the annual demand for the product over the next ten years as shown below. Using expected value criteria, what is the most suitable location?

Demand (units)	Probability
50,000	.40
80,000	.30
100,000	.20
150,000	.10

4. A company ships a product from three plants to three warehouses. The weekly warehouse demand, weekly plant capacities, and unit shipping costs are as follows:

Warehouse	Plant			Demand (units)
	Albany	Broad	Callis	
Durham	$10	$12	$ 9	40
Everett	4	5	7	50
Fango	11	8	6	60
Capacity (units)	70	50	30	150

What is the optimum routing schedule? What is the total weekly freight bill?

5. If in Problem 4 the Albany plant is enlarged to a weekly capacity of 80 units, how should the routing schedule change? How much weekly freight cost will be saved?

6. The Sunset Corporation produces fabricated parts in three plants and delivers them to regional warehouses in three cities. Demand has grown nationwide to such a point that another regional warehouse is being planned. On the basis of customer service, the alternative warehouse locations have been narrowed down to Garlin and Heel. The following data are available:

Plant	Distribution cost/unit To existing warehouses Denver	Eagle	Frontier	To proposed warehouse Garlin	Heel	Production cost/unit	Capacity (units)
Albany	$3.00	$4.00	$5.00	$6.00	$7.00	$14.00	5000
Boise	3.75	3.75	4.75	6.25	2.75	13.25	6000
Castle	3.25	4.25	2.25	1.25	2.25	15.75	6000
Expected demand (units)	6000	4000	4000	3000	3000		

Based on the above data, should the warehouse be located in Garlin or Heel?

7. As a location consultant you are planning Aquarius, a new satellite city, from scratch. You must determine where to locate the fire station. The city will be composed of four areas, A, B, C, and D. To protect these areas three potential fire station locations are being considered—W, X, and Y. The following data are available:

	A	B	C	D
Expected no. of fires/yr	20	40	10	20
Average building value	$20,000	$30,000	$40,000	$80,000

The average number of minutes from each location to each area is as follows:

	A	B	C	D
W	2	4	5	6
X	5	3	3	7
Y	6	7	3	2

The effectiveness of a fire station is estimated as follows:

Minutes to respond to fire	Average % of building value lost
2	5
3	10
4	20
5	30
6	50
7	60

What location would you select to minimize the expected annual fire loss?

8. A university is considering an expansion of its research facilities so it can bid on a government contract. The cost of the expansion is $2,000,000. If the expansion is made and

the government contract is received, a net gain of $800,000 will result. If the expansion is made and the contract is not received, the university can recover about $1,500,000 of the $2,000,000 investment by doing subcontract work for local industry. The research director feels there is a 70% chance of getting the contract if the facilities are expanded, and no chance without the expansion. However, without the expansion the university is guaranteed other subcontract work that will net $300,000. Should the university expand its facility?

CASE 1: EXECUTIVE PREFERENCE

A group of investors has decided to pool resources and establish a furniture manufacturing company. The members of the group are either experienced business people or skilled furniture craftsmen. They expect to provide about half of the required capital from personal funds or loans; the other half is to come from bank loans secured by the firm's assets and from the sale of stock to unsecured creditors (friends and relatives interested in nonmanagement ownership). The group plans to manufacture high quality furniture for homes and offices. Most of the anticipated sales will be to retail establishments such as fine furniture stores and dealers in prestigious office furnishings.

The raw materials for the fine furniture are varied in character and source. The American hardwoods like birch, maple, oak, and walnut will come from the northern states and Canada. Smaller quantities of mahogany and other tropical woods will be obtained from importers. Few softwoods will be used except for a few novelties and for crating. Most upholstering fabrics will be obtained from eastern and southeastern mills; some special order fabrics will be imported. Initially, the firm plans to produce traditional pieces to stock, but most of the wide array of finishes and coverings will be custom ordered.

Many of the plant operations are to be as mechanized as possible, but a large portion of the work will require skilled hand operations. Workers will include cabinetmakers, upholsterers, wood carvers, and finishers; also, unskilled or semiskilled labor for machine operations, sanding, packing, and similar jobs.

The owner/operator in charge of production hopes to store and season much of the lumber outdoors and in unheated open sheds. Kiln drying also will be required. The finished furniture will be stored in heated space. The varnishing and enameling operations are not exceedingly critical as to temperature conditions, but trouble is expected during hot, humid weather. Shipments of finished goods will be made principally by truck.

The manufacturing concern plans to start operations with not more than 100 employees in a plant of approximately 20,000 square feet. The owners envision rapid growth and hope to justify a plant with at least four times the initial square footage.

The group of founders has decided to use a committee approach to finding a location for their plant. Assume that you are a member of that committee. For personal reasons, you would like to locate the plant in an industrial community near your present home. To support this objective, proceed as follows:

1. List the information necessary to make a wise location decision.
2. Study the area in which you live and make a list of the pro and con factors that will affect the location of the plant.
3. If the above analysis seems favorable, select a plant site.

CASE 2: ENERGY CENTER

The Board of Regents and administrative faculty at Crude University are investigating four possible locations for higher education's first energy research center. The structure will house laboratories, lecture halls, meeting rooms, classrooms, offices, etc., and be used cooperatively by several of the schools within the university system, e.g. engineering, geophysical sciences, business. The governing board particularly is concerned with four location factors:

1. The most important consideration is the ease of access to faculty, students, and other university personnel. Since the center's activities will involve several disciplinary areas, close proximity to the schools which will utilize the facility most fully is the major priority. Most of the schools mentioned are segregated from each other on the main campus. It is a goal of the administrators to locate the center within a convenient distance to all of these areas and yet maintain the natural physical boundaries which segment the campus.

2. The cost to acquisition the land for the building site is not a minor factor. However, the university has received generous donations from interested alumni, industrial groups, energy conglomerates, scientific organizations, and research foundations; these funds have been matched by state appropriations. The cumulative total of public and private contributions exceeds all estimates for each of the properties under investigation, but any amount of the total not spent on land acquisition could be used for equipment, furnishings, new faculty positions, etc. While the administrators are not unconcerned about how the funds are expended, ease of access is held to be at least 50% more important than the cost of the property.

3. Adequate parking space and surrounding land area together are considered to be a necessary component. The energy center will draw frequent visitors and will require more parking space than most other university buildings. Furthermore, the plans for the energy center include subsequent expansion. Land initially used for parking later could be used as a building site; conversion from a parking lot into a research structure would create a new parking problem. Therefore, the board is giving utmost attention to surrounding land areas which are available now and to contiguous properties where the state easily could get title and the owners are predisposed to sell. The availability of surrounding land area is felt to be just as important as the cost of the initial acquisition.

4. Finally, public sentiment and support are deemed to be important for present and future operation of the center. The locations are being examined in terms of how residents and benefactors will react to the location choice. The public may have use of the facility, live next to it, or be moved to make room for its construction. Those who donated toward its creation will have reason to express pleasure or dissatisfaction over its accessibility to industry and public use. This consideration is the least important of all, perhaps only half as important as the cost of the land acquisition.

The four locations being considered are: (A) a relatively accessible area where the old University Hall stands; (B) a vacant property near the University Sports Arena which is situated at a far end of the south campus; (C) a residential area, Solar Brook, which borders the main campus; and (D) a property on the North Campus which lies eight miles from the main campus and is readily accessible from the Interstate system leading to the Metropolitan Airport.

The Board of Regents has decided to evaluate the location alternatives on each of the four factors. It has decided to use a five-point scale on which 1 represents "poor" and 5 represents "excellent." The rating points assigned to each of the alternatives for each of the factors are shown below. The Board now must reach a conclusion determining the best location for the energy center.

	Locations[a]			
Factor	A	B	C	D
1. Accessibility to students & faculty	4	2	5	1
2. Acquisition cost	4	3	1	2
3. Surrounding land area	1	4	1	5
4. Public support	3	2	1	4

[a]Five-point scale: 5 = excellent, 4 = good, 3 = average, 2 = below average, 1 = poor.

1. Evaluate the location alternatives based on a weighted score technique.
2. Discuss the complication of multiple criteria in making location decisions.
3. What other factors or considerations could be involved in the energy center location decision?

SELECTED BIBLIOGRAPHY

Beckman, M. *Location Theory,* New York: Random House, 1968.

Collins, L. *Locational Dynamics of Manufacturing Activity,* New York: Wiley, 1975.

Greenhut, M. *Plant Location in Theory and Practice,* Chapel Hill, NC: University of North Carolina Press, 1956.

Karaska, G. and D. Bramhall. *Locational Analysis for Manufacturing,* Cambridge, MA: MIT Press, 1969.

Reed, R., Jr. *Plant Location, Layout, and Maintenance,* Homewood, IL: Irwin, 1967.

Whitman, E. S. and W. J. Schmidt. *Plant Relocation,* New York: American Management Associations, 1966.

13
Plant Layout

LAYOUT INPUTS

LAYOUT CONSTRAINTS
Production Goals
Equipment and Capital Availability
Human Factors

LAYOUT DESIGN CONSIDERATIONS
Building Design
Materials Handling
Work Place Design
Support Services

LAYOUT OUTPUTS
Capacity
Layout Types
Process Layout
Product Layout
Fixed Position Layout

Group Technology (GT)
Equipment Requirements

CONCLUSION

APPENDIX A. LINE BALANCING
Trial and Error Technique
Ranked Positional Weight Technique

QUESTIONS

PROBLEMS

CASES

SELECTED BIBLIOGRAPHY

The major objective of plant layout is to develop a productive system that meets the requirements of capacity and quality in the most economical fashion. Plant layout establishes the spatial configuration for the physical facilities. Layout must integrate machines, support services, work places, manpower, logistical subsystems, and storage areas so that feasible operating schedules can be formulated. Layout engineers attempt to utilize facility space, equipment, and manpower in the most orderly and efficient fashion.

Plant layout is necessary every time future building requirements are planned. However, it is more often encountered as a relayout of an existing facility. Every organization encounters a layout or relayout problem from time to time. This is true for warehouses, distribution centers, department stores, and hospitals as well as manufacturing installations. A substantial change in product mix, work methods, product design, process design, or equipment may dictate a need for a new layout in an existing facility. The scope of the layout problem can vary widely. It may involve a minor adjustment to a single department or work station, or it may encompass the entire facility.

Since change is a common occurrence in most organizations, the layout problem is encountered frequently. Change results in efficient layouts becoming poor ones. A good layout must therefore be a changing layout. It should be flexible enough to be changed quickly, inexpensively, and with as little disruption to operations as possible.

The layout problem concerns the rearrangement of an existing operating facility, movement to an existing new facility, or a new facility which has yet to be designed and constructed. The greater degree of flexibility is available when a new facility is

FIGURE 1
Layout of facilities.

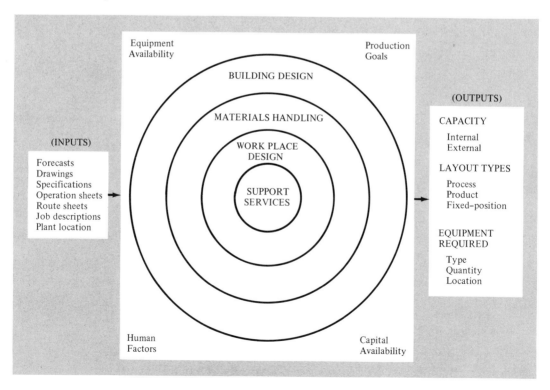

being designed. In this case, buildings and structures can be designed to accommodate the most desirable layout. When the facility already exists, the layout must accommodate its dimensional and structural constraints. The major considerations in plant layout are schematically represented in Figure 1.

The layout problem is to determine the best design from a multitude of possibilities that fits today's needs and is amenable to future expectations. Although the initial planning of a layout is demanding, it is more difficult to alter facilities once they are in place.

Poor layout can reveal itself in several ways. The simultaneous occurrence of bottlenecks and idleness within a facility might indicate the need for a relayout. A cluttered work area with materials stacked around machines and in aisles suggests possible improvement. Excessive cycle times, poor customer service, and lost orders are indications of inefficiencies. Poor safety records and high maintenance costs often point to weaknesses. It is difficult to establish conclusively a list of symptoms that indicate a poor layout, since many of these symptoms are associated with other operational problems. However, when these symptoms are present, the adequacy of the layout should be investigated.

LAYOUT INPUTS

The major inputs to plant layout come from the outputs of product decisions, process decisions, and plant location. The inputs are forecasts, drawings, specifications, operation sheets, route sheets, job descriptions, and plant location. Forecasts indicate the timing and structure of demand for the product. The engineering drawings and product specifications define all the physical and functional characteristics of the product. The operation sheets delineate the work activities to be performed at each work station. The route sheets outline the routing of the product to the work stations. The job descriptions specify the quantity and type of manpower required at each work station. Finally, the plant location indicates the location of the physical site for the facility. These inputs are usually necessary before the layout of the facility can be undertaken.

The layout decision requires information about the products to be produced, the processes to be used, and the expected levels of demand. It dramatically affects the efficiency, productivity, and operating costs of a production system. A good layout should

1. utilize space efficiently,
2. utilize human resources efficiently,
3. position equipment for maximum utilization,
4. provide a convenient, comfortable, and safe work environment,
5. provide easy access for equipment repair and maintenance, and
6. result in a smooth flow of materials or people through successive productive stages.

LAYOUT CONSTRAINTS

PRODUCTION GOALS

Production goals deal with the output capacity of a facility. A production planner is concerned with present and future levels of demand as well as the present and future mix of products. Frequently demand will exhibit pronounced variations because of seasonal or cyclical influences. A varying demand level can result in excessive costs. Various cost tradeoffs exist in establishing the capacity for a facility. An organization can vary its production rate, the size of its work force, or its inventory levels. With a varying production rate, inventory levels are kept low and there is considerable hiring and firing of personnel. With a fixed production rate, the work force does not vary but inventory levels do. Of course, if demand is fairly stable, it is much easier to establish plant capacity levels.

Capacity refers to the productive capability of a facility. When the units of output are identical or nearly so, it can be measured in units of output (tons of steel, number of television sets, gallons of paint, etc.). When the units of output are diverse and without commonality, capacity can be expressed in units of input (number of doctors, labor man-hours, hours per week, etc.). Capacity is always measured as the rate of output or input per time unit. Service organizations usually measure capacity in input terms.

The capacity level chosen is usually a compromise between the maximum possible demand and the average expected demand of the facility. Obtaining a quantitative estimate of capacity requires a suitable unit of capacity, such as number of men, machines, man-hours, units of product, tons, machine-hours, gallons, or customers. It can be established on a single or multiple shift basis. Capacity can be increased by adding extra shifts or overtime. Subcontracting is another source of increased capacity, this time from external sources.

For many organizations it is difficult to establish a single measure of capacity. Different units of production are not homogeneous and readily added to each other. The number, kind, and mix of products can vary substantially and complicate a direct translation into a common single measure of capacity.

Capacity levels set the maximum output for the production system. Capacity levels are influenced by the number of work shifts, overtime, growth capacity, subcontract capabilities, and seasonal demand levels. The resolution of the capacity problem will be dependent on forecasts of future demand. Capacity will determine total plant investment and future operating costs for the facility.

EXAMPLE 1

The city of Aquarius is planning a new hospital. The capacity of the facility will be measured by the number of patients receiving treatment per day. The planning committee has estimated the demand for patient treatment per day to be as follows:

Number of patients	Midpoint	Probability	Service level fraction
50–99	75	0.10	0.10
100–149	125	0.20	0.30
150–199	175	0.30	0.60
200–249	225	0.20	0.80
250–299	275	0.15	0.95
300–349	325	0.05	1.00
		1.00	

What patient treatment capacity should the hospital have if it is built to meet (a) average demand, (b) 150% of estimated average demand, (c) a 95% service level?

a:

Midpoint X	Probability P(X)	X · P(X)
75	.10	7.5
125	.20	25.0
175	.30	52.5
225	.20	45.0
275	.15	41.25
325	.05	16.25
		187.50

The average number of patients demanding treatment is 187.5, or 188.

b: For 150% of estimated average demand, a (1.5)188 = 282 patient treatment capacity is required.

c: A 95% service level would require a 300 patient treatment capacity.

EQUIPMENT AND CAPITAL AVAILABILITY

Once the capacity level is known, the quantity of each type of equipment must be determined. If unused equipment is available, it can be deployed. If insufficient equipment is available, capital must be allocated to acquire the needed capacity. Since plant decisions involve a huge investment, capital availability is an important constraint on a new facility.

A preliminary step in any plant layout analysis is the determination of what is to be laid out. It begins by ascertaining the kind and amount of equipment required for operations. The type of equipment will be indicated by the operation sheets developed in process decisions. The quantity of equipment is established by the selection of the capacity for the work station. For example, if 800 hours of grinder time are required each month, and each grinder provides 172 hours, the required number of grinders is

$$\frac{800 \text{ hr/month}}{172 \text{ hr/machine-month}} = 4.65, \text{ or 5 machines.}$$

EXAMPLE 2

An organization must install enough automatic processors to provide 800,000 good units per year. The processing time per unit is 30 seconds, but the processors are only 80% efficient due to scrap and maintenance allowances. How many automatic processors must be purchased if the firm operates 2000 hours per year?

$$\text{Individual processor capacity} = \frac{3600 \text{ sec/hr}}{30 \text{ sec/unit}} = 120 \text{ units/machine-hr}$$

$$\text{Required capacity} = \frac{800,000 \text{ units/year}}{(2000 \text{ hr/year})(0.8)} = 500 \text{ units/hr}$$

$$\text{No. of processors required} = \frac{500 \text{ units/hr}}{120 \text{ units/machine-hr.}} = 4.2 \text{ machines.}$$

The organization would probably plan for the installation of five automatic processors.

HUMAN FACTORS

Human factors relate to those aspects of the facility that support the human work endeavor. The temperature and humidity of the facility should be within the comfort range, so heat and air conditioning systems must be considered. Adequate lighting must be provided from natural or power sources. Industrial safety should be considered in the design phase, with protection from work hazards such as noise, chemicals, falling objects, overhead protrusions, vehicles, and accidents. Noisy, smoky, odor-producing, and hazardous areas should be isolated.

LAYOUT DESIGN CONSIDERATIONS

An initial phase of the layout analysis begins with a plot of new buildings, existing structures, and grounds. New structures must be located on the grounds. This requires consideration of rail sidings, highways, roadways, docks, receiving areas, and distribution points. The next step consists of floor plans of structures and facilities. Ceiling heights, load capacities of floors, and plant utilities (sewers, drains, water mains, electric power lines, air lines, and steam lines) must be situated. The floor plan should contain information on walls, columns, doors, windows, stairwells, elevator shafts, and sprinkler systems.

FIGURE 2
Layout logic.

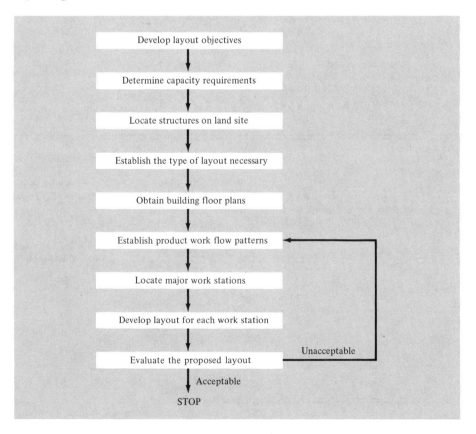

The operation and flow process charts developed in process decisions are a good starting point for the layout of operating facilities. They indicate the operations that must be performed on the product and their required sequence. They indicate the relative position of work stations and departments. Efficient flow of work is a major consideration. There is no fixed set of rules that will determine exactly the most efficient allocation of area. As a result, no two analysts are likely to recommend the same overall arrangement. There are likely to be several good layouts that are acceptable. It is more important not to select a poor layout than to select the very best.

From manufacturer specifications the analyst knows the number of square feet of floor space each piece of equipment will occupy. A study of existing layouts may indicate the percentage of total work station areas occupied by equipment. From these relationships a crude measurement of total work station areas can be ascertained. If existing layouts are congested or contain wasted space, appropriate corrections can be applied. Of course this type of procedure yields only rough approximations, which can be revised with a more detailed analysis. It is however a good starting point for space allocation. A great deal of judgment is usually involved. The basic layout logic for a new facility is outlined in Figure 2.

When a new plant is being contemplated, it is possible to build the plant around a proper layout rather than to lay out the plant within the restrictions of an existing building. It is more desirable to develop the layout and build the building around it, than to construct the building first and then attempt to fit the layout into it. The major layout design considerations are building design, materials handling, workplace design, and support services. Each will now be discussed in further detail.

BUILDING DESIGN

A new structure may be an addition to an existing building or an entirely new plant. The building is designed to protect the property and employees of an organization. For those plants where employees, materials, and processes do not require protection, no building is required. The petroleum and chemical industries frequently do not require enclosed facilities. However, most organizations need some type of protective structure.

If an organization is small, it may be able to rent or buy an existing facility. When extensive space is required, it is difficult to find suitable facilities for rent or purchase. This necessitates the design and construction of a new facility, which in turn requires the services of an architect and a contractor. Large industrial construction firms frequently will handle all the details associated with new construction. Plant design and construction is a specialized field outside the scope of this text.

Most industrial buildings are single story, multistory, or some combination. The most desirable type depends on the production processes, the cost of construction, and the cost of land. When land is available at a reasonable cost, the single story building is popular. Single story buildings require no stairs, elevators, elevator wells, or ramps. Materials handling is simplified because all the moving is horizontal. The single story provides the lowest overall cost per square foot of operating space. When land is expensive or not available, the multistory building provides maximum floor space per square foot of land. Construction costs are higher for multistory structures. Table 1 contains a qualitative comparison of single story and multistory buildings.

A structure should provide for flexibility so it can be adapted to changing needs without incurring excessive costs. Flexibility renders a facility less subject to obsolescence while providing greater operating efficiency as processes and technology

TABLE 1
Comparison of single story and multistory buildings

Characteristic	Type of building	
	Single story	Multistory
Layout flexibility	Good	Poor
Ease of ventilation	Good	Poor
Ease of expansion	Good	Poor
Use of natural illumination	Good	Poor
Floor load capacities	Unrestricted	Restricted
Fire danger	Less	More
Use of land	Poor	Excellent
Cost of construction	Low	High
Materials handling cost	Low	High
Heating cost	High	Low

change. Convertibility makes changes possible at lower costs. A facility should be designed with future growth needs in mind.

The services of a competent architect and building engineer are necessary in establishing building design, but the manager himself should be aware of major building design factors. He should work closely with the designers to ensure a facility that will meet the future needs of the organization.

MATERIALS HANDLING

Any organization that produces a physical product must be concerned with materials handling. The movement of supplies, materials, components, or products within an organization belongs to the province of materials handling. Whether the movement is by hand, truck, conveyor, or sophisticated transfer equipment, it is a major aspect of plant layout.

The method of materials handling can be decided only after the kinds and amounts of materials to be transported are known as well as the locations from and to which materials are to be transported. Thus, the location of work stations will influence the choice of the materials handling equipment, and the choice of materials handling equipment will influence the location of work stations. A good layout will minimize the cost and time required to move materials through the facility.

Frequently, materials handling costs are a major portion of product cost. Since transfer equipment costs are usually contained in overhead with other process equipment, they are considered a fixed cost. Organizations that are highly capital intensive tend to have sophisticated materials handling systems. Labor intensive organizations tend to have less sophisticated systems. Fixed path materials handling equipment is typically associated with continuous production, while variable path materials handling equipment is associated with intermittent production systems.

Materials handling equipment can dramatically affect space requirements and equipment arrangements. Hand or powered trucks require wider aisles than conveyors do. Overhead cranes require unencumbered overhead spaces free from supporting columns. Automated materials handling equipment tends to use space more efficiently. Each movement mode dictates certain spatial requirements for efficient operations.

When product demand is high, the product design is stable, and few products are produced, automated materials handling systems are common. When numerous variegated products are produced in the same facility, more labor intensive materials handling systems are usually found.

Materials handling is a major portion of any plant layout. It is important because of its large investment, its potential safety hazards to personnel, and its tremendous influence on operating efficiency. Materials handling will be covered in greater detail in the next chapter.

WORKPLACE DESIGN

In a previous chapter, process decisions established the scope of work effort at each work station via operation sheets. Workplace design takes the information on operation sheets and designs the spatial relationships for each work station. The workplace will consist of equipment, manpower, tools, benches, tables, chairs, or desks required to perform the work effort. The manpower element may be an individual or a team. The equipment may be as simple as a lever or as complex as a computer. The job may be as simple as an assembly line repetitive task or as complicated as a maintenance repair. For efficient plant operation, area and volume requirements should be allocated to each work station in proportion to its needs.

It is also necessary to locate each work station in relation to all other work stations. Route sheets will indicate the sequence of required operations on the given products. A study of route sheets will indicate the preferences of work stations in relation to each other. It is desirable to locate those work stations that have the most interactions close to each other. In this manner, materials handling costs tend to be minimized. Aisleways must be planned for maneuverability of manpower and transfer equipment between or through work stations.

SUPPORT SERVICES

A number of activities must be performed that do not directly contribute to the production of the product. These activities indirectly support the production process and are considered necessary. We will lump all of these activities into a category called support services. Space in the facility must be allocated to them. Support services vary from organization to organization; some of the more prevalent are restrooms, cafeterias, locker rooms, storerooms, security areas, medical facilities, recreation rooms, and maintenance areas. Some support services may be located in buildings other than the operating facility.

LAYOUT OUTPUTS

The outputs from plant layout are the designation of capacity, the type of layout, and a required equipment list. The configuration of the facility including all its equipment is thereby made known and spatially defined. These outputs will now be outlined in greater detail.

CAPACITY

The maximum level of output for a facility is its capacity. For organizations with a single or only a few products, capacity is most easily determined. For multiproduct organizations, capacity is more difficult to measure when the products share facilities. Capacity must be related to a time frame and is frequently stated as a rate (quantity of output in a given time). It can be on a single shift or multishift basis. It is only a theoretical level of output, which may or may not be attainable.

Organizations can operate 8, 16, or 24 hours a day. A facility operating 8 hours a day needs to be nearly three times as large as a 24 hour operation in order to produce the same daily output. Similarly, operations may run for 5, 6, or 7 days a week. The fewer the hours worked, the more plant capacity needed for a given output. Per-unit overhead expenses (depreciation, insurance, taxes) are lower when a small plant is used intensively. However, maintenance is easier for less intensive use of a facility (repairs can be performed in off hours with no production interference). Many organizations use part of their facility intensively (16 or 24 hours a day) and other parts extensively (8 hours a day).

Frequently as an organization approaches its capacity level of operations, its efficiency drops and costs increase rapidly. Operating at 100% capacity is a rare if not unattainable accomplishment because of equipment breakdowns, personnel vacancies, and absenteeism.

We have been discussing capacity as a design consideration. Actually there are several different meanings to the term. Three different capacity measures are as follows:

1. *Design capacity*—the maximum theoretical output level that can be obtained under ideal conditions.
2. *Effective capacity*—the maximum output level considering quality limitations, equipment maintenance, product mixes, and so forth.
3. *Actual capacity*—the demonstrated output level actually achieved. It cannot exceed effective capacity and usually is less because of breakdowns, resource shortages, absenteeism, defective output, scheduling difficulties, and so forth.

Actual capacity is determined by the factor in short supply or the bottleneck operation. It may be constrained by the number of personnel, equipment, or the size of the facility. Capacity expansion is based on increasing output in the bottleneck areas.

It is common to hire personnel and purchase equipment for current needs and to

FIGURE 3
Plant capacity.

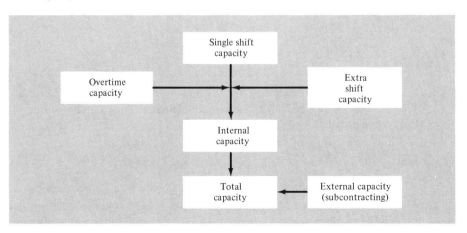

provide space in the facility for future needs. Space added later is usually more expensive and has a long lead time. In an expansionary period, a facility will have plenty of orders and may approach effective capacity. In a recessionary period, orders diminish and production levels are well below capacity. Cutting back on capacity is generally easier than adding capacity, which takes much longer.

Capacity can be subdivided into internal and external. *Internal capacity* is the output capability within the organization. *External capacity* is the output capability available from subcontractors or suppliers. Total capacity is the sum of internal and external capacities. Both types of capacities are shown in Figure 3.

LAYOUT TYPES

Layouts can be based on the work flow or the function of the facility. Based on work flow, the basic types are process layouts, product layouts, and fixed position layouts. A *process layout* groups work centers according to the general function they perform without regard to any particular product. Machine shops, department stores, universities, and hospitals are usually arranged in this manner. In a *product layout*, work stations are arranged according to the progressive steps by which the product

FIGURE 4
Work flow layouts.

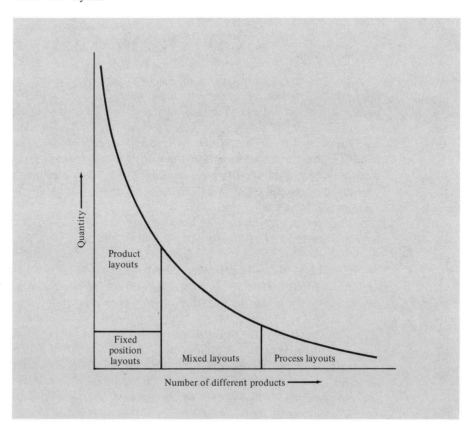

is produced. Assembly lines typify this layout category. A *fixed position layout* has a product that remains in a given location because of its bulk or weight. Typical examples are buildings, special projects, and huge structures.

Based on function of the facility, the basic types are storage layouts and marketing layouts. A *storage layout* performs an inventory function with no physical change in the product. Space utilization is frequently more important in storage layout than materials handling cost. Typical examples are warehouses, storerooms, and distribution centers. A *marketing layout* is an arrangement to facilitate the sale of the product. Marketing layouts attempt to maximize the net profit per square foot of display space. Similar products are grouped together for shopper convenience. Behavioral considerations or revenue generation influence this type of layout much more than cost considerations. Typical examples are retail stores, advertising displays, and supermarkets. Neither the storage layout nor the marketing layout involves any physical change in the product.

The layout problem is surprisingly large and complex when considered mathematically. It can involve millions of layout alternatives. This explains why intuitive and heuristic approaches have been widely used. The layout problem is further magnified when the facility must be shared by many products that require different flow paths and sequences through the system. In general, plant layouts based on work flow are process oriented, product oriented, or fixed position oriented. Continuous processes are product oriented, intermittent processes are process oriented, and special projects are fixed position oriented. The type of flow dictated by process selection is a dominant consideration in layout selection. As shown in Figure 4, the variety and volume of products influence the type of work flow layout.

Process Layout

A process layout (sometimes called a functional or job shop layout) results in machines, equipment, and processes of the same functional type being grouped together. It is employed when the same facilities must be used to fabricate and assemble a wide variety of products. With the process layout, the facilities and equipment are flexible so they can be used on numerous products. The location of departments or work centers with a process layout is usually based on minimizing materials handling costs. Since transportation per se adds no direct value to the product, it can be considered a wasteful expenditure. Thus, an efficient layout will reduce or minimize unnecessary flows among work centers.

With a process layout there is no fixed path through the system. Each job may have a different set of operations and a different sequence. Thus, work effort at each work center can vary considerably depending on the mix of jobs in the system. The central problem of layout design is the relative location of the work centers. It is desirable to locate those work centers with the most interaction adjacent to each other. This reduces the transportation of in-process materials from work center to work center. For organizations producing a physical product, adjacency lowers materials handling costs. For organizations producing a service, adjacency reduces process time in the system. Since different jobs have different requirements, it is necessary to aggregate all the job paths through the system to determine the most desirable relative locations. While the resulting location combination may be poor for some products, in aggregate it will be the best.

Layout design for intermittent operations can be approached quantitatively by determining the location of work centers (departments) which will minimize a stated objective function. The objective function is expressed in measurable terms of the work flow. Its criteria usually is either the minimization of materials handling costs in manufacturing operations or the minimization of employee or customer travel time in service organizations. The total cost of the materials or traffic flow for a given layout can be determined from the following formulation:

$$\text{Total cost} = \sum_{i=1}^{N} \sum_{j=1}^{N} T_{ij} C_{ij} D_{ij},$$

where

N = number of departments,

T_{ij} = number of trips between departments i and j,

C_{ij} = cost per unit distance per trip between departments i and j,

D_{ij} = distance from department i to j.

The number of trips between pairs of departments per time period (T_{ij}) can be estimated from route sheets and forecasts. The cost per unit of distance traveled on each trip (C_{ij}) may vary for exchanges between pairs of departments due to dissimilar work flow methods, but C_{ij} can be obtained from an analysis of the cost data for each method of transfer. Since both T_{ij} and C_{ij} can be determined prior to choosing a layout, they are held constant in the total cost formula and are assumed independent of the location of departments. The distance between pairs of departments (D_{ij}) does depend on the layout chosen. Once an initial layout is designed, values for D_{ij} are found and total cost is calculated. Improved layouts then are attained by considering exchanges between pairs of departments which lower total cost. The optimal solution by this approach cannot be derived unless every possible combination of departments is evaluated.

A graphical approach to locating work centers for a process layout is called *operations sequence analysis*. It requires the development of a load summary or travel chart (a "from and to" matrix), which indicates the flow between all combinations of prospective work centers for a given time period. The information from the load summary chart is included in a schematic flow diagram where circles represent work centers and connecting lines are labeled to indicate the intensity or number of transactions between centers. By a trial and error approach, the centers are moved (shifted) in an attempt to improve the locations by minimizing the number of non-adjacent trips, loads, or cost. The method tries to juxtapose centers between which there will be an expected heavy traffic flow. When a satisfactory arrangement is obtained, the circles are replaced with block templates so the specific arrangement will accommodate the various size (area) requirements of each work center. Variations in sizes and shapes may be necessary to fit the building.

Templates are two dimensional outlines of objects. Scale models are three dimensional outlines of objects. In a trial and error fashion, analysts move these devices about until they find a reasonable layout. Although such means are useful in approaching a satisfactory layout, they do not promise an optimal layout. It is more meaningful to talk about obtaining a satisfactory layout.

For a process layout, a feasible procedure might be summarized as follows:

1. Diagram the interdepartmental flow including the number of movements.
2. Establish an initial feasible layout.
3. Determine the layout cost by multiplying the number of loads by the materials handling cost per load.
4. Search for a different layout that will reduce cost.

The graphical approach to the determination of the relative location of work centers has obvious limitations. It depends too much upon the analyst's insight and it becomes extremely cumbersome as the number of work centers increases. Several computerized approaches such as CRAFT (computerized relative allocation of facilities technique), ALDEP (automated layout design program), CORELAP (computerized relationship layout planning), and PLANET (computerized plant layout and evaluation technique) have been developed to analyze numerous different work centers.[1] The CRAFT program requires as inputs an initial spatial array, matrices of the volume of interaction, and the interaction cost per unit volume per unit distance. The algorithm functions by computing the changes in interaction cost that result if locations are exchanged, making exchanges progressively for those switches with the greatest cost reduction potential. It can be used for both new design and redesign of facilities based on minimizing materials handling costs.

ALDEP, CORELAP, CRAFT, and PLANET are iterative heuristic programs that do not necessarily result in optimal solutions. They do usually result in a good layout. These computerized techniques have assumptions that limit their applicability, but when the assumptions are reasonable they can substantially improve the layout decision.

Product Layout

A product layout (sometimes called a line layout) has equipment arranged according to the sequence of operations to be performed on the product. Assembly lines are product layouts where specialized equipment is arranged so as to assemble large quantities of a product. Operations are often routine and highly repetitive, so wage rates are comparatively low and the jobs are not appealing to all workers.

With a product layout, the best configuration of tasks assigned to work stations (or work zones) is obtained by balancing the line. Balance refers to the equality of output of each successive work station in sequence along the line. Tasks are assigned to work stations so that ideally each work station takes the same amount of time to complete its work effort.

In a process layout the pattern or sequence of work flow is highly variable. In a product layout it is highly predictable and fixed. Although work center location is not a problem for product layouts, the achievement of a smooth flow of products between work stations is. This is the line balancing problem.[2]

Line balancing is a combinatorial problem that seeks a combination of task times that will maximize labor utilization, or equivalently, minimize labor idle time. A task or work element is the smallest unit of work that is separable from other activities

---

[1]For a detailed analysis of computerized approaches and other techniques see R. L. Francis, *Facility Layout and Location,* Prentice-Hall, 1974, pp. 95–141, and J. M. Apple, *Plant Layout and Material Handling,* Wiley, 1977.

[2]For a more detailed explanation of line balancing, see Appendix A at the end of the chapter. A summary of line balancing approaches can be found in E. J. Ignall, "A Review of Assembly Line Balancing," *Journal of Industrial Engineering,* Vol. 16, No. 4, July–August 1965, pp. 244–254.

TABLE 2
Comparison of product and process layouts

Characteristic	Layout type	
	Product (line)	Process (functional)
Production process	Continuous	Intermittent
Production equipment	Special purpose	General purpose
Equipment utilization	High	Low
Production volume	High	Low
Production by inventory	Make to stock	Make to order
Product design	Standardized	Specialized
Product demand	Stable	Lumpy
Number of products (product mix)	Few	Many
Transfer system	In-line (built-in)	Added on
Transfer equipment	Conveyors (fixed path)	Trucks (variable path)
Aisleways	Narrow	Wide
In-process storage space	Small	Large
Routing and scheduling	Easy	Difficult
Maintenance	Supercritical	Important
Department workload	Balanced	Variable
Staff skill	Specialist	Generalist
Worker skill	Semiskilled	Skilled
Worker job instruction	Little	Much
Worker learning time	Short	Long
Raw materials inventory	High	Low
In-process inventory	Low	High
Finished goods inventory	High	Low
Throughput time	Short	Long
Cost per unit	Low	High
Capital investment	Very large	Large
Major advantage	Low unit cost	Flexibility
Major concern	Line balancing	Department locations
Objective function	Minimum no. of stations[a]	Minimum materials handling costs

[a] Given the cycle time.

such that it can be performed independently and possibly in different sequences. However, an extremely small line balancing problem with only ten tasks has 10! different sequences, or approximately 3.63×10^6. Of course, technological sequencing requirements reduce the number of feasible sequences, but the enumeration problem is still unwieldy. The problem becomes one of grouping tasks into work stations that are feasible within technological sequence restrictions, while minimizing the number of work stations given the cycle time. To better visualize sequence relationships, a precedence diagram can be drawn showing the dependences among job tasks.

The choice of cycle time is related to the demand for the product and production output requirements established for the facility. The cycle time is the time required to complete the work tasks at each work station. A completed product will come off the line after each cycle time. With perfect balance, the work tasks at each work station will exactly equal the cycle time. If it is impossible to attain a perfect balance, there will be idle time at some work stations.

Given a cycle time, the initial step in balancing a line is to decide upon a rule by which tasks may be allocated to the different work stations. Tasks can be allocated so long as they do not violate technological sequence requirements and the total task times do not exceed the cycle time. Task times are usually assumed to be deterministic in line balancing. However, they are frequently stochastic when humans are involved.

Many organizations develop layouts that are neither pure product nor pure process but are some combination of both. Some operations may be performed continuously while others are intermittent. Product and process layouts represent the extremes of layout. It is desirable to extract the best features of each in developing an organization's particular configuration. A comparison of the pure product and process layouts is contained in Table 2.

Fixed Position Layout

Process and product layouts are the most common types of work flow layouts found in organizations. Another less common but basic type of layout is known as a fixed position layout. In this type the product is stationary while resources (men, equipment, and materials) are brought to it. This is often done for large, complex products that are built from the ground up and are not suitable for movement. Typical examples of fixed position layout are found in shipyards, heavy construction (buildings, bridges, dams, roads), aircraft, and special projects.

With a fixed position layout there are usually only a small number of units processed. Assembly is performed from the ground up, based on technological priority of operations. Since congestion can develop, the scheduling of operations is a major consideration. This layout is used when size, fragility, weight, cost, and other factors render it undesirable or impractical to move the product through a system.

GROUP TECHNOLOGY (GT)

A concept that is gaining increasing acceptance in the U.S. is group technology. It attempts to modify traditional process layouts to exploit the advantages of product layouts. GT groups similar parts into part families which have common characteristics based on their size, shape, or processing steps. By creating dedicated production cells in which only families of parts are produced, efficiencies associated with assembly line production are sought. It enables an organization to achieve the economies of product layouts without product standardization. Conversion to cellular production promises shorter lead times, reduced work-in-process and finished goods inventories, less materials handling, and simplified production planning and control. Further, GT is considered necessary for the successful application of computer-aided design and computer-aided manufacturing (CAD/CAM).

The majority of products manufactured in the U.S. are produced by intermittent processes laid out in functionally semiautonomous departments. Typically, 95% of a product's throughput time from work release to shipment out the door is wait or queue time. Only 5% of the time is work actually being performed on the product. Thus, a product with a lead time of 2 weeks may only require 4 hours of operations time. Because parts in a GT system can be produced in one area (cell) instead of being routed from department to department, throughput time is reduced dramatically. Since GT cells are dedicated to similar work, workers do not need to prepare as many special setups. So changeover costs go down as well as lot sizes and work-

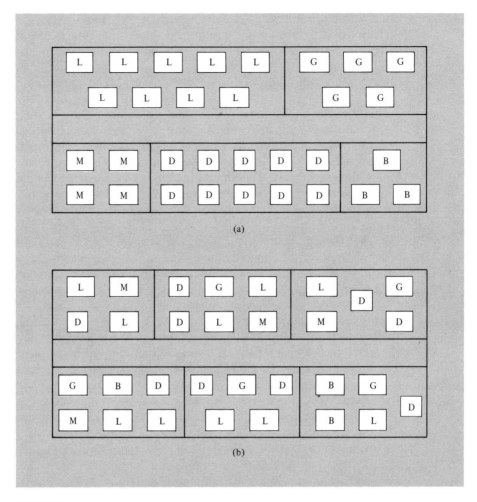

FIGURE 5
Process vs. group technology layouts: (a) process layout, (b) group technology cell layout. B: broaches; D: drills; G: grinders; L: lathes; M: mills.

in-process inventory. Additionally, the reduced setup time translates into higher equipment utilization.

The application of GT involves two steps. The first step is the determination of part families which require similar sequences of operations. The second step is to arrange processing equipment into cells, each containing the equipment used to process a particular family of parts. The result is a group of small plants within a plant. The processing required by each family can be performed within a cell to accommodate the common flow pattern. Thus, GT restructures the work flow within an organization so it is smoother and more continuous. Figure 5 illustrates a five department process layout that was converted to a six cell group technology layout.

Regardless of the eventual end product use, many component parts that are manufactured in an organization exhibit a number of similarities. These similarities may be in size, shape, processes, raw materials, and any number of other characteristics.

GT attempts to segregate the various component parts into groups exhibiting similar characteristics. There are several methods used to identify the members of a part family. One method relies on the product and shop knowledge of experienced company personnel. Another method requires that each component be assigned a code number in which the digits describe various important characteristics. Retrieval programs then allow the formation of part families by focusing on certain of those characteristics. Once identified, a family can be examined for a common process or cell.

The work cell concept physically creates a layout of dissimilar equipment necessary to process a particular family of parts. The equipment is dedicated to a particular group and is physically arranged in the sequence in which operations are performed on the family of parts. This arrangement allows the assembly line principles of balance and synchronization to be introduced. Internal lead times are reduced from weeks to hours, and work-in-process inventory between operations is all but eliminated.

The size and content of a cell are somewhat arbitrary. A cell can and oftentimes should be designed to produce more than one family of parts. This is necessary to justify the assignment of equipment to a cell when annual part requirements for one part family are not sufficient. However, there is a point in which too many families assigned to one cell can present complexities. There is no one way to implement GT, and there is a spectrum of possible applications. The applications and benefits are only limited by the imagination of the user.

GT is product independent. It indicates that a component part should be produced at the same time its "brothers and sisters" in the same family are being produced. It enables an organization to take advantage of common setups for similar parts. Since parts are produced in a given geographical area, there is much less materials movement and queue time, so throughput time is reduced. Cellular production enhances both schedule performance and equipment utilization, which translates into productivity improvement.

EQUIPMENT REQUIREMENTS

A complete equipment list will indicate the type and quantity of equipment required as well as its intended location. Equipment in this sense includes machinery, desks, chairs, tools, and support service items. The equipment list will be used by purchasing to acquire those items not currently available.

CONCLUSION

The most familiar tools for the solution of layout problems have been graphic and schematic models, particularly templates (two and three dimensional), assembly charts, operation process charts, and flow process charts. Quantitative models usually attempt to minimize materials handling cost or minimize worker idle time. The layout problem is multifaceted and difficult to solve by a model with a single objective function criterion. Before any model is applied to the layout problem, it is necessary to analyze its relevancy to the particular situation.

Process layouts characteristically have low volume production, numerous different products, changing product mixes, production to order, labor intensive operations, a skilled work force, general purpose equipment, variable routings, and flexible capacity. *Product layouts* usually have high volume production, little product variety, fixed product mixes, production to stock, capital intensive operations, a semi-skilled work force, special purpose equipment, fixed routings, and dedicated capacity. *Fixed position layouts* essentially are dedicated to special projects with unique processing requirements. It is not uncommon for organizations to combine desirable features from the above layouts into a hybrid layout adapted to their specific processing needs.

APPENDIX A. LINE BALANCING

The establishment of production rates for a continuous production system involves line balancing. An assembly line is the simplest example of a continuous production system. An assembly line consists of numerous work stations. The number of work elements (tasks) assigned to a work station is adjusted so that it takes the same amount of time to complete the work at each station. As the work is completed on a product at one station, it is passed on to the next station for further processing. The cycle time is the time the product is at each work station. The selection of a cycle time is dependent upon the desired output from the line. Once the production rate is established, the cycle time can be obtained. (Usually, the smallest possible cycle time is the duration of the longest work element.)

Balance is the major problem in a continuous production system. Balance refers to the equality of output of each successive work station on the assembly line. The maximum output of the line is dictated by its slowest operation. Perfect balance exists when each work station requires the same amount of time, and there is no idle time at any of the work stations. Because of bottleneck operations, perfect balance is seldom obtained.

To comprehend line balancing, the following terms must be understood.

Work element: A unit of work that cannot be divided between two or more operators without conflict between them.

Operation: A set of work elements assigned to a single work station.

Work station: An area alongside the assembly line where given tasks (an operation) are performed.

Cycle time: The time the product is at each work station.

Balance delay: The total idle time in the line as a result of unequal division of work between work stations.

The activities along a perfectly balanced line are synchronized to achieve maximum utilization of labor and equipment. The synchronous activities of the perfectly balanced line give the smoothest flow of work possible. The major obstacle to a perfectly balanced line is the inability to obtain work element bundles that have the same durations. The greater the flexibility in combining work elements, the higher the degree of balance and the smoother the flow of work.

Line balancing is combining work elements into work stations so that the amount of idle time is minimal for the entire line. To perform line balancing, information is needed concerning element performance times, element precedence requirements, and the cycle time. The performance times of work elements are obtained from work measurement systems such as stopwatch studies.

The line balancing problem is complicated by technological precedence requirements on work sequences. For example, a washer must go on before a nut, a hole must be drilled before it is reamed, and a wheel must go on before a hubcap.

Two types of lines that require balance are assembly and fabrication lines. There is little difference between the line balancing processes for these two types. Fabrication usually involves numerous fixed machine cycles that limit the freedom in achieving balance. Since assembly involves fewer fixed machine cycles and precedence requirements, there is more flexibility in achieving balance.

The simplest kind of line balancing involves a conveyor that moves a product past fixed work stations at a constant speed. A stationary operator removes the product from the conveyor and performs his operation, or he completes his tasks while the unit is still on the conveyor.

The choice of a cycle time is dependent on the demand for the product. Desired output rates place limitations on balance. Efficiency varies greatly with cycle time, so it is desirable to investigate a range of cycle times. With forecasts of expected future demand, an organization will determine the cycle time needed to meet demand within the limitations of the number of shifts to be worked. Suppose an organization that works a single 8-hr shift has a uniform yearly demand of 300,000 units. What would be the cycle time that would exactly match demand (assume 300 working days per year)?

$$\text{Cycle time} = \frac{1 \text{ year}}{300{,}000 \text{ units}} \cdot \frac{300 \text{ days}}{\text{year}} \cdot \frac{8 \text{ hr}}{\text{day}} \cdot \frac{3600 \text{ sec}}{\text{hr}}$$

$$= 28.8 \frac{\text{sec}}{\text{unit}}.$$

The theoretical minimum number of work stations is the total work element duration time divided by the cycle time:

$$n = \frac{\sum_{i=1}^{j} t_i}{C} = \text{theoretical minimum number of stations,}$$

where

j = number of work elements,
t_i = duration time of work element i,
C = cycle time.

Frequently the theoretical minimum number of work stations is impossible to attain because of precedence requirements and work element times that are not readily compatible. However, any balance that does result in the theoretical minimum number of work stations for a given cycle time is the best (most efficient) configuration even though it may contain idle time. Such a balance will contain the least total idle time. The maximum possible efficiency with the theoretical minimum number of stations is as follows:

$$e_{\max} = \frac{\sum_{i=1}^{j} t_i}{nC} = \text{maximum possible efficiency,}$$

where

t_i = duration time of work element i,
n = theoretical minimum integer number of stations,
C = cycle time,
j = number of work elements.

If it is impossible to attain the theoretical minimum number of stations, the actual efficiency of the line is

$$e = \frac{\sum_{i=1}^{j} t_i}{mC} = \text{actual possible efficiency,}$$

where

m = actual number of stations.

Note that e is always equal to or less than e_{max}. If $e < e_{max}$, attempt to increase efficiency by rearranging elements in a better configuration.

Line balancing concepts have been implemented in a number of practical methods for large-scale problems in industry. These methods include: (1) linear programming models, (2) dynamic programming, (3) heuristic methods, and (4) computer-based sampling techniques.

This appendix will look at two techniques. The trial and error technique and the ranked positional weight technique are both heuristic methods for obtaining a solution to the line balancing problem. A heuristic method is one based on trials with logical ground rules or policies to guide the assignment of job elements to work stations.

Trial and Error Technique

The trial and error technique simply adds work elements to stations so as not to violate the cycle time. The analyst adds work elements as he sees fit or in any fashion he believes to be best. If he is able to obtain the theoretical minimum number of stations, he knows an optimum assignment has been made. If the theoretical minimum number of stations is not obtained, he tries different arrangements until he comes as close as possible to the optimum number of stations.

EXAMPLE A-1

A company works an 8-hour day for 5 days per week. The production line is operated for only 7 hours per day to allow for rest, delays, etc. Given the information in the table below, determine the theoretical minimum number of stations if the line is designed for an output of 8400 units per week. Can the theoretical minimum number of stations be attained? Show a schematic of the minimum number of stations. What is the maximum possible efficiency? What is the actual possible efficiency?

Element	Performance time (seconds)	Element must follow element listed below
a	14	—
b	10	a
c	30	b
d	3	—
e	5	d
f	13	e
g	14	e
h	14	e
i	6	c,f,g,h
j	7	i
k	3	j
l	4	k
m	7	l
Total	130	

$$\text{Cycle time} = \frac{1 \text{ week}}{8400 \text{ units}} \cdot \frac{35 \text{ hr}}{\text{week}} \cdot \frac{3600 \text{ sec}}{\text{hr}}$$

$$= 15 \frac{\text{sec}}{\text{unit}},$$

$$n = \frac{\Sigma t_i}{C} = \frac{130}{15} = 8\tfrac{2}{3}, \text{ or 9 stations.}$$

EXAMPLE A-1—*continued*

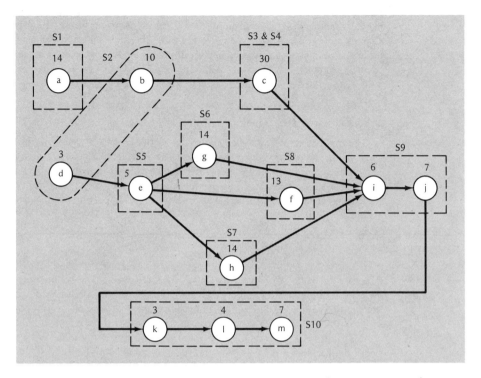

The above configuration shows 10 stations. Because of incongruent performance times, the least number of stations is 10. Element c takes 30 seconds, so it is broken into 2 stations, since it equals the cycle time. There are many configurations for 10 stations. The above configuration is as follows:

Station	Elements	Time
1	a	14
2	b,d	13
3	c	15
4	c	15
5	e	5
6	g	14
7	h	14
8	f	13
9	i,j	13
10	k,l,m	14

$$e_{max} = \frac{\Sigma t_i}{nC} = \frac{130}{9(15)} = 0.963, \text{ or } 96.3\%,$$

$$e = \frac{\Sigma t_i}{mC} = \frac{130}{10(15)} = 0.867, \text{ or } 86.7\%.$$

Ranked Positional Weight Technique

The ranked positional weight technique of line balancing assigns work elements to stations by choosing first those elements separated from final completion by the greatest time duration. This assignment is accomplished by the following steps:

Step 1. Determine the positional weight of each element by adding the element times of the task itself and all tasks that must follow it.

Step 2. Rearrange the elements in descending order of their positional weight with immediate predecessors indicated.

Step 3. Specify the cycle time.

Step 4. Assign tasks to stations on the basis of the highest positional weight. The sum of element times must not exceed the cycle time, and precedence restrictions must be observed. If an element violates either of the above restrictions, pass over it and take the next acceptable element. When a station's cycle time is filled, move on to a new station and proceed in the same manner until all tasks are assigned.

The ranked positional weight technique, like the trial and error technique, does not necessarily give an optimum balance. It is just a rule-of-thumb method that can systematically perform the balance function.

EXAMPLE A-2

Using the information from Example A-1, balance the line by the ranked positional weight technique.

Element	a	b	c	c	d	e	f	g	h	i	j	k	l	m
Element time	14	10	15	15	3	5	13	14	14	6	7	3	4	7
Positional weight	81	67	57	57	76	73	40	41	41	27	21	14	11	7
Preceding elements	—	a	b	b	—	d	e	e	e	c,g f,h	i	j	k	l

Station	Element	Time
1	a	14
2	d,e	8
3	b	10
4	c	15
5	c	15
6	g	14
7	h	14
8	f	13
9	i,j	13
10	k,l,m	14

Note that the ranked positional weight technique gave 10 stations, which is the same number as with the trial and error technique, although the stations have a different configuration.

As is illustrated in the example (see element c), sometimes a particular element exceeds the cycle time. In this situation parallel (duplicate) stations will be needed with each working every second or third unit; or several workers will operate the station. The specific design will depend on whether the worker is stationary and the conveyor brings the work to him, or he walks (or rides) along the line to perform the work and then walks back to the starting point past his co-worker.

QUESTIONS

1. What types of changes may necessitate a relayout of an existing facility?
2. What occurrences could be symptoms of a poor layout?
3. Name the major inputs and outputs of plant layout decisions.
4. List a few of the goals a good layout should accomplish.
5. How can variations in demand be handled without changing the size of the work force?
6. What information, charts, and other planning tools would be helpful in the initial phase of a layout analysis?
7. Under what conditions are multistory buildings superior to single story buildings?
8. Contrast the types of materials handling equipment most commonly used in continuous and intermittent production systems.
9. Give three different meanings for the term capacity and several examples which express capacity in measurement terms.
10. Name the layout types which are based on work flow and the types which are based on the function of the facility.
11. Describe a linear function model which can be used for improving intermittent production layouts.
12. How does the CRAFT program determine the location of work centers?
13. What are the major advantages of a process layout and a product layout?
14. Contrast the sequence of work flow in a process and a product layout.
15. What is group technology? What two major steps are involved in its application?
16. What constitutes a perfectly balanced assembly line?
17. How does the ranked positional weight technique differ from the trial and error technique for line balancing?
18. Discuss and classify the type of layout found in several organizations in your community.

PROBLEMS

1. A department is to be laid out on a process basis. The equipment to be located in the department will require 500 square feet of floor space. An analysis of a similar layout of a department reveals that it occupies a total space of 4000 square feet, of which 1000 is utilized by equipment. In general, the department does not appear to be congested, nor does it seem to contain wasted space. What might be a good estimate of the total space requirement for the department under consideration?

2. Material must be moved on pallets between two departments that are 0.1 mile apart. A loaded pallet weighs 500 pounds. The average speed of a forklift truck is 5 miles per hour, and each truck has a capacity of three loaded pallets. The average speed includes the return trip without load, the loading time, delays, and maintenance downtime. In an eight hour day, 200 tons of material must be moved between departments. How many forklift trucks are needed?

3. If the average loading (and unloading) time for each forklift truck in Problem 2 is 6 minutes, how many trucks will be needed with an average speed of 5 miles per hour?

4. It is necessary to produce 3000 units a month of a standard machine part. The machine operation time is 12 minutes per part. How many machines are needed if they operate 8 hours a day for 20 days a month at 100% efficiency with no downtime?

5. If machine utilization is 80% in Problem 4, how many machines are needed?

6. An organization has decided to make a component hitherto supplied by an unreliable vendor. It is necessary to produce 120 components during a regular 8-hr shift. The component requires three operations with standard times as follows:

Operation	Description	Time (min)
A	Mechanical assembly	12
B	Electrical wiring	8
C	Bench test	4

How many work stations will be required for each operation?

7. The assembly line described below has an 8-minute cycle time. Draw the precedence diagram and arrange the work elements into work stations in such a manner that idle time is minimized.

Element	Immediate predecessor	Duration (min)
a	—	3
b	a	2
c	b	4
d	b	3
e	c	6
f	c	1
g	d,e,f	5
h	g	2
		26

8. Balance the activities below for a cycle time of 6 minutes. What is the theoretical minimum number of work stations? What is the actual number of work stations? What is the maximum possible efficiency? What is the actual possible efficiency?

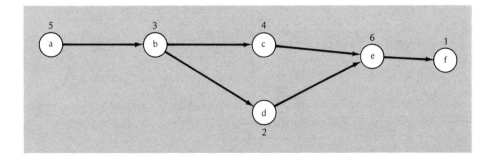

9. Balance the following activities for a cycle time of 1 minute. What is the actual possible efficiency?

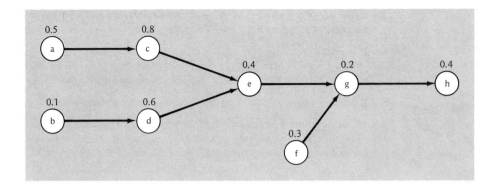

10. The average forecasted demand for a nasal spray product (production data tabulated below) is 4500 units per week. The firm works a single shift 40 hours a week. What will be the configuration of the work stations with the ranked positional weight technique?

Element	Immediate predecessor	Duration (sec)
a	—	10
b	a	14
c	b	23
d	—	16
e	c,d	19
f	e	12
g	f	11
h	f	4
i	—	6
j	h,i	15
k	g,j	8
		138

11. A firm desires to produce 96 units per day of a product on a five-day, two-shift operation (16 hours per day). From the information below, balance the line by the trial and error technique. What is the theoretical minimum number of stations? What is the actual possible efficiency of the line?

Element	Immediate predecessor	Duration (min)
a	—	4
b	a	8
c	a	4
d	—	4
e	c,d	3
f	b,e	5
g	f	4
h	f	7
i	g,h	3
		42

12. A firm that produces electronic surveillance devices has decided to mass produce a new product. A production quota of 600 units per 40-hr week has been established. The

relevant production data are listed below. What is the cycle time? What will be the station configuration if the line is balanced by the ranked positional weight technique?

Job element	Immediate predecessor	Performance time (min)
a	—	3
b	a	1
c	b	2
d	b	2
e	c,d	3
f	—	4
g	e,f	2
h	—	1
i	—	1
j	g,h,i	3
k	i	2
l	j,k	2
		26

13. The production quota for a product is set at 5760 units per three-shift operation (24 hours per day). From the following data, balance the line by the ranked positional weight technique.

Element	Immediate predecessor	Duration (sec)
a	—	2
b	a	2
c	a	4
d	a	3
e	a	7
f	b,c	6
g	d,e	4
h	f,g	6
i	—	9
j	h,i	6
		49

14. The production quota for an assembly line is set at 2400 units per day. The organization works a ten-hour single shift for a four day week. From the following data, balance the line by the ranked positional weight technique.

Element	Immediate predecessor	Duration (sec)
a	—	10
b	a	6
c	—	5
d	b,c	4
e	d	8
f	—	3
g	—	7
h	e,f,g	5
i	h	4
j	h	9
k	i,j	2
		63

CASE 1: A FACE LIFT

Dobbs Drug chain is a 35-unit drugstore chain. The chain recently made its third and most innovative design renovation of the Long Island store. The new layout is shown in Figure 6. The diagonal design of the layout was imposed on the existing rectangular building; its configuration was based on attaining desired traffic patterns, evening the flow of traffic throughout the store, and eliminating dead spots (areas with low customer activity) and corners.

In the original design, the tobacco, magazine, and photo development sales were handled at the checkout stations. The checkout area was directly inside the store entrance. The entrance was not slanted as it is now, but was flush with the face of the building. The cosmetics and perfumes were shelved with the other health and beauty aids; they now receive individual

FIGURE 6
Long Island drugstore layout.

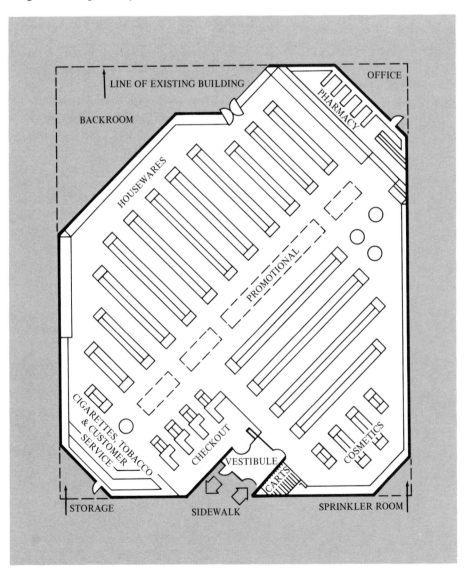

emphasis in their own floor space. The cosmetic display area has been given a thorough glamorizing, complete with plush lavender carpeting and a flashy ceiling treatment. The store has a perimeter valence—an aspect of the makeover which will definitely be added to other stores. The valence is painted with department defining colors and names; it hides the lighting system used to illuminate the walls and is used as an alternative to a brightly illuminated interior. A seasonal aisle which runs down the middle of the store is used for sale and promotional merchandise.

The beauty items have the highest percentage markup of any inventory category. The fastest turnover of goods occurs in the tobacco, snacks, and magazine sections. The promotional area generally displays the bulkiest inventory items. The merchandise on promotion often is seasonal: in the winter, Christmas giftwrap, snow shovels and brooms, antifreeze and rock salt, etc., and in the summer, lawn chairs, charcoal briquets, coolers, and other picnic and yard goods.

Rising energy costs at all thirty-five stores are a major consideration. Average costs have been increasing about 20% per year. Some energy-saving changes are under consideration for the new design and existing facilities. Dobbs intends to add insulation to the walls and ceilings of all its facilities. So far actions have included the closing up of excess storefront windows and the installation of recessed ''beehive'' ceiling fans over checkout counters to recirculate the warm air.

Dobbs is undecided whether to duplicate the high cost design of its Long Island store at other locations or to make selective adaptations in the design prior to additional renovations. The organization is anxious to begin work on another unit but wants to make any adjustments before future renovations are started.

1. What layout factors are important for Dobbs and for retail stores in general?
2. Mention any apparent advantages or disadvantages of the Long Island layout.
3. How should Dobbs evaluate the Long Island layout?

CASE 2: CHOW LINES

Two major fast-food competitors use different processing methods for preparing customer orders. Consequently, they adopt different customer service layouts for their restaurants. The two chains appear similar but not identical in many of the operational characteristics which influence layout planning. For example, the degree of product standardization and average volume of output per store are similar for the two chains. Still, there are some contrasts in detail. Some of these planning differences are apparent in the brief descriptions of their operations and customer service designs given below.

Chain A: Chain A is the fast-food industry giant. Most of its stores are similar in size even though the volume of business among stores shows significant variation. The peak business hours are similar for most of the stores and exhibit highly volatile demand patterns. Each store typically has four to six checkout stations located at the service counter, and stations are opened and closed according to the fluctuating demand. The service counter is situated at the front of the food preparation center. The preparation center usually occupies from one-fourth to one-third of the entire floor space and is in the rear of the facility.

Customers enter the facility from doors at each side of the service area (the floor space directly in front of the service counter). The doors are used as both entrances and exits from the service area and the store as well. The seating or dining area is located in the front of the facility and usually is separated from the service area by some type of partition. When a customer places an order at the counter, the person who accepts the order also prepares and takes payment for it.

Chain A started with a basic burger and has expanded the menu to include several other burgers, fish, chicken pieces, desserts, and various drink items. A breakfast menu is available during morning hours. The chain occasionally offers slight variations of the standard menu items as promotions and frequently runs market tests of proposed menu items.

Chain B: Chain B is a relative new comer but shows impressive early growth. Its stores also are similar in size and in architecture. Chain B generally has a lower volume output per store than Chain A, but demand fluctuates according to the same daily pattern.

Chain B's customers must enter a food service line which is queued according to "first come, first served." When customers reach the front of the line, their order is placed and payment is received. They are moved down the line as their order is being individually prepared. At the end of the line, they pick up their order and move into the dining area at the front of the facility Each store has only one service line, which leads to the service counter. Order preparation is specialized; that is, personnel are specifically assigned to handle only one phase of order preparation (i.e. order taking, assembly, delivery, and payment).

Chain B started with a basic burger patty, but sandwich variations could be made by stacking the patties and selecting a variety of condiments and relishes. Chili, milk shakes, and other drink items also were offered. Now the menu has been increased and includes chicken sandwiches and a few other special sandwich choices. Salads can be made by customers at the salad bar located in the dining area.

Both chains do the following: depend upon quick service of basic fast-food items, serve customers at inside counters and drive-in windows, and provide mass produced menus. Yet, the methods they have selected to serve their customers differ physically.

1. What are the advantages and disadvantages of the two types of service layouts?
2. Does the described layout suit the needs of the operation, or would another layout or combination of layout configurations be more suitable?
3. Given your experience in fast-food establishments, what suggestions do you have for improving their service through layout planning?

SELECTED BIBLIOGRAPHY

Apple, J. M. *Plant Layout and Material Handling,* New York: Wiley, 1977.

Buffa, E. S. *Modern Production Management,* 5th edition, New York: Wiley, 1977.

Buffa, E. S. et al. "Allocating Facilities with CRAFT," *Harvard Business Review,* Vol. 42, March/April 1964, pp. 136–159.

Francis, R. L. *Facility Layout and Location,* Englewood Cliffs, NJ: Prentice-Hall, 1974.

Helgeson, W. B. and D. P. Birnie. "Assembly Line Balancing Using the Ranked Positional Weight Technique," *Journal of Industrial Engineering,* Vol. XII, No. 6, November–December 1961, pp. 394–398.

Ignall, E. J. "A Review of Assembly Line Balancing", *Journal of Industrial Engineering,* Vol. 16, No. 4, July–August 1965, pp. 244–254.

Lee, R. C. and J. M. Moore. "CORELAP—Computerized Relationship Layout Planning," *Journal of Industrial Engineering,* Vol. 18, March 1967, pp. 195–200.

Mastor, A. A. "An Experimental Investigation and Comparative Evaluation of Production Line Balancing Techniques," *Management Science,* Vol. 16, July 1970, pp. 728–746.

Moore, J. M. *Plant Layout and Design,* New York: Macmillan, 1962.

Reed, R., Jr. *Plant Layout,* Homewood, IL: Irwin, 1961.

———. *Plant Location, Layout, and Maintenance,* Homewood, IL: Irwin, 1967.

Ritzman, L. P. "The Efficiency of Computer Algorithms for Plant Layout," *Management Science,* Vol. 18, January 1972, pp. 240–248.

Scriabin, M. and R. C. Vergin. "Comparison of Computer Algorithms and Visual Based Methods for Plant Layout," *Management Science,* October 1975, pp. 172–181.

Tonge, F. M. "Assembly Line Balancing Using Probabilistic Combinations of Heuristics," *Management Science,* Vol. 11, No. 7, May 1965, pp. 727–735.

Vollmann, T. E. and E. S. Buffa. "The Facilities Layout Problem in Perspective," *Management Science,* Vol. 12, June 1966, pp. 450–468.

14

Materials Handling

MATERIALS HANDLING INPUTS
Supply Demands
Production Demands
Distribution Demands
Flow Analysis

CONSTRAINTS
Flowability
Material Form
Process Requirements
Movement Dimensions
Distance
Direction
Intensity
Space
Cost

FLOW FACTORS
Movement Features
Continuity
Flexibility
Unitization
Packaging
Palletization
Containerization
Equipment Alternatives
Trucks and Tractors
Conveyors
Lifts
Special Systems and Aids

MATERIALS HANDLING DECISIONS

MATERIALS HANDLING OUTPUTS
Handling Efficiencies
Sourcing
Purchase
Lease
Rental

CONCLUSION

QUESTIONS
PROBLEMS
CASES
SELECTED BIBLIOGRAPHY

Handling material is a major portion of the cost of manufacturing, distribution, and marketing. Every time material is handled, costs are incurred. Movement and control generally add no value to a product, so handling operations should be minimized. The importance of materials handling to an organization is reflected in the ratio of materials handling cost to total product cost. In the production of low unit value, bulky or heavy items, the handling cost is usually a major cost factor; in the production of high unit value, compact or light-weight items, handling cost is usually a lower cost factor. Poor materials handling can lead directly to lost or damaged products, customer dissatisfaction, production delays, and idle employees and equipment. It plays a vital role in reducing inventory, lowering costs, and increasing productivity.

Materials handling is concerned with all aspects of the flow of material within an organization. The physical transportation of materials from receiving areas through production operations to final shipment undisputably is recognized as the domain of materials handling. More inclusively, materials handling consists of the network of activities that receive, store, transport, and deliver materials. In short, the handling, storage, and control of materials are its constituents.

Materials handling is an integral part of production in all manufacturing organizations and a vital concern in the operations of most wholesalers, distributors, and retailers. The objectives of materials handling are:

1. to eliminate handling wherever possible,
2. to minimize travel distance,
3. to minimize goods in process,
4. to provide uniform flow free of bottlenecks,
5. to minimize losses from waste, breakage, spoilage, and theft.

It is common to consider materials handling as an auxiliary activity of production, where the most intense material movement usually occurs. However, a brief review of a typical flow pattern reveals the presence of movement demands throughout an organization. As depicted in Figure 1, materials handling requirements are apparent in many areas:

1. Physical supply
   a. Receiving
   b. Counting
   c. Storing
   d. Order picking
   e. Sorting
   f. Shipping
2. Production
   a. Work station transfer
   b. In-process storage
3. Transportation and physical distribution
   a. Loading
   b. Unloading
   c. Staging
   d. Transporting

Conceptually, the materials handling function offers a cohesive mental framework for evaluating the functional influences of the flow of material. Because of its bearing

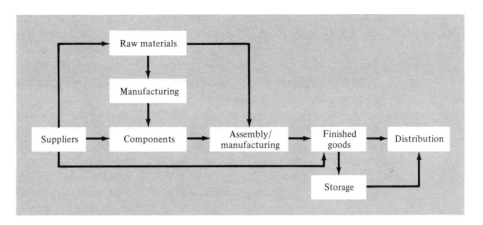

FIGURE 1
Flow of materials and products.

FIGURE 2
The materials handling function. [From Richard J. Tersine and John H. Campbell, *Modern Materials Management,* New York: North Holland, 1977, p. 196.]

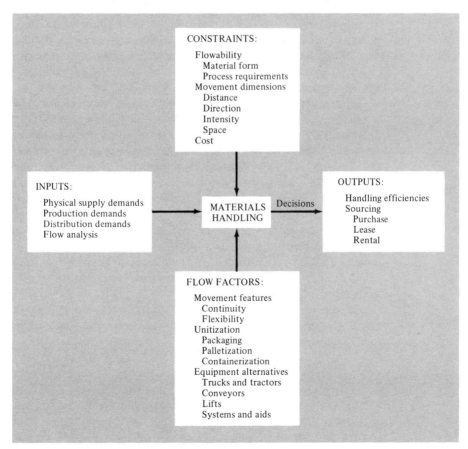

on organizational effectiveness and relationship to productivity, the materials handling function has recently begun to enjoy intensified managerial interest. Materials handling activities are essential to performance in other functions. Managed as discrete activities within individual functions, they become duplicative, costly, and ineffective. Treated as an integrated function, materials handling offers important opportunities for cost control and operational efficiencies.

The materials handling function is characterized by inputs, constraints, flow factors, and outputs as illustrated in Figure 2. Inputs include supply demands, production demands, distribution demands, and flow analysis. The inputs are complicated by the fact that they may originate from different sources with variable frequency.

Constraining the decision process are considerations of flowability, movement dimensions, and cost. Features of the decision environment which require attention are called flow factors and include movement features, unitization, and equipment alternatives. Ultimately materials handling decisions result in the functional outputs of handling efficiencies (related to system's definition) and sourcing (related to equipment selection).

MATERIALS HANDLING INPUTS

A major obstacle to understanding the materials handling function is the absence of a concise set of documents serving as functional inputs. In an effort to establish paper inputs, some documents from other areas have been designated as inputs. Obviously, the bill of lading has a role in materials handling with respect to receiving and shipping. Picking tickets play a part in order retrieval and transfer. Similarly, work orders may dictate handling procedures in production. However, concentration on inputs closely related to other functions forces a mistreatment of materials handling. Inputs are not necessarily defined as a convenient collection of common use documents.

While materials handling does exist as a unique and definable organizational function, it has qualities that broaden the scope of potential inputs. Materials handling facilitates flow and thereby serves other functions. To be effective it must be highly integrated with each function served. The requirement for integration causes materials handling to assume characteristics similar to those of the functions it serves. Thus, in receiving, shipping, and order processing, materials handling may appear as a part of the physical supply function. In manufacturing operations, materials handling takes on characteristics of the production function. In vehicle loading and unloading procedures, it appears as an element of the distribution function. However, materials handling does retain its functional identity. The relationships between materials handling and the functions it serves can be described as *functional transparency*. While its visibility is diminished by other more obvious activities, it still exists as an identifiable entity.

Major materials handling inputs are derived from demands originating from the physical supply, production, and distribution functions. Additionally, materials handling requirements are often specified in a flow analysis document.

SUPPLY DEMANDS

Since the physical supply function concerns material transfer, retrieval, and storage, it requires capabilities to move products among and within points of use. These requirements appear as demands placed on the materials handling function. The most visible means for satisfying movement demands is in the wide variety of handling equipment used to support physical activities. Mechanical handling aids are obvious in receiving, shipping, order picking, and storage.

Physical supply activities are interwoven throughout the material flow cycle. *Frequency* and *volume* parameters determine the service loads that must be met by materials handling. Likewise, materials handling offers service flexibility to respond to changes in the physical supply function. Materials handling methods and equipment may vary from activity to activity in the physical supply function; however, it is a normal objective to employ common and interchangeable methods and equipment. The potential for use of multipurpose methods and equipment is apparent in the similarity of demands originating in receiving and shipping, or storage and retrieval.

Receiving and shipping demands are usually met with equipment peculiar to the materials handling function. Fork trucks, conveyors, hand trucks, and dollies are common devices used in receiving and shipping. Equipment used to satisfy storage and retrieval demands is often more difficult to classify in such a fashion. Order picking equipment may appear to be a part of an order processing system, and storage devices may be seen only as warehouse facilities.

PRODUCTION DEMANDS

Production demands for materials handling capabilities are either expressed through the physical supply function or placed directly on the materials handling function. Expressed through the physical supply function, demands usually involve movement of raw material and components from a place of storage to the point of production or from the point of production to a place of storage or use. Common handling equipment such as trucks, conveyors, and dollies is used for these purposes. Job-shop and intermittent production systems usually place such simple demands on the materials handling function. It is also normal for additional handling support to be required for in-process storage and production stores. Such support may involve the use of bins, roll carts, racks, pallets, or tables. Mechanical handling aids may or may not be used.

Sophisticated production processes require closer support from materials handling. In continuous production systems, materials handling is often considered an integral element of the production process. Since material undergoes handling and production activities simultaneously, the operations must be in concert with one another. Good examples are in the production (and handling) of soft drinks and crushed stone. In the former case, raw materials (syrup and carbonated water) are gathered in hoppers for injection into containers (bottles and cans) as they move in the handling system. They are then sealed and packaged or crated. In the latter case, raw stone is usually fed by conveyors to the crushing mill, processed, and then packaged or conveyed to a storage location. Notice in each case the dependence on movement in the handling systems. Numerous other examples in television, glass, fertilizer, automobile, and tire manufacturing illustrate the interdependence between production and materials handling.

It is quite apparent that production capabilities have been greatly enhanced through technology. Almost unnoticed, materials handling has become a high technology industry. Changes in production systems have altered the related technology and design innovations of materials handling systems. As manufacturing technology, aided by computer assisted machines, has made strides in improving productivity, it has become apparent that new approaches to storing, disbursing, moving, and controlling materials are required to keep pace.

Complex and sophisticated production procedures generate corresponding handling requirements. As manufacturing processes become increasingly automated, materials handling support systems must provide a smooth, reliable, and efficient flow of materials with better control over the entire process. Just as computers are controlling more manufacturing equipment and integrating many aspects of the manufacturing process, computers and on-board microprocessors linked to computers are controlling the types of equipment which move materials through the integrated system. Much of this equipment is as much a carrier of information as it is a carrier of parts, components, and finished products. Automated storage and retrieval systems, automated guided vehicles, robotics, automatic material identification devices, and automated conveyor systems are new forms of this technology. Other advances include the updating of standard materials handling devices—for example, retrofitting lift trucks and order pickers with on-line terminals.

DISTRIBUTION DEMANDS

The most significant demand from distribution is for the handling capability to generate maximum-density load units compatible with vehicles of conveyance. The operational and cost effectiveness of the physical distribution function depends in large part on handling techniques providing optimal load characteristics. Here, handling equipment and handling aids are important. Handling equipment includes common devices such as trucks and conveyors; handling aids include devices to unitize loads. In the area of load unitization, the pallet and the container are primary handling devices. They not only establish characteristics for a load, but they also serve to consolidate items into units that can be easily handled by mechanical devices.

FLOW ANALYSIS

Flow analysis is a method for defining the functional demands placed on materials handling. Results are usually embodied in a chart using symbols to represent features of a procedure.

The most prominent chart types are *operation process charts* and *flow process charts*. Operation process charts graphically represent events during a series of operations, such as steps in the assembly of a product. Operation process charts offer graphic representations of operational sequences. They may include other information such as operator time requirements, machine requirements, and machine locations. While operation process charts are helpful in evaluating a process, materials handling requirements are usually more apparent in the flow process chart, which was introduced in the previous chapter on *Process and Operation Design*.

Illustrated in Figure 3, flow process charts graphically represent the sequence of all operations, including transportation, inspection, and storage events. Other information may include temporal requirements and movement distances. Notice the inclusion of important handling demands: material, time, place, and distance. Further, analysis often adds movement *intensity* to the flow process chart, expressed as volume and frequency of movement. With the flow process chart, the inputs to the materials handling function are interpreted and analyzed in an interdependent manner.

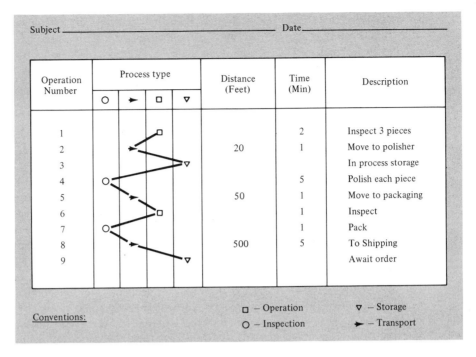

FIGURE 3
Flow process chart.

CONSTRAINTS

Materials handling is subject to several constraints that limit decisions. Their nature varies from organization to organization. To a large degree, the number and importance of constraints depend on the size of the organization, the particular type of enterprise, and economic conditions. However, there are several rather broad categories of constraints which are common to all organizations and are valuable reference points for evaluation. They include flowability, movement dimensions, and cost.

FLOWABILITY

Flowability refers to the affinity of materials and process characteristics to flow requirements. Given that material must move within and among points of use, the efficiency of movement is directly related to flowability.

Material Form

The form of the material limits the number of handling methods available to increase flowability. Material forms can be generally segregated into three categories, each possessing important relationships to flowability. *Bulk* material exists in a loose unpackaged state without constant dimensions. Material in a bulk state, such as stone, wheat, sand, and petroleum, is easy to move in a fixed flow pattern using conveyors and pipelines, but it is not efficiently moved in a variable flow pattern.

Itemized material exists as discrete parts, components, or assemblies with definite dimensions. It may be packaged or maintained in a loose state. Itemized material may be small or large. Small items are efficiently moved on an individual basis in a fixed flow pattern using conveyors or in a variable flow pattern using light mechanical aids such as dollies and carts. Obviously, small items can also be moved manually without mechanical aids. Large items can be moved over a fixed pattern using specialized equipment (overhead cranes, monorails, and underfloor tows) or over a variable path using manually operated trucks. *Unitized* material is a set of consolidated items grouped together to facilitate effective handling. Bulk or itemized material may be packaged, containerized, or affixed to a platform (pallet), or a combination of the three, to produce more flowable form characteristics. Units can be efficiently moved on either a fixed or a variable path. Containerized and palletized material can be moved with fixed path methods, but they have the added advantage of being efficiently moved by the most prevalent variable flow device, the fork truck. Regardless of the form of material, there are other physical characteristics that cannot be ignored. Characteristics such as fragility, hazard, and threat of deterioration can affect or even determine flowability.

Complicating the impact of material characteristics on flowability is the probability that material form will not be constant. For example, in most production and fabricating operations, the form of raw material and component parts is appreciably different from that of the finished product. Handling methods for raw material and component parts may not be appropriate for the finished product. Distribution (marketing) oriented organizations have a similar problem in that they must handle a multiple product mix to satisfy consumer demands. While the form does not change, it is different among the various products. Thus, form homogeneity plays an important role in determining the degree of difficulty in achieving effective flowability.

Process Requirements

Different production and distribution processes have different effects on flowability. In production organizations, the activity level (speed) and number of operations dictate flowability. A continuous production process requires a continuous material flow, usually served by fixed flow handling systems. High volume, repetitive handling operations result in fixed paths of material flow. On the other hand, intermittent and job shop processes usually require variable flow handling procedures. Very complex processes and those with demanding production tolerances may require a high degree of flexibility.

With numerous product types, distribution organizations depend on accessibility and selectibility. It is common for materials handling systems to support both fixed and variable flow capabilities. Because of similarity in operations, computer technology has enjoyed wide application in achieving access and selection efficiencies in distribution organizations.

MOVEMENT DIMENSIONS

Movement dimensions quantify the flow of material. They are physical quantities and lend themselves to analysis and measurement. The most important dimensions of a material flow are distance, direction, intensity, and space. Evaluation of movement dimensions usually begins with the flow analysis and its descriptive charts.

Once dimensions are established and measured, further analysis is necessary to determine their impact on handling decisions.

Distance

Material flow means movement between points of use over some geographic distance. Obviously, as distance increases, so does dependence on handling capabilities. Time is directly related to distance, since timing demands control the speed of movement between points of use. Geographical and temporal characteristics of distance constrain handling in several ways. As the distance between use points increases,

1. materials handling costs increase,
2. efficiency decreases, and
3. reliability decreases.

Costs include expenditures for equipment, labor, and indirect expenses. Efficiency decreases because of additional time involved in the flow of material, and also because material being handled is not usually involved in a productive operation. Finally, reliability is diminished when material is subjected to extensive travel time because of influences such as vibration, damage in handling, or handling system failure.

Materials handling must serve to make movement efficient when (as usual) it cannot be eliminated altogether. In general, one tries to optimize the flow of material by minimizing distance. With this end in mind, most handling equipment and systems are designed for movement over short distances. Less movement means less labor, less time, and less equipment; reducing any of these is usually desirable.

An interesting relationship among materials handling and the other functions it serves becomes apparent. As movement distances become very small, materials handling approaches production or physical supply as a function. Conversely, as distance increases, materials handling approaches transportation and distribution. For example, newsprint requires handling during printing, but that is accomplished as an integral part of the production operation; gravity fed picking racks are simple materials handling devices usually associated with physical supply activities. Material flow that entails movement over great distances, such as between plant locations, is referred to as distribution rather than materials handling. Thus, movement over a very short or a very long distance can be effectively accommodated by production or physical supply on the one hand, or transportation and distribution on the other. Between these extremes lies the realm of materials handling, in which the efficiency can be maximized through minimizing distance.

Direction

The direction in which material flows plays a major role in determining the efficiency and cost of a materials handling system. Frequently, direction is predetermined by existing facilities and operational (production, physical supply, or transportation) procedures. In such cases, efficiency depends on the availability of materials handling equipment.

Mechanical efficiency in the direction of flow is greatest when the amount of work required to effect movement is minimized. In diminishing order of directional efficiency, the directions are *downward, horizontal,* and *vertical.* Downward movement allows the flow of material to take advantage of gravity, a power source that is constant, requires no motorized aids, and (most importantly) is free. Unfortunately, gravity flow is unidirectional and thus cannot satisfy all movement requirements in the material flow cycle. Excellent use of gravitational forces is made in some conveyor applications, chutes, and gravity fed bins. Where downward movement is not possible, horizontal movement is most efficient. Horizontal flow requires artificial power (man or machine rather than gravity) to move material. In materials handling, horizontal flow is accomplished by pushing or pulling. The amount of work required is usually lessened by use of wheeled or rollerized equipment. Carts, dollies, some conveyors, and trucks are examples of equipment frequently used to move material in a horizontal direction. With vertical flow both downward and upward movement is necessary. Here, of course, lifting action is in direct opposition to natural forces and requires the greatest amount of work. It is important to appreciate the influence of direction on flow efficiency and cost.

Intensity

Intensity is the movement dimension that quantifies the amount of material handled. Often referred to as *flow loading,* intensity is specified in units of volume and frequency. Volume is a measure of the gross amount of material to be moved over a specified planning period. The planning period may encompass requirements for a single movement or the aggregate demand for a week, month, or year. Frequency is the measure of how often a constant volume is moved during a given period of time. Intensity is dictated by functions exogenous to materials handling and acts to constrain the selection of handling procedures and equipment. Interaction between production operations and other functions is frequently expressed as volume and frequency of interacting material flow. Preventing bottlenecks by balancing the flow between use points is a major responsibility of the materials handling function.

Space

The physical environment of an organization is an important restraint on the flow of material. Specifically, plant layout represents static confines to material flow, within which materials handling must seek to provide necessary dynamic flow capabilities. Available space in a facility is allocated to the various organizational functions according to priority of need. Thus the functions compete for space resources. Like other resources, space can be effectively used only if it is efficiently distributed. It has been noted that materials handling activities are apparent in other functions, primarily production, physical supply, and distribution. Thus, materials handling competes for space in two ways, directly for its own unique needs and indirectly through the sponsorship of other functions.

Direct demands for space include those for obvious needs, such as floor space for fixed equipment, operating room for mobile equipment (turn space and aisle width), and overhead clearance for equipment. Aisles must be wide enough so personnel and mobile handling equipment can safely move through the facility. The layout of the facility should permit an efficient flow of persons and materials.

Because of the accelerating cost of real estate, the type of spatial environment in many organizations is following a trend away from the single level, land intensive facility. Multilevel structures are often more economical to acquire or construct when land is expensive. This tendency has a major influence on the materials handling function. Multilevel facilities require vertical material flow, which is less efficient than horizontal flow. Thus, it is probable that materials handling will depend more on expensive mechanically powered equipment.

Items with dissimilar materials characteristics and flow requirements may have to be stored and handled differently. Fast moving and slow moving materials can be stored and retrieved differently using hybrid systems. It is difficult, if not impossible, to design a primary system to handle all material requirements. A primary system might be designed to meet 80 to 90% of the requirements, and a secondary system provided to accommodate the exceptions and serve as a backup to the primary system. In some cases, two or more secondary systems might be appropriate.

The lowest cost storage space in a facility is the space closest to the ceiling. By using this space, cube utilization is improved. Managers should investigate opportunities to store material higher, in a more compact manner. This is especially desirable for slow-moving items. It releases space for fast-moving items at more convenient, low locations.

Randomized storage minimizes space requirements, while dedicated storage tends to maximize throughput. With randomized storage material can be stored anywhere in the system. Randomized storage is also referred to as floating-slot storage, since the location of a given item can vary (float) over time. With dedicated storage each given item is assigned to a fixed location that does not change. Other terms for dedicated storage are assigned or fixed-slot storage. To improve throughput with dedicated storage, items with the most activity are assigned to preferred locations (fast movers are up front and slow movers are in the rear). Hybrid systems that combine randomized and dedicated storage concepts are frequently desirable. For example, dedicated storage can be used for the fastest movers while randomized storage is used for others.

COST

Investments in personnel and capital equipment are made with the intention of realizing some discernible economic return. From outlays for materials handling it is difficult if not impossible to isolate a measurable return. This function is therefore considered a cost center in most organizations. The cost is frequently an indirect accounting charge to production, physical supply, distribution, or operations, but most commonly it is subsumed in the general overhead of the organization. Regardless of its accounting classification, the materials handling cost is substantial, representing up to 50% of the total production cost in many basic processing industries.

To appreciate the full thrust of materials handling costs, it is useful to classify cost elements as direct and indirect charges. Some of the major cost elements are summarized in Figure 4. In evaluating expenditures for materials handling it is important to remember that an objective of the materials handling function is to minimize total cost. Increased materials handling expenditures (costs) may result in reduced overall organizational cost. Materials handling costs are not completely avoidable, only controllable.

Whether materials handling systems are manual, mechanized, or automated is another comparative cost consideration. *Manual systems* are highly labor intensive with little reliance on support equipment. *Mechanized systems* tend to reduce labor intensity and use a combination of labor and handling equipment. *Automated systems*

Direct	Indirect
1. Equipment	1. Downtime
2. Labor	a. Equipment
3. Maintenance	b. Labor
4. Operating	2. Damages
	3. Overhead
	4. Opportunity

FIGURE 4
Materials handling costs.

minimize the labor content and are highly equipment intensive. The selection of a handling system should be based on an incremental or cost-benefit analysis.

In high-volume, repetitive operations, materials handling systems are automated. With automation, direct supervision of handling activity is eliminated. Automation increases the importance of materials handling to an organization. A significant portion of the final cost of a product with an automated system will be the materials handling cost. Most automated handling systems are custom designed and constructed for each particular application.

FLOW FACTORS

In addition to constraints, several other considerations, called *flow factors,* influence materials handling decisions. An understanding of these factors broadens, rather than limits, the scope of decision alternatives. Three essential categories of flow factors are embodied in the materials handling function. *Movement features* describe the variability of material flow, *unitization* is concerned with methods of enhancing material flowability, and *equipment alternatives* encompass the vast array of hardware available to meet handling requirements.

MOVEMENT FEATURES

Movement features provide management with controls that can dampen the effects of flowability constraints. Two features universally descriptive of material flow are continuity and flexibility. Together they are primary operational considerations in equipment selection. A separate analysis of the role of each as a movement feature is necessary.

Continuity

Continuity refers to the regularity or frequency of material flow. Handling systems exert control over continuity by varying the flow frequency. It is important that these handling systems be compatible with the particular flow they serve.

Movement can be categorized as *continuous, intermittent,* or *discrete*. Each category describes a unique flow of material and is distinguishable by the type of materials handling equipment employed.

Continuous movement requirements usually originate from production. Materials handling equipment must be capable of facilitating a constant flow of material to and

Flow	Power	Equipment	Control system
Continuous	Mechanical	Conveyors, pipes, robots, AGVS	Automated
Intermittent	Mechanical, manpower	Conveyors, trucks,	Mechanized
Discrete	Mechanical, manpower	Trucks, handling aids, lifting devices	Mechanized/manual

FIGURE 5
Continuity characteristics.

from various operations at specified rates. Such demand normally necessitates the use of conveyor type equipment powered by mechanical means. Equipment supporting a continuous process (and thus continuous handling requirements) that is controlled by mechanical intelligence (a computer) is referred to as an automated materials handling system.

Intermittent movement can serve production, physical supply, or distribution. Flow is not constant, but occurs at relatively fixed intervals. Equipment used to furnish intermittent handling capabilities may be wheeled or of a conveyor type. Both powered and nonpowered devices are common. Handling systems using wheeled or conveyor type equipment without automated controls are called mechanized systems.

Discrete movement occurs in a random manner. Although such demands may develop in any function, they are most common in distribution. Equipment is usually limited to unitizing aids, nonpowered conveyors, lifting devices, and powered or nonpowered trucks. Because discrete movement procedures are labor intensive, they tend to be manual or mechanized systems.

A summary of the continuity movement feature is provided in Figure 5. Continuity has an important influence on materials handling decisions. Continuous movement represents long term commitment to rather static capabilities, and the decisions entail substantial risk if future demand for such capability is uncertain. Intermittent and discrete movements require more movement flexibility, and they are less sensitive to shifting operational demands.

Flexibility

Flexibility is dependent on the nature and constancy of the material flow, which is described by the path of movement. Paths of movement are *fixed, semifixed,* and *variable*. Each can be adequately distinguished by equipment types and sponsoring functions. Also, the several paths with associated handling requirements may appear in any mix within an organization.

Fixed path systems possess the least handling flexibility because they use stationary equipment and a constant movement pattern. In a continuous flow, fixed path equipment provides efficiency as a tradeoff for inflexibility. Such systems are common in automated or mechanized processes in production and physical supply. Examples of equipment employed are powered conveyors, monorails, underfloor tows, fixed cranes, elevators, automated sorting devices, and automated guided vehicles.

Semifixed path systems have similar characteristics to fixed systems, but they can be modified when not in operation. They are useful with fairly constant movement patterns requiring infrequent flow changes. Primary applications are found in inter-mittent processes that can tolerate the time necessary for making modifications be-tween operations. Semifixed equipment is usually mechanized rather than automated and is of greatest benefit in the production and physical supply functions. Movable conveyors and mobile cranes are prevalent types of semifixed equipment. However, newer technologies combine the benefits of automation with the advantages of flexi-ble operation. Computer operated carousels for storing and delivering work-in-pro-cess allow storage at remote locations and retrieval at operator stations.

When the pattern of material flow is not fixed, greater flexibility is needed. *Vari-able path* equipment is mobile in that it actually imitates or models the materials flow path. In essence, variable path equipment moves with the flow. Although it may be mechanized, it is not automated. Human operation or monitoring is essential. Vari-able path systems are found in production and physical supply, but they are most apparent in physical distribution, where operations are frequently discrete and non-standardized. Equipment examples include handling aids such as pallets, containers, carts, dollies, and powered equipment such as fork lift trucks and tractors.

UNITIZATION

Unitization consolidates material into bodies that offer optimal handling character-istics. Essentially, unitization seeks to adjust the form dimensions of material to enable application of effective handling techniques. Having common size, weight, and shape makes it possible to systematize handling procedures and use labor saving devices. With its effect on material form, unitization acts as a significant hedge against flowability constraints. Enhanced flowability is the objective of unitization. It is accomplished in three ways—packaging, palletization, and containerization.

Although the handling of materials as individual items or parts is not uncommon, items are usually combined into unit loads for transport efficiency. Unit loads refer to tote pans, boxes, pallets, or skids which are designed to carry multiple items or parts at a time.

The two categories of loads are unit and mixed. *Unit loads* are quantities of iden-tical items generally stored and retrieved from a central location. They are normally stored on skids, racks, pallets, bins, or wire containers. *Mixed loads* are quantities of different items such as parts, tools, and subassemblies stored and retrieved from several locations. They are normally stored in bins, drawers, or boxes.

Packaging

Packaging can be subdivided into two categories: commercial and industrial. *Com-mercial packaging* is geared to marketing objectives such as (1) offering package sizes to meet consumer demands, (2) differentiating products through unique pack-aging, (3) promoting the product through advertising, (4) identifying and protecting the product, and (5) serving as a utility producing extension of the product. *Industrial packaging* is concerned with achieving maximum flowability through efficient and economic movement. Commercial and industrial packaging are not mutually exclu-sive, since marketing and flowability objectives are both complementary and inter-dependent.

Packaging contains and confines materials to facilitate use or handling by stan-

FIGURE 6
Universal product code.

dardizing physical dimensions; it is a useful tool for control over the flow of material. For example, small electronic components are often boxed (with or without internal protective packing) to allow more efficient handling in areas of movement and storage. Packages are designed to withstand the hazards of materials handling.

Often packaging appears as part of the production process as finished goods are prepared for distribution. As an example, soft drinks are actually packaged during the production process. For operations that do not require integrated production and packaging, the packaging industry offers a wide assortment of mechanized devices.

Two final packaging considerations are identification and cost. The package usually permits visual recognition of the material it holds. While visual graphics are useful to identify and even promote package contents in marketing, they may not be sufficient for effective materials handling. Content identifiers are coded, often using numeric or mnemonic descriptors. Recently machine scannable graphic indicators have become popular. Called Universal Product Codes (UPC), they are sensed by an electronic reading device, which interprets the symbols to identify contents. The Universal Product Code, illustrated in Figure 6, is used on both commercial and industrial packages for item identification requirements in material locations, retrieval, counting (inventory), pricing, and sales.

While packaging is a useful tool to dampen the effects of flowability restraints, it can be an expensive tool. In general, it is common for packaging to represent as much as 20% of the final product cost. This is particularly true of very sensitive high technology material and small consumer items. Because of cost, packaging must be evaluated in terms of the benefits it provides to materials handling and other organizational functions.

Palletization

A pallet is simply a platform upon which material is placed to form a moveable collection of items. With the desired quantity of material placed on it, the pallet is called a *load unit*. A palletized load unit is desirable because several pieces of material or very heavy single items can be moved with minimum handling difficulty. Using pallets results in load units too heavy for manual movement, but the pallet is compatible with handling equipment such as fork trucks and large conveyors. This permits movement of large load units with convenient and efficient *terminal weights*.

Depending on its intended use, a pallet can be constructed of numerous materials and in various sizes. For example, metal is often required for very heavy material, but wood is used for lighter commodities. Another consideration is the number of times a pallet will be reused. Numerous attempts have been made to standardize the dimensions of pallets, but success has been limited because of the variety of func-

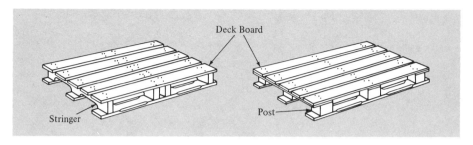

FIGURE 7
A typical pallet.

tional areas influencing pallet design. The typical warehouse pallet is four feet by four feet, but these dimensions may not be compatible with production, transportation, or physical supply activities.

While it is beyond our present scope to describe in detail the various pallet designs, it is important to recognize the basic components of a typical pallet. Depicted in Figure 7, the primary parts of a pallet include the face and the stringer. The *face* is made up of deck boards, which form the platform. Pallets have either single or double faces, the latter offering two interchangeable sides, one used for a platform and the other as a flat ground contact surface. *Stringers* support the platform, normally about six inches high. Being spaced off the ground allows entry of fork lift tines (blades). If the stringers run the entire length of the pallet, it can be approached by a fork truck from two sides and it is called a two-way entry pallet. Four-way entry is possible if stringers do not cover the full pallet length. Here, of course, the platform board must also be supported by edge boards.

Material is secured to a pallet using tiedown straps, metal bands, chains, nets, and shrinkable film. Tiedown devices serve to protect the integrity of the unit load. One of the more recent innovations in tiedown devices is shrinkable film: a plastic film that reduces in size when heated. It is placed over a palletized unit load and subjected to uniform heat, sealing the material configuration and pallet into a single unit. While useful, shrinkable film is limited to applications with fairly light material and to commodities that are not extremely heat sensitive.

Containerization

By providing materials handling efficiencies, containers offer benefits similar to packaging and palletization. Containerization is a method for confining material in convenient load units. Containers are designed to be easily handled in transport. Two categories of containers are distinguishable: those for internal use, and those for external use (shipping containers).

Internal use containers are used to hold material while it is awaiting use or movement. Common examples are boxes, bags, bins, drums, and carboys. The most frequently used box is constructed of fiberboard. Boxes are also constructed of wood, either as a crate, a frame for fiberboard, or as sides of a box pallet. Bags are often used for granular or powdered materials. Cushioned bags have recently become popular for holding small parts, books, and documents, particularly when they are shipped. Bins are usually stationary containers, although they can be mobile if they are on wheels. Similar to an open box, they hold frequently used materials such as parts and tools. Drums and carboys are used to hold liquids or other flowable material. Drums are usually made of metal, wood, or fibrous material, depending on their contents and the number of reuses intended. Carboys are ceramic or glass containers used for material with special characteristics such as acids or other sensitive substances.

Shipping containers are unitization devices designed for material consolidation and transfer. In distribution, they are intermodal (can be transferred between modes of transportation). In other areas, shipping containers are interfunctional (can be used in and moved among several functions).

Shipping containers can hold bulky, packaged, and palletized material. They are constructed of fibrous material, wood, and metal, metal being the most popular form. Containers are usually shaped as a rectangular solid. They may serve as a large box for consolidation, a mobile truck trailer, and a rail boxcar, all without modification. Other containers are designed for specific purposes, such as those built to fit passenger airliner cargo compartments (called igloos) and those for liquid and gases.

The metal container, though not universally applicable, has caused a revolution in the shipping industry. Containers are available in several standard sizes. They provide efficient unit loads, handling ease, economy, material security, environmental control, and multimodal capabilities. They survive many uses. They can be an effective part of a materials handling system.

EQUIPMENT ALTERNATIVES

Of major importance to the manager considering a materials handling system is an appreciation of the equipment alternatives available. The materials handling industry offers an enormous variety of labor saving devices, and just about any handling equipment need can be met with specially designed, unique purpose systems. Because of the sheer number of alternatives available, it is not possible to enumerate all of them. It is possible, however, to categorize alternatives and briefly discuss each. There are four basic categories of handling equipment:

1. trucks and tractors,
2. conveyors,
3. lifts,
4. special systems and handling aids.

Trucks and Tractors

Trucks and tractors are wheeled vehicles for moving material along a variable path, usually in an intermittent or discrete fashion. Trucks lift and carry, whereas tractors push and pull. A few examples of trucks and tractors are shown in Figure 8. Trucks may be manual or powered. The most familiar is the forklift. It is available in a number of sizes and styles to fit various needs. Forklift capabilities depend on such factors as terminal weight of material to be moved, reach (height) requirements, and space available for maneuvering. The forklift truck is not economically adapted to long distance horizontal movement because of its high demand for labor per unit of transfer. It is most commonly employed in shipping and receiving, as well as to

A

B

C

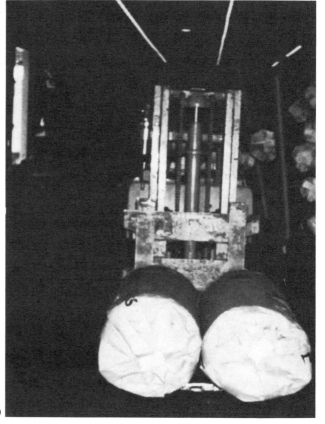

D

FIGURE 8
Trucks and tractors: (A) Lift truck interfacing with retrieval system; (B) special dolly for tote boxes; (C) cart for manual order picking; (D) lift truck with roll adapters. Photographs courtesy of American Chain & Cable Company.

place material in high cube storage. As the trend toward narrow-aisle high stacking grows, rotating fork assemblies will become more common. Their design enables them to operate in cramped quarters. Industrial trucks of various types are applicable to transporting nonuniform unit loads intermittently over varying routes.

Tractors are powered equipment used to move other equipment, usually without lifting. Dollies and carts are often pushed or pulled by a tractor. Vehicles not under power (trailers, vessels, and airplanes) are moved with tractors or related equipment.

Conveyors

Conveyors provide for continuous or intermittent movement over a fixed or semi-fixed path. Conveyor systems provide efficient flow, but they are inflexible. While many types of conveyors exist, two categories are readily discernible: those with stationary surfaces and those with moving surfaces. Stationary conveyor surfaces have rollers, wheels (casters), or bearings over which material moves. Such arrangements are common in gravity systems or where material is pushed or pulled along the conveyor's surface. Conveyors with moving surfaces employ power. Typical moving surfaces include belts, chains, slats, and buckets. Examples are illustrated in Figure 9.

Conveyor equipment includes tracked and pneumatic devices, which possess similar movement characteristics, benefits, and limitations. Monorails and underfloor tows are fixed tracks to guide the flow of material. Gravity and mechanical power sources are used in monorails, which are employed to move material suspended above ground level. Underfloor tows are also tracked, but they are generally mechanically powered to push or pull wheeled vehicles. Pneumatic materials handling equipment is essentially a pipeline through which material is forced. The pneumatic conveyor is a system of tubes or ducts through which material is moved by pressure or vacuum. Familiar examples are grain pumps used to load and unload grain elevators, vessels, and other vehicles. Pneumatic tubes are used to move capsules of material among use points in production, warehousing, or retail facilities.

Lifts

Trucks, tractors, and conveyors can of course provide vertical movement, either by lifting or moving on an incline. However, there is a category of equipment specially designed for vertical movement: *lifts,* including hoists, elevators, cranes, and derricks. Shown in Figure 10, lifts are mechanically powered and are frequently used in conjunction with other handling equipment. Elevators may be conventionally designed to provide discrete up and down movement, or they may employ conveyor techniques to allow continuous movement. Cranes and derricks usually lift by means of cables, chains, or pneumatic pumps. Cranes may be fixed or mobile; derricks are normally fixed.

FIGURE 9
Conveyors: (A) Belt conveyor; (B) underfloor tow; (C) roller conveyor; (D) extendible conveyor for shipping and receiving; (E) roller conveyor in order picking operation; (F) monorail yarn spool handling line; (G) pallet conveyor; (H) overhead hanging garment sorting system. Photographs courtesy of American Chain & Cable Company.

Special Systems and Aids

The final category of equipment includes an almost unlimited collection of custom designed handling systems and handling aids, some of which are depicted in Figure 11. Special materials handling systems are useful or necessary when materials handling is an integral part of another function. For instance, in beverage bottling operations, container and ingredient handling are a part of production; so also, complex sorting systems become part of the order processing activity of physical supply.

Because handling activities are necessary throughout the flow of material, and because not every activity fits into some arbitrary descriptive category, equipment must be available to serve as handling aids. Several handling aids, such as pallets and containers, have been mentioned. Other aids available are hand trucks, carts, dollies, jacks, flow racks, ball mats (for turning heavy and bulky material and pallets), and small hand tools. All are essentially labor and time saving devices used to make movements more efficient.

Automation of materials handling is beneficial for distribution centers and manufacturing facilities. The objective of automated materials handling is to integrate ma-

E   F

G   H

terials management into overall operations of an organization. These systems are a combination of materials handling equipment and computer control. It results in integrated materials handling rather than "islands of automation." Typical applications include robotics, automated guided vehicle systems (AGVS), automated storage and retrieval systems (AS/RS), palletizers, automated identification systems (optical and laser scanners), and automated sorting systems.

A prerequisite to the design of a materials handling system is a knowledge of the different kinds and types of handling equipment available. The selection of handling equipment will be based on several factors, some of which are:

1. functional adequacy of the equipment,
2. capital investment required,
3. equipment reliability and life expectancy,
4. cost savings potential,
5. safety considerations,
6. equipment flexibility,
7. maintenance requirements,

A

B

C

D

E

FIGURE 10

Lifts: (A) Construction cranes; (B) gantry crane; (C) bridge crane; (D) vacuum lift for sheet products; (E) jib crane and hoist. Photographs courtesy of American Chain & Cable Company.

FIGURE 11
Systems and aids: (A) Freight sorting system; (B) drum handling and storage retrieval system; (C) storage retrieval system for handling barstock; (D) control console for an automatic sorting system; (E) sorting system in a modern warehouse; (F) automatic sorting system; (G) palletizing units. Photographs courtesy of American Chain & Cable Company.

8. spare parts and service availability,
9. fuel and power requirements,
10. complexity of manpower training required.

Trucks are generally used for handling material in intermittent production. With intermittent operations, material has a variable path of travel, so variable-path equipment (trucks, forklifts, or tractors) is used. Conveyors are generally used for handling material in continuous production. With continuous operations, material usually follows a fixed path of travel, so fixed-path equipment (chutes, conveyors, elevators, or pipes) is utilized. Fixed-path equipment usually costs less to purchase and to operate. Variable-path equipment requires an operator and additional manpower. Usually fixed position transfer equipment is controlled by manufacturing or maintenance, and mobile transfer equipment without a permanent work location is controlled in a transportation pool.

MATERIALS HANDLING DECISIONS

Inputs, constraints, and flow factors fully define the decision environment of the materials handling function. Handling decisions are made subject to environmental influences and in concert with decisions of other organizational functions. Realization that the materials handling decision environment is shared by and interacts with other functions is a prerequisite to effective management. Additionally, materials handling is a dynamic area featuring rapid technological innovation. As technology improves, the manager must understand and anticipate changes to ensure that his decisions are responsive to both functional and organizational objectives.

Materials handling methods can be decided only after the following are known:

1. the kinds and amounts of material to be handled,
2. the locations to and from which materials are to be transported.

Work stations can't be established without considering the space for loading, unloading, and movement of handling equipment. Thus, the location of work stations will influence the choice of handling equipment, and the type of handling equipment will influence the location of work stations.

Manpower and equipment requirements can be estimated from flow charts and work analysis information. Work sampling and predetermined time studies (standard data) may be employed. Speeds, loads, distances, and technical data concerning the capability of equipment are usually available from manufacturers. Comparisons can be made between maximum and minimum flow requirements. It is usually desirable to design a system around the maximum possible capability (peak workload requirements). Allowances for growth should be considered, as well as maintenance and downtime. Typical quantitative tools that can improve decision making are flow analysis, work measurement, work sampling, predetermined time standards, incremental analysis, linear programming, queuing theory, and simulation.

The phases in the design of a materials handling system are:

1. Define the objectives/scope of the system.
2. Analyze the handling, storage, and control requirements.
3. Generate alternative system designs.
4. Evaluate alternative system designs.
5. Select the preferred system(s).
6. Implement the preferred system(s).

MATERIALS HANDLING OUTPUTS

Like the inputs, the outputs of materials handling decisions are difficult to identify with convenient descriptions. The ultimate objective of course is to facilitate an effective flow of material. Outputs should represent mechanisms for accomplishment of that objective. Appreciation of the environment and principles of materials handling is a necessity. It is also necessary to evaluate the availability of equipment resources and how they are acquired. Thus, the two primary outputs of the materials handling function can be classifed as *handling efficiencies* and *sourcing*.

HANDLING EFFICIENCIES

Handling efficiencies are the principles that are used to evaluate the materials handling function. Once accepted by the manager, they establish a conceptual framework for approaching any materials handling problem. Figure 12 contains a list of handling efficiencies which should be beneficial to the manager concerned with the materials handling function. They are drawn from considerations of inputs, constraints, and flow factors.

Caution must be exercised in using any list of principles or efficiencies. Neither this list nor any of its elements is universally valid. Every situation is unique in some way. It is important to remember that principles are useful if they fit situations; situations can seldom be made to fit principles. Nevertheless, appreciation of handling efficiencies as a part of the body of knowledge known as materials handling is invaluable to the manager.

When studying materials handling, safety aspects must be given consideration. Better methods and personnel training should result in fewer accidents as well as

FIGURE 12
Handling efficiencies.

1. Minimize material movement where possible.
2. Minimize manual handling and man movement.
3. Move material instead of men.
4. Maximize unit load size.
5. Maximize unit load terminal weight.
6. Where possible use gravity to move material.
7. Minimize idle time by reducing terminal time.
8. Use direct path movement schemes.
9. Minimize backtracking and parallel movement.
10. Use mechanized devices to ensure predictable activity rates.
11. Employ line production techniques if appropriate.
12. Ensure optimum use of space, particularly aisle areas.
13. Consolidate handling operations with production, physical supply, and distribution where possible.
14. Move larger weights short distances.
15. Combine operations whenever practical to eliminate handling between them.

lower costs. Handling equipment can be dangerous if misused or not properly maintained. Education, safety programs, and preventive maintenance can considerably reduce hazardous situations.

SOURCING

Sourcing is concerned with the methods of obtaining resources for materials handling. Acquisition involves an investment in manpower, equipment, and services. Manpower requirements are directly related to the labor intensity of the materials handling function, which is controlled by the mix of equipment and services rendered. Sourcing is equipment oriented when equipment is actually bought. It is service oriented when materials handling capabilities are leased or rented.

Purchase

Outright purchase of equipment represents a long term commitment of funds and an implicit assumption that future handling demands will remain fairly constant. These risks are balanced by the internal control exercised by the purchasing activity over employment of equipment capabilities. Because of the risks and costs, it is necessary to include materials handling in the equipment planning activities of an organization.

Although direct purchase can offer significant advantages, it must be carefully evaluated because of the magnitude of expenditure required for materials handling equipment. Contributing up to 20% of production cost, materials handling is a competitor for substantial portions of available resources. As a cost center, materials handling is not additive to profit; its contribution is to minimization of cost.

Lease

Risks can be lessened if a lease arrangement is used, so that commitment of funds is limited by a contract. With a lease, the responsibility for equipment upkeep and maintenance usually rests with the vendor. Control exercised by the lessee is subject to contractual terms. The lease payments are treated as expenses and charged to the period. (With direct purchase, depreciation methods are employed.) It is routine for handling organizations to offer lease-purchase agreements and consultant services, which can be valuable to organizations with limited handling expertise. Leasing is appropriate for a wide range of equipment requirements, from handling aids to the design and implementation of complex systems.

Rental

The minimum possible investment is under rental arrangements. It is beneficial to employ rental services if:

1. long term investment is limited by availability of funds,
2. alternative investment is more profitable,
3. future handling requirements are uncertain,
4. handling requirements occur in a cyclical fashion,
5. extensive operational changes are in progress or anticipated.

Upkeep and maintenance may be a part of the rental agreement or the responsibility of the sourcing organization. Rental equipment normally includes a limited range of equipment and aids such as common use trucks and conveyors.

CONCLUSION

Materials handling is a subtle function in many organizations. It can be seen both as an active participant in other functions and as a function itself. Its objective is to minimize costs. The most efficient handling system usually involves the least amount of handling. The materials handling function can be defined by evaluating functional inputs, constraints, flow factors, and outputs.

The key to efficient materials handling in the future is an integrated approach. Careful economic and engineering studies must be made to determine the system, facility, and equipment to use, considering the relevant constraints. A properly designed and implemented handling system will reduce costs, reduce waste, increase productive capacity, improve working conditions, and improve distribution. Cost savings are realized through lower inventory and production control cost, better space utilization, minimum handling, and shorter production cycle time. Waste is reduced by limiting damage through improved handling. Production capacity is increased because of better control of materials, handling system coordination, constant production rates, and lessened machine idle time. Thus, it is through the systems approach that materials handling becomes more controllable.

QUESTIONS

1. What are some of the objectives of materials handling?
2. In what areas of an organization are materials handling requirements apparent?
3. How are production demands for materials handling capabilities changing?
4. Define flowability.
5. Briefly describe the three categories of material form.
6. How do the geographical and temporal characteristics of distance influence materials handling?
7. Describe the relationships among materials handling and other functions as movement distances become smaller and larger.
8. What is movement intensity?
9. Differentiate between randomized and dedicated storage.
10. Relate the degree of materials handling sophistication to fixed and variable costs.
11. What type of control system and equipment are associated with the major categories of movement continuity?
12. What are the three most common paths of movement which describe the pattern of material flow?
13. Distinguish between commercial and industrial packaging.
14. Give a brief description of the four basic categories of handling equipment.
15. State several factors on which the selection of handling equipment should be based.
16. Identify five handling efficiencies.
17. Name several examples of activities other than manufacturing that must deal with the handling of materials.

PROBLEMS

1. A conveyor costing $6000 will save 30 minutes a day of labor time. The current labor rate is $10 per hour. The firm operates 300 days per year. How long would it take for the conveyor to pay for itself?

2. A contractor has just received a job to move earth from one site to another. Approximately 400 tons of earth are to be moved during every 10-hour day. The two locations are separated by 6 miles. The load capacity of the contractor's trucks is 15 tons. The average truck speed will be about 12 miles per hour, which includes loading and unloading, speed under load, speed without load on the return trip, and delays. How many vehicles must be committed to the job?

3. A special truck is being designed to transport material between two departments that are 0.2 mile apart. The average speed of the truck will be 6 miles per hour. The average speed includes return trip without load, load time, unload time, and delays. In a 10-hour day, 120,000 pounds of material must be moved between departments. What should be the load capacity of the truck for continuous operation?

4. An organization uses a single overhead crane and forklift trucks to unload fertilizer from railroad cars and move it into a warehouse. It takes the overhead crane 2 minutes to unload a unit load of fertilizer onto a truck. It takes a truck 10 minutes to travel to the warehouse, unload, and return for another load. How many forklift trucks are required to keep the crane operator working full time?

5. Two electric forklifts can be purchased for $9100; a single forklift costs $5000. Computations indicate that one forklift will save 5 minutes of labor per hour and two will save 8.5 minutes per hour. The present labor rate is $9.50 per hour. The organization operates 315 days per year on a two shift basis (16 hours/day). Considering no downtime for maintenance, what is the payback period for a single forklift? What is the payback period for two forklifts?

6. John Harris, the plant manager at Better Products, Inc., has developed the total monthly cost equations for production and distribution to be as follows:

   production cost $= 3X^2 - 20X + 40,000,$

   distribution cost $= 2X^2 - 30X + 27,000,$

   where X is the number of units in thousands. How many units should be produced monthly to minimize total costs?

7. Mary Hunchback is evaluating whether or not to adopt palletization for handling materials. The following data have been collected:

Cost of pallets (per 100)	$450.00
Cost of tiedown straps (per 1,000 ft)	550.00
Cost of tiedown clips (per 1,000)	50.00
Cost of banding tool (each)	25.00

   A total of 2000 pallets will be required. It is estimated that 25,000 feet of tiedown straps, 50,000 tiedown clips, and eight banding tools will be required. Labor costs will be reduced by 10% and breakage (damage) by 15% with the use of pallets. Breakage for the last three years was $45,000, $51,000, and $48,000 respectively. The firm operates 8 hours per day for 320 days a year, and the current labor rate is $20 per hour. Should pallets be purchased if a payback period of 36 months is required?

8. Sara Jones, vice president of High Quality Products, Inc., is considering the purchase of a new automated loading machine. Just last week a salesman from Automation Plus discussed the situation with her, and the following information was obtained:

1. The new machine will reduce the cost of labor by 25%, but increase the cost of electricity by 40%.
2. The new machine will cost $30,000 and have a $5000 salvage value at the end of five years.
3. The company's present expenses for the loading operation are $40,000 for labor and $2000 for electricity.

Assuming a cost of capital of 16% and ignoring tax considerations, should the automated loader be purchased?

CASE 1: CELLAR TO STELLAR

The Balder engine assembly plant in Buffalo began producing V-6 engines for passenger cars six years ago. It assembles 30 engine models and supplies all five divisions of Consolidated Motors. The assembly operation is busy sixteen hours a day, five days a week and produces about 24,000 engines a week. The manufacturing facility itself operates three shifts, seven days a week in order to support the heavy production pace.

Among the problems plaguing Balder's total operation are a shortage of floor space in the assembly area and an outdated storage system. Some production managers insist on having their work on the floor well before the material actually is scheduled to be used. Large inventories of in-process materials are stored in the assembly area to prevent production line stoppages. The present storage system forces lift truck drivers to search over 60,000 square feet of storage space to locate production parts. The amount of time the drivers spend stocking assembly lines has increased, while the throughput rate for material movements has decreased from 22 to 18 pallets per hour. The drivers now have less time remaining for other storage system tasks which they previously performed. More personnel are needed to handle the restocking of the storage system or to assist with shipping and receiving. Finally, shortages periodically are discovered during the line stocking operation, and some shortage occurrences critically impair the plant's production performance.

One operations manager proposes the construction of an automated storage and retrieval system (AS/RS) to alleviate certain inefficiencies and lessen the burden on lift truck drivers. He suggests that the 60,000 square feet of storage space be converted into a narrow-aisle, high-rise system estimated to occupy only 10,000 square feet of floor space. He wants the AS/RS located near the receiving dock to decrease the requirement for lift truck traffic inside the plant and to avoid the need for a complete rearrangement of the plant's material flow and assembly patterns.

The proposed system is quite expensive; besides the four-aisle, all-welded structure which contains floor-to-ceiling bins, it includes the purchase of four storage/retrieval (S/R) machines, one for each aisle. The S/R machines under consideration have their own on-board microprocessors which make them computer-controlled, robotized material handlers. The machines are guided by optical sensors and can carry loaded pallets (unit loads) to and from the assembly facility's input-output conveyors.

Materials entering the AS/RS are placed on pallets by lift trucks at the "head" (beginning) of the system. Here each pallet is assigned an inventory control number. Each load (pallet) then travels to a weigh station. There its weight is taken and its dimensions are assessed by fixed-beam scanners to ensure it meets the specifications of its designated storage bin. From the weigh station each load moves to one of four input stations and is deposited in its assigned bin by an S/R machine.

The microprocessors on the S/R machines are controlled by a minicomputer. The minicomputer also is the base for the proposed stock locator control system. It assigns bin locations and spaces "critical" parts strategically in the storage area so that they can easily be retrieved in the event of an equipment failure. The stock locator control system operates as a slave to the inventory control system contained in the main frame computer. It is directed to store and issue material. It interfaces with the host system which controls inventory tightly. Material requisitions in the form of pick lists are received by the minicomputer, and material store/issue transactions are transmitted back to the host system after they are accomplished. Both the stock locator control system and the S/R machines can be operated manually.

Other managers are not satisfied with this proposal. One manager wants a more centralized real time management system. He recommends the acquisition of a material system which could perform receiving, quality control, unit load storage, mini (small parts) load storage, order processing, order consolidation, factory tracking, and shipping. His ideal system would be capable of controlling material from the moment it is received into the facility until it leaves the shipping dock. Instead of obtaining pick lists as the stock locator control system does, this would be a comprehensive inventory system which interfaces with the MRP system more directly; it would obtain scheduled orders and transmit inventory transactions relative to the orders. Furthermore, it would be totally automated and practically eliminate the need for lift trucks.

Another manager is altogether against installing automated systems. She would rather acquire more lift trucks and hire more personnel. Her rejection of automated systems comes from the problems she associates with system installations, field service of automated systems, centralized activities and functions, lack of flexibility, user requirements, etc. In short, she is resistant to unestablished methods which do not cater to the special needs of all operating personnel.

1. Discuss the problems and their probable causes at Balder.
2. What are the advantages and disadvantages of the AS/RS and stock locator system proposal?
3. What particular problems and issues do the other proposals address, create, or solve?

CASE 2: THE PATHFINDERS

Driverless vehicles were introduced in the mid 1950s. Those models were simple carts which were guided by a wire in the floor and operated in response to a single command from a dispatcher. They were not considered a rousing success; their acceptance was neither unqualified nor widespread, partly because of their high cost and operational inflexibility. When installed for conventional transportation systems, they were unable to provide acceptable uptime. In general, their operating difficulties diminished delivery system reliability.

Newer driverless vehicles (automated guided vehicles, AGVs) are considerably more sophisticated. Their conveyance is based on electronic guidance systems imbedded in the floor (guide paths), which are controlled largely by microcomputer technology. Most contemporary AGVs are equipped with more than one sensor to sense the electromagnetic field created through the wire guide paths. One system, for instance, has 18 wires placed in the floor. Seven of the wires are for frequencies which control the travel of the vehicle. The other eleven are for communications which tell the microprocessor-equipped vehicle what to do. The modern AGV systems range from a single vehicle which travels a simple route to more than 50 vehicles operating in a complex installation. Within the new systems, guide paths can be changed and vehicles can be added as required.

There also is a range of options available for the vehicles themselves. For example, units can be equipped to move forward, in reverse, and to the sides. Trailers can be included to increase carrying capacity. Load transfer equipment and other automatic features are options. In addition, vehicles can be fitted to form a mobile assembly platform with programmed height adjustments. With the use of on-board microprocessors, AGVs can be programmed with complete details of the travel route and work detail, and various levels of control are available.

In all AGV systems there is a degree of system complexity. The complexity is determined by information and communication requirements, layout complexity, traffic patterns, and cycle frequency and intensity. Increases in the complexity of a system place a higher demand on intelligence. Moreover, increasing complexity compromises the reliability with which the system performs. At the lowest level of sophistication, the AGV's destination is punched out in advance on its on-board keyboard. At the highest level, the vehicle responds to a completely automatic system with instructions coming from a central computer. On some centralized systems an illuminated routing display is used so that the precise location of each vehicle is known in the control center. Visual monitoring of these complex systems frequently is accomplished through a closed-circuit television system.

Futuristically, AGVs are considered part of the developing technology expected to address the demands of the automated factory. These demands include system integration in distribution, storage, manufacturing, and assembly operations; high up-time or reliability; fast throughput; good floor space utilization; reduced inventory levels; smooth implementation (possibly through a "building block" or component approach); vital communications between each function and the central control; and enhanced profitability.

Considering the past, present, and future of AGVs and using any outside research sources, answer the following:

1. What major advances distinguish each phase of AGV technology?
2. What are some of the current applications for AGVs? In particular, what are some of the diverse industries which use AGVs (especially for materials handling functions)?
3. How are AGV systems expected to change and/or be adapted to new uses?
4. What major issues or problems need to be resolved concerning AGV technology?

SELECTED BIBLIOGRAPHY

Apple, J. M. *Plant Layout and Materials Handling,* New York: Ronald Press, 1950.

Ballou, R. H. *Business Logistics Management,* Englewood Cliffs, NJ: Prentice-Hall, 1973.

Bowersox, D. J. *Logistical Management,* New York: Macmillan, 1978.

Davis, G. M. and S. W. Brown. *Logistics Management,* Lexington, MA: Lexington Books, 1974.

Heskett, J. L. et al. *Business Logistics,* New York: Ronald Press, 2nd edition, 1973.

Jenkins, C. H. *Modern Warehouse Management,* New York: McGraw-Hill, 1968.

Mathews, L. M. *Control of Materials,* London: Industrial and Commercial Techniques, 1971.

Sims, E. R. *Planning and Managing Materials Flow,* Boston: Industrial Education Institute, 1968.

Sussams, J. E. *Industrial Logistics,* Boston: Cahners Books, 1972.

Tersine, R. J. and J. H. Campbell. *Modern Materials Management,* New York: Elsevier North-Holland, 1977.

Tyler, E. S. *Materials Handling,* New York: McGraw-Hill, 1970.

Warman, J. *Warehouse Management,* London: William Heinmann, 1971.

VI

OPERATIONS DECISIONS

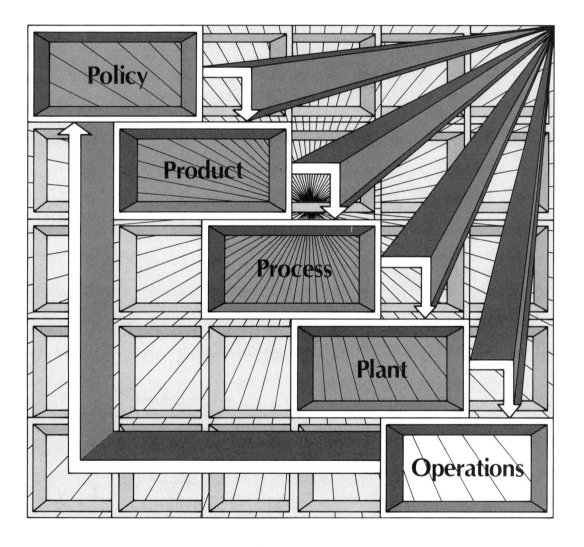

Up to this point, with the exception of prototypes, no resources (plant, manpower, material, or equipment) have been procured for production. Operations decisions will make the "go" or "no-go" decision on the product or project. A "no-go" decision will scrap the whole undertaking. A "go" decision will necessitate activation and organization to implement all the prior planning (product decisions, process decisions, and plant decisions). With activation, operations decisions will decide when and how many units of the product to provide. As shown by Figure I, the final output of operations decisions will be the goods and services provided to a customer or the public.

This section on operations decisions comprises nine chapters. The *Forecasting and Market Analysis* chapter determines the expected demand for the organization's products. The *Production Planning and Master Scheduling* chapter plans for the utilization and control of facilities, manpower, and materials. The *Material Requirements Planning* chapter introduces a computer-based system for scheduling and material control. The *Scheduling and Production Control* chapter provides for the short term (day-to-day) scheduling of resources into the production system. The *Inventory Control Models* chapter outlines the various control techniques for material. The *Inventory Control Systems* chapter establishes the macro systems for aggregate material control. The *Purchasing and Procurement* chapter deals with the acquisition of materials and services from external sources. The *Quality Control* chapter concerns assuring that inputs, processes, and outputs are in compliance with established standards. Finally, the *Maintenance* chapter discusses means for ensuring the continuing operation of the facility (plant and equipment).

FIGURE I
The operations function.

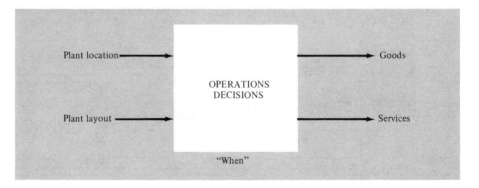

15

Forecasting and Market Analysis

THE FORECASTING FUNCTION

TIME SERIES ANALYSIS

Last Period Demand
Arithmetic Average
Moving Average
Regression Analysis
Exponentially Weighted Moving Average (EWMA)
EWMA with Trend Correction
EWMA with Seasonal Correction
EWMA with Trend and Seasonal Corrections
EWMA Overview
Box-Jenkins Models

SOLICITING OPINIONS

ECONOMIC INDICATORS

ECONOMETRIC MODELS

CONCLUSION

QUESTIONS

PROBLEMS

CASES

SELECTED BIBLIOGRAPHY

Man has always had a fascination with the future. Astrologers, prophets, wizards, and psychics have been looking into the future throughout recorded history. In organizations, forecasting is the window into the future, upon which most major activities are based, in particular, the allocation and use of resources.

Forecasting is the prediction, projection, or estimation of the occurrence of uncertain future events or levels of activity.[1] Since the future rarely is certain, some system of forecasting, implicit or explicit, is necessary. Managers are interested in the timing, magnitude, and effects of future events that influence their operations. The purpose of forecasting is to make use of the best available present information to guide future activities toward organizational goals.

Absolute accuracy in predicting the future is unachievable, so there are limits on its potential benefits. Should funds be expended on a venture that is almost always in error? The answer obviously is yes, since the alternative is making decisions in total ignorance. Organizations cannot foresee the future, but they desire strong inferences about it when large amounts of money and time are to be committed.

Forecasting pertains to more than predicting demand. It can be used to predict revenues, costs, profits, prices, rainfall, technological changes, and a host of other variables. While the focus of this chapter is on demand forecasting, it should be remembered that the same concepts and techniques apply equally well to these other variables.

There are many types of forecasting used in organizations. It is one input to many types of planning and control. Within the context of the structure of this book, master forecasting, as illustrated in Figure 1, relates to all the major decision categories at once. Functional forecasting, as shown in Figure 2, influences each of the business functions separately. Thus, there are many plans and decisions and many different types of forecasting requirements, involving different techniques.

Most organizations are not in a position to wait until orders are received before they begin to determine what production facilities, process, equipment, manpower, or materials are required and in what quantities. Few consumers would be willing to wait over such a time horizon. Most successful organizations anticipate the future demand for their products and translate that information into factor inputs required to satisfy expected demand. Forecasting (predicting the future) provides a basis for managerial planning. For a business to survive, it must meet its customers' needs at least as quickly as its competitors do. The better management is able to estimate the future, the better it should be able to prepare for it. In many organizations, sales forecasts are used to establish production levels, facilitate scheduling, set inventory levels, determine manpower loading, make purchasing decisions, establish sales conditions (pricing and advertising), and aid financial planning (cash budgeting and capital budgeting).

Many environmental factors influence the demand for an organization's products and services. It is never possible to identify all of the factors or to measure their probable effects. It is necessary in forecasting to identify the broad, major influences and to attempt to predict their direction. Some major environmental factors are:

1. General business conditions and the state of the economy
2. Competitor actions and reactions

---

[1]A substantial portion of this chapter is taken from Chapter 2 of Richard J. Tersine, *Principles of Inventory and Materials Management,* New York: Elsevier North Holland, 1982.

417

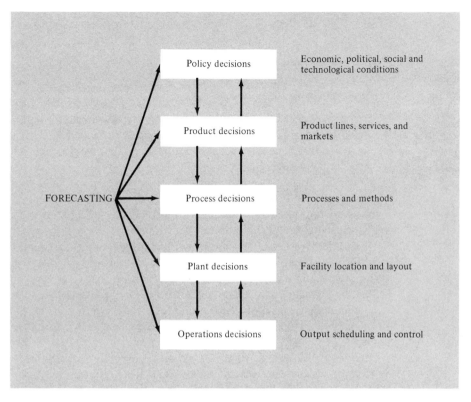

FIGURE 1
Master forecasting.

FIGURE 2
Functional forecasting.

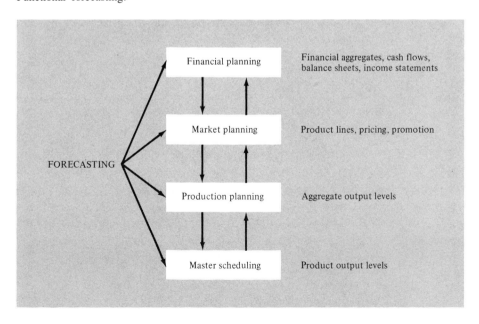

3. Governmental legislative actions
4. Marketplace trends
   a. Product life cycle
   b. Style and fashion
   c. Changing consumer demands
5. Technological innovations

For the purposes of this chapter, a forecast is an estimate of the level of demand expected in the future. It should be an unbiased estimation of what is expected to occur. It should not be confused with a plan, goal, or a performance measure, which indicates what is desirable.

Organizations may use many different forecasting bases. Sales revenue, physical units, cost of goods manufactured, direct labor hours, and machine hours are common forecasting bases. The selection of a forecasting base is dependent upon plans for establishing the necessary factor requirements.

Top-down forecasting and *bottom-up forecasting* are general forecasting patterns used for predicting product demand. Top-down forecasting begins with a forecast of general economic activity (GNP, national income, etc.) for the geopolitical unit where the organization operates. Industry forecasts are developed from the general economic activity forecast. The organization's share-of-the-market forecast is predicted from the industry forecast, and specific product group forecasts are developed from it.

Bottom-up forecasting begins at the product level. Forecasts are made for each product or product group summed to obtain the aggregate organizational forecast. The aggregate forecast can be modified in relation to the general business outlook and the competitive situation. Advertising and promotion may necessitate further forecast revision.

Forecasting, as we are referring to it here, is a short-run tool for establishing input-output levels. (By the short run, we mean that products, processes, equipment, tooling, layout, and capacity are essentially fixed.) All statistical forecasting techniques assume to some extent that forces that existed in the past will persist in the future. A forecast is the link between the external, uncontrollable environment and the internal, controllable affairs of an organization. Adequate forecasting procedures can go a long way toward solving many organizational problems.

THE FORECASTING FUNCTION

Frequently, forecasting is considered as a group of procedures for deriving estimates of future activity, the major emphasis being on the type of forecasting technique. However, it is more desirable to focus on the forecasting function itself than on the specific forecasting techniques or models. The forecasting function includes techniques and models, but it also highlights the significance of inputs and outputs (see Figure 3).

To develop the forecasting function, it is first necessary to determine the outputs. The outputs (and their format) can be specified by a delineation of the intended uses of the forecasts. This chapter has already mentioned numerous uses for forecasts in organizations. When the users obtain the outputs, specific actions will be taken to assure that future demand will be satisfied. The precision and accuracy of forecasting outputs should be conveyed, along with the intended uses, during the development of the forecasting function.

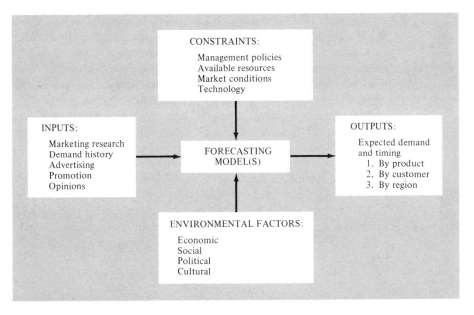

FIGURE 3
The forecasting function. [From Richard J. Tersine and John H. Campbell, *Modern Materials Management*, New York: North Holland, 1977, p. 49.]

The initial specification of outputs can simplify the selection of the forecasting model, but the forecasting function is not complete without the input considerations. No matter how long a system is studied, only a few of the many inputs can be isolated. Fortunately, most systems are relatively insensitive to most of their inputs. The size of the problem must be reduced by only including the most significant inputs to the forecasting models. These are the ones that will be closely observed for changes in the future.

The data needed to prepare a forecast can be obtained from internal and/or external sources. External sources may provide valuable information on environmental factors such as economic, social, political, and cultural conditions. The selection of forecasting models depends heavily on constraints imposed on the organization by management policies, available resources, market conditions, and technology.

Forecasting is a model-based information system, and there are many models from which to choose. Not only do they differ in techniques but also in effort and cost of implementation. Forecasting models can be classified as either qualitative or quantitative. Qualitative models rely on judgment, experience, and expertise; quantitative models rely on the use of historical data or associations among variables to develop forecasts. Some techniques are quite simple, while others are quite complex. Some work better than others, but no single technique works all the time. All forecasts include a degree of inaccuracy, and allowances should be made for it.

By knowing the desired outputs and significant inputs or variables that affect demand, different forecasting models can be analyzed. The forecasting model should be selected after consideration of user and system sophistication, time and resources available, specific use and decision characteristics, data availability, and data pattern (components). Sometimes a specific model will be indicated. When a single model is not apparent, several can be tested and the most reliable model adopted.

In general, the forecasting model should be matched to the knowledge and sophistication of the user. Some models require the user to analyze and interpret statistical measures. Managers are reluctant to use results from techniques they do not understand. Fairly crude techniques frequently enjoy widespread popularity because users are more comfortable using them. Thus, the forecasting approach should fit the organizational environment and the management expertise.

Many models require a substantial amount of historical data. If adequate and relevant historical data do not exist or are prohibitively expensive to accumulate, then many techniques automatically can be ruled out. All quantitative forecasting techniques depend upon the existence of adequate and accurate historical data. Elegant forecasting techniques applied to poor data cannot yield good forecasts. The choice of a forecasting technique is often constrained by the available data.

The demand pattern will affect the type of forecasting technique selected. If several components (trend, seasonal, cyclic) are apparent, more advanced techniques are needed. If the demand pattern is unstable over time, a qualitative technique may be needed.

Forecasting usually involves the following considerations:

1. items to be forecasted (products, product groups, assemblies, etc.),
2. top-down or bottom-up forecasting,
3. forecasting techniques (quantitative or qualitative models),
4. units of measure (dollars, units, weights, etc.),
5. time interval (weeks, months, quarters, etc.),
6. forecast horizon (how many time intervals to include),
7. forecasting components (levels, trends, seasonals, cycles, and random variation),
8. forecast accuracy (error measurement),
9. exception reporting and special situations,
10. revision of forecasting model parameters.

In most organizations, a small percentage of the material requirements represents a majority of the investment. These high cost or high usage items should receive the greatest degree of forecasting attention. There are also a great many low cost or low usage items that represent a small percentage of the total investment (although a high percentage of the number of items). Very little effort should be devoted to making forecasts for them. For low cost items, crude forecasts supplemented with large safety stocks are sufficient. Forecasting emphasis should be placed on those items that represent a significant investment.

Fortunately, many items produced by an organization do not need forecasts. Dependent demand items such as components, subassemblies, and services that are part of a finished product can be calculated from the forecasts for the end item. Forecasts should be made only for end items and services that have an uncertain demand.

The presence of randomness precludes a perfect forecast. Forecasts for groups (families) of items tend to be more accurate than forecasts for individual items, because forecasting errors among items in a group tend to cancel. Additionally, error potential increases as the time horizon of a forecast increases. It is well recognized that the accuracy of forecasts diminishes the further ahead in time they are projected. Thus, a short-term forecast is generally more accurate than a long-term forecast.

There are four basic demand forecasting models—*time series analysis, soliciting opinions, economic indicators,* and *econometric models.* These techniques are short-range forecasting devices, and their value diminishes as the time horizon increases. Many of the techniques are based on extrapolation into the future of effects that have existed in the past.

The forecasting approaches to new products and established products are dissimilar. For established products with a demand history, future activity can be based more quantitatively and objectively on past performance. The forecasting techniques of time series analysis, economic indicators, and econometric models can appropriately use conditions which prevailed in the past to approximate the future. New products with little or no history of past demand are unavoidably more interpretative and must rely more heavily on subjective phenomenon and solicitation of opinions. The direct survey approach—asking prospective customers of their buying intentions—is frequently used. An indirect survey approach may also be employed: information is obtained from people (salesmen, wholesalers, jobbers) who know how the customers respond. Also, if a comparable or substitute product exists, comparisons with similar products can be made. Finally, a limited market test of the new product can indicate product acceptability by potential customers.

There is no single forecasting technique that is superior in all cases, and the same organization can use different techniques for different products. It is difficult to ascertain the effect of changes in selling price, product quality, marketing methods, promotion, and economic conditions on forecasts. Regardless of the method adopted, the results provide the decision maker with nothing more than a starting point for making the final forecast. The final forecast usually requires an additional input in the form of judgment, intuition, and experience. Nor should any organization make a forecast and adhere to it blindly without periodic review.

TIME SERIES ANALYSIS

Time series analysis predicts the future from past internal data. A time series is a set of time ordered observations on a variable during successive and equal time periods. By studying how a variable (historical demand) changes over time, a relationship between demand and time can be formulated and used to predict future demand levels. In time series analysis, historical data are analyzed and decomposed to identify the relevant components which influence the variable being forecasted. Time series data may contain up to five interacting components—*levels, trends, seasonal variations, cyclical variations,* and *random variations*. Some or all components may be present. The components (except for the random variations) then are projected forward into the future. If historical components persist into the future, a reliable forecast will be obtained.

Levels indicate the scale or magnitude of a time series, while trends identify the rate of growth or decline of a series over time. As illustrated in Figure 4, the trend component indicates the long-term historical pattern between demand and time. It is given by a smooth trend line fitted to the historical data and rarely, if ever, coincides with the historical information. Instead, it depicts the general upward or downward movement of demand.

Seasonal variations consist of annually recurring movements above and below the trend line and are present when demand fluctuates in a repetitive pattern from year to year. The twelve month periodicity may be related to weather patterns, tradition, school openings, vacations, taxes, bonuses, model changeovers, or calendar oriented customs (Thanksgiving, Christmas). Examples of products with a seasonal pattern

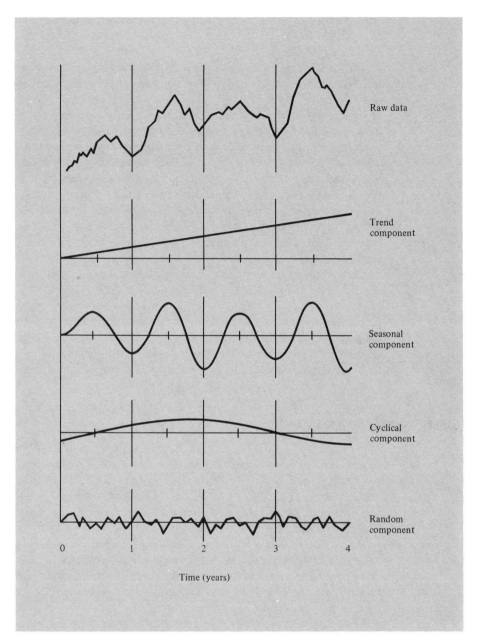

FIGURE 4
Time series components.

are antifreeze, soft drinks, ice cream, toys, snow tires, grass seed, textbooks, air conditioners, and greeting cards.

Before seasonal corrections are included in a forecast model, some conditions should be met. There should be some known reason for the periodic peaks and valleys in the demand pattern, and they should occur at essentially the same time every year. For the seasonal modification to be worth including, it should be of a larger magnitude than the random variations.

Cyclical variations are long term oscillations or swings about a trend line and account for some of the variation between the trend line and raw data points. The cycles may or may not be periodic, but they often are the result of business cycles of expansion and contraction of economic activity over a number of years. The familiar pattern of the business cycle, i.e. prosperity, recession, depression, and recovery, may vary as to the time of occurrence, the length of the phases, and the amplitude of the fluctuations. Although the business phases generally trigger some reaction in the plotted variable, the reaction to the cyclical influences within an organization also may be unique and inconsistent. Because the magnitude, timing, and pattern of cyclical movements vary so widely and may be attributed to several causes, there are no generally reliable methods of predicting their repetition. The available methods are beyond the scope of this section and too involved to be practical.

Random variations have no discernable patterns and usually are without specific, assignable causes. They represent all the influences not included in trend, seasonal, and cyclical variations. They include such things as measurement errors, floods, fires, earthquakes, wars, strikes, and unusual weather conditions. Many times an erratic occurrence may be isolated and removed from the data, but there are no general techniques for doing so. An averaging process will help eliminate its influence. Random variations are often referred to as noise, residuals, or irregular variations.

Past trends may be good indicators of the future, but the forecaster should be alert to factors that may cause severe abruption from the past. External factors frequently have a very pronounced effect on the future, and time series analysis tends to neglect them. Time series analysis is somewhat like driving your car down the road with the windshield blacked out, only being able to see through the rear view mirror. You cannot see where you are going, but only where you have been. If something is going to happen in the future which has not occurred in the past, there is no way time series analysis can be aware of it and respond accordingly.

There are many techniques for time series analysis. Some of the most common ones are last period demand, arithmetic average, moving average, regression analysis, and the exponentially weighted moving average. All of the techniques assume some perpetuation of historical forces and that past data are reliable predictions of the future. Inaccuracies result when past conditions change or cease to be operative.

The decision to adopt a new model or continue with the present one usually rests on some measure of forecast error. Each technique is tested on the historical data, and the one with the smallest forecast error is selected as the forecast instrument. Several measures of forecasting error are shown in Figure 5.

Forecast errors influence decisions in two different ways. One is in making the choice among various forecasting techniques, and the other is in evaluating the success or failure of a technique in use. Two commonly used measures for summarizing historical errors are the mean absolute deviation (MAD) and the mean squared error (MSE). The MAD is the average error, and the MSE is the average of squared errors. The difference is that one weights all errors equally, while the other weights errors according to their squared values. The MSE, unlike the MAD, penalizes a forecasting technique much more for larger errors than for smaller ones.

The MAD (*mean* is the statistician's term for average; *absolute* means the plus or minus sign is ignored; and *deviation* means the difference between actual demand

1. Mean absolute deviation (MAD) – extent:

$$MAD = \frac{\sum_{i=1}^{n} \left| Y_i - \hat{Y}_i \right|}{n}$$

2. Mean squared error (MSE) – extent:

$$MSE = \frac{\sum_{i=1}^{n} (Y_i - \hat{Y}_i)^2}{n}$$

3. Standard deviation of regression (S_r) – extent:

$$S_r^2 = \frac{\sum_{i=1}^{n} (Y_i - \hat{Y}_i)^2}{n-2}$$

4. Bias – direction:

$$bias = \frac{\sum_{i=1}^{n} (Y_i - \hat{Y}_i)}{n}$$

5. Tracking signal (TS) – revision:

$$TS = \frac{\sum_{i=1}^{n} (Y_i - \hat{Y}_i)}{MAD}$$

FIGURE 5
Forecast error measurement.

and the forecast) is obtained by dividing the number of observations into the sum of absolute deviations.[2] The MAD is calculated from the following formula:

$$MAD = \frac{\sum_{i=1}^{n} |Y_i - \hat{Y}_i|}{n},$$

where

$\hat{Y}_i$ = forecasted demand for period i,
Y_i = actual demand for period i,
n = number of time periods,
$Y_i - \hat{Y}_i$ = algebraic deviation or forecast error,
$|Y_i - \hat{Y}_i|$ = absolute deviation.

Forecasting is probably going to be wrong to some degree. It is useful to know how inaccurate the forecast is likely to be. The MAD can aid in this determination. It uses past history as the guide in trying to predict forecast error. When several different forecasting techniques are compared, the most desirable is the technique with the smallest MAD.

While the MAD expresses the extent of the forecast error, it does not indicate the direction. The direction of forecast errors is expressed by the bias, which measures the tendency to consistently overforecast or underforecast. An ideal forecast tech-

---

[2]For a normal distribution, the standard deviation is closely approximated by 1.25 times the MAD. The relationship between the standard deviation and the MAD is important in determining confidence limits for forecasts and in establishing inventory safety stock levels via computer routines.

nique would have zero MAD and bias. The bias is calculated from the following formula:

$$\text{bias} = \frac{\sum\limits_{i=1}^{n}(Y_i - \hat{Y}_i)}{n}.$$

A positive bias indicates a tendency to underforecast, while a negative bias indicates a tendency to overforecast. The inaccuracy (error) of a forecast is measured by its MAD and bias.

LAST PERIOD DEMAND

The last period demand technique simply forecasts for the next period the level of demand that occurred in the previous period. No calculations are required, and forecasted values lag behind actual demand by one period. Mathematically,

$$\hat{Y}_t = Y_{t-1},$$

where

$\hat{Y}_t$ = forecasted demand for period t,

Y_{t-1} = actual demand in the previous period.

The last period demand technique indicates that the immediate future is expected to behave much like the recent past. It works well if there is little variation in actual values from period to period. It responds fairly well to trends; it does not compensate very well for seasonals; and it overreacts to random influences.

ARITHMETIC AVERAGE

The arithmetic average simply takes the average of *all* past demand in arriving at a forecast. Mathematically,

$$\hat{Y}_t = \frac{\sum\limits_{i=1}^{n} Y_i}{n} = \frac{Y_1 + Y_2 + \cdots + Y_n}{n},$$

where

$\hat{Y}_t$ = forecasted demand for period t,

Y_i = actual demand in period i,

n = number of time periods.

The arithmetic average technique, unlike the last period demand technique, will smooth out random fluctuations; it will not adequately respond to trends in demand; and it neglects seasonals. Smoothing refers to the dampening or diminishing of random fluctuations and is synonymous with averaging.

The basic objection to the arithmetic average is that it takes too little account of recent data and is not responsive enough to changes in demand pattern. The arithmetic average works well in a stable situation where the level of demand does not change. It is appropriate for data that are stationary (horizontal) and randomly distributed.

MOVING AVERAGE

The moving average technique generates the next period's forecast by averaging the actual demand for the last n time periods. The choice of the value of n should be determined by experimentation. The objective of the moving average is to include a sufficient number of time periods so random fluctuations are canceled, but few enough periods so irrelevant information from the distant past is discarded. The moving average is computed over time, changing with the addition of new data and the deletion of old data. As data become available for each time period, the latest data are included and the oldest data are excluded from the computation of the mean. Mathematically,

$$\hat{Y}_t = \frac{\sum_{i=1}^{n} Y_{t-i}}{n},$$

where

$\hat{Y}_t$ = forecasted demand for period t,
Y_{t-i} = actual demand in period $t - i$,
n = number of time periods included in moving average.

This technique gives more weight to the more current time periods. How many periods to use in the average is difficult to say without examining the particular situation. If too few are used, the forecast fluctuates wildly, influenced by random variations in demand. If too many are used, the average is too stable and current trends are not detected. If there is a trend in demand, the moving average will always lag behind it. If the number of periods in the average is short, the lag will be small, and vice versa.

The moving average technique is a compromise between the last period demand and the arithmetic average technique with the advantages of both and the disadvantages of neither. If the demand rate is steady, the moving average will respond with fairly constant forecasts, as does the average method. However, when the average demand does change, the moving average forecast, like the last period demand forecasts, responds fairly quickly to the change, but without the extreme fluctuations that are characteristic of the last period demand forecast. Increasing the number of periods in the moving average will produce forecasts closer to arithmetic average forecasts. Decreasing the number of periods will produce forecasts closer to last period demand forecasts. The moving average dampens random effects, responds to trends with a delay, and does not compensate for seasonals.

EXAMPLE 1

Monthly demand in units for the last two years is listed below. Evaluate the forecasts with the last period demand, arithmetic average, and two-month moving average techniques. Utilizing the mean absolute deviation (MAD) as a criterion, determine the most desirable of the three forecasting techniques. What is the forecast for the twenty-fifth month with each of the three techniques?

Month	Demand	Month	Demand	Month	Demand
1	34	9	38	17	58
2	44	10	44	18	54
3	42	11	36	19	46
4	30	12	46	20	48
5	46	13	42	21	40
6	44	14	30	22	50
7	56	15	52	23	58
8	50	16	48	24	60
					Total 1096

The following table compares the three forecasting techniques:

Month	Demand	Last period demand Forecast demand	Absolute deviation	Arithmetic average Forecast demand	Absolute deviation	Two-month moving average Forecast demand	Absolute deviation
1	34	—	—	—	—	—	—
2	44	34	10	—	—	—	—
3	42	44	2	39	3	39	3
4	30	42	12	40	10	43	13
5	46	30	16	38	8	36	10
6	44	46	2	39	5	38	6
7	56	44	12	40	16	45	11
8	50	56	6	42	8	50	0
9	38	50	12	43	5	53	15
10	44	38	6	43	1	44	0
11	36	44	8	43	7	41	5
12	46	36	10	42	4	40	6
13	42	46	4	43	1	41	1
14	30	42	12	42	12	44	14
15	52	30	22	42	10	36	16
16	48	52	4	42	6	41	7
17	58	48	10	43	15	50	8
18	54	58	4	44	10	53	1
19	46	54	8	44	2	56	10
20	48	46	2	44	4	50	2
21	40	48	8	44	4	47	7
22	50	40	10	44	6	44	6
23	58	50	8	44	14	45	13
24	60	58	2	45	15	54	6
25		60		46		59	
	1096		190		166		160

The two-month moving average has the smallest mean absolute deviation, 7.27 (160/22); the arithmetic average has a MAD of 7.55 (166/22); and the last period demand has the largest MAD, 8.26 (190/23). The two-month moving average technique is the most desirable of the three techniques evaluated, and its forecast for the next month is 59 units.

REGRESSION ANALYSIS

Regression analysis establishes a temporal relationship for the forecast variable. The variable to be predicted (demand) is referred to as the dependent variable, while the variable used in predicting (time) is called the independent variable. A cause-effect relationship is implied. The simplest type of relationship is a linear association. Regression analysis by the least squares method will fit a straight line to a plot of data. The line fitted by the method will be such that the sum of squares of the deviations about the line is less than the sum of the deviations about any other line. The regression line will encompass the trend effect, but not the seasonal effect. The basic equation for a straight line that expresses demand (Y) as a function of time (t) is

$$\hat{Y}_t = \alpha + \beta t,$$

where α is the intersection of the line with the vertical axis when $t = 0$, and β is the slope of the line. The parameters α and β are estimated from the following formulas:

$$\beta = \frac{n\sum_{i=1}^{n} t_i Y_i - \left(\sum_{i=1}^{n} t_i\right)\left(\sum_{i=1}^{n} Y_i\right)}{n\sum_{i=1}^{n} t_i^2 - \left[\sum_{i=1}^{n} t_i\right]^2} = \text{slope},$$

$$\alpha = \bar{Y} - \beta \bar{t} = \frac{\sum_{i=1}^{n} Y_i - \left[\beta\sum_{i=1}^{n} t_i\right]}{n} = \text{intercept},$$

where n is the number of periods of demand data included in the calculation.

If the relationship between variables in regression analysis is not perfect, there will be a scatter or variation about the regression line. The greater the scatter about the regression line, the poorer the relationship. A statistic that indicates how well a regression line explains or fits the observed data is the correlation coefficient. The degree of linear association of the forecast variable to the time variable is determined by the correlation coefficient. The correlation coefficient ranges between -1 and $+1$. A high absolute value indicates a high degree of association, while a small absolute value indicates little association between variables. When the coefficient is positive, one variable tends to increase as the other increases. When the coefficient is negative, one variable tends to decrease as the other increases. Figure 6 illustrates typical scatter diagram correlations. The following formula for r^2, the coefficient of determination, is used to compute the correlation coefficient r:

$$r^2 = \frac{\left[n\sum_{i=1}^{n} t_i Y_i - \left(\sum_{i=1}^{n} t_i\right)\left(\sum_{i=1}^{n} Y_i\right)\right]^2}{\left[n\sum_{i=1}^{n} t_i^2 - \left(\sum_{i=1}^{n} t_i\right)^2\right]\left[n\sum_{i=1}^{n} Y_i^2 - \left(\sum_{i=1}^{n} Y_i\right)^2\right]}.$$

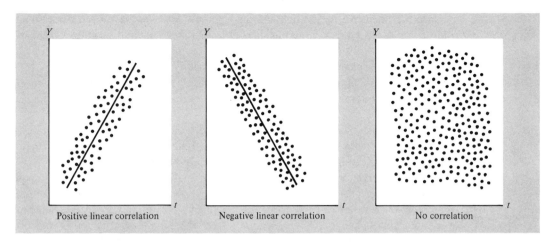

FIGURE 6
Typical scatter diagram correlations. [From Richard J. Tersine and John H. Campbell, *Modern Materials Management*, New York: North Holland, 1977, p. 57.]

The simple correlation coefficient measures the strength and direction of the relationship between two variables. The value of r^2 measures the proportion of the total variation of the dependent variable (Y) which is explained by the independent variable (t). The remainder of the variation $(1 - r^2)$ is due to chance or factors other than the independent variable. It is therefore desirable to have a value of r^2 as close to one as possible.

The following table represents a general rule of thumb for interpretation of the coefficient of correlation:

Absolute value of correlation coefficient	Interpretation
0.90–1.00	Very high correlation
0.70–0.89	High correlation
0.40–0.69	Moderate correlation
0.20–0.39	Low correlation
0 –0.19	Very low correlation

In linear regression analysis, it is assumed that demand is a normally distributed random variable whose mean is the Y coordinate on the regression line at that point in time. By knowing the standard deviation of the distribution, probability statements can be made about the reliability of the forecasts. It is assumed that the standard deviation S_r can be determined from the following formula:

$$S_r^2 = \frac{\sum_{i=1}^{n} Y_i^2 - \alpha \sum_{i=1}^{n} Y_i - \beta \sum_{i=1}^{n} t_i Y_i}{n - 2}$$

$$= \frac{\sum_{i=1}^{n} (Y_i - \hat{Y}_i)^2}{n - 2}.$$

Once the linear regression line and the standard deviation have been determined, control limits can be established at one, two, or three standard deviations from the mean. When the actual demand occurs, it can be compared with the control limits to determine if the demand is what could be reasonably expected. If the demand falls outside the control limits, there is reason to wonder if the cause system has changed. If it has, a new forecasting model should be developed to replace the inadequate model.

Frequently, time series data are autocorrelated or serially correlated. Autocorrelation occurs where one observation tends to be correlated with the next. Autocorrelation violates the conditions required to produce a valid regression estimate. To be valid, each observation on the data in regression analysis should be totally independent of any other observation. Time series data do not usually meet this condition, since most observations in the series can be forecasted by the last observation plus or minus a small change. This is especially true where a strong trend exists. Regression analysis requires that errors about the regression line be small and unrelated to each other and that their expected value be zero.

In some cases a high demand in one period may be an indication of a low demand to follow (the high demand could be due to advance stocking). This condition displays negative autocorrelation. In other cases, a high demand can arise from a cause which will also increase the following period's demand. This condition displays positive autocorrelation.

If autocorrelation exists, regression will underestimate the true variance and result in confidence limits that are too narrow. Autocorrelation may sometimes be corrected for by using first differences. With first differences, the observed datum Y_t is replaced with its first difference $Y_t - Y_{t-1}$. The extent of autocorrelation can be determined by the Durbin-Watson statistic or the von Neumann ratio, an explanation of which can be found in advanced statistics books.

EXAMPLE 2

Annual sales for the last seven years for an organization are given in the following table. Determine (a) the linear least squares regression line; (b) the standard deviation of the regression; (c) the correlation coefficient; (d) the forecasted demand for next year; and (e) the two standard deviation control limits for next year.

Year	Annual sales
1	$1,760,000
2	2,120,000
3	2,350,000
4	2,800,000
5	3,200,000
6	3,750,000
7	3,800,000

The following table develops the pertinent data:

Year t	Demand Y (10^6)	tY	t^2	Y^2
1	1.76	1.76	1	3.0976
2	2.12	4.24	4	4.4944
3	2.35	7.05	9	5.5225
4	2.80	11.20	16	7.8400
5	3.20	16.00	25	10.2400
6	3.75	22.50	36	14.0625
7	3.80	26.60	49	14.4400
28	19.78	89.35	140	59.6970

a:

$$\beta = \frac{n \sum_{i=1}^{n} t_i Y_i - \sum_{i=1}^{n} t_i \sum_{i=1}^{n} Y_i}{n \sum_{i=1}^{n} t_i^2 - \left(\sum_{i=1}^{n} t_i\right)^2} = \frac{7(89.35) - (28)(19.78)}{7(140) - 28^2} = 0.3654,$$

$$\alpha = \frac{\sum_{i=1}^{n} Y_i - \beta \sum_{i=1}^{n} t_i}{n} = \frac{19.78 - 0.3654(28)}{7} = 1.3641,$$

$$\hat{Y}_t = \alpha + \beta t = (1.3641 + 0.3654t) \times 10^6 = 1,364,100 + 365,400t.$$

b:

$$S_r^2 = \frac{\sum_{i=1}^{n} Y_i^2 - \alpha \sum_{i=1}^{n} Y_i - \beta \sum_{i=1}^{n} t_i Y_i}{n - 2}$$

$$= \frac{59.6970 - 1.3641(19.78) - 0.3654(89.35)}{5} = 0.01332,$$

$$S_r = 0.1154 \times 10^6 = \$115,400.$$

c:

$$r^2 = \frac{\left[n \sum_{i=1}^{n} t_i Y_i - \left(\sum_{i=1}^{n} t_i\right)\left(\sum_{i=1}^{n} Y_i\right)\right]^2}{\left[n \sum_{i=1}^{n} t_i^2 - \left(\sum_{i=1}^{n} t_i\right)^2\right]\left[n \sum_{i=1}^{n} Y_i^2 - \left(\sum_{i=1}^{n} Y_i\right)^2\right]}$$

$$r^2 = \frac{[7(89.35) - 28(19.78)]^2}{[7(140) - 784][7(59.6970) - 391.2484]} = 0.9824,$$

$$r = 0.991.$$

d: $\hat{Y}_8 = 1,364,100 + (365,400)8 = 4,287,300$

e: $\hat{Y}_8 \pm 2S_r = 4,287,300 \pm 2(115,400) = \$4,287,300 \pm 230,800.$

The two standard deviation control limits are $4,056,500 to $4,518,100.

EXPONENTIALLY WEIGHTED MOVING AVERAGE (EWMA)

The exponentially weighted moving average is a special kind of moving average that does not require the keeping of a long historical record. The moving average technique assumes that data have no value after n periods. Some value (although possibly very little) remains in any datum, and a model that uses all the data with appropriate weightings should be superior to a model that discards data.

Like most forecasting techniques, EWMA uses historical data as its prediction basis. It is a special type of moving average where past data are not given equal weight. The weight given to past data decreases geometrically with increasing age of the data. More recent data are weighted more heavily than less recent ones. The major advantage of the EWMA is that the effect of all previous data is included in the previous forecast figure, so only one number needs to be retained to represent the demand history.

The simplest EWMA model estimates the new average or forecast demand level for the current period from the most recent forecast plus a fraction of the error between the actual demand and the forecasted demand for the most recent period. In other words, a fraction of the difference between the previous period's actual demand (Y_{t-1}) and its forecasted demand $(\hat{X}_{t-1})$ is added to the previous forecast itself to obtain an updated forecast for the current period $(\hat{X}_t)$:

current forecast level $=$ (previous forecast)

$+\ a$(previous actual $-$ previous forecast)

$=\ a$(previous actual) $+\ (1\ -\ a)$(previous forecast),

$$\hat{X}_t = \hat{X}_{t-1} + a(Y_{t-1} - \hat{X}_{t-1}) = aY_{t-1} + (1 - a)\hat{X}_{t-1},$$

where

$Y_{t-1} - \hat{X}_{t-1} =$ error in previous forecast,

$a =$ exponential smoothing constant between 0 and 1.

For example, suppose you are attempting to obtain the forecast level of June sales by the EWMA. The relationships would be as follows:

$$\hat{X}_t = aY_{t-1} + (1 - a)\hat{X}_{t-1},$$

June forecast $=\ a$ (May actual) $+\ (1\ -\ a)$(May forecast).

The smoothing constant a lies between zero (no weight to recent actual data) and 1.0 (all weight to recent actual data). Small values of a put greater weight on historic demand conditions and have a greater smoothing effect (maximum stability with minimum responsiveness). Large values of a put greater weight on current demand conditions (maximum responsiveness and minimum stability). Stability is the ability to maintain consistency and not be influenced by random fluctuations, while responsiveness is the ability to adjust quickly to true changes in demand level. The appropriate value of a for a given set of data is determined by trial on a sample of actual past demand (retrospective testing). It is common to develop forecasting models on the first half of historical data and then test them on the second half.

Guideline values for a range from 0.1 to 0.3. Larger values of a may be used for short time periods when anticipated changes will occur such as a recession, an aggressive but temporary promotional campaign, introducing a new product, or discontinuing some products in a line. The value of a should allow the forecast model to track major demand changes while averaging the random fluctuations.

The general formula for the exponentially weighted moving average model is as follows:

$$\hat{X}_t = a[Y_{t-1} + Y_{t-2}(1 - a) + Y_{t-3}(1 - a)^2 + \cdots + Y_{t-k}(1 - a)^{t-1}]$$
$$+ (1 - a)^t \hat{X}_0,$$
$$= a\sum_{k=1}^{t}(1 - a)^{k-1}Y_{t-k} + (1 - a)^t \hat{X}_0$$

where

$\hat{X}_t$ = forecasted demand level for period t,

$\hat{X}_0$ = forecasted demand level for initial period,

Y_{t-1} = actual demand for period $t - 1$.

The EWMA attributes part of the difference between actual demand and forecasted demand to a real cause and the remainder to chance causes. The EWMA assigns to the demand values of the previous periods weights that decrease in an exponential manner (exponential decay) as the demand data are removed from the present (thus the name exponentially weighted moving average). The weight of past demands decreases exponentially because the fraction $1 - a$ is raised to a power. Notice that all the weights add up to one.

A general formula for expressing the weight of an individual demand value in a future forecast is as follows:

Weight = $a(1 - a)^{k-1}$,

where k is the number of time periods removed from the current period.

The table below shows the weight that is given to the actual demands of previous periods for a given exponential smoothing constant. When a is low, more weight is given to past data; when it is high, more weight is given to recent data. Note that when a is as low as 0.1, the three most recent periods account for only $0.1 + 0.09 + 0.081 = 0.271$ or 27.1% of the forecast value. However, if a is as high as 0.9, the three most recent periods account for $0.9 + 0.09 + 0.009 = 0.999$ or 99.9% of the forecast. If $a = 1$, the forecast is simply the last period demand.

Exponential smoothing constant a	Period weight				
	$k = 1$ a	$k = 2$ $a(1 - a)$	$k = 3$ $a(1 - a)^2$	$k = 4$ $a(1 - a)^3$	$k = 5$ $a(1 - a)^4$
0	0	0	0	0	0
0.1	0.1	.09	.081	.0729	.06561
0.2	0.2	.16	.128	.1024	.08192
0.3	0.3	.21	.147	.1029	.07203
0.4	0.4	.24	.144	.0864	.05184
0.5	0.5	.25	.125	.0625	.03125
0.6	0.6	.24	.096	.0384	.01536
0.7	0.7	.21	.063	.0189	.00567
0.8	0.8	.16	.032	.0064	.00128
0.9	0.9	.09	.009	.0009	.00009
1.0	1.0	0	0	0	0

With the basic EWMA model you can forecast more than one period into the future, but the more distant estimates are the same as the current estimate. The relationship to forecast n periods into the future when you are at the beginning of period t is thus simply

$$\hat{Y}_{t+n} = \hat{X}_t.$$

Of course the previous relationship assumes that there are no trend, seasonal, or cyclical effects in the data (only random effects need correction).

The exponential smoothing model without a trend correction reacts slowly to a big change in demand, since the change may be only a random variation. If the change reflects an actual increase or decrease in demand, it will continue in subsequent periods and the exponential smoothing system will track the actual demand and respond to it. The size of the smoothing constant a will determine the sensitivity of the response to changes in demand. Surges in demand can be satisfied by safety stock when a small value of a is used in the forecast system.

There is a direct relationship between the moving average technique and the EWMA without trend or seasonal effects. Just as the sensitivity of a moving average decreases as the number of time periods in the moving average increases, the sensitivity of an EWMA decreases as a decreases. In fact, if n is the number of periods in the moving average, then for the corresponding EWMA we have[3]

$$a = \frac{2}{n+1}, \quad \text{or} \quad n = \frac{2-a}{a}.$$

Thus, a moving average model with $n = 7$ is equivalent to an EWMA model with $a = 0.25$ and no trends or seasonal influences.

EXAMPLE 3

From the data below, determine the best forecasting method by using the smallest mean absolute deviation. Evaluate the last period demand, three-month moving average, and EWMA with $a = 0.3$. (Assume the initial LPD and EWMA forecast for month 1 = 185.)

	Demand		
Month	19X0	19X1	19X2
1	180	215	225
2	186	208	225
3	179	195	215
4	170	200	225
5	170	194	210
6	165	185	200
7	155	180	204
8	150	180	195
9	170	181	210
10	192	205	220
11	195	225	240
12	205	235	250

[3]See Robert G. Brown, *Statistical Forecasting for Inventory Control*, New York: McGraw-Hill, 1959, pp. 58–62.

The following table compares the three forecasting methods with fractions rounded to whole numbers:

Month	Actual demand	Last period demand		Three-month moving average		EWMA	
		Forecast demand	Absolute deviation	Forecast demand	Absolute deviation	Forecast demand	Absolute deviation
1	180	185	5	—	—	185	5
2	186	180	6	—	—	184	2
3	179	186	7	—	—	184	5
4	170	179	9	182	12	183	13
5	170	170	0	178	8	179	9
6	165	170	5	173	8	176	11
7	155	165	10	168	13	173	18
8	150	155	5	163	13	167	17
9	170	150	20	157	13	162	8
10	192	170	22	158	34	165	27
11	195	192	3	171	24	173	22
12	205	195	10	186	19	179	26
13	215	205	10	197	18	187	28
14	208	215	7	205	3	195	13
15	195	208	13	209	14	199	4
16	200	195	5	206	6	198	2
17	194	200	6	201	7	199	5
18	185	194	9	196	11	197	12
19	180	185	5	193	13	194	14
20	180	180	0	186	6	189	9
21	181	180	1	182	1	187	6
22	205	181	24	180	25	185	20
23	225	205	20	189	36	191	34
24	235	225	10	204	31	201	34
25	225	235	10	222	3	211	14
26	225	225	0	228	3	215	10
27	215	225	10	228	13	218	3
28	225	215	10	222	3	217	8
29	210	225	15	222	12	220	10
30	200	210	10	217	17	217	17
31	204	200	4	212	8	212	7
32	195	204	9	205	10	209	14
33	210	195	15	200	10	205	5
34	220	210	10	203	17	207	13
35	240	220	20	208	32	211	29
36	250	240	10	223	27	219	31
37		250		237		229	
			335		470		505

The last period demand has the smallest mean absolute deviation, 9.31 (335/36); the EWMA has a MAD of 14.03 (505/36); and the three-month moving average has the largest MAD, 14.24 (470/33).

EWMA WITH TREND CORRECTION

The simple EWMA model provides an adequate future forecast if no trend, seasonal, or cyclical effects exist. If a trend is present, the model can be extended to adjust two variables, the average level and the trend. First, the average level for the current period is expanded to include the previous trend:

Current forecast level $= a$(previous actual) $+ (1 - a)$

(previous forecast level $+$ previous trend)

$$\hat{X}_t = aY_{t-1} + (1 - a)(\hat{X}_{t-1} + T_{t-1}).$$

The current forecast level is then used to update the trend where the apparent trend for each period is the difference between the consecutive forecast levels $(\hat{X}_t - \hat{X}_{t-1})$. By smoothing the difference with the previous trend, the trend component for the current period is adjusted as follows:

Current trend $= b$(current level $-$ previous level) $+ (1 - b)$(previous trend)

$$T_t = b(\hat{X}_t - \hat{X}_{t-1}) + (1 - b)T_{t-1}$$

$$= \text{trend adjustment for period } t$$

where

$b = $ exponential smoothing constant between 0 and 1.

Using the calculations for the current level and the trend adjustment, the forecast for time period t is

$$\hat{Y}_t = \hat{X}_t + T_t.$$

Frequently a forecast of more than one period into the future is desired. Assuming a constant trend for future periods, the forecast for n periods beyond the current period t is determined from the following equation:

$$\hat{Y}_{t+n} = \hat{X}_t + (n + 1)T_t.$$

EXAMPLE 4

From the one-year record of monthly demand in the table below, develop a trend adjusted exponentially weighted forecast with $a = 0.1$, $b = 0.1$, $\hat{X}_1 = 40$, and $T_1 = 0$.

Month	Demand	Month	Demand	Month	Demand
January	47	May	38	September	47
February	42	June	34	October	54
March	16	July	45	November	40
April	47	August	50	December	43

The trend adjusted exponentially weighted forecast is derived in the following table:

Month	Demand Y_t	Level $\hat{X}_t$	Trend T_t	Forecast $\hat{Y}_t$	Deviation $Y_t - \hat{Y}_t$
January	47	40.00	0	40.00	7.00
February	42	40.70	.070	40.77	1.23
March	16	40.89	.082	40.97	−24.97
April	47	38.47	−.168	38.30	8.70
May	38	39.17	−.081	39.09	−1.09
June	34	38.98	−.092	38.89	−4.89
July	45	38.40	−.141	38.26	6.74
August	50	38.93	−.074	38.86	11.14
September	47	39.97	.037	40.01	6.99
October	54	40.71	.107	40.82	13.18
November	40	42.14	.239	42.38	−2.38
December	43	42.14	.215	42.36	0.64
January		42.42	.221	42.64	

In the above table, the forecast level for February is obtained as follows:

$$\hat{X}_t = aY_{t-1} + (1 - a)(\hat{X}_{t-1} + T_{t-1}) = 0.1(47) + 0.9(40 + 0) = 40.70.$$

The trend adjustment for February is subsequently obtained in the following manner:

$$T_t = b(\hat{X}_t - \hat{X}_{t-1}) + (1 - b)T_{t-1} = 0.1(40.70 - 40) + 0.9(0) = 0.070.$$

Finally, the forecast for February is

$$\hat{Y}_t = \hat{X}_t + T_t = 40.70 + .070 = 40.77.$$

All other values in the above table are determined in a similar fashion for the appropriate period. The process is very simple, although manually it is laborious and time consuming.

EWMA WITH SEASONAL CORRECTION

Seasonal demand patterns are characterized by recurring periods of high and low demand. Exponential smoothing models can be modified to account for seasonal variations. Seasonalization can be achieved by a set of seasonal index numbers which represent the expected ratio of demand for individual periods to an average demand.

The following example indicates how indices can be obtained from two years of past monthly data:

Month	Demand 19X0	Demand 19X1	Average	Seasonal index I_t
January	90	110	100	0.962
February	85	95	90	0.865
March	90	100	95	0.913
April	100	120	110	1.058
May	125	141	133	1.279
June	120	130	125	1.202
July	110	120	115	1.106
August	100	120	110	1.058
September	95	105	100	0.962
October	85	95	90	0.865
November	85	95	90	0.865
December	90	90	90	0.865
			1248	

$$\text{Average monthly demand} = \frac{1248}{12} = 104.$$

The indices in the above table are obtained by dividing the average monthly demand (104) into the respective average for each month. The seasonal index for the month of January is 100/104, or 0.961.

The most common methods of forecasting when there is a seasonal pattern depend on comparing the observed demand with that in a corresponding period in the previous year or with the average of the demand in the corresponding periods in several previous years. The standard for comparison is called a base series, and it has a value for each review period. The commonest base series is the actual demand during the corresponding months last year. If the peak demand shifts back and forth by a month or so from year to year, then the average of the demand in the three months surrounding the corresponding month last year may prove to be a more stable base series.

Exponential smoothing can filter out random effects for both deseasonalized demand and seasonal indices. Actual demand data are deseasonalized by dividing by the index numbers, and the resultant demand (with or without trend effects) is forecasted by a smoothing model. The index numbers also are updated by a smoothing routine:

$$I_{t+m} = \frac{cY_t}{\hat{X}_t} + (1 - c)I_t,$$

where

I_t = seasonal index for the period t,

c = exponential smoothing constant between 0 and 1,

m = number of periods in seasonal pattern ($m = 12$ for monthly data and $m = 4$ for quarterly data with an annual seasonal pattern).

If no trend exists, the forecast level with a seasonal adjustment is as follows:

$$\hat{X}_t = \frac{aY_{t-1}}{I_{t-1}} + (1 - a)\hat{X}_{t-1}.$$

The forecast for period t is the forecast level multiplied by the seasonal index or

$$\hat{Y}_t = \hat{X}_t I_t.$$

Dividing the actual demand by the seasonal index has the effect of deseasonalizing the demand. Multiplying the forecast level by the seasonal index provides the seasonal correction to the forecasted demand.

For forecasting more than one period into the future the forecast is determined as follows:

$$\hat{Y}_{t+n} = \hat{X}_t I_{t+n} \qquad \text{for} \quad n \leq m,$$

where n is the future period beyond the time period t for which a forecast is desired. Forecasts for future periods more distant than m can be made by reusing the appropriate seasonal index.

EWMA WITH TREND AND SEASONAL CORRECTIONS

If both trend and seasonal effects are evident, the EWMA model updates the level, the trend, and the seasonal index each time period. This process is accomplished using the following set of equations:

$$\hat{X}_t = \frac{aY_{t-1}}{I_{t-1}} + (1 - a)(\hat{X}_{t-1} + T_{t-1})$$

$$T_t = b(\hat{X}_t - \hat{X}_{t-1}) + (1 - b) T_{t-1}$$

$$I_{t+m} = \frac{cY_t}{\hat{X}_t} + (1 - c) I_t.$$

The updated results yield a forecast for period t when substituted into the following formula:

$$\hat{Y}_t = (\hat{X}_t + T_t) I_t.$$

For forecasting more than one period into the future the forecast is determined as follows:

$$\hat{Y}_{t+n} = [\hat{X}_t + (n + 1)T_t] I_{t+n} \qquad \text{for} \quad n \leq m,$$

where n is the future period beyond time period t for which a forecast is desired.

EXAMPLE 5

From the data given in Example 3 develop an EWMA model with trend and seasonal corrections for 19X2 from the data for 19X0 and 19X1. Assume $a = 0.1$, $b = 0.1$, $c = 0.3$, $\hat{X}_1 = 220$, $\hat{Y}_1 = 220$ and $T_1 = 0$. What is the forecast for March 19X3?

The seasonal indices are developed in the following table:

Month	Demand 19X0	Demand 19X1	Demand Average	Seasonal index I_t
January	180	215	197.5	1.049
February	186	208	197.0	1.046
March	179	195	187.0	0.993
April	170	200	185.0	0.982
May	170	194	182.0	0.966
June	165	185	175.0	0.930
July	155	180	167.5	0.889
August	150	180	165.0	0.876
September	170	181	175.5	0.932
October	192	205	198.5	1.054
November	195	225	210.0	1.115
December	205	235	220.0	1.168
Total			2260.0	

$$\text{Average monthly demand} = \frac{2260}{12} = 188.33.$$

EXAMPLE 5— *continued*

Month t	Demand Y_t	Level $\hat{X}_t$	Trend T_t	Seasonal index I_t	Seasonal index I_{t+m}	Forecast $\hat{Y}_t$	Deviation $Y_t - \hat{Y}_t$
January	225	220.00	0	1.049	1.041	220.00	5.00
February	225	219.45	−0.055	1.046	1.040	229.49	−4.49
March	215	218.97	−0.097	0.993	0.990	217.34	−2.34
April	225	218.64	−0.120	0.982	0.996	214.59	10.41
May	210	219.58	−0.014	0.966	0.963	212.10	−2.10
June	200	219.35	−0.036	0.930	0.925	203.96	−3.96
July	204	218.89	−0.078	0.889	0.902	194.52	9.48
August	195	219.88	0.029	0.876	0.879	192.64	2.36
September	210	220.18	0.056	0.932	0.939	205.26	4.74
October	220	220.74	0.106	1.054	1.037	232.77	−12.77
November	240	219.63	−0.016	1.115	1.108	244.87	−4.87
December	250	219.18	−0.059	1.168	1.160	255.93	−5.93
January		218.61	−0.110	1.041↵		227.46	

In the above table, the new seasonal index I_{t+m} for January of the following year is obtained as follows:

$$I_{t+m} = \frac{cY_t}{\hat{X}_t} + (1 - c)I_t = \frac{0.3(225)}{220} + (1 - 0.3)1.049 = 1.041.$$

The forecasted demand level for February is obtained in the following manner:

$$\hat{X}_t = \frac{aY_{t-1}}{I_{t-1}} + (1 - a)(\hat{X}_{t-1} + T_{t-1})$$

$$= \frac{0.1(225)}{1.049} + (1 - 0.1)(220 + 0) = 219.45.$$

The trend for February is obtained as follows:

$$T_t = b(\hat{X}_t - \hat{X}_{t-1}) + (1 - b)T_{t-1}$$

$$= 0.1 (219.45 - 220.00) + (1 - 0.1)0$$

$$= -0.055.$$

Thus, the forecast for February is

$$\hat{Y}_t = (\hat{X}_t + T_t)I_t = [219.45 + (-0.055)]1.046 = 229.49.$$

All other values in the above table are determined in a similar fashion for the appropriate period. The advantages of using a computer should be apparent from the tedium of the numerous computations.

The forcast for March 19X3 is

$$\hat{Y}_{t+n} = [\hat{X}_t + (n+1)T_t]I_{t+n} = \hat{Y}_{t+2} = [218.61 + 2(-0.110)]0.990$$

$$= 216.21.$$

A summary of the EWMA models outlined in this chapter is contained in Table 1.

TABLE 1
EWMA models

EWMA variable	Time series components			
	Random	Random/trend	Random/seasonal	Random/trend/seasonal
Forecast model $\hat{Y}_t$	$\hat{X}_t$	$\hat{X}_t + T_t$	$\hat{X}_t I_t$	$(\hat{X}_t + T_t)I_t$
Forecast level $\hat{X}_t$	$aY_{t-1} + (1-a)\hat{X}_{t-1}$	$aY_{t-1} + (1-a)(\hat{X}_{t-1} + T_{t-1})$	$\dfrac{aY_{t-1}}{I_{t-1}} + (1-a)\hat{X}_{t-1}$	$\dfrac{aY_{t-1}}{I_{t-1}} + (1-a)(\hat{X}_{t-1} + T_{t-1})$
Trend adjustment T_t	0	$b(\hat{X}_t - \hat{X}_{t-1}) + (1-b)T_{t-1}$	0	$b(\hat{X}_t - \hat{X}_{t-1}) + (1-b)T_{t+1}$
Seasonal adjustment I_{t+m}	0	0	$\dfrac{cY_t}{\hat{X}_t} + (1-c)I_t$	$\dfrac{cY_t}{\hat{X}_t} + (1-c)I_t$
Multiperiod forecast $\hat{Y}_{t+n}$	$\hat{X}_t$	$\hat{X}_t + (n+1)T_t$	$\hat{X}_t I_{t+n}$	$[\hat{X}_t + (n+1)T_t]I_{t+n}$

EWMA OVERVIEW

EWMA facilitates computation and reduces data storage requirements, which are important when many series are being forecasted. Exponential smoothing is computationally simpler and requires much less data retention than other techniques. In numerous instances, the forecast variable is serially correlated.[4] In other words, demand in the present period is closely and naturally related to demand in the previous period. EWMA is an excellent tool for treating serially correlated data, since it gives the heaviest weight to the most recent historical data.

EWMA is one of the simplest yet most flexible methods of forecasting demand from past observations. It is simple by comparison with the moving average in that it requires only two multiplications and one addition, and only two data in the simplest form. It is flexible in that the weight assigned can be easily changed or revised.

Considerable efforts have been made to obtain the best exponential smoothing constants *(a, b,* and *c)*. The techniques tend to involve enumerative computer programs that analyze past sales history and determine the best smoothing constants by a trial and error method. For data with no trend or seasonal effects, the only parameter needed is *a*. Since $1 \geq a \geq 0$, the best parameter value can be approximated by selecting the lowest mean absolute deviation (MAD) from testing *a* in 0.05 increments. Many analysts recommend that the smoothing factor be in the range from 0.05 to 0.30. When more than one smoothing factor is required, different possible combinations can be tested to obtain the combination with the least MAD. Manually, the process is very tedious, but with a computer it is not difficult.

In selecting a forecasting technique, it is common to apply numerous techniques to historical data and determine which technique best fits the data. A common criterion is to select the technique with the smallest MAD. The errors or deviations for each period are obtained by subtracting the forecasted demand from the actual demand. The *absolute* sum of deviations is used in place of the *algebraic* sum of deviations because it is possible to obtain zero as the sum of algebraic deviations even when the individual deviations are large. This situation is remedied by using the absolute deviation without regard to its sign. Once the specific technique is adopted, the algebraic sum of errors is also used to detect any positive or negative bias in the forecast.

The error in the forecast is defined as the difference between the actual demand level and the forecast demand level. If the error terms are plotted for a large number of forecasts, a frequency distribution is generated. The distribution for forecast errors should approximate the normal distribution. The dispersion (variability) of the error about the mean error (the mean error should be zero if forecast errors are normally distributed) can be expressed in a common form such as the variance, standard deviation, or mean absolute deviation. The mean absolute deviation is the most readily available measure of dispersion used in EWMA analysis.

The forecasting model having the lowest MAD over a period of time is most desirable. Concurrently, the algebraic sum of errors should cancel out (be at the zero level) over a period of time, so no bias remains in the distribution of forecast errors. The algebraic sum of errors helps to indicate how well the forecasting system is estimating demand. When the forecast fails to respond to changes in demand, the

---

[4]Autocorrelation analysis, which is beyond the scope of this chapter, will often reveal the existence of trends or seasonality in data.

sum grows larger and larger in a positive or negative direction. Positive errors indicate that demand is rising faster than the forecast, while negative errors indicate a decreasing demand.

After a forecasting model has been selected, it is necessary to monitor its performance. A tracking signal can be used to indicate when the forecasting model should be revised. A tracking signal will indicate when a basic change in demand dictates a revision in the forecasting model parameters. It is simply a method of evaluating when a forecast exceeds a tolerable error limit. The tracking signal is calculated by the following formula:

$$\text{Tracking signal} = \frac{\text{algebraic sum of forecast errors}}{\text{MAD}} = \frac{\Sigma(Y_t - \hat{Y}_t)}{\text{MAD}}.$$

The tracking signal is the ratio of cumulative forecast error to the corresponding value of the MAD. The resulting tracking signal is compared with predetermined limits, upper and lower. These usually range from ± 3 to ± 8. Errors that fall within limits are judged acceptable, while errors outside limits are a signal that corrective action is needed. The tracking signal is reviewed each period and a forecast revision issued if necessary.

Demand patterns for items are subject to change over a product's life cycle. Such changes dictate revisions of the forecasting model. There are many tests that can indicate the need for a permanent change, but usually a plot of the demand will suffice. Also, there are usually external environmental conditions that cause the demand changes, and managers are well aware of their existence and influence.

Sales promotions as well as other factors influence a forecast to such an extent that predictions based on intuitive judgments and experience may override a statistical extrapolation of past data. Forecasts cannot properly estimate future demand when promotional activities are involved. Special promotions and advertisements may produce an "artificial seasonal" effect. They can also borrow sales from the future and cause cycles. When past data contain unusual promotional effects, it is a good idea to "depromotionalize" the data to a normal level.

When the forecast is for many periods ahead, the EWMA can be a perilous technique. The use of a short term forecasting technique for a long time ahead assumes a stability that may not occur. The longer the projection, the less reliable the forecast becomes.

Time series analysis is best suited to items that have a continuous demand. For items with a discrete or lumpy demand, this mode of forecasting is inadequate. Lumpy demand exists when demand is nonuniform or occurs sporadically. It can range from high levels to very low levels or not occur at all during some periods (zero demand). Christmas trees, seasonal agriculture items, high fashion apparel, and repair maintenance items are examples. For such items a probabilistic approach based on expected demand or marginal analysis is appropriate.

In the EWMA only one way of handling trend and seasonality was considered. Trend was considered a linear or additive component, and seasonality was considered a multiplicative or index component. There are situations where trend might be considered as a constant percentage growth component, and seasonality might be applied as an additive component rather than a function of the level itself. There are other extensions that can be included in EWMA. The particular parameters to apply to the forecasting model are a function of demand behavior, and experimentation with the data is necessary before specific models are adopted. Forecasting model selection is a tailoring process.

BOX–JENKINS MODELS

The most sophisticated time series analysis method is that of Box and Jenkins. It is a systematic method that does not assume any specific model, but analyzes historical data in order to determine a suitable model. Their generalized model is called the *autoregressive integrated moving average model* (ARIMA). It consists of several possible separate model combinations. With statistical aids, an analyst rationally eliminates inappropriate model combinations until he is left with an appropriate model. The experience and judgment of the analyst are an important part of the selection process. The ARIMA methodology consists of three steps:

1. identification of a tentative forecast model,
2. estimation of parameters for the identified model,
3. diagnostic checking of the estimated model to determine its appropriateness.

An *autoregressive* model assumes that current data values are dependent on their past values. This means that current performance is a function of past performance. Such a model contains an autoregressive coefficient displaying the portion of the last period's performance affecting or explaining the current period's performance. The autoregressive coefficient is analogous to the slope in traditional regression analysis. A *moving average model* assumes that current data values are dependent on forecast errors of prior periods. The forecast error is the difference between the actual results and the forecasted value. This means that current performance is a function of the difference between the previous period's performance and its forecast. The moving average coefficient represents the proportional effect of deviations from the prior period's forecast on current performance. An *integrated model* is one for which the data have been adjusted for trend and/or seasonality. A given time series may be represented by an autoregressive model, a moving average model, or a mixed autoregressive integrated moving average model. The Box–Jenkins three-step procedure is designed to develop the ARIMA model that best describes the time series to be forecasted.

While the Box–Jenkins procedure can be effective in short-term forecasting, it has not been widely applied to individual item inventory control. The procedure requires large amounts of data for proper use, the tools are difficult to master, and the data must be transformed to achieve stationarity. It is more expensive than exponential smoothing. It is useful where only a few time series need to be forecasted and the extra expense is warranted.

SOLICITING OPINIONS

A subjective approach to forecasting involves the solicitation of opinions concerning future levels of demand from customers, retailers, wholesalers, salesmen, and managers. Through interviews and market research, estimates of future demand can be obtained from customers, wholesalers, and retailers. There are difficulties to this approach, since customers do not always do what they say they will, and it is not uncommon to obtain a broad spectrum of conflicting opinion.

If a sufficient history of past demand is not available, then forecasts must be based on market potential studies, general surveys, and whatever parallel experiences are available. These factors are then combined with selected experiences, insights, and intuitions. Internal opinions can be secured from salesmen and managers. Each salesman may be asked to estimate future volume in his territory, and the estimates of all salesmen can be added to obtain a forecast for the entire company. This collective opinion approach is frequently used for new products with no sales history, but it becomes ineffective as the length of the forecast horizon is increased.

This less elaborate and less technical approach makes use of the qualitative knowledge of people in the field and the home office. Forecasts of this type tend to be heavily influenced by immediate events. Also, when an estimate is developed from collective opinion, the final result may be more the opinions of a few influential or persuasive individuals rather than those of the group from which it was drawn.

The Delphi technique is designed to remedy some of the problems which arise in consensus forecasts. The technique attempts to maximize the advantages of group dynamics while minimizing the problems caused by dominant personalities and silent experts. An iterative procedure is employed to develop forecasts from forecasters (experts) on an individual by individual basis. Each expert develops his forecast for a well-defined event individually, without contact with other experts. The responses are summarized statistically and returned to the experts. The experts revise their forecasts, and the procedure is repeated until consensus is achieved. The Delphi technique has been used in forecasting future technological events, but it can also be adapted to other forecasting problems.

ECONOMIC INDICATORS

Economic indicators are frequently used to predict future demand. The knowledge of one variable is used to predict the value of another (prediction by association). The decision maker searches for an economic indicator (gross national product, personal income, bank deposits, freight car loadings, etc.) that has a relationship with the forecast variable.[5] A cause–effect relationship is not necessarily implied between the indicator and the forecast variable.

The simplest type of relationship is a linear association. Regression analysis by the least squares method will fit a straight line to a plot of data from two variables. The line fitted by the method of least squares will be such that the sum of squares of the deviations about the line is less than the sum of the squares of the deviations about any other line. A linear function has the form

$$Y = \alpha + \beta X,$$

---

[5]Sources of information on economic indicators include the Federal Reserve Board, Department of Commerce, Department of Labor, trade associations, and university bureaus of business research. Publications such as the *Survey of Current Business, Federal Reserve Bulletin,* and *Monthly Labor Review* are typical sources of economic indicators.

where

Y = dependent variable (variable to be forecasted),

X = independent variable (economic indicator),

α = intercept,

β = slope.

The parameters α and β are estimated from the following formulas:

$$\alpha = \overline{Y} - \beta\overline{X} = \frac{\Sigma Y - \beta\Sigma X}{n},$$

$$\beta = \frac{n(\Sigma XY) - (\Sigma X)(\Sigma Y)}{n\Sigma X^2 - (\Sigma X)^2}.$$

With the simple regression analysis, the forecaster seeks to discover those variables which have the greatest impact on the forecast variable. What linear regression analysis does is to compute a line which comes closer to connecting the observed points than any other line which could be drawn. It may be used to estimate the relationship between any two or more variables.

A statistic that indicates how well a regression explains or fits the observed data is the correlation coefficient, which ranges between -1 and $+1$. A high absolute value indicates a high degree of association, while a small absolute value indicates little association between variables. When the coefficient is positive, one variable tends to increase as the other increases. When the coefficient is negative, one variable tends to decrease as the other increases. The correlation coefficient is given by

$$r^2 = \frac{(\Sigma xy)^2}{(\Sigma x^2)(\Sigma y^2)} = \frac{\left[n\sum_{i=1}^{n} X_i Y_i - \left(\sum_{i=1}^{n} X_i \right) \left(\sum_{i=1}^{n} Y_i \right) \right]^2}{\left[n\sum_{i=1}^{n} X_i^2 - \left(\sum_{i=1}^{n} X_i \right)^2 \right]\left[n\sum_{i=1}^{n} Y_i^2 - \left(\sum_{i=1}^{n} Y_i \right)^2 \right]}$$

where

r = simple correlation coefficient,

$x = X - \overline{X}$,

$y = Y - \overline{Y}$.

The decision maker can verify the statistical significance of any derived simple correlation coefficient by using standard statistical tests found in many texts. A simple t-test can be used to verify if a correlation coefficient differs significantly from zero.

Similar to time series analysis, the standard deviation of regression S_r is obtained from the following formula:

$$S_r^2 = \frac{\Sigma Y^2 - \alpha\Sigma Y - \beta\Sigma XY}{n-2} = \frac{\Sigma(Y - \hat{Y})^2}{n-2}.$$

EXAMPLE 6

Find the least squares regression line and the coefficient of correlation of Y on X from the following data:

Y	68	66	68	65	69	66	68	65	71	67	68	70
X	65	63	67	64	68	62	70	66	68	67	69	71

We have

Y	X	X^2	XY	Y^2
68	65	4225	4420	4624
66	63	3969	4158	4356
68	67	4489	4556	4624
65	64	4096	4160	4225
69	68	4624	4692	4761
66	62	3844	4092	4356
68	70	4900	4760	4624
65	66	4356	4290	4225
71	68	4624	4828	5041
67	67	4489	4489	4489
68	69	4761	4692	4624
70	71	5041	4970	4900
$\Sigma Y = 811$	$\Sigma X = 800$	$\Sigma X^2 = 53{,}418$	$\Sigma XY = 54{,}107$	$\Sigma Y^2 = 54{,}849$

$$\alpha = \frac{\Sigma Y - \beta \Sigma X}{n} = \frac{811 - 0.476(800)}{12} = 35.85$$

$$\beta = \frac{n(\Sigma XY) - (\Sigma X)(\Sigma Y)}{n\Sigma X^2 - (\Sigma X)^2} = \frac{12(54{,}107) - (800)(811)}{12(53{,}418) - (800)^2} = 0.476,$$

$$Y = \alpha + \beta X = 35.85 + 0.476X,$$

$$r^2 = \frac{\left[n\sum_{i=1}^{n} X_i Y_i - \left(\sum_{i=1}^{n} X_i \right) \left(\sum_{i=1}^{n} Y_i \right) \right]^2}{\left[n\sum_{i=1}^{n} X_i^2 - \left(\sum_{i=1}^{n} X_i \right)^2 \right] \left[n\sum_{i=1}^{n} Y_i^2 - \left(\sum_{i=1}^{n} Y_i \right)^2 \right]}$$

$$= \frac{[12(54{,}107) - 800(811)]^2}{[12(53{,}418) - 640{,}000][12(54{,}849) - 657{,}721]} = 0.4937,$$

$$r = 0.702.$$

Many organizations are sensitive to broad economic trends, but finding a particular indicator of how operations will react to economic pressures can be a challenging task. Industrial sales tend to be sensitive to the GNP, but consumer sales are more sensitive to disposable income. There is even a class of products that behave opposite to the general movement of the national economy. The availability and cost of complementary and substitute products can complicate the economic indicator relationship.

An indicator is referred to as leading, coincident, or lagging depending on whether it precedes, parallels, or follows in time the demand it is being used to forecast. It is desirable to use leading indicators, since an economic indicator for a given period will be known only after the period has ended, too late to permit its use to predict sales for that period. If no lag exists, a forecasted value of the economic indicator can be used for prediction.

Multiple linear regression deals with the relationship between the dependent variable (variable to be predicted) and two or more independent variables (variables used to make the prediction). The difference between a simple linear regression and a multiple linear regression is in the number of independent variables used in the analysis. For example, for two independent variables the linear regression equation would be

$$Y = \alpha + \beta_1 X_1 + \beta_2 X_2.$$

In multiple linear regression analysis, more than one independent variable is used to forecast the dependent variable. An F-test is conducted on the multivariate model to determine if the model significantly forecasts the dependent variable.[6] In multiple linear regression analysis, the simple correlation coefficient is replaced with partial correlation coefficients. Partial correlation coefficients indicate the influence of each individual independent variable on the dependent variable while all other independent variables are held statistically constant. The significance of each independent variable is revealed by a t-test.[6] An insignificant t-test means that an independent variable does not significantly aid in the forecast of the dependent variable. A multiple correlation coefficient is analogous to the single correlation coefficient except it contains the contributions of several independent variables. In determining the multiple correlation coefficient, only those independent variables that have a significant partial correlation coefficient should be included.

With multiple regression analysis, the problem of multicollinearity can arise. Multicollinearity is the situation where there is intercorrelation between independent variables. When two or more of the independent variables are highly correlated, you are in effect using the same variable twice. In this situation, the forecaster simply deletes one of the related variables.

In many cases, the relationship between variables is nonlinear or curvilinear and a more complex type of analysis is required. Straight lines, polynomials, and logarithmic functions are frequently used when trends or growth patterns are present; trigonometric functions (sines and cosines) can be used when cyclic tendencies are present.

It is seldom practical to use economic indicators for item forecasts. They are usually used to forecast product groups or aggregate dollar demand for an organization. Time series analysis is much more practical for item-by-item forecasting.

Economic indicators are *associative:* they depend on the interaction of two or more variables. An important feature of economic indicators (as well as econometric models) is that they can be used to predict turning points in a demand function, based

---

[6]The F-test and t-test determine if the regression coefficients are significant. The F-test determines if $\beta_1 = \beta_2 = \beta_3 = \cdots = \beta_n = 0$, and the t-test individually determines separately if $\beta_1 = 0$, $\beta_2 = 0$, $\beta_3 = 0$, . . . , or $\beta_n = 0$.

on the changing values of known indicators. In contrast, time series analysis can only predict future demand based on the past demand; it cannot predict upturns and downturns in the demand level.

ECONOMETRIC MODELS

An econometric model is usually a set of simultaneous equations that explains the interactions of variables involved in a business situation. The models attempt to show the relationships between relevant variables such as supply, demand, prices, and purchasing power of the consumer. The models can become quite complex, since they analyze the causative forces operating on the variable to be predicted. Usually, they require forecasts of a number of structural variables.

The structural relationships of econometric models can be grouped into four categories—behavioral, technical, institutional, and identities. *Behavioral* relationships include supply curves, demand curves, and other curves that reflect the behavior of particular economic units (consumers, business firms). *Technical* relationships are mainly production functions that show input–output relationships as constrained by technology. *Institutional* relationships are specified by law or regulation and indicate the boundaries of acceptable social behavior (taxes, minimum wages). *Identities* specify balance relationships such as the definition of the gross national product (GNP), which is the sum of personal consumption expenditures, gross private capital formation, government purchases of goods and services, and net foreign trade.

A variant of econometric analysis is input–output forecasting models. These models consider intraperiod as well as interperiod dependences between sectors of the economy. Econometric textbooks treat model development in this area.

In order to capture all the interactions, the econometric model must have many equations. As more equations are added, the model becomes cumbersome in both the initial estimation and the required maintenance. Once a model is developed, its entire structure is known and its assumptions are in full view. Over a period of time, the model can be refined by new research. An econometric model may become very complex, because the phenomenon it is attempting to describe is not simple.

A possible way to estimate future product demand is to determine first the customers, their uses of the product, how much they need for each use, and when they will order the product. A mathematical model can then be built relating all the relevant factors. Because of the number and complexity of factors, a complete model is seldom possible. Approximate models can be built that are worthwhile. A difficulty with this approach is the cost as well as the time consumed in model development.

Econometric analysis usually requires a highly specialized professional staff as well as a computer. Thus it can be very expensive, and is usually confined to large organizations. Of course, the selection of a forecasting technique should not be based on cost alone, but on a cost-benefit analysis.

CONCLUSION

Forecasting is predicting, projecting, or estimating some future event or condition which is outside of an organization's control. While forecasting is not planning, it is an indispensable input into planning. Planning sets goals and develops alternative strategies to attain goals. Forecasting deals with the realm of matters outside of management's control. Organizations forecast so they can plan and help shape their future.

A demand forecast is the link between external factors in the organization's environment and its internal structure. The determination of the types of forecasts required and the establishment of procedures governing their generation are fundamental steps in the structure of a well-conceived organization. Forecast techniques depend very much on the number of items being controlled and on the type of operating system. Forecasts need to be made on a routine basis, so the techniques must accommodate the available staff skills as limited by the available computing facilities.

The forecasting of independent demand items is required for supply to be maintained in anticipation of demand. Forecasting is important when an advance commitment (to procure or to manufacture) has to be made. From the forecasts, operational plans are developed. The less flexibility there is in subsequently modifying original plans, the more important the dependability and accuracy of the forecast. There has been a substantial increase in the availability of sophisticated forecasting techniques, but increases in forecasting effectiveness have not been as pronounced. Unfortunately, poor forecasts are often a fact of life. Refinements in forecasting techniques are frequently less important than the development of operational flexibility to be able to live with poor forecasts.

Some useful generalizations about forecasting are as follows:

1. Forecasts are almost always wrong.
2. Long range forecasts are less accurate than short term forecasts.
3. Aggregate forecasts for families or groups of products are usually more accurate than item forecasts.
4. Only independent demand items should be forecasted; dependent demand items can be calculated.

A forecast is only an estimate of expected demand: actual and forecasted demand cannot be expected to agree precisely. Forecasts are only "ballpark" figures that permit the planning function to commence. Frustration should not result from the inability to predict the future precisely. With a properly designed forecasting system, uncertainty is kept to a measurable minimum.

Forecasters can be somewhat more confident about a range of values than about a single point forecast. A good forecast usually includes not only a single estimate, but an estimate of the magnitude of likely deviations as a guide to the comparative reliability of the forecast. Deviation is usually expressed by developing the best single estimate (expected value) and then establishing limits above and below that indicate the range of likely variation.

The tracking (forecast errors) of a forecast model is needed to verify the continued integrity of the model. Forecasting models must be revised when they are no longer appropriate. The tracking of a model can provide numerous benefits to management; it can

1. indicate the reliability of the existing model,
2. provide the criterion for forecast model selection,
3. facilitate selection of parameters (months in a moving average, or EWMA smoothing constants),
4. assist in establishing safety stock levels.

Reducing forecast errors requires increasing expenditures on forecasting techniques. Eventually one reaches a point of diminishing returns, and a perfect forecast is in any case an impossibility. Frequently, a much better investment is the development of operational and production flexibility that permits a rapid redeployment of resources in light of market changes.

Forecasting is an ongoing process that requires maintenance, revision, and modifications. The most obvious time to revise a forecast is when it is in error. Some techniques have built-in warning signals that indicate a departure from some predetermined tolerance range. Other techniques require personal surveillance to give the signal. Either way, the existence of the error should be communicated along with the causal relationships.

It is impossible to design decision rules and forecasting models that will cover every eventuality. The design is primarily concerned with routine, repetitive situations. Unusual situations that cannot be anticipated must result in a managerial override or interrupt. The computer can handle the routine occurrences, and the manager can devote his skill and experience to the nonroutine ones.

The techniques outlined herein are not intended to be exhaustive, but only to summarize prevalent categories. The imagination and ingenuity of a forecaster are vital ingredients in the design of forecasting systems. Although precise mathematical formulas give the impression that forecasting is a science, it still remains an art with a tenuous scientific superstructure.

QUESTIONS

1. List some factors which influence the selection of a forecasting model.
2. Discuss how the MAD, the bias, and the MSE are useful in evaluating a forecasting model. Which measure is the best?
3. Describe the areas of application for qualitative, time-series, and economic indicator forecasting techniques.
4. Name four components into which time series data usually are decomposed for analysis.
5. Cite some of the advantages and disadvantages of the last period demand, arithmetic average, moving average, and exponentially weighted moving average techniques.
6. Which exhibits a greater degree of linear association, a correlation coefficient of $+1$ or a correlation coefficient of -1?
7. Distinguish the methodology of economic indicator forecasting from time series methodology.
8. How does econometric forecasting differ from regression analysis?
9. Name two difficulties which occur when soliciting opinions for demand forecasting.
10. What independent variables might be used to forecast the following dependent variables: number of applicants to a medical college; annual beer sales for a brewery; demand for residential housing; and demand for farm fertilizer?
11. Distinguish between "fit" and "prediction" when used in a forecasting context.
12. How are the values of the smoothing constant a related to the number of periods in a moving average? How well do low values of a track rapidly changing demand?
13. In what instances would an organization choose to ignore available historical data and use a qualitative forecasting method?
14. Why does the exponentially weighted moving average (EWMA) not require the keeping of a long historical record?
15. What is meant by autocorrelated time series data?

PROBLEMS

1. From the data below, determine the MAD and bias for the following forecasting techniques: (a) last period demand, (b) arithmetic average, (c) two-month moving average. What is the forecast for period 7 using each technique?

Month	1	2	3	4	5	6
Demand	20	30	40	30	50	58

2. From the data in Problem 1, determine the linear regression equation. Determine the MAD and bias. What is the forecast for period 7?

3. Develop EWMA forecasts from the information in problem 1 using $a = 0.2$ and assuming the forecasted demand for the first month is the same as the actual demand. From the forecasts, determine the MAD and the bias for the EWMA model. What are the forecasts for periods 7 and 8?

4. Using exponential smoothing and the data in problem 1, forecast monthly demand if $a = 0.2$ and $b = 0.2$. Assume that the actual demand in the first month is the same as the forecasted demand and that the initial level and the initial trend for month 1 both are 10. From these results, forecast the demand for period 8.

5. From the analysis performed in Problems 1 through 4, which technique is most desirable?

6. If the simple exponential smoothing constant is 0.30, what weight is placed on the current period's demand after an elapse of four additional time periods?

7. Suppose a firm has been using a simple exponential smoothing constant of 0.25. You suspect that the model is overreacting to random fluctuations in demand. Should you try a larger or a smaller smoothing value of a? Why?

8. Suppose your organization has been using a six month moving average model and has been getting good results. Your boss recently purchased a desktop computer and an EWMA forecasting program. What simple exponential smoothing constant is equivalent to the old moving average model?

9. From the data below, determine the MAD and bias for the following forecasting techniques: (a) last period demand, (b) arithmetic average, and (c) three-month moving average. What is the forecast for period 13?

1.	93	7.	100
2.	105	8.	101
3.	114	9.	81
4.	111	10.	118
5.	106	11.	103
6.	116	12.	114

10. Based on the bias obtained for the techniques in Problem 9, is there a significant trend in the data?

11. From the data in Problem 9, determine the linear regression equation. Does there appear to be a trend? What is the correlation coefficient? What is the standard deviation of regression?

12. From the data in Problem 9, determine the MAD, the bias, and the tracking signal for an EWMA model with $a = 0.2$. Use a forecast for period 1 of 100.

13. From the data in Problem 9, determine the MAD, the bias, and the tracking signal for an EWMA model with $a = 0.1$, $b = 0.2$, an initial forecast of 100, an initial level of 100, and an initial trend of 0. (Assume period 1 as the initial period.) What is the forecast for period 13? Period 15?

14. From the quarterly data below, determine the linear regression equation.

1.	497	7.	821
2.	454	8.	1017
3.	624	9.	709
4.	764	10.	715
5.	631	11.	1794
6.	624	12.	1242

15. Using the data from the first eight quarters in Problem 14, compute the quarterly seasonal indices.

16. Using the data from the last four quarters in Problem 14 and the initial seasonal indices computed in Problem 15, determine the MAD and bias of an EWMA with $a = 0.2$, $b = 0.4$, $c = 0.5$, an initial forecast of 720, an initial trend of 65, and an initial level of 801. What is the forecast for quarter 13? For quarter 15? (Assume period 1 as the initial period.)

CASE 1: PAINT APPLICATION

Peacock Paint Supply is a full-service supplier of a wide range of home repair and construction products to homeowners and commercial contractors. Peacock carries a limited number of name brands and has exclusive privileges to market several brands in its immediate distribution area. The firm prefers to promote high quality merchandise and takes every step to remove itself from direct competition with discount supply houses. Peacock's product lines and personal level of service afford large and small customers a measure of quality unattainable at large discount houses.

The exterior paints Peacock stocks have both market recognition and distinct product advantages. Of its well-known brands, Peacock usually carries the manufacturer's base paint formula in gallon containers and colors it to customer specifications. Although some exterior paint is stocked throughout the year, there always are fluctuations in the demand for the highest quality paints, for two main reasons—first, the overall demand for exterior paint is by nature seasonal (even in Peacock's temperate weather location); and second, the particular brands Peacock carries have application directions which recommend use under specific weather conditions.

For example, Brand X is carried in large quantities during the milder months because of cold weather application problems and the increased demand for paint in general during warm weather periods. The manufacturer of Brand X also produces another exterior paint which has warm weather application problems and is suggested for conditions which run counter to those recommended for Brand X. Several products in Peacock's lines have such complementary demand patterns, but all of these products are considerably more expensive than year-round formulas.

Because of the undulating demand and relative expense of seasonal products, Peacock's manager, Art Plume, realizes that substantial holding cost savings can be gained during low periods of demand if unneeded stock is eliminated. In the case of the exterior paint, he would rather stock only enough paint to meet demand and not have excess paint on hand at the end of its peak season. Art also is aware that forecasting demand for each of the paints is critical to this goal.

The seasonality in demand always has substantially increased the difficulty of making a reliable forecast. Moreover, Art thinks the type of customer is particularly important in the forecasting process. Approximately 60% of paint sales is to local paint contractors, and 40% is to "do it yourself" homeowners. Past demand forecasts for commercial sales have proven to be much more stable than forecasts for homeowners. This contrast is accentuated by the preference of private consumers for prime weather conditions. A late fall or early winter can cause significant fluctuations in the demand.

So far, Art Plume has forecasted demand through experience. The accuracy of the experiential forecasting has been declining, and stocking has become a problem. Art's uneasiness about increased competition and the ever-growing need for efficiency have made him decide to improve upon experience. In addition to his direct observations and general knowledge of Peacock's customers, Art has decided to make specific forecasts. He has categorized past sales by month and customer type. The following table gives the compilation of three years of demand for Brand X:

	Brand X sales[a]					
	Contractors			Homeowners		
	19X3	*19X4*	*19X5*	*19X3*	*19X4*	*19X5*
Jan.	10	20	30	10	10	10
Feb.	20	25	30	10	10	16
Mar.	40	50	55	30	45	50
Apr.	55	70	80	75	60	65
May	110	120	140	80	70	80
Jun.	150	160	175	100	95	100
Jul.	170	190	210	100	90	110
Aug.	180	200	210	80	70	70
Sept.	160	170	165	90	100	110
Oct.	50	80	70	70	80	70
Nov.	30	35	60	20	15	20
Dec.	30	50	65	20	30	36

[a]In gallons of base paint.

Art still is flummoxed by the forecasting task. He wonders whether the same technique should be applied separately to each customer category or whether a single forecast should be made by integrating homeowner sales with contractor sales. Besides which forecast method is best in either case, he is concerned with what information other than past data might be useful to the forecasting process.

Use the information given, and:

1. List the points which are important to this forecasting situation in general.
2. Discuss whether Peacock should forecast for product groups or for individual items; whether Peacock should prepare forecasts for separate customer categories.
3. Subjectively analyze which forecasting techniques would perform best for Brand X. Experiment with different forecasting techniques, and check your empirical results against your untested judgments.
4. Discuss other techniques which could be applied if additional information were available. Include the applicability of economic indicators.
5. State what factors may affect and possibly bias forecasting based on historical data or qualitative input. What might be done to compensate for these?

CASE 2: ABBREVIATED DISCS

Hot Records had been a giant in the music industry since the industry's huge growth era of the '60s and '70s and was the undisputed leader in annual record sales in the rock categories. Hot had been the foremost representative for artists introduced in the U.S. on a nationwide scale until the tune changed and the record industry began its four-year decline of 13% of annual sales. The firm, which previously had spent lavishly on high living and frills, incurred serious financial setbacks when the boom went bust.

The music industry suffered for many reasons. A sluggish and inflation-ridden economy, fewer "mega" hits, record counterfeiting, limited radio-station play, high costs of producing and promoting records, poor quality recordings, and fierce competition from video games were blamed for driving music sales down. Hot executives believed their particular firm's losses stemmed not only from the causes cited by industry spokespersons but from the large prices charged for long-playing albums, from its inability to sign new artists or get signed artists introduced successfully, and most of all, from home taping. Hot's customers were wary of expensive albums, even those by major artists. The recordings by new artists aroused even more caution. The average customer, young and less able to afford luxuries during economically hard times, preferred to tape recordings and to spend money on video entertainment.

Hot executives now are excited by the apparent end to the downward trend of their maturing industry. While it is too early to label a music recovery a sure thing, a number of trends are running in the industry's favor. The recession is winding down, consumer spending is picking up, and an industry built on hits currently has a few "monster" successes. An important new source of support for records is unexpectedly coming from television. A cable channel which has become a big success is exchanging free air time for videotapes of artists performing their latest songs. The industry also has gone to records which come in more economical sizes and are of higher quality.

To undo the drop in its album sales and ride the crest of the music turnaround, Hot plans to introduce a line of twelve-inch "dance singles" called "shorts" which feature extended versions of hit songs and sell for as little as $3.49. It also plans mini-albums that carry half as many songs as regular albums, sell for $4.49 instead of $6.98, and contain some previously unreleased material. Hot hopes the shorter formats will overcome resistance to purchasing the long-plays. Figuring that these new records will be eye-catching in their reduced size, less expensive, and higher quality (with a cotton substitute for the expensive petroleum additive), Hot believes it has a winner.

The sole purpose of shifting attention to the "shorts" is to increase total sales. The expected increase, due in part to a perceived revival of pop music, is not precisely known. The Hot executives feel they can capture a large part of the album buyer's market and believe the new discs will serve to introduce artists who will later record on the long-plays. Though there is a consensus that the "shorts" are a solution to the sales problem, the management staff would like to know just how successful the undertaking will be. The staff has decided that forecasting should be done prior to the new releases. As to the type of forecasting technique, they are perplexed.

Since this is an entirely new line for Hot, the staff realizes an exact forecast is impossible. They cannot use any of the methods in practice for their established lines, but they wonder if a modification of one might suffice. One executive suggests that multiple linear regression, which is used with the regular album lines, would be suitable. She feels that the independent variables that affect regular discs, such as the general state of the economy, would be equally significant indicators for the new line. However, she welcomes more input from other record executives before she is prepared to declare an end to the sour trend and listen to the sweet music of success.

1. Discuss some difficulties in developing forecasts for new products.
2. Could multiple linear regression be a practical forecasting technique for the new line?

For total record sales? What other independent variables could be used in the predictions?

3. What new product features, technological changes, competitive forces, other external decisions or pressures, and industry as well as organizational factors affect the forecast and the selection of a forecasting method?

SELECTED BIBLIOGRAPHY

Box, G. E. P. and G. M. Jenkins. *Time Series Analysis: Forecasting and Control,* San Francisco: Holden-Day, 1976.

Brown, R. G. *Smoothing, Forecasting, and Prediction of Discrete Time Series,* New York: Prentice-Hall, 1963.

————. *Statistical Forecasting for Inventory Control,* New York: McGraw-Hill, 1959.

Chambers, J. C. et al. "How to Choose the Right Forecasting Technique," *Harvard Business Review,* July–August 1971.

Chisholm, R. K. and G. R. Whitaker, Jr. *Forecasting Methods,* Homewood, IL: Irwin, 1971.

Landau, E. "On the Non-Statistical Aspects of Statistical Forecasting," *American Production and Inventory Control Society Conference Proceedings,* 1976.

Makridakis, S. and S. Wheelwright. *Forecasting Methods and Applications,* New York: Wiley/Hamilton, 1978.

Tersine, R. J. and W. Riggs, "The Delphi Technique: A Long Range Planning Tool," *Business Horizons,* Vol. 19, No. 2, 1976.

Trigg, D. W. and A. G. Leach. "Exponential Smoothing With an Adaptive Rate," *Operations Research Quarterly,* March 1977.

Wheelwright, S. and S. Makridakis. *Forecasting Methods for Management,* New York: Wiley, 1977.

Whybark, D. C. "A Comparison of Adaptive Forecasting Techniques," *The Logistics and Transportation Review,* Vol. 8, No. 3, 1973.

16

Production Planning and Master Scheduling

FORMALIZED PRODUCTION PLANNING

PRODUCTION PLANNING METHODS
Charting Techniques
Linear Programming Techniques
Miscellaneous Techniques
Linear Decision Rule
Management Coefficients Model
Simulation and Search Models
Goal Programming

MASTER SCHEDULING
Master Scheduling Inputs
Capacity Constraints
Structural Features
Time Cycle Charts
Master Schedule Revision

CONCLUSION

QUESTIONS

PROBLEMS

CASES

APPENDIX A: MASTER SCHEDULE FORMAT

SELECTED BIBLIOGRAPHY

Production planning is concerned with the overall operation of an organization over a specified time horizon. It is also known by such names as aggregate planning, operation planning, and aggregate scheduling. From forecasts and customer orders, production planning determines the human and material resources necessary to produce the output demanded in an efficient manner. The goal is to effectively allocate system capacity (plant, equipment, and manpower) over a designated time horizon. The position of production planning in top-down planning is shown in Figure 1.

Production planning is an integral part of master planning in an organization. As indicated in Figures 2 and 3, various types of forecasting are necessary in master planning. The production plan indicates the organization's strategic position in response to the expected demand for its outputs. A good production plan should (1) be consistent with organizational policy, (2) meet demand requirements, (3) be within capacity constraints, and (4) minimize costs.

Production planning deals with output in broad terms. It usually uses a single overall measure of output or a limited number of product categories. Aggregates such as tons of output, hours of equipment time, hours of service, or number of customers are conglomerated. The conglomeration of products into a common output unit substantially simplifies the planning process. It permits top management to allocate resources in a general way without being engulfed in specific details. It is the big-picture approach to top-down planning.

After the product has been designed, the processes established, the plant laid out, and the demand forecasted, this combined portfolio of information is forwarded to production planning. Production planning assembles the engine of production by putting men, materials, and equipment together in an orderly fashion. Production plan-

FIGURE 1
Top-down planning.

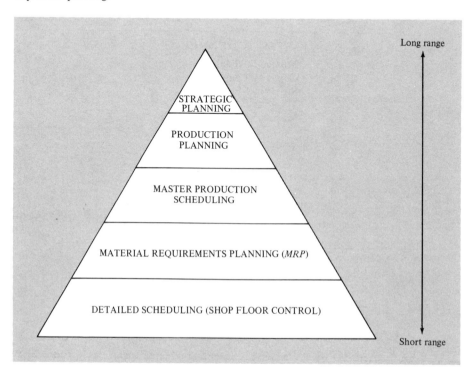

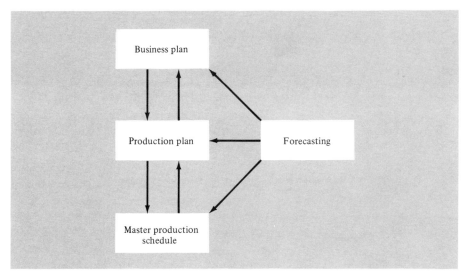

FIGURE 2
Master planning.

ning is confined to aggregates such as the total work force, output, and inventory. It is performed in broad and general terms usually at the product line level. Production planning establishes output levels for the forthcoming periods and projects the impact upon inventory, employment levels, and customer service.

The production planning function, as illustrated in Figure 4, devises production strategy in relation to aggregate levels of demand. If the demand for a product or service were constant, the planning activity would be trivial. With variability in demand, production planning takes on significance. The major strategy variables associated with production planning for variable demand are the production rate, the inventory level, the work force size, extra shifts, overtime, the product mix, and subcontracting. These strategy variables can be varied, modified, fixed, or nonexistent for any given organization, depending on its peculiarities and policies. Each organization is composed of an intricate and interdependent mix of labor, equipment,

FIGURE 3
Master planning levels.

PLAN	UNIT OF MEASURE	CAPACITY	TIME INTERVALS
Business plan	Financial aggregates	Plant	Quarters
Production plan	Product families	Plant	Months/quarters
Master schedule	Products	Depts./work centers	Weeks

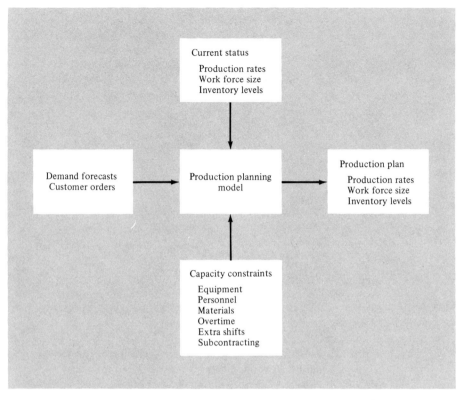

FIGURE 4
Production planning function.

and materials. Several potential responses to demand fluctuations are as follows:

1. Vary the size of the work force.
2. Carry finished goods inventory.
3. Utilize overtime.
4. Add extra shifts.
5. Vary the load by altering the product mix.
6. Subcontract work to other firms (the make or buy decision).
7. Vary the level of customer service.
8. Add contracyclical products to stabilize demand.
9. Vary marketing (price, advertising) to counterinfluence the demand pattern.

Demand variations can come from numerous sources. They may be random, or they may be predictable because of trend, seasonal, or cyclical influences. Most organizations do not follow precisely the ups and downs of actual demand. It is usually too costly to vary output levels substantially from time period to time period.

In production planning, the organization attempts to satisfy demand by manipulation of the size and combination of variables in its control. Pure and mixed strategies can be used to indicate how the variables are structured. A *pure strategy* means that output is changed by varying only one of the variables under management's control.

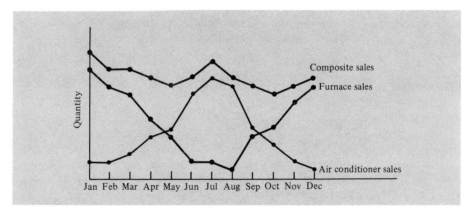

FIGURE 5
Demand effect of contracyclical products.

Four pure strategies for absorbing demand fluctuations are as follows:

1. Management may keep the work force and production rate constant, and allow fluctuations in inventory levels to absorb the fluctuations in demand.
2. The production rate may be altered by using overtime or idle time.
3. The production rate may be changed by hiring and firing, thus changing the size of the labor force.
4. Subcontracting may be used to meet peak fluctuations in demand.

A *mixed strategy* means that output is changed by varying two or more of the variables at a time.

More labor input will in principle generate more output, so work force increases, overtime, and extra shifts can expand capacity. Similarly, inventory can act as stored capacity in periods of slack demand and assist in smoothing the impact of demand fluctuations on employment levels. During periods of low demand, fixed production rates result in inventory level increases; during high demand periods, inventory is depleted while fixed production levels are maintained.

Every strategy has countervailing costs associated with it. Varying employment levels results in training, hiring, severance, and unemployment compensation costs. Idle time is an obvious waste, while shift work and overtime command a premium. Inventory has a high holding cost as well as a stockout cost. Subcontracting costs are usually above in-house costs, while capacity expansion involves a capital expenditure as well as a risk. The most favorable solution is usually a combination or mixed strategy that meets the objectives of the organization in light of its particular circumstances.

Organizations can respond passively or actively to their demand. A passive response means the organization takes demand as given. Many organizations, however, attempt to influence their demand in some manner. During normally low demand periods, increased demand can be generated through price cuts, increased promotion, and advertising. As shown in Figure 5, the adoption of contracyclical products can add stability to demand. Products that have peaked demand while other products are in off season can balance the capacity utilization of operations. Order backlogs are also used to maintain production stability.

FORMALIZED PRODUCTION PLANNING

A structured approach to production planning is as follows:

1. Determine organizational policy regarding controllable variables.
2. Establish the forecasting time period and the horizon of the production plan.
3. Develop the demand forecasting system.
4. Select an appropriate unit of aggregate capacity.
5. Determine the relevant cost structures.
6. Use an appropriate production planning method.

Aggregate planning methods are based on organizational objectives and strategies. An organization tends to develop an institutionalized value system that guides the decision process. Planning decisions are value-laden and full of conflicts and trade-offs. A typical goal is to develop a plan that will satisfy or meet demand within the limits of available resources at the least cost. However, there are usually other objectives to satisfy. The interests of various parties must be reconciled. For example, employment stabilization is important for many organizations as a matter of social responsibility.

All forecasts are made for time intervals or incremental periods of time. The horizon of a production plan usually comprises several time intervals. The time intervals are usually weekly, monthly, or quarterly. The length of the time horizon will tend to vary from organization to organization. However, it should be sufficiently long so that changes can easily be made in the controllable variables. The minimum time horizon is also constrained by the product line with the longest combined lead time.

There are numerous good forecasting techniques available. Management must select a demand forecasting system that meets their particular needs. The forecasting system should provide production planning with an aggregate forecast of demand based on a common overall unit of capacity. The overall unit of capacity may be production units, machine-hours, man-hours, tons, etc.

To analyze different alternatives, it is necessary to know the relevant costs. The criterion for judging the best plan is based on minimization of costs. The primary cost considerations are as follows:

1. Costs of production rate changes
   a. Undertime (underutilization of workers)
   b. Overtime (overtime and multiple shifts)
2. Costs of work force changes
   a. Work force increase (hiring and training)
   b. Work force decrease (severance and unemployment insurance)
3. Costs of inventory changes
   a. Inventory decreases (lower customer service and stockouts)
   b. Inventory increases (storage, obsolescence, deterioration, shrinkage, insurance, and opportunity costs)

PRODUCTION PLANNING METHODS

The production planning method will take the expected demand per period and develop a production plan from it. There are numerous methods available that range widely in sophistication and level of expertise. The methods range from simple charts, through linear programming (transportation) models, to sophisticated nonlinear and heuristic search techniques. There is no single, rigorous analytical method for solving such problems in real-world situations. Because several of the variables involved are interdependent and intangible, production planning methods usually do not yield truly optimal solutions.

CHARTING TECHNIQUES

Charting (graphical and tabular) approaches usually work with a few variables at a time on a trial and error basis. Various alternatives are tested, and the final selection is usually the alternative with the lowest cost. Unfortunately, there are theoretically thousands of mixed strategy combinations that can be investigated. The realities of the situation generally reduce the alternatives to a more manageable number. An evaluation of the alternative production plans is made on an incremental cost basis. A few examples will illustrate the charting approach.

EXAMPLE 1

You are supplied with a monthly demand forecast, an organizational policy of requiring 10% of a month's forecast as safety stock, and the number of operating days available each month. There is no inventory available at the beginning of the first month, January. The following table contains the demand requirements:

	January	February	March	April	May	June
1. Beginning inventory	0	1,000	1,500	3,000	2,700	3,000
2. Forecasted demand	10,000	15,000	30,000	27,000	30,000	16,000
3. Safety stock	1,000	1,500	3,000	2,700	3,000	1,600
4. Production requirements (2 + 3 − 1)	11,000	15,500	31,500	26,700	30,300	14,600
5. Operating days	22	19	21	21	22	20
6. Cumulative forecasted demand	10,000	25,000	55,000	82,000	112,000	128,000
7. Cumulative production requirements	11,000	26,500	58,000	84,700	115,000	129,600
8. Cumulative operating days	22	41	62	83	105	125

The costs for the organization are as follows:

Manufacturing cost/unit	$100
Inventory holding cost[a]	$2.00/unit-month
Hourly wage rate	$8.00
Stockout cost per unit	$5.00
Hourly overtime wage rate	150%, or $12.00
Subcontracting cost/unit	$104
Labor hours/unit	4 hours
Layoff cost/worker	$500
Hiring and training cost/worker	$400

[a]2% of manufacturing cost per month.

continued

EXAMPLE 1— *continued*

Three potential plans for the production are:

1. Produce to exact production requirements by varying the size of the work force on regular hours. Assume there are 250 workers available in January.
2. Maintain a constant work force of 518 workers. Assume no subcontracting is available and inventory will fluctuate with stockouts filled from the following month's production.
3. Produce with a fixed work force of 500 on regular time and subcontract all excess demand over the period production. Inventory will increase when production exceeds demand; no stockouts are permitted.

Each of the three plans is tabulated in Table 1, and a comparison is made in Table 2. Plan 2 with the constant work force and production rate with variable inventory and stockouts results in the lowest incremental cost, $102,176. There are obviously many other plans that could be evaluated.

TABLE 1
Three possible strategies

Plan 1

Month	1 Unit production required	2 Production hours required [(col. 1) × 4]	3 Available hours per month per worker [(no. of days) × 8]	4 Workers required [(col. 2)/ (col. 3)]	5 No. of workers hired[a]	6 No. of workers laid off[a]	7 Hiring cost [(col. 5) × $400]	8 Layoff cost [(col. 6) × $500]
Jan.	11,000	44,000	176	250	0	0	0	0
Feb.	15,500	62,000	152	408	158	0	$ 63,200	0
Mar.	31,500	126,000	168	750	342	0	$136,800	0
Apr.	26,700	106,800	168	636	0	114	0	$ 57,000
May	30,300	121,200	176	689	53	0	$ 21,200	0
Jun.	14,600	58,400	160	365	0	324	0	$162,000
							$221,200	$219,000

Plan 2

Month	1 Unit production required	2 Production hours available [(no. of days) × 8 × 518]	3 Units produced [(col. 2)/4]	4 Ending inventory[b]	5 Inventory holding cost[c]	6 Stockout cost[d]
Jan.	11,000	91,168	22,792	11,792	$23,584	0
Feb.	15,500	78,736	19,684	15,976	31,952	0
Mar.	31,500	87,024	21,756	6,232	12,464	0
Apr.	26,700	87,024	21,756	1,288	2,576	0
May	30,300	91,168	22,792	(−6,220)	0	31,100
Jun.	14,600	82,880	20,720	(−100)	0	500
					$70,576	$31,600

TABLE 1 *(continued)*

	Plan 3						
	1	*2*	*3*	*4*	*5*	*6*	*7*
Month	Unit production required	Production hours available [(no. of days) × 8 × 500]	Units produced [(col. 2)/4]	Units subcontracted[e]	Ending inventory[e]	Subcontracting cost [(col. 4) × $4]	Inventory holding cost [(col. 5) × $2]
Jan.	11,000	88,000	22,000	0	11,000	0	$22,000
Feb.	15,500	76,000	19,000	0	14,500	0	29,000
Mar.	31,500	84,000	21,000	0	4,000	0	8,000
Apr.	26,700	84,000	21,000	1,700	0	$ 6,800	0
May	30,300	88,000	22,000	8,300	0	$33,200	0
Jun.	14,600	80,000	20,000	0	5,400	0	10,800
						$40,000	$69,800

[a]If the difference (col. 4)$_{t+1}$ − (col.4)$_t$ is positive, it represents the number of workers hired. If negative, it represents the number laid off.

[b]Ending inventory is (beginning inventory) + (units produced) − (unit production required).

[c]Inventory holding cost is the positive ending inventory balance times 2.

[d]Stockout cost is the negative ending inventory balance times 5.

[e]Ending inventory is (beginning inventory) + (units produced) − (unit production required). When a negative number is obtained for ending inventory, it represents the units subcontracted, and ending inventory is recorded as zero.

TABLE 2
Comparison of the three plans

Cost item	Plan 1 (exact production; vary work force)	Plan 2 (constant work force; vary inventory and stockouts)	Plan 3 (constant work force; vary inventory and subcontract)
Hiring cost	$221,200	0	0
Layoff cost	219,000	0	0
Inventory holding cost	0	$ 70,576	$ 69,800
Stockout cost	0	31,600	0
Subcontract cost	0	0	$ 40,000
	$440,200	$102,176	$109,800

The previous example evaluated only three production plans. With most charting techniques it is impossible to know if an optimum production plan in terms of lowest cost has been obtained. There are just too many possibilities. If an organization has several of the variables fixed, it is possible to obtain an optimum production plan within the limits of its fixed contraints. The following example will illustrate such a possibility.

EXAMPLE 2

An organization uses overtime, inventory, and subcontracting to absorb fluctuations in demand. A production plan for 12 months is devised and updated each month. The expected demand for the next 12 periods is as follows:

continued

EXAMPLE 2— *continued*

Time period	1	2	3	4	5	6	7	8	9	10	11	12
Unit demand (10³)	10	15	30	27	30	16	12	10	18	26	30	15

The following costs and constraints are relevant:

Maximum regular production/period	19,000 units
Maximum overtime production/period	4,000 units
Regular production cost	$30/unit
Overtime production cost	$35/unit
Subcontracting cost	$37/unit
Inventory holding cost/period	$1/unit

What is the optimum production plan for the next 12 months (assume beginning inventory is zero, desired ending inventory is zero, and no stockouts can be tolerated)?

From the costs and constraints it is apparent that it is desirable to produce to inventory on regular time for five holding periods before overtime production is economic. Overtime production should be used for two holding periods before subcontracting is desirable. Production to inventory on regular time should be used for seven holding periods before subcontracting is desirable. If units are not used in the period in which they are produced, holding costs are incurred. With these cost tradeoffs in mind, the optimum production plan will be devised in the following table:

			Strategy variables[a]			
Period	Demand	Beginning inventory[b]	Regular production	Overtime production	Sub-contract	Ending inventory[b]
1	10	0	10(1),7(3),2(4)			9
2	15	9	15(2),4(3)			13
3	30	13	19(3)	2(4),2(5)		6
4	27	6	19(4)	4(4)		2
5	30	2	19(5)	4(5)	5(5)	0
6	16	0	16(6),1(11)			1
7	12	1	12(7),7(11)			8
8	10	8	10(8),6(10),3(11)			17
9	18	17	18(9),1(10)			18
10	26	18	19(10)			11
11	30	11	19(11)			0
12	15	0	15(12)			0

[a]The quantity to be produced is entered in the row associated with the production time period. The parentheses immediately after the production quantity indicate the time period in which it will be demanded.

[b]The beginning and ending inventory columns are determined after all the strategy variables are assigned.

The production plan is as follows:

	Period											
Strategy variable	1	2	3	4	5	6	7	8	9	10	11	12
Regular production	19	19	19	19	19	17	19	19	19	19	19	15
Overtime production			4	4	4							
Subcontract					5							
Total	19	19	23	23	28	17	19	19	19	19	19	15

Charting techniques are useful in evaluating previously proposed production plans. They do not necessarily suggest better plans, nor do they guarantee an optimal plan. It is necessary to try new plans or revisions to plans until a satisfactory one is found. Charting techniques are usually trial-and-error approaches to the problem.

LINEAR PROGRAMMING TECHNIQUES

Since production planning involves the allocation of capacity (supply) to meet expected requirements (demand), it should be no surprise that linear programming can develop the plan. Linear programming deals with the allocation of scarce resources among competing demands that have varying degrees of utility (desirableness). The supply consists of inventory on hand plus units that can be produced during the period. The demand consists of expected unit requirements plus any de-

TABLE 3
Linear programming tableau

Supply from		Demand for							Total capacity available (supply)
		Period 1	Period 2	Period 3	Period 4	Period 5	Period 6	Unused capacity	
Beginning inventory									
1	Regular								
	Overtime								
	Subcontract								
2	Regular								
	Overtime								
	Subcontract								
3	Regular								
	Overtime								
	Subcontract								
4	Regular								
	Overtime								
	Subcontract								
5	Regular								
	Overtime								
	Subcontract								
6	Regular								
	Overtime								
	Subcontract								
Demand									

sired ending inventory. The transportation method of linear programming developed in Chapter 5 can have direct application in production planning.[1]

A typical linear programming tableau for production planning is shown in Table 3. The sources of supply are beginning inventory and the units produced each period by regular time, overtime, and subcontracting. The demand for each period is simply the expected unit requirements. A simplified example will illustrate the use of the technique.

EXAMPLE 3

An organization with a stable work force uses inventory, overtime, and subcontracting to meet demand requirements. No shortages are permitted, and demand must be satisfied through in-house production or subcontracting. The following data are available for the upcoming periods:

Period	Expected demand (units)	Regular capacity (units)	Overtime capacity (units)	Subcontract capacity (units)
1	1,000	600	180	200
2	500	500	150	200
3	700	600	180	200
4	800	650	200	200
5	900	600	180	200
6	900	600	180	200
	4,800	3,550	1,070	1,200

The beginning inventory at the start of period 1 is 200 units and the desired ending inventory for period 6 is 100 units. The relevant cost data are as follows:

Regular cost/unit	$100
Overtime cost/unit	$125
Subcontract cost/unit	$130
Inventory holding cost/period	$2/unit

Determine the production plan that will satisfy demand at minimum cost.

The problem is attacked by starting with a linear programming tableau as shown in Table 3. The last column in the tableau (total capacity available) is filled in, as is the last row (demand). On an incremental cost basis, the regular cost per unit of $100 is assigned a zero value; the overtime cost becomes $25/unit, and the subcontract cost becomes $30/unit. The appropriate incremental costs are added to each feasible cell in the tableau. The next step is to assign available capacity to meet the demand requirement at the least cost. When all the demand has been satisfied without violating the capacity constraints, the problem is solved.

The optimum production plan is contained in Table 4. The following should be noted:

1. Total capacity exceeds demand, so a "slack" demand of unused capacity is added to achieve the required balance of supply and demand.
2. The beginning inventory of 200 units is available at no additional cost if used in

---

[1]E. H. Bowman, "Production Planning by the Transportation Method of Linear Programming," *Journal of Operations Research*, February 1956.

TABLE 4
Linear programming tableau

Supply from		Demand for — Period 1	Period 2	Period 3	Period 4	Period 5	Period 6	Unused capacity	Total capacity available (supply)
Beginning Inventory		200 (0)	(2)	(4)	(6)	(8)	(10)	(0)	200
1	Regular	600 (0)	(2)	(4)	(6)	(8)	(10)	(0)	600
1	Overtime	180 (25)	(27)	(29)	(31)	(33)	(35)	(0)	180
1	Subcontract	20 (30)	(32)	(34)	(36)	(38)	(40)	180 (0)	200
2	Regular		500 (0)	(2)	(4)	(6)	(8)	(0)	500
2	Overtime		(25)	(27)	(29)	(31)	(33)	150 (0)	150
2	Subcontract		(30)	(32)	(34)	(36)	(38)	200 (0)	200
3	Regular			600 (0)	(2)	(4)	(6)	(0)	600
3	Overtime			100 (25)	(27)	70 (29)	10 (31)	(0)	180
3	Subcontract			(30)	(32)	(34)	(36)	200 (0)	200
4	Regular				650 (0)	(2)	(4)	(0)	650
4	Overtime				150 (25)	50 (27)	(29)	(0)	200
4	Subcontract				(30)	(32)	(34)	200 (0)	200
5	Regular					600 (0)	(2)	(0)	600
5	Overtime					180 (25)	(27)	(0)	180
5	Subcontract					(30)	10 (32)	190 (0)	200
6	Regular						600 (0)	(0)	600
6	Overtime						180 (25)	(0)	180
6	Subcontract						200 (30)	(0)	200
Demand		1,000	500	700	800	900	1,000	1,120	6,020

period 1. Holding cost is $2/unit if units are retained until period 2, $4/unit until period 3, and so on.

3. Regular cost per unit is assigned a zero incremental cost if used in the month produced; otherwise a holding cost of $2/unit-period is added on for each month the units are retained.

4. Overtime cost per unit is assigned a $25 incremental cost if used in the month produced; otherwise a holding cost of $2/unit-period is incurred as in the regular situation.

5. Subcontract cost per unit is assigned a $30 incremental cost if used in the period produced. If unused in the period, a holding cost of $2/unit-period is incurred.

6. The desired ending inventory (100 units) must be available at the end of period 6,

continued

EXAMPLE 3— *continued*

and it has been added to the period 6 demand of 900 units to obtain the 1000 units.

7. Since no stockouts are permitted, production in any month to satisfy a preceding month's demand is not a feasible alternative. Infeasible cells in the tableau are crosshatched.

8. Unused capacity is assigned a zero value in this problem. If there were an opportunity cost to unused capacity on regular time, it would normally be assessed. For example, unused capacity on regular time might result in idle labor. In this situation the labor cost contribution to the product would be the cost of unused capacity.

The optimum production plan obtained from Table 4 is as follows:

Period	Regular production (units)	Overtime production (units)	Subcontract production (units)	Total production cost[a]
1	600	180	20	$85,100
2	500	0	0	50,000
3	600	180	0	82,500
4	650	200	0	90,000
5	600	180	10	83,800
6	600	180	200	108,500
	3550	920	230	$499,900

[a]Total production cost does not include holding cost, which is $4(70) + 6(10) + 2(50) + 2(10) = 460. Thus, total cost is $499,900 + $460 = $500,360$.

Simplex linear programming models can be built to include several more variables than in transportation linear programming. However, as more variables are included, the complexity of the model grows at a rapid rate.

Linear programming methods ignore nonlinearities and other considerations for the sake of computational efficiency. For this reason, they have not experienced widespread acceptance.

MISCELLANEOUS TECHNIQUES

Numerous other analytical, heuristic, simulation, and computer search techniques have also been developed for production planning. None of the techniques has gained widespread acceptance. Frequently, their input requirements and assumptions seriously limit their application. Many of them are only of theoretical or academic interest.[2]

---

[2]For a more detailed discussion of several approaches to production planning see Samuel Eilon, "Five Approaches to Aggregate Production Planning," *AIIE Transactions*, Vol. 7, No. 2, June 1975, pp. 118–131.

Linear Decision Rule

The linear decision rule (LDR) requires that cost functions of the variables be quadratic (contain one or more squared terms).[3] The relevant costs include regular payroll, hiring and layoff, overtime, and inventory (holding, backordering, and setup) costs. The model works by differentiating the quadratic cost function with respect to each variable to ultimately derive two linear decision rules for computing (1) the work force size for the forthcoming period, and (2) the number of units to produce for the forthcoming period.

The assumptions behind the LDR severely limit its application in industry. There are three specific drawbacks to it. First, the quadratic cost relationships (which must be tailor made for each organization) limit its application. Second, there is difficulty getting accurate cost information from a firm's operations to use the model. Finally, there are no limitations placed on the variables, so it is possible to generate negative work force and production schedules.

Management Coefficients Model

The management coefficients model is a heuristic approach to planning production levels based on the past performance of managers.[4] It attempts to incorporate experience and sensitivity into a formalized model. Regression analysis of past behavior in similar situations is used to smooth the erratic or variable behavior of managers and develop the coefficient of each variable in the model. This model assumes managers are knowledgeable and experienced, and it attempts to utilize their wisdom as revealed by past performance in developing the production plan. The article of faith required is that managers are basically good decision makers.

Simulation and Search Models

Simulation and search models are built on the structure of the models previously discussed. Simulation and search models simulate various possible production plans on a computer and attempt to find the coefficients of the model that result in the least cost. Unfortunately, these models do not ensure optimality. Although they explore and evaluate a large number of plans, they do not examine all possible plans. However, the general procedures of simulation and search models are very attractive for production planning. Three typical models are as follows:

1. Jones's parametric production planning is similar to the linear decision rule, but it uses a search technique to develop coefficients and it defines parameters in terms of central tendency and deviation.[5] A heuristic grid search technique is used to find the coefficients.

---

[3]Charles C. Holt et al., *Planning Production, Inventories, and Work Force,* Englewood Cliffs, NJ: Prentice-Hall, 1960.

[4]E. H. Bowman, "Consistency and Optimality in Managerial Decision Making," *Management Science,* Vol. 4, January 1963, pp. 100–103.

[5]Curtis H. Jones, "Parametric Production Planning," *Management Science,* July 1967, pp. 843–866.

2. Vergin's scheduling by simulation uses linear, quadratic, and step costs in its search for a minimum cost production plan.[6]
3. Taubert's search decision rule uses multiple cost structures in an attempt to find least cost coefficients.[7]

Goal Programming

Most mathematical programming models (linear programming, quadratic programming, integer programming, and stochastic programming) use a unidirectional (single value) objective function. This means one single measure is used to explain all the organization's objectives. Goal programming permits multiple goals to be expressed in a mathematical model.[8] It incorporates numerous objectives into the constraints of linear relationships. The goals are rank ordered in terms of priority. The technique builds on a linear programming framework. The highest priority goal is satisfied first, and then lower level goals are considered. The process continues until all the goals have been considered. When conflicts exist, the solution satisfies higher goals at the expense of lower goals.

MASTER SCHEDULING

A master schedule (also known as a master production schedule) shows the kinds and quantities of products to be provided in each time period in the future. It translates the production plan into specific products or product modules and specifies the time periods for their completion. Moreover, it can generate detailed material requirements and capacity planning information which enable it to balance demands against resources. The master scheduling function is illustrated in Figure 6.

In some organizations it may be difficult to differentiate between the production plan (PP) and the master schedule (MS). The master schedule is derived from the production plan but contains greater detail. The production plan deals with aggregate planning for total output (usually product groups or lines), while the master schedule usually relates to specific products or end items. Figure 7 depicts the role of master scheduling and its relationship to other activities.

Normally a production plan covers a time horizon from 6 to 24 months and is updated monthly. A master schedule is formulated within the time horizon of the production plan and usually is updated weekly. The master schedule should be somewhat longer than the sum of cumulative lead times of component parts, subassemblies, and final assemblies. The temporal correspondence of lead times to time horizons is diagrammed in Figure 8. Within the confines of the production plan, the master schedule must balance material and capacity requirements. In other words, it finite loads the facility by leveling the load within the available capacity.

The minimum planning horizon is usually based on the product with the longest lead time. It is frequently desirable to extend beyond the minimum planning horizon

---

[6]Robert C. Vergin, "Production Planning Under Seasonal Demand," *Journal of Industrial Engineering,* May 1966, pp. 260–266.

[7]William H. Taubert, "A Search Decision Rule for the Aggregate Scheduling Problem," *Management Science,* February 1968, pp. B353–B359.

[8]S. M. Lee and L. J. Moore, "A Practical Approach to Production Scheduling," *Production and Inventory Management,* Vol. 15, No. 1, 1974.

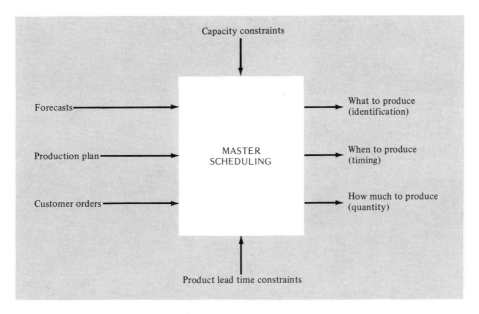

FIGURE 6
The master scheduling function.

FIGURE 7
Master scheduling relationships.

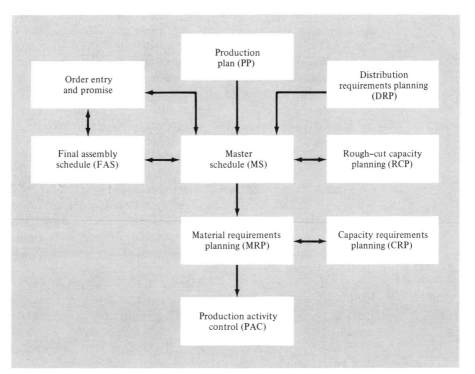

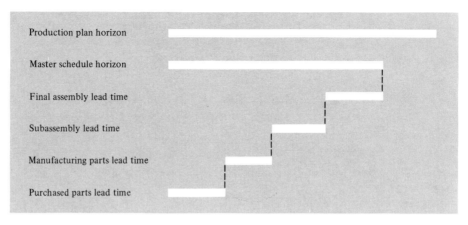

FIGURE 8
Time horizons and lead times.

for flexibility purposes. The number of time periods can be less than the minimum planning horizon, but those end items with a longer lead time will require special action to ensure their availability. If a few parts have extremely long lead times, they can be held in inventory so that the master schedule can extend over a shorter period of time. The planning horizon should be long enough to allow a close coordination of material and capacity. Providing material when capacity is not available results in excess inventory investment; providing capacity when material is not available results in low productivity. The planning horizon should provide sufficient time for synchronization.

The production plan is made operational through a master schedule that identifies specific products (usually end items) and their production dates. The master schedule is a major input into material requirements planning (MRP), which generates specific job orders and work releases at the component, part, and subassembly levels. Production planning is performed predominately by upper management; master scheduling, by middle management.

Priority and capacity are important master scheduling considerations. Priority (what to make and when) establishes when a product will be made available, while capacity (volume flowing per time period) indicates the output capability of a facility. Priority planning relates to material requirements and determines what material is required and when it is required. Capacity planning relates to labor and equipment requirements. It determines what labor and equipment capacity is required and when it is required. The master schedule must balance product demand (quantity and priority) with facility capacity. Priorities are derived from the master schedule and are established within the constraints of available capacity. If capacity is inadequate, a human decision must designate revisions to the master schedule or propose a means of capacity expansion.

These major problems in a production system—priority and capacity—are frequently confounded, muddled, and confused. Priorities indicate the sequence in which jobs should be worked, while capacity indicates the output rate of a facility. A capacity problem will not be solved by addressing priority; a priority problem will not be solved by addressing capacity. If the work load on a facility increases, it cannot be reduced with expediters who address the priority problem. If customer orders are delayed because the priority ranking system is ineffective (lower priority jobs are processed ahead of higher priority jobs), increasing capacity does not solve the problem. Frequently a priority problem is mistaken for a capacity problem and vice versa. Many organizations concentrate on priority to the exclusion of capacity. Both must be managed.

The steps required in developing a master schedule are:

1. Select the items and/or levels in the product structure to be included in the master schedule.
2. Determine the time horizon and time fences for the master schedule.
3. Obtain demand information for each item in the schedule over the time horizon.
4. Prepare a tentative master schedule.
5. Perform rough-cut capacity planning on the tentative master schedule.
6. Revise the tentative master schedule so it is capacity feasible.

MASTER SCHEDULING INPUTS

The major demand inputs to the MS are *customer orders* (firm orders booked but not available from inventory) and *product forecasts* (expected but unrealized demand). The *product lead time* includes the assembly, subassembly, and fabrication time as well as the time required to purchase all components, parts, or raw materials from suppliers. When products are to be supplied from inventory (make to stock items) or in less than their lead time, the master schedule is developed on the basis of product forecasts. The production plan is also an input to the master schedule. It indicates the overall boundaries within which the master schedule must operate.

CAPACITY CONSTRAINTS

Capacity is a major constraint on a master schedule. Capacity in this situation is the demonstrated ability to produce, and not a theoretical or maximum level. Capacity is controlled by the number of scheduled days per period (5, 6, or 7 days per week), the number of shifts scheduled, the overtime policy, manpower levels, and the available equipment. The emphasis is on a realistic or realizable capacity based on historical performance. Certain factors, such as absenteeism, equipment breakdown, lack of material, and yield tend to reduce capacity. Capacity is usually expressed in terms of output units, weight, size, or length for homogeneous products, or in time units such as man-hours for nonhomogeneous products.

It serves no useful purpose to schedule an output that exceeds the available capacity. The maximum output level is dictated by the capacity and not the inputs scheduled. As shown in Figure 9, a manufacturing facility is like a funnel. Once the input has filled the neck of the funnel, putting more in will not get more out. Output depends on capacity, not input, once full utilization is achieved. Scheduling 8000 hours of output into a facility with a 6000 hour capacity will only create frustration and poor service. Once full capacity utilization is achieved, additional inputs or loadings are only wasteful. If inputs exceed the output capacity, backlogs will increase which can result in excessive in-process inventory. When requirements exceed capacity in a work center, the master scheduled quantity may be reduced or moved into a later time period.

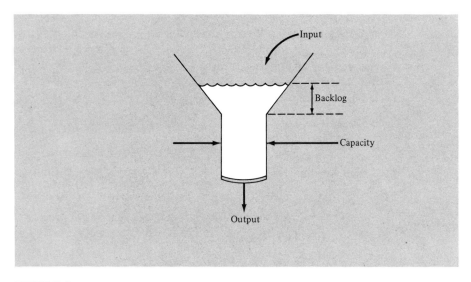

FIGURE 9
Capacity limitations. Input must equal or be less than output, or backlog will increase.

The production plan serves as a type of rough-cut capacity plan for the master schedule. Rough-cut capacity planning (RCP) is used to ensure the tentative master schedule does not exceed capacity requirements in critical work stations. It determines the resources required for planning periods by converting master schedule quantities into workload requirements. It macro measures the required capacity and provides a warning of infeasible or difficult scheduling problems. A load profile for each master scheduled item indicates the critical resources needed to produce a single unit. By multiplying the operation time for each item by the scheduled quantity per period, adding setup time, and summing for all items, the work load per work center for each period is ascertained. Thus, RCP converts the time-phased master schedule

FIGURE 10
Rough-cut capacity planning.

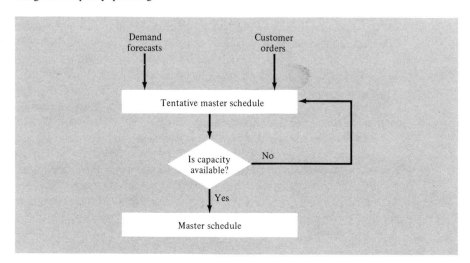

into equivalent load hours in work centers. If requirements exceed capacity in a work center, the master scheduled quantity may be reduced or moved into a later time period.

It is extremely important to locate the critical constraining production center or bottleneck operations. It might be a machine, a machine group, a department, or a manpower group (skilled operators). These critical centers should be loaded to capacity, but not overloaded. The bottleneck work center may change with the nature of the work to be performed in a given time period. As shown in Figure 10, the master schedule is finalized only when sufficient capacity is available at each work center.

STRUCTURAL FEATURES

The selection of product categories or end items will vary from organization to organization. For organizations with less than 100 products, all products can be included. As the number of products provided exceeds several hundred, some modifications are necessary. Some products may be combined into product groups based on their similarity. A common grouping might combine colors, packaging, or minor configuration changes that can be assigned later.

The actual items that are master scheduled will depend on the organization's product and bill of material structure. Three general product structures are shown in Figure 11. The idea is to plan at the point of greatest commonality—the narrowest part of the product structure. Item A represents an organization with a limited number of products made from numerous component parts. In this case, you would master schedule the finished product. Item B represents an organization with many products made from a smaller number of subassemblies, which are made from numerous component parts. In this case, you would master schedule the subassemblies. Item C represents an organization that makes numerous products from few component parts. In this case, you would master schedule at the component part level.

Master scheduling need not be restricted solely to end items. It may be necessary

FIGURE 11
General product structures.

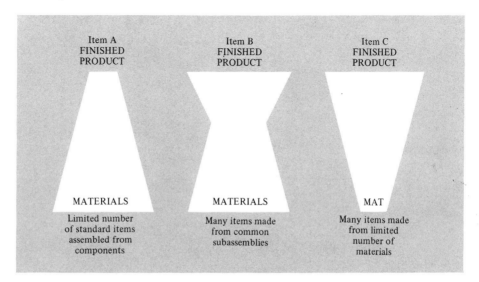

to master schedule at various levels within the product line. It may be at the top level, the bottom level, or somewhere in between. If a product has so many options that scheduling all end items results in too large a number to control, it usually is desirable to schedule at a lower level on the product structure. In such a case, a final assembly schedule (FAS) is required to transform the lower level items into final product configurations. End items are assembled to order, based upon actual customer orders through the FAS. Thus, a decision must be made whether to master schedule at the end item level or to utilize a planning bill and introduce an additional level into the planning process.

Manufacturing organizations can be characterized by one or more of the following three environments:

1. *Make-to-stock:* The firm knows exactly what end items to produce from inventory replenishment requirements and/or forecasts. The master schedule contains end items.

2. *Make-to-order:* The receipt of customer orders is necessary to ascertain end item demand. If the firm operates with an order backlog with delivery lead time greater than product lead time, the end item can be master scheduled; otherwise, neither the end item configuration nor end item demand pattern can be predicted. However, forecasting can be done at the product group or family level.

3. *Assemble-to-order:* A hybrid of the two environments above. Although end items can be defined, there usually are a vast number of them. End items can be assembled from a group of standard subassemblies that are far less than the total number of end items. The subassemblies are made to stock in anticipation of actual orders for end items which consume them in final assembly. Thus, subassemblies are forecasted and end items are built to customer order.

In make-to-stock, an organization sells units off the shelf from inventory; in make-

FIGURE 12
Master schedule levels.

ENVIRONMENT	FORECAST	MASTER SCHEDULE LEVEL	CLASSIFICATION
Make-to-stock	End items	End items	Single-level master schedule
Make-to-order 1. DLT ⩾ PLT	None required	End items from actual orders	Single-level master schedule
2. DLT < PLT	Families with planning bill	Family planning bill and percentage of end items	Two-level master schedule
Assemble-to-order	Generic end item with planning bill	Generic end item and percentage of options	Two-level master schedule

DLT = delivery lead time; PLT = product lead time

to-order or assemble-to-order, no inventory is maintained, so customers must place an order and wait for its completion. In the make-to-stock situation, the master schedule and the final assembly schedule are one and the same.

In the make-to-stock environment, the end items can be master scheduled from forecasts. In the make-to-order environment, the end item is master scheduled from actual orders if the delivery lead time exceeds the product lead time; otherwise it is necessary to master schedule from forecasts with planning bills of materials at the family level. The family level denotes a pseudo item, since it never exists physically. The percentage of family members is used to break down the forecast for the family.

In the assemble-to-order environment, the end item cannot be master scheduled and planning bills of material are used. The advantage here is that it is easier to forecast the total number of options than the number of option combinations. Percentages can be applied to extend the forecast to the option level. The logic for master scheduling level selection is contained in Figures 12 and 13.

FIGURE 13
Master scheduling level selection.

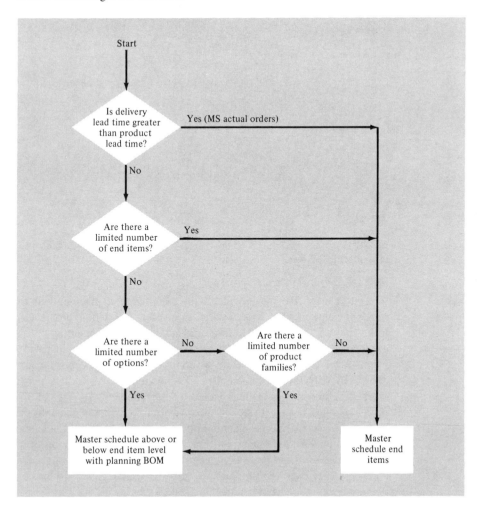

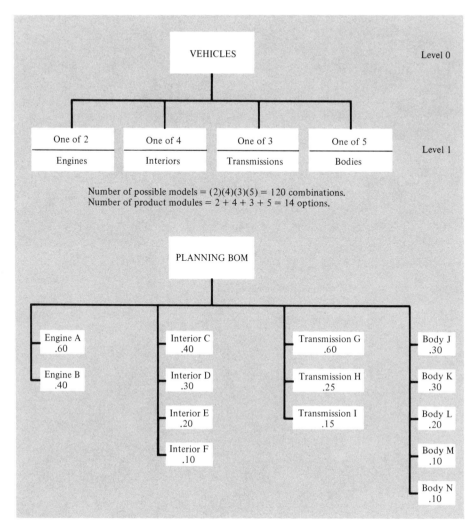

FIGURE 14
Planning bill of material: modular.

Restructuring the traditional bill of material to a planning bill of material is a standard solution to a wide variety of master scheduling problems, especially for make-to-order and assemble-to-order situations. The planning bill is an artificial group of items used to facilitate master scheduling and/or material planning. The parent level is always a pseudo assembly, while the component level is normally composed of buildable assemblies. The component quantities per parent are expressed as percentages rather than absolute numbers. This is called the popularity percentage and is used to define the probability of option selection or a specific end item within a family. The planning bill is not a single type but includes various bills which simplify the planning process. There are many ways of structuring bills of material. Some of the more popular planning bills are super bills, modular bills, and common parts bills. These planning bills are pseudo parts list made up of selected items which can be master scheduled, but *not* built.

A typical planning bill of material is contained in Figure 14. It depicts vehicles which are assembled to order from a limited variety of options. There are 120 different configurations of vehicles that can be built. If end items were forecasted, it would require 120 separate forecasts. With the planning bill, a single forecast for vehicles is made and decomposed into the popularity percentage for each option, which in turn is used to derive option forecasts. For example, if the vehicle forecast for a period is 100 units, the engine option forecast derived from it will be for 60 engine A and 40 engine B. In a similar manner, all the option forecasts could be obtained. This example shows 14 options which are master scheduled from forecasts derived from the pseudo parent. Each option has its popularity percentage determined from historical records or future expectations. The popularity percentage permits the breakdown of the pseudo parent forecast into the forecast for each optional feature.

A planning bill introduces an additional pseudo level into the planning process. The additional pseudo level may be a generic product (ignoring options) in which the buildable master schedule level consists of the modular options that make up the end item; it also may be a product family in which the buildable master schedule level is the specific end items within the family. The reason for not master scheduling the end item directly is the difficulty in forecasting individual members of a large population when demand for the members is small in a given time period. Forecasting becomes feasible only when relatively large numbers are involved, as would be likely for generic products or in family groups. The next chapter will discuss the formats, types, and uses of the BOM.

TIME CYCLE CHARTS

A time cycle chart shows how much time it would take to produce a product starting from scratch with no inventories available. It indicates lead time requirements as well as the minimum planning horizon for the master schedule. If customer delivery is to be made in less than the maximum time on the time cycle chart, inventories must be maintained.

Each material, component, and assembly requires some lead time. Starting with the final product, the time cycle chart works backwards through each manufacturing step, assembly operation, and purchase to map the time relationships. A typical time cycle chart is shown in Figure 15. Product 1 is assembled from subassemblies 2 and 6 and purchased part 21. Subassembly 2 consists of manufactured components 3, 4, and 5, which in turn are made from purchased parts 22, 23, and 24 respectively. Similarly, subassembly 6 consists of manufactured components 7 and 8 and purchased part 27. Manufactured components 7 and 8 are made from purchased parts 25 and 26 respectively. The bottleneck item is purchased part 25, which sets the no inventory lead time at approximately 22 weeks.

Obviously, an organization must have inventories if it is going to offer customer delivery in less than 22 weeks. If the organization is going to offer instantaneous customer services (delivery lead time is zero), it is a make-to-stock situation and end items are produced from a forecast. If delivery lead time is 22 weeks or more, it is a make-to-order situation where no forecasting is necessary; end items are produced and material needs determined only after the receipt of customer orders. Suppose a six week lead time is available to customers. An inventory of critical items must be available at the time of customer order receipt. The critical items are determined by drawing a horizontal line across the time cycle chart at six weeks. In Figure 15, the

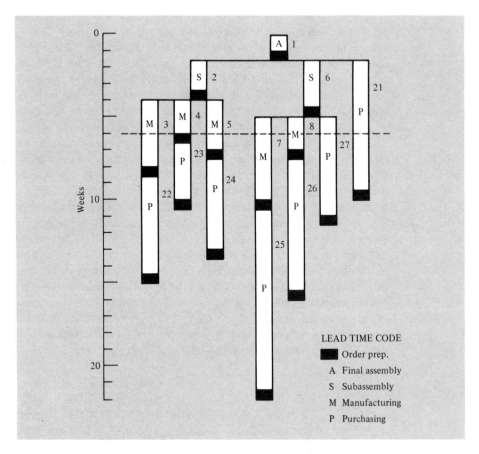

FIGURE 15
Time cycle chart. [From Richard J. Tersine, *Principles of Inventory and Materials Management,* New York: North-Holland, 1982, p. 361.] Lead time code: ■ = order preparation; A = final assembly; S = subassembly; M = manufacturing; P = purchasing.

critical items are 3, 4, 5, 7, 8, 21, and 27. Demand must be forecasted out to 22 weeks so critical items will be available for assemble-to-order in week 6. End items are assembled to order when customer orders are received. With different delivery lead times, the group of critical items can change.

MASTER SCHEDULE REVISION

A master schedule should be an up-to-date rolling schedule that is revised by adding periods and updating as necessary. As new information or new orders become available, the schedule will change. At the end of a period, any incomplete work must be rescheduled. If a work center becomes a bottleneck, there are only two alternatives—add more capacity or redo the master schedule. If a part or component will not be available, perhaps the product should be rescheduled to a later date.

As new forecasts or orders are received, they are loaded on the facility to the available capacity. If capacity is fully allocated and cannot be increased in the period, the work is scheduled to the nearest future period *or* a lower priority job is bumped to a future period to make room for it.

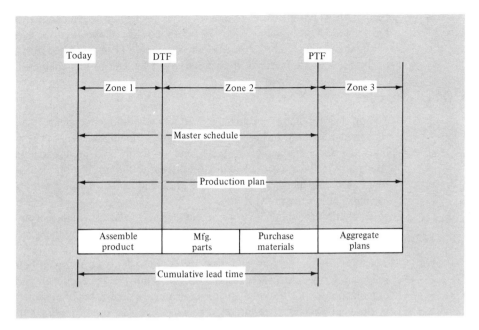

FIGURE 16
Master schedule time fences.

The master schedule should be realizable and not overstated. When scheduled production exceeds capacity, usually some or all of the following occur:

1. invalid priorities,
2. poor customer service (missed deliveries),
3. excess in-process inventory,
4. high expediting costs,
5. lack of accountability.

The master schedule should be a workable and realizable plan that is kept up to date. When properly maintained, it can reduce inventory, improve customer service, and increase productivity.

Time fences or zones are used in master scheduling to reveal the significance of potential schedule changes. They are established for each master scheduled item and can vary considerably among items. Figure 16 illustrates the time fence concept in three zones. Future planning is done in zone 3, where additions and changes to the master schedule can be made without affecting any lower level material or capacity planning. In zone 2, material has been ordered and work started on lower level items, so changes here can have a cost consequence. In zone 1, changes have a major cost impact and should be avoided except for emergency changes approved by top management. The first time fence at the end of zone 1 is called the *demand time fence* (DTF) and frequently is the final assembly lead time. The second time fence at the end of zone 2 is called the *planning time fence* (PTF) and usually is set at or beyond the cumulative lead time. Cost tradeoffs should be made on all changes within the time fences of zones 1 and 2. The time fences are boundaries of time horizon subperiods in which different guidelines govern schedule modifications. Within a given time fence, certain changes are not permitted. The closer a period is to the present, the tighter are the controls on schedule changes. Master schedule format and the uses of time fences are outlined in Appendix A at the end of this chapter.

CONCLUSION

The production plan is top management's handle on the business. It is management's statement of policy on how the organization should be run with respect to output, inventory levels, manpower levels, and so forth. The production plan becomes a constraint on the master schedule. Additionally, the production plan provides a basis for rough-cut capacity planning. The production plan must be valid with respect to capacity within the organization.

With the production plan as an input, the master schedule becomes a more detailed operation schedule that must balance both material and capacity requirements. Before a master schedule is finalized, it must be validated with respect to capacity constraints. Both priority and capacity conflicts must be resolved before the master schedule is released. The master schedule is universally applicable in manufacturing organizations, but it is vital for material requirements planning, which is the subject of the next chapter. The master schedule drives the entire production and inventory control system.

QUESTIONS

1. What are the major production strategy variables?
2. What is production planning?
3. How can an organization try to influence its aggregate demand?
4. What time horizons are associated with production planning and detailed scheduling?
5. Outline the basic steps in developing a master schedule.
6. What is the major limitation of charting techniques for production planning?
7. What advantage do linear programming techniques have over charting techniques?
8. What makes goal programming a desirable production planning technique?
9. Why have the sophisticated and mathematical production planning techniques not gained widespread acceptance?
10. Differentiate between a production plan and a master schedule.
11. Contrast priority and capacity planning.
12. What is the function of rough-cut capacity planning (RCP)?
13. What are the two major demand inputs to a master schedule?
14. Indicate what items generally are forecasted and/or master scheduled in make-to-order, make-to-stock, and assemble-to-order environments.
15. What planning situations generally favor two-level master scheduling?
16. Describe the concepts of pseudo assembly and popularity percentage as they apply to planning bills of material.
17. Why are end items often not master scheduled in a direct manner?
18. How are critical items identified from time cycle charts?
19. Define demand time fence and planning time fence; give their significance with respect to schedule changes.
20. Within the context of a typical master schedule format, what do available to promise (ATP) and projected available balance (PAB) indicate?

PROBLEMS

1. The production planner for a single product company is supplied with the following data:

Beginning inventory		250 units
Forecasted demand	1st qtr	9,000
	2nd qtr	14,000
	3rd qtr	14,500
	4th qtr	12,500
Safety stock (desired ending inventory)		200
Operating days	1st qtr	63 days
	2nd qtr	64
	3rd qtr	63
	4th qtr	62

The relevant costs are as follows:

Manufacturing cost/unit	$95.00
Inventory holding cost/unit-qtr	$1.50
Hourly wage rate	$12.00
Hourly overtime wage rate (150%)	$18.00
Subcontracting cost/unit	$100.00
Labor hours/unit	5
Layoff cost/worker	$120.00
Hiring and training cost/worker	$750.00
Stockout cost per unit	$4.75

Which of the following three production plans results in the lowest cost?
1. Produce to exact production requirements by varying the size of the work force on regular hours. There are 89 workers available at the beginning of the first quarter.
2. Produce to capacity with a constant work force of 124 workers.
3. Produce to capacity with a fixed work force of 100 workers on regular time, and subcontract all excess demand. No stockouts are permitted.

2. Troy Manufacturing Company uses overtime, inventory, and subcontracting to absorb fluctuations in demand. A production plan for 12 months is devised and updated each month. The expected demand for the next 12 periods is as follows:

Time period	1	2	3	4	5	6	7	8	9	10	11	12
Demand (10^3)	17	15	28	24	34	17	13	12	21	27	32	12

The following costs and constraints are relevant:

Maximum regular production	20,000 units/month
Maximum overtime production	4,000 units/month
Regular production cost	$25/unit
Overtime production cost	$30/unit
Subcontracting cost	$32/unit
Inventory holding cost	$1/unit-period

What is the optimum production plan for the next twelve months (assume beginning inventory is 4000, desired ending inventory is 2000, and no stockouts are tolerated)?

3. Brown Manufacturing maintains a stable work force by using inventory, overtime, and subcontracting to meet demand requirements. Stockouts are not permitted, and all demand is satisfied by in-house production or subcontracting. The following data are provided for the upcoming fiscal year:

Quarter	Expected demand	Regular capacity	Overtime capacity	Subcontract capacity
1	1200	700	150	300
2	700	600	125	300
3	900	700	150	300
4	1000	800	200	300

The beginning inventory at the start of quarter 1 is 150 units, and the desired ending inventory for quarter 4 is 100 units. The relevant cost data are as follows:

Regular cost	$50/unit
Overtime cost	$70/unit
Subcontracting cost	$75/unit
Inventory holding cost	$2/unit-period

Determine the production plan that will satisfy demand at minimum cost using linear programming.

4. Phillips Corporation manufactures air compressor pistons. The expected demand in thousands of units for piston PS-624-373 for the next year is given below:

Jan.	Feb.	Mar.	Apr.	May	Jun.	Jul.	Aug.	Sep.	Oct.	Nov.	Dec.
21	17	29	26	32	12	18	12	19	23	29	17

The following costs and constraints are relevant:

Maximum regular production	18,000 units/month
Maximum overtime production	5,000 units/month
Regular production cost	$20/unit
Overtime production cost	$30/unit
Subcontracting cost	$33/unit
Inventory holding cost	$1/unit-period

What is the optimum production plan for the next year (assume beginning inventory is 3, desired ending inventory is 2, and stockouts are not tolerated)?

5. The production supervisor of O'Fallon Manufacturing Company compiled the following data:

Beginning inventory (units)		164
Forecasted demand (units):	Jan.	7,200
	Feb.	6,100
	Mar.	8,900
	Apr.	7,400
	May	9,300
	Jun.	11,200
Required safety stock		150

Operating days:	Jan.	Feb.	Mar.	Apr.	May	Jun.
	21	19	23	20	22	22

The relevant costs are as follows:

Manufacturing cost/unit	$122.00
Inventory holding cost/unit-month	$4.88
Hourly wage rate (average)	$5.95
Hourly overtime wage rate (160%)	$9.52
Subcontracting cost/unit	$128.40
Labor hours/unit	4.5
Layoff cost/worker	$97.00
Hiring and training cost/worker	$435.00
Stockout cost/unit	$27.40

Which of the following production plans results in the lowest cost?

1. Produce to exact production requirements by varying the size of the work force on regular time. There are 193 workers available on January 1.
2. Produce to exact production requirements by varying the work force between 173 and 213 workers, working overtime, and producing to inventory.
3. Maintain a constant work force of 222 workers and produce to capacity on regular time.
4. Produce to capacity with a fixed work force of 200 workers on regular time, and subcontract all excess demand with no stockouts permitted.

6. St. Charles Foundry maintains a stable work force and uses inventory, overtime, and subcontracting to meet demand requirements. Stockouts are not permitted, and demand must be satisfied through in-house production or subcontracting. The following data are available for the next two quarters:

Period	Expected demand	Regular capacity	Overtime capacity	Subcontract capacity
1 (Jan.)	940	620	200	250
2 (Feb.)	475	500	150	250
3 (Mar.)	730	550	150	250
4 (Apr.)	790	575	150	250
5 (May)	895	600	200	250
6 (Jun.)	915	600	200	250
	4,745	3,445	1,050	1,500

The beginning inventory at the start of January is 350 units, and the desired ending June inventory is 300 units. The relevant cost data are as follows:

Regular cost/unit	$9.00
Overtime cost/unit	$13.50
Subcontracting cost/unit	$15.00
Inventory holding cost/unit-month	$0.50

Determine the production plan that will satisfy demand at minimum cost, using linear programming.

7. Yarmouth Manufacturing Corporation produces six standard products to customer order.
   a. Using the data provided in the following table, draw up a master schedule for the next six weeks in the matrix provided.
   b. What production problem do you foresee?
   c. What changes could be made?

Product	Standard mfg. hr/unit	Demand (units/period)					
		1	2	3	4	5	6
A	90	12	6	8	11	7	9
B	45	7	3	4	5	3	2
C	60	4	5	3	6	4	4
D	120	9	11	10	7	8	7
E	70	2	6	4	2	3	4
F	150	15	12	13	9	12	14

Product	Demand (standard mfg. hr/period)					
	1	2	3	4	5	6
A						
B						
C						
D						
E						
F						
Standard hours loaded						
Standard hours capacity[a]	4000	4000	4000	4000	4000	4000

[a]Capacity is set at 400 standard hours per period on a single shift without overtime.

8. For the item below, determine the projected available balance (PAB) and the available to promise (ATP).

Item _____ DTF __2__ PTF __6__		Period							
Part number _____ Lead time __2__ Lot size __25__ Safety stock __3__		1	2	3	4	5	6	7	8
Forecast		0	1	0	4	11	15	14	15
Actual Demand		15	9	14	6	4		1	
Master Schedule		25		25		25		25	
Projected Available Balance	6								
Available to Promise									

9. The Bass River Electric Corporation manufactures electric motors. The material list for motor stock number BR 1005 is displayed below with the procurement, manufacturing, assembly, and subassembly times.

a. Draw a time cycle chart for the motor.
b. If a lead time of five weeks is desired, what are the critical stock items?
c. If a lead time of ten weeks is desired, what are the critical stock items?
d. What is the minimum planning time fence for the master schedule if no inventory is stocked?
e. Where would you set the demand time fence for the master schedule? Why?

		Time
Assembly	A	1.0
Subassembly 1	S1	2.0
Manufacturing 1	M1	4.0
Purchasing 1	P1	6.0
Purchasing 2	P2	3.5
Manufacturing 2	M2	1.5
Purchasing 3	P3	2.0
Purchasing 4	P4	3.0
Purchasing 5	P5	8.5
Manufacturing 3	M3	13.0
Purchasing 6	P6	4.0
Subassembly 2	S2	3.5
Manufacturing 4	M4	2.5
Purchasing 7	P7	3.0
Purchasing 8	P8	6.5
Purchasing 9	P9	3.0
Purchasing for final assembly	PFA	7.0

10. For the two-level master schedule below, determine the projected available balance and the available to promise.

Item Family Part no. _____		Period							
		1	2	3	4	5	6	7	8
Master Schedule			20		20		20		20
Actual Demand			10	10	10	6	8		
Available to Promise									

Item Common (100%) DTF __0__ Part number _____ PTF __6__ Lead time __2__ Lot size __20__ Safety stock __0__		Period							
		1	2	3	4	5	6	7	8
Forecast									
Actual Demand			10	10	10	6	8		
Master Schedule			20		20		20		20
Projected Available Balance									
Available to Promise									

Item ___ Option (50%) ___ DTF __2__ PTF __5__ Part number _____ Lead time __2__ Lot size __10__ Safety stock __2__		Period							
		1	2	3	4	5	6	7	8
Forecast									
Actual Demand			6	4	5	3	5		
Master Schedule			10		10		10		10
Projected Available Balance	2								
Available to Promise									

CASE 1: ROOM AT THE INN

Sondra Waverly is provisionally in charge of all motel operations at the St. Louis Georgian House, one of sixty motels owned by the prestigious Wessex Hotel Corporation. Wessex general management claims that the St. Louis motel is its central region's worst discommodity and is denying Sondra permanent status until improvements in the profit-and-loss statement for lodging operations are evident. The ultimatum comes as a result of Wessex management's conviction that the seasonality of the tourist trade is not the singular or even the primary reason the motel is unprofitable during the long off-season. Management imputes the unacceptable off-season performance to unprogressive management policies and flagrant wastefulness: it ascribes fault in particular to extravagant use of supplies and consumable items, redundant and dawdling employees, inordinate labor costs, unenticing motel promotions, and high vacancy rates, and in general to immoderation in most cost categories. Similar censure is not taken against the motel's restaurant, banquet, and lounge businesses, since they consistently earn a profit.

Upon examination of cost components said to be excessive, Sondra finds that a substantial portion of costs are fixed. The large number of suites, sumptuous meeting rooms, and lavish room furnishings are already in place. Sondra concedes that many of the rooms go unoccupied during the off-season but is quick to point out the satisfactory occupancy rate when the tourist trade is flourishing. Consequently, Sondra segregates the fixed facility expenses from the more practical cost reduction alternatives.

The cost components she considers under her control include:

1. *Room provisions*—linens; stationary, post cards, etc.; toiletry items; paper hygiene products; and so forth.
2. *Room amenities*—cable television service; ice; soft drink and snack concessions; magazines; free local telephone calls.
3. *Housekeeping supplies*—cleaning agents; plastic bags; vacuum bags.
4. *Office supplies and variable expenses*—forms; telephone calls; rented equipment; duplicating materials; pens, pencils, and the like.
5. *Housekeeping personnel*—full- and part-time, hourly employees.
6. *Maintenance personnel and grounds keepers*—full-time, salaried help.
7. *Security officers*—full-time, salaried employees.
8. *Pool staff*—seasonal, hourly employees.
9. *Reservation clerks*—full- and part-time, salaried and hourly personnel.
10. *Office staff*—full-time, salaried personnel.

The inventories of supplies and room provisions basically are kept in accordance with company regulations. Orders for such items are placed with central supply, and charges are set by that office (emergency orders from local suppliers are a rare exception). Sondra has the authority to stock supplies within a specified range but is sure that tighter control of these low cost items is an inadequate cost restriction.

Labor costs are the most significant portion of costs Sondra classifies as manageable. The turnover rate for housekeeping personnel is extremely high; in contrast, the attrition rate for maintenance and security personnel is the lowest in the central region. Housekeepers essentially are unskilled and paid minimum or slightly above minimum wages; though remunerated as salaried personnel, maintenance and security employees receive weekly paychecks which are approximately the same as union scale for a similar job classification and length of service. Office clerks are trained employees and are given professional status. Their prescribed duties do not overlap with those performed by reservation clerks, but during peak periods their actual duties may be enlarged to give needed assistance. The reservation clerks typically are less skilled than the office personnel and are paid accordingly.

The Georgian House operates with a very high level of customer service. Housekeepers usually arive at 7:30 A.M. and stay, working overtime if necessary, until all rooms assigned to them are immaculate. Other housekeepers arrive later in the day in order to make service calls at lodgers' requests. Guests check in throughout the day and may have checkout times extended until 3:00 P.M. Maintenance personnel are scheduled around the clock; they each work 40-hour weeks and rotate weekend duty. Security is maintained 24 hours a day, 7 days a week. The pool staff is employed on a seasonal basis; staff members supervise activities at the outdoor pool from 9:00 A.M. until 9:00 P.M. daily and devise their own work schedules subject to Sondra's approval. The reservation desk is open at all times, but the number of on-duty clerks varies. Office personnel typically work 9:00 A.M.–5:00 P.M., five days a week, and average eight hours a month overtime.

The reservation clerks, maintenance and security personnel, and housekeepers all appear to have idle time. Sondra surmises that much of the idleness is due to the wide variation in their workloads but that a portion of the slack time is excess. She wants to lay off some of the workforce in a gradual manner; the layoffs would continue until motel operations begin to show adverse effects. At that point, the firings would cease. Sondra conjectures that the layoffs will not be widespread even though the system appears ''fat.'' Too many layoffs would be infeasible, because it would compromise the customer service and risk the loss of the motel's first-class reputation.

1. What options for improving operating performance are available to Sondra?
2. What information is necessary for evaluating these options?
3. What course(s) of action do you recommend? Why?

CASE 2: PROLIFERATION

National Motors, Inc. produces recreational vehicles. Its entire product line includes 12 models of various sizes in regard to passenger accommodation and payload. The emphasis at National is on large recreational vehicles which are equipped with a wide range of optional features. The total number of parts and components at the final assembly level for all models is about 5800; this figure is based upon an assembly planning level, where a complete gearbox represents one of the 5800 parts.

National Motors master schedules by product family (i.e., vehicle model) and by product option modules. Forecasting is performed monthly for each model in each of the market areas (foreign and domestic). In addition to forecasting for vehicle models, estimates are made for the optional requirements. The forecasting information pertaining to models and options is used to prepare the master schedule. However, the calculations which result from the master scheduling process are modified to provide buffer stocks. The buffer stocks serve as a hedge against unexpected changes from the present product and/or option mix.

The production environment is assemble-to-order, which allows National to build a highly customized vehicle. Just a partial list of product optional features would include 16 options or modules, which themselves consist of specified numbers of required items. The requirements (material and capacity) depend upon the modules which are consumed in the production of each customized vehicle, but they also depend upon the combination of modules (options) ordered by the customer. For example, a customer might choose a particular wheelbase (frame length) as one option, and a specific rear light arrangement as another. For the rear light option associated with the particular wheel-base there must be a combination option. This combination option might consist of extra cable of designated length and a specified number of cable fasteners. Although the combination option may be inexpensive compared to most of the customer selected options, it also must be master scheduled to ensure its availability. Consequently, the master schedule is comprised of modules associated with three different levels—(1) the vehicle model; (2) the customer selected options; and (3) the combination options.

With each option introduced, not only is a new module created but any number of combination modules for the different configuration possibilities. This is causing an exponential growth in master schedule modules. Since the introduction of National's present module system in the early sixties, the number of modules has doubled every five years. The number of modules is fast approaching the total number of parts and components.

When modules were few and easily recognizable, the scheduler could use his judgment to estimate, evaluate, buffer, and schedule. Now, because of the proliferation of modules, no scheduler can exercise good judgment. Instead, the module information is being left for the most part to data processing and is going uncorrected. The result is that schedulers no longer eliminate many modules from scheduling, are forced to master schedule everything, and are turning out infeasible master schedules.

1. Identify the problems and their apparent causes.
2. Suggest some practical solutions to the problems.

APPENDIX A. MASTER SCHEDULE FORMAT

Master scheduling can be performed with different formats. A generalized format is shown in Figure 17. Sometimes, when planning bills are used, the forecast line is broken into two categories, called the service forecast and the production forecast. In this case, the service

FIGURE 17
Typical master schedule format.

Item ___ DTF ___ Part number ___ PTF ___ Lead time ___ Lot size ___ Safety stock ___		Period							
		1	2	3	4	5	6	7	8
Forecast									
Actual Demand									
Master Schedule									
Projected Available Balance									
Available to Promise									

The column entries are self-explanatory. The row entries have the following meaning:

Forecast is the anticipated demand for the item for each period.

Actual demand is the quantity sold (or warehouse orders), recorded in the periods when shipments will occur.

Master schedule is the quantity of items scheduled to be available in a given period.

Projected available balance is the expected number of completed items on hand at the end of each period.

Available to promise is the number of units that are available for sale.

forecast is for independent demand spare part requirements, and the production forecast is generated from a master scheduled parent item (this is referred to as two-level master scheduling, and the item is a component in a planning bill).

The logic used herein is to consume the forecast with actual orders. When orders are received, they are entered in actual demand and the forecast is reduced by a like amount. The demand time fence (DTF) significantly affects the projected available balance (PAB). Within the DTF, the forecast is removed from consideration in the projected available balance; beyond the DTF, the forecast is included in the calculation of the projected available balance. For the initial (first) period within the DTF, the projected available balance is calculated as follows:

$$PAB(1) = PAB(0) + MS(1) - A(1) - S.$$

For subsequent time periods within the DTF, the projected available balance is calculated as follows:

$$PAB(i) = PAB(i - 1) + MS(i) - A(i).$$

Beyond the DTF, the projected available balance is calculated as follows:

$$PAB(i) = PAB(i - 1) + MS(i) - A(i) - F(i),$$

where

$PAB(i)$ = projected available balance for time period i,
$MS(i)$ = master scheduled quantity for period i,
$A(i)$ = actual demand for period i,
$F(i)$ = forecasted demand for period i,
S = safety stock quantity.

If the PAB becomes negative, it indicates a shortage of the item during the period.

The forecast is excluded from consideration in the PAB within the DTF, because it provides the master scheduler with the information to make an important decision. The PAB quantity within the DTF is what is expected to be available if the forecast is not realized. If the forecast is too optimistic, it may be desirable to reschedule out or reduce the lot size.

The available to promise (ATP) line indicates to marketing the number of items that are "for sale" to customers. It is the uncommitted portion of an organization's inventory or planned production based on the supply from the master schedule (the forecast is always ignored in the ATP). It helps marketing to respond to customer requests for delivery dates. If the ATP line becomes negative, more units have been promised to customers than can be delivered. The ATP is only calculated when a new replenishment in the master schedule line is found. For the initial (first) period, the ATP is calculated as follows:

$$ATP(1) = PAB(0) + MS(1) - \sum_{j=1}^{n-1} A(j).$$

For subsequent time periods, the ATP is obtained as follows:

$$ATP(i) = MS(i) - \sum_{j=1}^{n-1} A(j),$$

where

$ATP(i)$ = available to promise quantity in period i,
$MS(i)$ = master scheduled quantity for period i,
$A(j)$ = actual demand in period j,
$\sum_{j=1}^{n-1} A(j)$ = summation of actual demand from period i up to but not including the next period (n) in which there is a master schedule receipt.

Item _____ DTF _2_ Part number _____ PTF _7_ Lead time _2 weeks_ Lot size _20_ Safety stock _2_		Period							
		1	2	3	4	5	6	7	8
Forecast		O	O	12	2	10	2	18	2
Actual Demand		15	5	4	2	5			
Master Schedule		20		20		20		20	
Projected Available Balance	6	9	4	8	4	9	7	9	7
Available to Promise		6		14		15		20	

FIGURE 18
Example of MS computations.

Because marketing needs to know what is left to sell, based on actual demand and not theoretical demand, the forecast is excluded in the calculation of ATP. Since it is part of what can be sold to meet demand, safety stock is not deducted in determining ATP. An example of master schedule computations is contained in Figure 18.

The master schedule in Figure 18 is interpreted in the following manner: The item is produced in lot sizes of 20 units with a safety stock of 2 units, a lead time of 2 weeks, a demand time fence of 2 weeks, and a planning time fence of 7 weeks. Units are master scheduled for receipt in periods 1, 3, 5, and 7. As orders are received for a given period, (1) the quantity is added to the actual demand, and (2) the forecast is reduced by a like amount. In weeks 1 and 2, the forecast has been completely consumed by actual demand. In periods 3 to 5, actual demand has consumed only a portion of the forecast. No orders for periods 6 to 8 have been received at this time, so these forecast figures are unadjusted.

At the start of period 1 there are 6 units available in inventory. Up to the demand time fence (in periods 1 and 2), the forecasted demand is ignored in calculating the projected available balance (PAB). The forecasted demand is included in the PAB for each period thereafter (weeks 3 to 8). The specific PAB calculations for each period are:

$$PAB(1) = 6 + 20 - 15 - 2 = 9,$$
$$PAB(2) = 9 + 0 - 5 \qquad = 4,$$
$$PAB(3) = 4 + 20 - 4 - 12 = 8,$$
$$PAB(4) = 8 + 0 - 2 - 2 = 4,$$
$$PAB(5) = 4 + 20 - 5 - 10 = 9,$$
$$PAB(6) = 9 + 0 - 0 - 2 = 7,$$
$$PAB(7) = 7 + 20 - 0 - 18 = 9,$$
$$PAB(8) = 9 + 0 - 0 - 2 = 7.$$

The available to promise (ATP) is calculated only for those periods in which a master schedule receipt is expected. It is determined by reducing the available supply by the summation of actual demand from the relevant scheduled receipt up to the next master schedule receipt. For ATP(1), the available supply includes PAB(0); no PABs are pertinent in ensuing calculations. The actual quantities are derived as follows:

$$ATP(1) = 6 + 20 - 15 - 5 = 6,$$
$$ATP(3) = 20 - 4 - 2 \qquad = 14,$$
$$ATP(5) = 20 - 5 - 0 \qquad = 15,$$
$$ATP(7) = 20 - 0 - 0 \qquad = 20.$$

Item	Vehicles		Period							
Part no. _____			1	2	3	4	5	6	7	8
Master Schedule			40	40	40	40	40	40	40	40
Actual Demand			40	40	35	30	20	10		
Available to Promise										

Item Engine A (60%) DTF 2			Period							
Part number _____ PTF _____ Lead time 2 Lot size 48 Safety stock 2			1	2	3	4	5	6	7	8
Forecast			0	2	4	6	12	18	24	24
Actual Demand			26	22	20	18	12	6		
Master Schedule			48		48		48		48	
Projected Available Balance	5		25	3	27	3	27	3	27	3
Available to Promise			5		10		30		48	

Item Engine B (40%) DTF 3			Period							
Part number _____ PTF _____ Lead time 2 Lot size 32 Safety stock 2			1	2	3	4	5	6	7	8
Forecast			2	0	1	4	8	12	16	16
Actual Demand			14	18	15	12	8	4		
Master Schedule			32		32		32		32	
Projected Available Balance	2		18	0	17	1	17	1	17	1
Available to Promise			2		5		20		32	

FIGURE 19
Two-level master schedule.

Figure 19 is a presentation of a two-level master schedule for assemble-to-order vehicles. It uses the engine option depicted in Figure 14 as an example. The forecast is for 40 vehicles per week, and they are master scheduled. Engine A and B options for the vehicle have a popularity percentage of 60% and 40% respectively. Therefore, engine A is forecasted at 60% of the vehicle master schedule of 40 units, or 24 units per week. In a similar manner, engine B is master scheduled for 16 units per week. The lot sizes for engines A and B are 48 and 32 units respectively. The actual demand for 26 units of engine A completely consumes the forecast for 24, and the actual demand for 14 units of engine B leaves 2 units in the forecast unconsumed. For period 2, the actual demand for vehicles again is 40 (22 for engine A and 18 for engine B); for engine A, 2 (24 − 22) units are left in the forecast, while the forecast for engine B is totally consumed by an actual demand of 18. For period 3, the actual demand for vehicles is only 35 units (20 for engine A and 15 for engine B); for engine A, 4 (24 − 20) units are left in the forecast, while one unit remains in the forecast for engine B. There are declining actual demands for vehicles until periods 7 and 8 where customer orders are yet to be received. For periods 7 and 8, the forecasts for engines A and B are totally unconsumed.

The situation given in Figure 19 is only for the engine option. The same type of computer assisted computation must be made for all other options (interiors, transmissions, and bodies). The option levels (14 in this case) would all be exploded by MRP to determine lower level requirements. Lastly, a final assembly schedule (FAS) would combine the master schedule options into the final product configuration requested by each customer.

SELECTED BIBLIOGRAPHY

Bowman, E. H. "Consistency and Optimality in Managerial Decision Making," *Management Science,* Vol. 4, January 1963, pp. 100–103.

———. "Production Planning by the Transportation Method of Linear Programming," *Journal of Operations Research,* February 1956.

Chase, R. B. and N. J. Aquilano. *Production and Operations Management,* Homewood, IL: Irwin, 1981.

Eilon, S. "Five Approaches to Aggregate Production Planning," *AIIE Transactions,* Vol. 7, No. 2, June 1975, pp. 118–131.

Everdell, R. *Master Production Scheduling,* APICS Training Aid, Washington, DC.

Fogarty, D. W. and T. R. Hoffmann. *Production and Inventory Management,* Cincinnati, OH: South-Western, 1983.

Greene, J. H. *Production and Inventory Control Handbook,* New York: McGraw-Hill, 1970.

Holt, C. C. et al. *Planning Production, Inventories, and Work Force,* Englewood Cliffs, NJ: Prentice-Hall, 1960.

Jones, C. H. "Parametric Production Planning," *Management Science,* July 1967, pp. 843–866.

Lee, S. M. and L. J. Moore. "A Practical Approach to Production Scheduling," *Production and Inventory Management,* Vol. 15, No. 1, 1974.

Menipaz, E. "Overview of Production Planning," *Journal of Information and Optimization Sciences,* Vol. 4, No. 1, January 1983, pp. 65–72.

Monks, J. G. *Operations Management: Theory and Problems,* New York: McGraw-Hill, 1982.

Plossl, G. W. and W. E. Welch. *The Role of Top Management in the Control of Inventory,* Reston, VA: Reston Publishing, 1979.

Silver, E. A. "Medium Range Aggregate Production Planning: State of the Art," *Production and Inventory Management,* 1st Quarter, 1972, pp. 15–40.

Taubert, W. H. "A Search Decision Rule for the Aggregate Scheduling Problem," *Management Science,* February 1968, pp. B353–B359.

Vergin, R. C. "Production Planning under Seasonal Demand," *Journal of Industrial Engineering,* May 1966, pp. 260–266.

Wight, O. W. *Production and Inventory Management in the Computer Age,* Boston: Cahners Books, 1974.

17

Material Requirements Planning (MRP)

MRP INPUTS

MRP OUTPUTS

PRODUCT STRUCTURES
Low Level Coding

MRP COMPUTATIONS

MRP TYPES

MRP OVERVIEW

CAPACITY PLANNING AND CONTROL

CONCLUSION

APPENDIX A: BILLS OF MATERIALS (BOM)
Traditional Bills of Materials
Matrix BOM
Add/Delete BOM
Modular BOM
Pseudo BOM
Conclusion

QUESTIONS

PROBLEMS

CASES

SELECTED BIBLIOGRAPHY

Material requirements planning (MRP) is a computer-based production planning and inventory control system. It is also known as "time-phased requirements planning." MRP is concerned with both production scheduling and inventory control. It provides a precise scheduling (priorities) system, an efficient material control system, and a rescheduling mechanism for revising plans as changes occur. It keeps inventory levels at a minimum while assuring that required materials are available when needed. The major objectives of an MRP system are *simultaneously* to:

1. ensure the availability of materials, components, and products for planned production and for customer delivery,
2. maintain the lowest possible level of inventory,
3. plan manufacturing activities, delivery schedules, and purchasing activities.

It is the attainment of these objectives concurrently that makes MRP worthwhile.

Demand for an item may be independent or dependent. Independence means no relationship exists between the demand for an item and any other item, as in the case of end items or finished products. Independent demand tends to be continuous and fluctuates because of random influences; items with independent demands are subject to market conditions and are not contingent on operations requirements. In contrast, dependence means the demand for an item is directly related to or the result of the demand for a "higher level" item and has requirements generated for its use in the manufacture of another item. For example, raw materials, parts, or subassemblies are required for the manufacture of a finished product. Dependent demand is not random but tends to occur in a lumpy manner at specific points in time. The lumpiness occurs because most manufacturing is in lots, and all the items needed to produce the lots usually are withdrawn from inventory at the same time instead of unit by unit. Although the demand for the final product may be continuous and independent, the demand for lower-level, subordinate items composing the product tends to be discrete, derived, and dependent.

The lumpy demand pattern for dependent items is very unlike the constant demand rate assumption of the basic EOQ model. In principle, the EOQ replenishes inventory items when levels run low, so that inventory is available at all times. Except for the observance of lot sizing economies, dependent demand items should be available only when needed (not before and not after); they do not need to be replenished when no manufacturing requirement exists (demand is zero). In EOQ systems, independent demand for inventory items is forecasted and used to determine stock level replenishments. Dependent demand items need not be forecasted, because their requirements can be derived from the demand for "higher level" items. Demand should be forecasted only when it cannot be calculated. Independent demand items should be forecasted, while dependent demand items should be calculated by MRP via a bill of materials explosion.

The distinctions between independent and dependent demands are important in classifying inventory items and in developing systems to manage items within each demand classification. MRP systems were developed to cope better with dependent demand items than could previous systems based on unsuitable replenishment assumptions. MRP's role is to schedule all dependent components as required by the master scheduled items. The master schedule, as outlined in the previous chapter, develops the schedule for all independent demand items. MRP then determines what components will be required and when they will be required in order to execute the

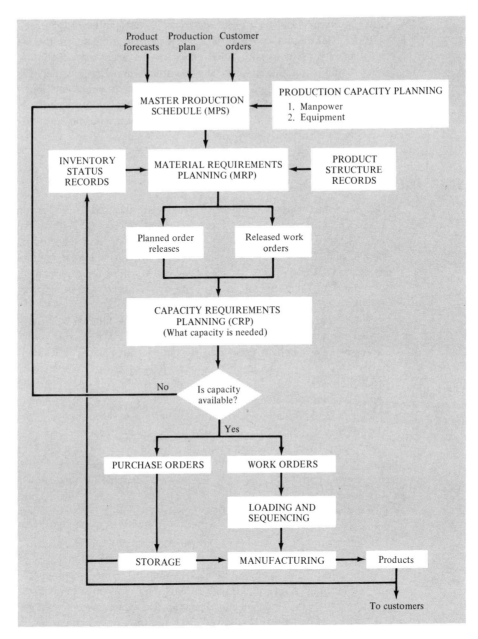

FIGURE 1
A closed-loop MRP system.

master production schedule. It systematically works backward from the scheduled completion dates of end items to derive the scheduled order quantities and order dates for dependent demand components. In manufacturing organizations, most inventory items are dependent and should be controlled by an MRP system.

The key features of an MRP system are the time-phasing of requirements, generation of lower-level requirements, planning of order releases, and rescheduling of orders to meet realistic commitments. Time-phasing of requirements simply establishes the time period in which work must be accomplished (or material made available) to meet the delivery date of the end item as stipulated in the master schedule.[1] Starting with the end item, MRP generates the necessary scheduling for all lower-level requirements (assemblies, subassemblies, and components). Planned order releases indicate when orders should be placed by purchasing and manufacturing. When work cannot be accomplished on time, MRP can reschedule planned orders so priorities are realistic and meaningful. A flow diagram of how a typical MRP system may function is shown in Figure 1.

MRP INPUTS

The three major inputs of an MRP system are the master production schedule, the inventory status records, and the product structure records. Without these basic inputs the MRP system cannot function. The master production schedule outlines the production plan for all end items. The product structure records contain information on all materials, components, or subassemblies required for each end item. The inventory status records contain the on-hand and on-order status of inventory items. A flow diagram of MRP inputs is contained in Figure 2.

The demand for end items is scheduled over a number of time periods and recorded on a *master production schedule* (MPS). The master production schedule expresses how much of each item is wanted and when it is wanted. The planning horizon of the MPS should be large enough to cover the cumulative procurement and production lead times ("stacked" lead times) for all components and assemblies composing the end items. One-week increments have been found to be the most practical, so the planning horizon can comprise several one-week planning periods. The MPS is developed from end item forecasts and customer orders. It must project a realistic plan of production that is leveled to accommodate the available capacity. The MPS is not the same as the forecast; they may differ because (1) the forecast may exceed the plant capacity, (2) it may be desirable to increase or decrease inventory levels, or (3) the firm may desire to operate uniformly using inventory as a buffer against demand fluctuations. Master scheduling is a basic input to and driving force behind the MRP system. MRP takes the master schedule for end items and translates it into individual time-phased component requirements.

The *product structure records,* also known as bill of material (BOM) records, contain information on every item or assembly required to produce end items. The master schedule shows how much of each end item must be available on particular dates to satisfy the independent demand. The quantities of components required to build the end items can be derived from the bills of materials. Information on each item, such as part number, description, quantity per assembly, next higher assembly, and quantity per end item, must be available. The product structure records contain the bills of materials for the end items in levels representing the way they are actually manufactured: from raw materials to subassemblies to assemblies to end items.

The *inventory status records* contain the status of all items in inventory. All inventory items must be uniquely identified. These records must be kept up to date,

[1]The term end item will be used in reference to the master schedule. The end item may be the final product, a product module, or a major assembly. When a product consists of numerous options, it is frequently desirable to master schedule below the product level at a lower level that disentangles the options.

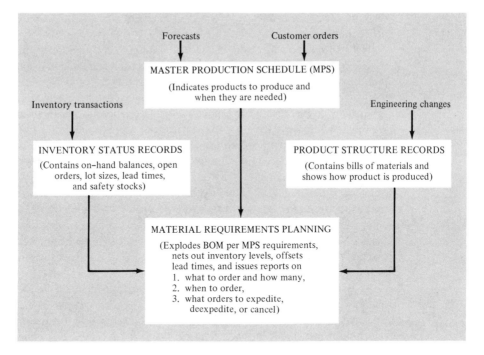

FIGURE 2
MRP inputs.

with each receipt, disbursement, or withdrawal documented to maintain record integrity. They should also contain information on lead times, lot sizes, or other item peculiarities. MRP will determine from the master production schedule and the product structure records the gross component requirements; the gross component requirements will be reduced by the available inventory (on-hand plus on-order) as indicated in the inventory status records. Quantities of items in inventory at the start of a planning horizon are available for use and are referred to as "on-hand." "On-order" quantities are those that are expected to become available during a planning horizon from open work orders or open purchase orders. MRP takes into account both on-hand and on-order quantities.

MRP OUTPUTS

As stated previously, MRP takes the master production schedule for end items and determines the gross quantities of components required from the product structure records. Gross requirements are obtained by "exploding" the end item product structure record into its lower level requirements. The exploding process is simply a multiplication of the number of end items by the quantity of each component required to produce a single end item. The explosion identifies *what* components are required, as well as *how many,* to produce a given quantity of end items (the term explosion is used because each level in the product structure tends to create more requirements than the previous one). By referring to the inventory status records, the gross quantities will be netted by subtracting the available inventory items. The actual order quantity for an item may be adjusted to a suitable lot size, or it may simply be the net requirement.

Just as important as "what" and "how many" is *when*. The timing of orders is based on scheduling order releases for the purchase or the manufacture of component parts in a sequence which assures their availability in proper conjunction with the total manufacturing process. The orders are planned for far enough ahead to allow adequate time for scheduled completion of the final product without having materials waiting unnecessarily for entry into a particular stage of the production process. Considering when components are scheduled to be purchased or produced and the lead times for their supply, MRP time-phases orders by lead time offsetting or setbacks. For purchased components, lead time is the time interval between placement of the purchase order and its availability in inventory. For manufactured items, it is the interval between the release of the work order and its completion. To make sure the component is available when needed, the planned order is offset (moved back) so that it is placed at the beginning of the lead time. Normally, all components to an assembly are planned to be available before the start date and therefore are set back at least to the beginning of their lead time period.

Thus, the material requirements for each component are phased over time in a pattern determined by lead times and parent requirements. MRP plans orders (planned order releases) for purchasing and shop scheduling for the quantity of items that must be available in each time period to produce the end items. The planned order release provides the quantity and time period when work orders are to be released to the shop or purchase orders placed with suppliers. A schematic of planned order releases as MRP outputs is contained in Figure 3. When the order (work or purchase) is released or placed, it changes from being "planned" to being "scheduled," "open," or "on order." The two basic purposes of planned orders are:

1. to generate material requirements at the next lower level,
2. to project capacity requirements.

Although MRP is an excellent planning and scheduling tool, its greatest benefit may be its ability to replan and reschedule in view of unforeseen contingencies. The

FIGURE 3
MRP outputs.

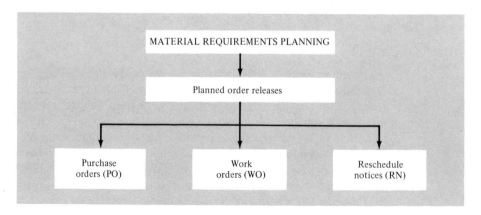

MRP system can predict shortages and overages soon enough so that something can be done to prevent them. It can keep order priorities up to date by planning and replanning order due dates. MRP provides exception reporting whenever a mismatch of timing between demand and supply exists. It is a priority system: typical messages are to delay, expedite, cancel an existing order, launch a new order, etc. It attempts to make the due date and need date coincide, so operations proceed as planned while inventory investment is minimized. If a component to an assembly will not be available when planned, MRP can reschedule all other co-components to the same assembly to a later date while rescheduling shop priorities. MRP will not actually reschedule orders, but it will print messages specifying exactly where changes are appropriate. The decision to make changes remains with management personnel.

PRODUCT STRUCTURES

MRP is well suited for fabrication and/or assembly type operations. A fabricated part has had manufacturing operations performed on it such as bending, cutting, grinding, milling, drilling, blanking, polishing, or coating. An assembly is a collection of parts and/or subassemblies that are put together. A subassembly is an assembly that is used at a higher level to make up another assembly. The term ''component'' in MRP refers to all inventory items below the product level, including subassemblies, parts, and raw materials, whether they are produced internally or obtained from suppliers. In MRP, only assembly and component relationships are considered; other terms such as subassembly, fabricated part, purchased part, or raw material are subsumed under ''components.''

A bill of materials (BOM) is a list of the items, ingredients, or materials needed to produce an end item or product. It lists all of the subassemblies, parts, and raw materials that go into a parent assembly, showing the quantity of each required to make an assembly. It shows how much of what materials is needed in what order to manufacture a product. An accurate formal bill of materials is needed for every product. The BOM will contain information on each input to the product, such as part numbers, descriptions, quantity needed for each part number, and the unit of measure. All items in the BOM must be uniquely numbered and identified.

When a product is designed, an engineering drawing (blueprint) is made, and the bill of materials is created at the same time. This initial design information is used by a process planner to develop route and operation sheets on how to make the product and by a purchasing agent to procure an adequate supply of parts for production. Originally, the function of a bill of materials was to define a product from a design point of view only. Unfortunately, a product may not be assembled the way it is designed. For MRP to be effective it is necessary to generate a BOM that represents the way the product is manufactured. Frequently, an existing BOM must be modified or restructured so it is a manufacturing as well as an engineering document.

Since MRP is product-oriented, bills of materials are an important basis for planning. Indeed, MRP is impossible without structured bills of materials. Without them, MRP could not successfully translate the master schedule into gross requirements below the end item level.

The traditional bill of materials for a product defines its structure by listing all the components that go into making it. A structured bill of materials specifies not only the composition of a product, but also the process stages in its manufacture. It defines the product structure in terms of levels of manufacture, each of which represents a completion state in the buildup of the product. It shows the "as built" as opposed to the "as designed" condition. In a schematic form, a structured bill of materials is known as a product structure, product tree, or Christmas tree. A more thorough discussion of the types of BOM is contained in Appendix A at the end of this chapter.

EXAMPLE 1

Suppose you are to produce 100 units of product A in period 8 with the product structure shown below. If no stock is on hand or on order, determine when to release orders for each component and the size of each order (Figure 4). Product A is made from components B and C; C is made from components D and E. By simple computation we can calculate our quantity requirements:

component B: (1) (number of A's) = 1(100) = 100,
component C: (2) (number of A's) = 2(100) = 200,
component D: (1) (number of C's) = 1(200) = 200,
component E: (2) (number of C's) = 2(200) = 400.

Now we must consider the time element for all the items. Table 1 creates a material requirements plan based on the demand for A, the knowledge of how A is made, and the time needed to obtain each component. It time-phases the requirements by offsetting the lead times. It shows which items are needed, how many are needed, and when they are needed.

A material requirements plan has been developed for product A based on the product structure of A and the lead time needed to obtain each component. Planned order releases of a parent item are used to determine gross requirements for its component items. Planned order releases generate a requirement in the same time period for its lower level components. In order to complete 100 units of product A in period 8 it is necessary to

FIGURE 4

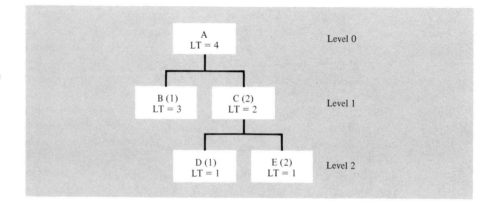

TABLE 1
MRP plan for 100 units of product A in period 8

Lead Time			1	2	3	4	5	6	7	8
4	A	Gross requirements								100
		Planned order releases				100				
3	B	Gross requirements				100				
		Planned order releases	100							
2	C	Gross requirements				200				
		Planned order releases		200						
1	D	Gross requirements		200						
		Planned order releases	200							
1	E	Gross requirements		400						
		Planned order releases	400							

release orders for 100 units of B in period 1, 200 units of C in period 2, 200 units of D in period 1, and 400 units of E in period 1. Planned order release dates are simply obtained by offsetting the lead times. A component's gross requirements time period is the planned order release period of its parent. Planned order releases indicated for the first period are those that are in "action buckets" where immediate action is mandatory. Planned order releases for two or more periods into the future do not require immediate action.

LOW LEVEL CODING

When a component is used on numerous products or appears in various levels in the BOM, it is necessary to use low level coding. Some components are used in two or more end items at various levels. When a component appears at more than one level, it is customary to assign it to its lowest level—i.e., the level farthest down the product structure (lower levels are indicated by higher numbers). Every item will have one and only one low level code. This code will indicate when to explode and net (subtract available inventory from the gross requirements) an item during MRP so it is netted only once during the generation of requirements.

The low level code determines when an item is eligible for netting (after all higher level items have been exploded and netted). It is necessary to explode the numbers of level 0 items needed in order to find out how many level 1 components are needed, because level 1 items are the ones that go directly into level 0 items. In a similar fashion, it is necessary to explode the numbers of level 1 items to find out how many level 2 components are needed. The above process is continued until all the product levels have been treated. The total gross requirement for an item is the sum of requirements from all its parents or sources.

FIGURE 5
The MRP process.

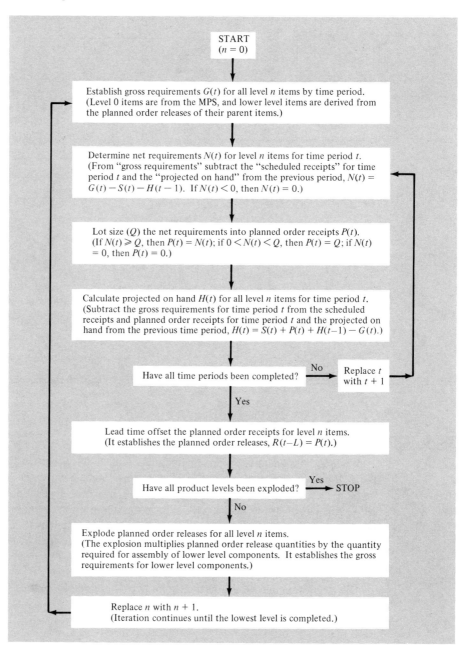

MRP COMPUTATIONS

The computations and steps required in the MRP process are not complicated. They involve only simple arithmetic. The MRP process is outlined in Figure 5. The format for a typical MRP matrix is shown in Figure 6 along with a description of the mean-

FIGURE 6
Typical MRP matrix.

Lot size	Lead time	On hand	Safety stock	Allocated	Low level code	Item

	Period							
PD	1	2	3	4	5	6	7	8

	PD	1	2	3	4	5	6	7	8
Gross requirements									
Scheduled receipts									
Projected on hand									
Net requirements									
Planned order receipts									
Planned order releases									

The column entries are self-explanatory. The row entries have the following meaning:

Gross requirements: the total anticipated production, use, or withdrawals during each time period. For end items, this quantity is obtained from the master production schedule (independent demand items); for components (dependent demand items) it is derived from the "planned order releases" of their parents.

Scheduled receipts: material that is already ordered (from manufacturing orders or purchase orders) that is expected to arrive (also known as on-order, open orders, or scheduled orders).

Projected on hand: the expected quantity in inventory at the end of the period, available for demand in subsequent periods. This is calculated by subtracting the "gross requirements" for the period from the "scheduled receipts" and "planned order receipts" for the same period as well as the "projected on hand" from the previous period.

Net requirements: the reduction of "gross requirements" by the "scheduled receipts" in the period plus the "projected on hand" in the previous period. This indicates the net number of items that must be provided to satisfy the parent or master schedule requirements.

Planned order receipts: the size of the planned order (the order has not been placed yet) and when it is needed. This appears in the same time period as the "net requirements," but its size is modified by the appropriate lot sizing policy. It shows when the order is needed in stock. With lot sizing, the planned order quantity will generally exceed the "net requirements." Any excess beyond the "net requirements" goes into "projected on hand" inventory. With lot-for-lot ordering, the "planned order receipts" is always the same as the "net requirements."

Planned order releases: when the order should be placed (released) so the items are available when needed by the parent. This is the same as the "planned order receipts" offset for lead times. "Planned order releases" at one level generate material requirements at lower levels. When the order is placed, it is removed from the "planned order receipts" and "planned order releases" rows and entered in the "scheduled receipts" row. "Planned order releases" show the *what, how many,* and *when* of MRP.

Lot size	Lead time	On hand	Safety stock	Allocated	Low level code	Item				Period						
							PD	1	2	3	4	5	6	7	8

								PD	1	2	3	4	5	6	7	8
25	2	10	0	0	1	Z	Gross requirements		10	15	25	25	30	45	20	30
							Scheduled receipts		10	25						
							Projected on hand	10	10	20	20	20	15	0	5	0
							Net requirements				5	5	10	30	20	25
							Planned order receipts				25	25	25	30	25	25
							Planned order releases		25	25	25	30	25	25		

Item Z with a low level code of 1 has an on hand quantity of 10, a lead time of 2 weeks, and a lot size of 25 units. The numbers in each time period are interpreted as follows:

In the past due (PD) period, the "projected on hand" is the present on hand quantity of 10.

In period 1, the "gross requirements" are 10, which are satisfied from the 10 "projected on hand" from the previous period. The "scheduled receipts" of 10 will then become the "projected on hand."

In period 2, the "gross requirements" for 15 are satisfied by the 10 "projected on hand" from the previous period and 5 of the 25 from "scheduled receipts." The rest of the "scheduled receipts" of 20 become the "projected on hand."

In period 3, the "gross requirements" for 25 are satisfied partially by the 20 "projected on hand" from the previous period. The "net requirements" for 5 generate the need for "planned order receipts" of 25, the lot size. Offsetting for two weeks of lead time, the "planned order release" is period 1.

In period 4, the situation is exactly the same as in period 3 except the "planned order release" is for period 2.

In period 5, the "gross requirements" for 30 are satisfied in part by the 20 "projected on hand" from the previous period. The "net requirements" for 10 generate the need for "planned order receipts" of 25, the lot size. Thus, the "planned order release" for 25 is planned for period 3. The rest of the "planned order receipts" of 15 become the "projected on hand."

In period 6, the "gross requirements" for 45 are satisfied in part by the 15 "projected on hand" from the previous period. The "net requirements" for 30 generate the need for "planned order receipts" of 30. Since the "net requirements" exceed the lot size, the "planned order receipts" are for the larger or the "net requirements." The "planned order release" is for period 4. Since the "planned order receipts" equal the "net requirements," the "projected on hand" becomes zero.

In period 7, the "gross requirements" of 20 become the "net requirements," since there are no units "projected on hand" from the previous period. The "net requirements" for 20 generate the need for "planned order receipts" of 25, the lot size. Thus, the "planned order release" is for period 5. The rest of the "planned order receipts" of 5 become the "projected on hand."

In period 8, the "gross requirements" of 30 are satisfied partially by the 5 "projected on hand" from the previous period. The "net requirements" for 25 generate the need for "planned order receipts" of 25, which is the lot size. The "planned order release" is for period 6. Since the "planned order receipts" equal the "net requirements," the "projected on hand" becomes zero.

FIGURE 7
Example of MRP component computations.

ing of each term. An example of MRP component computations is shown in Figure 7 along with an explanation of how the quantities were determined. A thorough understanding of the MRP matrix and component computations is necessary before MRP can be mastered.

EXAMPLE 2

In the MRP table below, indicate the projected on hand requirements, the planned order receipts, and the planned order releases. The lead time is two periods, and the lot size is the same as the net requirements (lot size = 1).

	PD	\multicolumn{8}{c}{Period}
	PD	1	2	3	4	5	6	7	8
Gross requirements		5	10	18	0	10	6	0	14
Scheduled receipts			20						
Projected on hand	20								
Net requirements									
Planned order receipts									
Planned order releases									

Solution:

	PD	\multicolumn{8}{c}{Period}
	PD	1	2	3	4	5	6	7	8
Gross requirements		5	10	18	0	10	6	0	14
Scheduled receipts			20						
Projected on hand	20	15	25	7	7	0	0	0	0
Net requirements						3	6		14
Planned order receipts						3	6		14
Planned order releases				3	6		14		

The preceding example illustrated how to net the gross requirements and establish planned order releases with lot-for-lot ordering (the order quantity is the same as the net requirements). The following example will require the same process except with a fixed lot size.

EXAMPLE 3

Redo Example 2 in the MRP table below with the lot size equal to 15 units.

	PD	\multicolumn{8}{c}{Period}

	PD	1	2	3	4	5	6	7	8
Gross requirements		5	10	18	0	10	6	0	14
Scheduled receipts			20						
Projected on hand	20								
Net requirements									
Planned order receipts									
Planned order releases									

Solution:

		1	2	3	4	5	6	7	8
Gross requirements		5	10	18	0	10	6	0	14
Scheduled receipts			20						
Projected on hand	20	15	25	7	7	12	6	6	7
Net requirements						3			8
Planned order receipts						15			15
Planned order releases				15			15		

The following example will illustrate the explosion process where gross requirements for a dependent item are derived from the parent which generates the demand for it. The planned order release of the parent is exploded into the gross requirements of its component items. It "lines up" (appears in same time period) with the gross requirements generated by it. Thus, the planned order release is responsible for the dependent item requirements.

EXAMPLE 4

Product K has the product structure shown below. Complete the MRP tables if the lot sizes are equal to one.

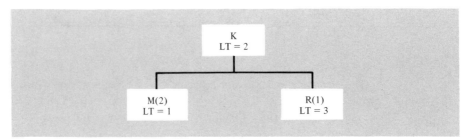

Period								
PD	1	2	3	4	5	6	7	8

K

Gross requirements		25	15	120	0	60	0	15	0
Scheduled receipts									
Projected on hand	50								
Net requirements									
Planned order receipts									
Planned order releases									

M

Gross requirements									
Scheduled receipts		30							
Projected on hand	225								
Net requirements									
Planned order receipts									
Planned order releases									

Solution:

K

Gross requirements		25	15	120	0	60	0	15	0
Scheduled receipts									
Projected on hand	50	25	10	0	0	0	0	0	0
Net requirements				110		60		15	
Planned order receipts				110		60		15	
Planned order releases		110		60		15			

M

Gross requirements		220		120		30			
Scheduled receipts		30							
Projected on hand	225	35	35	0	0	0	0	0	0
Net requirements				85		30			
Planned order receipts				85		30			
Planned order releases			85		30				

The preceding example illustrated the explosion process for a single product. The next example will show that a particular dependent item may have "needs" or gross requirements placed on it from more than one source. MRP will combine the gross requirements placed on items regardless of their source or number of parents.

EXAMPLE 5

Two products, *J*, and *K*, have the product structures shown below. Complete the MRP tables below with the lot sizes of $J = 1$, $K = 1$, and $M = 30$.

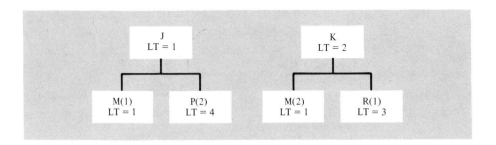

		Period							
	PD	1	2	3	4	5	6	7	8

J

Gross requirements		0	50	80	10	0	60	10	25
Scheduled receipts									
Projected on hand	15								
Net requirements									
Planned order receipts									
Planned order releases									

K

Gross requirements		25	15	120	0	60	0	15	0
Scheduled receipts									
Projected on hand	50								
Net requirements									
Planned order receipts									
Planned order releases									

		Period							
	PD	1	2	3	4	5	6	7	8

M

	PD	1	2	3	4	5	6	7	8
Gross requirements									
Scheduled receipts			30						
Projected on hand	225								
Net requirements									
Planned order receipts									
Planned order releases									

Solution:

J

	PD	1	2	3	4	5	6	7	8
Gross requirements		0	50	80	10	0	60	10	25
Scheduled receipts									
Projected on hand	15	15	0	0	0	0	0	0	0
Net requirements			35	80	10		60	10	25
Planned order receipts			35	80	10		60	10	25
Planned order releases		35	80	10		60	10	25	

K

	PD	1	2	3	4	5	6	7	8
Gross requirements		25	15	120	0	60	0	15	0
Scheduled receipts									
Projected on hand	50	25	10	0	0	0	0	0	0
Net requirements				110		60		15	
Planned order receipts				110		60		15	
Planned order releases		110		60		15			

M

	PD	1	2	3	4	5	6	7	8
Gross requirements		255	80	130	0	90	10	25	0
Scheduled receipts		30							
Projected on hand	225	0	0	0	0	0	20	25	25
Net requirements			80	130		90	10	5	
Planned order receipts			80	130		90	30	30	
Planned order releases		80	130		90	30	30		

EXAMPLE 6

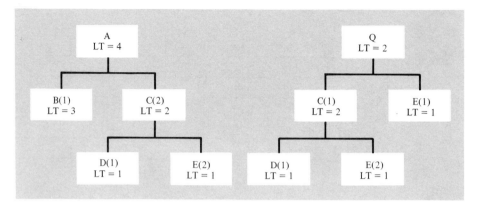

FIGURE 8

Develop an MRP plan for products A and Q with the product structures given in Figure 8. There are orders for 103 units of product A in period 8 and 200 units of product Q in period 7. The on hand inventory levels for each item are $A = 18$, $Q = 6$, $B = 10$, $C = 20$, $D = 0$, and $E = 30$. A safety stock of 5 units is maintained on product A and 6 units on product Q; there is no safety stock on other components. Additionally, 10 of the 18 units on hand of product A are already allocated. There are no open orders (scheduled receipts) on any item. The lot size for items A, Q, B, and C is the same as the net requirements (lot-for-lot ordering), while the lot size for D is 200 units and E is 500 units. What should be the size of the orders for each item, and when should the orders be released?

The low level code (LLC) for each item is as shown in Table 2. Since item E appears at level 1 and level 2 in product Q, and also at level 2 in product A, it is assigned the lowest level code of 2.

TABLE 2

Item	Low level code
A	0
Q	0
B	1
C	1
D	2
E	2

The MRP plan for 103 of product A and 200 of product Q is shown in Table 3. It shows *what* is needed, *how many* are needed, and *when* they are needed. The table was developed in the following manner.

1. The first step is to establish the gross requirements for items A and Q, which are given as 103 and 200 units. Items A and Q are netted, since they have low level codes of 0. By lead time offsetting, planned order releases for A and Q of 100 and 200 units in periods 4 and 5 are obtained.

2. The planned order releases for A and Q in periods 4 and 5 are exploded (multiplied by use quantities of items B, C, and E) and accumulated as gross requirements

TABLE 3
MRP plan for 103 product A and 200 product Q

Lot size	Lead time	On hand	Safety stock	Allocated	Low level code	Item		PD	1	2	3	4	5	6	7	8
1	4	18	5	10	0	A	Gross requirements									103
							Scheduled receipts									
							Projected on hand	3	3	3	3	3	3	3	3	0
							Net requirements									100
							Planned order receipts									100
							Planned order releases					100				
1	2	6	6	0	0	Q	Gross requirements								200	
							Scheduled receipts									
							Projected on hand	0	0	0	0	0	0	0	0	
							Net requirements								200	
							Planned order receipts								200	
							Planned order releases						200			
1	3	10	0	0	1	B	Gross requirements					100				
							Scheduled receipts									
							Projected on hand	10	10	10	10	0				
							Net requirements					90				
							Planned order receipts					90				
							Planned order releases		90							
1	2	20	0	0	1	C	Gross requirements					200	200			
							Scheduled receipts									
							Projected on hand	20	20	20	20	0	0			
							Net requirements					180	200			
							Planned order receipts					180	200			
							Planned order releases			180	200					
200	1	0	0	0	2	D	Gross requirements			180	200					
							Scheduled receipts									
							Projected on hand	0	0	20	20					
							Net requirements			180	180					
							Planned order receipts			200	200					
							Planned order releases		200	200						
500	1	30	0	0	2	E	Gross requirements			360	400		200			
							Scheduled receipts									
							Projected on hand	30	30	170	270	270	70			
							Net requirements			330	230					
							Planned order receipts			500	500					
							Planned order releases		500	500						

for items B, C, and E. Only items B and C have a low level code of 1. Items B and C are netted. A planned order release of 90 units is scheduled for B for period 1. Similarly, planned order releases for 180 and 200 units are scheduled for C for periods 2 and 3.

continued

EXAMPLE 6— *continued*

>   3. The planned order releases for B and C in periods 1, 2, and 3 are exploded (mul-
>   tiplied by use quantities of items D and E) and accumulated as gross requirements
>   for items D and E. Item E already has a gross requirement of 200 units in period 5
>   from item Q's explosion. Items D and E, with low level codes of 2, are netted.
>   Planned order releases for 200 units are scheduled for D for periods 1 and 2.
>   Planned order releases for 500 units are scheduled for E for periods 1 and 2.

The planned order release is exploded into gross requirements of its component items. It "lines up" (appears in same time period) with the gross requirements generated by it. Thus, the planned order release is responsible for the dependent item requirements. In Example 6, note how the planned order release for 100 units of product A in period 4 was exploded into gross requirements of 100 units for component B and 200 units for component C in the same period 4. Similarly, in Example 6, the planned order release for 200 units of product Q in period 5 was exploded into gross requirements of 200 units each of components C and E in the same period. The process of planned order releases creating requirements at the next lower level continues to the end of the product structure, when all the component requirements have been satisfied.

Planned order release quantities in MRP may be lot size quantities or identical to the net requirements for a given period. Ordering the same quantity as the net requirements, as in Example 1, is called lot-for-lot ordering. Safety stocks can be used with MRP, but it does not consider them available for regular use. Safety stock is recommended at the end item level but not the component level in MRP. The need for safety stock of components is reduced by MRP, since it calculates the exact quantities and when they are needed.

Reasons of economy or convenience may dictate the ordering of inventory items in excess of net requirements. Although MRP emphasizes the timing of orders more than the size of orders, lot sizing techniques based on balancing the costs of ordering and holding inventory commonly are used with MRP systems. There are several different types of lot sizing techniques, such as the economic order quantity (EOQ), the Wagner-Whitin algorithm, the Silver-Meal heuristic algorithms, and the part-period algorithm.[2]

Lot sizing which relies on forecasted demand may result in unstable lot sizes in dynamic situations. As the forecast signals change in response to irregular demand, the lot sizes are adjusted upward and downward. The ordering system becomes "nervous": it has frequent reactions to change and may initiate recomputation of MRP outputs in many of these instances. Lot sizing at upper levels of the product structure can cause aggravated "nervousness" in order sizes for lower level components, particularly for complex products with several levels. A "nervous" system typically has

---

[2]For a more detailed analysis of lot sizing see R. J. Tersine, *Principles of Inventory and Materials Management*, New York: North-Holland, 1982, Chapter 8.

a high volume of exception messages as manifestations of distorted or exaggerated lot sizing priorities.

Many exception messages will be generated if many orders are past due or scheduled too early or too late. With MRP logic, it is possible to have low level items scheduled "past due." However, it is not logical, operationally speaking, to schedule a component in a time period that has already passed. Therefore, the exception message will come to the attention of an analyst, who may revise the master schedule for the end item to a later period, or else compress the lead time by expediting the item if possible. Some managerial replanning is necessary when action is required in the past due time period.

When it is desired to supersede MRP logic, a *firm planned order* (FPO) is used. It freezes an order in a particular time bucket. It does not allow the normal MRP gross to net and lead time offset logic to take place. A firm planned order is a manual intervention mode to override typical MRP logic so a planner can expedite a past due order, compress lead time, change the lot size, or perform other changes.

MRP performs its procedures from the top of the product structure downward, exploding requirements level by level. There are times when it is desirable to identify the parent item that generated the component (dependent) requirement. This is possible through what is called "pegged" requirements. The pegging of requirements permits a retracing upward in the product structure to identify each parent that created the component demand. Single-level pegging locates the immediate parents; full pegging determines the end items that generated the component requirement. If a component will be delayed, it is then possible to indicate its impact on the delivery of the end item to the customer. Pegged requirements are very important in determining the significance of rescheduling alternatives.

It should be apparent by now that a manual MRP system is untenable except for very simple products. Computerized MRP systems are necessary because of the massive number of lower level items and the tedium of manual computations. Numerous organizations have highly sophisticated MRP systems, which have been implemented in the last decade. Software packages are readily available to ease the pain of conversion from other systems. However, MRP systems must be tailored to meet the specific needs of an organization.

MRP TYPES

There are two basic types of MRP systems, the regenerative and the net change systems, geared to different frequencies of replanning. With *regenerative systems,* the entire MRP (full explosions) is recalculated periodically (usually once a week), based on the latest master schedule requirements. The regenerative approach is designed for low-frequency replanning and employs batch-processing techniques. Regeneration starts over with a "new slate" and reexplodes the entire master schedule. After each planning period the planning horizon is extended one more period into the future. One advantage of the regenerative system is that it permits efficient use of data processing equipment. Another benefit is that fewer data errors are compounded over time, since it is checked and corrected on a regular basis.

With *net change systems,* the entire requirements for every component are not recalculated periodically; only additions and subtractions from the master schedule are entered. The requirements change is then calculated for only those components affected (partial explosions). Net change can be applied instantaneously or at the end of each day. Net change is designed for high-frequency replanning. In a stable environment (master production schedule) the regenerative MRP functions satisfactorily; in a volatile environment with constant change the net change MRP is more desirable.

MRP OVERVIEW

MRP originally was seen as a superior method of ordering inventory. As it evolved, its major emphasis shifted to scheduling (establishing and maintaining valid due dates on orders). Today, it has been expanded further into manufacturing resource planning (MRP II) to include the effective planning of all the resources of a manufacturing

FIGURE 9
Manufacturing resource planning.

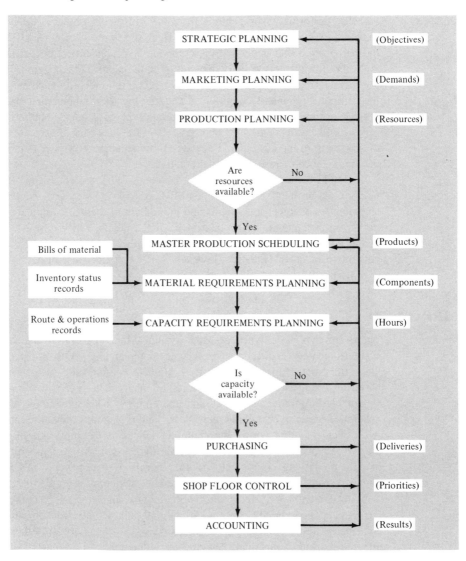

organization. As illustrated in Figure 9, manufacturing resource planning is a much more sophisticated system which incorporates information from manufacturing, marketing, engineering, and finance into a total operations plan for the organization. The evolution of MRP to closed-loop MRP to MRP II results in a single game plan to meet the overall goals of an organization. This is possible because it ties together strategic, financial, and capacity planning areas.

Thus, the term MRP has meant different things to different people at different times. Some think of it as an inventory system, others as a scheduling system, and still others as a complete closed-loop production system. It can be all of these things, depending on the organization and the stage of its development with MRP. Most would agree that MRP tends to foster systems thinking and it tends to become the cornerstone of the production system. Within the limits of its methodology, it will reveal (1) what is needed, (2) how many are needed, (3) when they will be needed, and (4) when they should be ordered.

The time horizon in MRP is composed of equal time periods called "time buckets." The "time buckets" are usually weeks or some other convenient time increment. The time horizon is usually longer than the longest sequence of component lead times of any product. It should be long enough to obtain all materials and produce all components before a planned order release for end items. It is also possible to have "bucketless MRP" where equal time periods are not used but specific dates are developed for every order.

The effective operation and efficiency of an MRP system depend on the integrity of the files and records of relevant data. The quality is directly influenced by data accessibility, up-to-dateness, and accuracy. Lack of record integrity is a major reason for the failure of MRP systems to live up to expectations. Computer-based MRP, even more than manual, will not perform satisfactorily with poor files and records. File integrity is not a one-time affair, but must have constant maintenance. The outputs from a computer-based MRP system cannot be better than its inputs.

When inventory decisions cannot be separated from production decisions, they must be considered part of aggregate planning for the total production system. Dependent demand inventory items are in this category, since they are production dependent. The function of an MRP system is to translate the overall plan of production (master production schedule) into detailed component requirements and orders. It determines what is to be manufactured and when, as well as what is to be procured and when. For end items, it is feasible to hold extra inventory to provide for customer service. To hold extra inventory of components with a dependent demand serves no function.[3] While the demand for end items may be uncertain, the demand for components is certain (deterministic) and dictated by the production schedule.

When the following conditions hold, MRP is usually superior to other inventory systems:

1. The final product is complex and contains several other items.
2. The specific demand for the product in any time period is known.
3. The final product is expensive.
4. The demand for an item is tied in a predictable fashion to the demand for other items.

---

[3]Safety stocks for components may be desirable to cushion uncertain lead times, scrap losses, and shrinkage.

5. The forces creating the demand in one time period are distinguishable from those in other time periods.

CAPACITY PLANNING AND CONTROL

Capacity planning determines how many persons, machines, and physical resources are required to accomplish the tasks of production. It defines, measures, and adjusts the levels of capacity so they are consistent with the needs of production. Capacity must be planned in terms of some unit of measure that is common to the mix of products encountered (units, tons, meters, standard hours, etc.). The unit of measure selected must translate all products into a common equivalent unit related to time.

There are many factors that affect capacity. Some factors are completely under management control, while others are not. The management controlled factors include:

1. land,
2. labor,
3. facilities,
4. machines,
5. tooling,
6. shifts worked per day,
7. days worked per week,
8. overtime,
9. subcontracting,
10. preventive maintenance.

Other, less controllable factors include:

1. absenteeism,
2. personnel turnover,
3. labor performance,
4. equipment breakdown,
5. scrap and rework.

Capacity can be affected by a change in any of the above factors.

Capacity refers to the production capability of a work center, department, or facility. It is important because (1) sufficient capacity is needed to provide the output for current and future customer demand, (2) it directly influences the efficiency (cost) of operations, and (3) it represents a sizable investment by the organization.

Operations managers must address the conflicting objectives of efficient plant operation, minimum inventory investment, and maximum customer service. They must answer the questions:

1. What should I be working on?
2. Do I have the capacity to work on it?

The first question deals with *priorities* and the second with *capacities*. It is necessary to plan and control both priority and capacity. Priority is the ranking by due date of an order relative to other orders. It determines what material is required and when it is required. MRP is a form of priority planning. Capacity is the quantity of work that can be performed at a work center and is frequently expressed in hours.

Capacity planning relates to labor and equipment requirements. It determines what

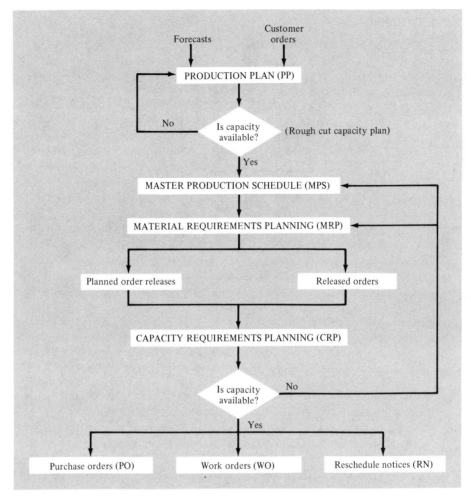

FIGURE 10
Capacity planning.

labor and equipment capacity is required and when it is required. It is usually planned on the basis of labor or machine hours available within the plant. Capacity has a direct influence on customer service. Excess capacity results in low resource productivity, while inadequate capacity may mean poor customer service.

Capacity decisions really start with the production plan, which establishes the output for each time period in aggregate terms. The production plan should be leveled so it is realizable within capacity constraints. The time horizon of the production plan is usually long enough that capacity can be changed (expanded or contracted) to meet expected demand. While the production plan deals in aggregate terms, the master schedule, which is derived from it, contains more specific detail on products and product modules. As shown in Figure 10, the production plan serves as a rough cut capacity plan within which the master schedule must be laid out.

The master schedule must also be a realizable schedule. MRP plans priorities, and

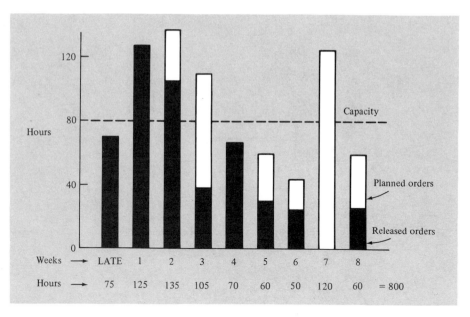

FIGURE 11
Capacity requirements plan.

it assumes that sufficient capacity is available to execute the master schedule. If the master schedule is overstated (overloaded), MRP priorities will be invalid and impossible to attain. For this reason, it is necessary to verify that sufficient capacity is available after the material requirements plan is obtained.

MRP is not a capacity plan, it does not solve capacity problems, and it does not level work loads in the shop. It tends to utilize capacity in a lumpy manner. Leveling the MPS can attenuate capacity fluctuations, but the netting of demands against existing stocks, previous order actions, and lot sizing policies tends to generate fluctuations in capacity requirements at the lower shop level.

The output from MRP will be planned order releases and released (open) orders, which are the inputs into capacity requirements planning (CRP). As shown in Figure 11, the combination of planned orders and released orders will be converted into their capacity requirements by time period. From route sheets, the operations required and their standard time can be ascertained. The capacity requirements plan will calculate the standard hours of production by work center and time period required to satisfy the master schedule. The objective is to indicate if existing capacity is adequate to support the master schedule. If sufficient capacity is not available, the master schedule must be revised or capacity expanded. If sufficient capacity is available, the material requirements plan can be executed.

The ability to see capacity requirements ahead of time is especially important in manpower planning. CRP enables an organization to anticipate overloads, underloads, or bottlenecks in work centers in time to take corrective action. It takes material requirements from MRP and converts them into standard hours of load on the labor and equipment in the various work centers for future time periods.

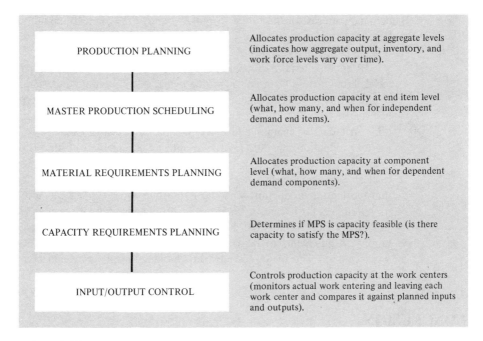

FIGURE 12
Production planning and control systems.

Thus, capacity planning is performed at various stages with different degrees of exactness. Before MRP, capacity planning is rough cut (performed in broad aggregate terms). After MRP, capacity planning, in the form of CRP, measures the work load at each work center, based on both planned and released orders. Capacity planning is really an iterative process of comparing available capacity with future capacity requirements. When there is an imbalance the following steps can be taken:

1. If available capacity is less than required capacity, either increase available capacity (utilize overtime, extra shifts, subcontracting, etc.) or reduce required capacity (reduce master schedule requirements, select alternate routings, etc.).
2. If available capacity is greater than required capacity, either reduce available capacity (shift or lay off manpower, reduce shift hours, etc.) or increase required capacity (increase master schedule requirements, release orders early, reduce subcontracting, etc.).

Frequently organizations have critical work centers that limit production. Critical work centers are bottleneck work centers where capacity is limited and flow restricted. In job shops, critical work centers may change from time period to time period. Frequently, work center loading is based only on released orders. With MRP, capacity requirements on work centers are based on planned orders as well as released orders. Thus, critical work centers can be planned more effectively.

An objective of capacity management is to match the level of operations to the level of demand. The uncertainty of demand gives rise to the need for capacity management. *Capacity planning* is a medium to long range problem based on expected demand patterns for the future. *Capacity control* is a short to medium range problem based on implementation of capacity plans and deployment of resources to accommodate temporary changes in demand.

MRP is a material-dominated scheduling technique which backward schedules material through time from end item due dates. After the time and quantity of material requirements have been determined, a capacity analysis (CRP) is performed to evaluate capacity feasibility. Problems are identified and solutions initiated by rescheduling materials or changing capacity. If either material or capacity is inadequate, the master production schedule is revised until an acceptable schedule is developed.

MRP is an input to capacity requirements planning, which must assess the workload at work centers and determine if capacity is sufficient. MRP systems assume that the master production schedule is feasible and adequate capacity exists to meet its requirements. If capacity is insufficient, changes must be made. Usually, capacities in key work centers are continuously monitored, for they indicate capacity limitations. Adjustments to labor and machine utilization may be necessary in critical work centers. The major modules in a production planning and control system are outlined in Figure 12.

CONCLUSION

Production planning and master scheduling establish the manufacturing plan of products or end items to be produced during a given time frame. MRP takes the master schedule for end items and calculates the plan for all dependent demand items composing the end items. Manufacturing and purchasing are responsible for executing the overall material plans as portrayed in Figure 13.

MRP combines product explosions, netting, lot sizing, time phasing, and other operations into one coordinated procedure. It can be compared to a person who makes a menu each day and buys groceries according to the menu. Items are purchased only as the menu requires them. Non-menu items are not purchased or prepared, so inventory is held very low.

Although MRP primarily calculates material requirements, it can be used to calculate machine time and labor needs. Once the MRP plan is established, route and

FIGURE 13
Material planning.

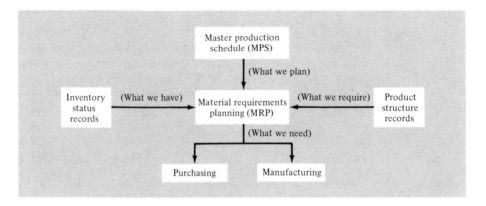

operation sheets can be utilized to determine labor and machine times. This additional extension is called capacity requirements planning. Thus, MRP is a valuable tool for (1) inventory control (time phasing orders to needs), (2) scheduling (setting priorities), and (3) capacity requirements planning (determining MPS capacity feasibility).

MRP is normally implemented as a computer-based system because of the quantity of transactions and simple calculations required. It is practically impossible to plan and replan hundreds of subassemblies with many-leveled product structures on a manual basis. Without a computer it is impossible to keep up-to-date records on the status of thousands of inventory items.

APPENDIX A: BILLS OF MATERIALS (BOM)

A bill of materials (BOM) is a list of the items, ingredients, or materials needed to produce a parent item, end item, or product. It can take several different forms and be used in many ways. It may be (1) a simple parts list, (2) structured to indicate how a product is produced, or (3) structured to simplify forecasting and master scheduling. The BOM is called a product structure when it indicates how a product will be produced. The specific format for the BOM depends upon its intended use. Some if its important uses are to:

1. define the product and distinguish it from other products,
2. facilitate the forecasting of optional product features,
3. permit the master schedule to be stated in terms of the fewest possible end items,
4. allow easy order entry from customers,
5. provide the basis for product costing,
6. facilitate material procurement,
7. aid manufacturing planning and final assembly scheduling,
8. permit efficient file storage and maintenance.

Bills of materials can be structured to provide information by either tracing down (exploding) or tracing up (imploding) a product structure. Explosion begins with the parent and breaks it into its lower level components; implosion begins with the component and builds into the parent or higher level items. The explosion of end item requirements or master scheduled items into component requirements is vital in MRP to establish all lower level component scheduling. When scheduling problems exist at the component level, implosion permits the identification of the parent item generating the requirement.

Traditional Bills of Materials

When product structure data are stored in a computer system, they can be retrieved and displayed in a variety of formats for the benefit of the various users. The objective is to load one bill that can generate numerous formats to satisfy different users in the organization. Six popular formats are:

1. single-level explosion,
2. indented explosion,
3. summary explosion,
4. single-level implosion,
5. indented implosion,
6. summary implosion.

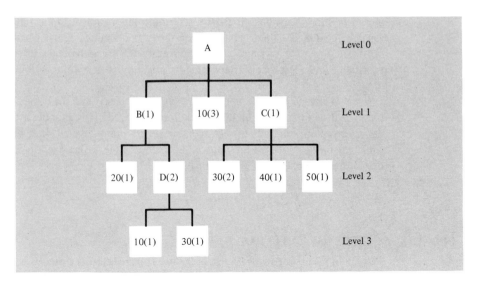

FIGURE 14
Multilevel product structure. The letters represent assemblies/subassemblies, and the numerals represent parts. The numbers in parentheses are the quantities required for assembly.

Each of the six formats is described briefly in this section. Following each general description is an illustration of the format style. All of the example illustrations use the information from the multilevel product structure for product *A* shown in Figure 14.

1. *The single-level explosion* format displays the components used at a specific level of assembly. Several single-level bills are designed to represent completely the product structure of a multilevel product. The four level product structure given in Figure 14 results in four single-level bills:

Single-level explosion BOM for assemblies *A*, *B*, *C*, and *D*

Assembly	Component part number	Quantity per assembly	Description
A	*B*	1	
	C	1	
	10	3	
B	*D*	2	
	20	1	
C	30	2	
	40	1	
	50	1	
D	10	1	
	30	1	

2. *The indented explosion* format lists components on all lower levels by indentation under their respective parents. Indentation signifies levels. All components of a given level are shown with their part numbers beginning in the same column. The indented format represents the product in the manner in which it is manufactured. Figure 14's product structure appears as follows when arranged in an indented explosion format:

Indented explosion BOM for product *A*

Part number			Description	Quantity per assembly	Unit of measure
Level 1	2	3			
B				1	
·	20			1	
·	D			2	
·	·	10		1	
·	·	30		1	
C				1	
·	30			2	
·	40			1	
·	50			1	
10				3	

3. *The summary explosion* format lists all items which go into an end item along with their total quantities. As can be seen from the example below, it includes all the components of an end item, irrespective of level, with the quantities reflecting use per end item rather than per immediate parent. When a component is used in more than one assembly, the summary explosion bill aids purchasing in the procurement of the proper quantity of items. This format does not indicate the way the product is produced, but it does assist in product costing, procurement, and other related activities:

Summary explosion BOM for product *A*

Assembly	Component[a]	Description	Quantity required	Unit of Measure
A	10		5	
	20		1	
	30		4	
	40		1	
	50		1	
	(B)		(1)	
	(C)		(1)	
	(D)		(2)	

[a]Subassemblies are indicated by parentheses. This listing of subassemblies is optional.

4. *The single-level implosion* format displays the assemblies that directly use a component at the next higher level. It is a where-used list that indicates all the immediate parents of an item. The items and their immediate parents for the multilevel structure of product *A* can easily be incorporated into the next example format:

Single-level implosion BOM for components 10, 20, 30, 40, and 50

Component part number	Assembly used on	Quantity per assembly	Description
10	A	3	
	D	1	
20	B	1	
30	C	2	
	D	1	
40	C	1	
50	C	1	

5. *The indented implosion* format indicates the usage of a component to all higher levels. It traces both the direct and indirect usage of a given component to all higher levels until the end product is reached. It is valuable in determining the parent that generated the component requirement as well as in evaluating the effects of engineering design changes. Component 30 from the product structure in Figure 14 is used to illustrate this format:

Indented implosion BOM for component 30

Component part number	Assembly used on	Quantity	Description
30	D	1	
	·B	2	
	··A	1	
	C	2	
	·A	1	

6. *The summary implosion* format shows all higher level items which contain the component along with the total quantity used in each. It is an expanded where-used list in which all higher levels that contain the component are listed. The "quantities per" are total quantities of the component used in each of the higher level assemblies. The identification of higher level requirements by summary implosion is depicted for components *D*, 10, and 30 of product *A*:

Summary implosion BOM for components *D*, 10, and 30

Component part number	Assembly used on	Quantity required	Description
D	A	2	
	B	2	
10	A	5	
	B	2	
	D	1	
30	A	4	
	B	2	
	C	2	
	D	1	

Matrix BOM

A matrix BOM is a consolidation of product summary data for families of items with a large number of common components. This format is used to identify and group the common parts found on the models in a family. The components are listed down the left hand side and the models or end items across the top. The numbers in the body of the matrix indicate the total number of components used to produce a single end item (it is the same information listed as "quantity required" in the summary explosion BOM for product *A*). An "X" is used to indicate a component is not used on a given item.

This bill is useful for products having many common components among products. The matrix format does not specify the manner in which the products are built. It cannot be used as manufacturing instructions for multilevel products, since it does not indicate the levels of assembly. An example for three products is as follows:

Matrix BOM for products *A*, *X*, and *Z*

Component part number	Description	Unit of measure	Product		
			A	*X*	*Z*
10			5	5	2
20			1	2	X
30			4	7	2
40			1	1	X
50			1	1	X
60			X	X	3
(B)			(1)	(2)	(1)
(C)			(1)	(1)	(X)
(D)			(2)	(1)	(2)

Add/Delete BOM

This bill, sometimes called a "comparative" or "same as, except" bill, defines a special product in terms of a standard product and specifies which components are to be added and which components are to be removed. New or unique products are stated as a standard product with some items added and others subtracted. Figure 15 shows the special product B15 is produced by putting together standard product B12 with components *F* and *G* and removing component *A*. It is an effective way to explain how one product differs from another. This bill cannot be utilized in making forecasts and is not well suited for MRP.

Modular BOM

Modular bills of materials are used for complex products that have many possible configurations and are made from a number of common parts. For example, in vehicle manufacturing, where choices of engines, transmissions, bodies, interiors, trim, and many other features are available, the several variations can be combined into a tremendous number of final configurations. Modularization provides a wide choice of products to the customer while keeping component inventories down. It has been used extensively in the automotive and farm equipment industries.

When a product line has many variations (optional features), their combinations can be astronomical and forecasting them for the master schedule becomes impossible. If a separate BOM were used for each unique end product for MRP purposes, the file records would be excessive (too costly to store and maintain). The solution to this problem is the modular bill of materials. A modular BOM is stated in building blocks or modules from which the final product is assembled. The process of modularizing breaks down the bills of products into

FIGURE 15
Add/delete BOM.

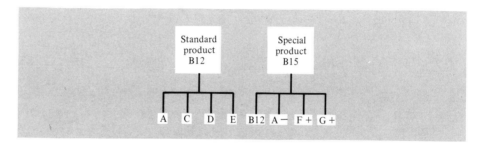

lower level modules. The demand for these modules can be forecasted separately with much more accuracy than the final configurations. Modules can achieve two different purposes:

1. to disentangle combinations of optional product features,
2. to segregate common parts from unique parts.

The first purpose facilitates forecasting, while the second minimizes inventory investment in components common to optional units.

An example will illustrate the concept of modularity. Suppose a manufacturer offers his customers 10 engines, 30 colors, 4 bodies, and 2 frames. By assembling the optional features in various combinations, it is possible to build $(10)(30)(4)(2) = 2400$ models or unique configurations:

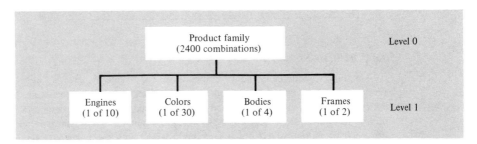

It would be irrational to set up separate bills for each end product (level 0); 2400 would be needed. Furthermore, the development of a master schedule showing the quantity of each model needed in specific time periods would be arduous. The solution is to disregard specific end item forecasts and proceed with a single forecast for the product family. From it, forecasts for each option can be derived from *popularity percentages,* defined as the probability of option selection based on past customer orders or expectations. These will make it possible to decompose the family forecast into the forecasts for each option. For example, past sales may

FIGURE 16
Product structures for four end items.

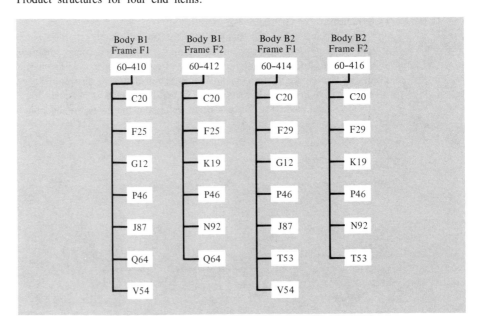

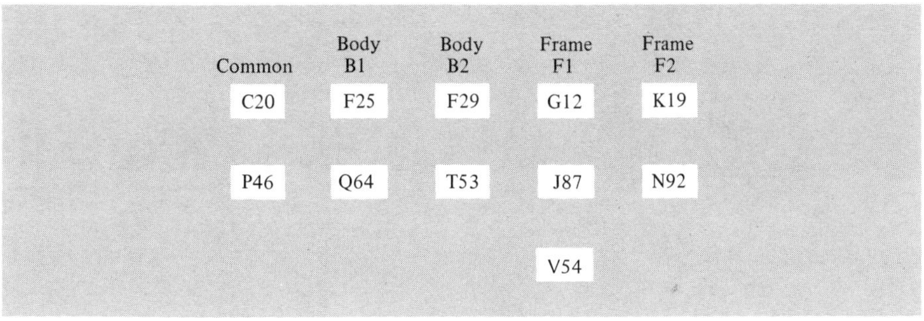

	Common	Body B1	Body B2	Frame F1	Frame F2
	C20	F25	F29	G12	K19
	P46	Q64	T53	J87	N92
				V54	

FIGURE 17
Modular bills of materials.

indicate that 75% of orders call for frame *A* and 25% for frame *B*. If the forecast is for 100 products per period, orders for 75 *A* frames and 25 *B* frames would be scheduled. In using the modular method, each of the options or modules would have a BOM, but there would be a total of $10 + 30 + 4 + 2 = 46$ bills instead of 2400.

If commonality of components within the product family exists, further analysis can reduce inventory investment by segregating common parts from unique parts. To illustrate this procedure, the previous example is scaled down so the restructuring process can be seen more clearly. Assume the product has only two optional features, the body and the frame, each with only two choices. The customer can select between body 1 and body 2, and between frame 1 and frame 2. Figure 16 represents the four bills of materials (B1 & F1, B1 & F2, B2 & F1, and B2 & F2). Only level 0 and level 1 are shown; lower levels are excluded for clarity. To restructure these bills into modules, they first are broken down into components. The components then are analyzed and compared with respect to usage on level 1 items (bodies and frames); they subsequently are grouped according to use. The analysis reveals that components C20 and P46 are common to all products, so they are assigned to the common group. Components F25 and Q64 are used only on B1F1 and B1F2, so they are unique to body option B1; components F29 and T53 are used only on B2F1 and B2F2, so they are unique to body option B2; components G12, J87, and V54 are used only on B1F1 and B2F1, so they are unique to frame option F1; and components K19 and N92 are used only on B1F2 and B2F2, so they are unique to frame option F2. Reorganization of the components according to their product options and common usages results in the modular bills shown in Figure 17.

Modularity does away with BOM at the product level (level 0) for purposes of MRP. Instead, assembly components (level 1 or lower) are promoted to end item status. This procedure establishes a new modular planning bill suitable for forecasting, master production scheduling, and MRP.

The BOM that cites the options necessary to build a specific end item is called a *manufacturing bill* or M-bill. It is simply a conglomeration of all the individual modular BOM that are selected by a customer or included in a specific warehouse order. This bill is not a direct part of the MRP system. It integrates with the MRP system by defining the items to be assembled against the final assembly schedule (FAS) given that these items use the components planned and provided by the MRP system.

Pseudo BOM

Pseudo BOM are imaginary components which are never actually produced. They sometimes are called ''phantom bills,'' ''super bills,'' or ''S-bills.'' As was illustrated in Figure 17 many assemblies and subassemblies become end items in modularizing the bills. This increases the number of items that will have to be forecasted and identified in the master schedule. The set

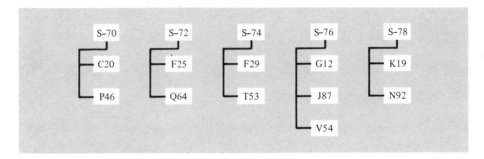

FIGURE 18
Super bills of materials.

of components in any related group is assigned an artificial part number. In Figure 18, the five groups of items in the modular bills of Figure 17 are assigned to imaginary part numbers S-70, S-72, S-74, S-76, and S-78. These artificial assembly numbers are not actually assembled, but are used in forecasting and master scheduling operations. The "quantity per" relationship of the pseudo bill is the popularity percentage of each module.

Another type of pseudo bill is the "K-bill". In building a product, a large number of small loose parts such as nuts, bolts, and fasteners frequently are used. Rather than identify each of the items individually, they are grouped together under an artifical part number called a kit. Thus, with one number an entire group of components that goes with a particular feature can be properly scheduled.

Conclusion

The BOM specifies the material content of an item, and multiple levels reflect the manufacturing processes for the item. Different BOM formats are used within an organization to explode requirements for MRP, prepare material purchase requisitions, assist product costing, make engineering changes, and so forth.

MRP information is usually stored in the single level format. It requires that the product be defined in such a manner as to express a valid master schedule in terms of BOM part numbers. It works with products and the relationship of their component items, using the BOM as the planning guide. Each component must be uniquely identified by part number. The BOM should signify the composition as well as the process stages in the product's manufacture in terms of levels. Without an accurate, up-to-date, complete, and properly structured file, MRP cannot work properly.

Restructuring of the traditional bill of material format can substantially simplify master scheduling for many organizations. If a firm order backlog does not cover the cumulative lead times, it is necessary to forecast master schedule requirements. Most organizations either make to stock, so that all planning is based on forecasts, or they use customer orders in the short range, and forecasts fill out the remainder of the planning horizon. Thus, the product must be defined in forecastable terms in the master schedule. It is simple to see that in a make-to-order environment, end items are not the best thing to forecast. Some specific BOM is needed to link the master schedule to its dependent components that have to be obtained prior to receiving the customer orders. Planning bills perform this function and substantially reduce the number of items to be forecasted and master scheduled.

QUESTIONS

1. What are the primary objectives of an MRP system?
2. Differentiate between independent and dependent demand items by pointing out the defining characteristics of each. To which category of items is MRP better suited?

3. What are the key features of an MRP system?

4. List and describe briefly the three major inputs to an MRP system.

5. Explain the phrase " 'exploding' the end item product structure record."

6. How does MRP time-phase net requirements?

7. To what items does the term "component" refer in MRP systems?

8. What is the purpose of low level coding? Does the product (end item) have the highest or lowest level code? Why?

9. Give the rules for lot sizing the net requirements into planned order receipts.

10. Distinguish between planned order receipts and planned order releases.

11. How are gross requirements obtained for end items? for components?

12. How does a net change system differ from a regenerative system?

13. What is the appropriate time horizon for an MRP system?

14. Give a concise discussion of the relationship of MRP to capacity planning.

15. What short-term steps can be taken to correct a capacity imbalance where available capacity is less than required capacity?

16. What are the uses for a bill of materials (BOM)?[4]

17. Why would a BOM generate both an explosion and an implosion format for the same product structure data? Give an example of both format types and the uses of each example.[4]

18. In what situation would a modular BOM be appropriate? Why?[4]

PROBLEMS

1. Compute the net requirements for the three items listed below:

	Item A	Item B	Item C
Gross requirements	175	30	140
On hand	35	5	70
On order	40	0	50
Safety stock	18	3	0

2. From the information given below for product A, draw the product structure:

Parent:	A	B	C
Components:	B(1)	E(2)	D(1)
	C(1)	F(1)	G(3)
	E(1)	G(1)	
	F(4)		

3. Make an indented bill of materials with low level coding for the product in Problem 2.

4. An indented parts list for product Z is given next. How many component F's are required? How many component 50's are required?

---

[4]Requires information contained in Appendix A.

Part number			Quantity/assembly
Z			—
·	A		1
·	·	80	6
·	·	110	6
·	·	F	3
·	G		2
·	·	50	4
·	·	70	4
·	·	90	1
·	K		2
·	M		2
·	Q		1
·	R		1
·	·	50	4
·	·	70	4
·	·	D	1
·	50		1

5. Subic Marine, Inc. manufactures power packages for the U.S. Navy. An order for 200 power packages has been received. Each power package contains two engines, each of which contains one gearbox; each gearbox contains five gears, and each gear is forged from high tensile strength steel. The available inventory is as follows:

Engines	13	Gears	215
Gearboxes	22	Steelforges	67

Determine the net requirements for each item.

6. After reviewing reliability data, the production manager in Problem 5 decides that a safety stock of five engines is necessary. What are the new net requirements for each item?

7. A manufacturer of one-half ton trucks offers its customers a number of options. The options available are as follows:

5 engines	15 colors
3 transmissions	4 bodies
2 rear ends	3 frames

How many unique truck configurations are possible? At what level of the product structure would the organization perform its master scheduling?

8. The lead time to purchase a steel spring from a supplier is four weeks. There are currently 42 springs available with an additional scheduled receipt of 20 springs in four weeks. The gross requirements for the steel spring over the next eight weeks are as follows:

Week	1	2	3	4	5	6	7	8
No. of units	12	17	0	14	2	28	9	18

If the order quantity is 20 units, when should orders be released for the spring?

9. An order has been received for 200 units of product A with the product structure shown next. If no stock is available or on order, determine the size of each order and when to release each order.

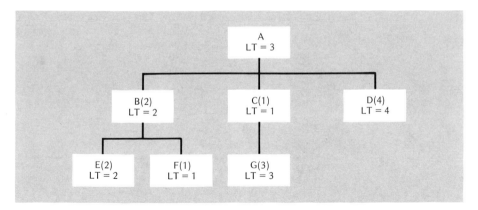

10. An order has been received for 150 units of product *A* with the product structure shown below. If no stock is available or on order, determine the size of each order and when to release each order.

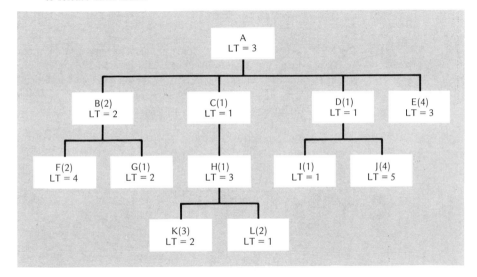

11. Orders have been received for 20 units of product *A* and 50 units of product *R* with the product structures shown below for period 8. The on hand stock levels are $A = 1$, $R = 4$, $B = 74$, $C = 19$, $D = 190$, and $E = 160$. What is the low level code for each item? If components are ordered as required (no fixed lot sizes), what should be the size of each order? When should orders be released for each item?

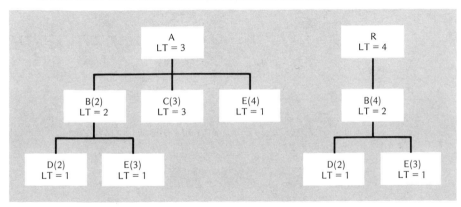

12. The A and B Manufacturing Company produces two products with the product structures shown below. It has orders for 150 units of product A in period 8 and 135 units of product B in period 7. The on hand inventory levels for each item are $A = 5$, $B = 2$, $C = 135$, $D = 300$, and $E = 356$. When should orders be released for each item, and what should be the size of the order?

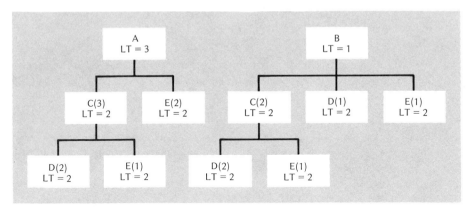

13. The XYZ Corporation assembles three products as shown in the product structures below. It has orders for 50 units of product X for period 8, 20 units of product Y for period 6, and 10 units of product Z for period 7. The on hand stocks of each item are $X = 7$, $Y = 3$, $Z = 2$, $A = 3$, $B = 12$, $C = 30$, $D = 3$, and $E = 40$. When should each order be placed, and what should be the size of each order?

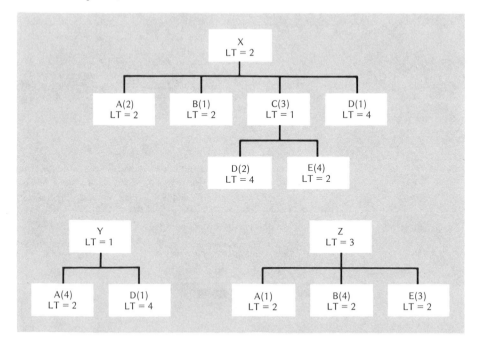

14. Joe Breakdown, the maintenance manager for XYZ Corporation, has just informed you that he will need ten item E in period 4. How would this change affect the orders planned in problem 13?

15. The supplier of item E in Problem 13 indicates that its lead time will be one period longer (3 periods) due to strike difficulties. What impact will this change have on the delivery of the product orders?

CASE 1: WILDCAT OPERATIONS

Gulf Coast, Inc. is a Texas manufacturer that engages in the production and distribution of equipment for the oil-producing industry. Gulf Coast is regarded as a competent manufacturer by the petroleum industry and especially so by the front-line production employees, who boast a high rate of success with G.C. products. The confidence shown in Gulf Coast is attributed to the generally faultless field installation of the company's pumping units and the outstanding performance and maintenance records of both the pumping units and the well heads. The major product lines are these two critical pieces of equipment: well heads (casing and tubing types and Christmas-tree assemblies) and pumping units (hydraulic-powered sucker-rod pumps, sub-surface hydraulic pumps, and plunger lifts). Gulf Coast is adding another artificial lift to the pump line this year, an electrical submersible centrifugal pump. Production design changes are occurring very rapidly due to technological advances, and additions to the major lines are being made frequently as a result of the dynamic nature of the industry.

The petroleum industry and all its subsections are presently undertaking projects that could drastically alter current operating methods. The industry is in perpetual motion and is investing ever more capital in research and development in order to promote further technological advance. Gulf Coast is an active participant in the change process. The company is dedicated to improving oil-producing equipment both to retain its competitive edge and to keep abreast of methods that extract the precious resource by the most efficient means.

Other changes occurring in oil-producing equipment and practices are less voluntary but an outcome of external regulations. The EPA, for instance, is becoming a very strong voice against the numerous and disastrous accidents that are plaguing drilling operations. Legislation governing the allowance for depletion is being scrutinized with a view to a reduction in the percentage rate of depletion. Laws are also being enacted to regulate exploration, transport, refinement, and sale of oil products; these newer and stricter measures could have adverse effects. Further, Congress has passed legislation to levy taxes on the income of the producers, i.e. windfall profits. Those particularly vulnerable to such taxation laws appear to be the integrated companies and the independent producers, who are Gulf Coast's largest customers.

Some legislation is on the horizon that could benefit the industry. One such act that could mitigate the onslaught of deleterious regulations is a proposed measure to support secondary recovery methods. Legislation of this type could foster the acquisition of new equipment and supplies. A second move to improve conditions is the American Petroleum Institute's increasing leniency regarding the specifications that have been set as to size, grade, weight per foot, type, etc. of the many casings used throughout the industry.

All factors considered, the industry is experiencing phenomenal growth. The growth of the independent producers is unprecedented. Gulf Coast is in the remarkable position of having sold all the pieces of equipment that it could possibly produce under present conditions for the next two years. With capacity and supplier constraints both being critical, the firm is unable to promise any more equipment within this two year period. However, the firm's management is in hope of increasing the supply by the implementation of an MRP system to replace the fixed order size system now in use.

Gulf Coast executives feel that an MRP system could be a more efficient way to order and control inventory. The present method of ordering every item—even valves, gauges, casings, tubings, etc.—independently is unsatisfactory. Computerized reports are seen as better control devices. In addition, the MRP system is considered to be a superior method for production scheduling. Given the frequent design changes, the increasing costs in the oil-producing industry, and the volatility of the energy related fields, MRP seems to be the safeguard that Gulf Coast management desires. Therefore, a shift to an MRP system appears to be a solution to Gulf Coast's problems of having parts on hand at necessary times and of being able to schedule and deliver by customer due dates.

However, in conjunction with the MRP system, Gulf Coast is also considering a companion system for the spare parts division. Because of the need for a large stock of spare parts, i.e. tubings and casings, for field installations and repairs, Gulf Coast knows it would be an impossibility to supply these needs from a dependent demand system. Thus, it is expected that a scaled-down version of the present EOQ system would be operational for spare parts after implementation of an MRP system to handle orders for finished products.

1. Does Gulf Coast management seem to be considering many of their circumstances as exceptional?
2. What effects does the demand side of the industry have on Gulf Coast's situation?
3. Is an MRP system a practical solution to the capacity and supply problems?
4. What purposes could an MRP system serve at Gulf Coast?

CASE 2: PROMISES, PROMISES

Sinthetics Corporation has two separate product lines. In one of the product lines, there are four "major" products, each composed of over six subassemblies of varying value. Most of the subassemblies have multiple configurations; in other words, the customer may select different product options (subassemblies) and hence define his own final product configuration. Because of the seemingly infinite number of possible end items (final product configurations), Sinthetic does no demand forecasting for this product line. Instead, it fabricates options and assembles end items after receipt of customer orders. The options are fabricated from parts which are planned using reorder point techniques. Consequently, the customer is given a delivery date based on the cumulative lead time of subassembly and final assembly processes (lead times are derived from actual average throughput times for unexpedited components and orders).

For the line of products with optional features, Sinthetic has excellent engineering drawings and reasonably accurate parts lists. Every drawing has a part number, and every part and assembly has a drawing. Whenever two or more parts are joined together, an assembly drawing is made and a unique part number assigned. Many of the "assemblies" have different part numbers but consist of the same components. A vast majority of subassemblies never flow in and out of the stockroom. The skilled assembly technicians, for example, will cut tubing, drill holes, mount fittings, etc. as they "build up" the end item (carry out the sequence of manufacturing steps). Wiring harnesses and other electrical assemblies similarly are prepared during the final assembly process. Because Sinthetics already possesses detailed engineering drawings of its uniquely identified parts and components, the production manager, Jim Wickersham, has decided that their incorporation into a computerized MRP system would facilitate inventory control and improve customer service. After these bills of materials are properly input into the system, it is thought that the outcomes from lead time offsetting and lot-for-lot ordering will be simplified scheduling and more economical parts ordering.

The second line of products is not composed of customer selected options, but still is not forecasted, due to low and irregular levels of demand. This line has five products, each with a set of uniquely numbered parts and components. Figure 19 represents the engineering product structure for one of the items belonging to this line, a power supply assembly. This item's lead time is based on "stacked" lead times, but in this case delivery lead time is the accumulation of purchase, fabrication, and assembly lead times. Judging from its product structure, delivery cannot be promised any sooner than 15 weeks from order receipt. Even with excessively long lead times quoted to customers, scheduled delivery dates commonly are protracted. Not only do the long lead times invariably result in unreliable delivery promises, but they indirectly are blamed for insufficient components. The shortages frequently are traced to the chaotic cannibalization of parts from one order to another in an effort to speed up the lengthy delivery process for preferred customers.

The assembly supervisor, John Brody, does not agree with the practice of stacking lead times. He sees the lengthy process as creating increased inventory levels, proliferating work orders, and adding unnecessary indirect costs. He would rather shorten the cumulative lead times by eliminating the separate fabrication of some of the assemblies shown on the engineering BOM. He asserts that the entire product practically could be put together at final assembly. The wiring harnesses, presently used in the fabrication of the fan housing assem-

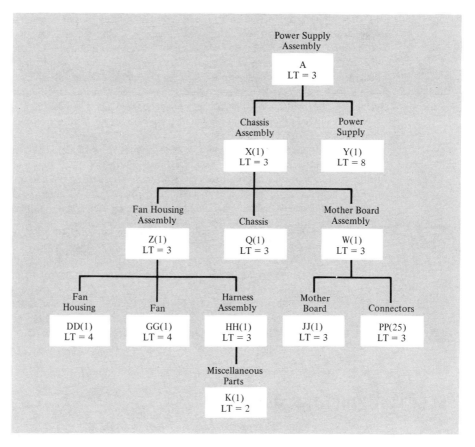

FIGURE 19.
Engineering product structure for power supply assembly.

blies, could be scheduled for completion prior to the actual start of the final assembly process. The harness subassemblies could be delivered directly to final assembly. The power supply component also would be delivered to final assembly by virtue of an automatic issuance policy whereby power supplies are given priority at the receiving dock and sent immediately to the power assembly area. The wiring harness and the power supply would become level 1 items along with a newly created power supply subassembly. The power supply subassembly is to be composed of items promoted to low level code 2—namely, the fan housing, fans, chassis, connectors, and mother board. The items to be designated as level 2 would retain their original part numbers, but the power supply subassembly would be assigned a unique number.

All purchased parts would still have purchase lead times, but a possibility exists where individual lead times could be shortened due to new methods for receiving, releasing, staging, and issuing parts for assembly orders. Three assembly lead times would be eliminated by the removal of the three assemblies from the present product structure (the fan housing, mother board, and chassis assemblies). In place of these separate processes will be a power supply subassembly with a lead time of two weeks. The final assembly lead time is estimated to be shortened by one week due to superior policies regarding the issuance of components directly to the final assembly area. For example, the power supply, given priority because of its high value, is expected to be ready for assembly in six weeks from order release rather than eight weeks, due to improved and speedier receipt and acceptance policies.

Thus, three assemblies will be eliminated and replaced by one. Fewer separate assembly processes will have to be scheduled, and the new assembly will not have to be moved in and out of storage as with the present subassembly processes. Production is expected to flow more in a continuous fashion, reducing waiting and lead times. For instance, the fan housing components now pass from storage to fan housing assembly to chassis assembly to final assembly, with storage sequences in between. Under the proposed sequence, the fan housing component would be delivered almost immediately to the power supply subassembly and then to final assembly; this could change its minimum total time in the facility from nine weeks to only four weeks.

John Brody calculates a considerable time savings in order deliveries and a reduction in inventory levels and their associated carrying costs. Furthermore, he foresees an unprecedented flexibility for Sinthetics in both of its product lines. Transferring the concept to the line with optional features, John anticipates that Sinthetics finally will be able to react to changes in final product demand for individual configurations which use certain multiple use components.

1. Will the reliance upon the engineering BOM as inputs to an MRP system lead to the outcomes Jim Wickersham expects?
2. What else should be done in conjunction with the implementation of MRP to bring about system improvements? Be sure to consider the forecasting and parts numbering aspects of the situation.
3. Comment on the workability of John Brody's proposal for reducing lead times. Include what assumptions must be made and what tasks must be carried out to execute his plan (do not ignore forecasting, supplier, and MRP input considerations).
4. If John's technique is applied to the power supply assembly, how should the modified BOM be structured?

SELECTED BIBLIOGRAPHY

Brown, R. G. *Materials Management Systems,* New York: Wiley, 1977.

Fogarty, D. W. and T. R. Hoffmann. *Production and Inventory Management,* Cincinnati: South-Western, 1983.

Orlicky, J. A. *Material Requirements Planning,* New York: McGraw-Hill, 1975.

Orlicky, J. A. et al. ''Structuring the Bill of Materials for MRP,'' *Production and Inventory Management,* December 1972, pp. 19–42.

Plossl, G. W., and O. W. Wight. *Production and Inventory Control,* Englewood Cliffs, NJ: Prentice-Hall, 1967.

Tersine, R. J. *Principles of Inventory and Materials Management,* New York: North-Holland, 1982.

Wight, O. W. *MRP II: Unlocking America's Productivity Potential,* Boston: CBI Publishing, 1981.

Wight, O. W. *Production and Inventory Management in the Computer Age,* Boston: Cahners Books, 1974.

18

Scheduling and Production Control

PRODUCTION CONTROL SYSTEMS
  Flow Control
  Special Project Control
  Service Control
  Order Control

FLOW SHOP SCHEDULING

JOB SHOP SCHEDULING

Shop Loading
  Charts
  Index Method of Loading
  Assignment Method of Linear Programming
  Transportation Method of Linear Programming

Sequencing
  Charts
  Priority Rules
  Critical Ratio Technique
  Optimization Methods
  Simulation

Input/Output Control
Revision

IN-PROCESS INVENTORY

JUST-IN-TIME

CONCLUSION

QUESTIONS

PROBLEMS

CASES

SELECTED BIBLIOGRAPHY

Scheduling allocates resources or capacity to orders, jobs, activities, or customers. Its purpose is to ensure that available capacity is used efficiently and effectively to achieve organizational goals. Scheduling is concerned with the timing of occurrences (arrival to and departures from a system). It means deciding where and when activities are to take place. Scheduling is a pervasive and ubiquitous process in any organization.

Organizations tend to have two general types of scheduling. Master or aggregate scheduling plans the level of production (output) for the total facility and usually has a time horizon of three months to a year. Detailed scheduling plans at a much lower organizational level and deals with day-to-day operations. The time horizon differentiates between the two types of scheduling. Master scheduling plans for and procures the necessary inputs, while detailed scheduling allocates the inputs. Detailed scheduling operates within and is confined by the master schedule.

The master schedule contains the overall (macro) plan for production for the entire operating facility. After the master schedule is developed, it is necessary to perform detailed (micro) scheduling for the various work centers (machines, equipment, departments, or areas) that compose the operating facility. Detailed scheduling disaggregates the master schedule into time-phased activities. It plans work activities in the very short run. In this chapter the primary concern is with detailed scheduling.

PRODUCTION CONTROL SYSTEMS

Scheduling regulates the work flow through the system. The key factor that dominates scheduling strategy is the type of flow allowed by the process design. Thus, the choice of scheduling method depends on whether it is a continuous process, intermittent process, or special project. Different types of production systems have different scheduling problems and needs. A brief relative comparison of continuous and intermittent systems is contained in Table 1.

The production control system for continuous production is called *flow control;* for intermittent production it is called *order control*. Intermittent production is more complex with respect to production control, since a greater number of products are involved. Thus, order control is more complicated than flow control.

Production control implements prior planning activities and is the focal point of daily production decisions. It converts plans into action notices that identify specific operations to be performed in a time-phased manner. It must discover and correct irregularities so output is completed as promised or scheduled.

FLOW CONTROL

In flow control, the primary purpose is to control the rate at which a product flows through the facility. Products, equipment, and work assignments are standardized. Since standard products are produced, they are produced to stock and not to customer order. The sequence of operations is fixed, so scheduling considerations are designed into the layout of the facility. There is no need to work with route sheets and operation sheets for each item. Since the process is essentially fixed and repetitive, the availability of materials and purchased parts is extremely important. Lack of even a single item can halt production. Less scheduling paperwork is required for flow control, and progress reports consist of the actual output of the facility.

TABLE 1
Production system features

Feature	Production system	
	Continuous	Intermittent
Product	Standardized	Nonstandardized
Number of products	Few	Many
Layout type	Product	Process
Production control	Flow control	Order control
Raw materials inventory	High	Low
In-process inventory	Low	High
Finished goods inventory	High	Low
Worker skill	Low	High
Process flexibility	Low	High
Equipment	Special purpose	General purpose
Work flow pattern	Fixed	Variable

SPECIAL PROJECT CONTROL

Special project control is reserved for distinctive or particularly important undertakings with unusual features, such as construction projects. A project is a series of related jobs that are directed toward some major output and require an extensive period of time to perform. Projects produce a specific output and often require that workers and materials be brought to a fixed job site. For special projects some type of network analysis is appropriate. Network scheduling establishes the schedule of interdependent activities taking into account precedence constraints. PERT and CPM are commonly used to identify project duration time and the critical activities. Special project control was covered in Chapter 8 on Network Programming and Project Planning.

SERVICE CONTROL

One major difference between production control in manufacturing and service industries is that services cannot be stockpiled. Empty seats on yesterday's airplane flight are not available today. Empty motel rooms cannot be used for future reservations. An idle policeman's services are gone forever. Therefore, control of services is directly related to service capacity and thus to the design of the facility. If there is no demand, the service is lost; if there is excess demand, customers must wait or go somewhere else. Approaches to solving service problems are discussed under queuing theory and simulation in Chapter 23.

Reservation and appointment systems are used extensively in service industries to balance the flow of customers with service capabilities. These are intended to control the timing of customer arrivals in order to minimize customer waiting time and achieve a high degree of facility utilization.

ORDER CONTROL

A job shop handles a variety of independent orders. Each order usually requires distinctive processing, with individual and separate records required. A job shop is difficult to control, because an order is usually small and the routing can differ substantially from order to order. Each order or lot tends to be unique and require separate attention. It is characterized by a diversity of operations (tasks) to be accomplished. Functionally equivalent machines are usually grouped into work centers. Because of the large number of orders and work centers, and the diversity of order routings, scheduling is a paramount problem. Job shops do not only occur in manufacturing; hospitals and restaurants are classic examples of job shops in the service sector.

In order control, the major concern is with getting the particular order for a given product through the facility. From route sheets and operation sheets, the flow pattern and scope of work on each product can be ascertained. These sheets provide the processing instructions for each item. Route sheets indicate the flow pattern for an item; the operation sheets indicate the scope of work required at each work center. Before any work actually takes place, production control must check the availability of the factors of production. Material, manpower, and work center availability should be verified. Material requirements are obtained by exploding the bill of materials. Material requirements are withdrawn from inventory or purchase orders are issued from them; work center requirements are obtained from route sheets; manpower requirements are determined from operation sheets. Existing work loads on the work centers are obtained from work center load reports. Production control releases work orders to the shop, which authorize production. Once jobs are released, progress reports are maintained on the status of each job until it is completed.

In order control, the two principal methods of scheduling are *backward scheduling* to meet a deadline and *forward scheduling* to produce as soon as possible. Forward scheduling starts with the first operation as soon as factors of production are available and works forward by scheduling each succeeding operation until the completion of the last operation is reached. Backward scheduling begins with the desired delivery date and the last operation and works backward by scheduling each preceding operation until the first operation is reached. Lead times must be determined for every part, subassembly, and assembly whether it is purchased or performed within the organization. Lead times consist of administrative time, process time, transit time, and queue time.

Organizations vary in their approach to authorizations for producing a product. Such authorizations may originate from a sales order, a manufacturing requisition, or the master schedule. In an MRP system, requirements are derived from the master schedule through explosion of the bills of materials.

The titles and activities of production control vary substantially among as well as within industries. The nature and size of an organization affect the production control methods. However, the fundamental activities that must be performed are almost identical in all organizations.

FLOW SHOP SCHEDULING

Continuous processes are found in assembly lines and the so-called process industries. If only one product is produced, the scheduling problem is at least partially solved by the design of the process, i.e., the work flow may be smoothed by line balancing (as outlined in Chapter 13). When several different products or models are produced within the same facilities, processes are less repetitive, calling for greater consideration in scheduling and flow control. Each product typically is produced in a batch, and a changeover is required before the next product is processed. Lot sizes are developed for multiple products, and runout time calculations can be used to determine the schedule which allocates capacity among products. Although a variety of products is made, the features of multiproduct facilities distinguish their recurrent processes from the changing mix of tasks found in job shop operations; generally, the lot sizes are larger, and standard items are made to stock on a rotation basis.

The two basic questions for multiproduct facilities are what order size (also referred to as lot or run size) to use and in what sequence products should be processed. The order size can be obtained by using a fixed order size model as illustrated in Chapter 19 on inventory control models, or by physical limitations such as equipment capacity. Once the order sizes for each product have been determined, on economic grounds or otherwise, the sequence of products can be ascertained by the runout time method.

The runout time method is a simple heuristic for computing the production sequence for a group of products produced on the same equipment. The runout time is calculated for each product sharing the equipment. The runout time is the inventory position divided by the period demand. The decision rule is to schedule first the product with the lowest runout time and then include additional products in the order of increasing runout times. The lower the runout time, the more crucial it is to replenish the supply of a product. The following example illustrates the runout time method.

EXAMPLE 1

An assembly line makes five different products to stock. The inventory levels, forecast demands, order sizes, and production rates for the products are listed below.

(a) Calculate the runout times and determine the tentative schedule sequence.
(b) Simulate 5.5 weeks of production. Use projected inventory levels and runout times to determine the 5.5 week production schedule.
(c) Do any real or potential scheduling problems occur during the 5.5 week period?

Product	Inventory (units)	Forecast weekly demand (units)	Order size (units)	Production rate (units/week)	Production time per order (weeks)
A	1600	500	1000	1000	1.0
B	1200	300	1500	3000	0.5
C	600	300	2000	1000	2.0
D	1500	300	1800	1800	1.0
E	1600	200	1000	1200	1.2
					5.7

Solution:
(a) The initial step is to determine the runout times and the tentative processing sequence for the products. The following table shows the tentative sequence based on the runout time rule:

continued

EXAMPLE 1— *continued*

Product	Inventory (units)	Forecast weekly demand (units)	Runout time = (col. 2)/(col. 3) (weeks)	Tentative processing sequence
A	1600	500	3.20	2
B	1200	300	4.00	3
C	600	300	2.00	1
D	1500	300	5.00	4
E	1600	200	8.00	5
	6500			

The table indicates that product C will be the first product sequenced for production.

(b) The next step is to simulate 5.5 weeks of production using projected inventory levels and runout times to sequence the production schedule. It is assumed that the first product to be processed is product C as indicated in part (a). It is produced for two weeks (the length of its production time per order). At the end of week 2.0, projected inventory levels and runout times are calculated for each product. The runout times are reevaluated; based on the lowest runout time, the next product processed is product A. It is produced for 1 week; at the end of week 3.0, projected inventory levels and runout times again are calculated. Based on a reevaluation of runout times, product B is produced during the next 0.5 weeks. At the end of week 3.5, the process is repeated. It continues until the completion of 5.5 weeks of production. The remainder of the processing schedule is product D for 1 week and finally product A for 1 week. The schedule can be simulated as far into the future as desired. The following table summarizes the simulation process described for the 5.5 week production period. [Note that the simulated production schedule differs from the tentative sequence indicated in part (a).]

Product	End of week 2.0 Projected inventory	Runout time	End of week 3.0 Projected inventory	Runout time	End of week 3.5 Projected inventory	Runout time	End of week 4.5 Projected inventory	Runout time	End of week 5.5 Projected inventory	Runout time
A	600	1.20	1100	2.20	850	1.70	350	0.70	850	1.70
B	600	2.00	300	1.00	1650	5.50	1350	4.50	1050	3.50
C	2000	6.67	1700	5.67	1550	5.17	1250	4.17	950	3.17
D	900	3.00	600	2.00	450	1.50	1950	6.50	1650	5.50
E	1200	6.00	1000	5.00	900	4.50	700	3.50	500	2.50
	5300		4700		5400		5600		5000	

In determining projected inventory, it is assumed that demand is exactly equal to the forecast. For example, for product A the projected inventory at the end of week 2.0 is the initial inventory minus two weeks of forecasted demand, or $1600 - (2 \times 500) = 600$ units. Similarly, for product C the projected inventory at the end of week 2.0 is the initial inventory plus two weeks of production minus two weeks of forecasted demand, or $600 + 2000 - (2 \times 300) = 2000$ units. The projected inventory is only a simulated value. In reality, demand will not be exactly equal to the forecast, so inventory levels will vary from the projected amount.

(c) The table in part (b) indicates a potential problem for product A. At the end of week 4.5, product A has a runout time of 0.70 weeks. Because its runout time at that point is less than its production time per order (1.0 weeks), the potential for a stockout exists.

A stockout is unlikely to occur given the probable circumstances. Product A is scheduled for production from the end of week 4.5 until the end of week 5.5. During that period it is possible to produce 1000 units, while only 500 units are expected to be demanded. The runout time means that 0.70 weeks of supply are available at the beginning of production, assuming that demand is continuous and equal to the forecast. If the production rate also is assumed to be continuous and predictable, and the units can be supplied before the entire order is completed, a runout will be averted.

A stockout is more likely to occur if the demand assumptions do not hold, i.e. demand is not continuous but occurs at the beginning of the production run and/or at a rate faster than predicted. A stockout also is more probable if supply cannot be provided before order completion or the production rate is subject to greater discontinuities. In either case, capacity might be expanded or order sizes might be reduced in previous periods to avert a runout. The simulation calculations provide some future visibility, so such problems can be solved before they reach crisis proportions.

The runout time is a dynamic heuristic that is revised as actual demand data are accumulated and new forecasts are made. One schedule is not made for all products and followed throughout a complete cycle. It is revised as each product order is completed. It can adjust to changing levels of demand and indicate if inventory is building too fast or being reduced too low.

JOB SHOP SCHEDULING

Order control is the type of production control system used in job shops. The objective is to process each order efficiently as it moves through the facility. Job shop scheduling involves (1) allocating jobs to specific work centers, (2) prioritizing all jobs at each work center, (3) revising priorities as changes occur, and (4) monitoring the progress of jobs. The job shop scheduling process is illustrated in Figure 1. It should be realized that it is a dynamic process which changes with the passage of time. The goals of job shop scheduling usually are:

1. high percentage of orders completed on time,
2. high utilization of workers and facilities,
3. low in-process inventory,
4. low overtime.

Job shop scheduling applies to intermittent operations of all types, whether in a factory, hospital, office, courtroom, or restaurant. For service operations, the term "job" is replaced by patient, customer, client, or whatever flows through the facility. The work center may be a desk, office, room, or skill specialty. Each unit in a job shop typically moves through the facility with many starts and stops, not smoothly as in a continuous process.

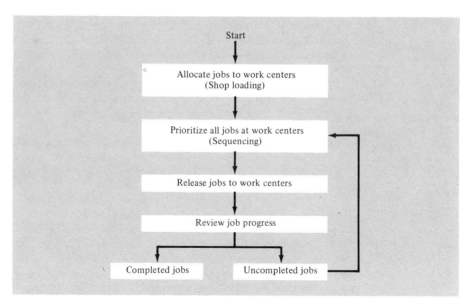

FIGURE 1
Job shop scheduling process.

SHOP LOADING

The allocation of jobs to work centers is called shop loading. Loading determines the work centers to receive the jobs. It assigns jobs to the work centers, but it does not necessarily specify the order in which jobs will be performed. Loading is a problem when several work centers are capable of performing the same job and several jobs are available. The preferred center must be identified.

Infinite and finite loading are the two types of loading methods. *Infinite loading* assigns jobs to work centers without regard to capacity limitations. *Finite loading* assigns jobs to work centers so as to never exceed their capacities. Figure 2 illustrates the difference between finite and infinite loads. The infinite load case shows both overloads and underloads. The infinite load method identifies and measures the overloads, indicating the time periods in which they will occur. It indicates what capacity is really needed. The finite load method, in contrast, does not permit overloads; it reschedules jobs to other time periods. Updating and revising an infinite loading is simple: completed jobs are removed and new jobs are added. A finite loading update requires a deletion of completed jobs, but also a rearrangement of all new and remaining jobs into a new priority sequence for reloading. Infinite loading is also called capacity requirements planning when it is based on both open orders and planned order releases from an MRP system.

Finite loading is supposed to develop realistic dates based on priorities assigned and the capacity limitations assumed for the various work centers. Before finite loading can begin, priorities must be established for all jobs. Obviously, the highest priority jobs should get first claim on the available capacity. As soon as a work center is filled to its limiting capacity, additional jobs are rescheduled to another time period or rerouted to work centers with available capacity.

Finite loading is not considered by many to be a valid loading technique. If an overload exists with dependent demand items, it is more realistic to revise the master

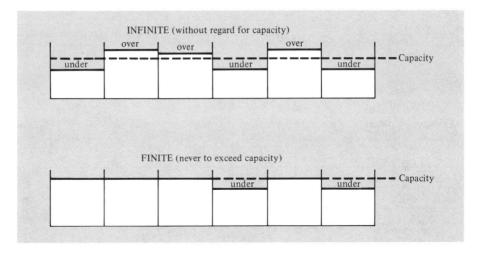

FIGURE 2
Loading methods.

schedule that generated the end item requirements. It makes little sense to reschedule a component when the real overload comes from the end item requirements. When jobs cannot be finished on time in a work center, it makes more sense to load level (revise) the master schedule.

A work center is overloaded when the total amount of work assigned for a given period is more than can be completed with its current capacity. Overloading can be handled by rerouting work to other work centers with unallocated capacity, by operating men and equipment on overtime, by subcontracting, by purchasing additional equipment, or by revising the schedule of jobs with lowest priority. Underloading can be handled by acquiring more jobs, by scheduling work in anticipation of future orders, or by reducing the level of available resources. The response to an overload or underload condition depends on whether it is temporary or permanent. Because of fluctuating loads on different work centers, the most economical equipment and methods for processing jobs may not always be available. Splitting a job into two or more batches can reduce the lead time (cycle time) and sometimes alleviate overloading at the cost of additional setups. Conditions conducive to job splitting include a low ratio of setup time to total run time and idle duplicative equipment.

When there are few, if any, choices in the selection of work centers to perform certain jobs, loading is very simple. When two or more work centers are available and capable of doing the same job, the choice of work center is more complex. The choice among work centers may depend upon setup and operating costs, operator skills required, or other jobs which must be loaded. The usual methods for job shop loading include charting, the index method, the assignment method of linear programming, and the transportation method of linear programming.

Charting

There are various types of loading charts available. They may take the form of graphs, tables, or boards. Also, they may be manual or computerized. The simplest form of charting is the Gantt load chart. Henry Gantt developed a chart with time on

TABLE 2
Load chart

Week of _____

Job order number	Work center							
	#10		#20		#30		#40	
	Hours reqd.	Hours available	Hours reqd.	Hours available	Hours reqd.	Hours available	Hours reqd.	Hours available
14	3	80	2	40	4	80	1	60
17	6	77	1	38	8	76	3	59
18	4	71	1	37	7	68	6	56
19	5	67	3	36	6	61	5	50
20	7	62	—	33	5	55	—	45
22	8	55	4	33	—	50	4	45
23	2	47	1	29	3	50	2	41
24	6	45	2	28	4	47	3	39
25	—	39	—	26	3	43	1	36
26	8	39	4	26	6	40	7	35
		31		22		34		28

the horizontal axis and work centers on the vertical scale. Bars and lines running from left to right convey various types of information. A tabular load chart is shown in Table 2 for assigning job orders to four work centers. As each job order is assigned to a work center, the available hours remaining are recorded.

Charts are widely used and easy to understand. They are an excellent aid in monitoring the load on a facility. They are not very helpful, however, in deciding the work center to be loaded when alternative centers can do the same job. With charts alone, the choice of where to load a job is left to the discretion of the scheduler. Therefore, they tend to be more of a record-keeping device than a decision-making tool.

Index Method of Loading

Sometimes, when several work centers can perform similar operations, management must decide how to schedule a great number of orders to achieve low production cost. The index method is a heuristic technique that permits a rapid, inexpensive

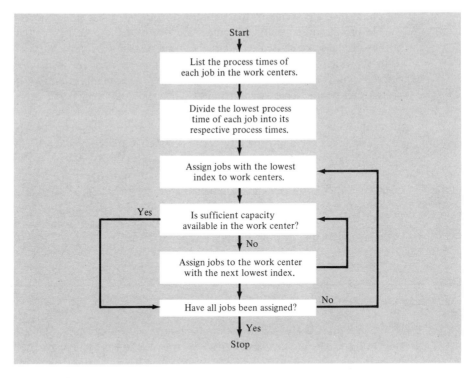

FIGURE 3
Index method load diagram.

solution to the loading problem. However, it is an approximation technique that does not promise an optimum solution.

Ideally, it is desirable to assign a job to a work center that takes the shortest amount of time or results in the lowest cost (depending upon the performance criterion). Because of capacity limitations, this is not always possible. When a job cannot be performed at the fastest work center, the next fastest center is to be chosen. The index method of loading provides a systematic procedure for assigning jobs on this basis.

The procedure assigns jobs within capacity limitations, based upon their relative desirability at particular work centers; it attempts to assign jobs to the most desirable work centers first and then reassigns some jobs to alternative centers when capacity prohibits preferred assignments. A row of index numbers is computed for each job with respect to its performance in each work center. Specifically, the procedure divides the shortest processing time of the job at any of the possible centers into the processing time of each respective center; the result is an index for each job that indicates its relative desirability at each center. The lowest possible index number, 1, indicates the most desirable assignment for the job. Index numbers greater than 1 indicate relative penalties associated with not assigning the job to the preferred center; e.g., an index of 1.3 means that the job will take 30% more time at that center than it would at the fastest work center.

First assignments always are made to the center with the index 1; that is, jobs initially are assigned to the fastest work centers. Capacity allocations at the work centers then are examined to determine if aggregate job assignments exceed the available processing capacity. If centers are overloaded, some jobs initially assigned to those centers are shifted to alternative centers. The jobs chosen to be reassigned are those which have the next lowest index in a center with available capacity. The procedure is continued in order of increasing index numbers until all jobs have been assigned within capacity limitations. When the final assignments are made, they are indicated by placing parentheses around the time required for the job. The procedure for the index method is shown in Figure 3.

The index method generally does not give an optimum solution in terms of minimum total processing time. It will, however, give reasonably good results. It usually is better than solutions obtained solely by intuition or visual inspection. Manipulation and/or visual inspection can be applied after the work centers are loaded by the index method. It may be possible to improve the load by examining other solutions which are capacity feasible. An improved solution will have an aggregate allocation with fewer total hours of production assigned.

EXAMPLE 2

The jobs listed below can be performed in any of the three work centers. No job splitting between centers is permitted. Using the index method, load the work centers for the next week.

Job	Work center		
	#1	#2	#3
10C	100	150	125
20A	200	100	220
30G	25	50	20
40B	40	30	—
50E	60	50	70
Hours available	160	110	150

The following table contains the indexes for each job. Jobs assigned are shown with parentheses around the number of hours required at the work center.

Job	Work center					
	#1		#2		#3	
	Hours	Index	Hours	Index	Hours	Index
10C	(100)	1.00	150	1.50	125	1.25
20A	200	2.00	(100)	1.00	220	2.20
30G	25	1.25	50	2.50	(20)	1.00
40B	(40)	1.33	30	1.00	—	—
50E	60	1.20	50	1.00	(70)	1.40
Hours assigned	140		100		90	
Hours available	160		110		150	

All of the jobs except 40B and 50E were assigned to the center with an index of 1.00. Job 40B was assigned to center #1, since sufficient hours were not available in center

#2 and the work could not be performed at center #3; job 50E was assigned to center #3 because of capacity limitations in centers #1 and #2. The table indicates that jobs 10C and 40B are assigned to center #1, job 20A is assigned to center #2, and jobs 30G and 50E are assigned to center #3. All of the work centers still have hours available. Additional jobs can be scheduled if they do not exceed the capacity requirements.

When setup time or setup cost is insignificant, job splitting is possible. This simply divides a job among more than one work center. Whether that is feasible will depend on the nature of the job under consideration.

When time is used as the criterion in the index method, it is assumed the lowest process time will also be the lowest cost. In the typical job shop where the same worker can be assigned to several different machines and the hourly rate of pay is approximately the same among workers, the index method can be very useful. When time is not a valid surrogate for cost, it should be replaced with the cost of each job. The cost indexes will then be determined in the same manner as the time indexes.

Assignment Method of Linear Programming

The assignment method of linear programming can be used to assign jobs to work centers on the basis of cost, performance, time, or efficiency. Jobs cannot be split with this method: each job must be assigned to one and only one work center. If the number of jobs is not equal to the number of work centers, dummy rows or columns are added to ensure a square matrix (the number of rows must equal the number of columns). If any job–work center assignments are impractical or unfeasible, the cell is assigned an exorbitant cost that will prohibit its assignment. The procedure for the assignment method is outlined in Chapter 5 on Resource Allocation and Linear Programming. The assignment method does result in an optimum solution. It is simple and fast to do, and it can be done easily without a computer.

EXAMPLE 3

A scheduler has four jobs that can be performed in any of four work centers. The time per part is listed in the table below. Determine the allocation of jobs to work centers that results in the least time.

	Work center			
Job	#1	#2	#3	#4
A	9	4	5	9
B	5	1	3	6
C	6	5	4	5
D	8	4	3	9

The basic steps are as follows:

continued

EXAMPLE 3— *continued*

1. Column subtraction:

	1	2	3	4
A	4	3	2	4
B	0	0	0	1
C	1	4	1	0
D	3	3	0	4

2. Row subtraction:

	1	2	3	4
A	2	1	0	2
B	0	0	0	1
C	1	4	1	0
D	3	3	0	4

3. Cover all zeros:

	1	2	3	4
A	2	1	0	2
B	0—0—0			1
C	1—4—1—0			
D	3	3	0	4

4. Modify matrix:

	1	2	3	4
A	1	0	0	1
B	0	0	1	1
C	1	4	2	0
D	2	2	0	3

5. Cover zeros again:

	1	2	3	4
A	1—	0 — 0—	1	
B	0 — 0 — 1 — 1			
C	1 — 4 — 2 —	0		
D	2 — 2 —	0 — 3		

Optimum assignments:

Job A to work center 2.

Job B to work center 1.

Job C to work center 4.

Job D to work center 3.

The final allocation of assignments begins with the column or row with only one zero in it, such as centers 1 and 4. So job B is assigned to center 1 and job C to center 4. This results in job A being assigned to center 2 and job D to center 3. The final optimal assignment is as follows:

Assignment	Time
A to #2	4
B to #1	5
C to #4	5
D to #3	3
Total	17

Although Example 3 was very simple and dealt with only four jobs, the procedure is the same for much larger problems. For a more thorough explanation of the assignment algorithm, review the material in Chapter 5. The major weakness of the method is that each job can be assigned to only one work center (no job splitting).

Transportation Method of Linear Programming

The transportation method of linear programming can be used to load jobs on work centers. Unlike the assignment method, it will split jobs, and a square matrix is not required. The transportation method assumes setup and fixed costs are insig-

FIGURE 4
Transportation method of shop loading.

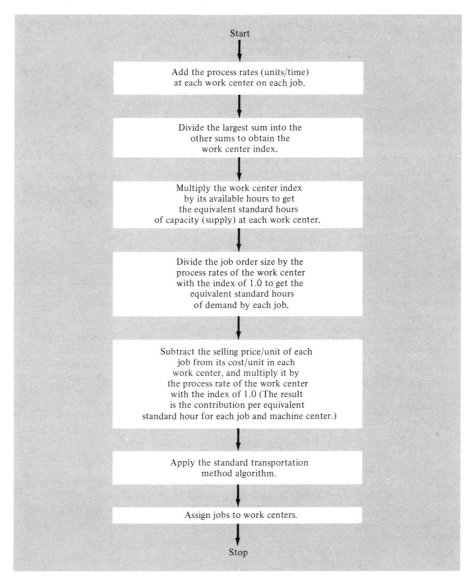

nificant or the same for all jobs. The procedure for the transportation method is outlined in Chapter 5 on Resource Allocation and Linear Programming.

Before the transportation method can be applied to shop loading, the data must be made suitable for the algorithm. When the transportation method was previously developed, the units of supply and demand were the numbers of identical products. In loading, the units of supply are hours available at a work center, and the demand is the quantity of output. This difficulty is overcome by converting both supply and demand to a common unit: equivalent standard hours. This is done by assigning the work center with the largest output an index number of 1.0. The standardized supply requirements (rim conditions) are obtained by multiplying the appropriate index by the hours of capacity available in each work center. The standardized demand (rim conditions) requirements are obtained by dividing the job order sizes by the process rates of the work center with the index of 1.0. Finally, the contribution per unit (objective function) is standardized by multiplying it by the process rates of the work center with the index 1.0. After the standardization process is completed, the standard transportation method algorithm is applied. The solution will indicate the preferred assignment of jobs to work centers. The above procedure is flow diagrammed in Figure 4. To change from standard hours to actual work center hours, simply divide each number of standard hours by its index number.

EXAMPLE 4

From the information in the table below, assign job orders to work centers using the transportation method.

			Work center					
			W1		W2		W3	
Job order number	Job order size (units)	Selling price ($/unit)	Process rate (units/hr)	Cost ($/unit)	Process rate (units/hr)	Cost ($/unit)	Process rate (units/hr)	Cost ($/unit)
J1	520	10.00	40	8.00	36	5.00	28	4.00
J2	320	20.00	10	16.00	9	12.00	7	10.00
J3	900	5.00	90	3.00	81	4.00	63	3.00
J4	480	12.00	60	9.00	54	10.00	42	11.00
			200		180		140	
Time available (hr)			24		20		30	

The first step is to calculate the work center index numbers:

Work center	Total output rate (units/hr)	Index number
W1	200	200/200 = 1.0
W2	180	180/200 = 0.9
W3	140	140/200 = 0.7

The second step is to convert work center capacities into equivalent standard hours by multiplying the time available by the appropriate index numbers:

Work center	Index number	Time available (hours)	Supply (equivalent standard hours)
W1	1.0	24	24
W2	0.9	20	18
W3	0.7	30	21

Next, the job order sizes are converted to equivalent standard hours of demand by dividing by the process rates of the work center with the index 1.0:

Job order number	Job order size	Process rate of W1	Demand (equivalent standard hours)
J1	520	40	13
J2	320	10	32
J3	900	90	10
J4	480	60	8

The last conversion yields the contribution per equivalent standard hour in the following manner:

Assignment	Selling price/unit	Cost/unit	Contribution/ unit	Process rate of W1	Contribution per equivalent standard hour
J1–W1	$10.00	$ 8.00	$ 2.00	40	$ 80
J1–W2	10.00	5.00	5.00	40	200
J1–W3	10.00	4.00	6.00	40	240
J2–W1	20.00	16.00	4.00	10	40
J2–W2	20.00	12.00	8.00	10	80
J2–W3	20.00	10.00	10.00	10	100
J3–W1	5.00	3.00	2.00	90	180
J3–W2	5.00	4.00	1.00	90	90
J3–W3	5.00	3.00	2.00	90	180
J4–W1	12.00	9.00	3.00	60	180
J4–W2	12.00	10.00	2.00	60	120
J4–W3	12.00	11.00	1.00	60	60

At this point all the data are dimensionally compatible and ready for the transportation matrix.

continued

EXAMPLE 4 — *continued*

Job order	Work center			Demand (ESH)
	W1	W2	W3	
J1	80	200	240	13
J2	40	80	100	32
J3	180	90	180	10
J4	180	120	60	8
Supply (ESH)	24	18	21	63

After applying the transportation algorithm as illustrated in Chapter 5, the following optimum tableau is obtained:

Job order	Work center			Demand (ESH)
	W1	W2	W3	
J1	80	200	240 / 13	13
J2	40 / 6	80 / 18	100 / 8	32
J3	180 / 10	90	180	10
J4	180 / 8	120	60	8
Supply (ESH)	24	18	21	63

The optimum job assignment in hours to work centers is as follows:

Assignment	Equivalent standard hours	Index number	Actual hours [(col. 2)/(col. 3)]		
			W1	W2	W3
J1–W3	13	.7			18.57
J2–W1	6	1.0	6.00		
J2–W2	18	.9		20.00	
J2–W3	8	.7			11.43
J3–W1	10	1.0	10.00		
J4–W1	8	1.0	8.00		
Total	63		24.00	20.00	30.00

The number of units to be processed at each work center is obtained by multiplying the actual hours by the corresponding process rate as follows:

Job order	Work center			Total units
	W1	W2	W3	
J1			18.57(28) = 520	520
J2	6.00(10) = 60	20.00(9) = 180	11.43(7) = 80	320
J3	10.00(90) = 900			900
J4	8.00(60) = 480			480

All 520 units of J1 would be assigned to W3; 60 units of J2 would be assigned to W1, 180 units to W2, and 80 units to W3; 900 units of J3 would be assigned to W1; and all 480 units of J4 would be assigned to W1.

SEQUENCING

Once jobs are loaded on the work centers, the next task is to sequence them.[1] Loading assigns jobs to work centers, but it does not necessarily specify their order of precedence. Sequencing, frequently referred to as dispatching, establishes the priority of jobs at a given work center (the order in which they will be processed). Loading is concerned with work center capacity control, while sequencing is concerned with work center priority control. A job shop is like a network of waiting lines in which the relative urgency of orders is constantly shifting.[2] Precedence restrictions must be observed. As jobs progress through work centers, they compete with other jobs for scarce resources.

A major consideration in sequencing is the number of jobs, n, that must be processed through the number of work centers, m. As the numbers of jobs and work centers increase, sequencing becomes more tedious and complex. With n jobs to pass through only two work centers ($m = 2$), there are $n!$ alternatives. The usual methods of sequencing include charts, priority rules, optimization methods, and simulation.

Charts

There are various types of sequencing charts available. Just as in job shop loading, several variations of Gantt charts are used. The Gantt chart is useful in showing planned work activities versus actual accomplishments on the same time scale. Typical sequencing charts are shown in Figures 5 and 6. Although charts provide for work schedule control, they offer little help in determining what the best work sequences might be.

Large and elaborate scheduling boards are available commercially with such names as "Boardmaster," "Sched-U-Graph," and "Produc-trol." Color coding is frequently used to show distinguishing characteristics. Colored strings, pegs, tabs,

---

[1]This is particularly true for infinite loading. For finite loading, loading and sequencing are really performed concurrently as a combined operation.

[2]Although queuing theory is helpful in describing the flow of jobs through a facility and delineating problem areas, it is not an effective order control technique.

560

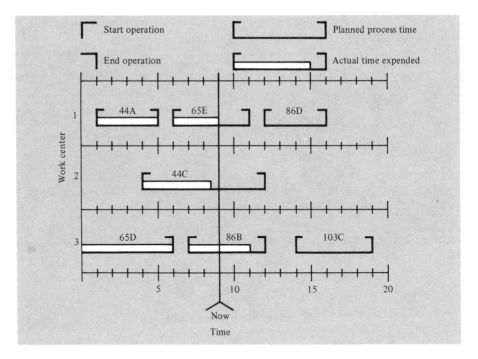

FIGURE 5
Gantt chart.

FIGURE 6
Sequencing chart.

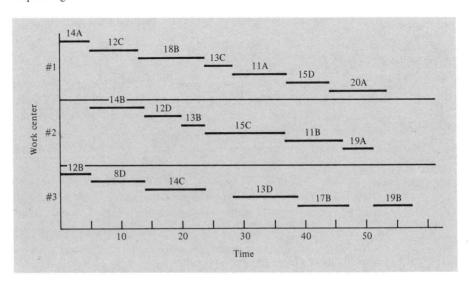

revolving disks, plastic slide inserts, and similar devices are used to indicate scheduling status. Manual charting methods become impractical as the numbers of jobs and work centers increase.

Priority Rules

Priority rules for the sequencing of orders are common in job shops. The purpose of a priority rule is to rank the jobs waiting in some way so a decision can be made about the next job to perform when the work center becomes available. Priority rules are heuristics (rules of thumb) that provide simplified guidelines for determining the sequence in which jobs will be worked.

Several different priority rules are listed in Table 3. The use of priority rules involves the calculation of a priority index for each job. Depending upon the specific rule, the next job selected will have the largest or smallest value. A *static priority rule* results in relative priorities that are impervious to time, while a *dynamic priority rule* results in relative priorities that can change simply by the passage of time. Priority rules are a practical way at arriving at schedules, but they do not, in general, generate optimal schedules.

When numerous jobs are sequenced on one work center $(n, 1)$, the shortest processing time rule (SPT) has certain advantages. The mean flow time, mean completion time, and mean waiting time are minimized with this rule. Additionally, work center idleness is frequently minimized. Under SPT, few jobs may be late, but those that are tend to be very late. The SPT rule totally ignores due dates. This problem can be overcome by imposing a limit on the amount of time a job is allowed to wait.

Priority or sequencing rules can be devised to favor the movement of orders on the basis of any desired criteria. Favoring certain orders results in delays to others. Selection of priority rules involves tradeoffs among customer service, order urgency, order profitability, and impact on capacity utilization. No single rule is best for every situation. The overall performance of priority rules will depend on the work center load. With a heavy load, most orders will finish late; with a light load, most orders will finish early. Priority rules are usually evaluated by the mean and variance of flow time, average job lateness, and average in-process inventory. Each organization should perform internal research and try to develop priority rules that best suit its needs.

TABLE 3
Priority rules

Rule	Symbol	Use
First come first served	FCFS	Job that arrives the earliest is first
Due date of job	DD	Job with earliest due date is first
Shortest processing time	SPT	Job with shortest processing time is first
Longest processing time	LPT	Job with longest processing time is first
Slack	S	Job with smallest amount of slack (time remaining to due date less processing time) is first
Slack per remaining operation	S/O	Job with smallest slack per remaining operation is first
Random selection	RS	Job selected at random is first
Preferred customer order	PCO	Job from preferred customer is first

No single rule can achieve everything. Priority rules tend to be based on only one objective at a time. Hybrids with multiple objectives have been developed, but their results have been less than spectacular. They tend to be myopic with respect to a work center and neglect downstream work center loads. They usually assume jobs are completely independent of each other, though some jobs may have common or similar setups. One rule may perform admirably under one criterion, yet poorly under another.

EXAMPLE 5

Sequence the jobs listed below by the priority rules of first come first served (FCFS), due date (DD), shortest processing time (SPT), longest processing time (LPT), and slack (S).

Job	Process time (days)	Due date (days hence)
A	6	8
B	4	7
C	1	2
D	3	3
E	2	4

The following table contains the job sequence for each priority rule:

FCFS	DD	SPT	LPT	S
A	C(2)	C(1)	A(6)	D(0)
B	D(3)	E(2)	B(4)	C(1)
C	E(4)	D(3)	D(3)	A(2)
D	B(7)	B(4)	E(2)	E(2)
E	A(8)	A(6)	C(1)	B(3)

Critical Ratio Technique

The critical ratio is a dynamic priority rule that facilitates the constant updating of priorities. It is used in conjunction with MRP systems and has broad industrial application. The critical ratio is a measure of urgency of any order compared to the other orders for the same facility. The ratio is based on when the completed order is required and how much time is required to complete it. The critical ratio is a dimensionless index that is calculated as follows:

$$\text{critical ratio} = \frac{\text{demand time}}{\text{supply time}} = \frac{\text{time remaining until needed}}{\text{time needed to complete work}}$$

$$= \frac{(\text{date required}) - (\text{today's date})}{\text{days needed to complete the job}}.$$

From the critical ratios, it is possible to determine the orders that are behind schedule, the orders that are ahead of schedule, the orders that are on schedule, the orders that should be processed next, and whether processing rates should be increased. Orders with the lowest critical ratio are processed before orders with higher ratios. If the critical ratio is greater than one, the order is ahead of schedule; if it is equal to one, the order is on schedule; and if it is less than one, the order is behind schedule. The lower the critical ratio, the more critical the order is. However, when there are several orders with negative critical ratios, it is desirable to rank these overdue orders by the amount of time behind schedule rather than the critical ratio. Negative critical ratios tend to distort priorities.

EXAMPLE 6

Sequence the jobs listed below by the critical ratio technique. Today is day 43 on the production calendar.

Job	Date required	Process time remaining (days)
A	50	3
B	45	2
C	44	2
D	53	5
E	46	4

The following table lists the jobs in the order in which they should be performed according to their critical ratios.

Job	Critical ratio
C	$(44 - 43)/2 = 0.50$
E	$(46 - 43)/4 = 0.75$
B	$(45 - 43)/2 = 1.00$
D	$(53 - 43)/5 = 2.00$
A	$(50 - 43)/3 = 2.33$

Jobs C and E are behind schedule and must be speeded up if they are to be completed by the date required; job B is on schedule; and jobs D and A are ahead of schedule.

When the critical ratio is used to schedule warehouse operations or determine what items should be shipped on the next delivery truck, the appropriate formula is as follows:

$$\text{critical ratio} = \frac{\text{days of supply}}{\text{lead time remaining}},$$

$$\text{days of supply} = \frac{(\text{stock on hand}) - (\text{safety stock})}{\text{average daily demand}}.$$

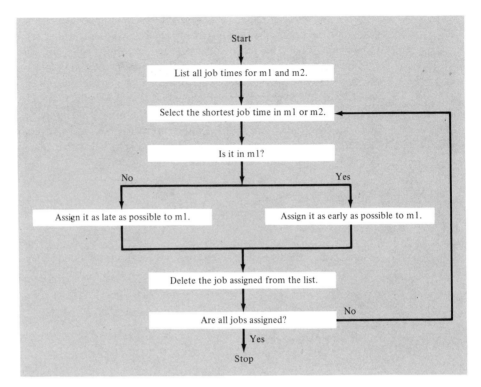

FIGURE 7
Johnson's rule for two work centers.

In practice, all the items being shipped should have their critical ratio calculated and ranked. All items with a critical ratio less than one should be shipped on the next truck. To obtain a full truckload, the next items in order of criticality should be shipped.

Optimization Methods

Optimization methods give the best solution based on the value criteria chosen. Unfortunately, optimization methods are available for only the smaller problems. When more than three work centers are encountered, the problem becomes difficult and exact analytical approaches that ensure optimality are not available.

When n jobs must be processed through one work center ($m = 1$), the shortest processing time (SPT) rule yields an optimum solution based on the minimization of mean flow time, mean waiting time, and mean completion time. This rule simply selects jobs in increasing order of their process time. It assumes that all jobs are of equal importance.

When n jobs must be processed through two work centers ($m = 2$) in a given technological sequence, Johnson's rule yields an optimum solution based on minimum completion time.[3] The technique results in the minimum total idle time at both

[3]S. M. Johnson, "Optimal Two- and Three-Stage Production Schedules with Setup Time Included," *Naval Research Logistics Quarterly,* Vol. 1, No. 1, March 1954, pp. 61–68.

work centers when all jobs must follow the same sequence through the two work centers ($m1$ to $m2$). It works well when there are no in-process storage problems or overriding individual priorities (all jobs of equal importance). It is optimal for any number of jobs through the same two-step process.

Johnson's rule requires that all jobs be listed showing processing times in each work center. As depicted in Figure 7, the jobs are scanned for the shortest processing time. If the shortest time is in $m1$, the job is placed as early as possible; if it is in $m2$, the job is placed as late as possible. Once a job is scheduled, it is eliminated from further consideration and the decision rule is applied to the remaining jobs. Any ties are broken by selecting the job with the lowest cumulative processing time.

EXAMPLE 7

A job shop processes all orders serially through two work centers. The process times in hours for five orders are given below. Sequence the jobs so there is minimum idle time in the work centers. How much idle time will there be in the work center 2?

	A	B	C	D	E
$m1$	3	6	9	4	7
$m2$	2	3	8	6	4

The smallest time is 2 for job A. Since it occurs in $m2$, it is placed last in the sequence and depleted from further consideration:

				A

The next smallest time is 3 for job B. Since it occurs in $m2$, it is placed as late as possible:

			B	A

Now a tie exists between jobs D and E for the next smallest time of 4. Job D is selected and placed as soon as possible:

D			B	A

The above process is continued until all the jobs are assigned and the following job sequence is obtained:

D	C	E	B	A

As shown below, there will be 8 hours of idle time in $m2$. No other sequence will result in less idle time for the facility:

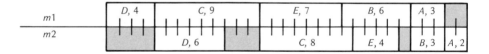

Unfortunately, there is no general solution for sequencing problems with more than two work stations ($m > 2$). There are heuristic approximations of the optimal solution, but they are beyond the scope of this chapter.[4] Complex problems can be treated by simulation techniques.

Simulation

Simulation permits sequencing methods to be tested before being applied. It can compare the relative benefits of different priority rules when it is infeasible or impractical to experiment with the real system. Management can test the effectiveness of scheduling concepts with computer simulation and select those methods which seem to yield the best results. Simulation models contain fewer restrictions and assumptions than analytical models.

In practice, precise schedules are seldom if ever achieved, because of variations in material flow and work center operations. Typical realities include breakdowns, spoilage, rework, emergency orders, lack of tools, mechanical difficulties, labor difficulties, absenteeism, lost orders, material shortages, and so forth. Computer simulation attempts to provide a reasonable duplication of actual operations. Such factors as absenteeism, breakdowns, and rejection of parts are included in simulation models by using actual distributions from past data or assumptions about such factors. Simulation models permit the testing in a few minutes of alternatives that could take years in the actual system. A large number of methods can be tested quickly, fairly, and inexpensively without disrupting operations. Analytical solutions to scheduling in job shops have been of limited usefulness. Most useful results have been obtained from simulation research. In particular, Monte Carlo simulation is developed in Chapter 23 on Maintenance.

INPUT/OUTPUT CONTROL

Input/output control regulates (1) the flow of work into a work center by comparing actual input with planned input, and (2) the flow of work from a work center by comparing actual output with planned output. The objective is to highlight deviations before they become acute. Minor divergences are to be expected as work progresses. Delays and disruptions are corrected so the *average input* of new jobs does not differ substantially from the *average output* of completed jobs. If work is released that exceeds the output of completed jobs, backlogs will develop and lead times will increase. If work is released that is less than the output of completed jobs, the backlog will drop and the lead time will be reduced.

It should be noted that the input rate cannot really be "controlled" at any work center except an entry (gateway) work center. Here, work is fed in, and it is possible to increase or decrease the input rate. At subsequent work centers, the input rate is controlled by regulating the output rates at the feeding work centers.

Figure 8 shows an input/output report for a typical job shop work center. The *planned input* of jobs to a work center includes both released ("open") orders that have not arrived yet and unreleased ("planned") orders. The *planned output* is the

---

[4]H. G. Campbell et al., "A Heuristic Algorithm for the *n* Job, *m* Machine Sequencing Problem," *Management Science,* Vol. 16, No. 10, June 1970, pp. B630–B637.

Work Center 5

Week	12	13	14	15	16	17	18	19	20	21
Planned input	540	540	540	540	540	540	540	540	540	540
Actual input	540	530	500							
Cumulative deviation	0	−10	−50							
Planned output	600	600	600	600	540	540	540	540	540	540
Actual output	610	520	600							
Cumulative deviation	+10	−70	−70							
Planned backlog	180	120	60	0	0	0	0	0	0	0
Actual backlog	170	180	80							

FIGURE 8
Input/output report. All quantities are in standard hours. There was a released backlog of 240 hours at work center 5 at the beginning of week 12.

objective or available capacity for the period, and it equals the planned input plus or minus any desired change in the backlog. The *actual input* is simply the standard hours of work that have arrived. The *actual output* is simply the standard hours of work completed. The *planned backlog* is the previous period's planned backlog plus the planned input minus the planned output. The *actual backlog* is the previous period's actual backlog plus the actual input minus the actual output.

The report in Figure 8 is in abbreviated form: in practice it typically would extend for 12 or more weeks. The planned output rate is 600 hours per week for the first four weeks and thereafter 540 hours per week. The planned input rate is 540 hours per week as far as the plan goes. The planned output of 600 for the first four weeks is higher than the planned input of 540. This is intended to reduce the existing backlog by 240 standard hours. The latest week for which data are available is week 14. The report clearly indicates whether or not the backlog is building. It measures capacity in total hours rather than late orders in the work center.

Figure 9 shows an input/output report for another work station. Work center 11 is not an entry point (a starting or gateway work center) for orders, but receives its inputs from the outputs of other work centers. It is a secondary or downstream work

FIGURE 9
Input/output report. All quantities are in standard hours. There was a released backlog of 60 hours at work center 11 at the beginning of week 21.

Work Center 11

Week	21	22	23	24	25	26	27	28	29	30
Planned input	220	220	220	220	220	220	220	220	220	220
Actual input	110	150	140	130						
Cumulative deviation	−110	−180	−260	−350						
Planned output	220	220	220	220	220	220	220	220	220	220
Actual output	150	140	160	140						
Cumulative deviation	−70	−150	−210	−290						
Planned backlog	60	60	60	60	60	60	60	60	60	60
Actual backlog	20	30	10	0						

center. Against a planned average output rate of 220 standard hours, actual output has fallen short by a cumulative total of 290 standard hours. From reviewing output figures only, a logical conclusion would be that work center 11 needs more capacity. However, input figures reveal the real problem lies in the work centers feeding work center 11. The actual input has fallen short by a cumulative total of 350 hours behind the plan. The work is not arriving at work center 11. To expand capacity would only compound the problem.

Figure 10 shows an input/output report for a different work station. Work center 13 is not an entry point for orders, but receives its inputs from numerous other work centers. Actual inputs have been fairly close to planned inputs, but actual output has consistently fallen short of planned output. The work center suffers from a capacity constraint. Something should be done to improve the capacity problem. The key to using input/output techniques is to establish a planned backlog and a tolerance level, such as $\pm 15\%$, for each work center. When the backlog tolerance level is exceeded, the work center's capacity should be altered.

Problems in input force the examination of upstream work centers, or in the case of gateway or primary work centers, the examination of the order release system. The gateway work centers are easier to control in terms of input. The input to secondary or intermediate work centers is more difficult to control because input is coming from multiple sources. Problems in output are usually associated with capacity unless they are the direct result of input problems. Selection of appropriate orders for processing in earlier work centers can result in desired adjustment in downstream work center backlogs. Orders are selected whose next operation is at work centers with little or no work.

Input/output control is essential at critical (bottleneck) work centers whether they are gateway, intermediate, or the final work centers. There is little reason to have a long backlog (queue) at gateway work centers. The input to and backlog at downstream work centers are controlled by order sequencing at upstream work centers. It is common to have planned backlogs at downstream work centers, particularly when they are bottlenecks. Improving performance in bottleneck work stations can substantially improve efficiency and productivity. It increases throughput, which reduces lead time and inprocess inventory.

FIGURE 10

Input/output report. All quantities are in standard hours. The released backlog at work center 13 at the beginning of week 5 was 200 hours.

Work Center 13

Week	5	6	7	8	9	10	11	12	13	14
Planned input	100	100	100	100	100	100	100	100	100	100
Actual input	110	105	95	95						
Cumulative deviation	+10	+15	+10	+ 5						
Planned output	100	100	100	100	100	100	100	100	100	100
Actual output	75	85	75	70						
Cumulative deviation	−25	−40	−65	−95						
Planned backlog	200	200	200	200	200	200	200	200	200	200
Actual backlog	235	255	275	300						

Input/output control deals with the throughput (the flow in and the flow out) rather than focusing only on backlogs. MRP plans priorities but does not address capacity. Capacity requirements planning (CRP), which was discussed in the previous chapter, is used to plan capacity; input/output control is used to control capacity.

REVISION

Because many changes can occur in job shops, schedules can become obsolete quickly. Priorities are subject to revision with the passage of time or as jobs progress in relation to other jobs. Replanning and rescheduling are common occurrences in production control systems. The adoption of loading and sequencing methods requires that they be flexible and capable of revision as changes occur. This revision and turnaround capability make computerized systems very desirable in production control.

IN-PROCESS INVENTORY

In-process goods are an inventory category peculiar to organizations that manufacture or produce a physical product. In organizations that manufacture products to order, in-process goods may represent 50% of the total inventory investment. In-process inventory is the accumulation of direct material, direct labor, and applied manufacturing overhead costs of products in the manufacturing process. The accumulation of these costs *begins* with the transfer of the raw materials to production and *ends* with the movement of completed products into storage or the shipping dock.

In-process inventory provides production economies in terms of capacity utilization. It protects against underutilization of manpower and facilities. Idle workers and facilities represent a loss of productivity. There are opposing costs involved: too little work in process results in underutilization costs, while too much results in excessive inventory costs.

To reduce in-process inventory levels, under the assumption that material cost and labor cost are adequately controlled, it is necessary to reduce the *manufacturing cycle time*. The cycle time is the time a job or order spends in the manufacturing process.[5] If the cycle time is reduced, the in-process inventory investment will be decreased in direct proportion.

As shown in Figure 11, the manufacturing cycle time is comprised of the following five elements:

1. *Setup time:* material, machine, or work center is prepared for performance of an operation.
2. *Process time:* the productive operations are performed.
3. *Move time:* transportation occurs from storage, to storage, or between operations.
4. *Inspection time:* testing or inspection occurs.
5. *Idle or queue time:* material waits for one of the above to take place.

Process time represents a small fraction of the manufacturing cycle time for most orders. Much of the time is spent waiting in queues for other orders to be processed.

---

[5]Cycle time is also referred to as "flow time" or "manufacturing lead time" by some authors.

Setup time	Process time	Move time	Inspection time	Idle or queue time

FIGURE 11
Manufacturing cycle time.

Idle time is usually larger than the combination of all the other time elements. The major opportunity for reducing cycle time is to reduce idle time. Typical reasons for orders being idle are as follows:

1. waiting for machine or work center availability,
2. waiting to be moved,
3. waiting to be inspected,
4. hot jobs get priority,
5. shortages of tools, materials, or information,
6. machine breakdown,
7. absenteeism.

All of the above reasons for idle time are directly or indirectly related to inadequate planning and scheduling. To reduce idle time, it is necessary to plan and schedule operations more efficiently.

For a specific order or job, the idle time is also a function of its priority. A high priority order will spend less time in queues and have a shorter manufacturing cycle time. Thus, priorities can dramatically affect an order's manufacturing cycle time in either direction. High priority orders leapfrog all or part of existing queues, which compresses their cycle time but tends to expand the cycle time of lower priority orders.

Reduction in investment for in-process inventory is directly proportional to manufacturing cycle time. Idle time, the major constituent of manufacturing cycle time, can best be reduced by eliminating physical backlogs in production. Backlogs can be reduced by better scheduling of operations and planning of the release of work to production. Reduction of the backlog or queue at each work center results in parts waiting less time for their "turn" to be worked, and the final effect is improved turnover of the cash investment in inventory.

The actions that can reduce the in-process inventory levels for an organization are as follows:

1. Schedule delivery of purchased materials as near as possible to the required first operation start date. Refuse to accept delivery of items that arrive in excess of defined reasonable limits.
2. Withdraw materials from storerooms as late as possible before their required operation date. This action delays material cost from being applied to work in process and keeps material under control until it is needed by production.
3. Balance the input rate of orders with the output rate of completed orders. If the input rate exceeds the output rate, backlogs will increase as well as cycle time.
4. Do not release work to production unless personnel, material, tooling, and support services are available in the needed quantities.

5. Schedule work to the shortest possible cycle time that does not result in excessive underutilization of facilities. Do not prerelease orders (the backlog) unless serious underutilization of resources will occur.

6. Use time increments that are compatible with actual requirements. The use of weeks is not appropriate for routings that actually require a day or two. Too large a time increment can inflate the cycle. It is not uncommon for the time scheduled to be the time taken.

7. Reduce setup times to an absolute minimum.

The reaction to large visible backlogs is frequently an attempt to increase capacity in some way. If the backlog consists of early release of orders or jobs for which there is no immediate demand, the result is an artificial backlog that can only be aggravated by increasing capacity. If schedules are not being met, the bottleneck work centers can be expanded by additional manpower, more shifts, overtime, subcontracting, or more equipment. A consistently high backlog can indicate the need for capacity expansion when it is predicated on an increase in demand for the product.

JUST-IN-TIME

The just-in-time (JIT) concept, developed by the Japanese, applies primarily to a repetitive manufacturing process. It does not necessarily require large volumes, but it is restricted to those operations which produce the same parts over and over again. It requires the production of precisely the necessary units in the necessary quantities at the necessary time with the objective of plus or minus zero performance to schedule. This means producing one extra piece is just as bad as being one piece short. Anything over the minimum amount necessary is viewed as waste, because effort and material expended for something not needed now cannot be utilized now (later requirements are handled later). The JIT concept is counter to American manufacturing philosophy, since good performance has been to meet or exceed the scheduled requirements "just-in-case" something goes wrong.

Waste is considered anything other than the absolute minimum resources of material, machines, and manpower required to add value to the product. Value is added only by the actual work performed on a product. Machining, assembling, painting, and packaging add value to a product. Other activities such as moving, storing, counting, sorting, and scheduling add cost to a product but not value. Fork trucks, expediters, and safety stocks add cost but not value. Cost without value is waste. Anything which does not directly add value to the product is waste and should be minimized if not eliminated.

With JIT, the ideal lot size is *one*. The manufacturing process can be viewed as a network of work centers wherein the perfect arrangement would be to have each worker complete his task on an item and pass it directly to the next worker just as that person is ready for it. The idea is to drive all queues toward zero in order to:

1. minimize inventory investment,
2. shorten production lead times,
3. react faster to demand changes,
4. uncover any quality problems.

TABLE 4
Comparison of conventional and JIT attitudes

Conventional	Just-in-Time
Large lots are efficient (more is better)	Ideal lot size is one unit (less is better)
Faster production is more efficient	Faster production than necessary is a waste (balanced production is more efficient)
Scheduling and queues are necessary tradeoffs to maximize output from equipment and manpower	Tradeoffs are bad; they trade one waste for another and prevent the proper solution of problems
Inventory provides safety	Safety stock is a waste
Inventory smoothes production	Inventory is undesirable

Since it is impossible to have all the workers in a network adjacent to one another and it must include outside suppliers, the system must allow for transit time between work centers. However, transfer quantities are kept as small as possible, and lot sizes are a fraction of a day's production. There are no allowances for contingencies. Every item is expected to be correct when received; every machine is expected to be available when needed to produce the item; every delivery commitment is expected to be honored at the precise time it is scheduled. Consequently, there is heavy emphasis on quality, preventive maintenance, and mutual trust between all participants in the manufacturing network.

JIT disavows the value of inventory. It is viewed in a negative fashion, not as an asset. It is considered a deterrent to product quality that hides (covers up) problems. Without inventory, problems are exposed, so they can be remedied before they cause trouble. Anything that unnecessarily occupies space consumes a valuable resource. Inventory occupies space so it can be regarded as a waste. To reduce this waste, it is necessary to plan efficient layouts and material flows.

For JIT to be feasible, there are certain preconditions to be met. JIT takes a number of seemingly unconnected concepts and techniques and binds them together in such a way that they not only begin to pull together toward a common goal, but they multiply, with each one building on and amplifying the results of the others. They include uniform plant loading, group technology, quality control at the source, minimized setup times, and a kanban type production control system. A comparison between conventional and JIT attitudes is contained in Table 4.

Uniform plant loading is accomplished by establishing a firm production plan for which output is frozen (usually for a month). The same mix of products are produced every day, even though the total quantities are small. For example, with a monthly requirement for 100 units, five might be built each day (presuming a 20 day month). Those five units would be intermixed with other products and not necessarily produced in exact sequence. Every day's schedule must be very nearly the same, or JIT will not work efficiently. The rated speed of equipment is ignored and only daily requirements are produced.

Uniform plant loading attempts to produce products at the rate they are demanded.

There are costs and side effects from producing more than is demanded. If products are produced faster than the demand rate then containers are needed to put them in, trucks are needed to move them, warehouse space is needed to store them, money is needed to finance the inventory, cycle counters are needed to count it, accountants are needed to keep track of it, and schedulers are needed to indicate when to produce more. All this because it was produced faster than the demand rate.

Group technology, which was discussed in Chapter 13, clusters dissimilar machines into work centers for a given part or family of parts. One operator may run several machines, which eliminates the move and queue time between operations in a given cluster or cell. Group technology is used to physically link and overlap as many operations as possible. Equipment are placed very close to each other similar to an assembly line. Balance, synchronization, and smooth flow are achieved, while lead times are reduced from days to minutes, which all but eliminates work-in-process inventory.

Quality control at the source means each worker is the quality inspector of his or her tasks. Every individual is responsible personally for the quality of the work that he or she produces. If a quality problem develops, the work is stopped and everybody in the area concentrates on resolving the problem. Work is not started again until the problem is corrected. Workers are responsible for feeding only good quality parts to the downstream operations they supply. Unacceptable quality is not tolerated; the emphasis is on quality instead of quantity. Quality circles frequently are used to improve quality and productivity. Quality at the source is predicated on three principles: (1) defect-free output is more important than mere output, (2) defects, errors, and breakdowns can be prevented, and (3) prevention costs less than doing things a second time.

Minimized setup times aim for single digit (less than ten minutes) setup times on every machine. Small lots cannot be run if setups take hours. Time saving devices like hinged bolts, roller platforms, and folding brackets are used to reduce setup times. Time and motion studies are helpful in meeting this goal. A large number of setups must be made with JIT, so unless setup times are at an absolute minimum, its benefits falter.

Kanban type production control systems are simple, self-regulatory, and paperless systems for scheduling and shop floor control. (Kanban is a Japanese word meaning card.) Kanban is a "pull" type of reorder system where authority to produce or supply comes from the final assembly schedule (usually the master production schedule). It is a material flow control system that functions in the following manner:

1. Production control gives a final production schedule to final assembly.
2. Final assembly withdraws parts in small quantities at the time required from the work centers which feed final assembly.
3. The work centers feeding final assembly then manufacture parts to replace those withdrawn by final assembly.
4. In order to do this, these work centers withdraw small quantities of parts as required from the upstream work centers which feed them.
5. Continuing in this manner, each work center withdraws parts at the time needed and in the quantities required from the work centers feeding them. Thus, the entire network is engaged in production synchronized to final assembly.

Kanban provides JIT production without the use of work orders for parts. In the Toyota kanban system, two types of cards are attached to the standard containers used to move parts. The conveyance kanban (cards) are used to move parts from feeding work centers to the using work centers (they are a form of move ticket); production kanban (cards) are used to authorize the production of parts to replace those which are withdrawn. These cards are prepared by hand and always circulated between the work centers and stock points for which they are designated.

Not every part can be controlled by kanban. Large components and irregular optional parts require special attention, but repetitively used parts are regulated by kanban.

The flow of kanban cards between two work centers is simple. When an assembly center starts to use part X, a worker takes the conveyance kanban and travels to the machine center storage area, where he finds a full container of part X. He removes the production kanban and replaces it with the conveyance kanban which authorizes him to move the container. The liberated production kanban is then placed in a rack by the machine center as a work authorization for another lot of material. Parts are manufactured in the machine center in the order in which cards are placed on the rack (the sequence of cards in the rack indicates the priority list for the machine center). No more parts are built than called for by the kanban cards in circulation. When the container of parts is completed, the production kanban is inserted into the container and it is moved into a storage area. The result is essentially a "pull" system. Each action by the assembly center results in a ripple effort back through the feeding work centers.

If a work center does not have any production kanban cards, no parts are produced. No parts are built in anticipation, so in-process inventory is kept low.

With JIT, it is desirable to have reliable local (nearby) suppliers. The quality control at the source concept is extended to suppliers. They are expected to deliver quality materials in smaller and more frequent batches as close to their use in production as is possible. This avoids costly inventory buildups and permits rapid responses to changes in market demand. The result is usually closer supplier relations, fewer suppliers, sole sources, and large contracts. Since contracts are larger and for longer time duration, supplier economies should be achieved that result in lower unit cost. The clustering of suppliers nearby shortens the logistical chain, with attendant economies.

JIT can be thought of as a logistical linking or chaining of the production operations that results in a steady, even flow of material similar to that found in an assembly line. The logistical chain reduces in-process inventory and lead times. JIT applies to a repetitive manufacturing process with a limited product line and where most of the parts must be repetitively manufactured. Inventory is stored in standard containers which are used to convey parts, one container at a time, through the production process with the fewest parts possible in each container.

CONCLUSION

Scheduling is the process of deciding when and where events will take place. Scheduling problems and methods differ substantially among organizations. The most complex scheduling problems tend to occur in job shops. In this chapter, several basic approaches to scheduling have been introduced.

QUESTIONS

1. Differentiate between master scheduling and detailed scheduling.
2. What type of production control system is used with each of the major production processes?
3. Describe the two principal methods of scheduling used in order control.
4. State briefly the decision rule used for the runout time method of production sequencing.
5. What are the goals usually associated with job shop scheduling?
6. Distinguish between shop loading and sequencing.
7. Explain the basis for the index method of shop loading. Does the index method result in an optimal load?
8. What is the major weakness of the assignment method?
9. How must data be structured for shop loading by the transportation algorithm logic?
10. What are the disadvantages of manually prepared charts in job shop scheduling?
11. Give the purpose of priority rules. What priority rule results in the least mean waiting time of jobs at a work center?
12. Should jobs with a critical ratio greater than one be delayed?
13. State the conditions for the use of Johnson's rule. Based on what criteria does Johnson's rule give an optimal solution?
14. What are the functions of input/output control?
15. What is manufacturing cycle time? List its five components.
16. How does cycle time influence in-process inventory?
17. What preconditions should be met for just-in-time (JIT) to be feasible?
18. Contrast the fundamental attitudes taken by proponents of conventional and just-in-time operations.
19. From your experience, name several manufacturing situations where job shop scheduling techniques could be applied.

PROBLEMS

1. For the next week, the work center capacities are as follows:

Work center	A	B	C	D
Capacity (hours available)	70	45	60	55

The following jobs have been loaded on the work centers:

Job number	Hours required per work center			
	A	B	C	D
10	5	6	4	2
12	6	2	—	4
14	2	6	2	2
15	7	8	4	—
16	4	—	6	2
17	8	5	2	3
18	14	11	9	5
19	3	9	4	—
20	6	—	5	7

Is sufficient capacity available to perform all the jobs? Are any work centers overloaded?

2. The jobs listed below can be performed on any of the four work centers. Using the index method, load the work centers for the next week.

	Work center			
Job	#1	#2	#3	#4
A	300	150	450	600
B	25	35	70	40
C	50	55	35	15
D	20	45	75	25
E	180	160	100	210
F	65	50	300	175
Hours available	325	100	110	65

3. If scheduled maintenance reduced the hours available for work center #1 in Problem 2 to 300 hours, how would it influence the job assignments?

4. A scheduler has four jobs that can be performed in any of four work centers. The cost per job is listed in the table below. Determine the allocation of jobs to work centers that results in the least cost if jobs cannot be split.

	Work center			
Job	#1	#2	#3	#4
A	19	14	17	16
B	12	15	18	19
C	16	22	14	13
D	17	19	20	15

5. The scheduling supervisor for Kirby Manufacturing Company has compiled the following data:

			Work center					
			W1		W2		W3	
Job order number	Job order size (units)	Selling price ($/unit)	Process rate (units/hr)	Cost ($/unit)	Process rate (units/hr)	Cost ($/unit)	Process rate (units/hr)	Cost ($/unit)
J1	650	10.00	50	7.00	45	4.00	40	3.00
J2	780	25.00	20	17.00	18	15.00	16	12.00
J3	960	8.00	80	4.00	72	5.00	64	3.00
J4	600	12.50	60	9.50	54	10.50	48	8.50
			210		189		168	
Time available			28		20		35	

Using the information compiled above with the transportation method, advise the scheduler on which jobs to assign to which work centers. What is the maximum contribution possible?

6. Sequence the jobs listed below by the rules of first come first served (FCFS), due date (DD), shortest processing time (SPT), longest processing time (LPT), and slack (S). Are the due dates being met?

Job	Process time (days)	Due date (days hence)
A	10	3
B	7	9
C	2	7
D	6	4
E	5	2
F	4	1

7. Today is the 175th day of the year on the production calendar. Sequence the jobs listed below by the critical ratio technique. Are any of the jobs behind schedule?

Job	Production calendar date required	Process time remaining (days)
A	190	5
B	178	2
C	184	10
D	181	3
E	205	17
F	187	15
G	184	9

8. Groton Small Boat Company manufactures sailboats to order. The company processes all orders serially through two work centers. At the beginning of the week the process times in hours for six orders are: $A = 7, B = 14, C = 9, D = 4, E = 10$, and $F = 6$ in work center 1; and $A = 8, B = 12, C = 11, D = 3, E = 13$, and $F = 2$ in work center 2. Sequence the jobs so there is minimum idle time in the work centers.

If each hour of production costs $250 in work center 1 and $180 in work center 2, what is the cost of idle time (assume new jobs will arrive so no idle time results in work center 1 at the end of the scheduling period)?

9. The E. J. Harris Manufacturing Company of O'Fallon, Missouri, has just completed a value analysis of the costs associated with their in-process inventory. The following data have been compiled:

Setup time: 10 hours per setup.

Process time: 24 hours per production run of 100 units.

Move time: 8 hours per production run of 100 units.

Inspection time: 5 hours per production run of 100 units.

Queue time: 150 hours per production run of 100 units.

The waiting (queue) time was further analyzed and the data below compiled:

Waiting to be moved	15%
Waiting to be inspected	10%
Hot jobs getting priority	30%
Shortages of material	40%
Machine breakdown	5%
	100%

Ted Jones, a recent graduate of the University of Missouri, computed that the following reductions in queue time could be achieved if a master production schedule and a material requirements planning system were installed:

Waiting time to be moved	20%
Waiting time to be inspected	50%
Hot jobs getting priority	10%
Shortages of material	90%

For 100 units what is the manufacturing cycle time at present? What would the manufacturing cycle time be if the master production schedule and MRP system were installed?

10. The following data are available on product AC 440–220–3P:

Selling price	$450/unit
Variable selling cost	$10/unit
Fixed cost	$60,000/year
Setup time	20 hr/lot at $30/hr
Process time	40 hr/50 units at $100/hr
Move time	50 hr/50 units at $20/hr
Inspection time	60 hr/50 units at $10/hr
Idle time	200 hr/50 units at $4/hr

How many units must be produced and sold to break even if only one production run is made per year?

11. A job shop has eight jobs, which must be processed in a sequential order through two departments. Apply Johnson's rule to determine the optimal sequence. The following table contains the number of hours required by each job in each department.

	Department	
Order	X	Y
A	14	6
B	8	10
C	9	5
D	10	12
E	5	3
F	24	8
G	3	15
H	7	8
Total	80	67

12. A company has five orders on hand, and each must be processed in sequential order through two departments. Determine the idle facility time by the first come first served rule (FCFS) and then by the shortest processing time rule (SPT). The following table lists the number of hours required by each job in each department.

	Department	
Order	X	Y
A	6	3
B	8	2
C	7	5
D	3	9
E	5	4

13. What sequence results in Problem 12 when Johnson's rule is used? How long does it take to complete all jobs, and what is the idle facility time?

14. An operations manager wishes to maximize the profit he can make on a mix of three products. There is a bottleneck in production, since the products utilize milling and drilling processes. Two mills and two drills are available, but each product requires a different amount of time on the various combinations of the equipment. The data are as follows:

	Product			Hours
	X	Y	Z	available
Mill 1 (hr/unit)	1.7	—	0.8	40
Mill 2 (hr/unit)	0.8	0.4	0.3	20
Drill 1 (hr/unit)	0.6	0.5	—	40
Drill 2 (hr/unit)	0.4	0.3	—	20
Profit ($/unit)	3.00	2.50	2.00	

The data indicate that product X can be made on either mill or either drill. Product Y can only be made on mill 2 but on either drill. Product Z need only be milled on either milling machine.

Assume that the firm can sell all the products it produces, setup time is negligible, and orders can be split. Set the problem up for solution by the simplex method by writing the constraint equations and the objective function.

Hint: Use subscripts with each variable $(X, Y,$ and $Z)$ to indicate the mill and drill combination. The first subscript indicates the mill and the second subscript the drill. For example, X_{12} indicates the number of units of product X produced on mill 1 and drill 2. Y_{22} indicates the number of units of product Y produced on mill 2 and drill 2. Z_{10} indicates the number of units of product Z produced on mill 1.

15. Complete the input/output report in Figure 9 using the following data, and analyze the results.

Week	21	22	23	24	25	26	27	28	29	30
Actual input	110	150	140	130	180	170	200	200	190	210
Actual output	150	140	160	140	150	170	180	210	210	220

16. Complete the input/output control report in Figure 8 using the following data, and analyze the results.

Week	12	13	14	15	16	17	18	19	20	21
Actual input	540	530	500	520	540	540	560	550	540	530
Actual output	610	520	600	580	530	520	540	540	530	530

17. A manufacturer presently is using a trial and error method to schedule its multiproduct assembly line but is considering converting to the runout time method for product sequencing. The most current information on the products being processed on the single assembly line follows:

Product	Inventory level (units)	Demand forecast (units/week)	Production rate (units/week)	Lot size
A	3000	750	3000	3000
B	6000	2000	4000	4000
C	1000	500	2000	1000
D	1600	500	1500	1500

(a) Using the information given, determine the tentative schedule sequence that the manufacturer would use according to the runout method.

(b) Assuming the information is correct, simulate production on the single assembly line for a five week period. Use projected values for inventory level and runout time calculations.

(c) Judging from the projected inventory level and runout times found in part (b), does the manufacturer seem to have scheduling and/or planning problems? If so, how might they be corrected?

CASE 1: MULTIFACETED

Octagon was founded in 1968 by John Tuxley, who was an established builder and general contractor. He developed the idea of a prefabricated home which could be built cheaply and assembled easily. The home was extremely heavy and awkward to move, so John came up with the idea of a tower crane. He built a prototype which performed excellently and soon found that people were far more interested in his crane than his prefab house. As a result, he started Octagon Manufacturing Company and began to produce tower cranes for industry.

When Octagon first went into production, operations ran smoothly. In more recent years the plant has experienced a rash of bottlenecks, late deliveries, customer cancellations, increased costs, reduced quality, and increased manufacturing cycle times (the usual four weeks increased to seven or eight weeks). The updated load reports continually revealed increased backlogs. What worsened the work load status was the rise in the volume of customer orders and government contracts. Orders had risen by approximately 25% in each of the preceding two years, but firm orders for the first production period of the current year were down for the first time in over ten years.

When operations were progressing methodically, most jobs were dealt with on a first-come, first-served basis. Nowadays orders often accumulate over several weeks. The accumulated orders plus any incoming orders are classified by type and size and then assigned to the work centers. The loading or assignment of tasks to a particular work center is done so as to minimize the number of times the machinery has to be set up. For each machine center (i.e. cutting, welding, casting, etc.), a list is prepared of all orders to be processed in the next two week period. The sequencing of orders at each work center is arranged to reduce setups and to shorten queue time with the saving of setup costs as the number one priority.

Setups have an average cost of $250, so any rush jobs which require additional setups are deemed too costly. The setup priority schedule is rarely altered once it is completed, and tampering with it is protectively disallowed. However, some members of Octagon management think that the tight schedules are the primary cause of delays and bottlenecks. Manufacturing lead times have become excessively long, and they assert this is due to the large accumulations of in-process inventory. It is also their assertion that proper scheduling could reduce in-process inventory by at least 30%. Although limiting setups may have kept production economical from one standpoint, it is causing inefficient compromises of competing goals, e.g. reduction of inventory costs.

This group of adversaries is pushing for a new scheduling system based on a restructuring of goals and priorities. Their position rests with the following assumptions: first, Octagon's situation is faltering due to poor scheduling, and second, Octagon is failing due to the adoption of misdirected goals. It is their belief that the basic criteria on which job shops compete—specifically cost, deliver, and quality—are not receiving sufficient focus. These adversaries have issued a challenge: ''All of the competitive criteria will be improved within a trial phase of a scheduling technique that incorporates unprecedented setups.''

As preliminary steps to devising the new schedule, studies are being performed on various aspects of plant activity, and process times are being computed at the work centers. A mean time for each job shop center is to be formulated by averaging a sample of the activities. These estimates will determine capacity. Plant personnel are being questioned as to which operations have proven to cause bottlenecks, and these particular operations will receive isolated study with subsequent closer estimation of time ranges. Job completion dates will be based on forward scheduling, but the actual way to sequence the orders is still under consideration. Lastly, the new scheduling method will reflect the following policies: changing priorities, use of overtime, tracking of progress, and necessary revisions.

1. How is competition affected by the old policies? Could the ''challenge'' be more effective?
2. Are the dispatching rules acceptable under the old plan? What are some suggestions for the new plan?
3. Since it is practically impossible to develop ''the'' optimal schedule in a job shop, would the new plan at least be satisfactory?
4. How will in-process inventory be affected by any changes?

CASE 2: THE UNCONTROLLABLE SHOP JUNGLE

Dave Conservative was reviewing the year-end financial statements of Wilson Manufacturing Company, a job shop operation which recently moved into a spacious new facility. Dave noted with alarm the changes that occurred in current assets during the first accounting period following the move. Specifically, he was alarmed by the decline in the cash balance and the growth in inventory.

Dave realized that as the company financial manager, he viewed things differently from John Lathe, who was vice president for production. He recalled John insisting on large stabilization stocks in order to keep production levels high. John scheduled long production runs in centers where frequent production changes had proven expensive. He also realized the disruption of production because of inventory shortages could be more costly than the extra holding costs. Furthermore, the large stocks allowed John to continue the use of flexible scheduling. He felt it important to maintain different input/output rates at work centers so as to maximize the efficiency and productivity of each center. So as a consequence of stabilization stocks, the centers enjoyed independent planning, and the firm as a whole could have flexibility in scheduling different products through the facility.

On Friday morning at the weekly department head meeting, Dave broached the subject of cash and inventory control with John. John proceeded to highlight areas where he saw problems. He said certain costs had definitely increased since the move, but most of these would be remedied in due course. Large cash outlays had gone to compensate the maintenance crew for overtime. The new machinery had many operational problems that were not covered under the purchase warranties. Another enlarged expense was the rise in materials handling costs. The materials handlers were slow in acquainting themselves with the new facility and its more spacious layout. The materials personnel were still confused on the locations of partially processed goods; more in-process goods were going to temporary storage so the accumulation on the shop floor would be reduced. The storage and retrieval of in-process goods were unfamiliar to the materials handlers.

John also thought that his direct labor costs were up, but he was sure this would also be self-correcting. The employees were having a hard time adjusting their pace to their workload. The employees had always formed notions about the amount of work to be processed through their center by judging the inventory coming in and going out. With the new layout they were

having difficulty estimating workloads, and their actual workload was greater than they perceived. For instance, as the firm reduced the input to some centers by leaving more inventory
in storage, the workers were slackening their pace to meet the reduced inventory coming to
the center. Also contributing to the slower pace was the relative absence of waste and damaged
goods, which gave the appearance of little in-process inventory.

In defense of other inventory control areas, John was quick to point out that a new purchasing and raw materials inventory control system installed this year had reduced raw material
inventory levels. The finished goods inventories were also down. "Look, Dave, marketing is
doing a superb job of forecasting demand. To reduce the finished goods any more will only
result in excess stockouts, and with the competition we have, we just can't afford that."

Dave, after reviewing the figures on the raw materials and finished goods inventory, had
to agree that they were both down. "You're right. The problem is with the in-process inventory. John, I guess you are doing all you can. In-process inventory is just part of the manufacturing process and beyond our control. We can only deal with these labor and maintenance
costs that will improve with some training and adjustment. Have a nice weekend, John, I'll
see you Monday."

1. Discuss how such diverse things as maintenance, scheduling, and materials handling
   affect in-process inventory.
2. How do behavioral considerations affect Wilson's cash or inventory problems?
3. Should Dave overlook the inventory problem and concentrate on the cash outlays, or is
   there some overlap?
4. What recommendations would you make to Dave?

SELECTED BIBLIOGRAPHY

Baker, K. R. *Introduction to Sequencing and Scheduling,* New York: Wiley, 1974.

Campbell, H. G. et al. "A Heuristic Algorithm for the *n* Job, *m* Machine Sequencing Problem," *Management Science,* Vol. 16, No. 10, June 1970, pp. B630–B637.

Conway, R. W. et al. *Theory of Scheduling,* Reading, MA: Addison-Wesley, 1967.

French, S. *Sequencing and Scheduling: An Introduction to the Mathematics of the Job Shop,*
New York: Wiley, 1982.

Johnson, L. A. and D. C. Montgomery, *Operations Research in Production Planning, Scheduling, and Inventory Control,* New York: Wiley, 1974.

Johnson, S. M. "Optimal Two- and Three-State Production Schedules with Setup Time Included," *Naval Research Logistics Quarterly,* Vol. 1, No. 1, March 1954, pp. 61–68.

Muth, J. F. and G. L. Thompson, eds., *Industrial Scheduling,* Englewood Cliffs, NJ: Prentice-
Hall, 1963.

O'Brien, J. J. *Scheduling Handbook,* New York: McGraw-Hill, 1969.

Starr, M. K. *Systems Management of Operations,* Englewood Cliffs, NJ: Prentice-Hall, 1971.

Wantuck, K. A. "The Japanese Approach to Productivity," *Inventories and Production,* Vol.
3, No. 1, 1983.

19

Inventory Control Models

TYPES OF INVENTORY

INVENTORY COSTS

INDEPENDENT VERSUS DEPENDENT DEMAND

CONTINUOUS AND INDEPENDENT DEMAND ITEMS

Fixed Order Size System (Q-System)

Economic Order Quantity (EOQ)
Economic Production Quantity (EPQ)

Fixed Order Interval System (T-System)

Economic Order Interval (EOI)

Sensitivity

Risk and Uncertainty

DISCRETE AND DEPENDENT DEMAND ITEMS

Material Requirements Planning (MRP) Systems

An EOQ–MRP Comparison

Discrete Lot Sizing

Part-Period Algorithm

TIME-PHASED ORDER POINT

SINGLE ORDER QUANTITIES

Marginal Analysis
Cost Analysis

CONCLUSION

QUESTIONS

PROBLEMS

CASES

SELECTED BIBLIOGRAPHY

The control and maintenance of inventory is a problem common to all organizations in any sector of the economy. The problems of inventory do not confine themselves to profit making institutions. The same problems are encountered by social and non-profit institutions. Inventories are common to agriculture, manufacturers, wholesalers, retailers, hospitals, churches, prisons, zoos, universities, and national, state, and local governments. Indeed, inventories are also relevant to the family unit: food, clothing, medicines, toiletries, and so forth. On an aggregate national basis, the total investment in inventory represents a sizable portion of the gross national product.

For many organizations, the investment in inventories is therefore important. A review of American industry balance sheets reveals that a large percentage of the assets in a company lie in inventories. Poor control of inventory can create a negative cash flow, tie up large amounts of capital, limit the expansion of an organization due to lack of capital, and reduce the return on investment by broadening the investment base. Many businesses have 15–40% of their total assets tied up in inventory. The pressure for capital and the effective utilization of resources has made decision makers more aware of its significance. Cash invested in inventories could be used somewhere else for profit, debt servicing, or dividend distribution.

TYPES OF INVENTORY

Inventory is material held for future sale or use. It may consist of supplies, raw materials, in-process goods, and finished goods. Supplies are inventory items consumed in the normal functioning of an organization that are not a part of the final product. Typical supplies are pencils, paper, light bulbs, typewriter ribbons, and facility maintenance items. Raw materials are the inputs into the production process that will be modified or transformed into finished goods. Typical raw materials for a furniture manufacturer might be lumber, stain, glue, screws, varnish, nails, paint, and so forth. In-process goods are final products that are still in the production process but have not been completed. Finished goods are the completed final product which is available for sale, distribution, or storage.

The assignment of inventory to any of these categories is dependent on the specific entity under study: one entity's finished product may be another entity's raw material. For example, a refrigerator manufacturer considers copper tubing as a raw material, but the firm that produces the tubing considers it as a finished good. The customer for finished goods inventory may be the ultimate consumer, a retail organization, a wholesale distributor, or another manufacturer.

Inventories are a kind of lubrication for the supply-production-distribution system that protects it from excessive friction. Inventories isolate one part of the system from the next to permit each to work independently, absorb the shock of forecast errors, and permit the effective utilization of resources when demand undulations are experienced.

INVENTORY COSTS

The objective of inventory management is to have the appropriate amounts of raw materials, supplies, and finished goods in the right place, at the right time, and at low cost. Inventory costs result from action or lack of action of management in establishing the inventory system. The inventory system cost factors include the following:[1]

1. purchase cost,
2. order/setup cost,
3. holding cost,
4. stockout cost.

Inventory costs are basic economic parameter inputs to any inventory decision model. For a particular item, only those cost elements that are incremental (out of pocket) are relevant in an inventory analysis.

The *purchase cost (P)* of an item is the unit purchase price if it is obtained from an external source, or the unit production cost if it is produced internally. The unit cost should always be the cost of the item as it is placed in inventory. For purchased items, it is the purchase price plus any freight cost. For manufactured items, the unit cost is the sum of direct labor, direct material, and factory overhead. The purchase cost is modified for different quantity levels when a supplier offers quantity discounts.

The *order/setup cost (C)* originates from the expense of issuing a purchase order to an outside supplier or from internal production setup costs. The order/setup cost is usually assumed to vary directly with the number of orders or setups placed and not at all with the size of the order. The order cost includes making requisitions, analysis of vendors, writing purchase orders, receiving and inspecting materials, following up orders, and the necessary paperwork to complete the transaction. The setup cost is the cost of changing over the production process to produce the ordered item. It usually includes preparing the shop order, scheduling the work, preproduction setup, expediting, and quality acceptance.

The *holding cost (H)*, frequently referred to as the carrying cost, originates from many sources. It includes such cost items as capital cost, taxes, insurance, handling, storage, shrinkage, obsolescence, and deterioration. Capital cost reflects lost earning power or an opportunity cost: if the funds were invested elsewhere, a return on the investment would be expected. Capital cost is a charge that accounts for this unreceived return. Many states treat inventories as taxable property; so the more you have, the higher the taxes. Insurance coverage requirements are dependent on the amount to be replaced if the warehouse is destroyed; thus insurance premiums will vary with the size of the inventory investment. Obsolescence is the risk that an item will lose value because of shifts in styles, technology, or consumer preference. Shrinkage is the decrease in inventory quantities over time from lost or stolen items. Deterioration involves a change in properties due to age or environmental degradation. Many items are age-controlled and must be sold or used before an expiration date (food items, photographics, and pharmaceuticals). The usual range of annual holding cost is from 15% to 40% of the inventory investment.

A *stockout cost* (depletion cost) results from external and internal shortages. An external shortage occurs when a customer of the organization does not have his order filled; an internal shortage occurs when a group or department within the organization

---

[1]Particularly those related with supplies, raw materials, and finished goods. See Arnold Reisman, *Industrial Inventory Control,* New York: Gordon and Breach, 1972, Chapter 5, for procedures for developing relevant cost parameters.

does not have its order filled. External shortages result in backorder costs, present profit loss (potential sale), and future profit loss (goodwill erosion). Internal shortages can result in lost production (idle men and machines) and a delay in completion date. The stockout cost depends on the reaction of the customer to the out-of-stock condition. If demand occurs for an item out of stock, the economic loss depends on whether the item is backordered, the need is satisfied by substitution of another item, or the order is canceled. In the first situation, the sale is not lost but only delayed in shipment. Typically, however, a company will institute an emergency expediting order to get the item. This results in expediting costs, handling costs, and frequently special shipping and packaging costs. In the last situation, the sale is lost. The stockout cost in this case consists of the profit loss on the sale plus an unknown loss connected with goodwill: the customer may not return in the future. A stockout cost due to an internal shortage can be extremely high if the missing item forces a production line to shut down. From these situations, it can be seen that the stockout cost can vary considerably for different items, depending on customer or internal needs and responses.

INDEPENDENT VERSUS DEPENDENT DEMAND

Production systems can be classified according to the manner in which demand is supplied and the impact the related supply method has on inventory requirements. The functions and nature of inventory vary as a consequence of the type of production system in use—on whether it is

1. production to order, or
2. production to stock (inventory).

With production to order, no production is initiated until a firm demand for an item exists. With production to stock, production commences in anticipation of demand. Continuous demand items tend to be associated with production to stock as end items produced for finished goods inventory. Discrete demand items characteristically are linked to production to order as raw materials, parts, and components required to produce customer-ordered end items. In a broader sense, discrete demand items can be connected to production-to-stock systems where the production process is periodic or intermittent. Here, the demand for the end item may be continuous, but the demand for the components making up the end item is discrete; the discrete pattern occurs because production typically is scheduled in lots.

For continuous demand items, demand is reasonably smooth while also responding to random influences stemming from customer preferences. The demand for such items usually is unrelated to the demand for other items and hence is termed "independent." Due to the usage traits of independent demand items, it is feasible to stock them at all times and to replenish their stock according to forecasted quantities.

Discrete demand items have contrasting qualities and usage patterns. Their discreteness implies that demand occurs at intervals (in a lumpy pattern). The occurrence of the intervals can be traced to intermittent usage in the manufacture of end item lots. Demand for such items is not independently determined but is *dependent* upon the demand for an end item. The order for component items is placed so that the quantity required for the end item's production schedule will be available when needed; there is no need to carry inventory of components during periods when they are not required by the production process. The timing of stock replenishment, therefore, is critical. For dependent demand streams, the traditional continuous and independent demand assumptions are invalid because:

1. individual demands are not independent,
2. demand is not uniform or continuous,
3. variations in demand are not caused by random fluctuations.

Manufacturing organizations are concerned with producing finished products that are assemblies of a number of separate components. The manufacturing process involves the production of component items followed by assembly in one or more stages into the final product. The only forecast of demand necessary is at the end item level; all other component demands can be inferred from it. It may be necessary for these organizations to have inventory of end items at all times but not inventory of the dependent demand components.

CONTINUOUS AND INDEPENDENT DEMAND ITEMS

The choice of an inventory system is predicated on whether the items to be controlled have dependent or independent demand patterns. It is a mistake to use systems designed for independent demand items to control dependent demand items and vice-versa. However, this should not be construed as an either-or decision for inventory system adoption. Since organizations, such as firms which fabricate parts and manufacture finished products, may have items from both demand classifications, successful ones will use systems in partnership. Distinct systems may be selected to control different demand categories of items, but the systems operating conjointly would be used to manage the entire inventory of the organization. The systems are designed to be complementary.

This section deals with systems used to control independent demand items.

FIXED ORDER SIZE SYSTEM (Q-SYSTEM)

The two fundamental questions posed to any inventory system are *how many* and *when* to order. Again, the answers depend on the nature of inventory demand. In the fixed order size system, demand is continuous. The same number of units (how many) always is ordered, but the time between orders (when) is allowed to vary according to fluctuations in usage. Furthermore, the stock level is reviewed continuously; hence, the system also is referred to as a perpetual inventory system. Whenever the inventory position reaches a predetermined point, an order for a fixed number of units is placed. Thus, the two defining parameters of the system are the reorder point *(B)* and the size of the order *(Q)*. The Q-system also is termed a reorder point system. A typical example is depicted in Figure 1.

Economic Order Quantity (EOQ)

The size of an order that minimizes the total inventory cost is known as the economic order quantity (EOQ). The classical inventory model assumes the idealized situation shown in Figure 2, where Q is the order size.[2] Upon receipt of an order,

---

[2]The classical inventory model is frequently referred to as a sawtooth model because of the series of right triangles.

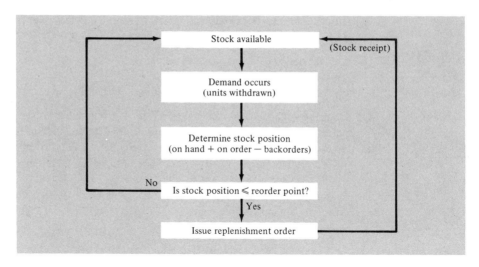

FIGURE 1
Fixed order size system logic.

the inventory level is Q units. Units are withdrawn from inventory at a constant demand rate, which is represented by the negative sloping lines. The inventory position is reviewed continuously. When the inventory reaches the reorder point B, a new order is placed for Q units. After a fixed lead time period, the order is received all at once and placed into inventory. The vertical lines indicate the instantaneous receipt of a lot into inventory. The new order is received just as the inventory level reaches zero, so the average inventory is $(Q + 0)/2$ or $Q/2$.

FIGURE 2
Classical inventory model.

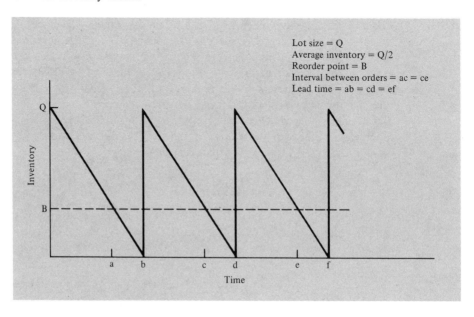

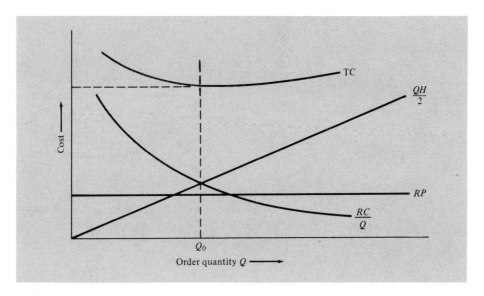

FIGURE 3
Annual inventory costs.

If stockouts are not permitted, the total inventory cost per year is graphically depicted by Figure 3 and given by the following formula:[3]

Total annual cost = purchase cost + order cost + holding cost,

$$TC = RP + \frac{RC}{Q} + \frac{QH}{2},$$

where

R = annual demand in units,

P = purchase cost of an item,

C = ordering cost per order,

$H = PF$ = holding cost per unit per year,

Q = lot size or order quantity in units,

F = annual holding cost as a fraction of unit cost.

In effect, the total annual cost equation determines the annual purchase cost, which is the annual demand times the purchase cost per unit. The annual order cost is obtained as the number of orders per year (R/Q) times the cost to place an order (C). The annual holding cost is the average inventory $(Q/2)$ times the annual unit holding cost (H). The sum of the three costs (purchase, order, and holding) will be the total inventory cost per year for any given purchased item.

---

[3]Although we have selected a time period of one year, any time period can be used as long as R and H are on the same time basis. The model does assume that stockouts will not occur.

To obtain the minimum cost lot size (EOQ), take the first derivative of total annual cost with respect to the lot size (Q) and set it equal to zero.

$$\frac{d\text{TC}}{dQ} = \frac{H}{2} - \frac{CR}{Q^2} = 0.$$

Solving the equation for Q, we get the EOQ formula:

$$Q_0 = \sqrt{\frac{2CR}{H}} = \sqrt{\frac{2CR}{PF}} = \text{economic order quantity.}$$

The reorder point is obtained by determining the demand that will occur during the lead time period. When the stock position (on hand + on order − backorders) reaches the reorder point, an order will be placed for Q_0 units, the economic order quantity. The following formula gives the reorder point when the lead time L is expressed in months:

$$B = \frac{RL}{12} = \text{reorder point in units.}$$

If the lead time L is expressed in weeks, the reorder point is expressed as

$$B = \frac{RL}{52} = \text{reorder point in units.}$$

The order is assumed to be received when the 'last item leaves the inventory, and the inventory level is then restored to a level equal to the amount ordered. If the lead time is less than the average order interval $(L < T)$, there will never be more than a single order outstanding. If the lead time is greater than the average order interval $(L > T)$, there will always be at least one order outstanding.

The minimum total cost per year is obtained by substituting Q_0 for Q in the total annual cost equation. The following formula results:

$$\text{TC}_0 = RP + HQ_0.$$

The classic EOQ results in items with high unit cost being ordered frequently in small quantities (the saving in inventory investment pays for the extra orders) and items with low unit cost in less frequent, large quantities (the inventory investment is small and the repeated expense of orders can be avoided). The EOQ formula is based on the following assumptions:

1. The demand rate is known and constant.
2. The lead time is known and constant.
3. The entire lot size is added to inventory at the same time.
4. No stockouts are permitted; since demand and lead time are known, stockouts can be avoided.
5. The cost structure is fixed; order/setup costs are the same regardless of lot size, holding cost is a linear function based on average inventory, and no quantity discounts are given on large purchases.
6. There is sufficient space, capacity, and capital to procure the desired quantity.
7. The item is a single product; it does not interact with any other inventory items.

EXAMPLE 1

The Williams Manufacturing Company purchases 8000 units of a product each year at a unit cost of $10.00. The order cost is $30.00 per order, and the holding cost per unit per year is $3.00. What are the economic order quantity, the total annual cost, the number of orders to place in one year, and the reorder point when the lead time is two weeks?

$$Q_0 = \sqrt{\frac{2CR}{H}} = \sqrt{\frac{2(30)8000}{3}} = 400 \text{ units,}$$

$$TC_0 = RP + HQ_0 = 8000(10) + 3(400) = \$81,200,$$

$$m = \frac{R}{Q_0} = \frac{8000}{400} = 20 \text{ orders/year,}$$

$$B = \frac{RL}{52} = \frac{8000(2)}{52} = 307.7 \text{ units.}$$

Economic Production Quantity (EPQ)

The assumption that the entire order is received into inventory at one time is often not true for in-house production runs.[4] Frequently, replenishment is continuous and the stock of inventory is being depleted even while the production of an order takes place (finished goods go into inventory gradually). The major decision involves the determination of the size of the production run. The size of the production run that minimizes the total inventory cost is known as the economic production quantity (EPQ).

Figure 4 depicts a typical cycle for the replenishment of inventory over a time period t_p. Production starts at time zero and ends at time t_p. For the time period $t - t_p$, no production occurs and the inventory stock is depleted. At time t, a new production run is started. If there had been no demand during the period zero to t_p, inventories would have risen at a rate p. Hence, $t_p = Q/p$. Since there is a demand at rate r, inventories will increase at a rate $p - r$, where p is greater than r.[5] During the production period (zero to t_p), inventories accumulate at a rate equal to the production rate minus the demand rate, $p - r$. The maximum inventory level is $t_p(p - r)$, or the time of production times the rate of inventory buildup. The average inventory is one-half of the maximum inventory, or $t_p[(p - r)/2]$. Since $t_p = Q/p$, the average inventory is given by the following formula:

$$\text{average inventory} = \frac{Q(p - r)}{2p}.$$

The average inventory is not just $Q/2$, but is $Q(p - r)/2p$. The factor r/p represents the fractional amount of the lot size withdrawn from stock during the time the

---

[4]When the entire purchase or production order quantity is received into inventory at one time, the replenishment rate is infinite. If the entire order quantity is not received at the same time, the replenishment rate is finite.

[5]When $p = r$, the rate of production equals the demand rate. In this situation, there are no setup or holding costs, since production is continuous and perfectly matched with demand.

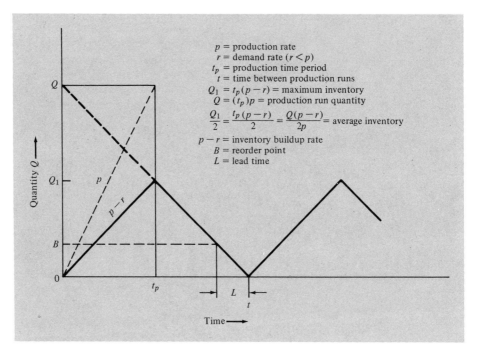

FIGURE 4
Production order quantity.

item is being produced. The factor $(p - r)/p$ represents the fractional amount of the lot size remaining in stock at the end of the production period. Since the stock level ranges between a minimum of zero and a maximum of $Q(p - r)/p$, the average inventory is simply one-half the maximum inventory. If stockouts are not permitted, the total annual inventory cost is as follows:[6]

Total annual cost = production cost + setup cost + holding cost,

$$\text{TC} = RP + \frac{RC}{Q} + \frac{Q(p - r)H}{2p},$$

where:

R = annual demand in units,

P = unit production cost,

Q = size of production run or production order quantity,

p = production rate,

r = demand rate,

C = setup cost per production run,

H = holding cost per unit per year.

---

[6]The model assumes that stockouts will not occur.

To obtain the minimum cost production order quantity (EPQ), take the first derivative of the total annual cost with respect to the production order quantity (Q) and set it equal to zero:

$$\frac{dTC}{dQ} = -\frac{RC}{Q^2} + \frac{(p-r)H}{2p} = 0.$$

Solving the equation for Q, the EPQ formula is obtained:

$$Q_0 = \sqrt{\frac{2CRp}{H(p-r)}} = \text{economic production quantity.}$$

Once the economic production quantity is known, the optimum length of the production run can be obtained as well as the production reorder point. If it is assumed that there are N operating days per year, the following relationships apply:

$$\text{optimum length of production run} = t_0 = \frac{Q_0}{p},$$

$$\text{production reorder point in units} = B = \frac{RL}{N} = rL,$$

where L is the scheduling and production setup time in days and r is the daily demand rate.

Replacing Q in the total annual cost formula by Q_0, the following formula results for the minimum total cost per year:

$$TC_0 = RP + \frac{(p-r)HQ_0}{p}.$$

EXAMPLE 2

The demand for an item is 20,000 units per year, and there are 250 working days per year. The production rate is 100 units per day, and the lead time is 4 days. The unit production cost is $50.00, the holding cost is $10.00 per unit per year, and the setup cost is $20.00 per run. What are the economic production quantity, the number of runs per year, the reorder point, and the minimum total annual cost?

$$r = \frac{R}{N} = \frac{20,000}{250} = 80 \text{ units per day,}$$

$$Q_0 = \sqrt{\frac{2CRp}{H(p-r)}} = \sqrt{\frac{2(20)(20,000)(100)}{10(100-80)}}$$
$$= 632 \text{ units,}$$

$$m = \frac{R}{Q_0} = \frac{20,000}{632} = 31.6 \text{ runs per year,}$$

$$B = \frac{RL}{N} = \frac{20,000(4)}{250} = 320 \text{ units,}$$

$$TC_0 = RP + \frac{(p-r)HQ_0}{p} = (20,000)(50) + \frac{(100-80)10(632)}{100},$$

$$TC_0 = \$1,001,264.$$

594

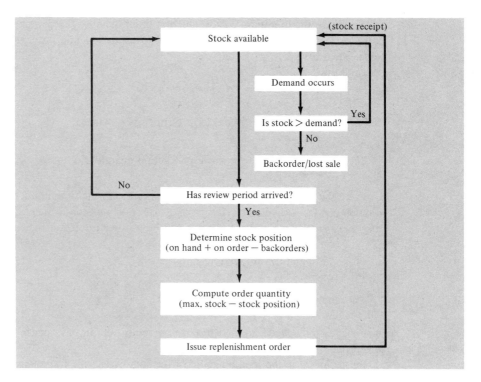

FIGURE 5
Fixed order interval system logic.

FIGURE 6
Fixed order interval system.

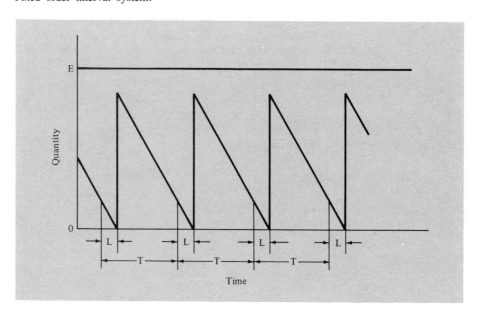

FIXED ORDER INTERVAL SYSTEM (*T*-SYSTEM)

The fixed order interval system, also called a periodic inventory system, is based on a periodic rather than a continuous review of the inventory stock position. It is a time based inventory system in which orders are placed at equally spaced, predetermined points in time (when to order). The order quantity (how many to order) varies according to the fluctuations in usage between order review periods.

A maximum inventory level for the item is developed, based on usage during both the lead time and the order interval. After a fixed period of time (*T*) has passed, the stock position of the item is determined. An order is placed to replenish the stock, and the size of the order is sufficient to bring the present stock level up to the maximum inventory level. Thus, the size of the order for the item is the difference between its maximum inventory level and its inventory position at the time of the review. The system, therefore, contains only two parameters to be chosen: the fixed review period *T* and the maximum inventory level *E*. From these, all replenishment orders are calculated.

The fixed order interval system is termed a *T*-system, since the order interval or "when" to order is constant (in the fixed order size system, the size of the order or "how many" was stationary). A typical fixed order interval system is shown in Figures 5 and 6.

Economic Order Interval (EOI)

The basic problem in this system is determining the order interval *T* and the desired maximum inventory level *E*. The economic order interval can be obtained by the minimization of total annual cost. If stockouts are not permitted, the total annual inventory cost is given by Figure 7 and the following formula:

Total annual cost = purchase cost + order cost + holding cost,

$$\text{TC} = RP + mC + \frac{RFP}{2m} = RP + \frac{C}{T} + \frac{RFPT}{2},$$

where

$$m = \frac{1}{T} = \text{number of orders or reviews per year,}$$

$$\frac{R}{2m} = \frac{RT}{2} = \text{average inventory in units,}$$

$$T = \frac{1}{m} = \text{order interval in years.}$$

To obtain the minimum cost order interval, the first derivative of the total annual cost with respect to the order interval *T* is set equal to zero:

$$\frac{d\text{TC}}{dT} = -\frac{C}{T^2} + \frac{RFP}{2} = 0.$$

Solving the equation for *T*, the following formula results:

$$T_0 = \sqrt{\frac{2C}{RFP}} = \text{economic order interval (EOI) in years.}$$

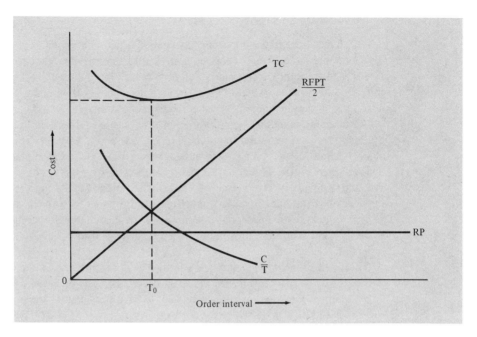

FIGURE 7
Annual inventory costs.

The minimum cost number of reviews per year is simply the reciprocal of T_0, or

$$m_0 = \frac{1}{T_0} = \sqrt{\frac{RFP}{2C}}.$$

In practice, the order interval tends to be determined by such factors as the number of clerks available to inspect stock records, or it is fixed at some convenient standard interval such as a week or a month.

In deterministic situations, there is no difference between the fixed order size system and the fixed order interval system. The order quantity for the fixed order interval is simply $Q = RT$, or

$$Q_0 = RT_0 = R\sqrt{\frac{2C}{RFP}} = \sqrt{\frac{2RC}{FP}} = \sqrt{\frac{2RC}{H}}.$$

The maximum inventory level E must be large enough to satisfy demand during the subsequent order interval T and also during the lead time L. The following formula gives the maximum inventory level when the order interval and lead time are expressed in years:

$$E = RT + RL = R(T + L) = Q + B = \text{maximum inventory level}.$$

The following formula gives the maximum inventory level when the order interval and lead time are expressed in days and there are N operating days in the year:

$$E = \frac{RT}{N} + \frac{RL}{N} = \frac{R(T + L)}{N} = Q + B.$$

The minimum total cost per year is obtained by substituting T_0 for T in the total annual cost equation. The following minimum total cost per year formula results:

$$TC_0 = RP + RHT_0.$$

EXAMPLE 3

From the information given in Example 1, determine the economic order interval and the maximum inventory level. The lead time is two weeks (10 working days) until an order is received, and there are 250 working days in the year.

$$T_0 = \sqrt{\frac{2C}{RH}} = \sqrt{\frac{2(30)}{(8000)3}} = 0.05 \text{ year, or } 12.5 \text{ days,}$$

$$E = \frac{R(T + L)}{N} = \frac{8000(12.5 + 10)}{250} = 720 \text{ units,}$$

$$TC_0 = RP + RHT_0 = (8000)(10) + 8000(3)0.05 = \$81,200.$$

Every 12.5 days the inventory position would be determined and an order initiated. Note that the optimum total annual cost is exactly the same for the fixed order interval system as for the fixed order size system.

SENSITIVITY

Basic inventory models (EOQ, EPQ, and EOI) are sometimes viewed with suspicion because of their restrictive assumptions. Rarely can a situation be found where demand is constant and known with certainty while costs are known precisely. Fortunately, basic inventory models are not oversensitive to errors in the measurement of parameters. Wide variations in demand level and cost parameters do not result in wide variations in model outputs.

Over a considerable range, the total variable cost curve is fairly flat, which indicates that substantial changes in demand, order cost, or holding cost will be attenuated. When the EOQ, EPQ, and EOI are computed with imprecise estimates, the errors are dampened or muted by the presence of the square root function. Therefore, the usefulness of these models is not diluted if exact precision is not available. Within a range of 0.4 to 2.5 times the parameter, the total variable cost changes by less that 11%.[7]

The insensitivity of the basic inventory models to parameter errors is a very advantageous property. Since total cost is only slightly increased by substantial departures from optimum conditions, the basic models do not require frequent revision (recalculation). Many components of cost parameters are difficult to measure, but the

---

[7]See R.J. Tersine, *Principles of Inventory and Materials Management*, New York: North-Holland, 1982, pp. 95–100.

insensitivity renders broad estimates operationally useful. All that is needed is to get into the "right ballpark."

RISK AND UNCERTAINTY

Risk and uncertainty enter an inventory analysis through many variables, but the most prevalent are variations in demand and lead time. These variations are absorbed by provision for safety stocks, also referred to as buffer stocks or fluctuation stocks. Safety stocks are extra inventory kept on hand as a cushion against stockouts. Safety stock has two effects on cost: it decreases the cost of stockouts, and increases the holding cost.

In a deterministic fixed order size system (EOQ), the average inventory is approximated as $Q/2$. When safety stock S is held, the approximate average inventory becomes $S + Q/2$. Thus, safety stock is a fairly permanent investment in inventory.

The reorder point establishes the frequency of exposure to risk of stockout. Stockouts can only occur after the reorder point is reached and before stock replenishment (during the lead time). The reorder point contains the safety stock and is defined as the average demand during the replenishment period plus the safety stock.

There are two approaches to establishing safety stocks (and thus the reorder point).[8] The first approach is based on known stockout costs (explicit costs that can be allocated to shortages). The second approach deals with unknown stockout costs where management specifies a service level (percentage of replenishment periods without a stockout) based on some probability distribution of demand. Usually stockout costs are difficult to ascertain, so the service level approach is the most widely used. Risk in inventory analysis is a highly involved topic. The interested reader should consult the references for detailed treatment.

DISCRETE AND DEPENDENT DEMAND ITEMS

A finished product is usually composed of many raw materials and components that are transformed during production into the desired end item. When a demand exists for a finished product, there is a concomitant demand generated for each of the finished product's input materials. Every raw material or component going into the final product will have a derived demand. Before production can commence, the necessary material inputs to the final product must be available and in inventory. The determination of the order quantity for input material is derived from the production levels, which are determined from product forecasts or customer orders for finished products.

If the demand for an item is continuous and independent of the demand for any other item, a fixed order size (EOQ or EPQ) or fixed order interval (EOI) system can be adopted. If the demand for an item is discrete and dependent on the demand for a product in which the item is a component, the inventory system can be a material requirements planning (MRP) system. For a manufacturing organization, the number of items that can be best controlled by an MRP system is substantially greater than the number that can be controlled by a fixed order size system.

---

[8]For a detailed treatment of risk and safety stocks see R.J. Tersine, *Principles of Inventory and Materials Management,* New York: North-Holland, 1982, Chapter 4.

MATERIAL REQUIREMENTS PLANNING (MRP) SYSTEMS

The MRP system is a means of coordinating manufacturing decisions involving production plans for finished products, control of raw material and component part inventory levels, and the scheduling of components in fabrication and assembly departments.[9] MRP can substantially reduce production costs and inventory investment while improving customer delivery performance. It is a time-phased quantity and due date planning system based on higher level time-phased requirements.

MRP is primarily a component fabrication (and subassembly) planning system applicable to items, purchased or manufactured, that are subject to dependent demand. It applies to materials and components that are not end products themselves, but are fabricated and assembled to become end products. It relates to groups of components rather than treating each component as a statistically separate item. The treatment of dependent demand items in an independent manner results in massive excess inventory with high safety stocks. Safety stock is not planned at the component level in MRP, but at the end item level.

The term component is used in material requirements planning to include all inventory items other than products or end items. Requirements for end items are stated in a master production schedule and are derived from forecasts or customer orders. Requirements for components and their timing are derived from the master production schedule by the MRP system. In manufacturing organizations, the bulk of inventory items tends to be at the component level.

The MRP system has numerous advantages over the fixed order size system for control of production items. A comparison of the fixed order size and the MRP systems is contained in Table 1. Some disadvantages of the fixed order size system are as follows:

1. It requires a very large inventory investment.
2. It is unreliable with a highly varying demand rate.
3. It requires a large investment in safety stock.
4. It requires forecasts for all items.
5. It is based on past demand data.
6. Material obsolescence is more likely.

TABLE 1
Comparison of fixed order size and MRP systems

Fixed order size system (EOQ/EPQ)	MRP system
Part oriented (every item)	Product/component oriented
Replenish supply	Actual requirements
Independent demand	Dependent (derived) demand
Continuous item demand	Discrete/lumpy item demand
Random demand pattern	Known lumpy demand pattern
Continuous lead time demand	No lead time demand
Reorder point ordering signal	Time-phased ordering signal
Historic demand base	Future production base
Forecast all items	Forecast master schedule items
Quantity-based system	Quantity- and time-based system
Safety stock for all items	Safety stock for end items
End items/spare parts	Raw materials/work-in-process
Just-in-case	Just-in-time

[9]For a more thorough and extensive treatment of MRP consult Joseph Orlicky, *Material Requirements Planning,* New York: McGraw-Hill, 1975.

An EOQ-MRP Comparison

The use of EOQ or EPQ when demand is dependent can create serious operational problems and excessive inventory investment. For dependent demand items, demand should be calculated from a bill of materials explosion. Demand should not be forecasted when it can be calculated. Independent demand items must be forecasted, but dependent demand items should be calculated. It is much more efficient to order components from product requirements and to drive the component inventory to zero between requirements. MRP will substantially reduce inventory investment in dependent demand items while improving operational efficiency by removing the automatic (built-in) risk of shortages associated with the EOQ or EPQ. Independent demand inventory models when used for dependent demand items generate excessive inventory when it is not needed and insufficient inventory when it is needed. A few examples will illustrate the benefits of the MRP system.

EXAMPLE 4

A toy manufacturer assembles a small wagon composed of the following components (quantities): frame (1), wheels (4), axles (2), body (1), and handle (1). All of the components are maintained on an EOQ system with the following service levels.[10]

Component	Service level
Frame	.90
Wheels	.90
Axles	.90
Body	.90
Handle	.90

What is the probability that all the components will be in stock when production is scheduled to commence? What must be the component service level to maintain a 90% service level for the complete wagon?

Since the EOQ system assumes independent component demand, the probability of all the components being available is obtained as follows:

$$(0.90)(0.90)(0.90)(0.90)(0.90) = (0.90)^5 = 0.5905, \text{ or } 59.05\%.$$

While service appears to be high at the component level, it is not high at the assembly (product) level. Very few production managers would agree that a service level of 59% is acceptable. To maintain a 90% service level on the wagon, each component must have a service level as follows:

$$\sqrt[5]{0.90} = 0.98, \quad \text{or } 98\%.$$

Now the production manager may be pleased with being able to produce a complete wagon 90% of the time, but the financial manager would argue relentlessly against a 98% service level on components because of the large quantity of safety stock required to maintain such a high service level. An extremely high level of investment would be

---

[10]The service level may be viewed as that fraction (percentage) of time components are available in the storage area (90% of the time the frame is available, and 10% of the time it is out of stock).

required in safety stock. Thus, the example illustrates the operational difficulties in using independent demand EOQ as well as the large inventory investment required to make the system work. When the final product is composed of many components (many more than the five used in the example), the EOQ is practically impossible to use.

EXAMPLE 5

An end item is fabricated from a single component supplied by a local distributor. The end item is produced on a cycle every fourth week, or 13 times per year, during weeks 3, 7, 11, 15, 19, 23, 27, 31, 35, 39, 43, 47, and 51. Annual demand for the end item is 52,000 units. Each component costs $3.50, and the order cost is $125 per lot. The annual inventory holding cost is 20% of the unit cost, and the lead time is a constant one week. What is the total annual cost with EOQ? What is the total annual cost of MRP with lot-for-lot ordering? Compare the EOQ and MRP costs.

With the EOQ model, the inventory policy would be as follows:

$$EOQ = Q_0 = \sqrt{\frac{2CR}{PF}} = \sqrt{\frac{2(125)(52,000)}{0.20(3.50)}} = 4310 \text{ units,}$$

$$\text{reorder point} = B = \frac{RL}{52} = \frac{52,000(1)}{52} = 1000 \text{ units.}$$

The performance of the EOQ model on inventory levels is shown graphically in Figure 8, based on production runs of 4000 units. Note how inventory levels go through a cyclical pattern every 20 weeks, with a stockout occurring at least twice and sometimes three times in a year. Instead of inventory peaks there are plateaus (for three weeks after each order is received, inventory lies dormant in the storage area awaiting production).

FIGURE 8
Inventory levels for EOQ model.

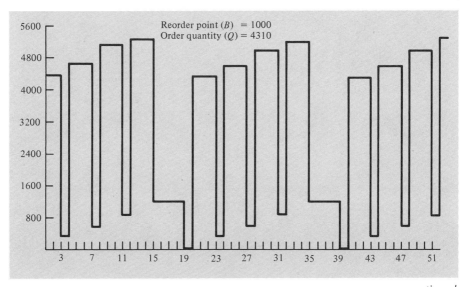

continued

EXAMPLE 5— *continued*

The following tabulation develops the average inventory level for the EOQ model:

Week	Inventory level	Week	Inventory level
1	4,310	27	620^a
2	4,310	28	4,930
3	310^a	29	4,930
4	4,620	30	4,930
5	4,620	31	930^a
6	4,620	32	5,240
7	620^a	33	5,240
8	4,930	34	5,240
9	4,930	35	1,240
10	4,930	36	1,240
11	930^a	37	1,240
12	5,240	38	1,240
13	5,240	39	0^a
14	5,240	40	4,310
15	1,240	41	4,310
16	1,240	42	4,310
17	1,240	43	310^a
18	1,240	44	4,620
19	0^a	45	4,620
20	4,310	46	4,620
21	4,310	47	620^a
22	4,310	48	4,930
23	310^a	49	4,930
24	4,620	50	4,930
25	4,620	51	930^a
26	4,620	52	5,240
		Total	172,610

^{a}Order placed.

$$\text{Average inventory} = \frac{172,610}{52} = 3319 \text{ units.}$$

Neglecting stockout cost, the total annual cost using the EOQ model is as follows:

Total annual cost = purchase cost + order cost + holding cost

$$= (52,000)\,(3.50) + (125)\,(11) + (3319)\,(0.20)\,(3.50)$$

$$= 182,000.00 + 1375.00 + 2323.30$$

$$= \$185,698.30$$

Now consider an MRP system with the same variables except that orders are scheduled to arrive the day before they are needed for production. The performance of the MRP system on the inventory levels is shown graphically in Figure 9. The following tabulation develops the average inventory level for the MRP system:

Week	Inventory level[a]	Week	Inventory level[a]
1	0(7)	27	4,000(1); 0(6)
2	0(7)	28	0(7)
3	4,000(1); 0(6)	29	0(7)
4	0(7)	30	0(7)
5	0(7)	31	4,000(1); 0(6)
6	0(7)	32	0(7)
7	4,000(1); 0(6)	33	0(7)
8	0(7)	34	0(7)
9	0(7)	35	4,000(1); 0(6)
10	0(7)	36	0(7)
11	4,000(1); 0(6)	37	0(7)
12	0(7)	38	0(7)
13	0(7)	39	4,000(1); 0(6)
14	0(7)	40	0(7)
15	4,000(1); 0(6)	41	0(7)
16	0(7)	42	0(7)
17	0(7)	43	4,000(1); 0(6)
18	0(7)	44	0(7)
19	4,000(1); 0(6)	45	0(7)
20	0(7)	46	0(7)
21	0(7)	47	4,000(1); 0(6)
22	0(7)	48	0(7)
23	4,000(1); 0(6)	49	0(7)
24	0(7)	50	0(7)
25	0(7)	51	4,000(1); 0(6)
26	0(7)	52	0(7)
		Total	52,000

[a]The number of days in the week at the given level follows in parentheses.

FIGURE 9
Inventory levels for MRP model.

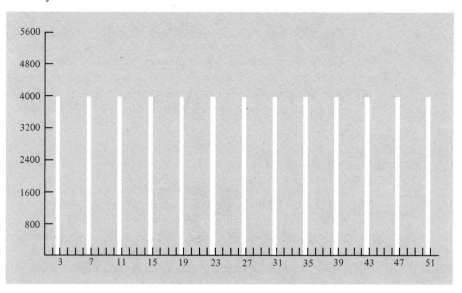

continued

EXAMPLE 5— *continued*

$$\text{Average inventory} = \frac{52,000}{365} = 143 \text{ units.}$$

To avoid complicating the computations, no attempt will be made to determine if savings could be realized by combining some orders and reducing the number of orders required from 13 to some lesser amount. However, discrete lot sizing techniques could be applied. Note that with MRP no stockouts occurred. The total annual cost with MRP is as follows:

$$
\begin{aligned}
\text{Total annual cost} &= \text{purchase cost} + \text{order cost} + \text{holding cost} \\
&= (52,000)(3.50) + (125)(13) + (143)(0.20)(3.50) \\
&= 182,000.00 + 1625.00 + 100.10 \\
&= \$183,725.10,
\end{aligned}
$$

$$
\begin{aligned}
\text{MRP cost savings} &= \text{EOQ annual cost} - \text{MRP annual cost} \\
&= 185,698.30 - 183,725.10 \\
&= \$1973.20.
\end{aligned}
$$

In this example, a cost saving of \$1973.20 was realized through the use of MRP when compared with EOQ. In addition, no stockouts occurred with MRP. Our example dealt with only one end item with only one component; evidently, far greater savings can be obtained with numerous products with several components. The advantages of MRP for dependent demand items should now be apparent.

As was previously illustrated in Table 1 an MRP system has several advantages over an EOQ system. However the systems are not really competing, for each has a different area of application. For continuous, uniform, and independent demand the EOQ system is desirable. For discontinuous, nonuniform, and dependent demand the MRP system is desirable. For production, manufacturing, fabrication, or assembly industries the majority of inventory items dictates an MRP approach.

DISCRETE LOT SIZING

The lot sizing systems developed for continuous and independent demand items (EOQ, EPQ, and EOI) assume that demand occurs with certainty at a constant rate. Discrete and dependent demand items exhibit time varying demand patterns. Although the static EOQs, EPQs, and EOIs are insensitive (robust) to variations from their underlying assumptions (including demand variations), there are situations where time variations in demand are so pronounced that the constant demand rate assumption is seriously violated. Discrete lot sizing deals with the deterministic, dynamic (nonconstant demand) order size problem.

Various approaches have been devised to handle varying demand rates.[11] Lot-for-lot ordering is the simplest: items are purchased in the exact quantities required for each period. Another approach is the part-period algorithm, which derives varying order sizes for varying demand patterns.

Part-Period Algorithm

The part-period algorithm can determine order sizes under conditions of known, but varying, demand rates. While the algorithm does not ensure optimality, it does approach optimal techniques. Whereas traditional order size formulas equate holding cost and order cost to determine the order size, this algorithm equates the part-period value derived from order and holding costs to the generated part-period value.

The generated part-period for an item is the number of parts held in inventory multiplied by the number of time periods over which the parts are held. If one part is held in inventory for one period, it incurs a particular holding cost; if it is held two periods, it incurs twice the holding cost. Two parts held one period incur the same holding cost as one part held two periods, and so forth. In calculating the generated number of part-periods, it is assumed that no holding costs are incurred for items consumed in the period in which they arrive.

To express order cost and holding cost in part-periods, it is necessary to divide the order cost by the holding cost per part per period. The order cost and holding cost part-periods are referred to as the derived part-period value. The derived part-period value is the number of part-periods it takes to make order cost and holding cost equal. A generated part-period value is obtained by accumulating part-periods over the demand time horizons for one or more periods. When the generated part-period value is first greater than the derived part-period value, an order should be placed. The order quantity will be the accumulated demand up to the time period for the next order. The following example illustrates the procedure.

EXAMPLE 6

The ordering cost for an item is $25 per order, and the holding cost per unit per period is $.25. Determine the order quantities by the part-period algorithm from the following demand forecast:

Period	1	2	3	4	5	6	7	8	9	Total
Demand	15	20	25	35	30	10	12	16	25	188

Derived part-period value $= \dfrac{25}{0.25} = 100$ part-periods.

The following table develops the part-period strategy assuming a nearly zero lead time:

continued

---

[11]See R.J. Tersine, *Principles of Inventory and Materials Management,* New York: North-Holland, 1982, pp. 340–354.

EXAMPLE 6— *continued*

Period	1	2	3	4	5	6	7	8	9	Total
Demand	15	20	25	35	30	10	12	16	25	188
Generated part-periods	0	1(20)	2(25)	3(35) 0	1(30)	2(10)	3(12)	4(16) 0	1(25)	
Cumulative part-periods	0	20	70	175	30	50	86	150	25	
Order size	60			87				41		188

Whenever the cumulative generated part-period value is greater than the derived part-period value (100), an order is indicated.

The cumulative number of part-periods exceeds 100 in periods 4 and 8. The first order quantity for period 1 is for 60 (15 + 20 + 25) units. The second order quantity for period 4 is for 87 (35 + 30 + 10 + 12) units. The third order quantity for period 8 cannot be determined until further forecast data are available, so it is set at the remaining demand of 41 units. The different order sizes indicate the dynamic nature of the algorithm.

TIME-PHASED ORDER POINT

The time-phased order point (TPOP) applies the logic of MRP to independent demand items. The MRP format can be used whether demand is independent or dependent. The use of TPOP for independent demand items at distribution centers is called distribution requirements planning (DRP). The conventional reorder point reacts to demand and has limited capabilities, since it indicates only when to place the next order. The TPOP indicates when to place orders, but has an additional feature that indicates when to reschedule an order to an earlier or later time period. TPOP also can accommodate unusual demand conditions (promotions, export orders, or any kind of lumpy demand can be put in a time-phased format as opposed to a conventional reorder point that assumes continuous demand during every period). Time-phasing transforms the ordering decision from a quantity (stock level) to a time dimension and is designed to plan ahead so action can be taken before problems arise.

TPOP is an outgrowth and extension of MRP, and it may be used along with MRP. By using the same technique in both distribution and manufacturing, only one system is needed with one set of data. TPOP uses an item's forecast directly as gross requirements. The future orientation of TPOP provides a rescheduling capability to deal with forecast errors and demand undulations so inventory levels are kept low. It shows well into the future the probable timing of each replenishment order.

With TPOP, an entire schedule of planned replenishment orders is developed rather than one order at a time. Actually, the name is a misnomer, since no order point as such is used. MRP logic takes over and provides for ordering at the right time. When the stock position drops down to the safety stock level, a lead time offset schedules the order correctly. TPOP constantly reexamines the need dates on orders to determine if they need to be rescheduled to another date based on changing requirements. Schedule changes can be implemented up until an order is actually shipped.

EXAMPLE 7

Develop the time-phased order point for an end item with a forecasted weekly demand of 30 units, a lot size of 100 units, a safety stock of 10 units, a lead time of 2 weeks, and a stock level of 80 units.

Solution:

		Period							
	PD	1	2	3	4	5	6	7	8
Gross requirements		30	30	30	30	30	30	30	30
Scheduled receipts									
Projected on hand	80	50	20	90	60	30	100	70	40
Net requirements				20			10		
Planned order receipts				100			100		
Planned order releases		100			100				

The forecast of 30 units per week is projected over the entire planning horizon of 8 weeks and represents gross requirements. The current quantity on hand of 80 will drop below the safety stock of 10 in period 3, and a replenishment order of 100 is planned to arrive at that time. Offsetting for lead time, a planned order release is scheduled for period 1. In period 6, there is a net requirement for 10 units to replenish the safety stock, so another planned order is scheduled for replenishment by ordering in period 4. Notice the results are the same as would result with a reorder point of 70 units, but with TPOP an entire schedule of planned replenishment orders is developed instead of one order at a time. It indicates when orders for an item are likely to be placed during the entire planning horizon.

SINGLE ORDER QUANTITIES

The single order is concerned with the planning and control of inventory items that are either purchased only once during a time period or produced in only one production run. The familiar inventory models (EOQ, EOI, and EPQ) do not readily apply to the single order because (1) demand is not continuous, (2) the demand level may change drastically from time period to time period, or (3) the product's market life may be very short due to obsolescence or perishability. The single order quantity problem is frequently referred to in the literature as the Christmas tree problem or the newsboy problem. Christmas trees, high fashion apparel, some perishable items, and seasonal agricultural products are examples that fall into the single order category.

The single order quantity model is applicable when (1) a demand exists for an item at infrequent intervals or (2) an uncertain demand exists for a short-lived item at frequent intervals. The first situation is typified by promotional and fad items ordered by retail stores, or spare parts for maintenance repair. The second situation is typified by highly perishable items (fresh fish, flowers) and short-lived, obsolescent items (newspapers, periodicals).

Within a time period, there are no repeat orders. If demand is greater than the order size, an opportunity profit loss results, since there is insufficient time to replenish the stock. If demand is less than the order size, the overstock is usually disposed of at a loss.

To determine the optimum single order quantity, it is necessary to balance two opposing costs. Order costs are irrelevant, since only one order will be placed and only one order cost incurred. Holding costs are not important, since an ongoing demand for the item is not apparent. The two relevant costs for the single order are obsolescence (overage) costs and opportunity (underage) costs. Obsolescence costs are incurred when all of the stock is not sold. Excess stock may be sold at less than cost, or the stock may be discarded for a total loss. Opportunity costs result from not being able to satisfy customer demand. Opportunity costs include lost profit from potential sales when demand exceeds supply. If demand exceeds the single order quantity, there is no obsolescence cost but only an opportunity cost; if demand falls short of the single order quantity, there is no opportunity cost but only an obsolescence cost. The optimum condition is when demand equals supply and no opportunity or obsolescence costs are incurred.

MARGINAL ANALYSIS

Marginal analysis can be used to solve the single order problem with variable demand. Given any inventory level (single order quantity), an additional unit should be added as long as its expected marginal profit plus its expected marginal stockout cost saving is equal to or greater than its expected marginal loss. The expected marginal stockout cost saving is added to the expected marginal profit, because the stocking of an additional unit will increase expected profit if the unit is demanded (the stockout cost is avoided on this unit).

When an additional unit is obtained, there are two possible outcomes: either

1. it will be demanded—it has a probability p of being sold—or
2. it will not be demanded—it has a probability $1 - p$ of not being sold.

The sum of the two corresponding probabilities must be one. The expected marginal profit plus the expected marginal stockout cost saving is found by multiplying the marginal profit plus the marginal stockout cost by the probability of the unit being sold. Likewise, the expected marginal loss is found by multiplying the marginal loss for the additional unit by the probability that the unit will not be sold. As stated previously, the additional unit should be stocked (added to the single order quantity) as long as

$$p\ \text{MP} + pA \geq (1 - p)\ \text{ML}, \qquad \text{or} \quad p \geq \frac{\text{ML}}{\text{MP} + \text{ML} + A},$$

where

$$MP = \text{marginal profit,}$$

$$ML = \text{marginal loss,}$$

$$p = \text{probability of selling one or more additional units,}$$

$$1 - p = \text{probability of not selling one or more additional units,}$$

$$A = \text{stockout cost per unit (marginal stockout cost),}$$

$$pA = \text{expected marginal stockout cost savings,}$$

$$p\,MP = \text{expected marginal profit,}$$

$$(1 - p)\,ML = \text{expected marginal loss.}$$

The probability p obtained by solving the preceding equation represents the minimum probability of selling at least an additional unit that justifies the stocking of the additional unit. In other words, it is the probability such that the expected marginal profit plus the expected marginal stockout cost saving just equals the expected marginal loss; as long as the probability of selling at least one more unit is equal to or greater than p, the marginal extra unit should be included in the single order quantity. If the probability of selling at least one more unit is less than p, but the unit is stocked anyway, it is expected to result in an obsolescence cost based on insufficient demand for the unit. Conversely, if the probability of selling at least one more unit is equal to or exceeds p, but the unit is not stocked, an opportunity cost is expected to result, based on demand in excess of supply. Frequently in single order problems there will be no stockout cost saving associated with excess demand. In this situation, the stockout cost per unit (A) is zero.

EXAMPLE 8

A merchant wishes to stock Christmas trees for sale during the Christmas season. He must determine how many trees to order, since only one order can be filled during the short time. He pays $5.00 for each tree delivered, and he sells the trees for $15.00. His ordering costs are negligible, and he can sell any tree left over for $2.00 as firewood. The merchant's probability distribution for Christmas tree demand during the season is as follows (he must order trees in multiples of ten):

Demand M	Probability P(M)
10	0.10
20	0.10
30	0.20
40	0.35
50	0.15
60	0.10
	1.00

continued

EXAMPLE 8— *continued*

How many trees should the merchant order?

$$p \geq \frac{ML}{MP + ML + A} = \frac{3}{10 + 3 + 0} = 0.23.$$

Demand M	Probability P(M)	Probability of demand $\geq M^a$
10	0.10	1.00
20	0.10	0.90
30	0.20	0.80
40	0.35	0.60
50	0.15	0.25
60	0.10	0.10
	1.00	

*a*Probability that demand will be this level or greater. These values indicate the probability of *at least* selling at that level M, and are compared with p to ascertain the order quantity.

From the above table, the probability of selling 50 or more units is 0.25, and the probability of selling 60 or more units is only 0.10, so 50 trees should be ordered.

EXAMPLE 9

The Evergreen Company owns acreage of shrub trees to be harvested and sold each spring. The company estimates the costs of cutting and trimming the trees to be $2.50 per tree. The average shipping cost to the retailer is about $.50 per tree. He receives about $5.00 per tree ordered by the retailer. However, if the trees are cut and not sold to the retailer, they are a total loss. Shipping costs are not incurred if trees are not sold. The following historical demand distribution exists:

Level of demand M (thousands)	Probability P(M)
10	0.10
20	0.20
30	0.25
40	0.30
50	0.15

How many trees should be cut in order to maximize profit if demand occurs in lots of 1000?

$$p \geq \frac{ML}{MP + ML + A} = \frac{2.50}{2.00 + 2.50 + 0} = 0.55$$

Level of demand M (thousands)	Probability P(M)	Probability of demand ≥ M
10	0.10	1.00
20	0.20	0.90
30	0.25	0.70
40	0.30	0.45
50	0.15	0.15

From the above table, the probability of selling 30 or more trees is 0.70, and the probability of selling 40 or more trees is 0.45. Since 0.55 is less than 0.70 but more than 0.45, 30,000 trees should be cut to maximize profits.

COST ANALYSIS

When items are intended for internal use with no generation of revenue, the selection of the single order size is based on the lowest expected cost. The cost components are the order cost, purchase cost, stockout cost, and salvage value. The following formula is for the expected cost of a single order for a continuous distribution:

Expected cost = order cost + purchase cost

+ expected stockout cost − expected salvage

$$EC = C + PQ + A \int_Q^\infty (M - Q)f(M) \, dM - V \int_0^Q (Q - M)f(M) \, dM,$$

where

C = order cost per order, or setup cost,

P = unit cost,

Q = single order quantity in units,

A = stockout cost per unit,

M = demand in units (a random variable),

$M - Q$ = size of stockout in units,

$f(M)$ = probability density function of demand,

V = salvage value per unit.

To determine the minimum expected cost for a continuous distribution requires taking the derivative of expected cost with respect to order size and setting it equal to zero. The following expression results:

$$\frac{dEC}{dQ} = P - A\, P(s) - V\,[1 - P(s)] = 0.$$

Solving the equation for $P(s)$, the following formula is obtained:

$$P(s) = \frac{P - V}{A - V} = P(M > Q) = \text{optimum probability of a stockout.}$$

TABLE 2
Standard normal distribution

Standard normal deviate Z	Probability of a stockout $P(s)$	Standard normal deviate Z	Probability of a stockout $P(s)$
−3.00	.999	1.10	.136
0.00	.500	1.15	.125
0.05	.480	1.20	.115
0.10	.460	1.25	.106
0.15	.440	1.30	.097
0.20	.421	1.35	.088
0.25	.401	1.40	.081
0.30	.382	1.45	.073
0.35	.363	1.50	.067
0.40	.344	1.55	.060
0.45	.326	1.60	.055
0.50	.308	1.65	.049
0.55	.291	1.70	.045
0.60	.274	1.75	.040
0.65	.258	1.80	.036
0.70	.242	1.85	.032
0.75	.227	1.90	.029
0.80	.212	2.00	.023
0.85	.198	2.25	.012
0.90	.184	2.50	.006
0.95	.171	2.75	.003
1.00	.159	3.00	.001
1.05	.147		

Observe that if the purchase cost is equal to or greater than the stockout cost, the desired stockout probability is one. Under these conditions, no orders will be placed until a known demand exists. Also, if an item has no salvage value, the optimum probability of a stockout is $P(s) = P/A$. For discrete distributions where the optimum probability of a stockout is not exactly attainable, select the stock level with the next lowest probability of a stockout. Thus, the above optimum expression can be used for both discrete and continuous distributions.

The quantity $1 - P(s)$ is the service level, and $P(s)$ is the stockout probability. Thus, if demand is normally distributed for the item with a known mean $\overline{M}$ and standard deviation σ, the following expression determines the lowest expected cost single order quantity:

$$Q_0 = \overline{M} + Z\sigma = \text{optimum single order size,}$$

where Z is the standard normal deviate obtained from the normal table for a stockout probability of $P(s)$. Table 2 gives the standard normal distribution, which permits conversion from stockout probabilities to standard normal deviates.

EXAMPLE 10

A large department store has just purchased a new central air conditioning unit. The lifetime of the air conditioner is estimated at twelve years. The manager must decide how many spare compressors to purchase for the unit. If he purchases the compressors now, they will cost $100 each. If he purchases them when the units fail, they will cost $1000 each. The manufacturer has supplied the following probability distribution of the number of failures of the part during the life of the air conditioner:

Failures (M)	Probability P(M)	Probability of failures > M P(s)
0	.30	.70
1	.40	.30
2	.25	.05
3	.05	.00

The installation costs of the compressor, as well as salvage value, are assumed to be negligible. How many compressors should be purchased if the holding costs are neglected?

$$P(s) = \frac{P - V}{A - V} = \frac{100 - 0}{1000 - 0} = 0.1.$$

There are two failures with probability 0.05 and one failure with probability 0.30, so two compressors should be purchased.

EXAMPLE 11

If the demand for an item is normally distributed with a mean of 100 and a standard deviation of 20, what should be the size of the single order if unit cost is $100 and stockout cost is $1000?

$$P(s) = \frac{P - V}{A - V} = \frac{100 - 0}{1000 - 0} = 0.10.$$

$$Q_0 = \overline{M} + Z\sigma,$$

$$Q_0 = 100 + 1.29(20) = 126 \text{ units.}$$

CONCLUSION

The significance, relevance, and organizational stature of materials management will continue to increase. Numerous forces are dictating changes in this direction. One force is the trend towards increasing the number of highly specialized and complex products. As a result, organizations in the future will make fewer and buy more of their material requirements. Consequently, materials will represent an increasing percentage of total product costs, and their control will be even more important than it is today. A second major force is the increasing trend toward automation. An uninterrupted flow of materials is required for an automated facility. Failure of supply on a single item can close the facility down. A third major force is the burgeoning cost of materials. An expanding world population with an almost insatiable demand for goods and services is creating shortages in supply, which are causing costs to sky-rocket. The days of cheap and abundant raw materials appear to be past. These forces and many others indicate that the management of materials is no longer a trivial matter to be relegated to lower managerial levels.

Pressures of the marketplace force organizations into broader product coverage and greater delivery capabilities. As product variety increases, so do the problems of materials management. Greater product variety increases the complexities of fore-casting future demand, which escalates the inventory investment required to maintain customer service levels. Expanded delivery capabilities necessitate branch ware-houses, which also escalate inventory complexity and investment.

All organizations have difficulty managing their inventory. The usual reason is the inability to forecast adequately. When materials are added to inventory, it is in antic-ipation of demand. If the demand is later than expected or never materializes, the result is excessive stock. If the demand is sooner or stronger than anticipated, the result is inadequate stock. Factors that tend to reduce inventory are better forecasts, improved transportation, improved communications, improved technology, better scheduling, and standardization.

QUESTIONS

1. Characterize the different types of inventory.
2. Give a brief delineation of the four inventory cost factors.
3. What are some of the elements of independent and dependent demand items?
4. Describe how a fixed order size system functions; indicate its defining parameters in your description.
5. What are some of the basic assumptions of the economic order quantity (EOQ)?
6. Differentiate between the EOQ and the economic production quantity (EPQ).
7. How does the fixed order interval system differ from the fixed order size system?
8. Relatively speaking, how sensitive are the basic inventory models to errors in estimation of the input parameters?
9. Through what two variables do risk and uncertainty enter an inventory analysis?
10. Compare fixed order size systems with MRP systems on the basis of their key features and areas of application.
11. What is the purpose of discrete lot sizing? On what basis does the part-period algorithm determine lot sizes?
12. How is the time-phased order point used?
13. Why are the familiar inventory models (EOQ, EOI, and EPQ) not readily applicable to the single order?
14. What is the premise of marginal analysis when used to solve single order problems?
15. Can you cite any instances where materials management has influenced your consumer purchases?

PROBLEMS

1. The Star Equipment Company purchases 54,000 bearing assemblies each year at a unit cost of $40. The holding cost is $9 per unit per year, and the order cost is $20. What is the economic order quantity? How many orders will be placed in one year?

2. The Hercules Machine Company purchases 38,000 units of a component each year at a price of $4.00 per unit. The ordering cost is $9.00 per order, and the holding cost is

estimated at 25% of the unit value. What is the economic order quantity? What is the total annual cost?

3. What is the reorder point for Problem 1 if the lead time is one month? What is the reorder point for Problem 2 if the lead time is two weeks?

4. The Never-Say-Die hospital purchases gauze in lots of 1500 boxes, which is a 6 month supply. The cost per box is $10; the ordering cost is $25 per order; and holding cost is estimated at 25% of unit value. What is the total cost of the existing inventory policy? How much money could be saved if the economic order quantity were applied to the purchase of gauze? What should be the reorder point if the lead time is 2 weeks?

5. If the hospital in Problem 4 decides to use a fixed order interval system, what will be the economic order interval and the maximum inventory level?

6. Assume that an organization currently is using a deterministic fixed order size system. The annual demand for a particular inventory item is 9000 units, and the item is ordered in economic order quantities of 300 units. If the firm changed to a fixed order interval system,
    (a) What would the EOI for the item be in years?
    (b) What maximum inventory level would be established if the lead time for the item is one week and there are 52 operating weeks per year?
    (c) How much inventory would be on hand at the time of the order review?

7. A tire manufacturer plans to produce 40,000 units of a particular type of tire next year. The production rate is 200 tires per day, and there are 250 working days available. The setup cost is $200 per run, and the unit production cost is $15. If holding costs are $11.50 per unit per year, what is the EPQ? How many runs should be made per year? If the production lead time is five days, what is the reorder point?

8. The ordering cost for an item is $15 per order, and the holding cost per unit per period is $0.30. Determine the order quantities by the part-period algorithm if forecasted demand follows the pattern below:

Period	1	2	3	4	5	6	7	8	9	Total
Demand	7	5	9	8	11	10	9	7	10	76

9. A firm manufactures and assembles metal bookshelves. Based on forecasts, a production level of 1000 bookshelves per week has been scheduled for the major selling item, a three-shelf bookcase. The following bill of materials information is available from the engineering drawings on the three-shelf bookcase.

Bill of Materials

Product: Bookcase, metal, 3 shelves
Part No.: 1

Part No.	Name	Description	Quantity required	Source
2	Shelf	3 sq. ft., 1/16" aluminum	3	Mfg.
3	Leg	2 sq. ft., 1/16" aluminum	4	Mfg.
4	Inserts	3/8" plastic	8	Purchasing
5	Screws	3/8" carbon steel	12	Purchasing

The firm purchases sheet aluminum in 18 square foot sheets, from which it fabricates the shelves and legs prior to assembly of the bookcase. A local supplier provides all of the items with a lead time of two days. What quantity of items should be ordered on Wednesday of the week prior to production so that all the items are in inventory on Monday morning of the week of the scheduled production?

10. The Parker Flower Shop promises its customers delivery within four hours on all flower orders. All flowers are purchased on the prior day and delivered to Parker by 8:00 the next morning. Parker's daily demand for roses is as follows:

Dozens of roses	Probability
7	.1
8	.2
9	.4
10	.3

Parker purchases roses for $5.00 per dozen and sells them for $15.00. All unsold roses are donated to a local hospital. How many dozens of roses should Parker order each evening to maximize its profits? What is the optimum expected profit?

11. Parker Flower Shop must stock some orchids for the upcoming high school prom. Most of the boys will purchase gardenias, but a few orchids will be requested. An orchid costs Parker $10.00 and sells for $25.00. Only one orchid order can be placed, and any unsold orchids will have no salvage value. Past prom sales records reveal the following data:

Orchid demand	Number of occurrences
12	5
13	5
14	10
15	15
16	30
17	20
18	15
	100

How many orchids should be ordered for the prom?

12. As president of the senior class you are responsible for planning activities for the ten-year class reunion. The planning committee has decided on a steak dinner cookout. It is your task to determine the number of one-pound steaks to purchase for the event. Demand for the dinner is normally distributed with a mean of 200 people and a standard deviation of 40. An out-of-town supplier will sell you steaks at $1.50 per pound for large orders placed two weeks in advance. If you do not have enough steaks you will have to purchase additional steaks from a local supplier at $2.00 per pound. What should be the size of the steak order to the out-of-town supplier?

13. A food broker is trying to decide how many bushels of apples to purchase from the orchards to maximize his profits. His potential sales are estimated to be normally distributed with a mean of 1000 bushels and a standard deviation of 100 bushels. The apples can be purchased for $5.00 per bushel and sold for $7.00. Any unsold apples can be sold for $4.00 per bushel for cider. Determine the quantity of apples to purchase by marginal analysis.

14. You have a new furnace installed. The dealer offers to sell you spare fuel pumps at $20 each if you buy them during installation. The pumps sell for $50 retail. Manufacturer's

records indicate the following probability of fuel pump failures during the furnace's lifetime:

Failures	Probability
0	.1
1	.3
2	.4
3	.1
4	.1

Ignoring installation and holding costs, how many spare fuel pumps should be purchased during installation?

15. A firm fabricates a part that is used in a continuous assembly line operation in another area of the plant. The part is scheduled intermittently for fabrication for 20 day processing periods. During processing periods, 300 parts can be fabricated each day. The assembly line operation uses the part at a consistent rate of 200 units per operating day.

(a) What is the production run size for the item?

(b) What is its maximum inventory level? its average inventory level?

(c) If it takes two days to set up the fabrication process, what is the production reorder point in units?

CASE 1: HARBORFEST

Harborfest is the summer gala event in San Mateo, in which the local residents and businesses participate in a sea-oriented extravaganza. Each year tens of thousands of people congregate at the downtown harbor to view a water spectacle. Locals and tourists come to converse, view art works and displays, watch sailing craft of all types, and witness the largest fireworks show on the coast. The event has become so famous that crews of foreign ships join American seamen in the festivities.

The highlight of the celebration is the Harborfest Seafood Feast. Large crowds come to sample crabs, scallops, shrimp, oysters, and clams. The seafood is prepared at the waterfront and distributed from booths scattered throughout the main harbor area. Only one seafood item is available at each booth, but there are usually several booths serving each item. The food is eaten in covered or open picnic areas or as one walks the boardwalk. One admission price is charged, and the customer can eat all he wants.

Until this year all the clams were shipped from a northern seaport. The festival officials have not been pleased with their size or flavor and have decided to buy the clams from a local bay fisherman. The problem of selecting the vendor and ordering the bay clams rests with Anne Cooney, the Regional Seafood Commission's home economics expert.

Anne is familiar with Captain Ben Edwards, an old-timer in the clam business. He knows the bay waters better than most and manages to locate the most succulent clams. Anne is positive that Captain Ben's catches are not overrated and a pound of his clams would contain fewer but larger and tastier clams than pounds purchased elsewhere. Anne, however, is unsure of the correct number of pounds to order.

Anne is to receive $1.50 from each ticket sold. Captain Ben has quoted her a price of $2.50 per pound. Based on past consumption, Anne estimates that one-third pound of clams will be consumed for each ticket sold. However, her estimate is based on a correlation of past tickets sold and the number of pounds purchased. She is unable to locate statistics on the number of pounds overage or on the frequency or level of dissatisfaction due to insufficient clams. Anne does have accurate data on the number of tickets sold. She has rounded the numbers and plotted the following distribution of ticket sales for the past 25 festivals:

Tickets sold	Probability
17,500	.10
20,000	.10
22,500	.40
25,000	.20
27,500	.15
30,000	.05

Because of his large contract with a leading soup company, Captain Ben has only a two-day opening left in his fishing schedule. The opening, however, is just prior to the festival and would enable him to provide fresh clams for the feast. Captain Ben promises Anne that he can provide up to 12,000 pounds if he allocates his fleet of resources to the project. Captain Ben needs a firm commitment from Anne within the week.

Anne's extreme apprehension over the correct number of pounds to order is not unfounded. The Harborfest Seafood Festival and the Regional Seafood Commission have both come under severe criticism. The community and the media have not been laudatory, and the credibility of both groups is at stake. Inclement weather has caused extensive overages and waste on some occasions; on others, there have been complaints of insufficient quantities. One newspaper article called the feast a hoax, because those who did not attend early went home hungry.

Because of the difficulties experienced in past Harborfests, the Festival Commission is declaring strict accountability. Each seafood item will be handled as a separate profit unit. If some items show a considerable loss this year, they may be dropped in upcoming feasts. Anne is determined to protect her reputation as well as the Commission's. She is desperate to find a quantitative method to calculate the number of pounds of clams so that she can show a profit and protect the clams from cancellation as a festival seafood item.

1. Taking into account statistical changes, do Anne's 25 years of data give a good indication of ticket sales?
2. How reliable are Anne's portion estimates?
3. What impact will adversities such as foul weather, more competition from other profit units, or strict accountability have on ordering practices?
4. What method should be used to order the clams, and what quantity should be ordered?

CASE 2: DEFENSIVE PURCHASING

The Propulsion Division of Tinker Air Force Base is a government operated facility for reworking military aircraft engines. The division supports five families of engines plus component parts. The disassembled engines flow through a series of continuous and intermittent process shops by means of an automated conveyor system with selected inventory control and feed points. The actual route and replacement work of an individual part entering the overhaul process is dependent on its condition as determined by nondestructive inspection techniques.

The purchasing function to support the rework facility is encumbered with several obstacles. The quantities of required parts have wide variability. Not only do work loads tend to be sporadic (partly a budgetary decision), but the types of rework necessary to repair or rebuild the incoming engines are also subject to extreme variation. Furthermore, purchasing, as a legislated procurement procedure, is done by contract with the recipients promising least cost delivery of federally specified parts. Many suppliers are becoming reluctant to submit bids. Other peculiarities are also increasing supplier reluctance, e.g. fear of short-term agreements after expensive setups, tight governmental guidelines, costs that restrict profit potential, and worse yet, the recent wave of favoritism. Therefore, as either a cause or an effect, an extension of the already successful in-house production of replacement parts is expected.

Tinker has an excellent staff of six civil service purchasing agents, skilled in public purchasing and experienced in make-or-buy decisions. The total budget for the purchasing department is $425,000 annually, with 50% allocated to staff salaries. The agents typically process 12,500 purchase orders per year, amounting to a total annual expenditure of $60 million. A work measurement study conducted in the purchasing department disclosed that preparation and follow-up on orders is required at the 90% performance level for rework operations.

There are other costs of particular importance to the purchasing department. Materials and expediting expenses are $12 per order for phone calls, forms, etc. Obsolescence costs are approximated at 3% of total inventory value, and costs for insurance, deterioration, and warehouse space are roughly 6%. Presently, the annual expense to operate the stores for inventory storage is budgeted at $125,000, the interest rate the military is assumed to pay on borrowed capital is 10%, and the required return on investment used for performance evaluation is set at 15%. These costs are used as in private enterprise to determine operating and inventory policies. The purchasing department calculates EOQs for purchased replacement parts and orders.

These costs are expected to change as the nation confronts an economic crisis. The administration and congressional bodies are formulating a comprehensive revitalization program. A significant part of the program is massive Federal restraint. Tinker is not certain how this will affect operations directly, but cutbacks in personnel and operating budgets seem imminent. With drastic cutbacks, the purchasing department feels it will have to cope in the short run by cutting some variable costs.

However, there is another administrative program that appears to be receiving popular support—increased defense spending. Provided this program receives approval, activity at Tinker could increase measurably. The not so invisible hand of the government could change rework orders substantially.

With operations so tightly predicated on government policies, the purchasing department cannot predict future circumstances. If cutbacks are severe, are changes in ordering strategies necessary or are changes in inventory systems preferred, e.g. from EOQ to two-bin? If defense spending is a priority item, are EOQs changed proportionately and are fixed costs likely to increase? If either or both situations occur, how is inventory management affected? These and more unanswered questions abound.

1. What ordering costs and holding costs are relevant prior to a revitalization program?
2. How might purchasing and inventory management change with stringent budgetary controls? With military proliferation?
3. What operating practices might come into play with the new program? Could another inventory control system be better in the deployment of the revitalization plan?
4. What effect could the federal programs have on suppliers and on in-house production?

SELECTED BIBLIOGRAPHY

Brown, R. G. *Decision Rules for Inventory Management,* New York: Holt, Rinehart, and Winston, 1967.

Lewis, C. D. *Scientific Inventory Control,* New York: North Holland, 1970.

Love, S. F. *Inventory Control,* New York: McGraw-Hill, 1979.

Orlicky, J. *Material Requirements Planning,* New York: McGraw-Hill, 1975.

Peterson, R. and E. A. Silver. *Decision Systems for Inventory Management and Production Planning,* New York: Wiley, 1979.

Plossl, G. W. and O. W. Wight. *Production and Inventory Control,* Englewood Cliffs, NJ: Prentice-Hall, 1967.

Reisman, A. et al. *Industrial Inventory Control,* New York: Gordon and Breach, 1972.

Riggs, W. E. and R. J. Tersine. ''New Product Inventory Levels: Introduction and Revision,'' *Production and Inventory Management,* Vol. 19, No. 3, 1978.

Starr, M. K. and D. W. Miller. *Inventory Control: Theory and Practice,* Englewood Cliffs, NJ: Prentice-Hall, 1962.

Tersine, R. J. *Principles of Inventory and Materials Management,* New York: North-Holland, 1982.

Tersine, R. J. and J. H. Campbell, *Modern Materials Management,* New York: North Holland, 1977.

Tersine, R. J. et al. *Problems and Models in Operations Management,* Columbus, OH: Grid, Inc., 1980.

20
Inventory Control Systems

TYPES OF CONTROL SYSTEMS

Perpetual Inventory System
Two-Bin Inventory System
Periodic Inventory System
Optional Replenishment Inventory System
Distribution Requirements Planning Inventory System
Single Order Quantity Inventory System
Material Requirements Planning Inventory System
Just-in-Time Inventory System

SELECTIVE INVENTORY CONTROL

INVENTORY SYSTEM DEVELOPMENT

INVENTORY SYSTEM IMPROVEMENT

AGGREGATE INVENTORY MEASUREMENT

CONCLUSION

QUESTIONS

CASES

SELECTED BIBLIOGRAPHY

Inventory is ubiquitous in today's organizations but may vary widely in the number and nature of materials held. Inventory in a manufacturing firm may take the form of raw materials waiting to enter the production process, work in process in some intermediate form of transformation, finished goods already completely transformed by the production system, or supplies used to support the process. It also may be found as retail and wholesale finished goods located at distinct parts of a distribution system or as service industry material or supplies. Its diffuse appearances are reminders of the sundry functions inventory performs throughout any organization. Production/operations, distribution, marketing, and financial activities rely heavily upon established inventory operating doctrine vis-à-vis the interplay of what and when to order. Inventory control doctrine and other major planning and control activities systematically interact; poor inventory control can intensify the variability of decision making at many levels and increase costs and operating inefficiencies organization wide. Inevitably, the type of inventory control system selected will have an impact on almost all other organizational activities.

The starting point in developing a control system is an analysis of the objectives of the intended system. This procedure discloses the critical activities in the operation where control can be most effective. It is imperative that the control mechanism satisfy the service and operating objectives of the institution at the lowest possible cost. For this reason it is the responsibility of top management to select the control system (or systems) and to establish aggregate inventory levels. However, an inventory control system, with guidelines on inventory policies, often is converted to rules for specific items by the operations personnel who implement and monitor the system.

By definition the operating system should indicate how routine and nonroutine situations are to be treated via predetermined rules and procedures. A good control system provides for self-control and only requires attention to exceptions. Adjustments are made as the system operates to

1. ensure that sufficient goods and materials are available,
2. identify excess and fast- and slow-moving items,
3. provide accurate, concise, and timely reports to management,
4. expend the least amount of resources in accomplishing the above.

The establishment of inventory operating policies usually is based on cost analysis which is rational, logical, and unemotional. It involves factors which can be analyzed and set forth in precise mathematical formulations. In spite of their apparent exactness, the use of sophisticated mathematical techniques does not necessarily result in an effective system. Precise techniques are of little value unless the information to feed into the models is available at a realistic cost. On these grounds, an inventory control system may vary in complexity and accuracy from an absence of any noticeable control to a highly sophisticated data processing system. Systems that select approximate, reasonable levels with low data processing costs often are preferable.

Without minimizing the importance of quantitative techniques, it should be understood that a comprehensive inventory system involves much more than refined inventory models. All aspects of the system must be considered and not just the specific model(s). Six areas are vital in the development and maintenance of the system, and a breakdown in any one can undermine the efficiency of the entire system:

1. the development of demand forecasts and the treatment of forecast errors,
2. the selection of inventory models (EOQ, EOI, EPQ, DRP, and MRP),
3. the measurement of inventory costs (order, holding, stockout),
4. the methods used to record and account for items,
5. the methods for receipt, handling, storage, and issue of items,
6. the information procedures used to report exceptions.

TYPES OF CONTROL SYSTEMS

There are various types of inventory control systems, and there are special hybrids of the common ones. It is difficult to classify them in an orderly fashion and still demarcate their defining characteristics. Nevertheless, a depiction of the systems used most frequently is given in Figure 1. It segregates the major systems by demand situation and operating doctrine. Included in the diagram are the perpetual, two-bin, periodic, optional replenishment, and distribution requirements planning systems, which usually apply to end items, in addition to the material requirements planning and just-in-time systems, which apply to materials and components used to produce end items. The single order quantity system also is categorized but remains unique in that it lacks a reorder dimension.

The perpetual and two-bin systems are referred to as fixed order size systems (quantity-based). The periodic and optional replenishment systems are referred to as fixed order interval systems (time-based). The distribution requirements planning system is a time-phased system for replenishments of items in a distribution network (distribution-based). The material requirements planning and just-in-time systems are derived order quantity systems for production environments (production-based). Quantity-based systems are checked continually (with each demand) to determine if an order should be placed. With time-based systems, a count of stock is only made on designated review dates, and orders are placed at that time. A distribution-based system predicts distribution requirements and schedules orders to meet them. Production-based systems order stock only to meet manufacturing requirements.

PERPETUAL INVENTORY SYSTEM

A perpetual system keeps a running record of the amount in stock. Each time a unit (or units) is issued from stock, the withdrawal is logged and the stock position is compared with the reorder point. If the stock position is equal to or less than the reorder point, an order is prepared for a fixed number of units. If the stock position is more than the reorder point, no action is taken.

This system is based on the economic order quantity (EOQ) and the reorder point. The perpetual system is completely defined by knowing the order size (Q) and the minimal stock level that signals the placing of an order (B). Under this system the reorder point and order quantity are fixed, the review period and demand rate are variable, and the lead time can be fixed or variable. Figure 2 describes the behavior of the perpetual inventory system for a single item.

The major disadvantage of the perpetual system is that it requires perpetual auditing of the inventory in stock to know as quickly as possible when the reorder point is reached. The review may consist of analyzing perpetual records (manual or com-

624

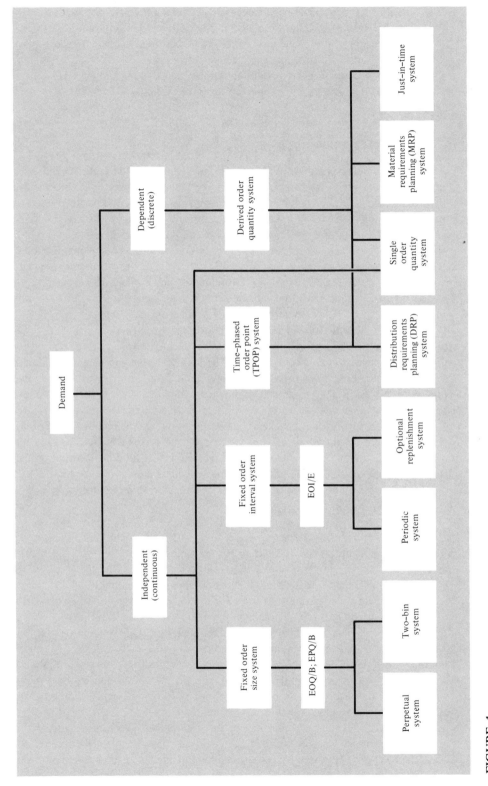

FIGURE 1
Demand-based inventory systems.

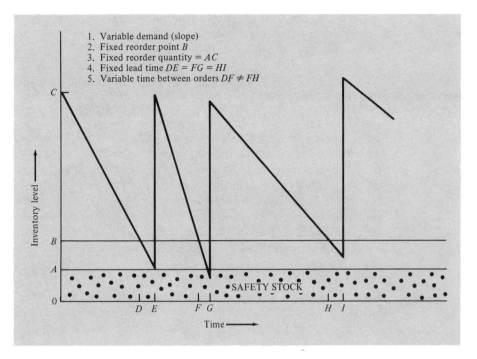

FIGURE 2
Perpetual inventory system.

puterized) as they are posted, or looking at the physical stock when it reaches the reorder point (the two-bin system is based on physical identification without additional records). Since an order can occur at any time, this prevents the economies that result from the amalgamation of several items from one supplier into one order. The potential savings from consolidated orders can be considerable.

Further weaknesses of the perpetual system may become evident if:

1. Managers do not take the time to study inventory levels of individual items and allow order quantities to be established by clerical personnel alone.
2. Reorder points, order quantities, and safety stocks are not restudied or changed for years.
3. Delays in posting transactions render the system useless for control.
4. Clerical errors or mistakes in posting transactions make the system impotent.
5. Numerous independent orders result in high transportation and freight costs.
6. Supplier discounts based on the dollar volume of individual orders are forfeited.

On the positive side, the fixed order size system with perpetual records is excellent for high cost items needing close control. It is extremely useful in these situations as well as others, because:

1. An efficient, meaningful order size is used.
2. Safety stock is needed only for the lead time period.

3. The system is relatively insensitive to forecast and parameter changes.
4. Inventory checks are related to usage; slow moving items receive less attention.

TWO-BIN INVENTORY SYSTEM

As indicated before, the two-bin system is a version of the fixed order size system which operates without perpetual record-keeping. Inventory usually is stored in two bins; upon order receipt, an amount equal to the reorder point is put into one bin, and the remainder of the order is placed in another bin. Stock is taken first from the bin which contains the difference between the order quantity and the reorder point. When stock in this bin is depleted, an order is released. Demands then are filled from the second bin containing the expected lead time quantity plus any safety stock (reorder point quantity). Due to this procedure, records need not be maintained of each withdrawal, and the signal for a replenishment order comes about by visual observation. Hence, it represents an obvious reduction in clerical work.

The system actually can be used with only one bin. An order can be triggered when the inventory level reaches some attention-getting device. The device may be a physical mark, such as a line painted at the reorder volume level on a tank of gasoline or other liquid, or it may be a partition placed in front of or on top of the reorder point quantity when stock is stored in a bin or container. Any similar markings or apparatus can be used to signal when stock is drawn down to the reorder point quantity.

The two-bin is suited best for items of low value with fairly consistent use and short lead times, such as office supplies, nuts, bolts, and so forth.

PERIODIC INVENTORY SYSTEM

In a periodic inventory system the number of items in storage is reviewed at a fixed time interval (T). A count must be taken of the goods on hand at the designated inventory review date.[1] The size of the replenishment order depends upon the number of units in stock at that time. Therefore, the order quantity varies from period to period, and the decision maker changes the quantity ordered to reflect changes in the demand rate.

Figure 3 describes the behavior of the periodic inventory system for a single item. A maximum inventory level E is established for each item. The order quantity is the maximum inventory level minus the inventory position on the review date (review dates are at points F, H, and J in the illustration). Under this system, the review period is fixed; the order quantity, demand rate, and the reorder point are variable; and the lead time can be fixed or variable.

The presumption in the periodic system is that some sort of physical count is made at the time of review. In many instances records of transactions (sales slips) are available, but the accuracy of the information system may require an actual count for

---

[1]The count may be from an information system relying on a perpetual inventory record, or through an inspection that includes an actual physical count. New point of sale registers and business machines maintain inventory records as well as register sales. The new machines serve many functions and are part of a management information system.

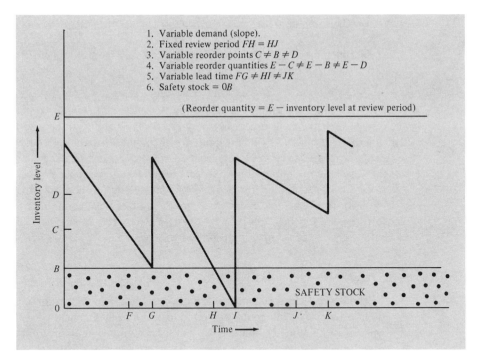

FIGURE 3
Periodic inventory system.

verification (lost or stolen items are not apparent from transaction records). Automatic data processing equipment can provide perpetual inventory records with order decisions still being made on a prescribed basis without the need for an actual physical count of items. Some accommodation must be made in these systems for the return of sale items, errors in transaction accounting, lost items, and stock shrinkage.

In the perpetual (continuous review) system, a replenishment order is initiated as soon as the inventory level drops to the reorder point; an actual count is not required, since the inventory records contain receipts, issues, and balances on hand. In the periodic (discrete review) system, the inventory position is checked only at specified time intervals. Thus, the perpetual system treats inventory item reviews continuously and independently, while the periodic system treats item reviews discretely and dependently.

Frequently, it is worthwhile to handle items in a dependent manner and consolidate their orders. Because of its discrete and dependent treatment of inventory review periods, the periodic system is well suited for consolidated ordering and particularly appropriate for situations where the supply sources are few or centralized (e.g. central warehouse locations). Consequently, the periodic system can provide the following benefits of joint orders:

1. A reduction in ordering cost may be possible because items are processed under a single order.
2. Suppliers may offer discounts for purchases exceeding a given dollar volume.

The lumping of several items into a single order can make the discount more attainable.

3. Shipping cost may be significantly decreased if an order is of a convenient size such as a boxcar. This can often be accomplished by the simultaneous ordering of several items.

The manner (or timing) in which the perpetual and periodic systems customarily initiate replenishment orders not only affects their ability to engage in consolidated ordering but also holds implications for their safety stock requirements. In the perpetual system, safety stock represents protection against demand fluctuations during the lead time period.[2] With a fixed order period, the periodic system requires safety stock for protection against demand fluctuations during both the review period and the lead time. This means that the periodic system will require a larger safety stock for a given item than the perpetual system. However, some or all of the additional safety stock expense may be justified by the economies achieved from joint orders.

OPTIONAL REPLENISHMENT INVENTORY SYSTEM

The optional replenishment inventory system is a hybrid of the perpetual and periodic systems. It commonly is referred to as a min-max system or as the s, S system, where s is the reorder point and S is the maximum inventory level (synonymous with B and E, respectively, in our notation). Figure 4 typifies the optional replenishment system for a single item with its three defining parameters:

1. the length of the review period T,
2. the maximum inventory level E,
3. the reorder point B.

A maximum inventory level is established for the item. If the inventory position is above the reorder point on the review date (e.g. at points F, I, L, and M in the illustration), no order is placed. If the inventory position is at or below the reorder point on the review date (e.g. at points G, J, and N), an order is placed. The order quantity is the maximum inventory level minus the inventory level at the review date.

Remember that both the perpetual and the periodic systems are defined by only two parameters, in contrast to three for the optional replenishment system. The instatement of the reorder point as a third defining parameter permits orders to be placed in efficient quantities; it reduces the costs which may result from frequent placements of small orders in the two-parameter periodic system. Coincidentally, the optional replenishment system is indistinguishable from the periodic inventory system when the review period is so long that an order is triggered at almost every review.

The review period is established by the procedures delineated for periodic systems. Likewise, the reorder point consists of the safety stock and the expected demand over the lead time and the review period. The safety stock is determined by analyzing the demand variation occurring for the period covered by the lead time L and the review period T. Unique to the optional replenishment system, no order is released if the inventory level at the time of the review, T, is slightly above the reorder point. In this case, safety stock must provide coverage for two order intervals

---

[2]It can be shown that the average inventory will be lower if orders are placed when needed rather than only at set times. However, the cost of operating the continuous record system may far exceed the advantages to be gained from it.

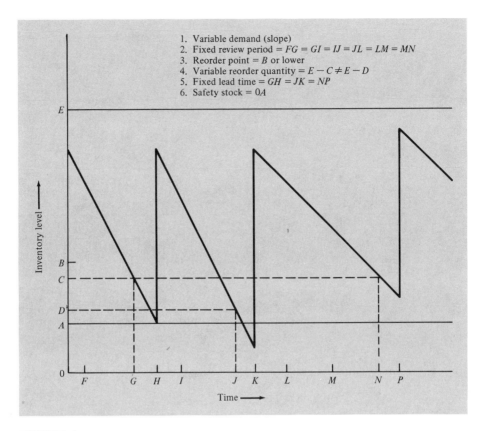

1. Variable demand (slope)
2. Fixed review period = $FG = GI = IJ = JL = LM = MN$
3. Reorder point = B or lower
4. Variable reorder quantity = $E - C \neq E - D$
5. Fixed lead time = $GH = JK = NP$
6. Safety stock = $0A$

FIGURE 4
Optional replenishment inventory system.

plus the lead time period. For this reason, the optional replenishment system can require substantially larger safety stocks.

DISTRIBUTION REQUIREMENTS PLANNING INVENTORY SYSTEM

A distribution network usually is characterized by multiple levels or echelons. When one organization is in control of more than one level of distribution, it is a multiechelon distribution system or network. The example of a trilevel distribution network shown in Figure 5 illustrates numerous local distribution centers fed from regional distribution centers, which in turn are fed from a master or central distribution center. The master distribution center places orders with suppliers or the organization's manufacturing facilities and disseminates the products throughout the distribution network. The system's local distribution centers may be retail outlets, and its master distribution centers may be plant warehouses.

Distribution network inventory systems can be classified as "pull" or as "push" systems. The *pull system* derives its name from its multiple subsystem centers which draw or "pull" stocks from their parent supply sources. Within a pull system arrangement, each distribution center acts independently of other distribution centers in the network and replenishes stock without regard to the inventory at any other location. In that respect, each center, despite its level in the network, performs its own

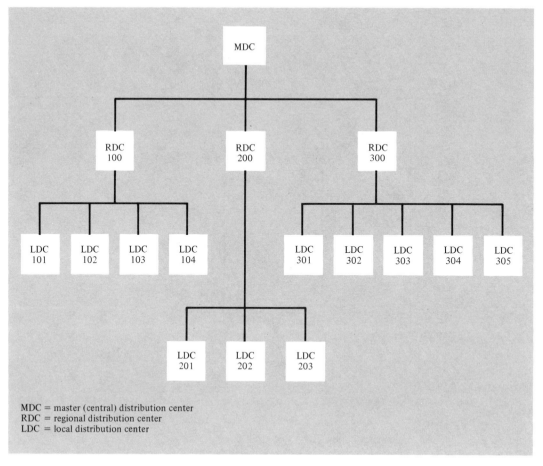

FIGURE 5
Trilevel distribution network.

forecasting and planning and usually maintains an individual safety stock. Acting to isolate themselves even further, similar centers generally engage only in limited stock transfers if they transfer inventory at all. Traditional pull systems include the perpetual, two-bin, and periodic inventory systems, all of which operate on an independent replenishment principle, treat demand as continuous, and require some form of forecasting.

Overall, a pull system reacts to demand without anticipating it properly. In the typical operation of a pull system, the parent centers receive erratic demands from the distribution centers they supply. For example, local centers might operate for several weeks without placing a replenishment order for an item and then impose a large demand on the parent center. Sometimes several different centers order the same item at about the same time and deplete the stock at the source. This results in a requirement for relatively large safety stocks at the source of supply to protect against stockouts. Obviously, communications in this type of system tend to flow in one direction, from the bottom up to the parent level. This inhibits parent centers from efficiently planning replenishment needs.

In the actual operation of a distribution network, demands at local distribution centers may be independent, continuous, and quite unlike demands placed for item replenishment at parent supply centers. Because stock actually leaves the distribution network from the local distribution centers, it is only at these outlets that demand is truly independent and subject solely to market influences. At higher levels in the network, e.g. at the master (central) and regional distribution centers, the demand pattern is lumpy and discontinuous. Because of its time-varying nature, demand at the parent centers (those which feed other centers) could be calculated rather than forecasted.

Pull inventory systems, which are based on average demands, do not operate satisfactorily when demand in discontinuous, discrete, or lumpy. In such cases the timing of requirements rather than an appropriately held inventory level is the paramount consideration. When the timing and magnitude of peaks can be anticipated, it is economical to keep minimal inventory in stock and schedule the amount and timing of requirements to meet peak conditions. As was shown in the example of parent centers receiving erratic demands, pull systems are unable to adequately or efficiently establish requirement order policies at levels faced with dependent demand.

In contrast, "push" systems have certain advantages when operating in distribution networks. A *push system* results in replenishments that are centrally planned at the master distribution center. In this arrangement, communications flow in both directions as the master distribution center decides what to send (push) through the network. Basically, a push system is an extension and a simplification of MRP, lacking a bill of materials explosion, and applicable to the whole distribution spectrum of a business. Because of its kinship with MRP, it can treat dependent demand on a network level as adequately as MRP does on the shop floor level.

Distribution requirements planning (DRP) is a popular push system. It uses time-phased order point (TPOP) logic as developed in Chapter 19 to determine network requirements. Items are pushed through the network to meet anticipated demand, rather than pulled through by decreases in actual demand. Gross requirements for items are developed from forecasts in a time-phased manner at all local distribution centers in a TPOP format. The planned order releases for a given item in each time period at the local centers are accumulated and become gross requirements at the parent center. Thus, parent centers no longer have to forecast lumpy requirements, but accumulate them from their demand sources. TPOP logic indicates when replenishments should occur. Disproportionate stock levels at local centers can be leveled through inter-center transfers.

The accumulation of planned orders for items from TPOP reports from the master distribution center are a major input to the master schedule as illustrated in Figure 7 in Chapter 16. This linking meshes the customer service goals of distribution with the production priorities at the master scheduling level. DRP uses the TPOP logic to accumulate item requirements for replenishment from outside suppliers or from an organization's manufacturing facilities. DRP efficiently replenishes what has been consumed in succeeding levels of a distribution network, based on its future visibility of requirements. It can improve procurement and inventory practices in a wholesale or retail business. For manufacturing organizations that function through a distribution network, it can significantly improve performance by an integrated system that combines DRP and MRP. Tangible benefits from DRP primarily are improved service, reduced inventory levels, and lower handling costs.

SINGLE ORDER QUANTITY INVENTORY SYSTEM

The single order quantity system is not really an inventory system but a general category for handling the variety of items that are ordered infrequently or only once. They tend to be unique and require special attention. Items fall in this category when (1) demand is nonrepetitive and occurs at infrequent intervals or (2) an uncertain demand exists for a short-lived item. The first situation is typified by promotional, fad, or seasonal items ordered by retail outlets; occasionally needed spare parts for maintenance; and materials required in the construction of special projects. The second situation is typified by highly perishable items (fresh fish, flowers) or short-lived, obsolescent items (Christmas trees, newspapers, periodicals). Lot sizes for single order items are determined by marginal analysis, cost analysis, calculation from specific project requirements, or management judgment.

MATERIAL REQUIREMENTS PLANNING INVENTORY SYSTEM

Most classical inventory systems assume that inventory items should be available at all times. They replenish inventory with a lot size that is triggered by a reorder point or a time interval. These systems are appropriate for items that exhibit a continuous and independent demand. Items sold by retailers, wholesalers, and distributors usually meet these requirements as well as products sold by manufacturers.

For items that exhibit a discrete and dependent demand, classical systems are less desirable. These items are more appropriately controlled under a material requirements planning (MRP) system. This system does not try to make inventory items available at all times. It plans inventory lot sizes so they are time phased to when they are needed. Inventory levels can be lower, and holding costs reduced substantially, if inventory is not held during time periods of zero demand. In order to achieve these economies, MRP must develop an elaborate scheduling system that indicates when each dependent demand item is needed. Items suitable for MRP are components of products that are listed on a product's bill of materials; they usually constitute the majority of items held in inventory by a manufacturing organization.

Time phasing is the essential ingredient of an MRP system. Time phasing requires *known future requirements* and *sufficient time to react* (lead time). MRP is impossible without these conditions, but even these conditions are not sufficient to ensure its success.

Known future requirements are ascertained from forecasts and customer orders that are translated into a capacity-feasible master production schedule (MPS). The master schedule indicates those products that should be produced in future periods. It applies predominately to the end items that the organization produces for its customers. It does not include all the components that are necessary to make the end item. Once the MPS is established, the exact quantities of these dependent or derived demand components needed to make the end items can be calculated from the bills of materials for end items. Thus, all of these components will have known future requirements.

The number of end items will be small in comparison to the number of components in a manufacturer's inventory. This is desirable, since forecasts need not be developed for dependent demand components but only for independent demand items. All dependent demand is derived and can be calculated from its parents' requirements. All components that make up an end item have dependent demand.

The demand for a component is dependent in the sense that the end item demand generates a known, exact requirement for each of its components. Thus, once the master production schedule is developed for end items (products), the specific number of its components can be deterministically calculated from bill of materials explosions.

Sufficient time to react is another vital ingredient for an MRP inventory system. Lead times must be established for every material order, fabrication, subassembly, and assembly. If a sufficient time horizon exists, it is possible to start without any inventory for end items and purchase exactly what is needed, fabricate just those components needed, and assemble the precise requirements with no surpluses or shortages. The lead times of all items and their interrelationships are vital to the success of time phasing.

MRP is a backward scheduling system that starts with the finished product. It then works back to the raw materials, through all levels of subassembly and fabrication. Its goal is to plan inventory so it is available when needed (not before and not after).

JUST-IN-TIME INVENTORY SYSTEM

The just-in-time (JIT) inventory system, developed by the Japanese, is used in repetitive manufacturing. As outlined in Chapter 18, it controls raw materials and in-process inventory levels for dependent demand items. It logistically links work centers so there is an even flow of material similar to that found in an assembly line. It attempts to drive all queues toward zero and achieve an ideal lot size of one unit.

For JIT to be feasible, the preconditions are uniform plant loading (usually for one month), group technology, quality control at the source (zero defects), minimized setup times (less than ten minutes), a kanban type production control system, and local (nearby) suppliers. JIT is a philosophy of production where inventory is considered undesirable.

SELECTIVE INVENTORY CONTROL

Materials management involves thousands or even millions of individual transactions each year. To do their job effectively, materials managers must avoid the distraction of unimportant details and concentrate on significant matters. Inventory control procedures should isolate those items requiring precise control from other items that can be controlled with less precision. Selective inventory control can indicate where the manager should concentrate his efforts.

It is usually uneconomical to apply detailed inventory control analysis to all items carried in an inventory. Frequently, a small percentage of inventory items accounts for most of the total inventory value. It is usually economical to purchase a large supply of low cost items and maintain little control over them. Conversely, small quantities of expensive items are purchased, and tight control is exercised over them. It is frequently advantageous to divide inventories into three classes according to dollar volume (the product of annual quantity and the unit purchase cost or production cost). This approach is called ABC analysis. The A class are high value items whose dollar volume typically accounts for 75–80% of the value of the total inventory, while representing only 15–20% of the inventory items. The B class are lesser value items whose dollar volume accounts for 10–15% of the value of the inventory,

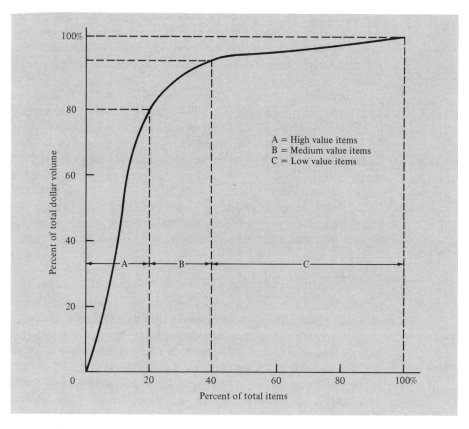

FIGURE 6
Typical ABC inventory analysis.

while representing 20–25% of the inventory items. The C class are low value items whose volume accounts for 5–10% of the inventory value but 60–65% of the inventory items. Figure 6 shows a typical ABC inventory classification. The breakdown into A, B, and C items is arbitrary, and further divisions may be established.

The inventory value for each item is obtained by multiplying the annual demand by the unit cost. Annual demand is used to avoid distortions from seasonal changes. The entire inventory is listed in descending order of value. The items are then classified as described above.

The same degree of control is not justified for all items. The class A items require the greatest attention, and the class C items the least attention. Class C items need no special calculations, since they represent a low inventory investment. The order quantity might be a one year supply with a periodic review once a year. Class B items could have EOQs developed with a semiannual review of the variables. Class A items could have EOQs developed with a review of the variables each time an order is placed. The major concern of an ABC classification is to direct attention to those inventory items that represent the largest annual expenditures. If inventory levels can be reduced for class A items, it will result in a significant reduction in inventory investment.

The purpose of classifying items into groups is thus to establish appropriate levels of control over each item. The ABC analysis is useful for any type of independent demand system (perpetual, periodic, optional replenishment, and so forth). With the periodic system, the ABC analysis can be subdivided so high-volume items receive a short review and low-volume items receive a much longer review. On a periodic basis, class A items might be ordered weekly, B items might be ordered biweekly, and C items might be ordered quarterly or semiannually. Note that the unit cost of an item is not related to the classification. An A item may have a high dollar volume through a combination of either low cost and high quantity or high cost and low quantity. Likewise, C items may have a low dollar volume because of low demand or low cost.

The A, B, and C classes are artificial strata. Each organization should tailor its inventory system to its own peculiarities. Organizations may choose to group their inventory into more than three classifications, but the principle is the same: high value items receive the most attention and low value items the least.

Before items can be classified, factors other than financial ones must be evaluated. Additional considerations can drastically change an item's classification as well as its control procedure. Some important factors might be:

1. a difficult procurement problem (long and erratic lead time),
2. the likelihood of theft,
3. a difficult forecasting problem (large changes in demand),
4. a short shelf life (due to deterioration and obsolescence),
5. a large storage space requirement (very bulky),
6. the item's operational criticality.

The ABC system does not apply directly to demand items controlled under MRP or JIT systems. Its primary application is to end items with demand independent of other end items. Dependent demand items tend to be of equal operational importance for continuity of the production function. Lack of even the lowest cost item can totally disrupt dependent organizational activities. Therefore, operational criticality overrides the item's financial influence.

INVENTORY SYSTEM DEVELOPMENT

The development and implementation of an inventory control system to meet the needs of a specific organization is a customizing operation. Since inventory management is not an island unto itself, the system must serve the goals of the organization as well as the service objectives of other departments. It is usually easier to develop an inventory system for a new company. If a revised system is planned for an existing company, the period of change can be traumatic. When a new system is introduced, operational procedures must be revised, new forms and reporting techniques are changed, employee work patterns are disrupted, and operating efficiency is usually diminished.

The decision to implement and, subsequently, to redesign an inventory system rests with top management. However, the ultimate fate of an inventory control system usually lies in the hands of lower level operations personnel. To avoid resistance to change and implementation difficulties, the affected departments should be included in the design of the inventory system. Their inclusion usually results in a better system with fewer behavioral problems when it is installed. Departments that help create the inventory system tend to nurture it during the implementation phase and correct unanticipated design flaws. Without employee support, any inventory system is subject to demise or at least a turbulent future.

Should the system be manual or computerized? Just as with any prospective investment, a cost-benefit analysis should be conducted. The decision will be influenced by many factors, the most important probably being the volume of work to be handled. Microcomputers and similar business machines are making electronic control a viable alternative for more and more organizations. Since electronic systems are providing additional benefits (accounting, control, and administration) beyond stock control, it is no surprise that they are popular.

A popular retail and wholesale device is called a point-of-sale terminal. There are two types: code readers and keyboards. The code reader automatically inserts information in a terminal by reading magnetic strips on specially designed tapes when the product is passed over a sensing device. The keyboard is similar to a cash register, but it maintains records of inventory status with each sale or withdrawal.

The use of the computer in materials management is growing rapidly. Manual methods (in many cases) have reached their limit. The computer can perform and develop forecasts, reorder points, order quantities, order intervals, product explosions, record maintenance, customer billing, inventory status, and supplier payments. However, manual systems with clerical control are still appropriate for small organizations with fewer material needs.

When initiating an inventory system, the following hints can be helpful:

1. Inventory will invariably increase very quickly. Items whose order quantity is increased will be ordered at once, and the stock will increase. Items whose order quantity is decreased will take time for their level to be worked off.
2. Forecasting should be based on daily or weekly data, since lead times are frequently shorter than a month. Monthly forecasting data can conceal patterns of demand occurring during the month and complicate estimates of lead time of shorter duration.
3. The system should be tried on a limited number of items initially to solve any unforeseen problems before it is implemented totally.
4. Run the initial pilot study manually (with a calculator) on a small number of items so personnel can understand it thoroughly. If the final system will be computer-based, the pilot can be studied manually as well as on an automated basis.
5. Before the total system is to be implemented, verify that all personnel involved understand it and are committed to its success.

There are many approaches to designing an inventory system; this section will cover a single approach that can provide a general framework. The general procedure is outlined in Figure 7.

A necessary precondition for developing the inventory system is forecasts of all end items produced or used by the organization. Item forecasts are developed from forecasting models that were covered in Chapter 15. After item forecasts are obtained, an ABC analysis of the inventory will indicate what system or systems would be preferable. If a perpetual or two-bin inventory system is indicated, the EOQ and

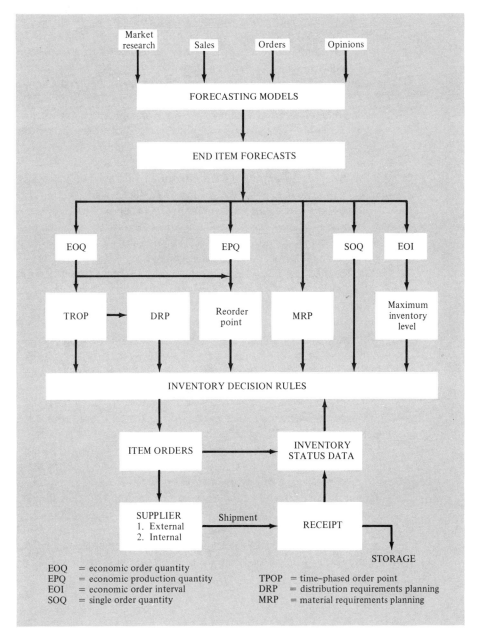

FIGURE 7
An inventory control system.

EPQ models can be employed. If conglomerate orders are necessary, the EOI model can be utilized for the periodic or optional replenishment inventory systems. If items fall into the single order category, the SOQ model can be used. If items are needed to support scheduled production operations, the MRP model can be applied.

From the various models and an understanding of the peculiarities of the organization, inventory decision rules can be established for all items. When inventory decision rules indicate items should be ordered, purchase requisitions are transmitted for the appropriate supplier. For external suppliers, purchase requisitions are transmitted to the purchasing department which contracts for the items. With internal suppliers, production requisitions are transmitted to the production control department which schedules the production of items.

When ordered items are received from the suppliers, they are quality accepted and put into inventory. Needless to say, all of the transactions involve the generation of paper for accountability and control. Inventory systems are best maintained from a central control location that can indicate the status of any item. These records become the data base for forecasting models. Because of the quantity of items and the proliferation of paperwork, inventory systems are natural candidates for computer control.

The ultimate success of an inventory system depends on turning inventory theory into workable detailed procedures. Any inventory system requires the collection and processing of vast quantities of data. The design of forms and procedures can be as important as precise quantitative accuracy.

The foundations of any inventory control system are input data and control records, which must be current and accurate. Inventory control is based on the accuracy of records of inflows and outflows. Poor records and data can destroy a perfectly designed control system. Inadequate records result in operating personnel finding informal methods (usually to the subversion of the formal procedures) for satisfying inventory needs (hoarding, stockpiling, overordering, early ordering, and so forth). Accurate and up-to-date records permit an inventory system to function efficiently and effectively.

Modern analytical techniques have taken much, but not all, of the guesswork out of inventory management. No longer need stock levels be determined solely by habit, hunch, or accident. Formulas are available to establish order quantities and order intervals, while statistical probability theory can be applied to safety stock determination. Intelligent and informed management judgment has not been replaced, but only supplemented. Both qualitative and quantitative evaluations, involving considerable study and collaboration, are usually required before intelligent decisions can be made and effective systems implemented.

The design of inventory systems must include sufficient flexibility to permit growth, expansion, and internal change without upsetting the operational system. The system must be able to cope with the exceptional item or event. The inventory system should be capable of being integrated into the other organizational systems with little difficulty.

INVENTORY SYSTEM IMPROVEMENT

Each purchase or production situation must be preceded by a decision making process. The number of items involved can range from scores to millions, and the number of transactions is far in excess of the number of items. The decision making process may be simple or complex, programmed or nonprogrammed, intuitive or mathematical, hasty or deliberate. There are many ways an inventory manager can reduce costs. Some of the more apparent methods are as follows:

1. *Reduce lead times:* By selecting local suppliers or suppliers close to the organization's geographical location, substantial reductions in cost can be

achieved. Local supply can reduce lead times, which lowers the reorder point and safety stock. Frequently, it is worth paying a higher unit cost for a local supply, since inventory can be maintained at a lower level. Local supply can eliminate purchase order preparation, since one can phone in orders.

2. *Inform suppliers of expected annual demand:* If suppliers are aware of annual needs, they can plan their production to have sufficient inventory available to meet the expected demand. This action can reduce lead time and permit the supplier to better plan and schedule production operations.

3. *Contract with suppliers for minimum annual purchases:* Contract to purchase a fixed annual quantity from suppliers with payment to coincide with the receipt of materials. Quantity discounts can be obtained in this manner while materials are ordered and received in economic quantities. This approach can also be a hedge against future price increases.

4. *Offer customers a discount on preordered items:* If customers order items before they need them, inventory reductions can be achieved by specially ordering components. If customers receive a discount on items ordered before they are needed, the price reduction can frequently offset the increase in holding costs associated with higher inventory levels.

5. *Use fewer suppliers:* Multiple suppliers can increase costs by reducing bulk purchases. With fewer suppliers, there can be greater provision for quality, price, and inventory control. Frequently, reliability and quality of supply are more important than short-term, minor price differences. Smaller order quantities with more frequent deliveries are more likely with "favored suppliers."

6. *Buy on consignment:* Arrange with suppliers to pay for their items as they are sold or used. This action will transfer a large portion of the holding costs to the supplier.

7. *Consider transportation costs:* Failing to consider transportation costs and the most economical mode of transportation can increase unit cost considerably.

8. *Order economical quantities:* Overbuying in relation to needs results in excessive holding costs.

9. *Control access to storage areas:* Protect against losses from theft, spoilage, unauthorized withdrawals by employees, and the ravages of the elements.

10. *Obtain better forecasts:* More reliable and precise forecasts can substantially reduce safety stocks.

11. *Standardize stock items:* Inventories can be reduced by a reduction in the quantities of each item or by a reduction in the number of different items used in stock. Inventory investment can be lowered by carrying one standard item instead of five different items that are used for essentially the same purpose.

12. *Dispose of inactive stock:* On a regular basis all stock should be reviewed to identify obsolete, poor quality, surplus, and slow-moving items. Disposal alternatives include return to vendor, scrap, rework, salvage, and reduced-price sale.

Frequently the quickest, most effective way to reduce inventory is better priority planning and control of operations. A poorly devised operating system may appear efficient with the aid of excessive inventory. Improved planning and scheduling of operations can reduce the investment in inventory.

Organizationally, the inventory control function is usually assigned to the purchasing or the production control department. Purchasing feeds the inventory reservoir, while production control draws from it. Because department managers tend to neglect the significance of costs outside their own departments, the materials management concept has developed. The materials manager consolidates purchasing, inventory control and production control into a single operating unit. The materials management concept grew out of the frustration of many companies at not being able to control inventory effectively. It is not uncommon for departments to continually find fault with each other, when the true culprit is an inadequate organizational structure.

The number of items in inventory has been growing because of the increasing technical nature of the items, a demand for greater variety by customers, and requirements for better service. The number of dollars invested in inventory is growing at a faster rate than the number of items. Computerization may hold the key to the solution of these problems. The computer aspect of materials management has been intentionally downplayed so as not to divert the reader from the really important subject matter. The computer's contribution lies in its power to execute a multitude of straightforward procedures in a very short time. The computer, while an essential tool of materials management, is not essential to understanding the subject.

Decisions to add new products, purchase foreign components, and add distribution points can have a dramatic effect on inventory investment. Likewise, uncontrolled product proliferation, errors in transaction documentation, and outdated bills of materials create serious problems. Computer routines and analytical techniques do not eliminate the need for good management.

AGGREGATE INVENTORY MEASUREMENT

Aggregate inventory measurement relates to the overall level of inventory and the techniques for its measurement. In essence it "looks at the forest and not each tree." Four common ways to measure aggregate inventory are as follows:

1. aggregate inventory value,
2. ratio of aggregate inventory value to annual sales,
3. days of supply,
4. inventory turnover.

An organization may use one or more of the above for aggregate inventory measurement.

Aggregate inventory value is simply the total value of inventory at cost. Many organizations set dollar limits or budgets on the amount which can be invested in each general class of materials. They are usually applied to broad classes and not to individual items. The dollar limits indicate the upper investment limit which aggregate inventory value should not exceed. Aggregate inventory value is very simple and easy to use, but it neglects the dynamic nature of inventory and its other financial interactions.

The *inventory to sales ratio* is the aggregate inventory at cost divided by annual sales. This ratio recognizes the dynamic relation between inventory and sales, but it can vary substantially due to cost and/or selling price changes. If profit margins change, the ratio can become distorted for comparison purposes.

The *days of supply* is the total value of inventory at cost divided by the sales per day at cost. The time supply of inventory is dynamic in nature, but it can become confounded if the cost of sales is not maintained and controlled.

Inventory turnover refers to the cycle of using and replacing materials. It is the ratio of the annual cost of goods sold (annual sales at cost) to the average inventory. It indicates the number of "turnovers" of the investment in inventory for a given time period (usually a year). If an organization has sales such that its cost of goods sold are $600,000 a year and has an average inventory valued at $300,000, it has two turnovers per year. If the organization could generate the same sales with an average inventory worth $150,000, it would have four turnovers per year. High turnover reduces the inventory investment and also saves holding costs. But it can be harmful if the low inventories cause frequent stockouts. A high inventory turnover at the cost of customer service and manufacturing expense is of dubious value. Inventory turnover recognizes the dynamic nature of inventory, but like most ratios it can easily become distorted.

Aggregate inventory measurement techniques usually reduce inventory items to a common financial denominator of dollars. The techniques measure results in absolute terms or ratios. The desirable range of performance is established historically by industry data, or by management judgment. While measurement in financial terms is desirable, inventory should also be viewed through other dimensions (composition, flexibility, contribution to organizational objectives).

CONCLUSION

An effective inventory system should be relative, dynamic, and truthful. *Relative* refers to meeting the needs of other organizational functions or departments. The system is dependent on the needs of others. *Dynamic* refers to the time variation of inventory needs. Any system must react to expected and unexpected changes. *Truthful* refers to the ability to report accurately the stock or position of inventory when required.

Management's responsibility is to manage the organization's assets, both human and nonhuman, in the light of preconceived goals and objectives. Inventory tends to have an impact upon all the functional areas. Thus it should not be surprising that inventories are troublesome and controversial.

The inventory function is outlined in Figure 8.

Control can be a two-edged sword. Intense overcontrol is just as undesirable and costly as undercontrol. A *carte blanche* attitude towards new sophisticated control systems can be costly. New systems that save hundreds and cost thousands of dollars are unhealthy investments. A control system (or systems) should be installed on the basis of its cost-benefit relationship and not to achieve control as an end in itself.

The design of aggregate materials management systems can be approached from different angles. It is common for emphasis to be put on specific control models rather than the relevant systems. A broad based aggregate program should include at least the following elements:

1. determination or delineation of organizational goals,
2. assessment of the significance of materials management to organizational goals,

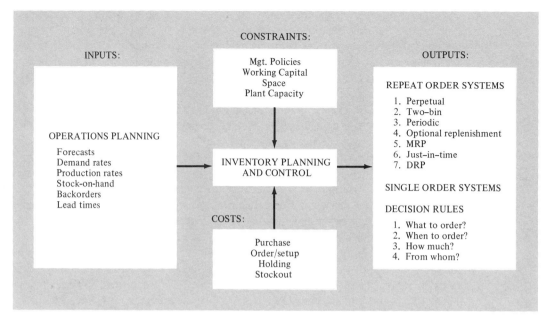

FIGURE 8
The inventory function.

3. determination of aggregate material needs,
4. design of appropriate material control models,
5. design of forecasting models,
6. measurement and collection of model parameter inputs,
7. model testing and implementation,
8. variable reporting and model redesign,
9. operationalization of the materials management system.

The decision to institute a materials management system can be just as important as the choice of the particular models for the system. Too frequently an organization is adapted to a mathematical model rather than vice versa. The system designers must tread a strait and narrow path between the pitfalls of oversimplification and the morass of overcomplication.

The problems of inventory and materials management are ubiquitous and complex. No simple formula takes into account all of the variables encountered in real situations. The value of good approximations in permitting a practical and understandable solution to a problem is often far greater than any loss caused by a lack of accuracy or precision. Aggregate inventory analysis is not a precise science.

QUESTIONS

1. What should an effective inventory control system accomplish? What vital areas should be considered in developing a comprehensive control system?

2. Identify the most frequently used inventory systems, and indicate the basis on which each operates.

3. What is the major disadvantage of the perpetual inventory system? What other problems may occur with the use of this system?

4. How does the two-bin inventory system differ from the perpetual system?

5. Compare the potential ordering practices and safety stock requirements of the periodic inventory system with those associated with the perpetual system.

6. What is the benefit derived from using a reorder point parameter in conjunction with the two other parameters of the optional replenishment system?

7. Define multiechelon distribution system.

8. What aspects of the "pull" system make it unsuitable in some distribution network situations?

9. State why a "push" system tends to operate well in multilevel distribution networks.

10. How does a distribution requirements planning system use time-phased order point logic?

11. Name some of the vital ingredients for an MRP inventory system.

12. What considerations can drastically affect an item's classification as well as its control procedure in an ABC inventory analysis?

13. With what organizational group does the ultimate success of an inventory system lie? Why?

14. Give two or three hints which might be useful information when initiating an inventory control system.

15. How can reducing lead times, offering customers a discount on preordered items, and using fewer suppliers reduce inventory costs?

16. Discuss the types of inventory control systems used in your home for food, clothing, medicines, and other household items.

CASE 1: SECOND-HAND GOODS

The Pickard Motor Company is imperiled by the contemporary problems that have nearly destroyed much of the American automobile industry. With the critical domestic economic situation, sales are falling dramatically, and ability to compete with foreign auto makers is seriously hampered. Proof of their financial jeopardy comes with the announcement of the latest quarterly earnings; Pickard is declaring the largest losses in corporate history. Witnessing the rapid decline of solvency, Pickard is undertaking a recovery program whereby drastic changes are being instituted in product offerings. Pickard is converting a large portion of passenger car production to energy efficient cars. To do so, Pickard is paying enormous re-tooling and inventory replacement costs with capital borrowed at record high interest rates.

The Louisville Assembly Plant of Pickard Motors is nearing the production "launch" of the newly engineered S-cars, Pickard's first energy efficient compacts. Since the Louisville plant is the site for finalizing engineering and production changes, the model year changeover to introduce the new line to production precedes operations at the other assembly plants by three months. Current model year production ends company-wide in four months, and all aspects of capital and procedural modification at Louisville must occur within that time.

Currently, Louisville has over $2.6 million worth of parts that are technologically acceptable for the present production year. Calculations show that these parts will carry over well beyond the final four weeks of scheduled production. Unfortunately, most of these parts are obsolete for the S-line, which is the only line to remain in production at the Louisville site. The number of obsolete parts becomes inordinately high after subtraction of the few "carryover" parts. The only possibilities of parts that could carry over to next year's line are certain sizes of tires and sparkplugs, a few incidental nuts and bolts, some standard paint colors, and other parts with dollar values that exclude even their mention.

Pickard headquarters is greatly disturbed about the dollar value of excess materials and is demanding prompt disposition of all surplus parts. The Louisville staff also recognizes the need for immediate disposition in order for the plant to attain operational status for the S-car "Launch Program." Louisville is more interested in getting the parts "off the books" than in the losses that will be suffered through quick disposition. The corporate headquarters, on the other hand, is taking an opposing view; headquarters is stressing reasonable cash recovery from the disposition of the goods.

Customarily, Pickard's initial disposition step would be return of the excess parts to the supplier and assumption of a small loss on the transaction. The present difficulty with this disposition route is time consumption and the predatory attitude the suppliers have taken in the current automobile producer dilemma. Pickard feels there has been systematic and conspired erosion of supplier repurchase prices, and therefore would rather choose an alternative route.

In the past, Pickard has also sold excess materials to employees. Recently, the company has considered forbidding this practice, because it has been used discriminately and has become a perquisite of top management. Furthermore, many of those who have participated in employee surplus sales have used the materials to start side-line businesses rather than for personal repairs or avocations.

Jim Jones, Louisville's scrap materials manager, seems to have been left with the bulk of the disposition task and has been instructed to get rid of as much dollar value of inventory as possible. As his first sources of solutions, he has been phoning friends in scrap materials businesses in automobile related fields. However, most of his hopes lie internally with great expectations of his counterpart at the San Jose Assembly Plant; he is sure he can ride to laurels on the proven disposition paths of the San Jose expert.

Ironically, San Jose, Louisville's sister plant, is found to seldom face excesses but chronically experience shortages. So, with little assistance from surplus materials personnel with understandably good track records and given headquarter's apprehensions concerning customary routes, Jim may have to push to pursue the old disposition means or quickly find new ones.

1. What disposition options are available?
2. Given their orientation, what would Louisville and the corporate headquarters most likely want done?
3. Should Louisville sacrifice sell and take the tax writeoff?
4. Could an ABC approach be applicable to Jim Jones's task?

CASE 2: MRP OR BUST

Rollo Fishbein, President of Alpha Electronics, has recently become a member of APICS, an organization for production and inventory control professionals. Through APICS, Rollo has gained considerable knowledge about modern production and inventory control systems. He has become particularly interested in material requirements planning (MRP) systems as solutions to many present day inventory problems—the types of problems which exist at Alpha.

Alpha Electronics is a small but rapidly growing manufacturer of electrical meters and test equipment such as voltmeters, potentiometers, ohmmeters, and galvanometers. All of the end products are high quality, expensive items sold primarily to industrial firms or to educational institutions. Alpha purchases over 1000 parts and manufactures approximately 1500 parts and assemblies of its own. Some of the parts are used on more than one instrument, and a few simpler parts are used on at least 40% of the finished items. Production lots are mostly small, as usual for precision instruments. Alpha is using a fixed order size system to control inventories of both parts and end items. EOQs and reorder points are calculated for all items.

Because of the rapid expansion of the firm, there is a recurrent cash crunch. In order to improve the liquidity position, Rollo would like to see inventories minimized. He has become enthusiastic about MRP's capability of substantially reducing production costs and inventory investments. His convictions about the relative advantages of MRP systems are so strong that he has declared that Alpha will implement an MRP system immediately with a target completion date of less than one year.

Judging from what he has heard and read, Rollo has determined that Alpha meets all the product requirements for successful implementation of an MRP system. The other requirements of the organization dictate computerized data processing methods, and the functional requirements of the production and inventory departments require a sophisticated MRP system. Rollo has deemed further investigation of alternative systems unnecessary and has chosen to bypass some of the system design phases. For instance, he has overridden the material manager's request for detailed systems design proposals from competing firms; Rollo has requested a design for an entirely new system and requisitioned information pertaining only to conversion to an MRP system. His short-cut procedure stipulates that the only detailed design is to be the selection of an MRP package. Rollo is so confident of his decision and so eager to begin the process that he has already contacted a software consultant to come in and tailor an existing MRP package to Alpha's needs.

The selection of the software consultant has anticipated the selection process for computer hardware. Rollo is circumventing the tedious process of choosing hardware and is ready to match the computer configuration to his stated system requirements and MRP software needs. Rollo has decided that the power and capabilities of the computer configuration should exceed the present system requirements by a wide margin. Thus, he is prepared to purchase more computing power for the firm and will simply select a system that is compatible with the MRP system undergoing development. Rollo is pleased that his software consultant is affiliated with a company well known for general purpose equipment. Not only is the computer company respected for its highly versatile equipment, but Rollo's APICS associates have informed him that this company could best meet his selection criteria—low cost and familiarity with the software.

As a further step toward a speedy implementation Rollo is proposing a direct conversion. This "cold turkey" approach is based on two important considerations. First, there should be an abrupt discontinuation of the old system, as it is obsolete and so drastically different from the new system that nothing could be gained from its continuation. Second, the conversion should be made quickly and inexpensively.

Rollo has assured his personnel that there will be an educational program, but it will have to come subsequent to the developmental phase. All system operators will receive on-the-job training, and all management and staff personnel will attend a session designed to explain the system outputs. In addition, management and staff will be required to attend an acceptance meeting near project completion and a follow-up meeting at project termination. Rollo has also promised that he will allocate funds for new positions; people with computer backgrounds and experience will be hired to execute a smoother transition and to ensure optimum operating efficiency.

1. Is the proposed system a good way of handling the firm's expansion problem? Realizing that perfect results are unlikely, have the potential benefits of the redesign been exaggerated?
2. What are the behavioral implications of this system conversion? Has Rollo Fishbein initiated the change in a manner that will lessen resistance?
3. What implementation approach would you suggest?
4. Is it essential that Alpha undergo a system redesign? If so, what needs to be redesigned?

SELECTED BIBLIOGRAPHY

Brown, R. G. *Materials Management Systems,* New York: Wiley-Interscience, 1977.

Buchan, J. and E. Koenigsberg. *Scientific Inventory Management,* Englewood Cliffs, NJ: Prentice-Hall, 1963.

Enrick, N. L. *Inventory Management,* San Francisco, CA: Chandler, 1968.

Greene, J. H. *Production and Inventory Control,* Homewood, IL: Irwin, 2nd edition, 1974.

New, C. *Requirements Planning,* New York: Wiley, 1973.

Plossl, G. W. and W. E. Welch. *The Role of Top Management in the Control of Inventory,* Reston, VA: Reston, 1979.

Tersine, R. J. *Principles of Inventory and Materials Management,* New York: North-Holland, 1982.

Tersine, R. J. and J. H. Campbell. *Modern Materials Management,* New York: North Holland, 1977.

Tersine, R. J. and R. A. Toelle. "Optimum Stock Levels for Excess Inventory Items," *Journal of Operations Management,* Vol. 4, No. 3, May 1984, pp. 245–258.

Wight, O. W. *Production and Inventory Management in the Computer Age,* Boston: Cahners, 1974.

21

Purchasing and Procurement

PURCHASING INPUTS
  Purchase Requisitions
  Product Specifications

  CONSTRAINTS
    Legalities
    Management Policies
    Resource Limitations
    Cultural Influences
    Market Conditions

    DEMAND FACTORS
      Items Used Continuously
      Large Single Orders
      Small-Value Purchases
      Normal Purchases

    PURCHASING DECISIONS

      PURCHASING OUTPUTS
        Supply Sources
        Supplier Selection
          Price Determination
          Quality Control
          Discounts
          Local Buying
          Reciprocal Buying
          Shipping Terms
        Timing of Purchases
        Contracts and Legal Considerations
        Purchase Records
        Surplus Disposal
        Value Analysis

          CONCLUSION

            QUESTIONS

            PROBLEMS

            CASES

            SELECTED BIBLIOGRAPHY

Every organization to varying degrees depends on materials and services supplied by other organizations. Since no organization is self-sufficient, purchasing and procurement are common functions of every organization. Purchasing is the exchange of money for goods or services, while procurement is the total responsibility for acquiring goods and services. The changing supply scene, with cycles of shortage and abundance complicated by varying prices, lead times, and availabilities, has buoyed purchasing and procurement to a prominent organizational position. It is of paramount importance when purchased items account for a high proportion of the unit cost of a product.

Procurement, or the purchasing function, can make a substantial contribution to the efficiency and effectiveness of an organization. To attain maximum benefits, it is necessary that it be treated as a functional area along with finance, production, and marketing. The purchasing function is vital to any organization. The ability of the purchasing department to obtain the required materials, equipment, services, and supplies at the right prices and at the right times is a key to successful operations. The largest expenditures made by most organizations are for materials, supplies, equipment, and services. The primary function of a purchasing department is to secure all the material inputs needed for sales or the production function. Such expenditures usually account for more than half of an organization's total.

Because purchasing involves large sums of money, even a small percentage saving can amount to a large dollar figure. Any reduction in material costs exerts a high leverage on profits. Since many items are purchased repetitively, any saving tends to accumulate year after year. A simple example will illustrate how profits can be increased in a variety of ways. In a small manufacturing organization, the following major relationships exist:

Total sales	$1,000,000
Purchased goods and services	500,000
Labor and salaries	300,000
Overhead	150,000
Profit	50,000

To double profit to $100,000 the following actions could be taken:

1. Increase sales 100%.
2. Increase prices 5%.
3. Decrease labor and salaries $16\frac{2}{3}\%$.
4. Decrease overhead $33\frac{1}{3}\%$.
5. Decrease purchase costs 10%.

A review of the above figures reveals the leverage of purchased goods and services. Every 1% decline in purchased goods and services results in a 10% increase in profit. For every dollar the sales department makes, only a small percentage falls through to the bottom line (profit). But all of every dollar the purchasing department saves falls through to the bottom line. It is frequently difficult (if not impossible) to increase prices, substantially increase labor productivity, or reduce overhead. Thus, a major opportunity for reducing costs and improving profit lies in purchasing and procurement.

Purchasing has the responsibility of procuring the kinds and quantities of materials authorized by requisitions issued by engineering, maintenance, production control, inventory control, or any other entity requiring materials. Purchasing means procur-

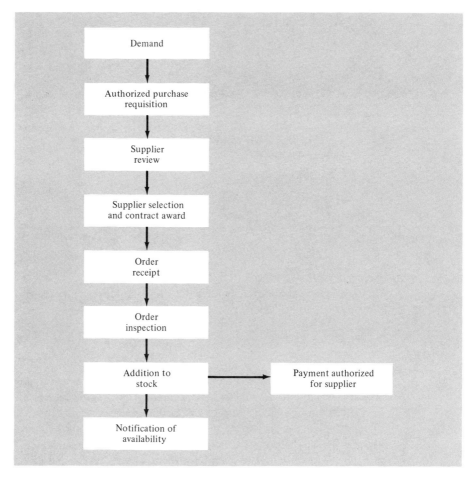

FIGURE 1
The purchasing cycle. [From Richard J. Tersine and John H. Campbell, *Modern Materials Management,* New York: North Holland, 1977, p. 84.]

ing goods and services from outside the organization in return for a price. What price (cost) is acceptable depends on quality, quantity, and time considerations. Quality, quantity, and time are usually established for purchasing, while cost and source are established or affected by purchasing.

Purchasing can be viewed through the purchasing cycle, which is a series of events occurring in almost all purchases (see Figure 1). To initiate the cycle, purchasing usually receives purchase requisitions from other functional areas of the organization. The requisitions are reviewed for authorization, for proper description, and to determine if an available lower cost alternative could do the job. Before writing the purchase order, suppliers must be selected on the basis of price, quality, and delivery schedule. After supplier selection, the purchase contract is signed and shipping dates confirmed. When the order arrives, it is inspected to verify quality and quantity. Supplier invoices for the accepted order are transmitted to purchasing and to the requisitioner of the order. The accepted order is placed in stores and becomes inventory until consumed in a production process or sold to a customer. With the fulfillment of the contract, purchasing must review the invoice, adjust it as needed

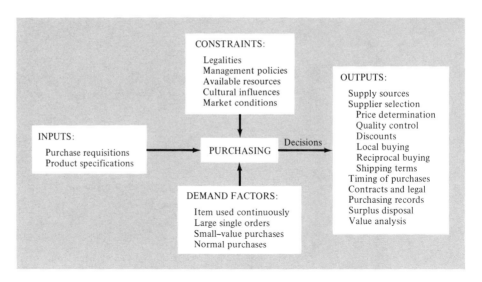

FIGURE 2
The purchasing function. [From Richard J. Tersine, and John H. Campbell, *Modern Materials Management,* New York: North Holland, 1977, p. 85.]

and agreed, and process it for payment, considering any discounts. The purchasing cycle stretches from the receipt of the purchase requisition to the point at which the order is available to the requisitioner and payment is authorized to the supplier.

Viewed through the purchasing cycle, purchasing appears to be a simple, straightforward function. This narrow view can be misleading to those with little purchasing experience. To help dispel simplistic notions, purchasing should also be viewed through the purchasing function, shown in Figure 2. The purchasing function describes purchasing in an input-decision-output framework with organizational constraints and demand factors influencing the final outputs.

The inputs to the purchasing function are also outputs from other organizational sources or functions. Inputs include purchase requisitions (authority for procurement) and product specifications. Purchasing is conditioned by organizational constraints and demand (market) factors. Organizational constraints are limitations imposed by the organization on the purchasing decision. Although they differ from entity to entity, some common limitations are legalities, management policies, available resources, cultural influences, and market conditions. Demand factors (both current and future) influence the quantity, amount, and type of purchase that will be consummated. For example, an impending unit price rise for a component might economically justify a larger purchase for an item with a continuous demand. The outputs of purchasing include approved supply sources, supplier selection, timing of purchases, contracts and legal matters, purchasing records, surplus disposal, and value analysis.

The significance of studying purchasing as a purchasing function is the systems (total) perspective obtained. A more shallow analysis would treat inputs, organizational constraints, demand factors, and outputs as independent, unrelated influences. Since dependence is readily apparent, it is more fruitful to study the interaction of the varied influences on the purchasing decision. The analysis of the purchasing function can result in economical, rational, consistent policies in regard to all the purchasing department's activities. It permits the role of purchasing to be more readily integrated into overall organizational purposes and goals.

Purchasing is in a state of transition from what was largely a clerical activity to a demanding analytical and intellectual function. A purchasing agent is no longer merely a clerk who receives requisitions from managers and catalogs from suppliers, and simply selects the lowest price alternative. Purchasing's role in organizational effectiveness requires that it no longer be perceived as an isolated, trivial activity.

PURCHASING INPUTS

The inputs to purchasing come from outside the purchasing department. They are necessary ingredients required before action can be initiated by purchasing personnel. The most important inputs are purchase requisitions and their accompanying product specifications.

PURCHASE REQUISITIONS

A purchase requisition describes the needed item(s), and it is the legal basis for action. This form is signed by the requisitioner and those whose authorization may be required to avoid irresponsible expenditures. The originator of a purchase may be from any operating department or functional area. Most organizations use a standard requisition form, but the format varies considerably because of differing communication patterns.

The authorization to purchase may take different forms. The three most common are: (1) standard purchase requisition, (2) traveling purchase requisition, and (3) bill of materials. Most organizations use standard purchase requisitions, but for special categories of repeat items, the traveling purchase requisition and the bill of materials may be used.

The *standard purchase requisition* is only standard in relation to a given organization. There is no standard requisition form in common use. Although various formats can be developed, a requisition should provide space for the following:

1. purchase requisition number (identification),
2. originator,
3. date of request,
4. account to be charged,
5. description and quantity of items,
6. date items are needed,
7. purchase order number,
8. delivery date,
9. shipping instructions,
10. buyer's name.

A *traveling purchase requisition* is used to procure material needs that originate from stores or the inventory control section. Traveling requisitions are used for recurring requirements for materials and standard parts. A traveling requisition is a card maintained for each item stocked continuously. Since information is on a single card which can be reused many times, the entire transaction can be handled without delay and with a minimum of clerical paperwork. When the stock level drops to the reorder point or a replacement order is initiated from stores, the card is sent to purchasing (no new purchase requisition need be made). The card contains information on the item, potential sources, record of use, order quantities, and so forth from which the purchasing agent can order. To indicate that the item has been requisitioned, a colored signal clip is attached to the inventory record card by stockroom personnel. When the purchase order is placed, the card is returned to the stockroom for reinsertion in the stock files until another order is signaled. Upon receipt of the order, the colored signal clip is removed and the cycle can start over again. Automated systems may function with different procedures, but the end result is the same.

A *bill of materials* is a list of all items incorporated into a finished product that the organization produces. The bill of materials is prepared at the time engineering drawings are made, and it is usually an integral part of the engineering drawings. The bill of materials and the upcoming production schedule can be sent to purchasing, which ascertains from it the quantity of all the needed production materials. The bill of materials indicates how much of each material is needed to produce a single finished product. By multiplying the production schedule quantity by the bill of materials, the size of the purchase order for each item is obtained. For MRP and similar computerized systems, the bill of materials is bypassed and planned order releases for each item indicate the quantity and timing for purchased items. These methods are primarily applicable to the purchase of standard production items.

Items reaching their reorder point, a periodic review of inventory, or planned order releases from an MRP system may reveal the need for additional purchased items and trigger a purchase requisition. A computerized system may automatically generate purchase requisitions when the need is recognized.

PRODUCT SPECIFICATIONS

Specifications are a detailed description of the characteristics and features of an item. Product specifications perform three main purposes:

1. further describe items on the purchase requisition,
2. let the supplier know exactly what the buyer wants,
3. permit verification of items upon order receipt.

There are many different types of specifications used to describe and grade products. Some common types of specifications are blueprints, market grades, commercial standards, material specifications, performance specifications, and so forth.

A *blueprint* or engineering drawing can accompany a purchase requisition. It is most appropriate where close tolerances or a high degree of mechanical perfection is required. *Market grades* are a common method of determining the quality of commodities such as wheat, cotton, tobacco, lumber, and meats. Trade associations, commodity exchanges, and governmental agencies establish and regulate market grades.

Commercial standards have been developed for items above the commodity level because of their widespread use. All nuts, bolts, pipes, motors, and electrical items are made to standard specifications as dictated by governments, trade associations, or engineering societies. Without commercial standards, mass production systems would be virtually impossible.

Material specifications usually define the physical or chemical properties desired in an item. Items such as metal (aluminum, steel, copper), drugs, oils, and paints are examples of products with material specifications.

Performance specifications do not describe an item physically or chemically, but in terms of what the item is to do (how it is to function). The supplier is told the performance that is required and not its content or how it should be manufactured. Performance specifications are based on the principle that the product should pass tests that indicate its performance in service. Performance specifications are common for complex systems where function and reliability are paramount, as in military, space, and sophisticated technological equipment.

Product specifications may emanate from (1) individual standards developed by the buyer, (2) standards established by private agencies (either other users, suppliers, or professional societies), and (3) governmental standards. Individual standards developed by the buyer can be arduous and expensive to establish. Standard specifications for many items have been developed by nongovernmental private agencies such as the American Standards Association, American Society of Mechanical Engineers, American Society for Testing Materials, American Institute of Electrical Engineers, and the Underwriters Laboratories. Governmental agencies such as the National Bureau of Standards, the General Services Administration, and the Defense Department also develop standards.

Many products cannot be adequately described by a single type of specification. In such cases, a combination of specifications may be used. If a nonstandard product is desired, engineering must compose in detail its own particular specification. Of course, the preparation of specifications for small-lot purchases can be economically prohibitive. Brand or trade names can be very economical for low-cost lot purchases. Buying by brand or trade names indicates a reliance upon the integrity and reputation of the supplier to provide consistent quality.

CONSTRAINTS

Constraints limit the alternatives available to a purchasing manager in making his decisions. These limiting factors narrow the decision space of acceptable solutions. Organizational constraints are manifold and vary from organization to organization. Organizations are constrained by legal considerations (statute and common law), management policies, resource limitations (money, machines, manpower), cultural influences (holidays, operating hours, operating days), market conditions, and so forth.

LEGALITIES

Although a legalistic approach to purchasing is in most cases unnecessary, the purchase contract is a legal document and the organization must be protected from legal problems. All purchasing agents are heavily affected by the Uniform Commercial Code, which has been adopted by all but one of the states. The Uniform Commercial Code determines right and obligations on the basis of fairness and reasonableness according to accepted business practice. However, there are variations in interpretations of laws by various states. Other federal and state laws control purchasing activities to varying degrees. Antitrust legislation holds any business practice that hinders competition or restrains trade to be illegal. The purchasing agent must understand basic legal concepts well enough to detect potential legal problems before they become serious.

MANAGEMENT POLICIES

Management policies influence the effectiveness of the purchasing department. The organizational structure within which procurement activities take place can limit its efficiency. However, there is no one best form of organization. Structure is usually shaped by tradition and operating needs stemming from the nature of the organization.

In particular, management may choose between centralized and decentralized methods. Centralized purchasing has economic advantages for multiplant organizations, since greater buyer specialization and input standardization can result. But centralization also tends to be slow, rigid, and rule-bound, as well as very costly for low-value purchases. To overcome these shortcomings, mixtures of centralized and decentralized techniques are often adopted.

Centralization is worthwhile when an organization uses generally related products in several locations. The advantages of centralization are lessened when a multiplant organization has broad unrelated items and its plants are widely scattered. Advantages of centralized purchases include:

1. the development of specialized purchasing skills,
2. the consolidation of order quantities, which can result in quantity and cash discounts,
3. better control over inventory investment,
4. less overlapping and duplication of purchasing effort,
5. uniform quality and less variety of materials.

RESOURCE LIMITATIONS

Resource limitations can seriously alter purchasing activities. The most apparent resource limitation involves finances. Purchasing must operate with the working capital and cash flow positions developed by the finance department. The right time to buy based on economics (price advantage) is not always the right time to buy from the standpoint of the organization's treasury. If purchasing places orders to take advantage of unusually low prices while neglecting finances, the entity can find itself paying for these purchases with funds needed for other purposes. Purchasing must strive for overall organizational goals, and this means that it must sometimes subvert its own subgoals. Other resource shortages such as available manpower, storage space, and handling equipment can also place limitations on the purchasing department.

CULTURAL INFLUENCES

Cultural influences refer to the time-honored methods and procedures by which organizations conduct their business. Usually these influences are not even thought about, since they become ingrained in a society. When interfacing with organizations in foreign countries, the cultural differences are readily apparent. Typical differences relate to attitudes toward work, hours of operation, holidays observed, methods of payment for services, and approaches to contract settlement.

MARKET CONDITIONS

Market conditions relate to short term market situations, which are influenced strongly by supply and demand as well as the state of the national economy. For example, during periods of shortage of strategic items, reliability of supply may be considerably more important than price. The purchasing agent must function in a changing environment, and he must be able to change his strategies as prevailing market conditions dictate. What might have been sound judgment at one time becomes irresponsible at another, and vice versa.

DEMAND FACTORS

The type of purchasing procedure adopted is dependent upon the type of demand that exists for the product. Quite obviously, the procedures for high volume, continuously used products will be different from those for one time, single purchases. Products can be grouped into four basic categories based on demand—items used continuously, large single orders, small-value purchases, and normal purchases (items not falling into any of the first three categories). Different categories will receive substantially different treatment by the purchasing agent.

ITEMS USED CONTINUOUSLY

Items that are used continuously in production processes, for which there is a fairly predictable demand, can be handled under a blanket purchase order. Blanket purchase orders, also referred to as open-end purchase orders, permit the requisition to go directly to the supplier, and it is not processed by the purchasing department. With a blanket purchase order, individual purchase orders need not be written each time. Purchasing negotiates a contract for a fixed period of time (perhaps a year), with delivery dates, quantities, and prices open. If the price is not specified, it is the price in effect when the quantity is purchased. Notification of delivery dates and desired size of shipments is sent to the supplier by the production control department. The purchasing agent is not involved in placing individual orders, but he does negotiate the basic contract.

With blanket purchase orders, discounts are usually obtained from the supplier based on the total annual purchases. The size of such a discount can be substantial. Such arrangements also make the releasing of purchase orders during the year a routine matter that can be delegated to less technical personnel. This conserves the time of the purchasing agent and his staff for more important duties.

LARGE SINGLE ORDERS

Large single orders are usually for special machinery or other unique types of capital goods (computers, vehicles, new buildings, military hardware, spacecraft). Many months of planning and evaluation are involved in the effort. Suppliers usually are requested to submit bids for the special order that include the cost of any design work. These purchases are negotiated on a one-time basis.

SMALL-VALUE PURCHASES

At the opposite end of the spectrum from the large single orders are the small-value purchases. Low-cost items that are used infrequently are small-value purchases. It is not uncommon for the process cost of the purchase order to exceed the cost of such a purchase. To reduce the cost of purchasing these inexpensive items, petty cash accounts or open-end orders with suppliers are established. Here also, purchasing does not do the actual buying but only establishes the conditions and monitors the system.

NORMAL PURCHASES

Any purchases that do not fit into any of the above categories are termed normal purchases and are handled by the normal purchasing routine. Normal purchases are handled through the purchasing cycle previously delineated. The purchasing agent does all the buying, and he coordinates the total activity from purchase requisition to delivery of goods.

PURCHASING DECISIONS

By taking into account the purchasing inputs from other functional areas, the organizational constraints emanating from the environment, and the demand factors, the purchasing manager must make a host of decisions. These decisions will functionally, operationally, or financially have an impact on every department in the organization. The decisions will ultimately result in outputs that establish purchasing policies and procedures for the future. These decisions are transfer functions that take data and information and transform them into actions necessary to acquire goods and services.

PURCHASING OUTPUTS

From purchase requisitions, the purchasing department will generate purchase orders. Purchase order forms vary in their format and their routing through the organization. The purchase order is essentially a legal document. It should contain at least the following:

1. purchase order number (identification),
2. date of issue,
3. name and address of supplier receiving the order,
4. quantity and description of item(s),
5. required delivery date,
6. shipping instructions,
7. price and terms of payment,
8. conditions governing the order.

The outputs of the purchasing function do not just select the supplier and award the contract. They establish policies, data, and procedures for the purchasing department on future purchases. Each contract award provides additional information to a data bank for improving future purchasing activities. The data bank (purchasing records) has many useful purposes, such as providing:

1. a list of supply sources for future purchases,
2. an appraisal of supplier performances,
3. a source of cost and price data,
4. a data base for make/buy/lease decisions,
5. an evaluation of purchasing agents' effectiveness.

SUPPLY SOURCES

There are two primary sources of supply for an item: internal (the organization itself) and external (outside suppliers). The make or buy decision is one of internal versus external supply. In one situation (make), the organization supplies itself, and in the other (buy), the source is another organization. The make or buy decision can involve numerous factors, but a major factor must be an incremental cost analysis.

The make or buy decision is multidimensional, and most organizations are faced with it continually. Being one's own supplier presents an opportunity for diversification. Most organizations do not have a consciously expressed policy with reference to this issue, but prefer to decide each case on its own merits. The "make" decision leads to largely independent and self-sustaining industrial entities that are vertically integrated. The "buy" decision leads to largely dependent industrial entities that are horizontally integrated.

Information on external sources of supply can be obtained from numerous references. Industrial advertisements of suppliers appear in many periodicals. Supplier catalogs that are quite comprehensive in product listings are often available upon request. Supplier salesmen and trade journals provide information on new products and processes. Trade directories, or trade registers, such as *Thomas' Register of American Manufacturers,* give listings of suppliers for different product classifications. The yellow pages of telephone directories list local suppliers. Records of an organization's past purchases indicate supply sources and their capabilities.

International trade tends to widen supply horizons to the development of foreign sources of supply. Industrial buyers tend to seek domestic sources of supply where possible. However, licensing agreements, joint ventures, acquisitions, and mergers have led many organizations into world-wide operations. Competitive pressures force organizations to consider new and lower cost sources of supply.

Suppliers are the "outside shop" managed by the purchasing department. Their products are brought into the organization as materials and are its livelihood. Few organizations can operate without them. If materials are not properly available, costs escalate and profits fall.

Though all suppliers and orders are important, it is wise to classify suppliers into the traditional ABC categories based on the dollar volume of orders and relative importance of each supplier. Usually 10 to 20% of suppliers represents 80% of purchases. It pays to establish special communication with the top 20% of suppliers.

SUPPLIER SELECTION

When selecting a supplier, the buyer is trying to find an organization that will meet his needs in quality, quantity, and timing at the lowest cost. The starting point is to compile a list of organizations that can make the needed item. The proficiency of each potential supplier must then be assessed. Only sources that meet performance standards are considered acceptable. Purchasing departments should compile a list of acceptable suppliers for each class of item procured.

When a purchase requisition is received, the purchasing agent can choose a few likely candidates from the approved supplier list. After contacting them, the final selection can be based on comparative quotations of price and delivery. The development of an approved supplier list is a cumulative process. With each purchase, additional data are developed for inclusion in the record.

The search for new suppliers to add to the approved list is a continual process. Once a source is added to the approved list, continual monitoring and evaluation of performance are necessary. The supplier's card in the approved list should indicate performance in such areas as price, quality, service, and delivery. Since late delivery or poor quality can have serious repercussions on operations, price is only one of the relevant variables in selecting a supplier. Other relevant variables are the supplier's management capability, technical (engineering) ability, production capacity, depth of service, and financial stability. Information can be obtained from personal visits, financial reports, credit reports, and historical performance.

Frequently, foreign supply can result in substantial cost savings. However, problems in communication, language, long lead times, and cultural background can cause difficulties. Small organizations can use the services of importers, trading companies, or agents representing foreign manufacturers to ameliorate foreign entanglements.

Should an organization use a single source or multiple sources? It is believed that multiple sourcing keeps prices down and service up through competitive bidding. However, advocates of single sourcing insist that economies of scale provide a stronger negotiating position and lower prices. Often single source contracts are longer term and include learning curve concepts which require prices to decline as the supplier becomes more efficient. Increasingly, organizations are using single sourcing with just-in-time (JIT) purchasing that requires suppliers to deliver components frequently in small lots as they are required. Suppliers often are located nearby the facility and deliver items several times a day under a long-term contract.

Supplier selection is a major purchasing responsibility. The shortage of many basic raw materials in recent years has had serious effects on organizations ignoring the development of good vendor relations. Good sources of supply should be cherished and protected.

Price Determination

Depending on the item, the market may vary from almost pure competition to oligopoly to monopoly. Obviously, prices will vary accordingly. Suppliers tend to set their prices on either a cost or a market basis. In the cost approach, a supplier sets price by covering costs plus a certain margin for profit. In the market approach, the price is set by the market place and may not be directly related to cost. A fair price should be paid to suppliers. A fair price is the lowest price that ensures a continuous supply of the proper quantity and quality. A continuous supply is not possible in the long run unless a supplier is making a reasonable profit.

A basic objective of purchasing is to obtain low prices. Published price lists, competitive bidding, and negotiation are the typical approaches to price determination. For many industrial products, prices are predetermined and not questioned. This is particularly true for low value items that are purchased infrequently in small quantities. Suppliers provide published *price lists* to prospective customers. The published prices are called asking prices, and they may or may not be the actual selling price.

With *competitive bidding,* requests for bids are sent to several vendors. A request for a bid asks the seller to quote a price at which he will perform in accordance with the terms and conditions of the order or contract should he be the successful bidder. Usually, the lowest bidder receives the order. Normal industrial practice requires at least three competitive quotes wherever possible. Obviously, the number will vary. Generally, competitive bidding is most applicable to standardized products and services that are widely used and produced to stock. Bids are normally secured when the size of an order exceeds some minimum dollar amount. Governmental purchases are commonly on a bid basis with the award made to the lowest responsible bidder. Some of the reasons why the lowest bidder may not get the order are as follows:

1. Low bidder may be unresponsive to purchase requirements.
2. Higher bid may provide more after-the-sale service.
3. The closest geographical supplier may receive preferential treatment (lead time may be critical or transportation costs lower).
4. Reciprocity may be a factor.
5. Local suppliers may be preferred for community goodwill.

In competitive bidding, the mode of purchase results in the selection of the vendor and price determination. *Negotiation* is another important approach to price determination. When time is too short, the number of bidders is small, the dollar value of the order is high, willingness to compete is lacking, or the specifications are vague, the buyer is driven to negotiate. The purchasing agent begins by analyzing cost, profit, and price and then negotiating with the source for a fair price. In the short run, nothing can be done to avoid paying a sole source's price, but in the long run, alternative sources can usually be developed. The mere fact that a buyer is searching for another source often makes the sole source willing to negotiate a better price.

There are a number of erroneous beliefs associated with negotiation. Among these, the most common are:

1. Negotiation is a win-lose confrontation game.
2. The idea is to overcome the other party.
3. Each negotiation is an independent, isolated transaction.

There are three phases to a successful negotiation. In the initial phase, issues are presented. The factors where agreement exists are defined, and those that require further negotiation are clarified. The second phase involves discussions or arguments and the movement by the parties toward some area of compromise. During the final phase, agreement is reached.

Successful negotiations in which everybody wins are to a great degree dependent on advanced planning and analysis. During the prenegotiation stage, the following questions must be addressed:

1. What do we hope to achieve?
2. What does the other party require?
3. What are we prepared to concede?

A thorough understanding of the other party's position, as well as its strengths and weaknesses, can improve a negotiator's position. The other party should always be allowed to "save face" or to have an "avenue of retreat" rather than being forced into a take-it-or-leave-it situation. Small concessions can be presented when the other party must concede a great deal. To maximize a position while yielding nothing can seriously jeopardize current as well as future negotiations.

Quality Control

A supplier who has the lowest price but furnishes materials of substandard quality may actually be a high price source. Interruptions of production and customer service caused by lack of material meeting quality standards can be very expensive. The type of inspection and quality techniques will depend on the circumstances and quality costs. If considerable variations of quality are acceptable, inspection will not be very important.

When quality is important, purchasing becomes an information source. Questions of quality on maintenance items should be decided by the maintenance department, on operating supplies by the production department, and on office supplies by the office manager. Materials for manufacturing are the responsibility of the engineering and production departments. Although purchasing will not make the final quality decision, it should be instrumental in making the decision.

The purpose of inspection is to verify that the supplier is delivering items per contractual requirements. There is little point in developing specifications without provisions to assure compliance. When an organization has any reason whatsoever to question an incoming shipment, inspection is necessary. Frequently, inspection and testing are included in specifications provided to the supplier. By specifying quality procedures, future difficulties with suppliers on acceptable quality can be averted.

Occasionally, inspection may be performed by an organizational representative in the vendor's plant. On-site inspection can save time and money while minimizing operational delays from inferior quality. When inspection is complicated, the services of testing laboratories may be solicited. Commercial testing laboratories usually employ capable staffs and the most modern X-ray, photometric, electrical, chemical, and physical testing equipment.

Procedures should be established for handling inferior quality. Should the shipment be returned to the supplier and the contract canceled? Should the buyer rework the item to an acceptable quality and bill the supplier? Should only rejected items be returned for replacement and acceptable items retained? Who absorbs transportation charges for returned items? Prior stipulation of the treatment of substandard quality with the supplier can do much to maintain an amicable long term relationship.

Quality is becoming more important as organizations move toward MRP, JIT, and zero inventory techniques. There is not time for rework or replacement of materials that do not meet specifications. The trend is toward quality standards so high that inspection is not required when the shipment arrives. More prevalently, organizations are developing long-term relationships with selected vendors who can supply the required quality, price, and delivery.

Discounts

An important aspect of price determination involves discounts that are available or can be secured by the purchasing agent. Buyers should be familiar with discounts. Trade, quantity, seasonal, and cash discounts are the types most frequently encountered.

Trade discounts are given to a purchaser on the basis of his classification. A product may be discounted in different amounts depending on whether the buyer is a manufacturer, wholesaler, or retailer. Ordinarily, the list price is considerably higher than the actual selling price. A trade discount represents the compensation of the buyer, who assumes certain distribution functions for the seller. The discount is granted to protect a certain channel of distribution. This is achieved by making it more economical for certain classes of customers to buy from the distributor than from the manufacturer.

Quantity discounts are given to a buyer for purchasing increasingly larger quantities of an item, or purchasing a specified dollar total of any number of different items. The cost is lowered as the quantity or dollar expenditure increases. The discount is justified because of the savings resulting from reduced selling, shipping, handling, and accounting cost per unit when larger amounts are purchased.

Quantity discounts may be based on a single order or on purchases made over a period. Period quantity discounts are granted as an incentive for continued patronage. They are frequently offered by suppliers with the aim of becoming a primary source.

Seasonal discounts exist because of the seasonal variation in the demand for some items. Suppliers offer discounts for purchases made in the off season. Consumer products in this category are bathing suits, snow tires, greeting cards, air conditioners, and so forth.

Cash discounts are given by suppliers for prompt and full payment of bills. When such discounts are given, they are offered as a percentage of the net invoice price. Although the terms vary, a typical cash discount policy is 2/10, net 30. This means that the buyer can deduct 2% of the bill if he pays the bill within ten days after the date of invoice. After ten days, the discount is rescinded and full payment is required before thirty days. Although the 2% may not seem like much at a first glance, it should be noted that it is based on a short duration. If the discount is not taken, the 2% is equivalent to a loss of 36% per year.[1] Cash discounts are commonly granted by suppliers; the actual terms are largely a matter of trade custom and vary considerably among industries.

Local Buying

The geographical location of suppliers can be very important to an organization. Many large organizations tend to buy directly from the manufacturer instead of going through a local middleman. Even with direct purchases, a substantial number of items can be bought from local suppliers. Operating supplies can be readily procured on a local basis. A local source can frequently offer more dependable service than a more distant source.

There are advantages from buying from local sources. Frequently, the local source can render better service because of personal knowledge of the buyer's needs. Freight cost savings can result from small quantity deliveries over a shorter distance. Prompt deliveries are possible because of the short distances involved and the use of truck transportation. Buying locally generates good public relations because the organization contributes to the welfare of its community.

To improve their public image, some organizations adopt a policy of local buying as well as playing an active role in community affairs. Local buying is more common in small towns with sparse industrialization and low economic activity. While local buying has definite social merit, it seriously restricts the buyer. It is necessary to weight the effects of local buying in each case.

---

[1] $365(0.02)/(30 - 10) = 0.365$, or 36.5%.

Reciprocal Buying

Reciprocal buying, or reciprocity, is the practice of giving preference in buying to those suppliers who also are customers of the buying organization. When an organization makes a point of buying from its customers, it is practicing reciprocity. Two organizations' buying from each other does not constitute reciprocity unless each entity's buying can be explained by the other's buying. It can be argued that if all factors are equal, it is good business to purchase from suppliers who are also customers because it strengthens both companies. Reciprocity is perfectly legal as long as it does not become an unreasonable restraint of trade. If a large organization uses reciprocity in a coercive manner by forcing its suppliers to purchase its products or be dropped as vendors, it can be violating the antitrust laws. In the absence of threats or other types of coercion, the use of reciprocity is not regarded as illegal.

On a national level, reciprocity is considered a vicious, inefficient practice. When firms can sell on some other basis than price, quality, and service, there is bound to be waste. Reciprocal buying practices are more pronounced in producer goods industries (industries selling to other industries) than in consumer goods industries. In producer goods industries, there are more opportunities for large-scale buying and selling. In spite of its negative connotation, reciprocity is a global phenomenon.

Although reciprocity is usually legal when practiced by smaller firms, its image has been tarnished and so its name has been changed to "trade relations" in the industrial community. Do not be fooled.

Many purchasing agents are opposed to reciprocal buying because of the inflexibility of such agreements. It can be argued that freedom of supplier selection is mandatory if the agent is to purchase materials on the most favorable terms. Top management should carefully weigh the pros and cons of all reciprocal buying agreements before entering into them. In the final analysis, the specifics of the particular case will determine the advisability of such agreements.

Shipping Terms

The cost of materials is not determined solely by the unit price of the material and the quantity. Someone, usually the buyer, must pay for transporting the material to the buyer's location. Careless purchasing with respect to delivery terms is a constant source of legal and practical difficulties. It costs money to load, transport, unload, and insure goods. If goods are lost or damaged in transit, someone must bear the loss. Furthermore, if goods arrive before or after the buyer needs them, storage costs or costly delays will result. If possible, purchase orders should specify the shipping terms and routing desired in transporting the material. The choice between equal suppliers is often determined by delivery costs.

The shipping terms contained in a contract will determine who will specify the carrier and the routing. A contract that does not include shipping terms requires the buyer to arrange and bear all the delivery costs. The shipping terms will establish the following:

1. when the buyer takes legal title to the goods,
2. who will pay the freight charges,
3. who will prosecute loss and damage claims against carriers.

An authorization or requirement for the supplier to ship goods does not mean he must pay the cost of shipment or that he is responsible for shipment loss or damage. There are numerous terms of shipment, but the most common are:

1. F.O.B. buyer's plant,
2. F.O.B. seller's plant,
3. F.O.B. seller's plant—freight allowed,
4. C.I.F. contracts,
5. F.A.S.

The F.O.B. (free on board) indicates who pays freight and handling charges as well as when title is passed on the goods. With *F.O.B. buyer's plant,* the buyer takes title to the goods when they are delivered to the loading dock at his plant; the supplier pays all transportation charges and processes all claims against the carrier for damage or loss of goods. With *F.O.B. seller's plant,* the buyer takes title when the supplier loads the goods onto a common carrier, and he pays all transportation charges as well as negotiating all freight damage claims with the carrier. With *F.O.B. seller's plant—freight allowed,* the legal liability is the same as for F.O.B. seller's plant, but the supplier reimburses the buyer for freight charges.

The *C.I.F.* (cost-insurance-freight) *contracts* and *F.A.S.* (free alongside ship) are commonly used in international trade. The C.I.F. contract price includes cost of the material, insurance, and freight. An export shipment from Paris might be listed as C.I.F. New York. In this case, the foreign supplier is responsible for the goods and all charges until the goods arrive at the New York destination. The buyer is responsible for seeing that the goods are unloaded and delivered to their final destination in the United States. With F.A.S. terms, the buyer designates port, berth, and vessel. The supplier is responsible for getting the goods to the ship, and the buyer takes title as well as all responsibility thereafter.

TIMING OF PURCHASES

The time at which some purchases are made determines the price paid and influences the total purchasing operation. In reference to the timing of purchases, a buyer is primarily interested in an adequate supply of material at the best price consistent with quality requirements. Timing is not a critical concern when the purchases are made in a stable price market; it is critical when purchases are made in unstable price markets. Although the purchasing agent cannot usually influence the market, he can control to some extent the price he pays.

Purchasing agents can purchase according to current requirements or purchase according to market conditions. If the first policy is adopted, the purchasing schedule adheres to the volume of current needs and disregards the behavior of the market in which the purchase is made. With the second policy, in addition to current needs, purchasing decisions are based on market conditions. Organizations that try to time their purchases in response to market conditions may adopt any of four approaches:

1. hand-to-mouth buying,
2. averaging down,
3. forward buying,
4. speculative buying.

The *hand-to-mouth* buying policy procures items only to meet immediate short-term requirements, and purchases not immediately needed are deferred. The quantities obtained are much smaller than those normally considered economical. Hand-to-mouth buying is rational when prices are expected to drop, engineering design changes may render materials obsolete, and financial liquidity dictates the release of cash for more pressing organizational needs. The disadvantages of this policy include the excessive ordering costs for numerous small purchases, inability to obtain quantity discounts, higher freight costs for small shipments, excessive stockout costs, and the risk of prices rising instead of falling. Handling costs increase because of the additional time spent in packing and unpacking in the shipping and receiving departments. Lead times can lengthen with small orders if suppliers give lower priority to them. Of course, any unanticipated delays with hand-to-mouth buying can stop scheduled organizational activities and increase costs. Hand-to-mouth buying should be used for exceptional circumstances only; it is not a recommended policy for normal operations.

Averaging down on the market means buying at a moment when the market dips sharply in the course of a gradual price change. Prices rarely rise or decline evenly, but tend to follow a saw-tooth pattern of ups and downs over a time period. The buyer waits until the price is below the market average for the period before placing his order. For example, assume a buyer expects the price of an item to average $.50 a pound during a time period. If the price is $.50 or higher, he will buy only the absolute minimum of items required. If the price is below $.50, he buys in much larger quantities. This approach encourages stock accumulation when prices are low and discourages it when they are high.

Forward buying is the procurement of materials in economical quantities exceeding current requirements, but not beyond actual foreseeable requirements. The approach is often used when prices are stable over time. It can also be used when prices are about to increase, and bulk buying offers substantial savings. Forward buying is adopted to obtain a favorable price, to get quantity discounts, to purchase in economical transportation units, to secure items when they are available, and to protect against prospective shortages. The forward buyer assumes the risk of a dip in price, and he increases inventory levels, which ties up working capital.

With *speculative buying,* items are purchased in excess of foreseeable requirements in order to make a profit from rising prices. Opportunities for purchases of this kind occur just before a price increase or when the market price drops temporarily and the buyer has sufficient working capital to finance the speculation. Here the objective is not only to have the needed items available, but also to earn profits from buying low and selling high. Speculative buying looks directly for a profit; the other three approaches are more defensive in that they seek to prevent or minimize losses that may occur as a result of unfavorable price movements.

Hand-to-mouth buying, averaging down, forward buying, and speculative buying all influence the timing of purchases. There are inherent risks in all these approaches, and the purchasing agent cannot be on the "right" side of the market at all times. Instead, a buyer may want to protect the organization from potential loss due to unanticipated price fluctuations of an unstable market. To negate the significance of the timing of purchases on commodities, he can engage in *hedging* in futures markets. When commodities must be purchased long in advance of the final product being available to the market, hedging takes away the risk of profit or loss on inventories and permits the organization to concentrate on its job without worrying about market fluctuations.

Hedging amounts to entering simultaneously into two transactions of a like amount (one a purchase and the other a sale). The buyer enters into a *cash* transaction and a *futures* transaction. The cash transaction is the current exchange of the buyer's cash for the physical commodity; the futures transaction involves the buyer's sale of a futures contract on the item with promised delivery at a specified date in the future. With the passage of time, the cash price and the futures price should fluctuate together, approximately paralleling one another. If prices go up, the buyer realizes an inventory profit on the commodity he bought, but since prices move together in like amount, he will suffer a loss of like amount on the futures contract. If prices go down, the buyer will lose on his cash purchase, but he will gain a like amount on the futures contract. A hedger simply takes one position (purchase or sale) in the cash market and the opposite position (purchase or sale) in the futures market. Hedging provides reasonable assurance that gains or losses in one market will be offset by losses or gains in the other market. Hedging can be viewed as a form of insurance against price risks. It protects against unforeseen major movements in price.

As already mentioned, the significance of purchase timing is dependent upon the type of market in which the purchase is made. In stable markets, purchasing according to current requirements is prevalent. With less stable markets, purchasing is based upon market conditions, and a buyer may hedge his purchase if a futures market exists for the item.

CONTRACTS AND LEGAL CONSIDERATIONS

Once a purchase order is accepted by a vendor, it constitutes a contract for delivery of the items in accordance with the terms of the purchase agreement. This legal document contains many other terms in addition to quantity, quality, delivery, and price. Both federal and state laws influence purchase contracts. Most organizations have printed purchase order forms that comply with the laws under which they operate. To promote fair trade, free from restraint and undue favoritism, statute laws such as the Sherman Act, Clayton Act, and Robinson-Patman Act have been passed and must be understood by purchasing agents.

Purchasing enters into contracts (binding agreements) every day. These written and spoken agreements commit the organization to approximately half of each year's expenditures. The results can be costly unless the organization is legally protected in its transactions. Contracts and legal documents should be drafted by lawyers, and routine commitments approved by legal services.

Few purchasing managers become involved in legal actions, since contractual disputes can normally be resolved without litigation. However, a basic knowledge of relevant legal principles is essential. Without an understanding of the legal implications of the job, legal entanglements become much more likely. Litigation is very expensive, and most organizations utilize it only as a last resort. The purchasing agent should use knowledge of the law in such a way as to avoid litigation.

The functions of procurement involve many legal facets which can only be explained and interpreted by a lawyer. The buyer must know enough about the law to know when to consult an attorney. Lawyers should draft all clauses used for routine purchase orders and approve all nonroutine agreements. The written purchase contract should take precedence over the oral agreement.

While lawsuits involving buyers and sellers are common in commerical transactions, they are surprisingly rare in industrial purchasing. In most cases, industrial buyers and sellers can amicably resolve their disputes through negotiation. A purchasing agent can minimize litigation by investigating a new supplier's ability to perform financial responsibilities and record of performance with other concerns.

The terms and conditions of each purchase contract must be precisely defined to prevent misunderstandings and to avoid potential liabilities. Each purchase contract should be satisfactorily drawn and legally binding on the supplier.

Although there are numerous modifications and subcategories, there are two basic types of purchase contracts. Business and government utilize fixed-price contracts and cost-type contracts. In selecting the best contract to use, the buyer must consider all available contract types and the factors influencing the use of each. The *fixed-price* contract is preferred by most buyers, but rapid change can render it costly and wasteful on some purchases.

When a fair and reasonable price can be established by competition or cost analysis, the fixed-price contract should be used. The financial risks are then borne almost entirely by the supplier, and he has the maximum incentive to produce efficiently. Fixed-price contracts do not always have a firm fixed price. They can include an escalation clause for either an upward or downward change in price as a result of changes in material costs and labor rates. They can also include a redetermination clause when the amount of labor and material are now known precisely. Other fixed-price contracts may have a ceiling price (maximum price) with a variable profit formula whereby every dollar the vendor reduces below his anticipated cost will be shared by the buyer and seller.

Sometimes, a purchase contract is for something that is so novel that neither the buyer or seller knows what the cost will be. Cost-type contracts are then used. The buyer assumes most of the financial risk with this type of contract, which is also known as a cost-plus contract. The supplier is guaranteed all his costs up to a predetermined figure as well as a fee in addition to his costs. The fee may be a percentage of cost, a fixed amount, or an incentive. With a percentage of cost fee, the supplier has the least incentive to control costs. With a fixed amount fee, the supplier receives his defined and itemized costs plus a definite sum of money (called a fixed fee). With an incentive clause, cost reductions below target costs are shared by the buyer and seller.

Because of the variety of contracts, the purchasing agent must exercise care in selecting one. Business practices in specific industries provide clues to the best contract instrument. The specific nature of the goods or services to be procured can often point up advantages of one contract type over another. The type of contract adopted for a purchase can substantially affect pricing. Although it is not always possible, a firm fixed-price contract should be used when conditions permit.

PURCHASE RECORDS

Purchase records provide a history of what has been done in the past, what costs were involved. and who the major suppliers were, as well as the costs, discounts, quality levels, and delivery on specific items. Since purchasing is a repetitive process, accurate records are a necessity for efficient operation. Past experiences in the form of records can contain a wealth of information upon which to base future decisions. Maintaining a good record system will increase operating costs, but it usually costs less than the savings received from aiding the purchasing agents in their buying activities. The unique needs of each purchasing department will dictate the specific structure of its records system. Most purchasing departments maintain the following basic records:

1. purchase order log,
2. open order file,
3. closed order file,
4. vendor record,
5. commodity record,
6. contract file.

The *purchase order log* contains a numerical record of all purchase orders issued. The record is usually not elaborate, but it should contain the purchase order number, the supplier's name, a description of the purchase, and the total value of the order. The log is a convenient record from which to summarize administrative data such as the number of small orders, rush orders, purchases from various suppliers, total orders issued, and so forth.

The *open order file* contains the status of all outstanding orders. Each open folder contains the purchase requisition, purchase order, any contracts, followup data, and correspondence pertaining to the order. The *closed order file* contains a historical record of all completed purchases. The closed order file is a useful reference when historical data are needed to guide future purchases.

The *vendor record* provides quick access to information about suppliers. A separate file is maintained for each supplier. In the file is recorded the supplier's name, address, telephone numbers, and other specific matters relating to the source. Many organizations summarize the vendor's delivery and quality performance. A buyer can obtain a wealth of information about a supplier by referring to the vendor record.

A *commodity record* is maintained on each major material or service that is purchased repetitively. It can be combined into a single file with perpetual inventory records (traveling purchase requisition). The commodity record consists of a separate file for each item, showing orders placed, receipts, and disbursements. The part name, part number, specification, vendor, order quantity, last price, and so forth may also be included in the file.

The *contract file* contains the purchase records of items under a term contract. This file is important if the contract is an open one against which orders may be placed. The contract file also contains special items that are not normally procured by a regular purchase order.

Purchasing work or activities can be analyzed, simplified, and improved by work simplification techniques. Flow charts can be used to analyze purchasing procedures and documentation flow. Improvement and the reduction in the number of forms used will increase efficiency while reducing the cost of the purchasing function. Information may be kept on cards, a ledger, or in computer files. Current trends are toward the mechanization of purchasing records and transactions via computerization.

SURPLUS DISPOSAL

The disposal of surplus materials and equipment is usually assigned to the purchasing department because of its knowledge of the markets. Surplus can result from overprocurement, wasteful production processes, and inefficiencies in general. Surpluses do not necessarily indicate inefficiency, and indeed all organizations have some surplus. It is not uncommon for the sale of surplus materials to represent a significant contribution to cash flow. Surplus materials may come from many sources, such as:

1. scrap,
2. waste,
3. obsolescence,
4. damage or deterioration,
5. forward or speculative buying.

Scrap is the residue of process materials left after efficient production operations have been completed (there are few production processes that utilize 100% of materials). *Waste* is the result of inefficient, careless production and items rejected because of poor quality. *Obsolescence* causes good material to be no longer needed because of design or model changes. *Damaged* or *deteriorated* items occur because of limited shelf life or improper materials handling. Surplus materials also result from overexuberant purchasing practices (forward and speculative buying) that prove to be in error.

Surplus materials and equipment should be sold when there is no longer any need for them. Periodic checks can be made to determine inactivity for each item carried in inventory. Usually, an arbitrary rule on surplus material is adopted, such as that any material not active for a year or two is automatically subject to disposal. With computerized inventory control, it is a simple matter to determine inactive items. These items are investigated, and anything that is surplus is sold for the best possible price. Without computerized inventory control, the process is more awkward and slow, but still very necessary.

Regardless of how efficiently an organization is managed, surplus materials will accumulate, and they must be periodically disposed of. The holding costs of inactive materials can be excessive. For economic reasons, all surplus items should be sold at their best price or discarded. Some of the possible disposal routes are as follows:

1. circulation within the organization,
2. return to supplier,
3. direct sale to another firm,
4. sale to dealer or broker,
5. sale to employees,
6. discard.

The salvage of surplus items can represent a significant contribution to cash flow. Not only does the salvage of items result in additional cash flow; it prevents pollution and serves to conserve raw material resources and energy. It is not uncommon for the excess or scrap items of one organization to be valuable operating items to another.

VALUE ANALYSIS

Value analysis is the organized, systematic study of the function of a material, part, component, or system to identify areas of unnecessary cost that can be eliminated without lessening the capacity of the item to serve its intended function. Value analysis is concerned with function, cost, and value; it attempts to identify savings that can be made in any way. It identifies unnecessary costs that do not add value, and it develops acceptable performance at a lower cost.

Value analysis possesses tremendous income potential. If an organization's after tax income is 10%, then obviously every $100 saved is equivalent to $1,000 sold. It can be far easier to save $100 than to sell $1,000 more. Thus, slight changes in material costs can exert a great influence (leverage) on an organization's income.

Value analysis measures the functional usefulness of items, processes, or procedures so the greatest value is obtained for the money spent. Better value is obtained by improving the functional aspect without increasing the cost, or by reducing the cost without impairing the function. The emphasis is not only on cost (paying the least for what you get), but on value (getting the most for what you pay). A typical value analysis of an item would ask a series of questions: What is it? What is its function? What does it cost? What is it worth? What else could perform the function? Can it be simplified? Is it necessary? This approach usually uncovers areas for improvement through substitution, elimination, standardization, combination, or simplification.

The value analyst seeks to improve performance by quality-price analysis, market-supplier analysis, and design-process analysis. *Quality-price analysis* seeks the minimum price for an item that meets the minimum quality standards. Extra quality in an item beyond performance requirements usually involves an extra cost, so a quality reduction may result in cost savings. *Market-supplier analysis* focuses on finding the lowest cost supplier consistent with quality and service requirements. *Design-process analysis* determines if an item is adequately designed for the function it performs, or if the item lends itself to more economic manufacture by standard production techniques.

Design-process analysis and quality-price analysis entail a methodical step-by-step study of all facets of the design of a given item in relation to the function it performs. The use of standardized parts, methods, and procedures is one goal. The value analyst determines which functions are necessary and how they might be fulfilled if different materials, tools, supplies, and processes were used. Competitive or substitute products are examined to see how they perform the same or similar functions.

Value analysis is used to detect items whose prices appear excessive and to uncover items whose costs are disproportionate to the function served. A design-process analysis may result in a new design, substitute materials, or improved production techniques. A market-supplier analysis may result in a substitute product or a revised product design. All of the analyses will be used in the make-or-buy decision. Although purchasing will probably not make the final decision by itself, it does play an integral part in the decision and accumulates the facts for it.

Value analysis can be very effective in dealing with shortages of materials. Emphasis is placed on the availability of alternatives or substitutes. The following checklist can be helpful when dealing with shortages:

1. Have suppliers been consulted for alternatives or modifications?
2. Have unusual forms of material (common and available) been considered?
3. Have technology developments rendered parts or processes unnecessary?
4. Is every item absolutely necessary?
5. Can a different item do the job?
6. Are wider tolerance ranges feasible?
7. Can items or subassemblies be combined?
8. Can a single item serve more than one function?
9. Can processes be combined?
10. Is the item overdesigned?
11. Are specifications and standards too tight?

Value analysis concentrates on cost reduction associated with product and materials redesign, revision of specifications, more effective purchase or conversion of materials, make-or-buy reanalysis, and related material cost saving activities. Value analysis pertains mainly to existing products, but it can be expanded to new or proposed products. It searches for alternative products, procedures, sources, techniques, and processes for improving performance.

Both large and small institutions are adopting value analysis. It may reside in purchasing or production. In smaller organizations it may be handled by a committee or team with representatives from the various organizational areas.

CONCLUSION

The role of purchasing and procurement in modern organizations has increased substantially in the last few decades. Material costs are frequently the largest proportion of a product's total cost. Inflation, shortages, and unstable markets make purchasing decisions important influences on overall performance of an organization. No longer can purchasing be considered a routine service function where money is spent and not made. Purchasing is a cost-saving or profit-making organizational function.

The typical steps involved in the purchasing process include (1) obtaining information on products and their specifications, (2) finding suitable suppliers, (3) obtaining competitive bids or negotiating with suppliers, (4) analyzing bids and proposals, (5) preparing purchase orders, (6) expediting and following up orders, (7) verifying proper receipt of material and invoice validation, (8) processing claims, and (9) disposing of surplus materials and equipment.

The purchasing department must be staffed by qualified, well-trained personnel. Professional training beyond that obtained on the job is important. Capable people can make a significant difference. The goal should not be to operate the purchasing department at the lowest cost. It should be to attain organizational objectives at the lowest cost. The buying clerk should be replaced by the value-conscious purchasing agent skilled in the latest techniques of materials management.

QUESTIONS

1. Why is it more beneficial to view purchasing through the purchasing function rather than through the purchasing cycle?

2. Explain what is meant by the "leverage of purchased goods and services."

3. Describe the various forms that purchase requisitions and product specifications may take.

4. What constraints other than resource limitations can confine the alternatives available to the purchasing manager? What is the most important resource limitation? Why?

5. Identify the types of purchasing procedures commonly adopted for items used continuously, large single orders, small-value purchases, and normal purchases (or items not fitting any of the other three categories listed).

6. What usually is the major factor involved in a make-or-buy decision?

7. Name some of the relevant factors considered in supplier selection. List some places where information about supplier performance on relevant factors can be obtained.

8. Give a brief account of the three approaches frequently used to determine purchase prices.

9. In what particular production situations is quality considered more important than price?

10. Name the three criteria that are established when shipping terms are specified.

11. In what industries is reciprocal buying most often found? What are its pitfalls?

12. Outline the bases on which the most familiar types of price discounts are given.

13. What conditions would be favorable for each of the following buying policies: hand-to-mouth buying, averaging down, forward buying, and speculative purchasing?

14. When should fixed-price and cost-type contracts be used?

15. Differentiate among the categories of surplus materials. Does the presence of surplus necessarily indicate inefficiency?

16. Define value analysis.

17. Each consumer is really a purchasing agent when he spends his funds. Suggest some practical purchasing practices that might lower the cost of operating the single family unit.

PROBLEMS

1. A manufacturing firm is adding an optional accessory to its product line and is faced with a make-or-buy decision. The cost accounting section has provided the following data:

Unit cost item	Existing plant capacity available	Expanded plant capacity
Variable mfg.	$3.40	$3.40
Additional plant & equipment	.00	.60
Additional factory overhead	.00	.10

A local manufacturer will supply the item at a delivered price of $3.80. Should the item be purchased if idle plant capacity is available? Should the item be purchased if the plant must be expanded?

2. An instrument manufacturer has decided to add a carrying case to its list of optional equipment. A local supplier has offered to supply a satisfactory case for $7.20 each. The sales projections and cost accounting data are shown below. If the existing plant capacity for the case is 6000 units, should the firm make or buy the case?

Sales (units)	Probability
3,000	.15
5,000	.40
8,000	.30
10,000	.15

Unit cost item	Existing plant capacity available	Expanded plant capacity
Variable mfg.	$5.80	$4.80
Additional plant & equipment	.00	1.50
Additional factory overhead	.20	1.20

3. One method of comparing suppliers is by a weighted-point plan. A total of 100 points are allocated among those factors considered important. The supplier with the largest number of weighted points is the most desirable. One organization uses the following weights to compare suppliers: quality 40 points, price 35 points, and service 25 points. Based on the data listed below, rank the three suppliers by the weighted-point plan.

Supplier	Shipments received	Shipments accepted	Unit price	Fraction of commitments fulfilled
A	500	480	$1.00	0.94
B	600	560	.96	0.90
C	80	78	1.20	1.00

4. From the following information compare the four suppliers by the weighted-point plan. The quality weight is 40, the price weight is 35, and the service weight is 25.

Supplier	Shipments received	Shipments accepted	Unit price	Fraction of commitments fulfilled
A	200	192	$.89	0.98
B	240	220	.86	0.90
C	60	48	.93	0.95
D	10	9	.90	1.00

5. What is the equivalent annual interest rate that would be lost if a firm failed to take the cash discount under the following terms:
   (a) 1/15, net 30.
   (b) 2/10, net 60.
   (c) 3/10, net 60.
   (d) 2/10, net 40.
   (e) 1/10, net 30.
   (f) 1/10, net 40.

6. Would you make or buy the item in the following example? It can be purchased for $22,000. The organization can make it for $25,000 with the following cost breakdown:

Materials	$7,500
Labor	3,750
Variable overhead	10,000
Fixed overhead	3,750
Total	$25,000

The plant is operating well below capacity and could easily make the item.

7. An organization that requires 2200 units of a product has received quotes from three suppliers of the product. From the information given below, determine the supplier with the lowest total cost (assume all cash discounts are taken).

	Firm A	Firm B	Firm C
Cost/unit	$.75 each up to 1,000 .65 each, next 500 .50 each over 1,500	$.70 each up to 2,000 .50 each over 2,000	$.72 each (no minimum)
Freight cost	$10.00/100 units	$5.00/100 units	F.O.B. buyer's plant
Cost discount	2/10 net 60	3/10 net 60	1/10 net 60

8. If the organization in Problem 7 cannot take advantage of the cash discount, what supplier should be chosen?

9. An organization must expand its facility and is negotiating with two contractors. One contractor offers a fixed-price contract for $925,000. The other offers a cost-plus 15% profit contract. The estimated cost of the facility is as follows:

Estimated cost	Probability
$700,000	.10
750,000	.20
800,000	.40
900,000	.30

Which contract should be selected?

10. A purchasing agent has received bids from three suppliers of an identical item. The freight cost for the item is standardized at $50 per hundred miles. Which supplier will result in the lowest total cost?

	Supplier		
	X	Y	Z
Unit cost	$5000	$4800	$4900
Shipping distance	300 miles	500 miles	800 miles
Shipment terms	F.O.B. buyer's plant	F.O.B. seller's plant	F.O.B. seller's plant (freight allowed)

CASE 1: THE PAPYRUS EXCHANGE

Papyrus Products is in the forefront of the school and office supplies industry. The company, which easily surpasses $200 million in sales annually, specializes in converting paper, metals, and other widely assorted materials into a product mix that spans ordinary bookstore items such as looseleaf binders and metal furnishings such as work station and storage pieces for data information centers. Papyrus produces in five manufacturing divisions which also operate as strategic distribution centers. The output from the manufacturing divisions is shipped as components to other manufacturing divisions or as finished goods to Papyrus's commercial and consumer mass markets.

Full operational planning and accountability are held at the divisional production level. Taking a look at just one of the operating divisions partially discloses the scope of Papyrus's manufacturing and distribution system. The Metalworks Division, the largest division still essentially captive to the company's manufacturing needs, has:

1. several hundred employees on three shift operations,
2. high speed fabrication equipment and several state-of-the-art assembly machines,
3. 40 separate work centers (stations) situated along standard assembly lines,
4. in-house fabrication of over 2000 parts supported by over 500 externally purchased items,
5. average inventory of $1.3 million in steel and assorted wire raw materials,
6. annual raw material purchases of 10,000 tons (annual raw material turnover of 3.0),
7. the status of major supplier to the Papyrus Bindery Division and secondary supplier to outside original equipment manufacturers,
8. a local purchasing staff.

These attributes make purchased material control and inventory control difficult. Divisional buyers have trouble forecasting raw materials, planning estimated purchase commitments, and following up on orders. The purchasing function in essence is executed through informal channels. Purchasing personnel have to be long on experience; it is only through familiarity with the system that the cost of materials is held down at all or that material is ever slated for on-time delivery.

The preponderance of buyers' efforts is directed toward purchase order modification—otherwise termed "expediting." Because the buyers spend the majority of their time launching and expediting orders, there is little time left for monitoring the commodity marketplace or in-depth analysis of outside vendor capabilities or capacities. For order writing the single most popular tool of the buyers is the discrete purchase order; as a rule, the purchasing staffs negotiate few annual contracts and only isolated blanket purchase orders.

Much of the information input to the purchasing function is output from the production planning process. An unmethodical master scheduling process at the production planning level precedes a single level product explosion. The master scheduled items are "exploded" all at once into an aggregation of the components required for their manufacture. Every component is given a priority based on the final product's manufacture, and no account is taken of subassembly or fabrication phases in the designation of priorities. The component requirements are interpreted as purchase requisitions when sent to the purchasing staff, and the buyers place orders for required components with other production divisions and/or external suppliers. Besides providing buyers with requisition outputs from the planning process, divisional production planners (usually through shop floor control) inform buyers when materials difficulties arise. The buyers must schedule or reschedule orders with vendors in response to these problems—communicating changes back and forth between production planners and vendors and using the planning schedules and reissue notices as primary communication vehicles.

In the eyes of the vendors, they are given too short and too unreliable down-range information. This is leading them to assume that most due dates are invalid in the first place. Feeling that they have scant time to reschedule their own operations, the vendors sense no real pressure to deliver on time. In the microperspective of the buyers, they are forced to "fire fight" lead time surprises sprung from the vendors. The buyers generalize that the vendors are developing the "galloping lead time syndrome" (a pattern of protracting lead times when faced with requests and changes). The buyers feel at the mercy of vendor whims. Sensing that they have neither the time nor the need to attend to alternate suppliers, the buyers self-defensively try to maintain good relations with the present vendors.

The upshot is that the production planner/buyer/vendor's main function—to support the manufacturing task—is being performed at too high a cost. Both administrative and production materials costs are grossly excessive. Currently, measurement of plan versus actual is not shared with vendors, on-time performance of vendors is not kept, nor is budgeting under tight control. Papyrus management feels that if current measurements are shared and other measurements of critical areas are kept, those involved in the acquisition, delivery, and use of materials will be forced into self-improvement once their poor performance is discovered and made public. If there is no self-generated improvement, the company plans to resort to a material cost cutting project whereby temporary buying teams are set up from within or outside of purchasing in an attempt to improve deliveries and materials costs as a short-term treatment.

1. Why might costs be too high? Outline the problems and their symptoms.
2. What would you advise for Papyrus in regard to materials acquisitions? Comment on the company plan and/or devise your own.
3. What improvements could be expected from your response to question 2?

CASE 2: A BREAK WITH TRADITION

Foreign competitive challenges are directing the attention of Bygone Industries toward the ideal of "stockless" production, i.e. manufacturing with virtually no buffers of in-process or raw materials inventory. At first the prospect of "stockless" production seemed thoroughly impractical to the organization's production analysts. For years Bygone analysts followed the timeworn principle that repetitive manufacturing should be done in long, infrequent production runs with buffer stocks inserted between stations and fabrication processes to cushion the shocks of irregularities and cut down on costly setups. Concurring skeptical impressions were voiced by the company's purchasing/inventory staff, who built a functional strategy upon an EOQ cornerstone—laying the classic model in place as the fundamental basis for ordering (producing) in lot sizes large enough to offset ordering (setup) costs.

After practicing Western large-lot production and economic lot acquisition for over a decade, only hard evidence could induce these skeptics to abandon their venerated principles. Both purchasing and production staffs were alarmed to find that Bygone typically carries $800 of in-process inventory for each unit produced, compared to an average of $170 per unit manufactured at a "stockless" production facility, and holds almost a 30 day supply of major parts, compared to a 2 or 3 day supply held by foreign counterparts. Operating efficiently with such low levels of inventory seemed impossible until managers were shown examples of facilities which strive for "zero" lead times and "zero" inventory as a consequence of a "pull-type" system of production/inventory control (a system in which requirements of the final assembly operation draw material along—see Chapter 18 for further explanation). Since becoming informed of competitors' successes with just-in-time production and the integrated procedures for accomplishing the JIT approach, Bygone management is committing itself to a JIT experiment.

As indicated, present operations at Bygone are far afield of the piece-at-a-time flows underway in JIT repetitive manufacturing. Bygone typifies many American MRP approaches (those which utilize the system's basic logic but take liberties with its execution). End items (product models) are scheduled in job lots for delivery in a given week. The master production schedule is exploded into parts requirements properly offset for lead times. Since high setup costs always have dictated making at least one week's supply of any item or component at one time, there are sizable lot-size inventories at every level of the product structure. Lot sizing at every stage of the process increases Bygone's inventory levels and leaves irregular lot quantities for further processing.

Production schedule cycles for product models seldom are repetitive. Only eight days of a planned schedule usually is firm, and the final assembly schedule used to determine actual production is set only three days in advance. Because of the high scrap rate for production parts, spare parts production also is thrust into the final schedules with little advance notice. The mixture of material called for on an average production day often varies by 25% or more from the requirements originally planned. Therefore, order expediting is a common practice of the purchasing staff; purchasing agents stand ready to shift priorities to cover larger or new requirements for any particular item.

The purchasing staff generally deals with large suppliers who are fiercely competitive for Bygone's business. Bygone takes advantage of the competition and uses multiple sourcing for most of its purchased parts, especially for parts critically hard to produce or for which delivery is sometimes difficult. Bygone buyers feel that they have good relations with suppliers due to the market forces. Most suppliers are amenable to Bygone's strictly dictated parts specifications and frequent specification changes. Bygone sets quality standards for each purchased part, and the suppliers themselves determine the means by which they will meet the established quality levels. When specifications are extremely hard to meet or just recently changed, most suppliers are quick to take back any inferior or noncompliant parts. Furthermore, the suppliers are a willing market for the materials which endlessly accumulate as scrap.

The total number of suppliers that Bygone uses surpasses 1000. Fortunately, those located the greatest distance away are all within a centralized industrial area. Because of Bygone's advanced software developments, the buyers can track materials over wide geographical areas and monitor the progress of even its most scattered suppliers. Additionally, the close communications allow Bygone to consolidate orders from suppliers grouped in certain regions through its sophisticated trafficking system. Bygone transmits purchase orders (usually for economic lot sizes) and shipping date requests electronically to its major suppliers and uses the trafficking system to synchronize some of the supplier activity for transportation reasons.

None of the Bygone suppliers runs on "stockless" production, and few of the members of the Bygone workforce have even heard of the term. Bygone management is making the first hints about "stockless" production to its employees and vendors, even though it already has rethought the course of the organization's future. While eager to embark on the promising experiment which lies ahead, the Western industrialists are beginning slowly, aware that old habits and cherished principles can die hard.

1. What technological and organizational problems might help or hinder reaching a goal of "stockless" production?
2. Describe a purchase/supply system that theoretically could support "stockless" production.
3. What preliminary or modest improvements could be made at Bygone to move (even slowly) in the stated direction?

SELECTED BIBLIOGRAPHY

Aljian, G. W., ed. *Purchasing Handbook,* New York: McGraw-Hill, 1973.

Ammer, D. S. *Materials Management,* Homewood, IL: Irwin, 3rd ed., 1980.

Ballot, R. P. *Materials Management,* New York: American Management Associations, 1971.

Dobler, D. W. et al. *Purchasing and Materials Management,* New York: McGraw-Hill, 1984.

Heinritz, S. F. and P. V. Farrell. *Purchasing Principles and Applications,* Englewood Cliffs, NJ: Prentice-Hall, 1971.

Lee Jr., L. and D. W. Dobler. *Purchasing and Materials Management,* New York: McGraw-Hill, 1977.

Leenders, M. R. et al. *Purchasing and Materials Management,* Homewood, IL: Irwin, 7th ed., 1980.

Schary, P. B. *Logistics Decisions,* Chicago: Dryden Press, 1984.

Tersine, R. J. and J. H. Campbell. *Modern Materials Management,* New York: North Holland, 1977.

Westing, J. E. et al. *Purchasing: Materials in Motion,* New York: Wiley, 1969.

22
Quality Control

CONTROL CHARTS
- Control Charts for Variables
- Control Charts for Attributes

ACCEPTANCE SAMPLING
- Operating Characteristic (OC) Curves
- Average Outgoing Quality (AOQ)
- Double Sampling Plans
- Sequential Sampling Plans

QUALITY CIRCLES

CONCLUSION

QUESTIONS

PROBLEMS

CASES

SELECTED BIBLIOGRAPHY

Organizations usually compete for customers on the basis of price, availability, and quality. Quality of products is an important consumer concern. Poor quality is unproductive and costly because of the initial cost of producing defectives, the cost of inspecting and reworking or scrapping products, and the potential cost of customer ill will. Loss of customer confidence occasioned by poor quality can have serious consequences for an organization. Public institutions such as universities, hospitals, and governments are also subject to quality problems. Management's responsibility is to establish standards on appropriate quality levels for their products and to design quality control systems to ensure compliance.

Quality can be interpreted in several ways. Consumers tend to view quality from three dimensions—appearance (how it looks), operation (how well it functions), and reliability (how long it will function). Quality begins with product design, continues through the transformation processes, and can extend to use after delivery to the customers. Organizations tend to be concerned with design quality, performance quality, and production (conformance) quality. Quality of design and performance was introduced in Chapter 7 on product decisions. The focus of this chapter is on production quality, which also is called quality of conformance or quality control.

The quality of a product is the result of many management decisions. Tradeoffs must be made among theoretical perfection, low selling price, and manufacturing capabilities as well as many other factors. A firm must decide what the characteristics of a product should be, and then have the engineers design a product that embodies these characteristics. The engineers must describe the product's design in drawings and specifications that can be understood in the factory. From these requirements, limits of acceptability can be established for incoming raw materials, processes, and outgoing final products. The quality control function in depicted in Figure 1.

Quality is a measure of how closely a good or service conforms to specified standards. The standards may relate to time, performance, materials, reliability, or any quantifiable characteristic of the product. The established limits of acceptability for a product are the basis for the control of quality. The determinants of product quality are design specifications, raw materials, manufacturing processes, and employee workmanship. Usually quality is designed in and not added on in the processes.

The purposes of quality control usually are to

FIGURE 1
The quality control function.

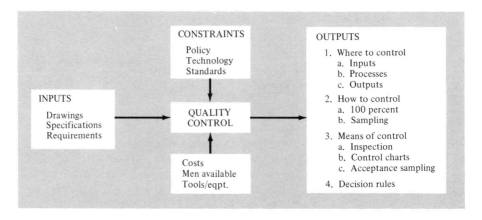

1. maintain design standards,
2. meet customer specifications,
3. spotlight and correct process discrepancies,
4. determine department and personnel effectiveness,
5. find and correct defective products.

The major sources of quality discrepancies are poor product design, defective raw materials, inadequate machines and tools, inadequate environment (noise, lighting, vibration), and human error (boredom, low skill, mistakes, fatigue). Quality control can do little about a poor product design, but it can influence the other sources of deviation. Quality control strives to maintain conformance to predetermined product specifications and performance standards. A typical quality control system is illustrated in Figure 2.

Quality control checks for conformance. It may range from inspection of all items to only a few items. With 100% inspection every item is checked for conformance, with sampling, less than every item. Most organizations use both sampling and 100% inspection to varying degrees. One hundred percent inspection can be costly and time consuming, but it is necessary where risks of unacceptable quality are high. One hundred percent inspection frequently is not desirable, because it may be destructive, expensive, and not even necessarily error-free, and it may induce poor performance in the belief that poor work will be detected later. Sampling is less fatiguing and may result in fewer errors in judgment that 100% inspection. In some cases, it is believed that the monotony of inspecting every item may result in passing more defective items than would random sampling. The amount of inspection to be used will depend on the type of product, the process variability, the variability of materials, and the nature of the inspection. Cost tradeoffs are important considerations.

The timing, location, and amount of inspection should be governed by the expected cost or probable loss from passing defectives at any stage of a process. The-

FIGURE 2
The quality control system.

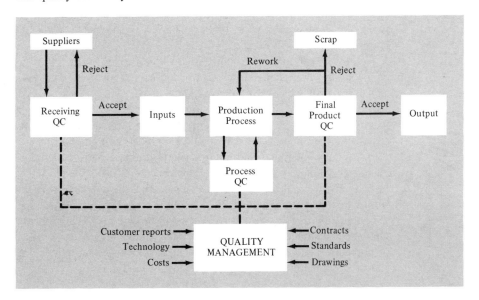

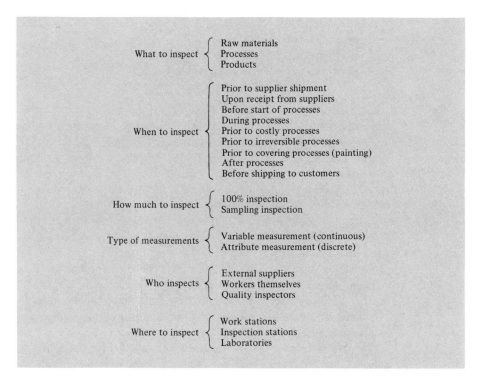

FIGURE 3
Inspection decisions.

oretically, the optimum amount of inspection is when the cost of inspection plus the expected cost of not inspecting is at a minimum. The precise determination of where an inspection should occur can be made from operation process and flow process charts outlined in Chapter 9 on process and operation design. Some organizations, particularly those using just-in-time production, establish quality programs with their suppliers, so inspection of incoming materials is eliminated. Typical inspection decisions are outlined in Figure 3.

Control over quality is established in three general ways: (1) control the quality of incoming raw materials, (2) control the actual processes that make the product, and (3) control the level of the outgoing final product. Usually quality control involves all three in some combination. The general set of methods for controlling incoming raw materials and outgoing final products is known as acceptance sampling. Process control is usually maintained by control charts.

Acceptance sampling and control charts are powerful statistical weapons in the pursuit of quality control. Statistical quality control deals mainly with the analysis of samples and the making of inferences concerning the characteristics of the population from which they are drawn. If the sample is a random sample in which each item in the population has an equal chance of being selected, then inferences about the population can be made from the sample. Statistical quality control is based on the theory of probability and is an application of management by exception. The basic categories of statistical quality control are shown in Figure 4.

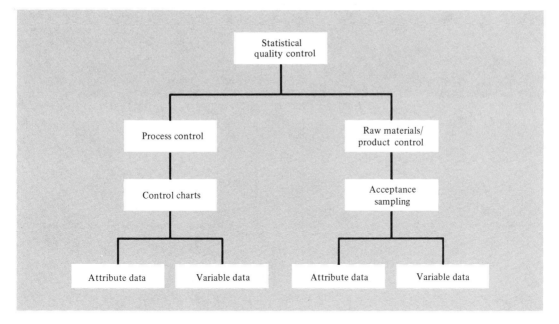

FIGURE 4
Statistical quality control classification.

CONTROL CHARTS

In contrast to acceptance sampling, control charts measure variation of a process during operations, rather than the acceptability of materials or products before or after operations. Control charts help to ensure that only acceptable products are produced by monitoring the process average so it stays within upper and lower statistical limits. If the process average falls outside the acceptable limits, the process is deemed out of control and corrective action is taken.

Variations occur in a process due to chance variations and assignable causes. *Chance variations* occur at random, and little can be done about them. Variations due to *assignable causes* are relatively large and can be traced. Control charts are maintained so that variations due to assignable causes can be detected and changes made to correct their influence. Assignable causes are differences among workers, machines, and materials as well as any combination of these factors. Control charts are graphic aids for detecting assignable cause variations in the output from a process.

A control chart looks like a distribution turned on its side, with each subsequent sample plotted against time. Control charts are used to determine process capabilities, monitor process outputs, and warn of deviating process conditions. Statistical control theory is designed to separate large assignable cause variations from chance cause variations. When a process is in a state of control, variations that occur are due only to chance variations and tend to be normally distributed. When variations due to one or more assignable causes are superimposed, it becomes obvious that something basic has changed.

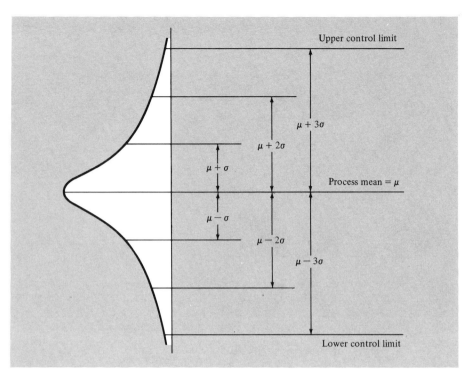

FIGURE 5
Control chart—normal distribution.

Control charts are constructed for sample means rather than for individual measurements. One important reason is the central limit theorem, which allows a distribution to depart radically from normality but states that the distribution of means of random samples will be approximately normal if the sample size is large. For a normal distribution, precise statements can be made about the probability of occurrence associated with measurements that are a given number of standard deviations (σ) from the mean (μ). Specifically:

68.26% of the values normally fall within $\mu \pm \sigma$,

95.45% of the values normally fall within $\mu \pm 2\sigma$,

99.73% of the values normally fall within $\mu \pm 3\sigma$.

The natural tolerance of a process is frequently taken as $\mu \pm 3\sigma$ (see Figure 5). The selection of control limits is a management policy decision. If the penalty is high for not recognizing when a process is out of control, it is desirable to utilize less than $\pm 3\sigma$ limits. As long as the sample mean stays within the control limits, the process is allowed to continue without interference. If a point falls outside one of the control limits, the variation is attributed to an assignable cause and the process is discontinued until corrective action is taken.

Control charts are usually kept right at the work station. A worker or an inspector checks a small sample periodically and plots its mean on a chart. The range or possibly the standard deviation may also be posted. If any of the measures are beyond the permissible limits, the process is unacceptable and the operation should be

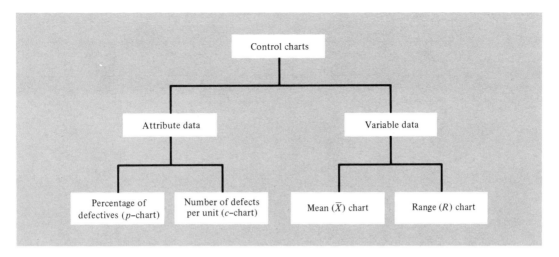

FIGURE 6
Control chart classifications.

stopped. If they are still within limits, but are steadily getting closer to one limit or the other, the operation may soon be turning out inferior work (maybe the tools are wearing or a machine may be getting out of adjustment).

Before we proceed, it is worthwhile to differentiate between attribute and variable data. *Attribute data* deal with a yes or no (go or no go, pass or fail) criterion; they are obtained by counting or classification. *Variable data* deal with a measurement of how much, how big, how thick, how round, and so forth. It is necessary to make this distinction because attributes and variables require different statistical procedures. Attributes deal with the percentage of defectives or number of defects per unit, while variables deal with averages of measurements and with the extent of deviations. Since attributes are obtained by counting, they form a discrete distribution and usually are treated by the binomial or Poisson distribution. Variables, which are obtained by measurement, have a continuous distribution, and are usually treated by the normal distribution.

The two basic types of statistical control charts are control charts for variables and control charts for attributes. The best-known control charts for variables record the process average $\overline{X}$ and the range R. The $\overline{X}$ charts show how the means of samples compare with the process mean; the R charts record the variability of individual readings within a sample. The best-known control charts for attributes include charts for the percentage of defectives (p-charts) and charts for the number of defects per unit (c-charts). The basic categories of control charts are shown in Figure 6.

CONTROL CHARTS FOR VARIABLES

In most production situations both the range and the mean can change. Therefore, it is necessary to maintain both a mean chart and a range chart for effective quality control. The $\overline{X}$ chart monitors the *accuracy* of a process, while the R chart monitors the *precision* of a process. Lack of accuracy is revealed by excessive variability between samples, and lack of precision by excessive variability within samples. Control charts for variables are based on the normal distribution.

TABLE 1
Control limit factors ($\pm 3\sigma$)

Sample size n	(Mean factor) A	(Upper range factor) B	(Lower range factor) C
2	1.880	3.267	0
3	1.023	2.575	0
4	0.729	2.282	0
5	0.577	2.115	0
6	0.483	2.004	0
7	0.419	1.924	0.076
8	0.373	1.864	0.136
9	0.337	1.816	0.184
10	0.308	1.777	0.223
11	0.285	1.774	0.256
12	0.266	1.716	0.284
13	0.249	1.692	0.308
14	0.235	1.671	0.329
15	0.223	1.652	0.348
20	0.180	1.586	0.414
25	0.153	1.541	0.459

In practice, the calculation of control limits is simplified by the use of the range rather than the standard deviation. The range is an easier obtained measure of variability than the standard deviation. It can be used with a table of factors to obtain upper and lower control limits. These predetermined factors are based upon the sample size (n) as shown in Table 1. The A factor is used for sample means, while the B and C factors are applied to sample ranges. The $\bar{X}$ and R control charts are constructed as follows:

$$\text{upper control limit for the mean} = \bar{\bar{X}} + A\bar{R},$$
$$\text{center line for the mean} = \bar{\bar{X}},$$
$$\text{lower control limit for the mean} = \bar{\bar{X}} - A\bar{R},$$
$$\text{upper control limit for the range} = B\bar{R},$$
$$\text{center line for the range} = \bar{R},$$
$$\text{lower control limit for the range} = C\bar{R},$$

where

$$\bar{X} = \frac{\Sigma X}{n} = \text{sample mean},$$
$$\bar{\bar{X}} = \frac{\Sigma \bar{X}}{N} = \text{grand mean},$$
$$\bar{R} = \frac{\Sigma R}{N} = \text{mean range},$$
$$X = \text{a single observation},$$

$$n = \text{size of sample,}$$

$$N = \text{number of samples,}$$

$$R = \text{range for a sample,}$$

$$A, B, C = \text{factors for control limits.}$$

If any future samples fall outside the control limits, it is probable that there is an assignable cause for the unusual observation. The cause of the variation should be identified and corrected.

EXAMPLE 1

From the information in the following table, develop the 3σ control limits for the mean and the range (the observations are stopwatch readings of the time required to perform a repetitive task).

Sample no.	Observation (seconds)					Sample mean $\bar{X}$	Sample range R
	a	b	c	d	e		
1	772	802	779	721	777	770	81
2	756	787	733	742	734	750	54
3	756	773	722	760	745	751	51
4	744	780	754	774	774	765	36
5	802	726	748	758	744	756	76
6	783	807	791	762	757	780	50
7	747	766	753	758	767	758	20
8	788	750	784	769	762	771	38
9	757	747	741	746	747	748	16
10	750	730	740	725	745	738	25
11	716	730	752	735	751	737	36
12	746	727	763	734	730	740	36
13	749	762	778	787	771	769	38
14	771	767	787	772	763	772	24
15	771	758	769	770	771	768	13
16	767	769	767	794	789	777	27
Total						12,150	621

$$\bar{\bar{X}} = \frac{12{,}150}{16} = 759,$$

$$\bar{R} = \frac{621}{16} = 39;$$

upper control limit for mean $= \bar{\bar{X}} + A\bar{R} = 759 + (0.577)(39) = 782,$

lower control limit for mean $= \bar{\bar{X}} - A\bar{R} = 759 - (0.577)(39) = 736,$

upper control limit for range $= B\bar{R} = (2.115)(39) = 82,$

lower control limit for range $= C\bar{R} = 0.$

continued

EXAMPLE 1— *continued*

The control limits for the mean are from 736 to 782 seconds. The control limits for the range are from 0 to 82 seconds. If any of the sample means or ranges had fallen outside the control limits, it would have been necessary to recalculate the limits with those samples deleted. In the example above, this situation did not occur.

Sometimes the computed lower control limit for a control chart is negative. Then the effective lower limit is zero.

CONTROL CHARTS FOR ATTRIBUTES

Control charts for attributes on the percentage of defectives occurring are based on the binomial distribution. Control charts for attributes on the number of defects per unit are based on the Poisson distribution. A p-chart is used when individual items are judged acceptable or defective. A c-chart is appropriate when the quality is measured by the number of defects in a constant unit of output. The p-chart and c-chart are constructed in the following manner:

For percentage of defectives,

$$\text{upper control limit} = \bar{p} + 3s_p,$$

$$\text{center line} = \bar{p},$$

$$\text{lower control limit} = \bar{p} - 3s_p.$$

For number of defects per unit,

$$\text{upper control limit} = \bar{c} + 3s_c,$$

$$\text{center line} = \bar{c},$$

$$\text{lower control limit} = \bar{c} - 3s_c.$$

where

$$\bar{p} = \frac{\Sigma p}{N} = \text{average percentage of defectives,}$$

$$s_p = \sqrt{\frac{\bar{p}(100 - \bar{p})}{n}} = \text{standard error of the percentage,}$$

$$\bar{c} = \frac{\Sigma c}{N} = \text{average number of defects per unit,}$$

$$s_c = \sqrt{\bar{c}} = \text{standard error of the defects per unit,}$$

p = percent of defectives in a sample,

n = sample size,

N = number of samples,

c = number of defects per unit in a sample.

If any future samples fall outside the control limits, it is probable that there is an assignable cause for the unusual observation. The cause of the variation should be identified and corrected. In most cases, the sample size is fixed. When the sample size n is variable, it is necessary to calculate different control limits to account for the effect of n on the standard error.

EXAMPLE 2

Fifteen samples of 50 observations each yield the information in the table below. Determine the 3σ control limits for the percentage of defectives.

Sample no.	Sample size n	Number of defectives np	Percent defective p
1	50	4	8
2	50	2	4
3	50	1	2
4	50	4	8
5	50	5	10
6	50	1	2
7	50	1	2
8	50	2	4
9	50	3	6
10	50	3	6
11	50	1	2
12	50	4	8
13	50	2	4
14	50	2	4
15	50	3	6
Total	750	38	76

$$\bar{p} = \frac{76}{15} = 5.1\%,$$

$$s_p = \sqrt{\frac{\bar{p}(100 - \bar{p})}{n}} = \sqrt{\frac{(5.1)(94.9)}{50}} = 3.11,$$

upper control limit = $\bar{p} + 3s_p$ = 5.1 + 3(3.11) = 14.4%,

lower control limit = $\bar{p} - 3s_p$ = 5.1 - 3(3.11) < 0.

The process average is 5.1% with control limits from 0 to 14.4%.

EXAMPLE 3

Ten assemblies were inspected, and the defects per assembly are shown in the table below. Determine the 3σ control limits for the defects per assembly.

Sample no.	Defects per assembly, c
1	6
2	4
3	1
4	4
5	8
6	0
7	2
8	0
9	4
10	3
Total	32

$$\bar{c} = \frac{32}{10} = 3.2,$$
$$s_c = \sqrt{\bar{c}} = 1.79,$$
$$\text{upper control limit} = \bar{c} + 3s_c = 3.2 + 3(1.79) = 8.57,$$
$$\text{lower control limit} = \bar{c} - 3s_c = 3.2 - 3(1.79) < 0.$$

The process average is 3.2 defects with control limits from 0 to 8.57 defects per assembly.

The following table summarizes the major quality control charts based on plus and minus three standard deviations.

Type	Central line	UCL	LCL	Distribution	Data
$\bar{X}$	$\bar{\bar{X}}$	$\bar{\bar{X}} + A\bar{R}$	$\bar{\bar{X}} - A\bar{R}$	Normal	Variable
R	$\bar{R}$	$B\bar{R}$	$C\bar{R}$	Normal	Variable
p	$\bar{p}$	$\bar{p} + 3s_p$	$\bar{p} - 3s_p$	Binomial	Attribute
c	$\bar{c}$	$\bar{c} + 3s_c$	$\bar{c} - 3s_c$	Poisson	Attribute

Attribute inspection normally requires less time and skill to make. It usually uses lower cost equipment than the exact measurements of variable inspection. Thus, control charts for attributes tend to be less expensive than control charts for variables. However, larger sample sizes are required for attribute inspection.

ACCEPTANCE SAMPLING

Acceptance sampling determines whether to accept or reject an entire lot of goods. It may be used at any point in an operation, but it is most often found in incoming inspection of vendor goods and outgoing inspection of the final product. In the simplest form of acceptance sampling, a random sample of size n is drawn from the total lot of size N. The decision to accept or reject the lot is based on the number of defectives in the sample. If the sample signals a decision to reject the lot, the lot may be subjected to 100% inspection and defective items discarded. In general, acceptance sampling is appropriate when

1. inspection destroys the product,
2. handling is likely to induce defects,
3. time does not permit 100% inspection,
4. the cost of inspecting is high, and the loss due to passing defective items is small,
5. fatigue or boredom from 100% inspection leads to errors.

Just as in statistical control charts, acceptance sampling procedures are available for sampling by attributes (classifying items as good or bad) and sampling by variables (actually taking measurements of some kind). Inspection and recording costs will normally be higher with variable sampling. However, for a given level of protection, variable sampling will require smaller samples and less total inspection than does attribute sampling. These smaller sample sizes can be very important when the inspection process destroys the part. The data generated by variable sampling provide more valuable diagnostic information for controlling production processes. The major disadvantage of variable sampling is that a separate acceptance plan must be developed for each variable being measured. In attribute sampling, numerous types of defects can be lumped together into one acceptance plan. For this reason, most acceptance plans involve attribute sampling. In general, the acceptance plan developed should minimize the combined cost of inspection and the cost of passing defectives. In this chapter, we shall confine the analysis to acceptance plans using attributes. The acceptance sampling procedure is outlined in Figure 7.

The inspection procedure for attribute sampling results in the simple classification of parts as good or not good. For part dimensions, this can be accomplished by the use of snap or plug gages with a go/no-go feature. The statistical methods used are based on discrete distributions, such as the binomial distribution or the Poisson distribution.

Acceptance sampling means accepting or rejecting whole lots of completed products on the basis of what the sample shows. With acceptance sampling, in contrast with control charts, you don't have to make up your own tables of sample sizes and rejection numbers. Statisticians have tabulated sets and published them in books. The two main sets of published tables are the Dodge-Romig sampling tables and Military Standard 105D.[1]

The consumer would like the lot to be free of defectives, but it is inevitable that lots will contain some defectives. The producer and consumer usually get together and agree on some maximum proportion of defectives in a lot that constitutes satisfactory quality. Rejection of a lot by the consumer may mean returning the lot to the producer or 100% inspection by the consumer with the producer bearing the cost.

When decisions are made based on samples, it is possible to make mistakes, even

---

[1]H. F. Dodge and H. G. Romig, *Sampling Inspection Tables—Single and Double Sampling*. New York: Wiley, 1959. U.S. Department of Defense, *Sampling Procedures and Tables for Inspection by Attributes*, MIL-STD-105D, Government Printing Office, Washington, DC.

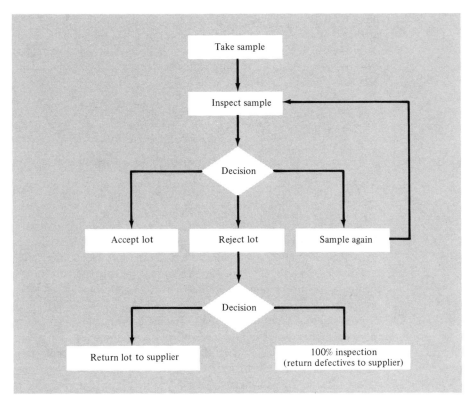

FIGURE 7
Acceptance sampling.

in controlled experiments. In acceptance sampling there are two types of errors that can be made. You can reject a good lot or you can accept a bad lot. The following decision matrix shows this point.

| Strategies | States of nature | |
	Lot satisfactory	Lot unsatisfactory
Accept lot	Good (correct decision)	Type II error, β (consumer's risk)
Reject lot	Type I error, α (producer's risk)	Good (correct decision)

The rejection of a satisfactory lot is called a type I error or producer's risk. It is so named because the producer absorbs the loss if such a decision is made. The acceptance of an unsatisfactory lot is called a type II error or consumer's risk. The consumer must absorb the cost of this decision. The only way of reducing both producer's and consumer's risk simultaneously is to increase the sample size.

Once it has been decided that a given lot will be accepted or rejected based on a sample taken from the lot, a specific sampling plan must be designed. This requires the determination of the sample size (n) and the maximum number of defectives (c)

permitted in the sample. If the number of defectives in the sample is c or less, the lot is accepted; if the number of defectives is more than c, it is rejected. Thus a sampling plan is simply a decision rule that specifies how large a sample should be taken and the allowable number or percentage of defectives.

OPERATING CHARACTERISTIC (OC) CURVES

An operating characteristic (OC) curve shows how well a particular sampling plan (combination of sample size n and acceptance number c) discriminates between good and bad lots. The OC curve is a graph depicting the probability of acceptance of a lot versus the percent defectives in the lot. The discriminating power of a sampling plan depends heavily on the size of the sample and the acceptance number. The OC curve becomes steeper as the sample size increases and as the acceptance number decreases. Larger samples tend to represent the lot more accurately, and a decrease in the acceptance number tightens the restrictions. An ideal OC curve can be obtained only by 100% inspection of the entire lot without any inspection errors. The discrimination ability of 100% inspection without inspection errors when the acceptable quality level is 3% is illustrated in Figure 8. An OC curve for a sampling plan will not be as discriminating as 100% inspection without inspection errors. Since sam-

FIGURE 8
OC curve: perfect discrimination.

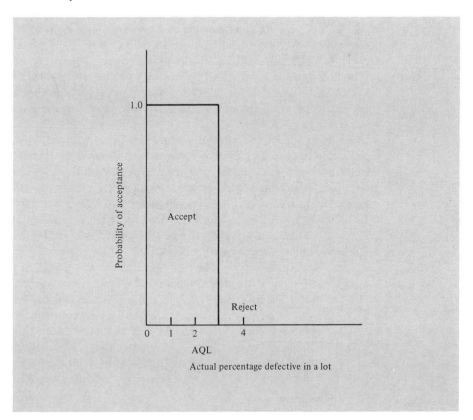

pling cannot guarantee 100% accuracy, there is some risk to the producer that good products will be rejected and some risk to the consumer that defective products will be accepted.

In developing a sampling plan for acceptance sampling, an appropriate operating characteristic curve must be selected. To select the operating characteristic curve, the producer and consumer must reach a decision on four variables:

1. *Acceptable quality level (AQL):* the smallest percentage of defectives that will make the lot definitely acceptable. This is the quality level that the customer prefers.
2. *Lot tolerance percent defective (LTPD):* the largest percentage of defectives that will make the lot definitely unacceptable. The customer cannot tolerate more than this amount of defectives.
3. *Producer's risk* (α): the probability that lots of AQL will not be accepted. This is the risk of getting a sample that has a higher proportion of defectives than the lot as a whole and rejecting a good lot, i.e., a type I error. It is frequently set at 5%.
4. *Consumer's risk* (β): the probability that lots of LTPD will be accepted. This is the risk of getting a sample that has a lower proportion of defectives than the lot as a whole and accepting a bad lot, i.e., a type II error. It is frequently set at 10%.

Once these four variables are determined, the operating characteristic curve can be established. The operating characteristic curve will indicate the sample size and the acceptance number to maintain the quality level specified by the above four variables. Lots of higher quality than the AQL will very seldom be rejected, and lots of poorer quality than the LTPD will seldom be accepted. The range of quality levels between the AQL and the LTPD is the "indifference" range.

The four variables (AQL, LTPD, α, and β) define two points for the OC curve: (AQL, $1 - \alpha$) and (LTPD, β). The producer and consumer agree that any acceptance plan whose OC curve passes through these points will be satisfactory. Figure 9 shows a typical OC curve.

Both the binomial and the Poisson distribution assume the lot size is infinitely large. In industrial practice, items for acceptance sampling are usually taken from a finite lot, without replacement, and with no regard to the order in which they are drawn. The hypergeometric distribution appropriately defines this situation, but it is cumbersome to manipulate. The Poisson distribution yields satisfactory approximations of the hypergeometric distribution for population percentages of defectives up to 20%. The Poisson distribution is much simpler to use, and its OC curves can be determined from statistical tables such as Table 2. In practice, sampling plans to fit producer and customer specifications are determined by utilizing specially prepared statistical tables and charts such as Dodge and Romig's *Sampling Inspection Tables*.

To use Table 2, divide the AQL into the LTPD and find the value in the table that is equal to or next larger than it. Determine the acceptance number by reading the value in the left column that corresponds to the quotient. The sample size is obtained by dividing the AQL into the corresponding value in the right column. If the LTPD/AQL quotient is not exactly as shown in Table 2, the value of β is not exactly 10% but just a close approximation. An exact fit is unlikely, since n and c must be integers.

693

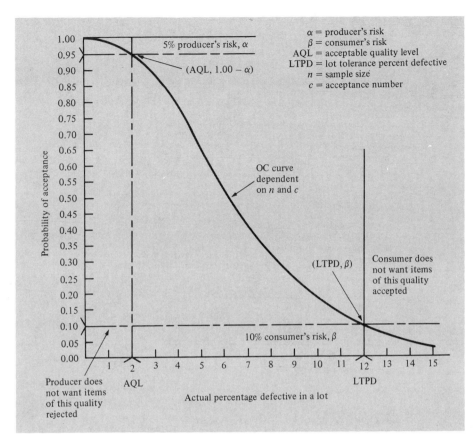

FIGURE 9
Operating characteristic curve ($\alpha = 5\%$, $\beta = 10\%$, AQL $= 2\%$, LTPD $= 12\%$).

TABLE 2
Single sampling plan for $\alpha = 5\%$ and $\beta = 10\%$

Acceptance number c	LTPD/AQL	$(100)(n)$(AQL)	Acceptance number c	LTPD/AQL	$(100)(n)$AQL)
0	44.890	5.2	13	2.240	846.4
1	10.946	35.5	14	2.177	924.6
2	6.509	81.8	15	2.122	1003.5
3	4.890	136.6	16	2.073	1083.1
4	4.057	197.0	17	2.029	1163.3
5	3.549	261.3	18	1.990	1244.2
6	3.206	328.6	19	1.954	1325.4
7	2.957	398.1	20	1.922	1407.2
8	2.768	469.5	21	1.892	1489.4
9	2.618	542.6	22	1.865	1571.9
10	2.497	616.9	23	1.840	1654.8
11	2.397	692.4	24	1.817	1738.2
12	2.312	769.0	25	1.795	1821.8

EXAMPLE 4

Determine the sampling acceptance plan when AQL $= 2\%$, LTPD $= 8\%$, $\alpha = 5\%$, and $\beta = 10\%$.

$$\frac{\text{LTPD}}{\text{AQL}} = \frac{8}{2} = 4.0$$

From Table 2 we find that 4.0 is near 4.057, which has an acceptance number of 4. The sample size is determined in the following manner from the last column in Table 2:

$$n = \text{sample size} = \frac{(100)(n)(\text{AQL})}{100(\text{AQL})} = \frac{197.0}{2} = 98.5$$

The sampling plan that approximates the conditions of the problem has $c = 4$ and $n = 99$. Therefore, a lot from which a sample of 99 items is taken will be rejected when over 4 items are found defective, and approximately 5% of the time the rejected lot will have fewer than 2% defective. Similarly, there is a probability of about 0.10 that fewer than four items in the sample of 99 are found defective when the lot actually contains more than 8% defective items.

AVERAGE OUTGOING QUALITY (AOQ)

A given acceptance sampling plan can be described in terms of the operating characteristic curve it generates. Another method of describing an acceptance sampling plan is by its average outgoing quality (AOQ). This second method requires that rejected lots be screened and all the defectives replaced by good items. As de-

TABLE 3

% defective p	Probability of acceptance P_a	$(N - n)/N$	AOQ = (Col.1)(Col.2)(Col.3)
0.00	1.00	.966	0.00
0.50	0.99	.966	0.48
1.00	0.99	.966	0.96
1.50	0.96	.966	1.39
2.00	0.90	.966	1.74
2.50	0.78	.966	1.88
2.75	0.75	.966	2.00 AOQL
3.00	0.66	.966	1.91
3.50	0.54	.966	1.83
4.00	0.40	.966	1.55
4.50	0.29	.966	1.26
5.00	0.20	.966	0.97
5.50	0.14	.966	0.74

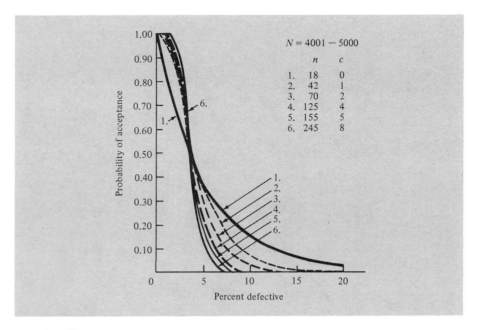

FIGURE 10
Operating characteristic curves—single sampling plans (AOQL = 2.0%). [From Dodge, H. F. and H. G. Romig, *Sampling Inspection Tables,* New York: Wiley, 1959, p. 84. Copyright 1959, Bell Telephone Laboratories. Reprinted by permission.]

fectives are replaced, the AOQ will improve in relation to the percent defective without replacement.

The AOQ is very near the defective percentage of a lot when it is small. The reason is that should few defectives be found in such sampling, few lots are rejected, and therefore few units replaced with acceptable units. As the defective percentage increases, more defectives are found through sampling and are replaced, and the AOQ becomes somewhat smaller than the defective percentage in the lot. At some value of the defective percentage, depending on the sampling plan, many lots are rejected and subjected to 100% inspection. As all defective units are replaced with acceptable units, rejected lots will have theoretically zero percent defectives. The AOQ with defective replacement (lot is returned to its original size) is determined as follows:

$$\text{AOQ} = pP_a \frac{N - n}{N}.$$

Table 3 is developed from the OC curve in Figure 10 with AOQ for $N = 4500$, $n = 155$, $c = 5$. The probability of acceptance figures are picked off the OC curve using the defective percentage as the entering argument. A process with 0.5% defective units has a probability of 99% of the lots being accepted. One percent of such lots are rejected and the defectives replaced. The average outgoing quality of the process is $(0.5)(99)(4500{-}155)/4500 = 0.48\%$ defective. This is the AOQ of the

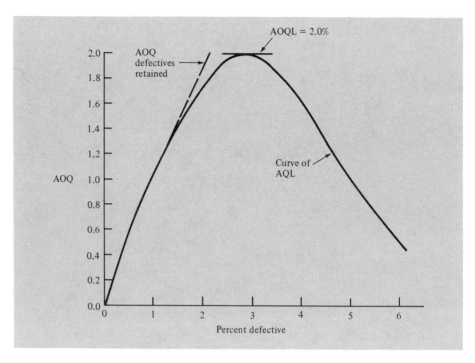

FIGURE 11
AOQL.

process with rectification during inspection. The AOQ for other process defective percentages is computed in a like manner.

Figure 11 is a plot of the AOQs developed in Table 3 against the percentage of defectives. The AOQ reaches a maximum point where the defective percentage is 2.75%. This maximum point is the *average outgoing quality limit*, AOQL. This limiting value is the worst AOQ possible from the rectifying inspection process, regardless of incoming quality.

The AOQL method is in wide use in industry today. The Dodge-Romig tables are a good statistical source for this type of plan. For this reason these tables have been chosen to demonstrate the application of AOQL type acceptance sampling.

The use of Dodge-Romig tables requires knowledge of the process average. As used in the tables, this quantity is the normal percentage of defectives that is to be expected from the process being sampled. It is usually determined by summarizing the results of the first samples or by examining the records of previous inspection results. Also, the process average may be tentatively determined by random sampling of the current production run. No matter what method is used to initially determine the process average, it should be periodically redetermined. In each redetermination, only data collected since the last one are considered.

If the process average selected is in error, it will not affect the AOQL. The only harm will be in not having the most efficient inspection plan. Additional inspection will be required, either on the first sample or on the second sample. Needless rejection of acceptable lots will cause these lots to be given 100% inspection. This too will cause less efficient inspection.

EXAMPLE 5

Develop a single sampling plan using Dodge-Romig tables that satisfy the following criteria:

$$AOQL = 2\%,$$
$$\text{process average} = 1.4\%,$$
$$\text{lot size} = 4{,}500.$$

Select the table titled Single Sampling Tables for AOQL = 2.0% (reproduced as Table 4). Entering the table with lot size 4500 and process average 1.4% yields the following information:

n	c	p_t (%)
155	5	6.0

A sample of 155 units is selected at random and inspected. If five or less units are defective, the lot is accepted. If six or more units are defective, the lot is rejected, given 100% inspection and all defectives replaced. (Here p_t is the lot tolerance percentage of defectives with consumer's risk of 0.10.)

continued

DOUBLE SAMPLING PLANS

Double sampling is different from single sampling in that the decision to accept a lot is not necessarily made on the first sample. As the name implies, two samples may be selected before the decision is reached. The primary advantage in using double sampling is the possible reduced cost of inspection. The reduced cost is effected by making the accept-reject decision on the first sample. The first sample of a double plan is much smaller than a sample specified under a single plan with the same AOQL or OC curve. If the lot is either very good or very bad, a decision can be made on the basis of the smaller sample at a lesser cost.

Another advantage of a double plan is the psychological effect on the individuals controlling the process under inspection. With double sampling, if the lot does not pass on the first sampling, there is a second chance. This assumes the defective quantity in the first sample has not exceeded an upper limit.

Increased administrative work and relative complexity are the principal disadvantages of double sampling.

In double sampling, one sample is taken and the number of defects recorded. The number of defects is compared with three standards. If it is equal to or less than the acceptable level, the lot is accepted. If it is greater than a certain higher acceptable level, the lot is rejected. However, if the number of defectives is between the acceptable level and the higher acceptable level, a second sample is taken with a new acceptance level. If the total number (first plus second sample) of defectives is equal to or less than this level, the lot is accepted; otherwise it is rejected. Figure 12 outlines the procedure for double sampling plans.

As can be seen from examining Tables 4 and 5, the Dodge-Romig tables are easy to use. Once the AOQL has been assigned, the sampling plan is simple to adjust if the lot size should vary. Also, it is easy to alter the sampling plan with updated information on the process average. This involves only changing columns.

Example 5—*continued*

TABLE 4
Single sampling table for average outgoing quality limit (AOQL) = 2.0%[a]

Lot size	Process average 0 to 0.04%			Process average 0.05 to 0.40%			Process average 0.41 to 0.80%		
	n	c	p_t(%)	n	c	p_t(%)	n	c	p_t (%)
1–15[b]	All	0	—	All	0	—	All	0	—
16–50	14	0	13.6	14	0	13.6	14	0	13.6
51–100	16	0	12.4	16	0	12.4	16	0	12.4
101–200	17	0	12.2	17	0	12.2	17	0	12.2
201–300	17	0	12.3	17	0	12.3	17	0	12.3
301–400	18	0	11.8	18	0	11.8	38	1	10.0
401–500	18	0	11.9	18	0	11.9	39	1	9.8
501–600	18	0	11.9	18	0	11.9	39	1	9.8
601–800	18	0	11.9	40	1	9.6	40	1	9.6
801–1000	18	0	12.0	40	1	9.6	40	1	9.6
1001–2000	18	0	12.0	41	1	9.4	65	2	8.2
2001–3000	18	0	12.0	41	1	9.4	65	2	8.2
3001–4000	18	0	12.0	42	1	9.3	65	2	8.2
4001–5000	18	0	12.0	42	1	9.3	70	2	7.5
5001–7000	18	0	12.0	42	1	9.3	95	3	7.0
7001–10,000	42	1	9.3	70	2	7.5	95	3	7.0
10,001–20,000	42	1	9.3	70	2	7.6	95	3	7.0
20,001–50,000	42	1	9.3	70	2	7.6	125	4	6.4
50,001–100,000	42	1	9.3	95	3	7.0	160	5	5.9

[a] n = sample size; c = acceptance number, p_t = lot tolerance percentage of defectives with a consumer's risk of 0.10. Source: Dodge, H. F. and H. G. Romig, *Sampling Inspection Tables*, New York: Wiley, 1959, p. 201. Copyright 1959, Bell Telephone Laboratories. Reprinted by permission.

FIGURE 12
Double sampling plans.

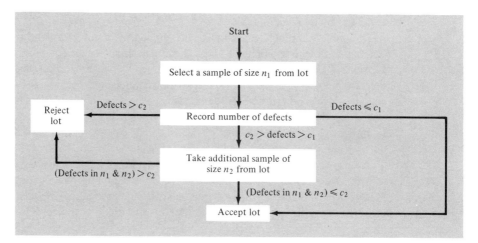

Process average 0.81 to 1.20%			Process average 1.21 to 1.60%			Process average 1.61 to 2.00%		
n	c	$p_t(\%)$	n	c	$p_t(\%)$	n	c	$p_t(\%)$
All	0	—	All	0	—	All	0	—
14	0	13.6	14	0	13.6	14	0	13.6
16	0	12.4	16	0	12.4	16	0	12.4
17	0	12.2	35	1	10.5	35	1	10.5
37	1	10.2	37	1	10.2	37	1	10.2
38	1	10.0	38	1	10.0	60	2	8.5
39	1	9.8	60	2	8.6	60	2	8.6
39	1	9.8	60	2	8.6	60	2	8.6
65	2	8.0	65	2	8.0	85	3	7.5
65	2	8.1	65	2	8.1	90	3	7.4
65	2	8.2	95	3	7.0	120	4	6.5
95	3	7.0	120	4	6.5	180	6	5.8
95	3	7.0	155	5	6.0	210	7	5.5
125	4	6.4	155	5	6.0	245	8	5.3
125	4	6.4	185	6	5.6	280	9	5.1
155	5	6.0	220	7	5.4	350	11	4.8
190	6	5.6	290	9	4.9	460	14	4.4
220	7	5.4	395	12	4.5	720	21	3.9
290	9	4.9	505	15	4.2	955	27	3.7

[b]"All" indicates that each piece in the lot is to be inspected.

EXAMPLE 6

Using the sampling inspection tables by Dodge and Romig, develop and describe a double sampling plan with AOQL of 2%, normal lot size of 6000, and process average of 1.5%.

Select the table from Dodge and Romig titled Double Sampling for AOQL = 2.0% (reproduced herein as Table 5). Entering the table with lot size of 6000 and a process average of 1.5% yields the following information:

Trial 1		Trial 2			
n_1	c_1	n_2	$n_1 + n_2$	c_2	p_t (%)
125	2	320	445	14	4.8

The first sample size is 125 units. On inspection of this sample, if zero, one, or two units are found defective, the lot is accepted. If more than two units are defective, but not more than 14, a second sample of 320 units is drawn. If either the first sample or the combined first and second samples have 15 or more defectives, the lot is rejected. Realistically, the lot would be rejected when 15 defectives have been found, rather than when the designated sample size has been inspected. The lot tolerance percentage of defectives with consumer's risk of 10% is 4.8%.

TABLE 5
Double sampling table for average outgoing quality limit (AOQL) $= 2.0\%^a$

Lot size	Process average 0 to 0.04%						Process average 0.05 to 0.40%						Process average 0.41 to 0.80%					
	Trial 1		Trial 2				Trial 1		Trial 2				Trial 1		Trial 2			
	n_1	c_1	n_2	$n_1 + n_2$	c_2	p_t (%)	n_1	c_1	n_2	$n_1 + n_2$	c_2	p_t (%)	n_1	c_1	n_2	$n_1 + n_2$	c_2	p_t (%)
$1–15^b$	All	0	—	—	—	—	All	0	—	—	—	—	All	0	—	—	—	—
16–50	14	0	—	—	—	13.6	14	0	—	—	—	13.6	14	0	—	—	—	13.6
51–100	21	0	12	33	1	11.7	21	0	12	33	1	11.7	21	0	12	33	1	11.7
101–200	24	0	13	37	1	11.0	24	0	13	37	1	11.0	24	0	13	37	1	11.0
201–300	26	0	15	41	1	10.4	26	0	15	41	1	10.4	29	0	31	60	2	9.1
301–400	26	0	16	42	1	10.3	26	0	16	42	1	10.3	30	0	35	65	2	9.0
401–500	27	0	16	43	1	10.3	30	0	35	65	2	9.0	30	0	35	65	2	9.0
501–600	27	0	16	43	1	10.3	31	0	34	65	2	8.9	35	0	55	90	3	7.9
601–800	27	0	17	44	1	10.2	31	0	39	70	2	8.8	35	0	60	95	3	7.7
801–1000	27	0	17	44	1	10.2	32	0	38	70	2	8.7	36	0	59	95	3	7.6
1001–2000	33	0	37	70	2	8.5	33	0	37	70	2	8.5	37	0	63	100	3	7.5
2001–3000	34	0	41	75	2	8.2	34	0	41	75	2	8.2	41	0	84	125	4	7.0
3001–4000	34	0	41	75	2	8.2	38	0	62	100	3	7.3	41	0	89	130	4	6.9
4001–5000	34	0	41	75	2	8.2	38	0	62	100	3	7.3	42	0	88	130	4	6.9
5001–7000	35	0	40	75	2	8.1	38	0	62	100	3	7.3	44	0	116	160	5	6.4
7001–10,000	35	0	40	75	2	8.1	38	0	62	100	3	7.3	45	0	115	160	5	6.3
10,001–20,000	35	0	40	75	2	8.1	39	0	66	105	3	7.2	45	0	115	160	5	6.3
20,001–50,000	35	0	40	75	2	8.1	43	0	92	135	4	6.6	47	0	148	195	6	6.0
50,001–100,000	35	0	45	80	2	8.0	43	0	92	135	4	6.6	85	1	185	270	8	5.2

Lot size	Process average 0.81 to 1.20%						Process average 1.21 to 1.60%						Process average 1.61 to 2.00%					
	Trial 1		Trial 2				Trial 1		Trial 2				Trial 1		Trial 2			
	n_1	c_1	n_2	$n_1 + n_2$	c_2	p_t (%)	n_1	c_1	n_2	$n_1 + n_2$	c_2	p_t (%)	n_1	c_1	n_2	$n_1 + n_2$	c_2	p_t (%)
1–15[b]	All	0	—	—	—	—	All	0	—	—	—	—	All	0	—	—	—	—
16–50	14	0	—	—	—	13.6	14	0	—	—	—	13.6	14	0	—	—	—	13.6
51–100	21	0	12	33	1	11.7	21	0	12	33	1	11.7	23	0	23	46	2	10.9
101–200	27	0	28	55	2	9.6	27	0	28	55	2	9.6	27	0	28	55	2	9.6
201–300	29	0	31	60	2	9.1	32	0	48	80	3	8.4	32	0	48	80	3	8.4
301–400	33	0	52	85	3	8.2	33	0	52	85	3	8.2	36	0	69	105	4	7.6
401–500	34	0	56	90	3	7.9	36	0	74	110	4	7.5	60	1	90	150	6	7.0
501–600	35	0	55	90	3	7.9	37	0	78	115	4	7.4	65	1	95	160	6	6.8
601–800	38	0	82	120	4	7.3	38	0	82	120	4	7.3	70	1	120	190	7	6.4
801–1000	38	0	87	125	4	7.2	70	1	100	170	6	6.5	70	1	145	215	8	6.2
1001–2000	43	0	112	155	5	6.5	80	1	160	240	8	5.8	110	2	205	315	11	5.5
2001–3000	75	1	115	190	6	6.1	115	2	195	310	10	5.3	160	3	310	470	15	4.7
3001–4000	80	1	140	220	7	5.8	120	2	255	375	12	5.0	235	5	415	650	20	4.3
4001–5000	80	1	175	255	8	5.5	125	2	285	410	13	4.9	275	6	475	750	23	4.2
5001–7000	85	1	205	290	9	5.3	125	2	320	445	14	4.8	280	6	575	855	26	4.1
7001–10,000	85	1	210	295	9	5.2	165	3	335	500	15	4.5	320	7	645	965	29	4.0
10,001–20,000	90	1	260	350	11	5.1	170	3	425	595	18	4.4	395	9	835	1230	37	3.9
20,001–50,000	130	2	300	430	13	4.7	205	4	515	720	22	4.3	480	11	1090	1570	46	3.7
50,001–100,000	135	2	345	480	14	4.5	250	5	615	865	26	4.1	580	13	1460	2040	58	3.5

[a]Trial 1: n = first sample size; c_1 = acceptance number for first sample. Trial 2: n_2 = second sample size; c_2 = acceptance number for first and second samples combined. p_t = lot tolerance percentage of defectives with a consumer's risk of 0.10. Source: Dodge, H. F. and H. G. Romig, *Sampling Inspection Tables*, New York: Wiley, 1959, p. 212. Copyright 1959, Bell Telephone Laboratories. Reprinted by permission

[b]"All" indicates that each piece in the lot is to be inspected.

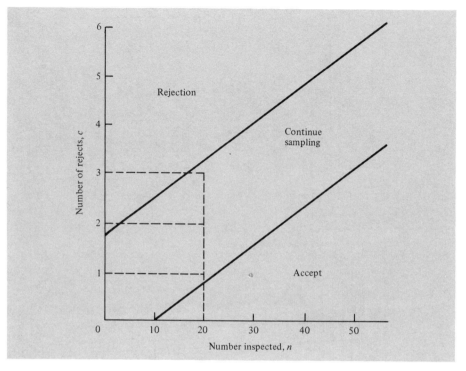

FIGURE 13
Sequential sampling plan.

SEQUENTIAL SAMPLING PLANS

Sequential or multiple sampling is an extension of double sampling. In such a plan, the random sample is drawn and inspected and the cumulated results analyzed. The possible decisions after analyzing the cumulated results of the plan are (1) reject the lot, (2) accept the lot, or (3) draw another sample. A graphical presentation of sequential sampling is shown in Figure 13. This plan indicates that a minimum of 10 units must be inspected before the lot may be accepted. For example, after 20 units have been inspected, the lot will be accepted if zero defectives have been found. If four or more defectives have been found, the lot will be rejected. With one, two, or three defectives, sampling will be continued.

Sequential sampling plans use even smaller samples sizes than double sampling plans. They allow for drawing whatever number of samples are necessary to reach a decision. However, the disadvantages of double sampling plans are multiplied in sequential plans. The statistical determination of the functional requirements based on the specifications, such as AQL, α, LTPD, and so forth, can be difficult. Here too, though, tables are available.[2]

---

[2]*Sequential Analysis of Statistical Data: Applications,* Statistical Research Group, Columbia University, 1960.

QUALITY CIRCLES

In recent years, organizations have given a great deal of thought to the establishment of more effective quality control programs. One of the quality programs, which had its origin in Japan, is commonly referred to as quality circles. It is based on the philosophy that quality can be improved through the participation of employees. Quality circles usually are composed of 5 to 15 volunteers from the same work area. They usually meet for one hour per week to discuss quality problems, to investigate causes, to recommend action, and to take corrective action on approved recommendations. Group members receive training in problem analysis, brainstorming, data collection, information display techniques, and general problem solving approaches. The goals of quality circles are to improve quality, productivity, and motivation. Many organizations have reported substantial improvements in operational performance after implementing quality circles.

Increasingly, organizations are recognizing the importance of having their workers in the mainstream of their quality control programs. If these efforts are to succeed, a sincere trust and loyalty must exist between the worker and management. Such a relationship cannot be developed overnight, and it usually takes years to establish. Quality circles are only one approach in the attempt to harness the energies and intellect of those most responsible for the creation of quality.

CONCLUSION

Quality is a measure of how closely a product conforms to specified standards. When 100% inspection is not practical, samples are the best way of measuring quality. Random samples give each item an equal chance of being selected and permit logical inferences about the population quality on the basis of sample evidence.

In general, two types of statistical methods are used in quality control when 100% inspection is not followed. Both control charts and acceptance sampling (sampling plans) are in common use. This classification is further divided into methods which measure attributes and methods which measure variables. Control charting measures the performance of a process in meeting output objectives. Acceptance sampling measures the quality of inputs and outputs.

The statistics involved in quality control can become quite complex. Fortunately, standard charts and tables have been developed that make it much easier to apply.

While sampling can substantially reduce quality control costs, there are always risks of error associated with decisions based on samples. However, the risks can be controlled.

QUESTIONS

1. Define product quality and state its usual purposes.
2. What are the major sources of quality discrepancies?
3. Discuss the use of sampling versus 100% inspection.
4. At what times are quality inspections desirable?
5. By what methods are incoming raw materials and final products statistically controlled? By what techniques is process control maintained?
6. Describe briefly how control charts are constructed. Once constructed, outline how control charts are used.

7. Why can't job shops with order sizes of less than 20 units use control charts?

8. Differentiate between chance variations and assignable causes.

9. Would you use 2σ or 3σ control limits on a potentially lethal drug?

10. Differentiate between attribute and variable data and how they are treated statistically.

11. How is between-sample and within-sample variation detected?

12. Define acceptance sampling and briefly describe its general procedures.

13. What is producer's risk? consumer's risk?

14. Upon what does the discriminatory power of an acceptance sampling plan depend?

15. What does an average outgoing quality (AOQ) explain about an acceptance plan?

16. How does the size of the first sample in a double sampling plan compare with the sample size in a single sampling plan?

17. Discuss any products (goods or services) you have purchased whose quality level was unacceptable. What could have been done to improve the quality level?

PROBLEMS

1. Inspection of 10 assemblies during December revealed the following numbers of defects:

    38, 41, 42, 34, 36, 43, 41, 38, 40, 35

    In January, after the holidays, the first assembly had 47 defects. What should this number of defects indicate to the line manager?

2. Groups of 6 of a certain manufacturing product yield the following data:

Group	$\overline{X}$	R
1	177.6	23
2	176.6	8
3	178.4	22
4	176.6	12
5	177.0	7
6	179.4	8
7	178.6	15
8	179.6	6
9	178.8	7
10	178.2	12
	1780.0	120

Develop the $\overline{X}$ and R control chart limits.

3. Specifications for manufacture of a shaft call for a diameter of $2.050 \pm 0.005''$. Samples of 5 of these shafts were taken every half hour. The results are shown below in thousands of an inch. Determine the $\overline{X}$ and R control chart limits for control of future production.

1	2	3	4	5	6	7	8	9	10	11	12	13	14	15	16
47	50	47	48	45	50	46	50	54	59	56	54	47	57	48	51
54	45	55	48	52	46	44	49	54	55	51	50	50	53	49	51
51	49	49	49	51	49	52	54	59	52	49	56	50	52	51	45
56	46	55	52	54	52	55	52	50	56	50	47	47	49	50	54
54	53	55	49	51	53	50	48	50	53	47	51	51	53	57	44

4. The number of defects found in 20 samples of five units each is as follows:

Sample	No. of defects	Sample	No. of defects
1	40	11	21
2	62	12	53
3	52	13	91
4	49	14	71
5	80	15	65
6	91	16	50
7	110	17	29
8	54	18	26
9	87	19	59
10	39	20	75
			1204

Set up a control chart for the number of defects.

5. 100 units of production are examined every day. The number of defectives found during the first 20 days are:

Day	No.	Day	No.	Day	No.	Day	No.
1	16	6	23	11	13	16	24
2	10	7	8	12	12	17	19
3	18	8	17	13	14	18	10
4	16	9	18	14	15	19	8
5	7	10	19	15	14	20	19

Develop the UCL and LCL for the percentage of defectives.

6. Develop the control chart limits based on the percentage of defective units from the following data:

Period:	1	2	3	4	5	6	7	8	9	10
Sample size:	50	100	50	75	50	80	50	50	25	50
No. of defects:	7	11	3	8	4	9	7	5	3	8

7. Determine the single sampling acceptance plan where AQL = 3%, LTPD = 10%, α = 5%, and β = 10%. (Use Table 2.)

8. Determine the sampling plan where AQL = 2%, LTPD = 6%, α = 5%, and β = 10%. (Use Table 2.)

9. The average percentage of defective items in a lot of products is 4%. Every defective item results in a loss of $10. What inspection cost per unit will justify 100% inspection?

10. Develop a single sampling plan using the Dodge-Romig tables that satisfies the requirements of AOQL = 2%, process average = 0.65%, and lot size = 5500.

11. Develop a double sampling plan using the Dodge-Romig tables that satisfies the requirement of AOQL = 2%, normal lot size = 10,000, and process average = 1.75%.

CASE 1: HOLDOUTS

Mercantile National Bank and Trust built a productivity program on a formal quality assurance framework. It issued a mission statement to all employees acknowledging their essentiality in providing high-quality services—namely, that "quality is everyone's service." To carry out its mission, Mercantile formed a Quality Assurance Division (QAD) to assist management and employees at all corporate levels in developing quality strategies. Quality was defined within the banking institution as the highest grade of accurate and timely service as perceived by the customer.

Since Mercantile had moved into a decentralized corporate structure, the responsibility for managing quality also was decentralized. Under the guidance of QAD, each user division had to establish its own program for improving quality. The steps in the development of the various quality programs generally were the same. The employees of each user division charted the flow of work through the area and then brainstormed for deviations (nonconformities) that occur in the work flow. The deviations believed by the employee groups to affect quality the most were stipulated as "key" and used for developing quality measures. The groups gathered data on their measures and supplied them to QAD. In turn, QAD reported back on the measures and typically sent each division charts and graphs of its quality performance measures and service volumes for the past twelve months. Along with these, QAD formulated monthly quality costs for the user divisions. QAD preferred to measure quality in terms of quality costs, i.e. how much the current level of quality is costing. Quality cost ranges also were used to alert QAD to high failure operations, which then became earmarked for quality improvement projects.

During its analyses of user divisions, QAD found that Area G was experiencing high quality costs. Area G processed computer tickets of customer transactions. The determination that the quality costs for Area G's service were too high was based on the following quality assurance measure that QAD had devised for Area G:

$$\frac{\text{tickets processed}}{\text{labor} + \text{systems use} + \text{forms}}$$

The numerator of the measure was the number of computer tickets processed correctly in one month. The denominator was the resources consumed in that month's ticket processing—labor expense, computer system run time (including other incidental user charges), and user ticket forms. The resources were assigned base rates at the time the measure was devised: the standard base rate for labor was $12.00 per hour (using the wages of processors and supervisors); system run time was set at a fixed cost of $500 per month; and processing forms were priced at $.05 apiece. The base rates were not changed for subsequent calculations so that future indices would change with the levels of resources used. At the time that measure was classified as unacceptable, it stood at 2.12 as indicated below:

$$\frac{21,000}{\$8,000 + \$500 + \$1,400} = 2.12$$

Along with the unacceptable quality costs, QAD had been alerted to operating problems through one of Area G's quality measures. The employees of Area G had cited "holdouts" as one of their serious deviations. "Holdouts" were defined as computer tickets that were rejected during daily processing. The employees felt that the holdouts severely hampered their processing productivity in that they substantially reduced the number of transactions which could be processed per unit of time. The holdouts (nonconforming tickets) had to be processed on the morning of the work day following their rejection. The processing of holdouts involved classification, sorting, correction of nonconformities, preparation of new tickets, and reprocessing. Although holdouts represented 30% of all tickets processed, there was one consolation. The processing of holdouts was an internal failure activity, as opposed to an external failure activity where a nonconformity is corrected after its discovery by a customer.

The employees of Area G began an improvement project on holdout processing. It began with data collection to determine accurately why the processing was slow and inefficient. A log was kept to identify which reprocessing activities caused the longest delays and the most frequent errors and which employees were the slowest and the most error prone. In addition, a matrix was compiled to see if there was a correlation between the two, and there was some but not significant correlation. After the two supervisors in charge of the log determined which activities and which employees most needed improvement, a solution to the problem was developed. It included additional training in holdout processing, improved descriptions of holdout processing procedures, and more supervisory assistance during reprocessing.

Six months after the unsatisfactory quality costs had been calculated and three months after the improvement project had been in effect, the quality costs were recalculated. There were shifts in the costs of the resources and the number of transactions processed per monthly period such that the productivity index improved to 2.33 as shown below:

$$\frac{22,000}{\$7,750 + \$500 + \$1,200} = 2.33$$

The index represented a 10% increase in productivity. The number of holdouts per period remained at approximately 30% of total processing, but the total number of transactions being processed and the resources consumed in processing both had moved in desirable directions. The employees of Area G and QAD were satisfied with the results. To them the index confirmed that their quality improvement program was a good foundation for productivity improvements.

1. Comment on the measures used in the quality improvement program in relation to the goals of the service institution.
2. Did the cost improvement program address the quality problems from the most reasonable perspective?
3. What other activities or programs could have been utilized to improve quality and productivity?
4. What quality control techniques could be applied to banking institutions?

CASE 2: ON THE SPOT

Marjorie Meddleson supervises two spot welding operations on subassembly A. The welding operations occur at two contiguous work stations on an unautomated subassembly line. The subassembly line in point is undergoing management appraisal in company-wide automation studies. Marjorie is involved in the appraisal in addition to her routine supervision and quality control of the welding stations and three other work stations on the same line.

Lately, final inspection has been rejecting increasing numbers of the product built with subassembly A because of faulty welds in the subassembly. Responding to the increase in finished products rejected for welding nonconformities, the operations manager, Joe Dragoo, is recommending replacement of the welders by a programmable robot. Joe maintains that the robot is commensurate with the two welders together in terms of output per unit of time but is superior to them both in regard to quality and operating conformity. His robot replacement has proven quality workmanship and, without watchdog superivsion, will produce less than one defective in every 100 spot welds.

Aware of the robot's potential takeover, Marjorie wants to find out if the welding operations actually are in control before any worker displacement occurs. If they are not, she wants to see what can be done to bring them into control aside from automating the jobs. She is frustrated by the fact that the only formal inspection records available are those belonging to the teams of inspectors who check incoming raw materials and outgoing finished products. There are no aids used to monitor partially completed outputs nor any specific subassembly quality standards. Without exact statements of quality characteristics, only her supervisory instinct and opinion are used to discover when processes are going astray and how process malfunctions should be corrected.

Marjorie's experience is satisfactory in cases where subquality outputs are obvious, but she has no evidence that her employees are doing an acceptable job overall. Consequently, she has decided to do her own quality testing. In order to do this, she plans to construct a control chart of the welding operations to determine for sure if the process is in control. She intends to construct the chart from the 20 daily samples she withdrew as the inprocess subassemblies left the last of the two welding stations. Each of her 20 samples includes five subassemblies which have 10 welds apiece at this stage of their processing. The sampling data show the following number of defectives contained in each of the daily samples:

Sample number	Number of defective welds	Sample number	Number of defective welds
1	3	11	3
2	3	12	3
3	2	13	2
4	4	14	3
5	3	15	2
6	3	16	2
7	2	17	2
8	4	18	1
9	2	19	0
10	3	20	1

Marjorie has chosen to plot the data points on a control chart constructed from control limits computed for the twenty daily samples. The control limits she has selected are $\pm 3\sigma$. If the plotted points show that the process is in control, Marjorie plans to plead for the workers' continued employment on that basis. If the process is shown to be out of control, she has in mind to provide training and counseling to help correct the problem. Along with her thinly laid plans for remedial instruction, Marjorie intends to build a case for a training program on the cost of instructing workers versus the cost of acquiring a robot. Finally, if the outcome of the quality testing reveals that the process is much better than acceptable, she plans to recommend that the employees receive bonus pay and company apologies for their regrettable personal upheaval. In addition to a vote of confidence for the employees, Marjorie intends to present her test results to Joe as a strong implication that the unequivocal quality of his robot would not only be unnecessary for these operations but would be excessively costly.

1. Establish the control limits from the sampling data, draw the control chart, and plot the data points.
2. Discuss the development of a control chart in this manner. Point out any assumptions which have to be made under this approach.
3. Analyze any findings (i.e. trends, extremes, etc.). What factors, behavioral or otherwise, could be influencing the welding operations' quality now and before the threat of replacement?
4. In order to evaluate a robot acquisition, what quality control issues must be appraised?

SELECTED BIBLIOGRAPHY

Belz, M. H. *Statistical Methods for the Process Industries,* New York: Wiley, 1973.

Dodge, H. F. and H. G. Romig. *Sampling Inspection Tables: Single and Double Sampling,* New York: Wiley, 1959.

Duncan, A. J. *Quality Control and Industrial Statistics,* Homewood, IL: Irwin, 1974.

Grant, E. L. and R. S. Leavenworth. *Statistical Quality Control,* New York: McGraw-Hill, 1972.

Hayes, G. E. and H. G. Romig. *Modern Quality Control,* Encino, CA: Benziger, Bruce, and Glencoe, 1977.

Kirkpatrick, E. G. *Quality Control for Managers and Engineers,* New York: Wiley, 1970.

Sequential Analysis of Statistical Data Applications, Statistical Research Group, Columbia University, 1960.

U. S. Department of Defense. MIL-STD-105D, *Sampling Procedures and Tables for Inspection by Attributes,* U. S. Government Printing Office, Washington.

U. S. Department of Defense. MIL-STD-414, *Sampling Procedures and Tables for Inspection by Variables for Percent Defective,* U. S. Government Printing Office, Washington.

23
Maintenance

TYPES OF MAINTENANCE
Breakdown Maintenance
Preventive Maintenance

INDIVIDUAL VERSUS GROUP REPLACEMENT

INTERNAL VERSUS EXTERNAL MAINTENANCE

CREW SIZE

QUEUING THEORY
Input Characteristics
Queue Characteristics
Service Characteristics
Mathematical Approach

MONTE CARLO SIMULATION

CONCLUSION

QUESTIONS

PROBLEMS

CASES

SELECTED BIBLIOGRAPHY

Anyone who has experienced the inconvenience of a breakdown in a vehicle (automobile, bus, train, or aircraft) can understand the frustration, delays, and expenses it can cause. These same consequences can occur for almost every aspect of an operating system. Because facilities and equipment are continually wearing out, they need repairs and replacement. Maintenance is the function that keeps the production system operable. It is aimed at keeping or restoring any asset to satisfactory operating status. Maintenance is primarily concerned with plant, machinery, and equipment. It usually involves such tasks as replacing worn-out parts, servicing equipment, keeping up buildings, making emergency repairs, and so forth. Without proper maintenance, costly production delays can be experienced, excessive idle time incurred, and unsafe working conditions encountered. It is an important, if not vital, function for any production system.

Maintenance activities in reference to an organization's outputs were introduced in Chapter 7 on Product Decisions. Reliability and maintainability of products are properly addressed in product design. These topics will not be discussed in this chapter, but the reader may wish to review Chapter 7.

Maintenance, which is sometimes referred to as facilities management or plant engineering, can encompass a host of responsibilities in different organizations. Table 1 lists several typical maintenance responsibilities found in organizations. The list is not exhaustive, but it does indicate the range of necessary activities. Frequently, the maintenance department is delegated those responsibilities that are not wanted by other departments.

The maintenance function may be centralized, decentralized, or a combination in a given organization. With centralization, workers are in one location and are assigned responsibilities as need arises. With decentralization, workers are located in different areas of the plant, and responsibilities are confined to their own areas. The degree of decentralization depends on the specific demand for maintenance services, the travel time from a central shop, the seriousness of downtime, and the degree of specialization required. Centralization results in a better utilization of personnel, but decentralization results in faster service.

Maintenance costs tend to be lower when an asset is new, and they tend to increase with equipment age as more effort is needed to maintain a given level of performance. Numerous assets tend to exhibit a disk-shaped curve (sometimes called a bathtub curve) for malfunctions. Early failure (infant mortality) is associated with

TABLE 1
Typical maintenance responsibilities

Item	Typical responsibilities
Machinery/equipment	1. Installation, replacement, and relayout
	2. General purpose (motors, pumps, etc.) and special purpose (computers, electronics, etc.)
	3. Shafts, bearings, belts, gears, and parts
Transportation devices	Elevators, conveyors, trucks, hoists, and cranes
Plant services	Power, light, gas, water, steam, sewage, garbage, heating, air conditioning, and housekeeping
Buildings/structures	Roofs, windows, walls, floors, foundations, and fences
Grounds	Grass, snow, shrubs, parking lots, and landscaping
Special services	Safety, fire prevention, machine shops, pollution control, and security

malfunctions in break-in operations. If the asset survives the break-in period, it usually operates satisfactorily for an extended period of time (normal operating period). Finally, a wearout period is encountered at the end of the cycle, where repairs or replacement are required. Of course, different assets exhibit different malfunction patterns, so no single curve can be used to describe all behavior.

The major operational choice is whether to repair equipment before it malfunctions (preventive maintenance) or wait and repair it after it malfunctions (breakdown maintenance). An asset that breaks down can be repaired immediately or placed in a queue of work to be accomplished. Preventive maintenance is performed prior to breakdown; it may be minor, or as major as complete overhaul or replacement. Preventive measures do not stop breakdowns, but they do reduce them. Preventive maintenance requires planning and scheduling of activities, while breakdown maintenance is management by exception.

TYPES OF MAINTENANCE

Breakdown and preventive maintenance are the two major types of maintenance. Breakdown maintenance takes no action until an asset has failed. Preventive maintenance involves actions designed to delay or prevent major breakdowns. The best type of maintenance to pursue is the one that provides the lowest total cost. Typical breakdown costs include the cost of repairs, equipment downtime, idle labor, loss of output, schedule delays, and customer dissatisfaction.

The objective of preventive maintenance is to reduce the total cost of providing a service. A cost analysis between breakdown and preventive maintenance can indicate the preferred alternative. To conduct a cost analysis, information must be available relative to:

1. cost of breakdowns,
2. frequency of breakdowns or failures,
3. cost of preventive maintenance to reduce or eliminate failures.

BREAKDOWN MAINTENANCE

Breakdown maintenance allows equipment or facilities to be used until failure. Since breakdown maintenance is of an emergency nature, breakdowns tend to occur at irregular intervals, which imposes variable workloads on maintenance personnel. Such irregularities force the maintenance department to operate at less than its peak efficiency so that the overall facility can function efficiently.

Inventories can serve as a buffer against the effect of equipment breakdowns. Excessive in-process goods can insulate the production system until breakdown repairs can be completed. However, excess stocks increase the asset investment as well as holding costs. Thus, this use of inventories can be an expensive policy.

Standby or backup systems are a method of maintaining service. They serve as insurance against service interruptions. As with an insurance policy, a premium must be paid. Backup systems represent an additional asset investment, and the additional expenditures must be justified. Furthermore, it cannot be assumed that a standby system will always function when placed in service.

EXAMPLE 1

The maintenance department must keep a fleet of 25 trucks in operation. It costs $50 a day to own a truck whether it is used or not. It costs the organization an average of $100 a day for every truck that breaks down. It takes an average of one day to return a truck to operation after a breakdown. Maintenance records indicate the following probabilities of breakdowns per day:

Number of breakdowns	0	1	2	3	4	5	6
Probability	.15	.30	.20	.15	.10	.08	.02

How many backup trucks should be purchased to supplement the existing fleet of 25? The following table develops the relevant cost relationships:

			Number of Backup Trucks							
			0		1		2		3	
Number of breakdowns	Cost	Probability	Expected cost	Cost	Expected cost	Cost	Expected cost	Cost	Expected cost
0	$ 0	0.15	$ 0	$ 0	$ 0	$ 0	$ 0	$ 0	$ 0
1	100	0.30	30	0	0	0	0	0	0
2	200	0.20	40	100	20	0	0	0	0
3	300	0.15	45	200	30	100	15	0	0
4	400	0.10	40	300	30	200	20	100	10
5	500	0.08	40	400	32	300	24	200	16
6	600	0.02	12	500	10	400	8	300	6
		1.00							
Breakdown cost			$207		$122		$ 67		$ 32
Backup cost			0		50		100		150
Total cost			$207		$172		$167		$182

The lowest cost policy of $167 involves the purchase of two backup trucks, which increases the fleet size to 27.

PREVENTIVE MAINTENANCE

Preventive maintenance means routine inspections and servicing. It is designed to detect potential failure conditions and make corrections that will prevent major operating difficulties. It is most effective when service requirements are known or failures can be predicted with some accuracy. Preventive maintenance is desirable when it can increase the operating time of an asset by reducing the severity or frequency of breakdowns. Preventive maintenance might include cleaning, lubricating, inspection, calibration, testing, critical part replacement before failure, or complete overhauls.

When equipment breakdowns occur, they idle men and machines, result in lost production time, delay schedules, and incur costly repairs. Thus, repairing assets after they fail is often not the best maintenance policy. Breakdown repair jobs are usually more costly than preventive repair jobs. It is frequently desirable to anticipate likely difficulties and perform expected needed repairs at a convenient time (weekends, holidays, slack periods), before the repairs are actually needed.

As a general rule, if a failure will harm an employee, stop production, or waste organizational assets, then it should be considered for preventive maintenance. As organizations become more highly mechanized, maintenance increases in significance. Excessive downtime in automated facilities is prohibitively expensive and frequently is justification for elaborate preventive maintenance activities.

Effective preventive maintenance requires trained personnel, an accurate record system, and regular inspections with servicing. By planning maintenance on a schedule (daily, weekly, monthly), perhaps during a second or third shift, more effective utilization of skilled personnel is possible. Good maintenance records provide substantial assistance in estimating the probability distributions of breakdown and repair times.

Preventive maintenance should only be undertaken when it provides a net benefit to the organization over breakdown maintenance. A cost tradeoff exists, and preventive maintenance can be carried too far. When immediate repair is not necessary and little harm is done by waiting, breakdown maintenance is satisfactory.

EXAMPLE 2

Every time a machine breaks down it costs the organization $2000. By performing preventive maintenance each week at a cost of $1500, the organization is protected against any major breakdowns. The breakdown records on the machine reveal the following:

Number of breakdowns/week	0	1	2	3	4
Number of weeks this occurred	25	18	4	2	1

Should the preventive maintenance program be installed?

The expected number of breakdowns per week is determined as follows:

$$\frac{0(25) + 1(18) + 2(4) + 3(2) + 4(1)}{50} = 0.72 \text{ breakdowns/week,}$$

$$\begin{aligned} \text{expected breakdown cost} &= (0.72 \text{ breakdowns/week})(\$2000/\text{breakdown}) \\ &= \$1440/\text{week.} \end{aligned}$$

Since the breakdown maintenance cost is $60 per week ($1500 − $1440) less than the preventive maintenance program, preventive maintenance should not be instituted.

If the expected cost of breakdowns per period without preventive maintenance is greater than the expected cost of breakdowns with preventive maintenance, preventive maintenance is the best policy. The expected cost of breakdowns per period, if there is *no preventive maintenance,* is the cost of breakdowns divided by the expected number of periods between breakdowns, or

$$\text{expected breakdown cost per period} = \text{TC} = C_b/E(n),$$

where

C_b = Nc_b = total cost of breakdowns,

N = total number of like items in the group,

c_b = cost of a single breakdown,

$E(n)$ = $\Sigma_n\, np_n$ = expected number of periods between breakdowns,

$1/E(n)$ = expected number of breakdowns per period,

n = time period,

p_n = probability of a breakdown in period n.

The expected cost of breakdowns per period *with preventive maintenance* must include both the cost of the preventive maintenance and the cost of those units that break down in spite of the preventive maintenance, or

$$\text{TC} = \frac{C_p + B_n c_b}{n},$$

where

B_n = $N(p_1 + p_2 + \cdots + p_n) + B_1 p_{n-1} + B_2 p_{n-2} + \cdots + B_{n-1} p_1$,

C_p = cost of preventive maintenance,

n = time periods between preventive maintenance,

B_n = expected number of breakdowns in n periods with preventive maintenance

performed every n time periods

= (number of machines expected to break down during the time period) plus (number expected to break down more than once).

Thus preventive maintenance is economical if

$$\frac{C_p + B_n c_b}{n} < \frac{C_b}{E(n)},$$

otherwise breakdown maintenance is more desirable.

EXAMPLE 3

An organization has 30 machines to keep in service. The breakdown repair cost is $900 per machine. Preventive maintenance at a cost of $200 per machine can reduce breakdowns. Experience reveals that the probability of a machine breaking down is as follows:

Months until breakdown	1	2	3	4	5	6	7
Probability of breakdown	.10	.05	.10	.20	.25	.15	.15

(a) What is the expected breakdown cost per month?

(b) If preventive maintenance is followed, how often should the machines be serviced?

(a): The average length of time a machine goes without a breakdown is

$$1(0.10) + 2(0.05) + 3(0.10) + 4(0.20)$$
$$+ 5(0.25) + 6(0.15) + 7(0.15) = 4.5 \text{ months.}$$

Thus,

$$\text{Expected monthly breakdown cost} = \frac{(30 \text{ machines})(\$900/\text{machine})}{4.5 \text{ months}}$$

$$= \$6000.$$

(b):   The expected number of breakdowns for each cycle is as follows:

$B_n = N(p_1 + p_2 + \cdots + p_n) + B_1 p_{n-1} + B_2 p_{n-2} + \cdots + B_{n-1} p_1;$

$B_1 = 30(0.10) = 3,$

$B_2 = 30(0.10 + 0.05) + 3(0.10) = 4.80,$

$B_3 = 30(0.10 + 0.05 + 0.10) + 3(0.05) + 4.80(0.10) = 8.13,$

$B_4 = 30(0.10 + 0.05 + 0.10 + 0.20) + 3(0.10) + 4.80(0.05) + 8.13(0.10)$
$\qquad = 14.85,$

$B_5 = 30(0.10 + 0.05 + 0.10 + 0.20 + 0.25) + 3(0.20) + 4.80(0.10)$
$\qquad + 8.13(0.05) + 14.85(0.10)$
$\qquad = 23.97,$

$B_6 = 30(0.10 + 0.05 + 0.10 + 0.20 + 0.25 + 0.15) + 3(0.25)$
$\qquad + 4.80(0.20) + 8.13(0.10) + 14.85(0.05) + 23.97(0.10)$
$\qquad = 31.16,$

$B_7 = 30(0.10 + 0.05 + 0.10 + 0.20 + 0.25 + 0.15 + 0.15) + 3(0.15)$
$\qquad + 4.80(0.25) + 8.13(0.20) + 14.85(0.10) + 23.97(0.05)$
$\qquad + 31.16(0.10)$
$\qquad = 39.08.$

The following table develops the preventive maintenance costs for each of the seven different cycle periods:

Preventive maintenance period n (months)	Expected breakdowns in n months, B_n	Expected no. of breakdowns per month, B_n/n	Expected breakdown cost per month, $(B_n/n) \times \$900$	Preventive maintenance cost per month, $\dfrac{30 \times \$200}{n}$	Expected total monthly cost, col. 4 + 5
1	3.00	3.00	$2700	$6000	$8700
2	4.80	2.40	2160	3000	5160
3	8.13	2.71	2439	2000	4439 ←
4	14.85	3.71	3339	1500	4839
5	23.97	4.79	4311	1200	5511
6	31.16	5.19	4671	1000	5671
7	39.08	5.58	5022	857	5879

Preventive maintenance on a 3-month cycle is the best policy. It saves 6,000 − 4,439 = $1,561 per month. Preventive maintenance is superior to breakdown maintenance.

If there are several machines or standby capacity, a single machine breakdown is not critical. Operations can be transferred to other machines with little difficulty. Excess capacity tends to favor breakdown maintenance over preventive maintenance. When equipment utilization approaches capacity, preventive maintenance tends to be more desirable.

Preventive maintenance is important for continuous and automated production facilities. Maintenance personnel are usually close by to take care of any emergencies. Interruptions to operations cannot be tolerated. The systems are under constant surveillance for any variations. Central monitoring stations and control consoles continually monitor operations, and adjustments are made as problems arise.

As an alternative to breakdown or preventive maintenance, equipment can sometimes be monitored to anticipate an impending failure. This is called predictive or diagnostic maintenance. Instrumentation is used to measure the condition of the equipment while it is operating and to indicate or predict when a failure mode is being approached. For example, sensors can measure high frequency noises and shaft vibration in rotating equipment as an indication of potential problems. Equipment then can be repaired or replaced on an as needed basis, avoiding a breakdown or unneeded preventive maintenance activities.

INDIVIDUAL VERSUS GROUP REPLACEMENT

Individual replacement applies to a single item that is replaced when it fails. Group replacement applies to a number of identical low cost items that are increasingly prone to failure as they age. The classic example of group replacement is street lights. When a single light burns out, little additional cost is incurred if all are replaced.

The analysis of periodic total quantity replacement versus failure replacement is similar to that above for preventive maintenance. Several types of replacement policies are possible, such as:

1. Replace only failed units as they fail.
2. Replace only failed units periodically.
3. Replace all units (both good and failed units) periodically.
4. Replace failed units as they fail and all units periodically.

EXAMPLE 4

A production process uses 1000 heating lamps. It costs $4.00 to replace an individual lamp when it expires. If all the lamps are replaced on the third shift, it costs $500 or $.50 per lamp. When a lamp fails, it must be replaced immediately. When group replacement is followed, all items in the group are replaced at one time regardless of age. The lamp manufacturer provides the following probability distribution for lamp failures:

Month	1	2	3	4	5	6
Probability of failure	.05	.10	.15	.30	.20	.20

(a) If group replacement is followed, what is the best cycle in months for replacement?

(b) Is individual or group replacement most economical?

(a): Group replacement consists of six possible subpolicies of replacement every 1, 2, 3, 4, 5, or 6 months. To determine the best cycle of replacement, we must calculate the expected total number of failures for each alternative. The following relationship gives the expected total number of failures if group replacement is performed every n months:

$$B_n = N(p_1 + p_2 + \cdots + p_n) + B_1 p_{n-1} + B_2 p_{n-2} + \cdots + B_{n-1} p_1$$

where

B_n = expected number of failures in month n,

n = number of cycle periods (months) considered,

N = total number of replacement lamps,

p_n = probability of a failure in month n.

The expected number of lamp failures during each cycle of replacement is as follows:

B_1 = 1000(0.05) = 50,

B_2 = 1000(0.05 + 0.10) + 50(0.05) = 152.5,

B_3 = 1000(0.05 + 0.10 + 0.15) + 50(0.10) + 152.5(0.05) = 312.6,

B_4 = 1000(0.05 + 0.10 + 0.15 + 0.30) + 50(0.15) + 152.5(0.10)

   + 312.6(0.05)

   = 638.4,

B_5 = 1000(0.05 + 0.10 + 0.15 + 0.30 + 0.20) + 50(0.30) + 152.5(0.15)

   + 312.6(0.10) + 638.4(0.05)

   = 901.1,

B_6 = 1000(0.05 + 0.10 + 0.15 + 0.30 + 0.20 + 0.20) + 50(0.20)

   + 152.5(0.30) + 312.6(0.15) + 638.4(0.10) + 901.1(0.05)

   = 1211.5.

The following table develops the maintenance costs for the six different cycle periods:

Group replacement period n (months)	Expected number of failures in n months, B_n	Expected number of failures per month, B_n/n	Expected failure cost per month, $(B_n/n) \times \$4.00$	Replacement cost per month, $500/n$	Expected total monthly cost, col. 4 + 5
1	50.0	50.00	$200.00	$500.00	$700.00
2	152.5	76.25	305.00	250.00	555.00←
3	312.6	104.20	416.80	166.67	583.47
4	638.4	159.60	638.40	125.00	763.40
5	901.1	180.22	720.88	100.00	820.88
6	1211.5	201.92	807.68	83.33	891.01

From the table above, the lowest expected monthly cost of $555.00 is obtained from a group replacement cycle of two months.

(b): The expected total monthly cost of individual replacement is obtained by dividing the replacement cost of all the lamps by the expected lifetime of the lamps:

expected lifetime = 1(0.05) + 2(0.10) + 3(0.15) + 4(0.30) + 5(0.20

   + 6(0.20)

   = 4.1 months,

expected total monthly cost of individual replacement

$$= \frac{(1000 \text{ lamps})(\$4.00/\text{lamp})}{4.1 \text{ months}}$$

= $975.61/month.

Group replacement on a two month cycle is the best policy, since it saves $975.61 − $555.00 = $420.61 per month. Thus group replacement is far superior to individual replacement.

INTERNAL VERSUS EXTERNAL MAINTENANCE

Organizations have to staff their maintenance departments with personnel having the necessary skills. When the needs are irregular and very high technical competence required, maintenance can be contracted to outside firms. Organizations frequently contract out their maintenance on elevators, telephones, or computers. Often lawn care, window washing, janitorial, and vehicle maintenance are performed by other organizations. An economic analysis will usually reveal the most desirable source of maintenance activities. Labor contracts may also indicate the sources for these services.

The decision to provide the necessary maintenance personnel within the organization or to utilize services external to the organization is primarily an economic decision. Neither policy is likely to be best for all facility maintenance. Queuing theory and Monte Carlo simulation can be used to arrive at the most desirable alternative.

CREW SIZE

Maintenance can be expensive, involving highly skilled personnel. Management would like to have sufficient personnel for immediate repair of any breakdown and for preventive maintenance at the exact prescribed time, but complete coverage can be prohibitively expensive. The situation involves a tradeoff of the cost of additional maintenance personnel against the cost of equipment downtime.

It is not uncommon for maintenance departments to be underutilized. If maintenance crews have high utilization, they may not be available when a critical breakdown occurs. The crew's idle time can be insignificant in relation to the cost of a critical breakdown. A maximization of output then dictates an underutilization of maintenance personnel.

QUEUING THEORY

Queuing theory is the science of waiting lines. Waiting lines occur when some customer, employee, part, machine, or unit must wait for service because the service facility is operating at full capacity and is temporarily unable to provide service. Our economic system is filled with situations in which both people and inanimate objects spend much valuable time waiting to receive service. Queues (waiting lines) form at bus stops, supermarket counters, doctors' offices, gas stations, airport runways, tool cribs, warehouse receiving docks, university registration desks, etc. Queuing theory is applicable to a wide variety of operational situations where there is imperfect matching between units requiring service and service facilities. In general, it can be used to determine the suitable number and type of service facilities.

Queuing theory has direct application to the maintenance function. If there are multiple machines with breakdown distributions, then breakdowns are comparable to arrivals to the waiting line, and the repair crews or centers are the service facility. Queuing theory can be used to determine the optimum capacity or operating level for maintenance support activities. The usual optimization approach is to minimize the combined cost of service and the cost of waiting (idleness).

Waiting lines must be expected to form by chance from time to time. If waiting lines never occur, the service facility is probably overstaffed. Since the times between arrivals and service time intervals are irregular, there will be periods when the

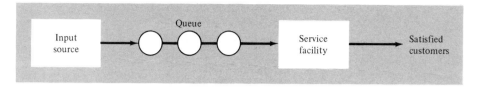

A. *Input characteristics:*
   1. Population size—finite or infinite.
   2. Arrival rate distribution—Poisson, uniform, hyperexponential, etc.
   3. Customer attitude—patient or impatient.
B. *Queue characteristics:*
   1. Queue size—finite or infinite.
C. *Service characteristics:*
   1. Facility design—series, parallel, or mixed (single channel, single phase; single channel, multiple phase; multiple channel, single phase; multiple channel, multiple phase; etc.).
   2. Service time distribution—negative exponential, uniform, etc.
   3. Service discipline—first come first served, random, priorities, etc.
D. *Objective functions:*
   1. Minimize the combined cost of idle time of customers waiting in line and the service attendants. (Minimize nonproductive time of employees.)
   2. Minimize the combined cost of lost time of customers waiting in line and the wages of the people providing the service.
   3. Heuristic criteria—the average customer will be served in an alloted time period, no customer will be required to wait longer than a specified time period, etc.
E. *Solution approaches:*
   1. Mathematical—arrival rate and service time distributions are approximated by a mathematically tractable distribution.
   2. Simulation—statistics concerning arrival rates and service times are iterated by Monte Carlo simulation from either historical or assumed distributions.

FIGURE 1
Queuing theory.

queue will become long even though the service facility is planned to accommodate the average arrival rate. There will also be time periods when the service facility will be idle. The manager must find the level of staffing that provides the best compromise between too much waiting time (customer inconvenience) and too little (high operating cost).

In its simplest form, queuing theory uses a body of mathematical formulas and theorems in explaining the formation of waiting lines and the movement through them. It constitutes an analytical method for balancing the cost of service against the cost of time-wasting queues. The solution approaches to queuing theory are either mathematical or simulated. In the mathematical approach, arrival rate and service time distributions are represented by known standard distributions. In the simulated approach, a standard distribution is not required, for any distribution can be used in Monte Carlo simulation. Figure 1 contains the general framework for queuing theory problems.

In this section, we will confine the rigorous treatment to the mathematical approach with the assumptions of Poisson distributed arrival rates and negative exponential distributed service times. This situation is referred to as the Poisson arrival–exponential holding time case. It can be shown that arrival rates and service rates approximated by a Poisson distribution have their reciprocal, the mean time between arrivals and the mean service time, distributed as a negative exponential. Specific formulas can then be developed to describe the waiting line situation.

The elements of a queuing process are defined in Figure 1 as the input source, queue, and service facility. An adequate understanding of all three elements is necessary to obtain a solution to a waiting line problem.

INPUT CHARACTERISTICS

The input source is the population of customers who utilize the service facility. It is defined by the size of the population, the arrival rate distribution, and the customer attitude. In many situations, the customers are not people, but orders waiting to be filled, trucks to be unloaded, jobs awaiting processing, or equipment in need of repair. The input source is either infinite or finite. The population can be considered infinite if the rate at which customers are generated is not appreciably affected by the number of customers already in the system. The customers in the system include those receiving service and those in the queue. If the number of customers in the system is a significant fraction of the population, the infinite population assumption is not valid.

In this section the arrival rate distribution is assumed to be a Poisson distribution. This is a discrete distribution completely defined by one parameter, the arithmetic mean. The Poisson distribution corresponds to completely random arrivals: it is assumed that each arrival is completely independent of others as well as of the condition of the waiting line. The Poisson distribution often applies when there are a large number of independent events, each with only a small, constant probability that a certain outcome will occur. Poisson distributions are skewed to the right, although they become more symmetrical as the mean value becomes larger. According to the Poisson distribution, the probability of x successes in n trials, when p is the probability of success in one trial, is approximately

$$P(x) = e^{-np} \frac{(np)^x}{x!} = e^{-m} \frac{m^x}{x!},$$

where

$m = np = $ mean of Poisson distribution,
$e = $ base of natural logarithms $= 2.71828$.

As applied to queuing theory, the relevant Poisson distribution is as follows:

$$P(a) = e^{-\lambda} \frac{\lambda^a}{a!} = \text{probability of exactly } a \text{ arrivals,}$$

where

$\lambda = $ mean arrival rate,
$1/\lambda = $ mean time between arrivals.

The customers' attitudes are described as patient or impatient. Patient customers will stay in the system after joining it no matter how long they must wait for service. Impatient customers will wait in line, but they will leave when their patience is exhausted. (It is difficult to estimate the dollar value of present and future sales lost due to customer impatience and subsequent loss of goodwill because of word of mouth disparagements.)

QUEUE CHARACTERISTICS

The queue refers to those customers waiting for service, but it does not include customers who are being served. A queue is characterized by its size, which may be infinite or finite. An infinite queue means anybody arriving for service will get in line; a finite queue means if a certain maximum number are in line the next arrival will not get in line. Queue size is usually controlled by the attitude of the customers.

Queues are a result of arrival and service variability. They arise because random, highly variable arrival and service patterns produce systems which are temporarily overloaded. If the variability of either or both can be reduced or eliminated, waiting lines can be shortened noticeably.

SERVICE CHARACTERISTICS

The service facility is characterized by its design, the service time distribution, and the service discipline. The facility design is in turn characterized by the number of facilities that are available and by the way in which the facilities are arranged: in series, parallel, or some mixture. Service facilities are commonly referred to as channels. In a multiple phase or series arrangement, the customer must be processed through many stations before service is complete. When a customer has a choice of waiting lines to enter, the system is referred to as parallel or multiple channel. A one-chair barber shop would be a single channel, single phase facility. A many-chair barber shop would be a multiple channel, single phase facility. A single product assembly line would be a single channel, multiple phase facility. Two or more parallel production assembly lines would be a multiple channel, multiple phase facility. The reason for breaking down the various waiting line situations into these basic structures is that the analytical methods available to study them differ. (See Figure 2 for a diagram of basic waiting line structures.)

In this section the service rate is assumed to be Poisson distributed, and this results in the service time, which is the reciprocal of the service rate, being distributed as a negative exponential. The negative exponential is a single parameter distribution completely defined by the arithmetic mean:

$$P(t) = e^{-\mu t} = \text{probability of (service time} \geq t),$$

where

e = base of natural logarithms = 2.71828,
μ = mean service rate,
$1/\mu$ = mean service time.

For the model to be realistic, the mean service rate must be greater than the mean arrival rate for a stable system. If $\lambda \geq \mu$, the length of the queue will theoretically become infinite.

The service discipline describes how customers are selected for service from the queue. It may be first-come first-served, random selection, priorities, last in first out, and so forth.

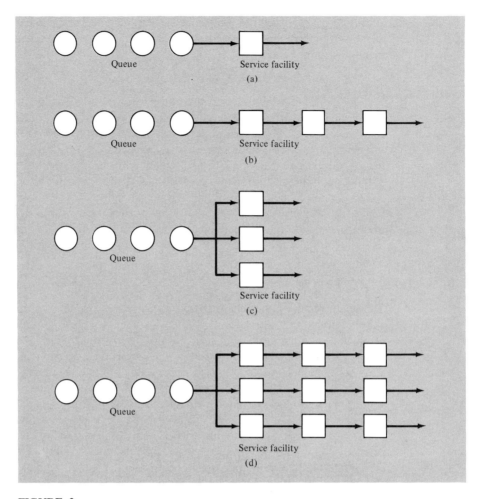

FIGURE 2
Basic waiting line structures: (a) single channel, single phase (SCSP); (b) single channel, multiple phase (SCMP); (c) multiple channel, single phase (MCSP); (d) multiple channel, multiple phase (MCMP).

MATHEMATICAL APPROACH

Table 2 contains a list of formulas derived for single channel, single phase and multiple channel, single phase queuing problems.[1] These formulas have been derived under the following assumptions:

1. infinite population and queue size,
2. Poisson arrival rates and negative exponential service times,
3. first-come first-served queue discipline,
4. mean service rate greater than mean arrival rate ($\mu > \lambda$).

Multiple phase is not considered, because the assumptions become too numerous, and it can be handled very readily by using simulation techniques. When arrival rates

---

[1] For a rigorous derivation of these formulas see Elwood S. Buffa, *Operations Management*, Wiley, 1968, Chapter 14.

TABLE 2
Queuing theory (Poisson arrivals and negative exponential service time)[a]

Variable	Symbol	Single channel	Multichannel
1. Mean arrival rate (units/time)	λ	λ	λ
2. Mean time between arrivals		$1/\lambda$	$1/\lambda$
3. Mean service rate (units/time)		μ	$M\mu$
4. Mean service time (time/unit)		$1/\mu$	$1/M\mu$
5. Traffic intensity	p	$\dfrac{L}{L+1} = \dfrac{\lambda}{\mu}$	
6. Relative traffic intensity	p_m		$\lambda/M\mu$
7. Probability of n units in system	P_n	$p^n P_0 = p^n(1-p)$	For $0 \le n \le M$: $\left(\dfrac{\lambda}{\mu}\right)^n \dfrac{P_0}{n!}$ For $n \ge M$: $\dfrac{P_0}{(M^{n-M})M!}\left(\dfrac{\lambda}{\mu}\right)^n$
8. Probability of a queue	P_q	p^2	
9. Probability of no units in system	P_0	$1 - p$	$\dfrac{1}{\left[\displaystyle\sum_{n=0}^{M-1}\dfrac{1}{n!}\left(\dfrac{\lambda}{\mu}\right)^n\right] + \left[\left(\dfrac{\lambda}{\mu}\right)^M \dfrac{1}{M!(1-p_m)}\right]}$
10. Mean or expected number in system[b]	L	$\dfrac{p}{1-p} = \dfrac{\lambda}{\mu-\lambda}$	$\dfrac{\lambda}{\mu} + \dfrac{\lambda\mu(\lambda/\mu)^M P_0}{(M-1)!(\mu M - \lambda)^2}$
11. Mean or expected number in queue[b]	L_q	$\dfrac{p^2}{1-p} = \dfrac{\lambda^2}{\mu(\mu-\lambda)}$	$\dfrac{\lambda\mu(\lambda/\mu)^M P_0}{(M-1)!(\mu M - \lambda)^2}$
12. Mean waiting time in system	W	$\dfrac{L}{\lambda} = \dfrac{1}{\mu-\lambda}$	$\dfrac{L}{\lambda} = \dfrac{1}{\mu} + \dfrac{\mu(\lambda/\mu)^M P_0}{(M-1)!(\mu M - \lambda)^2}$
13. Mean waiting time in queue	W_q	$\dfrac{L_q}{\lambda} = \dfrac{\lambda}{\mu(\mu-\lambda)}$	$\dfrac{L_q}{\lambda} = \dfrac{\mu(\lambda/\mu)^M P_0}{(M-1)!(\mu M - \lambda)^2}$

[a]Infinite queue, single phase.

[b]The number in the system refers to those being served as well as those waiting to be served. The number in the queue includes only those waiting to be served; it excludes those being served.

and service times cannot be adequately approximated by known distributions, the problem cannot be solved directly with equations. Before using distribution assumptions, it is advisable to collect data and verify the distribution by using the chi-square goodness of fit test. Simulation methods are necessary if mathematical methods cannot be used.

Any operation in which the units to be dealt with arrive at irregular intervals, and in which the operating facilities are of limited capacity, is a waiting line problem. A key characteristic of a queue is the random pattern of arrivals, which can only be described in probabilistic terms. The manager requires information about two frequency distributions, one describing unit arrivals and the other the length of time it takes to serve the units. The service facility must have excess capacity built into it if service is not to break down altogether (the average service rate must be greater than the average arrival rate). If the average arrival rate exceeds the average service rate, or even if they are equal, the queue will grow longer and longer without limit. If $\lambda = \mu$, the service facilities would be of sufficient capacity only if there were no oscillations in customer arrivals.

EXAMPLE 5

A single-clerk tool crib expects a customer every 4 minutes. Service takes, on an average, 3 minutes. Assuming Poisson arrival and negative exponential service times, answer the following:

(a) What are the mean arrival rate and mean service rate?

$\lambda = \frac{1}{4}(60) = 15$ customers/hr,
$\mu = \frac{1}{3}(60) = 20$ customers/hr.

(b) What is the probability that a customer will not have to wait in line for service?

$P_0 = 1 - p = 1 - \frac{15}{20} = 0.25.$

(c) What is the probability of one customer in the system?

$P_n = p^n(1 - p) = \frac{15}{20}\left(1 - \frac{15}{20}\right) = 0.1875.$

(d) What is the probability that there will be someone in the system (this is the probability of one or more people in the system)?

$1 - P_0 = 1 - 0.25 = 0.75.$

(e) What is the probability of a queue (this is the probability of two or more people in the system)?

$1 - (P_0 + P_1) = 1 - (0.25 + 0.1875) = 0.5625.$

(f) What is the mean number of customers in the system?

$L = \frac{p}{1 - p} = \frac{\frac{3}{4}}{1 - \frac{3}{4}} = 3$ customers.

(g) What is the mean number of customers in the queue?

$L_q = \frac{\lambda^2}{\mu(\mu - \lambda)} = \frac{225}{20(20 - 15)} = 2.25$ customers.

(h) What is the mean waiting time in the queue?

$W_q = \frac{\lambda}{\mu(\mu - \lambda)} = \frac{15}{20(20 - 15)} = 0.15$ hr.

(i) What is the mean waiting time in the system?

$W = \frac{1}{\mu - \lambda} = \frac{1}{20 - 15} = 0.2$ hr.

EXAMPLE 6

What changes occur in Example 5 if a second clerk is hired?
(a) What are the mean arrival rate and mean service rate?

$\lambda = \frac{60}{4} = 15$ customers/hr.
$M\mu = 2(60)/3 = 40$ customers/hr.

(b) What is the probability that a customer will not have to wait for service?

$$P_0 = \cfrac{1}{\left[\sum_{n=0}^{M-1} \frac{1}{n!}\left(\frac{\lambda}{\mu}\right)^n\right] + \left[\left(\frac{\lambda}{\mu}\right)^M \frac{1}{M!(1-p_m)}\right]}$$

$$P_0 = \cfrac{1}{(1+0.75) + \left[\cfrac{(0.75)^2}{2(1-0.375)}\right]} = 0.4545$$

$$P_1 = \frac{(\lambda/\mu)^n P_0}{n!} = \frac{(0.75)(0.4545)}{1} = 0.3409.$$

The probability of not having to wait is the probability of zero in the system plus the probability of one in the system, or

$$P_0 + P_1 = 0.4545 + 0.3409 = 0.7954$$

The probability of a customer not waiting for service increases from 0.25 to 0.7954.

(c) What is the probability of one customer in the system?

$$P_1 = \frac{(\lambda/\mu)^n P_0}{n!} = (0.75)(0.4545) = 0.3409$$

It increases from 0.1875 to 0.3409.

(d) What is the probability that there will be someone in the system?

$$1 - P_0 = 1 - 0.4545 = 0.5455$$

It decreases from 0.75 to 0.5455.

(e) What is the probability of a queue (this is the probability of three or more people in the system)?

$$P_2 = \frac{(\lambda/\mu)^n P_0}{n!} = (0.75)^2(0.4545)/2 = 0.1278$$

$$1 - (P_0 + P_1 + P_2) = 1 - (0.4545 + 0.3409 + 0.1278) = 0.0768$$

It decreases from 0.5625 to 0.0768.

(f) What is the mean number of customers in the system?

$$L = \frac{\lambda}{\mu} + \frac{\lambda\mu(\lambda/\mu)^M P_0}{(M-1)!(\mu M - \lambda)^2} = \frac{15}{20} + \frac{15(20)(15/20)^2(0.4545)}{(2-1)![20(2)-15]^2}$$

$$= 0.75 + 0.1227 = 0.8727 \text{ customers}$$

It decreases from 3 to 0.8727 customers.

(g) What is the mean number of customers in the queue?

$$L_q = \frac{\lambda\mu(\lambda/\mu)^M P_0}{(M-1)!(\mu M - \lambda)^2} = \frac{15(20)(0.75)^2(0.4545)}{(2-1)![20(2)-15]^2}$$

$$= 0.1227 \text{ customers}$$

It decreases from 2.25 to 0.1227 customers.

(h) What is the mean waiting time in the queue?

$$W_q = \frac{L_q}{\lambda} = \frac{0.1227}{15} = 0.00818 \text{ hours}$$

It decreases from 0.15 to 0.00818 hours.

continued

EXAMPLE 6— *continued*

(i) What is the mean waiting time in the system?

$$W = \frac{L}{\lambda} = \frac{0.8727}{15} = 0.05818 \text{ hours}$$

It decreases from 0.20 to 0.05818 hours.

This example illustrates a dramatic improvement in customer statistics (service) when an additional clerk is hired.

EXAMPLE 7

The tabulating department of a company is considering two alternative maintenance arrangements:

1. A small local group can repair 0.50 machines per hour at a cost of $10 per hour.
2. A large national group can repair 0.70 machines per hour at a cost of $15 per hour.

Both groups will charge for every working hour at the rate shown above. The average departmental rate of machine breakdown is 0.3 per hour, and the opportunity cost of down time is $12 per working hour. Which group should receive the contract?

The average time per machine in local repair is

$$W = \frac{1}{\mu - \lambda} = \frac{1}{0.5 - 0.3} = 5 \text{ hours.}$$

The average time per machine in national repair is

$$W = \frac{1}{\mu - \lambda} = \frac{1}{0.7 - 0.3} = 2.5 \text{ hours.}$$

The service time for local repair is $1/\mu$ or 2 hours, and similarly the service time for national repair is 1.43 hours. The cost per machine is the sum of downtime cost and repair cost.

$$\text{Cost per machine (local)} = 5(12) + 2(10) \qquad = \$80.00$$
$$\text{Cost per machine machine (national)} = 2.5(12) + 1.43(15) = \$51.45$$

Select the national outlet, since it has the lower cost per machine.

In this section, only the simplest cases of queuing models have been introduced. Many more elaborate models are available in the literature.

MONTE CARLO SIMULATION

Management decision approaches include pure intuition and judgment, experience and analogy with similar situations, analysis with the aid of analytical models, experimentation with real systems, and experimentation with a model of a real system.

Simulation is associated with the last approach. It uses a model of a system and manipulates it so as to imitate the system's behavior over time for the purpose of evaluating alternative design characteristics or decision rules. It is a systematic trial-and-error method for solving complex problems. Simulation makes available an experimental laboratory for the manager by permitting him to test various alternatives without risking or committing organizational resources. The effects of numerous alternative policies can be ascertained without tampering with the actual system. This form of system experimentation can reduce the risk of upsetting the existing structure with changes that would not be beneficial. Simulation gives the manager an opportunity to test and evaluate proposals without running the risk of actually installing new approaches and absorbing the costs associated with the changes. With simulation, "trial and error" need not become "trial and catastrophe."

When problems involve risk or uncertainty, an analytical solution may be difficult or impossible to obtain. Simulation is useful in situations where analytical solutions are not appropriate because the models are either too complex or too costly. A mathematical model using the analytical approach can become incredibly complex because of numerous interacting variables. Simulation offers an alternative for complex problems not suitable for rigorous analytical analysis.

Simulation develops a model of some phenomenon and then performs experiments on the model. It is a descriptive rather than an optimization technique, which means it does not yield optimal solutions. Monte Carlo simulation is a numerical technique that models a probabilistic system with the intention of predicting the system's behavior.

Monte Carlo simulation involves determining the probability distributions of the variables under study and then sampling from the distributions by using random numbers to obtain data. It is a probabilistic type of simulation that approximates the solution to a problem by sampling from a random process. A series of random numbers is used to describe the movement of each random variable over time. The random numbers allow an artificial but realistic sequence of events to occur. Monte Carlo simulation permits the manager to determine how varied policies or organizational conditions will be modified by the behavior of random or transient influences. A general approach to solving problems by Monte Carlo simulation is contained in Figure 3.

Monte Carlo simulation establishes a stochastic model of a real situation and then performs sampling experiments on the model. This technique generates a vast amount of data that might otherwise take a very long time to obtain. Following the generation of data, computations can be made and a problem solution derived.

The major steps in Monte Carlo simulation are as follows:

1. The probability distributions of certain key variables of the problem must be known distributions. They may be standard distributions such as the Poisson, normal, or exponential, or they may be empirical distributions obtained from historical records.
2. Convert the frequency distributions to cumulative probability distributions. This assures that only one variable value will be associated with a given random number.
3. Sample at random from the cumulative probability distributions to determine specific variable values to use in the simulation. A way to sample is to use numbers from a table of random numbers. The random numbers are inserted in the cumulative probability distributions to obtain specific variable values for

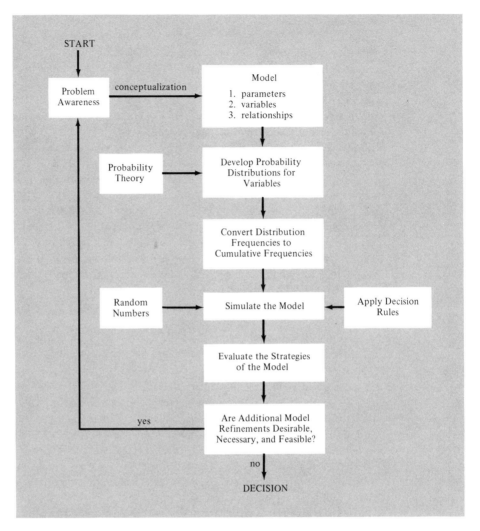

FIGURE 3
Monte Carlo simulation.

each observation. The sequence of assigned random numbers will imitate the pattern of variation expected to be encountered.

4. Simulate the operation under analysis for a large number of observations. The appropriate number of replications is determined in the same manner as the appropriate size of a sample in an actual experiment in the real world. The ordinary statistical tests of significance can be used. With computerized simulation the size of the sample can be increased without difficulty, and it is economical to run large samples with very small sampling errors.

Everything depends on the choice of frequency distributions. Unless there is some assurance they have been picked well, the entire simulation can be worthless. Distributions can be obtained from historical records or experimentation, or chosen *a priori* on a quasi-subjective basis.

Random numbers are numbers of equal long run frequency. They completely lack sequential predictability. The randomness of tabulated numbers can be validated by a chi-square test. The stream of random numbers can be obtained from a published table, or a computer can generate effectively random numbers (called "pseudo-random numbers") internally. Table 3 contains a typical random number table.

TABLE 3
Random number table

.6663	.0696	.6964	.6935	.3077	.6821	.8774	.1951	.9228	.9856
.8558	.8714	.9132	.3207	.6221	.8776	.9366	.5563	.6306	.2010
.8666	.5692	.0397	.7806	.3527	.5242	.3519	.8278	.9806	.9540
.4535	.3457	.0319	.6396	.0550	.8496	.8441	.2896	.5307	.2865
.7709	.0209	.1590	.1558	.7418	.6382	.7624	.8286	.4225	.7145
.7472	.0681	.9746	.4704	.5439	.7495	.4156	.4548	.4468	.7801
.5792	.0245	.8544	.2190	.6749	.6243	.9089	.5974	.4484	.8669
.5370	.4385	.9413	.4132	.8888	.9775	.8511	.6520	.1789	.0816
.4914	.1801	.9257	.3701	.3520	.0823	.5915	.5341	.2583	.0113
.6227	.8568	.1319	.0681	.8898	.9335	.3506	.4813	.5271	.5912
.7077	.0878	.1730	.0093	.9731	.6123	.6100	.0389	.0522	.7478
.8044	.7232	.7466	.0349	.3467	.0174	.1140	.5425	.2912	.7088
.4280	.3474	.3963	.5364	.7381	.8144	.7645	.5116	.0300	.6762
.8821	.4375	.9853	.9138	.0596	.6294	.3415	.4358	.2713	.8343
.8523	.5591	.3956	.3516	.8472	.2884	.8550	.3524	.3919	.3967
.6558	.3999	.0480	.3046	.8285	.1693	.2330	.7610	.2674	.3679
.1806	.3227	.9710	.8548	.5003	.6345	.6815	.9612	.3378	.5091
.9256	.0103	.1347	.8074	.4534	.0373	.9885	.1182	.0795	.7094
.6128	.2383	.9223	.4459	.8974	.4525	.0441	.7379	.0677	.6135
.4913	.6686	.4453	.0223	.7344	.6333	.8080	.1075	.5077	.2590
.3491	.9060	.0496	.5251	.2385	.3425	.7426	.0827	.7816	.3100
.1530	.7750	.1800	.5491	.4713	.3572	.8914	.3287	.3518	.4166
.5894	.9256	.1529	.4922	.7235	.9046	.5771	.3954	.6794	.1984
.7107	.7293	.5387	.9880	.4642	.6092	.4389	.3820	.4119	.5821
.5337	.8973	.0322	.7474	.5526	.7386	.3476	.0762	.9613	.8789
.9644	.9317	.7214	.9388	.5131	.7891	.6504	.8672	.4880	.1557
.3820	.4209	.4876	.6906	.9257	.4447	.8541	.5250	.8272	.9513
.7142	.7821	.9281	.0016	.4180	.2971	.7259	.3844	.3801	.5372
.3342	.0965	.3189	.7217	.0428	.6227	.8967	.1417	.4771	.0157
.7599	.6804	.3587	.7765	.9790	.5331	.8654	.5337	.8883	.1268
.5905	.5242	.3262	.2409	.1039	.8727	.2752	.3265	.1110	.6722
.9016	.0268	.2134	.8633	.9959	.8970	.2688	.9149	.8124	.3244
.3508	.3038	.3095	.6480	.3089	.7948	.7897	.4792	.9288	.5206
.9393	.2211	.6921	.8622	.2688	.7890	.1363	.1282	.9525	.5299
.8151	.0355	.0688	.3432	.8580	.9888	.2402	.0000	.1307	.1611
.6730	.6635	.9948	.3730	.5977	.6089	.6678	.7734	.1086	.1435
.1834	.3191	.4042	.7264	.9511	.0549	.4267	.2888	.9166	.1935
.9028	.7539	.3215	.9958	.7826	.7569	.0633	.4506	.0807	.5650
.6556	.7547	.1155	.1975	.7882	.5929	.1493	.7455	.4865	.2179
.4285	.8922	.8721	.3307	.6236	.6329	.5228	.7599	.6689	.1946

Monte Carlo simulation has many practical uses, such as waiting line problems where standard distributions for arrival rates and service rates are inadequate, layout problems of multiphase assembly lines, inventory problems (determining reorder points and order quantities), equipment replacement problems, and so forth.

EXAMPLE 8

Historical records reveal that two parts, A and B, have the following failure rates when tested individually:

Part A		Part B	
Days until failure	Frequency	Days until failure	Frequency
1	2	1	1
2	9	2	1
3	7	3	3
4	2	4	5
5	0	5	9
6	0	6	1
	20		20

It is necessary to know the failure pattern of a new product which consists of one part A and one part B. It is assumed that when the parts are combined no new failure element will be introduced. Predict the failure pattern of the new product by running 20 simulations with the following random numbers:

Part A:

68, 50, 88, 59, 06, 72, 44, 63, 83, 93, 83, 08, 13, 48, 71, 16, 34, 98, 12, 92.

Part B:

92, 27, 67, 28, 64, 83, 68, 94, 10, 80, 80, 48, 23, 27, 02, 30, 39, 27, 84, 42.

The first step is to develop the cumulative probability distributions for each part and their associated random numbers:

Part A

Day failed	Frequency of failure	Probability	Cumulative probability	Monte Carlo numbers
1	2	.10	0.10	01–10
2	9	.45	0.55	11–55
3	7	.35	0.90	56–90
4	2	.10	1.00	91–00

Part *B*

Day failed	Frequency of failure	Probability	Cumulative probability	Monte Carlo numbers
1	1	.05	0.05	01−05
2	1	.05	0.10	06−10
3	3	.15	0.25	11−25
4	5	.25	0.50	26−50
5	9	.45	0.95	51−95
6	1	.05	1.00	96−00

The next step is to stimulate the failures for each part with random numbers. The product is assumed to fail when either part *A* or *B* fails.

	Random nos.		Simulated activity: day of failure		Simulated results: combined parts
Simulation	(A)	(B)	(A)	(B)	failure (earliest day)
1	68	92	3	5	3
2	50	27	2	4	2
3	88	67	3	5	3
4	59	28	3	4	3
5	06	64	1	5	1
6	72	83	3	5	3
7	44	68	2	5	2
8	63	94	3	5	3
9	83	10	3	2	2
10	93	80	4	5	4
11	83	80	3	5	3
12	08	48	1	4	1
13	13	23	2	3	2
14	48	27	2	4	2
15	71	02	3	1	1
16	16	30	2	4	2
17	34	39	2	4	2
18	98	27	4	4	4
19	12	84	2	5	2
20	92	42	4	4	4

Frequency distribution of simulated results

Day	No. of failures	Probability of failure: A or B
1	3	0.15
2	8	0.40
3	6	0.30
4	3	0.15
5	0	0.00
6	0	0.00
		1.00

A simulation model does not produce an optimum solution. The manager selects the alternatives to evaluate by simulation, but he cannot be sure that he has included the best alternative. The simulation indicates possible solutions based only on the input of alternatives selected by the manager; it does not indicate which alternatives to evaluate. Simulation models usually develop heuristic rather than analytical solutions to a problem, but they can deal with very complex situations that defy solution by analytical methods.

No analytical solution can be extricated from its premises and assumptions. Simulation can investigate the effect of a relaxation of assumptions. Also, when no analytical solution is possible, simulation becomes important as a last resort. While simulation does not promise optimal solutions, it does allow picking out the best one tried. The ability of simulation to handle dependent variable interactions renders it a very powerful tool of systems analysis.

Simulation is used to reproduce a typical series of events (usually in mathematical form) which could have occurred in practice. If enough events are simulated and mean values determined, it can be assumed that they represent what would probably have happened in practice if the real situation existed. Standard statistical tests can be run on the output to determine when stability occurs.

Initial transient phenomena such as oscillations, rapid growth, and sudden decay are not unusual in simulation (or in reality). If system stability is desired, a sufficient startup period should be allowed for stability to develop. In real life such transient phenomena are commonplace occurrences. Whereas analytical methods are usually based on steady state conditions, simulation need not be limited by these assumptions.

EXAMPLE 9

An airline company uses many auxiliary power units that are exposed to severe service. Three bearings in the units are a source of trouble. In the past, the bearings have been replaced as they failed. With a new emphasis on cost control and preventive maintenance, management wants to evaluate the following three alternative plans:

    A. Replace a bearing when it fails.
    B. When a bearing fails, replace all three.
    C. When a bearing fails, replace it plus the other bearings that have been in use 1700 hours or more.

Pertinent data are as follows:

Mechanic time:	
Replace 1 bearing	5 hours
Replace 2 bearings	6 hours
Replace 3 bearings	7 hours
Mechanic wage rate	$9.00 per hour
Bearing cost	$15.00 each
Downtime costs	$6.00 per hour

Using the following random numbers, simulate 15,000 hours of service for each of the alternative policies:

Bearing #1—841, 584, 157, 599, 436, 255, 982, 525, 265, 247, 383, 188, 517, 883, 104

Bearing #2—848, 888, 534, 412, 059, 501, 084, 899, 836, 715, 887, 878, 896, 377, 703

Bearing #3—501, 921, 522, 870, 813, 446, 252, 378, 125, 316, 588, 522, 026, 616, 933

Given the actual service lives of 200 bearings as listed below, the first step is to develop the cumulative probabilities and their associated Monte Carlo numbers:

Bearing life (hours)	No. of bearings	Probability	Cumulative probability	Monte Carlo numbers
1100	3	.015	0.015	001–015
1200	10	.050	0.065	016–065
1300	12	.060	0.125	066–125
1400	20	.100	0.225	126–225
1500	27	.135	0.360	226–360
1600	35	.175	0.535	361–535
1700	30	.150	0.685	536–685
1800	25	.125	0.810	686–810
1900	18	.090	0.900	811–900
2000	15	.075	0.975	901–975
2100	4	.020	0.995	976–995
2200	1	.005	1.000	996–000
	200			

The bearing failure times (in hours) are:

#1	#2	#3
1900	1900	1600
1700	1900	2000
1400	1600	1600
1700	1600	1900
1600	1200	1900
1500	1600	1600
2100	1300	1500
1600	1900	1600
1500	1900	1300
1500	1800	1500
1600	1900	1700
1400	1900	1600
1600	1900	1200
1900	1600	1700
1300	1800	2000

continued

EXAMPLE 9— *continued*

Plan A

Individual bearing running time (hr)			Machine cumulative running time (hr)	Replace bearings #	Bearing cost	Wages	Down-time cost
#1	#2	#3					
1600	1600	1600	1,600	3	$ 15	$ 45	$ 30
300	300	300	1,900	1,2	30	54	36
1700	1700	1700	3,600	1,3	30	54	36
200	200	200	3,800	2	15	45	30
1200	1200	1200	5,000	1	15	45	30
200	200	200	5,200	3	15	45	30
200	200	200	5,400	2	15	45	30
1300	1300	1300	6,700	1	15	45	30
300	300	300	7,000	2	15	45	30
100	100	100	7,100	3	15	45	30
1100	1100	1100	8,200	2	15	45	30
100	100	100	8,300	1	15	45	30
700	700	700	9,000	3	15	45	30
800	800	800	9,800	1,2	30	54	36
800	800	800	10,600	3	15	45	30
500	500	500	11,100	2	15	45	30
800	800	800	11,900	1	15	45	30
200	200	200	12,100	3	15	45	30
900	900	900	13,000	2	15	45	30
500	500	500	13,500	1	15	45	30
200	200	200	13,700	3	15	45	30
1200	1200	1200	14,900	2	15	45	30
100	100	100	15,000	1,3	30	54	36
Total costs					$405	$1071	$714

Plan B

Individual bearing running time (hr)			Machine cumulative running time (hr)
#1	#2	#3	
		1600	1,600
1700			3,300
1400			4,700
	1600		6,300
	1200		7,500
1500			9,000
	1300		10,300
		1600	11,900
		1300	13,200
		1500	14,700
			15,000

There are no failures during the last 300 hours of operation for plan B. The cost per failure is as follows:

Labor	$ 63
Bearings	45
Downtime	42
Total	$150

($150 per failure) × (10 failures) = $1500.

Plan C

Individual bearing running time (hr)			Machine cumulative running time (hr)	Replace bearings #	Bearing cost	Wages	Down-time cost
#1	#2	#3					
1600	1600	1600	1,600	3	$ 15	$ 45	$ 30
300	300	300	1,900	1,2	30	54	36
1700	1700	1700	3,600	1,2,3	45	63	42
1400	1400	1400	5,000	1	15	45	30
200	200	200	5,200	2,3	30	54	36
1500	1500	1500	6,700	1	15	45	30
100	100	100	6,800	2	15	45	30
300	300	300	7,100	3	15	45	30
900	900	900	8,000	2	15	45	30
300	300	300	8,300	1	15	45	30
700	700	700	9,000	3	15	45	30
600	600	600	9,600	2	15	45	30
200	200	200	9,800	1	15	45	30
800	800	800	10,600	3	15	45	30
300	300	300	10,900	2	15	45	30
1000	1000	1000	11,900	1	15	45	30
200	200	200	12,100	3	15	45	30
700	700	700	12,800	2	15	45	30
700	700	700	13,500	1	15	45	30
200	200	200	13,700	3	15	45	30
1000	1000	1000	14,700	2	15	45	30
300	300	300	15,000	1	15	45	30
Total costs					$390	$1026	$684

Comparative total costs for plans A, B, and C are as follows:

Plan A: 405 + 1071 + 714 = $2190
Plan B: 450 + 630 + 420 = $1500
Plan C: 390 + 1026 + 684 = $2100

The best strategy of the three is plan B: to replace all three bearings when any bearing fails.

The use of simulation techniques would not be very feasible if it were not for the availability of computing equipment. While the design of many simulation models is not very complicated and does not involve a large amount of advanced mathematics, a large number of variables and equations is not uncommon. Thousands of simple manipulations and computations are usually required for each simulation, and the arithmetic operations are usually too numerous for hand computation. With the aid of the computer, simulation has become an important tool to the manager because it allows the manipulation of many variables and constants associated with a problem in an artificial environment.

CONCLUSION

All assets are susceptible to failure or deterioration due to the effects of use or natural causes. Failures result in repair or replacement expenses as well as losses in production. Costs also result from the idleness of equipment and personnel. Maintenance is necessary so that operations can continue.

Preventive maintenance is any maintenance performed to reduce the likelihood of failure. It may range from daily oiling of bearings to periodic removal from service for a complete overhaul. Breakdown maintenance is any maintenance performed after an asset has failed.

Maintenance usually involves decision making under risk. Expected value approaches to analysis are common when appropriate data are available. Cost analysis involves a minimization of opposing costs. Queuing theory and simulation have wide application in maintenance.

QUESTIONS

1. Name several commonplace maintenance department responsibilities.
2. What types of costs are associated with equipment breakdowns?
3. What information is needed to conduct a cost analysis between breakdown and preventive maintenance?
4. How can a production system be insulated or protected from the consequences of breakdowns without a preventive maintenance program?
5. Is preventive maintenance more applicable to equipment with a high or a low variability in its breakdown pattern?
6. When is breakdown maintenance preferred over preventive maintenance?
7. What is diagnostic maintenance?
8. How is individual versus group replacement similar to preventive maintenance?
9. As a rule, do many organizations use internal maintenance only?
10. Does high utilization of maintenance personnel indicate an efficient organization?
11. In queuing theory, what distribution is used frequently to describe arrival rates? service times?
12. Why must the average service rate be greater than the average arrival rate in the simplest single channel, single phase queuing model?
13. Why are frequency distributions converted to cumulative probability distributions in Monte Carlo simulation?
14. What determines the length of a simulation run?

15. Why doesn't a simulation experiment give an optimal solution?

16. Discuss the failure of any item in your home and the type of maintenance used to correct it.

PROBLEMS

1. The maintenance department of York Manufacturing Company is responsible for servicing 50 electric forklifts. It costs $30 per day to own a forklift whether it is used or not. It costs the company on the average 80% more a day for every forklift that breaks down. It takes on the average 1.5 days to return a forklift to operation after a breakdown. Maintenance records for the past 5 years indicate the following:

Number of forklifts broken down	Frequency (days)
0	150
1	300
2	450
3	300
4	180
5	105
6	15
	1500

How many backup forklifts should be purchased to supplement the existing fleet?

2. Barg-Wagner Corporation owns two large high pressure molding machines. Everytime one of the machines breaks down it costs $1350. By performing preventive maintenance each week at a cost of $1600 the corporation is protected against all major breakdowns. The breakdown records on the machines reveal the following:

Number of breakdowns per week	0	1	2	3	4
Number of weeks this occurred	22	17	4	2	1

Should the preventive maintenance be performed?

3. Manatock Machine Company has 40 lathes to keep in service. The breakdown repair cost is $1000 per lathe. Preventive maintenance at a cost of $300 per lathe can prevent breakdowns. Historical records indicate that the probability of a lathe breaking down is as follows:

Weeks until breakdown	1	2	3	4	5	6	7	8
Probability of breakdown	.10	.05	.10	.15	.20	.25	.10	.05

a. What is the expected breakdown cost per week?
b. If preventive maintenance is followed, how often should the lathes be serviced?

4. Mideast Electric Company operates three large baking ovens used to manufacture electric motors and generators. Each oven contains 2400 heating resistors. It costs $8.00 to replace an individual resistor when it burns out. If all the resistors are replaced (on Sunday night), it costs $7200. When a resistor fails, it must be replaced immediately. When group replacement is followed, all resistors are replaced at one time regardless of age. Statistical data provided by the research department of Mideast provide the following probability distribution for resistor failure:

Week	1	2	3	4	5	6
Probability of failure	.02	.08	.15	.30	.25	.20

Is individual or group replacement more desirable?

5. The B and P Manufacturing Company has a large hydraulic press. On the average, material arrives at the press every 8 minutes. The cycle time for the press is 5 minutes. Assuming Poisson arrival rates and negative exponential service times, answer the following:
   a. What are the mean arrival rate and mean service rate?
   b. What is the probability that a unit will not have to wait in line for service?
   c. What is the probability of one unit in the system?
   d. What is the probability of two units in the system?
   e. What is the probability that there will be some units in the system?
   f. What is the mean waiting time in the system?
   g. What is the mean waiting time in the queue?
   h. What is the mean number of units in the system?
   i. What is the mean number of units in the queue?

6. The maintenance manager for Holloway Tool Company is considering three bids for machinery repair:
   a. Offer from Rapid Repair to repair 1.5 machines per hour at a cost of $20 per hour.
   b. Offer from Reliable Maintenance to repair 1.1 machines per hour at a cost of $15 per hour.
   c. Offer from Fixit Right to repair 0.9 machines per hour at a cost of $11.50 per hour.
   The average rate of machine breakdown is 0.2 machines per hour, and the cost of downtime is $13 per work hour. Assuming Poisson arrival rates and negative exponential service times, what company should receive the contract?

7. If the cost of down time in Problem 6 were $55 per hour, what company should receive the maintenance contract.

8. Rogic Machine Company owns several high speed drilling machines. They are in continual use for 8 hours per day. The machines break down at an average rate of one per hour. Each inoperative machine represents a loss of $20 per hour. Three applicants applied for the job. A will cost $9 per hour, B will cost $12 per hour, and C will cost $17 per hour. Each applicant was hired on a three week trial basis. The following data were recorded:

Applicant	Average number of machines in system (L)
A	6.4
B	4.0
C	3.8

Which applicant should be hired?

9. A hydraulic actuating mechanism is made up of two different electric solenoids. The mechanism is designed so that if one solenoid fails the other will continue to operate the mechanism satisfactorily. Extensive reliability testing of each individual solenoid has provided the following failure rates:

Solenoid A		Solenoid B	
Cycles until failure (10^3)	Frequency	Cycles until failure (10^3)	Frequency
0–0.999	4	0–0.999	2
1–1.999	18	1–1.999	2
2–2.999	14	2–2.999	18
3–3.999	8	3–3.999	20
4–4.999	5	4–4.999	6
5–5.999	1	5–5.999	2

Assume that when the parts are combined no new failure element will be introduced.

a. Predict the failure pattern of the hydraulic actuating mechanism by running 20 observations with the random numbers listed below.

b. What is the probability that the product will fail in less than 3000 cycles?

Use the following random numbers:

Solenoid A: 89, 65, 01, 46, 64, 45, 01, 83, 32, 82, 35, 33, 69, 89, 09, 48, 64, 23, 04, 31.

Solenoid B: 60, 76, 82, 61, 61, 11, 92, 50, 30, 79, 19, 11, 35, 11, 71, 78, 34, 76, 66, 78.

10. Fairlanks-Norse manufactures diesel engines for Brown and Phillips Tug Boat Company. The diesel engines each have four valves. Brown and Phillips is interested in controlling maintenance costs and wants to evaluate the following three alternative policies:

a. Replace a valve when it fails.

b. When a valve fails, replace all four valves.

c. Replace all valves every 950 hours or whenever one valve fails.

Pertinent data are as follows:

Repair time:	
Replace 1 valve	12 hours
Replace 2 valves	20 hours
Replace 3 valves	25 hours
Replace 4 valves	30 hours
Maintenance wage rate	$18 per hour
Valve cost	$90 each
Unscheduled downtime costs	$75 per hour
Scheduled downtime costs	$50 per hour

Historical records show the service life of individual valves is as follows:

Valve life (hours)	No. of valves
500	6
600	25
700	30
800	50
900	64
1000	100
1100	95
1200	70
1300	45
1400	14
1500	1
	500

Using the random numbers below, simulate 8000 hours of service for each of the alternative policies. What alternative results in the lowest cost?

Valve 1: 276, 721, 487, 928, 318, 358, 326, 213, 309, 692, 068, 994, 404, 321, 115.

Valve 2: 223, 118, 425, 812, 988, 952, 130, 108, 916, 080, 486, 668, 985, 201, 954.

Valve 3: 173, 746, 396, 985, 395, 048, 971, 134, 842, 445, 049, 180, 152, 538, 032.

Valve 4: 500, 453, 897, 734, 238, 471, 723, 464, 552, 513, 925, 418, 042, 979, 103.

11. A piece of equipment must be overhauled or replaced every three years. The equipment was purchased three years ago. Replacement cost is $100,000, and annual operating expenses (including maintenance) are projected to be $10,000 the first year, $15,000 the second year, and $20,000 the third year. The first overhaul cost is $40,000, with operating expenses of $20,000 the first year, $30,000 the second year, and $50,000 the third year. The second overhaul cost is $40,000, with operating expenses of $24,000 the first year, $36,000 the second year, and $56,000 the third year. If the cost of capital is 10% and the equipment will be scrapped in 6 years with no salvage value, what is the most desirable overhaul-replacement cycle?

Hint: The four alternatives are replace now and in three years (R-R), replace now and overhaul in three years (R-O), overhaul now and in three years (O-O), and overhaul now and replace in three years (O-R).

CASE 1: KEEP IT COMING

On the premises of Disclaim Insurance Company Headquarters is the organization's main information processing center. The most active and highly utilized area of the expansive center is Data Section A. Working at twenty-five identical processing stations are individual, well-trained operators who sustain a breakneck pace to provide timely information to regional offices, and more importantly, to the company's 250,000 insured. Section A operates twelve hours each day on a four-hour shift basis. Employees rotate on three daily shifts so that accuracy is less likely to be impaired by worker fatigue or boredom. The processing jobs are extremely tedious because of an almost continuous flow of information, but the operators are compensated well for job strain and anxiety.

Because of high utilization of the information processing equipment, failures are frequent. When a machine or system in any station fails, operations in that station generally are stopped and the operator is idled. Out of the twenty-five stations, one station has a failure approximately every four hours. Disclaim has adopted a corrective maintenance program to handle the breakdown problem. A maintenance (systems repair) person is on hand during all operating hours to reduce the idle time (downtime) of the operator and the processing equipment. On average, the repair person will restore operations in about two hours, since spare parts and components are kept on the site.

The manager of Data Section A, Cy Borg, is unhappy with the current maintenance program. Because an operator is left idle while repairs are made, Cy is interested in changes that would result in better utilization of the specially trained operators. Since operators earn $20 an hour and repair personnel only $13 an hour, Cy is willing to engage two repair persons at all times instead of just one. The extra support staff should result in fewer stations in repair per unit of time and fewer operators involved in delay activities.

Cy assumes that queuing theory would be the way to analyze the extra support staff proposal. Repairs are done on a first come, first served basis, breakdowns are random, and breakdown occurrences and repair times can be estimated from past experience. Further, it can be assumed that repair work does not take place after working hours but that processing operations and repairs are happening concurrently.

1. Using breakdowns as arrivals and repair times as service times, analyze Cy's proposal from a maintenance and lost production time standpoint.
2. Besides maintenance and opportunity costs, what other factors may enter the decision process?
3. What other alternatives for dealing with the breakdowns could be analyzed?
4. What other technique(s) could be useful in establishing a maintenance program for Data Section A?

CASE 2: AN OUNCE OF PREVENTION

Pete Smith took over the position of maintenance manager for the Bland Company eighteen months ago. His predecessor, Larry Late, was released because of excessive downtime of shop floor machinery. Larry's maintenance policy was to give a complete overhaul of every machine that experienced a major breakdown at the time of the breakdown occurrence. Larry kept sketchy records of breakdown occurrences on 200 identical processing machines with similar breakdown characteristics. From Larry's records, Pete developed the following data on major breakdowns at intervals of 1000 hours of service:

Number of machines	Number of hours between major breakdowns
2	0001–1000
8	1001–2000
36	2001–3000
48	3001–4000
54	4001–5000
28	5001–6000
20	6001–7000
4	7001–8000

Also from the information in Larry's records, Pete estimated the typical cost to overhaul and make remedial repairs at each major breakdown to be $450 per machine.

Knowing about Larry's dismissal circumstances, Pete set a goal to improve machinery uptime. He was determined to keep shop machinery operable as much of the actual working day as was economically possible. As part of his plan to achieve high uptime, he instituted a preventive maintenance program for the processing machines mentioned previously. His policy was that each machine would be overhauled completely after 4000 hours of service. He figured that this maintenance interval would eliminate excessive downtime and keep maintenance costs at a reasonable level, since it was close to the average number of hours between breakdowns.

During the first year of Pete's preventive maintenance program, production delays were cut drastically. The major overhaul cost was reduced to only $100 per machine through the use of scheduling. Actual repairs of individual machines experiencing breakdowns under the program averaged $300 per machine and occurred less frequently. However, when cumulative end of the year costs were reviewed, they showed that the maintenance costs for the year were not as low as expected.

1. According to the data developed from Larry's records: (a) What was the average number of hours between breakdowns? (Assume that all breakdowns occurrred at the end of each interval.) (b) What was the maintenance cost per 1000 hours of service when overhauls were performed only at major breakdowns?
2. Under Pete's plan for overhauling each machine after 4000 hours of service, how many machines would be expected to break down before the scheduled overhaul?

3. At what, if any, service interval would you recommend preventive maintenance be performed on the 200 machines? Why?
4. What factors could account for the higher than expected maintenance costs? Be sure to consider the effect that failure records have on preventive maintenance programs.

SELECTED BIBLIOGRAPHY

Blanchard B. B. and E.E. Lowery. *Maintainability: Principles and Practice*, New York: McGraw-Hill, 1969.

Cooper, R. B. *Introduction to Queuing Theory*, New York: Macmillan, 1972.

Cunningham, C. E. and W. Cox. *Applied Maintainability Engineering*, New York: Wiley, 1972.

Gross, D. and C. M. Harris. *Fundamentals of Queuing Theory*, New York: Wiley, 1974.

Hardy, S. T. and L. J. Krajewski. "A Simulation of Interactive Maintenance Decisions," *Decision Sciences*, Vol. 6, No. 1, January 1975, pp. 92–105.

Lewis, B. T. and L. M. Tow. *Readings in Maintenance Management*, Boston: Cahners Books, 1973.

Mann, L. *Maintenance Management*, Lexington, MA: D. C. Heath, 1976.

Morrow, L. D. *Maintenance Engineering Handbook*, New York: McGraw-Hill, 1966.

Newbrough, E. T. *Effective Maintenance Management*, New York: McGraw-Hill, 1967.

Reed, R., Jr. *Plant Location, Layout, and Maintenance*, Homewood, IL: Irwin, 1967.

Shannon, R. E. *Systems Simulation: The Art and Science*, Englewood Cliffs, NJ: Prentice-Hall, 1975.

Turban, E. "The Complete Computerized Maintenance System," *Industrial Engineering*, March 1969, pp. 20–27.

Index

A

ABC inventory analysis, 633–635
Acceptable quality level (AQL), 692
Acceptance sampling
    average outgoing quality (AOQ), 694–697
    double sampling plans, 698–701
    operating characteristic (OC) curve, 691–694
    sequential sampling plans, 702
    statistical basis for, 688–691
Activity
    analysis, 227–228
    times in network programming, 227–232
Activity chart, 287, 289
Add/delete bill of materials (BOM), 529
Aggregate inventory measurement, 640–641
Aggregate planning, 458–472. *See also*
        Production planning
    costs, 462
    decision alternatives, 460–461
    and material requirements planning, 472–484,
        519–524
    mathematical models for, 462–472
ALDEP (Automated Layout Design Program),
        364
Allowance fraction, 310
Alternate optimal solutions, in linear
        programming, 125–126, 143
Analysis techniques
    breakeven, 79–84
    capital, 93–100
    cost, 79–89
    cost equalization, 84–85
    decision table, 44–46
    decision tree, 51–54
    linear programming, 113–157
    operations sequence, 363
    post optimality (sensitivity), 135–136
Annuities
    tables for, 94–95
Arithmetic average forecasting technique, 425
Arrow diagramming, 228–229
Artificial variables, 116–118
Assemble-to-order environment, 478–481
Assembly charts, 256–257, 286–287
Assembly lines. *See also* Continuous production
        systems
    analysis of, 364–367
    balancing of, 369–374
Assignable causes, in quality control, 681
Assignment method of linear programming, 152–
        157, 553–555

Attribute
    acceptance plans for, 688–703
    control charts for, 686–688
    date, 683, 689
Autocorrelation, 430
Automation, 215–216, 265–268, 391–394,
        400–401,
    as determinant of job design, 284–285, 293
Autoregressive integrated moving average model
        (ARIMA), 441
Available to promise (ATP), 492–495
Average outgoing quality (AOQ), 694–697
Average outgoing quality limit (AOQL), 695–697
Average rate of return, in financial analysis, 96
Averaging down, as purchasing strategy, 664

B

Backlogging, 461, 566–568, 570–571
Balance delay, 369
Balancing of assembly lines, 369–374
Beta distribution, as used in PERT, 230–232
Bias, of forecasts, 424–425
Binomial distribution, used in quality control,
        686–688, 692
Bill of materials (BOM), 652
    explosion, 501–502, 510–516, 525
    general structures for, 477–478
    manufacturing (M-bill), 531
    planning, 478–481, 528–532. *See also*
        Planning BOM
    traditional, 477–480, 503–505, 525–528
    uses of, 480–481, 503–504, 525
Bottom-up forecasting, 418
Bounded rationality, 60–61
Box-Jenkins models, for forecasting, 444
Breakdown maintenance, 711–712. *See also*
        Maintenance
Breakeven analysis
    linear, 80–82
    nonlinear, 82–84
Budgeting, 88
    zero-based, 185
Budgets, 184–186

C

c-chart, 686–688
Capacity, 11
    compared with priority, 474–475, 520–524,
        569
    constraints on master production scheduling,
        473, 475–477, 522–524

Capacity [*cont.*]
  factors affecting, 520
  input/output control of, 475–477, 566–568
  measures, 354, 359–361, 458
Capacity planning, 520–524
  intermediate range, 458–461
  leveling within, 482–483, 520–524, 548–549
  long range, 354–355, 359–361
  rough-cut, 473, 476, 522–523
  short range, scheduling, 542–574
Capacity requirements planning, 473, 522–524
  infinite loading or, 548–549
  leveling within, 521–524
Capital analysis, 89–106
  framework, 104–106
  disparities, 100–101
  present value concept of, 91–94
Capital investment analysis, 95–106
  techniques
    average rate of return (ARR), 96
    internal rate of return (IRR), 98–100
    net present value (NPV), 96–97
    payback period, 93
    payback reciprocal, 96
    uniform equivalent annuity, 98
Carrying (holding) costs, 585
Causal forecasting methods, 420, 445–449
Central limit theorem, 237, 682
Chance variations, 681
Charting techniques
  as approaches to aggregate planning, 463–467
  for job shop scheduling, 549–550, 559–561
  for materials handling analysis, 386–387
  for quality control, 681–688
  for work measurement and analysis, 286–292
Charts
  activity, 287, 289
  assembly, 256–257, 286–287
  flow process, 256–261, 286–289, 386–387
  Gantt, 549–550, 559–561
  operations, 273, 287–288
  quality control, 683–688
  Simo, 287, 290
Coefficient
  correlation, 428–429
  of determination, 428
  of optimality, in decision theory, 57
Competitive bidding, in price determination, 659
Component, defined, 503, 599
Computer aided design (CAD), 215–216, 267–268, 366
Computer aided manufacturing (CAM), 267–268, 366
Computer program applications
  facility layout, 364
  material requirements planning, 517
  simulation, 736
Consolidated orders, 627–628
Consumer's risk (β), 689–693
Containerization, 396–397
Continuous (repetitive) production systems
  characteristics of, 11, 268–270
  just-in-time, 571–574
  layout of, 364–366
  scheduling of multiproduct (flow scheduling), 544–547

Contracts, in purchasing
  types of, 665–666
Contribution margin, 82
Control
  of inventory systems, 621–642
  project, 225–243
  quality, 677–703. *See also* Quality control
Control charts, 681–683
  for attributes, 686–688
  for variables, 683–686
Control limits
  for quality control charts, 683–688
  for regression analysis forecasts, 430
Copyrights, 208
CORELAP (Computerized Relationship Layout Planning), 364
Correlation coefficient, 428–429
Cost analysis, 79–89
  of single order quantities, 611–613
  of reorder inventory situations, 587–597
  techniques
    cost equalization, 84–85
    incremental, 85–87
    linear breakeven, 80–82
    nonlinear breakeven, 82–84
Cost control, 87–88
Cost functions, 80–85
Cost recovery (depreciation), 101–104
Cost reduction, 88–89
Cost standards, 88
Costing systems, 87–88
Costs
  as criteria in decision making, 51–54, 56–57, 84
  direct, 87
  fixed, 8–9, 79–81
  of inventory management, 584–586
  obsolescence, 585, 607–609
  opportunity, 56–57, 125, 131, 152–157, 608–609
  variable, 8–9, 79–81
CRAFT (Computerized Relative Allocation of Facilities), 364
Criteria for decision making, 42
Critical items, on time cycle charts, 481–482
Critical path, 232–237
Critical ratio technique (scheduling rule), 562–564
Cycle time, 365, 369–370, 569–570
Cyclical variations, 421–423

D

Decision making, 40–62
  under certainty, 46, 75
  under conflict, 46–49, 75
  criteria for, 41–42
  features, 40–43
  group, 59–60
  process of, 41
  stances, 41
  strategic versus tactical, 183–184
  tradeoffs in, 42
  under uncertainty, 54–58, 75
Decision tables (matrices), 44–46
Decision theory, 39–77
  elements of, 44
  normative, 44–58, 73–74
  descriptive, 58–62

Decision trees, 51–54
Degeneracy, in linear programming, 126, 148–149
Delphi method, 445
Demand
    aggregate planning for fluctuations in, 459–461
    dependent, 498, 586–587, 630–631
    facility planning and, 329, 352–355
    forecasting, 415–449
    independent, 498, 586–587, 630–631
    during lead time, 590, 593, 595–596, 598–599
Dependent demand, defined, 498, 586–587
Depreciation (cost recovery)
    methods, 101–104
    tables, 102–103
Design
    process analysis, 253–274
    of products, 197–217
Detailed design, 201–210
Development, research and, 197–199
Discounts, purchase, 655, 660–661
Discrete
    demand, 586, 598–599
    lot sizing, 604–606
    movement, 393
Dispatching rules, 561–562. See also Sequencing, detailed; Scheduling, detailed
Distribution demands, 386
Distribution requirements planning (DRP), 606, 629–631
Distributions (probability), used in operations decisions
    beta, 230–232
    binomial, 686–688, 692
    negative exponential, 719–721
    normal (standard), 237–241, 429–430, 612, 682–685
    Poisson, 686–688, 692, 719–721
Diversification, 211
Division of labor (specialization), 283–284
Dodge-Romig's Sampling Inspection Tables, 692, 695, 696–697, 700–701
Double sampling plans, 698–701
Drawings, and specifications, 213–215, 503, 653
Dual method, of linear programming, 128–135
Dummy
    activities, 228–229
    locations, 145–148

E

Econometric models, 449
Economic indicators, 445–449
Economic order interval (EOI), 594–597, 626–628
Economic order quantity (EOQ), 587–591, 599–604, 623
Economic production quantity (EPQ), 591–593
Economies of scale, 8–9
Effectiveness, 174, 186
Efficiency
    contrasted with effectiveness, 11–12, 186
    of line balances, 370–371
Empty cell evaluation, 139–143
End item, defined, 477
Engineering
    as product design phase, 197, 199
    value analysis, 212–213, 668–669

Entering vector, determination of, 118–120, 141, 143
Equipment decisions, 265–272, 355–356, 393–394, 397–404. See also Technology
Events, defined, 51, 229
EWMA, exponentially weighted moving average. See Exponential smoothing
Expected value decision criterion, 49–51
Explosion process, in MRP, 501–502, 510–516, 525
Exponential smoothing. See also Forecasting
    basic exponentially weighted moving average, 432–435
    EWMA with seasonal corrections, 437–438
    EWMA with trend and seasonal corrections, 439–441
    EWMA with trend correction, 436–437
External environment, 26–29, 177–178
External maintenance, 718

F

Facilities decisions 32
Facility layout, 351–374. See also Layout decisions
    comparison, 365
    constraints, 353–356
    design considerations, 356–359
    line balancing techniques, 364–366, 369–374
    types
        fixed position, 361, 366
        group technology, 366–368
        process, 361–364
        product, 361, 364–366
Facility location, 327–345
    decision sequence, 329–333
    factor dependencies, 333–336
    qualitative factors affecting, 330, 335–336
    quantitative techniques for evaluating, 338–343
    trends, 337–338
Failure, product, 203–206. See also Maintenance
Families of items, 368, 480–481
Feasibility studies, in product design, 199–201
Feedback, 21
Final assembly schedule (FAS), 478
Financial analysis. See Cost analysis; Capital analysis
Firm planned order, defined, 517
Fixed cost, defined, 8–9, 79–81
Fixed order interval system (T-system), 594–597
Fixed order quantity system (Q-system), 587–593, 623–626
Fixed position layout, 361, 366
Flexibility, 392–393
    as characteristic of intermittent processes, 365
    tradeoff with efficiency, 364–366
Flow analysis, 256–260, 383–384, 386–387
Flow control (scheduling), 542
Flow factors, 392–404
Flow process charts, 256–261, 286–289, 386–387
Flowability, of materials, 387–388
Forecast accuracy, 420, 429
Forecast errors, 420, 423
    measurements of, 423–424

Forecast revisions, 423–425, 442–444
Forecasting, 415–449
    approaches, 421
    based on historical data, 420–423
    bottom-up, 418
    components, 421–423
    at different MPS levels, 475, 478–481, 492
    function, 417
    in inventory management, 477–481
    method selection, 418–421
    revisions, 423–425, 442–444
    top-down, 418
Forecasting techniques
    arithmetic average, 425
    Box-Jenkins models, 444
    econometric models, 449
    economic indicators, 445–449
    EWMA, 432–444. *See also* Exponential
        smoothing
    last period demand, 425
    moving average (simple), 426–427
    regression analysis, 428–429
    soliciting opinions, 444–445
    time series analysis, 421–444
    tracking signal for, 442–443
Form design, as phase of product design, 208–209
Forward buying, 664
Functional design, as phase of product design,
    201–208

G

Gantt chart, used in intermittent scheduling, 549–
    550, 559–561
Gauss-Jordan elimination procedure, 114–115
General purpose equipment, 265–268
Goal programming, 472
Goods and services, 4–6
    comparison of, 4–12
Government regulation, 26–29, 653–654
Gozinto (assembly) charts, 256–257, 286–287
Group replacement, in maintenance decisions,
    716–717
Group technology, 366–368, 573

H

Hand to mouth buying, 663
Handling efficiencies (principles), 405–406
Heuristics, 77
    assembly-line balancing, 371–374
    job shop layout, 364
    lot sizing, 605
    maintenance program, 726–736
    production planning, 463–467, 470
    scheduling, 545, 550–553
Human factors, as aspect of job design, 282, 296
Hybrid layouts, 366

I

Identity matrix, 116–117
Implosion, as used with bills of materials, 525
Incentive plans, 319
Incremental analysis, 86–87, 463
Independent demand
    defined, 498, 586–587
    inventory systems used for items with, 587–598

Index method of scheduling, 550–553
Industrial parks, 337–338
Informal time standards, 306–307
Information
    date availability and forecasting, 420–421
    importance of accuracy in, 519, 638
In-process inventory
    defined, 584
    control of, 569–571
Input/output control, 475–477, 566–568
Inputs to production systems, 4, 8
    linking environment, 25–26
    macro environment, 26–29
    micro environment, 23–25
    production function and, 8, 10
Intangible outputs from production systems, 5–7,
    9–10
Interest groups
    influence on policies and decisions, 23–28,
        174–176
Intermittent movement, 393
Intermittent (job shop) production system
    characteristics of, 11, 269–270
    choice of technology for, 266–268
    layout of, 362–364
    scheduling techniques for, 152–157, 547–566
Internal maintenance, 718
Internal rate of return (IRR), 98–100
International facility locations, 344
Inventory
    aggregate measurements of, 640–641
    costs
        holding (carrying), 585
        ordering/setup, 585
        purchase, 585
        Stockout, 585–586, 608–609, 611
    demand types
        dependent, 498, 519, 586–587, 606
        independent, 498, 586–587, 606
    requirements in operations environments
        assemble-to-order, 478–479
        make-to-order, 478–479, 586–587
        make-to-stock, 478–479, 586–587
    runout time, 545–547
    types of
        finished goods, 584
        in-process, 569, 584
        raw materials, 584
    used to offset demand fluctuations, 459–461
Inventory control models, 583–614
    based on type of demand, 587, 598, 604, 606,
        623
    discrete lot sizing, 604–606
    fixed order interval (EOI), 594–597, 626–629
    fixed order quantity
        instantaneous replenishment (EOQ), 587–
            591, 623–626
        gradual replenishment (EPQ), 591–593
    for distribution systems, 606–607, 623, 629–
        631
    for manufacturing systems, 599–604, 623,
        632–633
    risk and uncertainty in, 598
    sensitivity of basic, 597–598
    single order quantity, 607–613, 632
    time-phased order point, 606–607

Inventory control systems, 621–642
  ABC analysis of, 633–635
  behavior of, 623–633
  development of, 635–638
  distribution based, distribution requirements
    planning (DRP), 606, 629–631
  improvements in, 638–640
  production based
    just-in-time, 571–574, 633
    kanban, 573–574
    material requirements planning (MRP), 497–
      532, 632–633
    "pull" versus "push", 574, 629–631
  quantity based
    perpetual, 623–626
    two-bin, 623
  single order quantity, 623, 632
  time based
    optional replenishment, 623, 628–629
    periodic, 623, 626–628
  vital areas of, 622–623
Inventory status records, as input to MRP, 500–
  501

J

Japanese
  production control systems
    just-in-time, 571–574, 633
    kanban, 573–574
  quality practices, 573, 703
  technology, 366–368, 573, 633
Job design, 281–300. *See also* Work measurement
  affected by choice of technology, 284–286, 293
  establishment of
    job content, 283–285
    work methods, 283, 285–291
  job descriptions from, 300
  measures to increase satisfaction, 292–295
  physical factors influencing, 295–300
Job performance, measures of, 293–295
Job sequencing, in job shop scheduling, 559–561
Job shop. *See* Intermittent production system
Job splitting, to alleviate overloading of work
  centers, 555
Johnson's rule for scheduling, 564–565
Just-in-time systems
  concept of, 571–574
  compared to traditional production systems,
    572, 633

K

Kanban, production and material control, 573–574

L

Labor standards. *See* Time standards
Last period demand forecasting technique, 425
Layoff costs, in aggregate planning, 462
Layout decisions, 351–374. *See also* Facility
    layout
  computerized, 364
  constraints on
    production goals, 353–354
    equipment and capital availability, 355–356
    human factors, 356
Layout design considerations, 357–359
  buildings, 357

materials handling, 358
support services, 359
work places, 359
Lead time, in inventory planning, 474
Lead time offsetting, 502. *See also* Time-phasing
Leaving vector, determination of, 120–121, 141
Leveling, of production plans, 482–483, 520–524
Levels, of forecasts, 421
Life cycle, product, 195–197
Line balancing, 364–366, 369–371
  ranked positional weight technique, 373–374
  trial-and-error technique, 371–372
Linear decision rule, for aggregate planning, 471
Linear programming (LP), 113–157
  alternative optimal solutions in, 126, 143
  assignment method of, 152–157, 553–555
  assumptions, 114, 138
  degeneracy in, 126, 148–149
  dual method of, 128–135
  dummy locations in, 145–148
  economic interpretation of dual, 131–135
  formulation of
    constraints, 116, 121, 128–129, 145, 157
    objective function, 116, 121, 128–129, 145,
      157
  Gaussian elimination as basis of, 114–115
  notation, 115–117, 121, 128–129, 145, 157
  simplex method
    maximization, 114–121, 125
    minimization, 121–127
    unusual situations of, 126
  slack and artificial variables, 116–118, 144–
    145
  sensitivity (post optimality) analysis, 135–136
  transportation method
    modified northwest corner, 149–152
    northwest corner rule, 137–149
  uses
    aggregate planning, 467–470
    distribution, 137–149
    facility location, 341–343
    job shop scheduling, 553–559
    production mix, 113–137
Linear regression. *See* Regression analysis
Linking environment of production systems, 25–
  26
Load leveling, of master production schedule,
  476–477, 522–523, 549
Loading, 482–483, 474–477, 522–523
  defined, 476
  differences between finite and infinite, 548
  methods
    charting, 549–550
    indexing, 550–553
    linear programming, 553–559
    uniform plant, 574–575
Local buying, 661
Location decisions. *See* Facility location
Long-run, defined, 79
Lot sizing, 571–572
  algorithms used for, 516
  discrete, 604–606
  in MRP and MPS, 507–509, 516
  lot-for-lot, 509, 516
Lot tolerance percent defective (LTPD), 692–693
Low level coding, in MRP, 505–506

M

Machines
  numerically controlled, 265, 394
  robot, 266–267, 400–401
Macro environment of production systems, 26–29
Maintainability, 206–207
Maintenance, 709–736
  breakdown, 711–712
  group replacement, 716–717
  preventive, 712–716
  queuing models, 718–726
  simulation models, 726–736
Make or buy decision, 89, 261–264, 657
Make-to-order environment, 478
Make-to-stock environment, 478
Management coefficients model, in production
    planning, 471
Manufacturing, contrasted with service operations,
    4–13
Manufacturing bill of materials (M-bill), 531
Manufacturing cycle time, 569
Manufacturing resources planning, 518–519
Marginal analysis, 608–609
  in linear programming, 124–125, 131–135
Market quality level, 202
Marketing layout, 362
Master production schedule (MPS)
  formats
    typical, 492–493, 532
    two-level, 477–481, 492–495, 532
  as input to MRP, 474
  revisions in, 482–484, 517–518, 548–549
  steps in development of, 475
  time fences, 483–484, 492–495
Master production scheduling, 472–484, 631
  compared with production planning, 459, 472
  constraints, 475–476
  function, 473
  inputs to, 475
  leveling within, 482–483
  priority and capacity in regard to, 474–475
  in relation to other activities, 458, 472–474
  time fences used in, 483–484, 492–495
  time horizon of, 472–474
  two level, 482–484, 517–518, 548–549
  at various levels of product structure, 477–481
Master resources profile, 186–187
Material requirements planning (MRP), 497–532
  capacity planning in relation to, 520–524
  comparison with EOQs, 498–499, 599–604
  computations, 506–517
  features, 499–500
  inputs
    inventory status records, 500–501
    master production schedule (MPS), 500
    product structure records (BOM), 500, 503,
      525–532
  lead time offsetting, 502
  lot sizing in, 507–509, 516, 604–606
  matrix, 506–509
  modular BOM used in, 479–481, 493–495,
    529–531
  net change versus regenerative, 517–518
  objectives of, 498
  outputs from, 501–503
  overview, 518–520

parts explosion process, 501–502, 510–516
  terminology, 506–507
  time-phased order point extension of, 606–607,
    631
Material requirements planning MRP II
    (manufacturing resources planning), 518–
    519
Materials handling, 358–359, 381–407
  analysis of movement dimensions affecting,
    388–391
  automation in, 391–394, 400–401
  costs, 391–392
  demands placed on, 382, 384–386
  decisions, 404
  efficiencies (principles), 405–406
  flow factors that influence, 387–388, 392–404
Materials handling equipment, 358–359, 397–404
Materials selection, 202
Matrix bill of materials, 528–529
Maximax criterion, 58
Maximin criterion, 56
Maximum inventory level, 591, 595–596, 626,
    628
Mean absolute deviation (MAD), 423–424
Mean squared error (MSE), 423
Mean time between failures (MTBF), 205
Mean time to repair (MTTR), 206–207
Methods time measurement (MTM), 315–318
Micro environment of production systems, 23–25
Micromotions, 286–290
Minimax regret criterion, 56–57
Modeling process, 64–66
Models, 62–67
  classifications of, 64, 72–77
  validity of, 66
Modified northwest corner rule, 149–151
Modular bill of materials, 480, 529–531
Modular design, 212
Monte Carlo simulation, 726–736. *See also*
    Simulation
Motion economy, principles of, 290–291
Motion study, 286–291
Movement dimensions, 388–391
Movement features, 392–394
Moving average, simple, 426–427. *See also*
    Forecasting
MPS. *See* Master production schedule; Master
    production scheduling
MRP. *See* Material requirements planning
Multiphase decisions, 51–54

N

Negative exponential distribution, 719–721
Negotiation, in price determination, 659
Net cash flow, 90
Net present value (NPV) technique, 96–97
Net requirements, defined, 506
Network development, 227–230
Network scheduling. *See* Program Evaluation and
    Review Technique
Nonlinear breakeven analysis, 82–84
Node numbering, in PERT, 229–230
Normal (standard) distribution, 237–241, 429–
    430, 612, 682–685
Normal (standard) probability table, 238
Normal purchases, 656

Normal time
    defined, 310
    calculation of, 310–311, 314
Northwest corner rule, in transportation LP, 138–139

O

Objectives, 41, 173–174
    conflicting, 42, 174
    hierarchy of, 42, 174
    multiple, 41, 174
Obsolescence, 608
Operating characteristic (OC) curve, 691–694
Operation design, 272–273
    influence on job design, 282
Operation process charts, 256, 258, 287, 386
Operation sheets, 273, 544
Operations charts, 273, 287–288
Operations decisions, 14, 32–33
Operations sequence analysis, 363
Opportunity cost
    minimization using LP assignment method, 152–157
    minimization using minimax regret, 56–57
    minimization using single order quantities, 608–609
    or shadow price, 125, 131
Optimization models, 76, 114, 152, 564–566
Optimum probability of stockout, 611
Optional replenishment inventory system, 628–629
Order control, 543–544, 547–566
Ordering costs, 585
Organizational structure, 182–183
Outputs, from production systems, 4, 9–10, 20, 25, 27

P

p-chart, 686–688
Packaging, 209, 394–395
Palletization, 395–396
Parallel systems, 204
Parameters, of inventory systems, 587, 591, 595, 597–598, 623, 626, 628
Part-period algorithm, for lot sizing, 605–606
Patents, 208
Payback period, 93
Payback reciprocal, 96
Pegging, of requirements in MRP, 517
Performance, 12–13, 186
Performance, as in job design, 293–295
Performance rating, 309–310
Periodic inventory system (T-system), 623, 626–628
Perpetual inventory system (Q-system), 623, 623–626
PERT. See Program Evaluation and Review Technique
Physical factors, impacting job design, 295–300
Pilot operations, 198–199, 206
Planned order receipts, 502
Planned order releases, 502, 522
Planning bills of materials (BOM), 478–481, 528–536
    add/delete, 529
    matrix, 528–529

modular, 480, 529–531
    pseudo (super), 531–532
Plant layout. See Facility layout; Layout
Plant location. See Facility location
Poisson distribution, 686–688, 692, 719–721
Policy decisions, in operations management, 30, 170–186, 654
Popularity percentage, of planning modules, 479–480, 530
Post optimality (sensitivity) analysis, of LP, 131–136
Precedence diagram
    in line balancing, 369, 372
    in PERT, 227–230
Predetermined time study, 315–318
Present value
    of annuity, 94–95
    of single payment, 92–93
    use of, 90–91, 96–98, 100
Preventive maintenance, 712–716. See also Maintenance
Price determination, 658–659
Principle of insufficient reason (Laplace criterion), 55–56
Principles of motion economy, 290–291
Priority planning, in master scheduling, 474–475, 569
Priority rules, in intermittent scheduling, 561–562
Probability distributions. See Distributions
Process control, 681–688
Process decisions, 32
    choice of technology in, 11, 84–85
Process design, 253–274
    charts, 256–260
    by flow characteristics, 542
    interaction with
        product design, 254–260
        job design, 273–274
        operation design, 272–273
Process flow charts
    in flow analysis, 256–260, 386–387
    in scheduling, 544
    in work measurement, 286–287
Process layout, 361–364. See also Facility layout; Layout
Process requirements, in materials handling, 388
Process variations
    assignable causes, 681
    chance, 681
Processes, production, 11–12
    characteristics of
        continuous (line), 11, 268–270, 543, 586
        intermittent (job shop), 11, 269–270, 543, 586
        special project, 11, 225–243
    economic analysis of alternative, 84–85, 261–264
    environments
        assemble-to-order, 478–481
        make-to-order, 478
        make-to-stock, 478
    selection of, 253–271
Producer's risk (α), 689–693
Product decisions, 30, 192–217
Product design
    detailed, 201–210

Product design [cont.]
    development phase of, 197–199
    diversification, 211
    feasibility studies, 199–201
    interaction with process design, 253–274
    modular, 212
    preliminary, 201
    research phase of, 197–198
    in service organizations, 216–217
    simplification, 210–211
    value analysis, 212–213, 668–669
Product introduction strategies, 199
Product layout, 361, 364–366. *See also* Facility
        layout; Layout
Product life cycles, 195–197
Product specifications, 213–215, 503, 652–653
Product structures, 477–481, 503–505, 525–532
        See also Bill of materials
Production and operations management, 4–15
    defined, 4
    future challenges for, 12–14
Production capacity. *See also* Capacity
    alternative sources of, 460–461
    measures of, 354, 359–361
Production control, 541
Production control systems, 541–569
    continuous (flow control), 364–366, 542, 544–
        547
    intermittent (order control), 543–544, 546–571
    just-in-time, 571–574
    for services, 543
    special project, 543
Production demands, 353–355, 385–386
Production design, 210–213
Production function, 5, 8–12
    returns to scale, 8, 10
    returns to variable proportions, 8, 10
Production planning
    and control systems, 523
    costs of, 462
    and forecasting, 457–458, 462
    formalized, 462
    function, 460
    leveling used in, 482–483, 520–524
    models for, 462–472
    position in master planning, 458–460
    in relation to capacity planning, 520–521
    in relation to product design, 210–213
    in relation to variable demand, 459–461
    strategies, 459–462
Production run size, 591–593
Production scheduling. *See* Master scheduling;
        Scheduling
Production standards. *See* Time standards
Productivity, 12–14, 295
Profit maximization point, 83–84
Profitability index, 97
Program Evaluation and Review Technique
        (PERT), 225–243
    establishment of critical path, 232–237
    network development, 227–230
    PERT/COST, 242
    PERT/TIME, 226–241
Projected available balance (PAB), 492–495
Projects
    layout of, 366

planning and control of, 226–227, 241
probability statements concerning completion
        of, 237–241
scheduling methods for (PERT), 230–237
Prototype design, 201
Pseudo (super; phantom) bill of materials, 479–
        481
"Pull" inventory system, 629–631, 574
Purchase orders, 656–657
Purchase requisitions, 649, 651–652
Purchasing and procurement, 647–670
    according to demand factors, 655–656
    constraints, 650, 653–655
    decisions, 650, 656
    discounts, 660–661
    documents, 649, 651–652, 656–657, 666–667
    importance of, 648–651
    price determination in, 658–659
    records, 666–667
    in response to market conditions, 655, 663–665
    supplier selection, 657–663
    supply sources, 657
Purchasing cycle, 649–651
"Push" versus "pull" inventory systems,
        629–631

Q

Quality circles, 293, 713
Quality control, 677–703
    at source, 573, 660
    basis of, 681
    function, 678–680
    of processes
        control charts for attributes, 686–688
        control charts for variables, 683–686
    in purchase decisions, 660
    using acceptance sampling, 688–703. *See also*
        Acceptance sampling
Quality planning
    American and Japanese practices, 572, 703
    in just-in-time systems, 573
    price analysis and, 658–659
    in production design, 202–206
Quantity discounts, 661
Queue, characteristics of, 719–721
Queuing theory, 718–726
    applications, maintenance decisions, 718–726
    models
        single channel, 722–724
        multichannel, 722–725

R

R-chart, 683–686
Random number table, 729
Range, control charts for, 683–686
Ranging
    in linear programming sensitivity analysis, 135–
        136
    time series forecasts, 430, 443
Ranked positional weight technique, for line
        balancing, 373–374
Reciprocity, in purchase decisions, 662
Redundancy, as in parallel systems, 204
Regression analysis, in forecasting, 428–429
Reliability, 202–206

Reorder point, 587, 590, 623, 628
  time-phased, 606–607, 631
Replenishment versus requirements policy, in
    inventory management, 632–633, 586–
    587, 599–604
Research, 197–198
Resource allocation, 113–157
Resources, 176–177, 186–187, 654
Risk
  consumer's, 689–693
  producer's, 689–693
Risk and uncertainty, in decision making, 49–58,
    75, 105–106, 598, 727
Robotics, 266–267
Route sheets, 271–272, 544
Runout time method, for scheduling, 545–547

S

Saddle point, 47
Safety stock
  incorporated into inventory planning, 598, 630–
    631
  used in MRP systems, 516, 598–599
Sample size
  for stopwatch study, 308–309
  for work sampling, 312–313
Sampling, in quality control, 688–703
Scheduling, aggregate. *See* Master scheduling
Scheduling, contrasted with aggregate planning,
    472–475
Scheduling, detailed
  backward, 544, 633
  by flow characteristics of process design, 542
  forward, 544
  impact of route and operation sheets on, 542,
    544
  input/output control in, 566–569
  job shop
    loading, 152–157, 548–559
    sequencing, 559–566
Scheduling techniques, by process type
  continuous, 369–371, 544–547
  intermittent, 152–157
  special project, 225–243
Seasonal variations, 421–423
  correction for, 437–441
Sensitivity analysis
  of basic inventory models, 597–598
  in linear programming, 135–136
Sequencing, 559–566
  methods for job shops
    charts, 559–561
    critical ratio, 562–564
    optimization models, 564–566
    priority rules, 561–562
    simulation, 566
  in MRP, 500, 502, 520–524, 548, 569
Sequential sampling plans, 702
Service design, 216–217
Services and manufacturing, 4–14
  comparison of, 6–7, 255–256
Shadow price, 131
Shipping terms, 662–663
Short run, defined, 79
Simo chart, 287, 290
Simplex method, of linear programming, 114–127

Simplification, product, 210–211
Simulation, 77
  Monte Carlo, 726–736
  uses in operations
    aggregate planning, 471–472
    job sequencing, 566
    maintenance, 726–737
    scheduling, 545–547
Single order quantities, 607–613, 632
Single-phase versus multiphase decisions, 51
Site selection, 332–333
Slack, in PERT, 233–237
Slack variables, in linear programming, 116–118,
    144–145
Small-value purchases, 656
Soliciting opinions, 444–445
Special projects, defined, 11. *See also* Projects
Special purpose equipment, 265
Specifications, 652–653
  for product design, 213–215
Speculative purchasing, 664
Standard normal distribution, 238. *See also*
    Distributions; Normal distribution
Standardization, 211–212
  in operations, 89
Standards, cost, 88
Standards, time, 306–318. *See also* Work
    measurement
  determination of, 310–311, 314, 316–318
  uses of, 306
Standby equipment, 711–712
Strategies, 45, 47–48
  congruency of, 181–182
  for new product introduction, 199
  in operations, 179–182, 459–461
  versus tactics, 182–184
  in zero-sum games, 47–48
Stockout costs, 585–586, 608–609, 611
Stopwatch time study, 307–312
Storage layout, 362
Supplier selection, 657–663
Supply demands, 384–385
Supply sources, 657
Surplus disposal, 667–668
Systems, 18–19
  characteristics of, 20–21
  models of organization
    systemic environmental, 22–29
    systemic functional, 22, 29–33
    systemic operational, 22, 33
Systems theory, 20–33
  decision levels in, 29–33

T

Tactics
  organizational, 183
  versus strategic decisions, 183–184
Technological inputs, to production systems, 27–
    28
Technology. *See also* Group technology
  affects on operations decisions, 4, 27–28, 178,
    293
  choice of, 265–272, 366, 368
  financial analysis of, 79–106
  and productivity, 12–14
Therblig, 287

Time cycle charts, 481–482
Time fences, 483–484, 492–495
Time-phased order points, 606–607, 631
Time-phasing, 502–503, 632–633
Time series analysis, in forecasting, 421–444
Time standards, 306–318. *See also* Standards, time
Time study, 306–319
Time value of money, concept of, 90–94
Top-down forecasting, 418
Top-down planning, 458
Tracking signal, for forecasting methods, 442–443
Trademarks, 208
Tradeoffs
  in decision making, 678, 713
  in facility location, 329, 341
Transformation process
  in manufacturing and service industries, 4, 245–256
  in systems analysis, 23–25, 33
Transportation method, of linear programming, 137–152
  applications of, 137, 468, 555–559
  problem formulation, 138–139
  problem solution, 139–152
Trends, in facility location, 337–338
Trends, as components in forecasting, 421–423, 436–441
Turnover, inventory, 641
Two-bin inventory system, 625–626

U
Uncertainty
  decision theory methods for dealing with, 54–62
  degree of, 75
  in inventory analysis, 598

Uniform equivalent annuity, 98
Uniform plant loading, 574–575

V
Value analysis, 212–213, 668–669
Value of perfect information, 50–51
Variables data, in quality control, 683, 689
  control charts for, 683–686

W
Wage systems, 319
Waiting line analysis (queuing), 718–726
Warranties and guarantees, 207
Work analysis, 286–292, 306–318. *See also* Work measurement
  tools, 286–290
Work force changes, costs of, 462
Work measurement, 305–319
  methods study, 306–319
  purposes of, 306
Work measurement techniques
  informal time study, 306–307
  predetermined time study, 315–318
  stopwatch time study, 307–312
  work sampling, 312–315
Work sampling, 312–315

X
X-chart, 683–686

Z
Zero based budgeting, 185
Zero defects policy, 574
Zero-sum game, 46–49